Mediatization and Sociolinguistic Change

linguae & litterae

Publications of the School of Language & Literature
Freiburg Institute for Advanced Studies

Edited by
Peter Auer, Gesa von Essen, Werner Frick

Volume 36

Mediatization and Sociolinguistic Change

Edited by
Jannis Androutsopoulos

DE GRUYTER

ISBN 978-3-11-034357-1
e-ISBN 978-3-11-034683-1
ISSN 1869-7054

Library of Congress Cataloging-in-Publication Data
A CIP catalog record for this book has been applied for at the Library of Congress.

Bibliographic information published by the Deutsche Nationalbibliothek
The Deutsche Nationalbibliothek lists this publication in the Deutsche Nationalbibliografie;
detailed bibliographic data are available in the Internet at http://dnb.dnb.de.

© 2014 Walter de Gruyter GmbH, Berlin/Boston
Typesetting: epline, Kirchheim unter Teck
Printing: Hubert & Co. GmbH & Co. KG, Göttingen
♾ Printed on acid-free paper
Printed in Germany

www.degruyter.com

MIX
Papier aus verantwor-
tungsvollen Quellen
FSC® C016439

Contents

Section VI: **Mediatized spaces for minoritized languages**

Section I: **Framing the issues**

Jannis Androutsopoulos
Mediatization and sociolinguistic change. Key concepts, research traditions, open issues

1 Introduction

Despite a fair amount of relevant scholarship in sociolinguistics and neighbouring fields, the role of media in processes of linguistic change is not yet fully understood. Outside linguistics, the effect of the media – a term that often remains unpacked – on language is a common assumption. In linguistics, researchers from various subfields have approached the issue in quite different ways; however, dialogue across these subfields and their respective views has been limited. The predominant position in variationist sociolinguistics, i.e. that the media play no role in systemic language change (cf. Chambers 1998: 124; Labov 2001: 228), is increasingly perceived as unsatisfactory (cf. Boberg 2000: 23, Tagliamonte 2012: 356). This volume aims to contribute to this discussion in the following ways:

First, it introduces the notions of sociolinguistic change and mediatization in order to create a more inclusive theoretical space than the one offered by the notions of 'the media' and 'language change', which predominate in the discussion so far (Herring 2003). Moving from media to mediatization and from language change to sociolinguistic change is more than just rebranding. By introducing these concepts and exploring their relationship, this volume broadens the theoretical and empirical scope of studying language-media relations in sociolinguistics.

Second, this volume extends the conceptualization of language-media relations in sociolinguistics beyond the notions of 'influence' and 'effect'. Relations of language and media in communicative practice are highly complex, and the influence of television on spoken language change is only part of a larger picture. This volume contributes to a broader perspective on the relevance of media to language in society.

The third aim is to move the discussion beyond fixed boundaries between 'media language' vs. 'community language' or 'mass media' vs. 'interpersonal contact'. Media language has often been perceived as 'artificial' or thoroughly standardized, and therefore fully distinct from what is thought of as the genuine empirical object of sociolinguistics, i.e. conversational language in the community. There are problems with these dichotomies, as evidence across disciplines suggests that relations between media and community language are increasingly blurred. Media language becomes more conversational and vernacular, and media fragments are recycled in conversational interaction (cf. Androutsopoulos 2001, Coupland 2007, Stuart-Smith 2011). In media and communication studies, too, the traditional distinction between mass and interpersonal communication is being questioned.[1] The work presented in this volume focuses on interfaces of media language and conversational language and views their boundaries as synchronically fluid and historically shifting.

Fourth, this volume brings together various strands of current scholarship on language, media and socio-cultural change. The chapters present research in variationist sociolinguistics, interactional sociolinguistics, linguistic ethnography, media discourse studies, linguistic anthropology, language ideology, and minority language studies. All these lines of research are part of broadly-conceived sociolinguistics, yet have been largely unconnected so far. This is an attempt to examine their shared references and common lines of thinking, and to promote synergies in theory-building and empirical research.

This opening chapter begins by introducing the notions of sociolinguistic change and mediatization, which serve as conceptual brackets to the entire volume, and by reviewing some distinctions that seem necessary in order to transcend the blanket notion of 'the media'. Against this backdrop, it introduces five themes, or types of relations between sociolinguistic change and mediatization, which form the backbone to this volume. In brief, these are:

- Theme I – 'Media influence on language change' – covers research on the influence of mass media language, especially television, on language use and language attitudes.
- Theme II – 'Media engagement in interactional practice' – examines how media language and media experiences provide resources for social interaction.
- Theme III – 'Change in mass-mediatized and digitally mediated language' – shifts the perspective to changing language practices in the mass media and sociolinguistic change in computer-mediated communication.

---

1 Livingstone argues: "Society is witnessing a historic shift from a dualistic communication environment in which mass mediated communication variously gradually came to complement or undermine the traditional reliance on interpersonal communication. We are moving towards an environment characterized by diverse, intersecting, and still-evolving forms of multimodal, interactive, networked forms of communication" (Livingstone 2009: ix).

- Theme IV – 'Enregisterment of change in media discourse' – examines how media discourse represents processes of linguistic innovation and change, and how journalists themselves reflect on language change.
- Theme V –' Mediatized spaces for minoritized languages' – addresses the role of both 'mass' and 'new' media in the sociolinguistic development of small and endangered languages.

The remainder of this chapter introduces theoretical and methodological background to each theme – key concepts, research traditions and open issues – and offers a summary of the chapters in each section of the volume.

2 From language change to sociolinguistic change

The term 'sociolinguistic change' is not entirely new, but not firmly established either. It is sporadically found in the literature, referring both to processes that have been examined in language change research, especially standardization (cf. Deumert and Vandenbussche 2003), and to processes that are beyond the scope of structural language change.[2] This volume develops the notion of sociolinguistic change and elaborates on its theoretical distinction to language change, with the aim of going beyond certain limitations of the latter.

In his contribution to this volume, Nikolas Coupland argues that sociolinguistic change "challenges the dualism that underlies two traditions in the study of change (linguistic and social) and brings them together" (cf. also Coupland 2009a). It conceptualizes language and society "as mutually constitutive processes" and theorizes linguistic change as part of social change. The focus therefore "would be less in discovering change in language systems" and more in examining "changing relationships between language and society" with an emphasis on the linguistic or discursive character of social changes. Coupland (in this volume) distinguishes five dimensions of sociolinguistic change: discursive practices, language ideologies, social norms, cultural reflexivity, and media(tiza)

---

2 The Google search "sociolinguistic change" yields 2,640 hits (26 February 2013, including repetitions). A detailed inspection of the first 100 hits suggests that besides occasional use in the sense of 'language change in terms of sociolinguistic variables', the term refers to processes such as language shift, language death and loss, linguistic obsolescence, minority language revitalization, pidginization and creolization, the post-creole continuum, the study of language in urban areas, linguistic ideology, and vernacular writing.

tion. We return to his discussion of vernacularization as a process of sociolinguistic change below (Section 7).

Building on and extending Coupland's approach, I suggest that as a theoretical notion, sociolinguistic change transgresses five limitations of language change:

(1) Sociolinguistic change enables the study of changing language-and-society relations that are neither limited to specific linguistic features nor by definition restricted to a 'single' language. It encompasses change at the level of linguistic repertoires in multidialectal and/or multilingual communities, including processes of language shift, revitalization or loss and a reconfiguration of standard-dialect relationships.

(2) Sociolinguistic change focuses not on linguistic features but on language practices, that is, the socially situated use of linguistic resources in communicative action. For example, chapters in this volume examine change in terms of the conversational recycling of media resources, the organization of social interaction around media devices, the conversationalization of media genres, and crossmodal relations of language to other semiotic modes.

(3) Sociolinguistic change transcends the rigid boundary between language use and language ideology, focusing on their interaction in processes of change. This includes the role of the mass media in the homogenization of language attitudes (cf. Kristiansen and Ota and Takano, in this volume) and the language-ideological impact of representations of linguistic variability in media discourse (cf. Coupland and Pietikäinen, in this volume). Language-ideological change is deemed relevant not just to the extent that it might lead to changes in language use, but as a dimension of change in its own right.

(4) Sociolinguistic change is not limited to spoken language in the community, but also examines language practices and linguistic flows across media and institutional contexts. This is indeed necessary in order to understand the circulation of linguistic innovations and discourses in mediatized societies. For example, research on sociolinguistic change can examine the mediatized representation of 'new' varieties (cf. Kerswill, in this volume) and the circulation of minority language practices across media spaces (cf. Moriarty and Pietikäinen, in this volume).

(5) Sociolinguistic change offers a conceptual space in which to integrate institutional policies with individual agency. Standardization, revitalization and other large-scale processes of sociolinguistic change entail the planning and policing of language use by state institutions and corporate organizations, journalistic style guides, etc. But a single speaker's activities can also be influential to sociolinguistic change, to the extent these activities are disseminated and responded to by large audiences (cf. Moriarty and Deumert, in this volume).

These five aspects of sociolinguistic change have in common an interest in the interrelation of language practices and ideologies, institutional and individual agency, and an extension of scope beyond immediate spoken language to various communicative settings. While the notion of language change is tied to a structuralist perspective of language, then the notion of sociolinguistic change proposed here ties in with a post-structuralist view of language as a set of resources and practices (Blommaert 2010, Heller 2007, Pennycook 2007), and integrates change in language use and ideology with processes of socio-cultural change such as globalization, commodification and, indeed, mediatization.

3 The 'media' in sociolinguistics

The media is entirely missing from earlier publications on sociolinguistic theory (e.g. Chambers 2003, Coupland, Sarangi and Candlin 2001) and becomes more relevant in recent scholarship on language, globalization and transnational flows (e.g. Blommaert 2010, Pennycook 2007). However, the term 'the media' is still often used in an undifferentiated manner, which often boils down to mass media and especially television. Media and communications scholars are clear on the term's limitations. As Couldry points out,

> It is a basic point of media research that the term 'media', and notoriously the phrase 'the media' result from a reification. Indeed, media processes involve a huge complexity of inputs (what are media?) and outputs (what difference do media make, socially, culturally?), which require us to find another term to differentiate the levels within and patterns across this complexity (Couldry 2008: 379).

Couldry goes on to consider mediation and mediatization as such alternative terms. We return to these in the next section. First, let us specify what 'the media' refers to in sociolinguistic literature on language change. This is important because, as Spitzmüller (in this volume) points out, different notions of 'media' result in very different assumptions of the role of media in language change. It seems useful to distinguish four referents of 'the media' in sociolinguistic literature: mass media, new media, media representations, and media engagement. They are briefly discussed in turn.

The interest in mass media, especially television, in the context of language change is grounded both in the social function of mass media and in properties of media language. As Kristiansen (in this volume) points out, technologies and institutions of mass communication are fundamental to the production and reproduction of public spheres in modern society. Mass media produce and disseminate discourses that reach very large audiences; media language is professionally scripted and widely perceived as a "working definition of the standard language" (Bell 2011:178). Variationist approaches to the media and language change do not examine media language, but rather operationalize media consumption, exposure or engagement as an independent variable (see Section 5). However, the chapters in this volume that examine the influence of television on language use and attitudes (cf. Kristiansen, Stuart-Smith and Ota, Ota and Takano) suggest that taking various genres and styles of media language into account can help to understand which patterns of media language might have an influence on audiences. For example, it is important to distinguish between standardized news language and the stylistically more varied usage in television genres such as soaps, reality shows or anime series. Other chapters in this volume unzip the media, focusing on particular genres, discourses, language style and multimodal patterns (cf. Coupland, Kerswill, Luginbühl, Pietikäinen, Schmitz, Squires and Iorio). Like Bell's pioneering research on language style (Bell 1984, 1991), this line of research is not interested in the influence of media on spoken language, but in changes in the domain of media language and discourse. Findings reported in this volume suggest that certain types of programme promote the vernacularization of media language (cf. Coupland); changing patterns of multimodality in print and web texts reinforce linguistic economy (cf. Schmitz); and certain processes of sociolinguistic change first become visible in media for a niche audience (cf. Pietikäinen).

The shift of perspective from mass to new media challenges a number of earlier assumptions about language and the media. In particular, the assumption that 'media language' equates to standardized language just doesn't hold true for a lot of written language on the internet, which lies beyond institutional regulation and shows extensive variability. Having said that, it is also true that digital media extend the technologies of mass communication and enable hybrid combinations of public and private, institutional and participatory discourses. A number of chapters in this volume discuss the role of digital media in sociolinguistic change. Schmitz argues that the web accelerates tendencies of fragmentation and multimodality that are already evident in the design of print media, resulting in a loss of autonomy for written language. Squires and Iorio show how the language style of Twitter posts is re-contextualized into professionally produced newspaper copy. Deumert suggests that the participatory opportunities offered by the web favour digital literacy in indigenous languages. Pietikäinen finds that both mass and new media are involved in the circulation of linguistic resources and innovations in a minoritized language.

A third perspective on media in sociolinguistic literature focuses on media representations. In the tradition of cultural studies, representation is defined as the use of semiotic resources in practices of meaning making (Hall 1977). The study of representation entails a move beyond the formal analysis of media language and towards examining narratives, discourses, actors and characters in media text and talk. In sociolinguistic approaches to media performance and stylization, representation is key to the ways in which linguistic variability constructs identities in discourse (cf. Androutsopoulos 2010, Bell 2001, Bucholtz 2009, Hill 1995, Jaffe 2009; and papers in Bell and Gibson 2011, Androutsopoulos 2012). In the context of sociolinguistic change, "media representations of linguistic heterogeneity" (Jaffe 2009: 563), such as the use of local speech forms in the representation of a local community, are one aspect of the increasingly blurred boundaries between media language and community language (Stuart-Smith 2011). Another aspect is the metalinguistic discourse by which change in language and society itself becomes a subject of media representation (cf. Johnstone 2011, Kerswill in this volume). The mediatized performance of vernaculars can contribute to the construction of typical or 'exemplary' (Agha 2003) speakers and to a heightened reflexivity on language and identity.[3]

The fourth aspect of media in sociolinguistics, media engagement, shifts the focus back to language practices in conversational talk. Media engagement is understood here as cover term for interactional practices at the interface of media discourse and audience talk. It encompasses 'para-social interaction' during reception, talk about media experiences, orientation to media devices as focal points of interaction, and the creative recontextualization of media fragments. Unlike the rhetoric of 'influence', the focus on media engagement emphasizes the agency and creativity of audiences in how they deal with media language (see Section 6 of this chapter).

4 From media to mediation and mediatization

In current media and communication studies, mediation and mediatization are two concepts that transcend the limitations of 'the media' (Couldry 2008, Hepp in this volume).The focus of this discussion is on mediatization, and a full discussion on mediation would go beyond its scope. Suffice it to say that mediation is the broader concept of the two and already being used in linguistics, e.g.

---

3 Coupland and Kristiansen (2011: 31) argue that "modern media are increasingly flooding our lives with an unprecedented array of social and sociolinguistic representations, experiences and values, to the extent that (to put the case negatively) it is inconceivable that they have no bearing on how individuals and communities position themselves and are positioned sociolinguistically."

in the framework of mediated discourse analysis (cf. Norris and Jones, 2005). In broad terms, mediation refers to the cultural, material, or semiotic conditions of any communicative action. All symbolic communication is mediated by semiotic means (Agha 2011). In a narrower sense, some researchers limit mediation to writing as opposed to other technologies of communication (Kristiansen in this volume). In communication studies the two terms are not clearly distinguished, and some scholars use 'mediation' to refer to processes termed 'mediatization' by others (cf.Couldry 2008, Livingstone 2009, Lundby 2009).

The more recent concept of mediatization is used in communication studies for the critical analysis of interrelations between socio-cultural and media-communicative change (Hepp, in this volume). According to Lundby (2009: 1), mediatization "points to societal changes in contemporary high modern societies and the role of media and mediated communication in these transformations". The notion emphasizes the proliferation of media communication in all areas of social life. According to Livingstone (2009), we are moving from a society where mass media was one among many institutions of modern life to a stage where "everything is mediated" and no social process can be understood without taking (mass and new) media into account.

In his critical review of mediatization research in media and communication studies, Andreas Hepp (in this volume) distinguishes between an institutional and a social-constructivist version of the concept (see also Schulz 2004, Lundby 2009). The first focuses on changing relations between media and other social institutions such as politics, religion and sports, which gradually adapt to the "logic of the media" (Hjarvard 2008). Mediatization of society is, then, "the extension of the influence of the media (considered both as a cultural technology and as an organization) into all spheres of society and social life" (Lundby 2009:5). The social-constructivist version proposes a broader understanding of mediatization as a "meta process by which everyday practices and social relations are historically shaped by mediating technologies and media organizations" (Livingstone 2009: 10). It is closely associated with the work of German communications scholar Friedrich Krotz (2007, 2009) who draws on symbolic interactionism, ethnomethodology and cultural studies. Krotz defines mediatization as "a historical, ongoing, long-term process in which more and more media emerge and are institutionalized", so that "media in the long run increasingly become relevant for the social construction of everyday life, society, and culture as a whole" (2009: 24). He too distinguishes mediatization from 'mediated communication', which is roughly equivalent to mediation as defined above. Krotz argues that mediatization is a 'meta-process' at the same level of abstraction as globalization, individualization and commercialization, and therefore too multi-layered to be verified or falsified by any single research project.

In linguistic anthropology, Jaffe (2009, 2011) proposes an understanding of mediatization that "includes all the representational choices involved in the production and editing of text, image, and talk in the creation of media products" (Jaffe 2009: 572). Here mediatization is roughly equivalent to what is elsewhere described as 'staging'. Agha (2011: 163) defines mediatization as a "special case of mediation". While mediation refers to all semiotic means by which people relate to each other within frameworks of communicative activity, mediatization refers to "institutional practices that reflexively link processes of communication to processes of commoditization" (Agha 2011: 163). He writes:

> Today, familiar institutions in any large scale society (e.g., schooling, the law, electoral politics, the mass media) all presuppose a variety of mediatized practices as conditions on their possibility. In linking communication to commoditization, mediatized institutions link communicative roles to positions within a socioeconomic division of labor, thereby expanding the effective scale of production and dissemination of messages across a population, and thus the scale at which persons can orient to common presuppositions in acts of communication with each other. And since mediatization is a narrow special case of mediation, such links also expand the scale at which differentiated forms of uptake and response to common messages can occur, and thus, through the proliferation of uptake formulations, increase the felt complexity of so-called "complex society" for those who belong to it (Agha 2011: 163).

In Agha's sense, mediatized representations of cultural practices such as marriage differ from other forms of semiotic mediation in that they are designed for large audiences and thereby "provide massively parallel inputs to recontextualization" (2011:167). Even though people may respond to mediatized messages in many different ways, they all engage with the same messages and treat these "as indexical presuppositions of whatever it is they do or make" (Agha 2011: 67). So, whereas Jaffe's notion of mediatization focuses on media discourse as such, Agha's focuses on relations between mediatized messages and their recontextualization by audiences in everyday practices of semiotic mediation.

Which approach to mediatization is more productive from the viewpoint of sociolinguistic change? Not all chapters in this volume draw on the concept, and those which do adopt different readings. Kerswill draws on Jaffe's understanding of mediatization to explore metalinguistic discourse on 'Jafaican' in British newspapers. Kristiansen elaborates on the distinction between mediation and mediatization to theorize between direct and indirect influences of media on spoken language. He defines mediation as written representation of a language and mediatization as the process of "language being invested in the power and value hierarchies which support and are supported by the technologies and institutions of mass media communication". Coupland suggests that mediatization "creates affordances for sociolinguistic changes", which he locates both in media representation and speaker engagement with mass and new media.

In my own understanding, the social-constructivist approach to mediatization developed by Krotz and Hepp (in this volume) seems most promising for sociolinguistic theory. In this approach, mediatization is a facet of socio-cultural change that is specifically tied to the expansion and differentiation of communication media. Mediatization is constructed in analogy to other notions of socio-cultural change – other 'izations', as it where – which sociolinguists are already exploring in terms of their interrelation to language, such as globalization or commodification. Moreover, mediatization offers an alternative to the preoccupation with technology and its effects that shapes, more or less explicitly, a lot of earlier linguistic thinking about language and media.[4] Research on mediatization differs from media effects research in that it rejects a deterministic, cause-and-effect view of media technologies in relation to human behaviour (Hepp, in this volume). Mediatization research challenges the understanding of media as 'external' influence on social behaviour, focusing on institutional and community practices with media rather than media technologies themselves. Even though Krotz' and Agha's approaches on mediatization differ in their terminology, they are both interested in the interface between mediation (i.e. interpersonal communication in speech or writing) and the mass dissemination of standardized messages, Several several chapters in this volume adress this interface. Linguistics seems well positioned to investigate synchronic or diachronic relations between mediation and mediatization in processes of sociolinguistic change, for example how changes in technologies of writing played a role in standardization (Anderson 2006, Giesecke 1992, Ong 1982). A synchronic example is how changes in technologies of interpersonal literacy – from handwriting to typewriters to keyboards and screens) relate to the changing mediatization of interpersonal relationships.

To conclude this section, this volume argues that extending the theoretical scope from language change to sociolinguistic change immediately brings up issues of mediatization. The remaining sections of this chapter provide an overview of these issues in terms of their research traditions, methodologies, and empirical subjects.

---

4 Herring (2003) critically discusses approaches that rely on 'technological determinism', that is, the widespread assumption that media themselves affect or determine the communication they 'contain'.

5 Media influence on language change: Theme I

Theme I represents probably the most well-known approach to media and language change in sociolinguistics. As Herring (2003) points out, this approach conceptualizes the mass media, and in particular television, as a contextual parameter or independent variable whose impact on language variation and change can be studied in terms of single sociolinguistic variables. Different subfields and national traditions of linguistics have assessed the issue in quite diverse ways (cf. Stuart-Smith 2011, 2012). For example, German linguists have been quite receptive to the idea that mass media can have an impact on ordinary language use, although some of their suggestions are based on anecdotal evidence and lack solid empirical support.[5] Holly and Püschel (1993:148–152) suggest four types of influence of television on contemporary German:

1. *Popularization of the standard variety*: In the second half of the twentieth century, the spread of electronic mass media promoted the passive and then active competence of standard language across the German-speaking area and accelerated dialect levelling.

2. *Awareness of other (non-standard) varieties*: Through media representations, audiences gain access to regional and social dialects of German and thereby increase their awareness of non-standard varieties of language even in the absence of interpersonal contact to their speakers.

3. *Norm tolerance in spoken standard language*: The relaxation of norms of public usage that can be observed on television may act as a model for tendencies of norm relaxation in spoken language.

4. *Multiplication of linguistic trends*: Television can act as a multiplier and intensifier of neologisms and linguistic fads, which may have their origin in interpersonal language use but are disseminated via broadcast. Holly and Püschel argue that television discourse intensifies rather than creates linguistic innovations.

This approach casts the net widely: television influence encompasses here standardization (in the sense of dialect levelling), an impact on language attitudes, and the spread of neologisms and vogue words. By contrast, Anglophone variationist sociolinguistics has developed a much narrower perspective, in which most of these aspects are *a priori* excluded from investigation.

---

5 For example, Schmitz (2004: 30) claims that the media 'speed up and differentiate language change more than any other type of communication' (my translation). For further discussion, see Brand 2000; Holly 1996, Holly and Püschel 1993, Muhr 2003, Schmitz 2004, 2005.

The variationist perspective on language change is premised on the transmission of linguistic innovations by interpersonal accommodation during face-to-face interaction (Labov 2001, Trudgill 1986, Auer and Hinskens 2005: 336). As Stuart-Smith (2006: 140) points out: "The consensus seems to be that since we cannot interact with television characters in the same way as with our friends, neighbours and workmates, represented television dialects are unlikely to affect our own speech." The primacy of accommodation in interaction has often been understood as ruling out by definition any influence of television on the diffusion of innovations. In Trudgill's (1986: 40) words: "The point about the TV set is that people, however much they watch and listen to it, do not talk to it (and even if they do, it cannot hear them!), with the result that no accommodation takes place." In addition, systemic language change below the level of consciousness is sharply distinguished from change that involves 'superficial' (Chambers 1998) linguistic features. Trudgill argues that "highly salient linguistic features, such as new words and idioms, or fashionable pronunciations of individual words, may be *imitated* or *copied* from television or radio (rather than accommodated to)" (1986: 40–41, emphasis in the original). The role of media in lexical innovation and change (neologisms, new idioms, fashionable pronunciations of individual words, new variants in core vocabulary) is thus readily acknowledged, but excluded from analysis.[6] The same holds true for the impact of mass media on language awareness and attitudes. Milroy and Milroy point out that "although radio, film and television may not have had much influence on everyday speech, they are amongst the many influences that promote the consciousness of the standard and maintain its position" (1999: 31). Researchers of language variation and change have repeatedly observed that the stigmatization of on-going linguistic changes in media representations can prompt speakers of the stigmatized variant to modify their linguistic behaviour (cf. Pappas 2008, Zilles 2005). However, the variationist assumption has been that media representations reflect and reinforce language attitudes which already exist in the community (cf. Zilles 2005: 44, Pappas 2008: 495).

The three chapters in this section engage with four open issues in the current discussion on media influence on language change. First, the role of broadcasting in dialect levelling or de-dialectalization (cf. Kristiansen 2001). Included in

---

6 Trudgill (1986: 41) discusses the adoption of American English lexis and idioms into British English (e.g. *radio* for 'wireless', *toilet* for 'lavatory') and assumes that "radio and television play a major role in the diffusion of innovations of this type". Chambers (1998: 126) suggests that "mass communication diffuses catch-phrases" and "lexical changes based on the media are akin to affectations. People notice them when others use them, and they know their source."

Holly and Püschel's (1993) catalogue above, this is an issue repeatedly raised in non-Anglophone sociolinguistics and social dialectology, including Germany and Japan (cf. Ota and Takano, this volume; Auer and Spiekermann 2011, Brandt 2000, Hjarvard 2004, Lamelli 2004, von Polenz 1999: 457). I briefly discuss two studies which suggest that mass media language can serve as model for the adoption of standard forms. In the first, Lamelli (2004, 2006) found real-time shift from dialect to standard in the speech of town councillors in two German cities from the 1920s to 1960. Lameli finds a shift towards standard variants in the speech of councillors born in the 1930's and suggests it could have been driven by the spread of standard German via the radio since the 1920s (Lameli 2004: 108–111). Broadcasting influence is evoked here as a likely explanatory factor, though not investigated any further. The second study is Carvalho's (2004) research on language change in Uruguayan Portuguese, a border dialect of Brazilian Portuguese spoken as minority language by communities in Uruguay. Carvalho finds an orientation to features of mainstream Brazilian Portuguese among young female speakers, which "would be difficult to explain solely by frequency of contact with speakers of the standard dialect" (2004: 141). Based on interviews, Carvalho argues that her informants consciously orient to Brazilian television as a model in order to change their (stigmatized) dialect by a variety they deem urban, modern and prestigious. In some variationist literature, the role of broadcast media as a model for the adoption of standard variants has been explained away as an instance of individual "copying", just like the acquisition of new lexis via the media, and therefore as a process that is beyond the realm of systemic language change.[7] However, Kristiansen (in this volume) claims with regard to Denmark that "the view on media influence would have been less dismissive if the state-of-the-art view had been developed in a less Anglo-world focused discipline".

The second issue is the theoretical shift from the notion of 'exposure' to that of 'engagement'. The rare early variationist studies on media and language change were limited to correlations between linguistic variables and media exposure, which was measured in terms of hours of media consumption. Such correlations were either not found or not interpreted as causal (see discussion in Stuart-Smith 2012 and Stuart-Smith and Ota, in this volume). However, there is reason to doubt that the impact of media exposure on social behaviour can ever

---

7 Trudgill (1986: 41) suggests that an individual speaker's shift from dialect to standard is "one situation where core syntax and phonology *can* be influenced by the media (original emphasis)". People "may use the language of the media as a model", Trudgill continues, provided they make "a *conscious* decision to acquire the standard" and "there is considerable linguistic distance between a national dialect and local dialects" (original emphasis).

be scientifically established. In media and communication studies, it is now commonplace that the impact of media on social behaviour is much more complex and indirect than it was assumed in earlier media effects research (cf. Cormack 2007, Gauntlett 1998, Stuart-Smith 2012: 1081). The assumption that media exposure can be directly correlated to subsequent social behaviour is now viewed as unsuccessful and out-dated (cf. Gauntlett 1998) and has largely been replaced by more sophisticated models of media reception such as the'uses and gratifications' theory. Qualitative approaches to 'active audiences' emphasize people's motivation for media consumption, their interpretive practices and engagement with media texts (cf.Hepp, in this volume; Stuart-Smith and Ota, in this volume). The implication of this paradigm shift for the study of sociolinguistic change is that the search for a supposedly unconscious impact of the broadcast media on speech is doomed to fail. Instead, the motivation to engage with media discourse and orient to media language as a model is theoretically foregrounded.[8] As Ichiro Ota and Shoji Takano (in this volume), tellingly put it: "TV cannot change language by itself. The change needs to be caused by speakers when they want something more than what they have." The Glasgow project led by Stuart-Smith (2011, 2012, in press) finds robust correlations between language use (focusing on three consonantal variables that spread from Southern England English to Glasgow English) and media engagement, though not media exposure.

The third issue is the notion of "off the shelf" changes. Originally introduced by Eckert (2003: 395), it refers to cases of rapid linguistic diffusion such as the global spread of the quotative *like* from American English to the entire English-speaking world (Buchstaller 2008). "Off the shelf" changes "are transmitted with no or relatively little interpersonal contact" (Buchstaller 2008: 36). Milroy (2008) juxtaposes changes "off the shelf" to changes "under the counter" whose transmission requires regular social interaction. The notion thus signals a tentative departure from the premise that social interaction is a prerequisite to any transmission of linguistic innovations. However, the potential role of the media in spreading "off the shelf" changes is implied rather than empirically investigated in previous literature.

---

8 Carvalho (2004: 143) points out: "It is doubtful that exposure to television and adoption of standard features may ever be directly correlated, because for this relationship to happen there needs to be both psychological and social motives that instigate dialect assimilation. It is essentially the desire among the young, the middle-class, and women to replace UP [Uruguayan Portuguese] features with BP [Brazilian Portuguese] that motivates their use of television as a model for dialect acquisition".

The fourth issue is the premise of interpersonal accommodation as site of diffusion of linguistic innovations. Auer and Hinskens (2005) contrast the variationist 'change-by-accommodation' model to the 'identity projection' model from the 'acts of identity' theory of Le Page and Tabouret-Keller (1985), which views "the adoption of certain dialect features [as] the outcome of the speaker's wish to identify with a certain group" (Auer and Hinskens 2005: 337). In this model, "frequency of contact is not essential, and neither is face-to-face contact. Convergence rather proceeds towards an abstract image of the group"(338). Auer and Hinskens suggest that interpersonal accommodation "is better explained as accommodation of a stereotypical *persona* or mental representation (model) of a social group" (343). Likewise, Carvalho (2004: 141–2) suggests that "accommodation may not be in response to a particular interlocutor, but to stereotypes of the group the interlocutor belongs to, or of a socially attractive group not actually represented in the immediate context."

The three chapters in this section examine the potential influence of mass media on language attitudes and use, drawing on findings from Danish, English and Japanese. All chapters reject the simplistic assumption that media influence can occur by mere exposure to television and adopt the view that speaker motivation and engagement are prerequisites for their orientation to media language.

Tore Kristiansen suggests that the mass-media experience that shapes the modern Danish society has a decisive influence on covert or 'subconsciously expressed' language attitudes, which may subsequently influence language use. In Denmark, the indirect, i.e. ideologically mediated, influence of broadcast media consists in establishing a new standard language ideology, which reallocates sociolinguistic prestige from standard to Copenhagen Danish, the variety of Danish used by most media celebrities. Kristiansen shows that evaluative patterns for local, conservative standard and modern Copenhagen accents have a 'copy-like quality' across Denmark. This is unlike Norway, where the mass media strengthen the tolerance for (and even promotion of) regional variation, with dialect use not just accepted, but on the increase in many media genres. Kristiansen's argument, then, is that mediatization reinforces sociolinguistic attitudes that prevail in each particular society, thereby paving the way for sociolinguistic changes such as dialect levelling.

Jane Stuart-Smith and Ichiro Ota draw on the notion of 'the shelf' in their analysis of stylistic variation in Scottish English and Japanese. They advance the understanding of this notion by suggesting, first, that 'on the shelf' features can be of different kinds, including accent and tonal features in Japanese and consonantal features in Glasgow English. In Japanese, the phrasal pitch that can be heard in the standardized speech of Tokyo newscasters is found to occur in regional forms of standard Japanese across the country. Anime fictional characters offer another kind of 'media shelf' with their stereotyped prosodic features, which female speakers from one particular region, Kagoshima, draw on in their performance of standard Japanese. In Glasgow, the rapid diffusion of consonantal features associated with London English correlates with speakers' engagement with a London-based television series, East Enders. The authors suggest that this series serves as "one particular media shelf which offers ... features *and* associated local meanings." Thus 'media shelves' can vary considerably in terms of media genres, available linguistic features, and the way they tie in with existing indexical fields for particular sociolinguistic variables.

In their combined analysis of original data and meta-analysis of previous research on Japanese, Ichiro Ota and Shoji Takano point out the difficulties in separating media influence on speech from the impact of other processes of social change in the second half of the twentieth century. They locate potential media influences on Japanese in the standardization of local dialects and the spread of non-local, non-standard features across Japan. They suggest that media influence can result in either a more or less unconscious adoption of linguistic variants or in a conscious, stylized performance of media speech styles; the two are not rigidly separated in practice. Ota and Takano provide evidence for striking cross-regional similarities in the patterning of sociolinguistic variables from standard Japanese across distant regions, thus begging the question of how such patterns could have come up, if not through a common 'uptake and response' (cf. Agha 2011) to a joint reference style that is readily available in society at large via the mass media.

6 Media engagement in interactional practice: Theme II

The turn from Theme I to Theme II mirrors an earlier paradigm shift in media and communication studies, namely the turn from asking 'what media does to people' to 'what people do with the media'. Research on audiences and their everyday media practices originates in cultural studies as a response to media effects models and aims "to elucidate how media are recruited by audiences as resources to inform and enhance their actions in a variety of social contexts" (Jensen 2002: 164; Gillespie 1995; Gauntlett 1998; Talbot 2007). Since the 1980s, this line of research spread from cultural studies to interactional sociolinguistics and linguistic anthropology. It is by now well documented that audiences engage with media in various ways, including para-social interaction with show hosts; media talk (e.g. reanimation of jointly viewed films or series, comparison of real-life situations to media contexts, reference to media experiences as an occasion for talk); and recontextualization of media fragments, whereby "phrases and discourse styles are extracted from radio broadcasting and then recycled and reanimated in everyday usage, outside of the contexts of radio listening" (Spitulnik 1997: 95). Gillespie (1995) was one of the first cultural studies researchers to notice the appropriation of media phrases in everyday talk, and numerous sociolinguists have confirmed her observations:

> One of the most tangible examples of the way that the discourses of TV and everyday life are intermeshed is when jingles, catch-phrases and humorous storylines of favourite ads are incorporated into everyday speech. Ads provide a set of shared cultural reference points, images and metaphors which spice local speech. There are countless examples of this in the data on TV talk but to mention just one: a common refrain which accompanies a spectacular feat, such as a goal, is the slogan 'I bet *he* drinks Carling Black Label!' (Gillespie 1995: 178; original emphasis).

Sociolinguistic research on audience practices has mostly focused on young people and often from transnational, diasporic or minority communities. It uses various terms (e.g. media quotations, media phrases, media fragments; recycling, reanimation, incorporation, integration into everyday speech) and draws on a number of theoretical frameworks, including the Bakhtinian concepts of polyphony and double-voicing the notion of bricolage from anthropology and cultural studies de- and recontextualization (Bauman and Briggs 1990) and Anderson's (2006) notion of imagined communities.[9] Before we turn to the relevance of this research to sociolinguistic change, it is useful to summarize its findings in five points: origin and inventories of media fragments, interactional settings of their recontextualization, modification of media fragments, multilingual practices, and discourse functions.[10]

Media fragments are lifted from various media genres, including news stories, celebrity talk ("poaching from personalities", Spitulnik 1997: 108), stage performance, music and fiction. Some researchers distinguish between media material

---

9 Cf. Ayaß and Gerhardt 2012, Leppänen and Piirainen-Marsh 2009, Pujolar 2001, Rampton 1995, Spitulnik 1997, Spreckels 2006, Talbot 2007.

10 These categories are informed by, though not identical to the analytic categories used by individual researchers. For instance, Branner (2002) examines the use of commercial slogans by a female peer group in terms of the contextual trigger for quoting a slogan; alterations in linguistic form; individual animation as opposed to joint co-construction; and the embedding of slogans in the on-going conversation. Spitulnik (1997: 99) examines the de- and recontextualization of fragments from radio talk in terms of "the inherent reproducibility and transportability of radio phrases; the dialogic overtones that are carried over into new contexts of use; the formal, functional, and semantic alterations that occur in the recontextualization; the degree to which knowledge of the original radio source is relevant for understanding the recycled phrase".

from a particular source and the animation of a media register (e.g. 'acting like a show host').[11] Drawing on their media experience, people assemble inventories of media voices whose composition indexes the lifestyle and media consumption of a particular community or group. Birken-Silverman (2003) reports on a group of Italian-German youth whose inventory of media voices includes US-American hip-hop, Sicilian music, and German television. Lytra (2006) found that the media resources of Turkish-Greek schoolchildren draw on both the majority (Greek) and minority (Turkish) language and culture. Schlobinski (1989) shows how young people recontextualize media sources from mainstream television and punk music to index distance and identification, respectively. This suggests that the cultural origin of media fragments shapes their indexical value in recontextualization.

Besides informal interaction, the recontextualization of media fragments is attested in classroom talk (Lytra 2006, Keim 2003, Rampton 1999). Its contextual trigger can be external to the on-going interaction or part of it (Branner 2002), and media fragments can be reproduced as a solitary activity that is not taken up by others or jointly co-constructed and elaborated on (see also Georgakopoulou, in this volume). Shankar (2004: 326–7) emphasizes the intertextual relation between media reception and subsequent media talk by pointing out that "the type of talk that occurs during the film – especially reciting dramatic dialogues, enacting comedy routines, and singing along with songs – anticipates the incorporation of such verbal practices in talk outside these viewing contexts".

Recontextualization can involve formal, functional and semantic modifications of media fragments. They are typically set apart from speaker's own voice by means of prosodic and metapragmatic cues (e.g. higher pitch, metadiscursive markers or allusions to the reference media texts). By means of lexical modifications, a media fragment is creatively altered to fit into the on-going activity or current topic (Brenner 2002). Moreover, recycling often involves code-switching (or more specifically language crossing) whereby a media fragment that originates in another language or language variety is inserted into the base language of on-going talk. Examples from the literature include code-switching from Greek to Turkish song lines, from colloquial regional German to stylized ethnic German, from American English to mock Spanish or Hindi from Bollywood films, and from vernacular British English to stylized Asian English.[12] These findings suggest that

---

11 Cf. Birken-Silverman 2003, Dirim and Auer 2004, Hewitt 1986, Lytra 2006, Pujolar 2001.
12 Cf. Deppermann 2007, Hill 1995, Lytra 2006, Rampton 1995, Shankar 2004. Hewitt (1986: 135) and Rampton (1995: 60, 238, 250) discuss how language crossing draws on media fragments.

media engagement clearly transcends the monolingual context that shapes the discussion of television and language change in the first theme.

Media fragments have been found to act as contextualization cues that index a particular frame, which can disrupt or co-exist with the main on-going activity. In classroom interaction, media quotations can index a play frame and prompt funny talk that disrupts the institutional business of the classroom (Keim 2003, Lytra 2006). Others have focused on the double-voicing qualities of media fragments. Their creative recontextualization creates a tension between speaker and media voice, whereby a speaker can appropriate a media voice as part of their own contextually relevant identity or index a dissociation of speaker and voice for purposes of irony or parody. By drawing on media voices to accomplish conversational activities, speakers can distance themselves from the illocutionary force and/or the propositional content of their utterances and do things that would be considered transgressive or face-threatening if they were accomplished in their own voice (such as teasing, showing off, aggressive, sexist or racist comments etc.).[13] Media fragments can also serve as categorization devices by means of which a referent is indexed as member of a certain social category. Here media material evokes an implicit comparison between the referent (i.e. the person being categorized) and a shared media experience that entails certain category-bound properties. For example, singing a particular song as someone passes by can index a transfer of (stereotypical) attributes from the song's context to the passer-by (Spreckels 2006). Media resources can further be used to enact or reanimate a media performance (e.g. song, movie scene, commercial etc.) with varying degrees of modification and collaborative elaboration. Such impromptu performances have been reported to occur in transitional moments of an encounter, for example when conversationalists run out of steam or are uncertain about the further unfolding of the interaction (cf. Birken-Silverman 2003, Dirim and Auer 2004, Lytra 2006, Rampton 1995, Schlobinski 1989). At a higher level of abstraction, media fragments have been theorized as a resource for creating sociability, negotiating and displaying speakers' identities (Leppänen and Piirainen-Marsh 2009; Lytra 2006).In her study of how American teenagers of Indian heritage engage with Bollywood films, Shankar (2004: 317) points out that "the films provide narrative frameworks, prescripted dialogue, and socially recognizable

---

13 As Shankar (2004) points out, "Especially in the Desi context, where there are numerous social and parental restrictions placed on interacting with the opposite sex, [...] prescribed dialogues of flirting in movies are used by teens in their own conversations [...] certain dialogues can be especially instrumental to youth who are experiencing similar situations". Cf. Pujolar 2001 and Deppermann 2007 for similar findings.

registers and varieties of affect through which they enact their own dynamics of humor, flirting, conflict, and other types of talk".

The two chapters in this section further our understanding of media engagement as a practice with rich implications for socio-cultural and sociolinguistic change. Alexandra Georgakopoulou examines how (new) media experiences provide resources for everyday talk, thereby emphasizing that media engagement among young people is increasingly focused on digital media. In her case study of two girls, Georgakopoulou identifies two patterns of engagement with digital media: the popular girl, a leader in terms of media culture, is positioned by her stories as having 'media competence', for example being able to manage risk in new media spaces. Her talk about media experiences is positively assessed, e.g. frequently taken up by other participants. The less popular girl, a follower in terms of media culture, produces less media talk and is interactionally less successful with it in terms of uptake by others. Her stories position her as having experiences of trouble and being less able to handle new media. Georgakopoulou relates this difference to late-modern discourses about changing teenage femininities. The figure of 'girl power' is discursively constructed by, among other things, the ability to handle media engagement and be popular with it, whereas the opposite holds true for the 'the girl in trouble'.[14]

In her ethnography of language and communicative practices in a Turkish Saturday school in the UK, Vally Lytra examines the nexus of multilingualism, multimodality and media engagement in a transnational context. Lytra's analysis exemplifies the intersection between embodied multimodality in interaction and the mediatized multimodality of artefacts that integrate several modes and media. The pupils' engagement with mobile phones and rap music creates an alternative or background frame, which coexists with the discourses of ethnic identity and culture that predominate in official classroom activities. Lytra argues that media engagement offers resources for a dynamic coexistence of old and new cultural forms. It constitutes an alternative space of practice that proposes a "flexible, urbane response" to the tension between ethnic community and mainstream society.

The relevance of this research to sociolinguistic change might be less obvious at first sight. Indeed, this theme requires a radical departure from language change in the traditional sense and a different understanding of change altogether. It is about the mobility and 'mobilizability' (Spitulnik 1997) of language and its cir-

---

14 This also corresponds to the two sociolinguistic approaches to media reviewed so far: the figure of 'girl power' implies agency over media consumption, whereas the 'girl in trouble' figure evokes the powerless individual that is subject to media influence.

culation in society.[15] It is also about the change of the semiotic resources around which certain types of social interaction are organized. In a broader perspective, it is about shifts in interaction culture and the institutional practices by which certain types of identity are discursively constructed. I distinguish four ways in which the recontextualization of media resources is relevant to sociolinguistic change.

First, processes of conventionalization (or routinization) at the level of lexis and discourse. Media quotations are often ephemeral (Chambers 1998, Lytra 2006), and their fast pace of change is part of their social function, similarly to fashion and other trends. But some media phrases can "become normalized over years of repeated use" (Lytra 2006: 267), and this seems to hold true for quite specific categories of lexical and discourse items whose conventionalization is repeatedly attested. They include nicknames and categorizations derived from names of media celebrities or fictional characters;[16] metapragmatic discourse markers (expressions that regulate a communicative activity); and expressive interjections.[17] Conventionalized media items seem to feed into functional categories that are rich in social indexicality and undergo frequent renewal, as is indeed the case with social categorizations, intensifiers, evaluators and expressive interjections. However, the process by which media material is gradually integrated into a community or group's set of formulaic expressions is only poorly understood. It seems to entail a sort of intertextual bleaching, i.e. a decreasing interactional relevance of the fragment's intertextual link, so that its media origin is made ever less relevant in the actual instance of recontextualization.

Regardless of long-term conventionalization, the process of large-scale spread and circulation of media phrases is equally little understood. It remains to be examined how the creative recycling of media phrases in local, everyday interaction might be linked to the large-scale diffusion of media phrases that can

---

15 Spitulnik suggests "that the study of media discourse in popular culture is one such avenue for examining the dynamism and mobility of language, and that this mobility (and mobilizability) has far-reaching implications for both language change and the construction of public cultures and speech communities" (1997: 114).

16 Cf. Birken-Silverman 2003, Gillespie 1995, Spitulnik 1997, Spreckels 2006. Gillespie (1995:152) discusses how her London informants appropriated the term *Mangel* – derived from "Mrs Mangel, the key gossip character at Neighbours at the time of fieldwork" – "as a term of abuse for anyone who gossips". Spreckels (2006) discusses how a group of German female adolescents use the term *Britney* (i.e. pop star Britney Spears) as a categorization for a certain type of girls.

17 Spitulnik (1997) discusses radio phrases with the metapragmatic meaning of 'do you get it'. Examples from German include the expressive interjections *oops* originating in American English and *yoo-hoo*, which Spreckels (2006) attributes to the animation series, Simpsons.

be observed "sweeping through" a country, as Coupland (2007: 174) puts it on the example of the comedy-derived phrase *bovvered*, which illustrates the mediatization of a non-standard feature in British English, i.e. TH-fronting. When nationwide circulating media phrases include non-standard features, they act as hosts of sociolinguistic variability which gains symbolic or iconic status in the context of a particular mediatized performance.

A third aspect of change is the role of media engagement in shaping the interaction order. The key point here is that media resources of different kinds constitute increasingly common points of orientation for the establishment and management of social interaction. For example, media programmes and media devices provide typical occasions for small talk and offer conversationalists opportunities to index their group membership and lifestyle orientation. Media engagement carries considerable symbolic capital. There are followers and leaders in media engagement (Georgakopoulou, in this volume). Among young people, at least, the ability to perform with media voices and to spontaneously link media references to the topic of on-going interaction is a valued creative skill (Spreckels 2006). Not least, media devices are becoming increasingly important in establishing particular kinds of social action, as Lytra's (in this volume) parallelism of the mobile phone to the hopscotch illustrates.

These observations tie in well with the mediatization of interpersonal relationships as discussed by Krotz (2007). They make clear that the impact of media engagement practices reaches into the core empirical site of socially oriented linguistics, i.e. informal language use in private settings. To be sure, everyday talk has always been prompted by shared attention to some sort of significant object, be it media-related or not; the recycling of discourse fragments, in the broadest sense of the term, is certainly an older practice than electronic mass media. However, mediatization seems to bring a change of scale, a new order of relevance of media engagement for social interaction.

A fourth dimension of change is captured by Spitulnik's (1997) notion of "mediation of communities". Spitulnik argues that in large-scale societies, the type of communication required by the notion of speech community, (i.e. dense patterns of communication with frequency of interaction among speakers, only "occur in a vertical sense" (97), namely in people's everyday exposure to and consumption of mass media. Elements of these communication patterns are then instantiated at a horizontal level, i.e. in everyday talk, by means of people's "repeating, recycling, and recontextualizing of media discourse" (98). These recycling practices establish "an indirect connectivity or intertextuality across media consumers and across instances of media consumption" (98). Media fragments thus index joint frames of reference and thereby mediate societies into communities. Other researchers too have argued that the ability to recognize and recontextualize media quotes creates common ground and enables people to construct themselves as members of a community. Shankar (2004: 332) suggests that "the Bollywood language practices of quoting dialogue, using *filmi* registers for humor and flirting, and engaging with songs and lyrics create a media-based community". In research on the recontextualization of stylized *Türkendeutsch* (i.e. foreign-accented German associated with Turkish-background youth), Androutsopoulos (2001: 20) found that fragments of stylized speech lifted from comedy and other media genres "can be used to create an atmosphere of togetherness, in which interlocutors reassure each other that they belong to the same community of media consumption."

7 Change in mass-mediatized and digitally mediated language: Theme III

Theme III covers research that has been largely unrelated to the two preceding themes. Located in the fields of media linguistics and media discourse studies, this research focuses on change in the language and communicative norms of mass media (cf. Herring 2003). Sociolinguists interested in language change have often conceptualized the media as a centripetal domain whose potential influence basically amounts to promoting standardization (cf. Chambers 1998, 2005; Milroy and Milroy 1999: 29). This view originated in the 1970s and 1980s, a time of considerably more uniformity in media content and discourse. Today, the genres and styles of media language are much more diverse, and the hegemony of standard language is challenged by extensive sociolinguistic heterogeneity. It is by now well documented that vernacular speech styles and hybrid language forms proliferate in media discourse (cf. Androutsopoulos 2010, Coupland 2009b, de Houwer 2003), and that their spread historically coincides with processes of institutional and technological mediatization such as the diversification of target audiences, the fragmentation and multimodality of media products, and the rise of the web as a new domain of mediated communication. The chapters on Theme III link these processes to aspects of sociolinguistic change such as conversationalization, vernacularization, genre change, the multimodality of media texts, and the embedding of digital writing into professional newspaper language. These are briefly reviewed in this section.

The term conversationalization (Fairclough 1994, 1995) describes a process of change that involves "the modelling of public discourse upon the discursive practices of ordinary life" (1994: 253). By orienting to everyday styles of talk, journalists and institutional actors such as politicians or advertisers aim at symbolically bridging the gap between institutions and the everyday experience of audiences. Linguistically, this can manifest in innovative features of everyday conversational style that are used in contexts where more formal styles of speech or writing would have been expected, and in an increase of hybrid combinations of spoken and written or informal and formal features. Conversationalization promotes a restructuring of the boundary between private and public discourse and a relaxation of public language norms.

Although conversationalization was coined in a critical discourse approach that interrogates the economic and political interests and power relations behind mass-mediated discourse, its linguistic manifestations have been noticed by linguists working in other frameworks too.[18] For instance, Reynolds and Cascio (1999) show that English contracted forms (such as *it's* or *isn't*) increased in British newspaper language from the 1970s to the 1990s across newspapers with various target groups. Cotter (2003) suggests that the increase of sentence-initial connectors in American newspaper usage indexes journalists' changing strategies of relating to their audience. In her analysis, sentence-initial connectors are part of a shift from discourse to addressee orientation. They support understanding and transfer associations of informal conversation to written news discourse. As a cross-linguistically attested process of sociolinguistic change, conversationalization leads to stylistic pluralization in media language. Its directionality cannot be construed as an influence of media to community usage. Quite the opposite, it is media language that catches up with spoken language change (cf. Kristiansen, in this volume). However, the relaxation of broadcast norms can also trigger changes of usage in non-mediated contexts, as stipulated by Holly and Püschel (1993). There is evidence for such feedback concerning taboo expressions, for example, whose mediatized staging legitimizes their use in more formal face-to-face contexts (cf. Bell 2001).

The informalization of media language is itself embedded in and enabled by changes in media genres. Bell's (2003) comparison of news reports from the beginning and the end of the twentieth century suggests that immediacy of reporting enabled by audiovisual electronic media has had a dramatic impact on the development of news reporting towards conversational style. In this volume, Martin Luginbühl argues that television news offers a test bed for the study of change in media genres. Due to their complexity, television news are best regarded as a 'super genre' that is composed of different generic elements, whose configuration varies in time as well as across media channels and countries. In his study of American and Swiss television news shows during seven decades, Luginbühl coins the notion of 'genre profile' to describe the genre repertoires that make up

---

18 Cf. for German Burger (2005: 143), Schmitz (2005: 1617).

a news show, their frequencies, and their sequential order in the show. He finds only a few changes in the sequencing of the American news show, but a paradigm shift in the Swiss news show since the early 1980s. Some genre elements become obsolete, e.g. news items read by the newscaster; others gain in frequency, such as news presentation items and so-called 'packages', i.e. stories produced and told by a correspondent. The increasing segmentation of the Swiss *Tagesschau*, Luginbühl argues, is related to a changing orientation to the audience by which the structure of the news becomes more explicit, the style of reporting is more dialogue-oriented, and journalists are increasingly positioned as experts rather than just reporters. At the level of language style, these new genres create more space for conversationalization in the news.

The notion of vernacularization, as developed by Nikolas Coupland (in this volume), describes a process of sociolinguistic change by which vernacular linguistic features and speech styles gain access "into domains that have been the preserves of standardness". By this definition, vernacularization could also be understood as a part of conversationalization, and overlaps in the linguistic manifestation of the two are perhaps to be expected. However, the scope of vernacularization is narrower in terms of linguistic forms and their indexical values. The concept focuses on (regional or social) non-standard varieties of language whose indexical contrast to standardness is salient and loaded with socio-cultural associations that bear on the referent, the propositional content of the utterance, or other aspects of context.

Vernacular speech forms typically occur in certain media genres, in particular advertisements, fictional series, audience participation genres (especially reality television) and niche media for particular target groups, such as youth-oriented programmes and channels (cf. Androutsopoulos 2010a, Bucholtz 2009, Coupland 2007, 2009b). In these genres, vernacular elements are deployed in reflexive performances of identity. The language-ideological implications of vernacularization concern the impact of its higher visibility and the contextualized contrast between standard and vernacular voices within a media text or performance. Touching here on the interface to the next theme, the mediatization of vernaculars can boost their supra-regional awareness, offering opportunities for metalinguistic reflexivity and leading to "a more positive valorization of vernacularity as well as a weakening or restriction of standard language ideology" (Coupland, in this volume). However, the stylized representation of vernacular speakers and their speech is not always empowering in its indexical inferences and the audience uptakes it enables. The media stylization of vernaculars can also lead to increased social awareness of stigmatized features or speech styles, thereby further reinforcing their stigmatization (cf. Hjarvard 2004; Hill 1995; Zilles 2005; Pappas 2008).

The chapter by Ulrich Schmitz turns to a different aspect of mediatization: how changing communications technologies impact on the semiotic structure of space-bound (print and online) texts. Although Schmitz does not draw on the notion of mediatization, his argument resembles Krotz's understanding of mediatization as a process of increasing complexity and differentiation of communication means, which leads to a "highly complex and simultaneous interplay of all kinds of engineered and direct communication". Focusing on semiotic economy as a tendency of language change, Schmitz analyses the changing multimodal composition of texts across media types. Comparing issues of a local newspaper from 1946 and 2012, he suggests that the latter contains more, but shorter and syntactically less complex texts, and that the share of 'mini texts' of just a couple of sentences (such as front page teasers referring to longer reports in the same edition) has increased over time. Moving to the website of the same newspaper, Schmitz points out its multimodal structure: there is no "single conventional full text whose coherence is produced solely through written means". In interactive web services such as Google Maps, the traditional autonomy of the written text is entirely absent, and written language only comes embedded in multimodal environments. Schmitz extrapolates certain tendencies of written language change in media environments: decrease of "autonomously coherent main texts", decrease in text length, and increase of paratexts (i.e. accompanying smaller texts) and non-written elements (photographs, graphics, videos, pictograms).

The advance of digital media – computer-mediated communication – complicates the relation of mediatization and sociolinguistic change in far-reaching ways. In certain ways, digital media extends the repertoire of media organizations, which nowadays use the web to complement and in part replace their 'old' media technologies of print and broadcasting. For example, Schmitz (in this volume) argues that tendencies of written language change that are already detected in print media are taken to extremes on the web. In addition, computer-mediated communication has created new spaces of public written language communication, which originally emerged independently of the established mass media. The implications of these new public spaces for sociolinguistic change are far from clear. Certain innovations in the language of the new media, such as emoticons and abbreviations, are well documented cross-linguistically. However, hardly any of these constitute instances of structural language change (Crystal 2011), and evidence for a patterned 'spill-over' of digital written language features to other domains and modes of written or even spoken usage is limited to single lexical items and interjections. Androutsopoulos (2011) therefore argues that a structuralist understanding of language stops short from capturing the scale of sociolinguistic change that is brought about by computer-mediated communication.[19]

Drawing on the concept of *Ausbau*, Androutsopoulos (2011a) proposes to theorize sociolinguistic change in computer-mediated communication as an 'elaboration' of written language on three levels: a change of scale in the public circulation of vernacular written language; an increase in spelling variability; and a reconfiguration of written language repertoires.[20] I discuss these briefly in turn.

Computer-mediated communication makes vernacular written language – that is, language produced by non-professionals beyond institutional control– widely available in the public domain, for example in web forums and blogs, customer reviews and user comments. Ways of speaking that traditionally didn't find their way into public writing, such as regional or social dialects or minority and indigenous language, now gain opportunities of public representation (cf. Deumert, in this volume). This public vernacular writing is now often intertwined with professionally crafted and institutionally controlled written language and can thereby be transferred more easily into mainstream public written discourse (cf. Squires and Iorio, in this volume). We see here yet another take on the intermingling of the private and the public, a tendency that shapes sociolinguistic change in media discourse in general.

The massive change of scale in public vernacular written language has repercussions at a micro-level of spelling variability and a macro-level of written language repertoires. Digital writers transcend normative orthography, for example to represent allegro forms or vernacular speech, to simulate spoken language prosody, or to shorten the message. Spelling thus gains importance as a domain of sociolinguistic variation, thereby challenging the traditional sociolinguistic perspective on spelling as the most invariant level of linguistic structure (cf. Sebba 2007, Squires 2012). Unconventional spellings in digital writing neither replace standard orthography nor lead to a loss of normative awareness. Rather, evidence suggests that speakers broaden their written language repertoires by developing new styles of written language without entirely abandoning the formal written

---

19 The remainder of this section draws on Androutsopoulos (2011a).

20 The notion of elaboration differs from *Ausbau* (cf. Haarmann 2004). *Ausbau* describes an extension of written language use into new institutional domains as part of a broader language standardization process. However, the elaboration of digital written language is, at least in Europe, a 'post-standardization' process in the sense that it is carried out against the backdrop of fully standardized national languages. Moreover, *Ausbau* extends the written use of a language beyond the field of 'everyday prose' and towards increasingly abstract and technical written registers. By contrast, much digital written language is part of everyday language practices, which are being recontextualized and extended by means of digital media.

language that is required for non-digital, non-vernacular settings. In this process, the metapragmatic awareness of variability in written language changes too. The elaboration of digital written language thus implies a pluralization and localization of the ways in which written language can index social identity. Written language norms are pluralized to the extent distinct styles of writing are deemed appropriate for different communicative circumstances, and localized to the extent certain written language forms only circulate in specific online communities or networks. With regard to orthography and punctuation, the elaboration of digital written language can be thought of as a process of destandardization in the sense of status change (rather than structural change).[21] The normative claim of standardized orthography is challenged and partially replaced by smaller-scale conventions.

Two caveats are in order here. First, the elaboration of digital written language as a process of sociolinguistic change is more complex than a linear development towards greater destandardization or vernacularization. The small amount of available diachronic research on feature-based language change in CMC suggests that phases of innovative destandardization give way to more conventional, standard-oriented usage.[22] Second, interfaces of unregulated digital writing with standardized media language must be considered too. In this volume, Lauren Squires and Josh Iorio examine such an interface: how Twitter messages by celebrities are quoted in news reports. The authors examine the occurrence of 'netspeak' features and representations of prosody in reported tweets from 2009–2011. Their findings suggest that the non-standard orthography that is regarded as iconic of Twitter decreases over time. As a result, reported tweets gradually become less deviant from the orthographic norm of newspaper language. As the authors point out, "rather than the growth of new media pushing highly regulated spaces of discourse to relax their standards [...] the language of tweets is represented as being in closer alignment with the language of the standard news media itself." Squires and Iorio link this development both to editing practices by journalists and to the regulation of celebrity athletes' tweets by their professional institutions.

---

21 As described by Auer (1997) and Coupland (2009a), destandardization implies a language-ideological shift by which the standard variety loses (some of) its generally binding normative claim and is replaced in that regard by a number of smaller-scale standards (e.g. regional standards).

22 For example, a recent study on language change in French chat interaction (Strätz 2011) shows for a course of five years a decrease in performance mistakes (typos), increase in syntactic complexity and punctuation norms, decrease in abbreviations and a range of stylistic changes towards more communicative distance, i.e. more formal styles of writing.

8 Enregisterment of change in media discourse: Theme IV

Variability and change in language have long been subject to commentary and debate in the media (cf. Blommaert 1999; Milroy and Milroy 1999). Language changes in progress can be stigmatized in the media, thereby increasing the "overt social awareness" (Zilles 2005: 44) of the on-going change. The assumption that the media has an influence on language use is widespread and often put forward in media discourse itself, and media language is often held responsible for declining standards of usage (cf. Moschonas, in this volume; Thurlow 2006). Against this backdrop, Theme IV focuses on representations of linguistic change in media discourse. The three chapters examine how media discourse contributes to the enregisterment of sociolinguistic change, and how metalinguistic reflection among professional journalists constructs change in media usage.

Mass media – and increasingly also new media – are widely regarded as an influential site of metalinguistic discourse (see Blackledge 2005; Blommaert 1999; Johnson and Milani 2010; Johnstone 2011). As Milani and Johnson (2010: 4) put it, "the power of the media in language ideological processes lies to a considerable extent in their practices as gatekeepers in the regimentation of 'expert systems' (Giddens 1991) on language related issues." The media, they continue, open up discursive spaces, "thereby giving a public voice to a variety of social actors who compete with each other in staking various claims regarding what counts as *legitimate* knowledge in the domain of language" (Milani and Johnson 2010: 4). Metalinguistic discourse in the public sphere involves actors from various institutions and a range of discourse practices by which metalinguistic labels, classifications and distinctions are proposed, thereby often reproducing relations of social inequality and exclusion.

The chapters in this Section draw on three influential frameworks of language-ideological analysis that are widely used in sociolinguistic studies of metalinguistic discourses in the media. These are the semiotic processes of language ideology formation by Irvine and Gal, Silverstein's framework of indexical order, and Agha's framework of enregisterment. Irvine and Gal (2000) propose an analysis of language ideology formation in terms of three semiotic processes, i.e. iconization, fractal recursivity, and erasure. Their framework has been used to examine media representations of new varieties of national languages among migrants and migrant-background youth (cf. Androutsopoulos 2010b, Milani 2010). Silverstein's notion of orders of indexicality centres on the idea that indexical meanings in a community's linguistic repertoire are hierarchically organized (Silverstein 2003, Blommaert 2007, Johnstone, Andrus and Danielson 2006, Johnstone 2010). Orders of indexicality denote "a stratified general repertoire,

in which particular indexical orders relate to others in relations of mutual valuation – higher/lower, better/worse" (Blommaert 2007: 117). Three levels of indexical meaning are distinguished: first-order indexicality denotes observable correlations between linguistic forms and social categories, which are however not
deployed by speakers themselves in meaning-making. Second-order indexicality
occurs "when people begin to use first-order correlations to do social work, either
interpretive or performative" (Johnstone et al. 2006: 83). Third-order indexicality
is the stage at which enregistered speech forms become available for "reflexive
performances of local identities" (Johnstone et al. 2006: 83).

Enregisterment is defined by Agha (2003: 231) as the process by which "a
linguistic repertoire becomes differentiable within a language as a specially recognized register of forms". Discourse registers involve linguistic resources on
various levels of structure (lexis, prosody, constructions), which are associated
with social groups or practices (Agha 2007: 147–154). This association is established by means of metapragmatic stereotypes, which link speech forms with
recognizable speaker stereotypes and social contexts of use (Johnstone 2011).
The metapragmatic typification of a register can be found in "everyday reflexive behaviors" and "metadiscursive genres", including journalistic, literary and
pedagogic representations of language use. Genres of metapragmatic discourse
include "glosses of language use; names for registers and associated speech
genres; accounts of typical and exemplary speakers; propositions on usage;
standard of appropriate use; positive or negative assessments of the social worth
of a register" (Agha 2007: 150–1). In his work on the enregisterment of Received
Pronunciation, Agha distinguishes five "genres of accent metadiscourses" (2003:
245), each with a specific scale of circulation extending to recipients with specific demographic traits, among them popular handbooks, novels and "weekly
pennies". Enregisterment includes the discursive construction of typical or
'exemplary speakers', which can change in the course of time (2003: 265).[23] In
the framework of enregisterment, mass media "formulate models of language"
(Squires 2010: 471) by making metapragmatic typifications of registers available
to large audiences for recontextualization and response. As already pointed out
in the discussion on mediatization above (Section 4), Agha emphasizes the scale

---

23 Agha's (2003) notion of 'exemplary speakers' resonates with the sociolinguistic concept
of 'model speakers' proposed by Ammon (2003) in the context of standardization. However,
Ammon's conception of 'model speakers' focuses on agents of standard norm maintenance such
as newsreaders or other professional speakers. In the light of enregisterment theory, it seems
more useful to assume that broadcast in late-modern societies offers a variety of 'model speakers' for the typification of registers at various levels of formality or standardness. Mediatized
model speakers can also typify covertly prestigious speech styles (cf. Cutler 1999).

of collective response that mass-mediatization enable. Mediatized circulation is the aspect of the enregisterment process by which "some events within such processes set the initial condition for very large-scale forms of response" (2003: 269). Agha points out: "However particular audiences may respond, most of them are responding to the same thing" (2003: 266).

A recent study of sociolinguistic change that builds on indexicality and enregisterment is the research on Pittsburghese by Barbara Johnstone and associates (cf. Johnstone 2004, 2009, 2010, 2011). Framed as "a particularistic approach to linguistic and ideological change" (Johnstone et al. 2006: 77), this research links the public circulation of language ideologies to processes of sociolinguistic change in Pittsburgh's urban community. Its findings suggest that mediatization becomes relevant at the third level of indexical order, whereby features perceived as belonging to Pittsburghese are explicitly talked about and used in reflexive performances of identity. While second-order indexicality arises as a consequence of mobility, with speakers from Pittsburgh becoming aware of particularities in their own speech, third-order indexicality emerges as incomers to the city of Pittsburgh seek linguistic resources by which to position themselves towards established local identities. Pittsburghese features that are already enregistered become available for stylization to young locals whose own vernacular speech is less locally marked than the speech of their parents' generation. In this process, the indexical meaning of Pittsburghese features shifts from class to place: features that were previously perceived as signifiers of working class are now heard as indices of local urban identity. As Johnstone et al. (2006: 84, 94) point out, a range of media representations contribute to this process:

> Only a subset of the features of regional speech have been taken up into the third order of indexicality, in which using words and pronunciations from a highly codified repertoire is a way people who may have few of the resources for second-order indexicality can show that they know how Pittsburghers sound. [...] These people notice regional speech features, now as often in mass media representations like folk dictionaries and Web sites that metapragmatically link regional speech and local identity as by actually interacting with locals engaging in metapragmatic practices that link local forms with class and correctness. They use them in reflexive, self-conscious attempts to claim local identity by displaying local knowledge.

The mediatized representation of language varieties involves a multitude of genres (e.g. reports, radio features, online discussions, encyclopaedia entries, academic articles, folk dictionaries, merchandise); discourse spaces (e.g. newspapers, local broadcasting, web discussion forums); and 'ideology brokers', including journalists and language scholars (Androutsopoulos 2010b, 2011b; Kerswill, in this volume). Local and participatory media increasingly gain importance in the 'making' of new dialects (Johnstone 2011). Likewise, the enregisterment of 'net-speak' unfolds by means of speech chains that link mediatized representations to mediated responses, e.g. discussions in internet forums (Squires 2010).

In this volume, Paul Kerswill examines media representations of Jafaican ('fake Jamaican'), a recent label by which British newspapers refer to multi-ethnic vernacular forms of London English. Kerswill's account links a corpus and discourse analysis of 'Jafaican' to previous extensive research on Multicultural London English, thereby assessing mediatized representations against the backdrop of spoken language innovations. Kerswill uses the concept of mediatization in Jaffe's sense, i.e. the staging of metalinguistic discourse in media reports. He identifies a number of both positive and stigmatizing discourses which link Jafaican to social problems, entertainment culture, and socio-demographical change in London.

The notion of enregisterment seems particularly well suited to study the discursive construction of speech forms that are perceived as recently emerging in the context of socio-demographic and technological change. However, enregisterment processes are also at work when regional dialects – themselves the outcome of earlier processes of enregisterment – become anew the subject of metadiscursive awareness, with their indexical values being refashioned in the course of broader socio-economic and cultural changes such as regionalization and commodification. Johnstone's finding in the case of Pittsburghese is an indexical shift, or reindexicalization, of local features from meanings of class to those of place, would seem to hold true for other cases where regional dialects are metadiscursively transformed into emblems of commoditized places. Merchandise targeted to tourists and diaspora communities is a resource in this continuous reindexicalization (cf. Beal 2009, Johnstone 2009). The reinterpretation of indexical links between local speech forms, discursive practices and social identities can be observed in audio-visual performances too. For example, a study of the performance of German dialects in amateur videos on *YouTube* finds that "dialect discourses on *YouTube* destabilize existing mass-mediated regimes of dialect representation by pluralizing the performance and stylization of dialects"(Androutsopoulos 2013: 66). This study found that representations of the Berlin city dialect on *YouTube* transgress the traditional stereotype of the male, working class dialect speaker and stage new 'exemplary speakers' of the city dialect such as trendy young women and technologically savvy men. These representations are available for public evaluation and comment, illustrating how social media extend the authority to participate in enregisterment. We see here a topic worth in pursuing in further research: how mediatization induces shifts in the construction of public metadiscursive expertise (cf. Johnstone and Baumgart 2004).

Given the role of journalists in the production of mass media language, it is surprising that little attention has been paid to their practices in the context of language change. The second topic covered in this section is how journalists thematize linguistic change in and through the media.

The chapter by Colleen Cotter examines how an influential stylebook for professional journalists responds to linguistic and social change. Drawing on ethnographic research into journalistic practices and linguistic analysis of newspaper discourse, Cotter conceptualizes language attitudes in the professional community of journalists as a tension between the 'protection' of standards and the 'promotion' of innovations. News professionals see themselves as agents of the maintenance of language standards. They endorse a journalistic language ideology that builds on the principle of consistency and engage "in prescriptive routines at every level of practice" (Cotter, in this volume). At the same time, they act as promoters of innovations in language use and "consciously alter their usage patterns to reflect social change in progress". Cotter's analysis of several print editions and the online version of the Associated Press Stylebook suggests that the stylebook claims to feature "entries that reflect the language of our world". Its new or amended recommendations primarily concern 'socially sensitive' and 'politically correct' lexical items. However, its recommendations on grammatical rules remain consistent through time. The stylebook's responses to language change do not match actually observable patterns of structural change in the language of news, e.g. the frequency of determiner deletion (Bell 2011) or the general tendency of economy and fragmentation (cf. Schmitz, in this volume). Nonetheless Cotter concludes that journalists' awareness of change in language "is more attuned than one might think".

In his chapter, Spiros Moschonas asks how journalists and language experts conceptualize the effects of broadcast media on language change. While Cotter focuses on the community of news professionals, Moschonas emphasizes the fuzzy boundaries between lay, expert and academic metalinguistic discourse, pointing out that some folk conceptions of language change "are being propagated in and through the print media by linguists themselves". Based on a corpus of Greek newspaper data from 1986–2011, Moschonas outlines a "conceptual topology" of language-related issues, which include a strong belief in media-induced language change, language relativism, prescriptivism, and standardization. The metalinguistic discourse of Greek newspapers is predominantly prescriptivist and equates language change to deviation from written language norms. This discourse is also characterized by "an unequivocal belief in the reality of media-induced language change" (Moschonas, in this volume). Commenters share the assumption that mass media language creates standards by the mere reality of its large-scale reception and traditional authority. Interestingly, various types of media are assessed differently in terms of their assumed effects on language: print media are viewed as 'protectors' (in Cotter's sense) of language standards, whereas television and the internet are held responsible for introducing or propagating undesired linguistic changes.

As several chapters in this volume suggest, understanding the language-ideological processes that are associated with mediatization is in the centre of the current discussion of media and sociolinguistic change (cf. in particular the chapters by Coupland, Kristiansen, Stuart-Smith and Ota, Moriarty, and Pietikäinen). In a traditional sociolinguistic perspective on language change, metalinguistic discourse gains relevance only to the extent it correlates with language change at the feature level. However, Kristiansen (in this volume) and Johnstone maintain that "the existence of second-order indexical relations eventually influences the first-order 'facts on the ground', since the sociolinguistic value of a form affects the demographic distribution of its use" (Johnstone et al. 2006:84). For example, representations of German ethnolects in film, comedy and media discourse (Androutsopoulos 2001, 2010b, 2011b) have given rise to sociolinguistic knowledge, which is then indexed, by means of intertextual chains, in subsequent media representations. Metalinguistic representations in the media are readily available for recontextualization in various discursive sites. They can be thematized in pedagogic publications, stylized in talk shows or prompt an avoidance of enregistered features on the part of the speakers in their encounter with a fieldworker (cf. Auer 2013). Androutsopoulos (2011b) describes how schoolbooks on the German language recontextualize earlier media reports and comedy catch phrases in their representation of "the ethnolect" as a new variety of German. In a framework of sociolinguistic change, then, we can ask how mediatized represenations of language in society prompt subsequent mediatized representations and mediated responses in which audiences creatively recontextualize media fragments by exemplary speakers into their own performances.

9 Mediatized spaces for minoritized languages: Theme V

Theme V introduces a field of language-media relations in which several processes discussed so far are interrelated. It focuses on the role of (mass and new) media in the development of languages that can be regarded in certain ways as 'functionally incomplete'. By this I mean the opposite of what Moring (2007) calls 'functional completeness': a state where "speakers of the language, if they so choose, can live their life in and through the language without having to resort to other languages, at least within the confines of everyday matters in their community (Moring 2007:18).[24] Incompleteness in Moring's sense seems character-istic for languages which lack *Ausbau*, i.e. elaboration in function, in particular towards scientific prose (cf. Haarmann 2004). We can distinguish languages that never achieved 'completeness' from languages that are in the process of losing an earlier stage of 'completeness'. The former include for example indigenous lan-guages that lack codification and mass literacy (see Deumert, in this volume), the latter include so-called threatened and/or endangered languages that are losing public and institutional domains, Low German and Yiddish being examples.[25] In any case, languages characterized by 'functional incompleteness' are typically minoritized languages regardless of their historical trajectory and official status.

Media are implicated in the current development of 'incomplete' languages in ways that are historically distinct, but functionally related. As is well known, the media are often seen as an important part of the maintenance or revitalization of threatened and endangered languages (cf. Moriarty and Pietikäinen, in this volume). More recently, computer-mediated communication has been regarded as relevant to the functional expansion of indigenous languages towards liter-acy and public representation (cf. Lexander 2011 and Deumert, in this volume). The three chapters in this section discuss both developments. Before turning to a short summary, a brief overview of research in this field is given.

Probably the earliest sociolinguistic account of the role of media for minori-tized languages is Joshua Fishman's model of Reversing Language Shift (Fishman 1991, 2001), which represents the revitalization of a threatened language as an eight-step process that leads from the reconstruction of intergenerational trans-mission to the presence of the language in public and institutional domains. The media appear at the model's two "top stages": stage 1 features nationwide mass media; stage 2 includes local regional media. Fishman is critical of the relevance of media to RLS. Being part of a "high power" stage, mass media are in his view "particularly problematic for [threatened languages] because of the [majority group's] social control" (Fishman 2001: 473). Minority language media are in Fishman's view "often very pale imitations of [majority language] media" (473).[26] However, Fishman makes a distinction between mass media and what he

---

24 Discussing minority language media, Moring (2007) distinguishes 'functional completeness' (the actual use of minority language media by speakers) from 'institutional completeness' (the availability of a range of media types and media content to a minority language community).

25 The two types are not clear-cut. For example, Corsican combines aspects of both.

26 Fishman argues, "Black English media programmes have not made Black English speakers out of 'White English' listeners" (2001: 474). But in cases such as that of 'Mike' (cf. Cutler 1999), rap music and hip-hop media have had precisely this effect. Fishman's view seems grounded in a somewhat narrow, or perhaps simply outdated, perspective on 'ethnic' media content.

terms "self-regulated communications technologies", which he views as "content neutral" and "facilitators of any stage" (482). He suggests that "RLS-teachers must be linked to each other [...] via the most modern media that can be under their own regulatory management [...] and they must become skilled at using such media for RLS purposes". However, Fishman points out that media "only creates a 'virtual community'" and cannot substitute 'real' community relations and face-to-face interactions in the RLS process (2001: 458, 473, 482). We encounter here, I would suggest, a rigid distinction between 'media' and 'community' that also characterizes earlier variationist discussions.

Research on media and minoritized languages discusses the media as both a resource for and a potential threat to revitalization and maintenance (cf. Clyne 1991: 376, Cormack 2007, Cormack and Hourigan 2007, Cotter 2001, Jaffe 2007). According to Cormack (2007: 54–5), minority language media can offer 'language support' in three ways: it "puts large amounts of language use into public domain", can "function as a signifier that a community is fully modernized, capable of taking part in contemporary life", and can "meld people into a sense of a larger community". Cormack also distinguishes three types of media impact on language maintenance: active promotion of language use, "opportunities and motivations for language use", and "provision of a background against which language use can be developed" (2007: 60). However, such statements seem to be driven more by the instrumental and symbolic power of broadcasting than by empirical evidence. Critical voices point out that it is very difficult to empirically establish a direct positive effect by minority language media on actual language use. Cormack himself argues against expecting "to find direct evidence of how successful or not media use has been in encouraging language use" and points out that "the role that media can play in the more direct forms of language maintenance – that is, actually encouraging people to use a language – should not be over-estimated" (Cormack 2007: 62, 66). Media provision is a necessary, but not sufficient means of minority language support (cf. Moring 2007, Moriarty, in this volume). In order to be actually used by the minority language community, media must be attractive to audiences, but this is often not the case, especially with young audiences.

More recent 'ecological approaches' (Cormack 2007) to minority language media turn from the provision of minority language content to more fleeting and transitional processes of minority language circulation across media, thereby responding to the shift from traditional mass media to digital media and cross-media networks, in which boundaries between professional and participatory authorship dissolve (cf. Theme 3 above). A recent special issue on "Jewish languages in the age of the internet" (Benor and Sadan 2011) emphasizes "the role of the internet in the maintenance of endangered languages [and] in the negotiation of language ideologies and practices" (Benor 2011: 95). It suggests that the digitally-mediated use of Jewish languages such as Yiddish, Ladino and Judeo-Greek does not lead to a fully-fledged revitalization but to a "post-vernacular" stage of predominantly symbolic rather than practical communicative use. As a site of participatory discourse, the internet enables public metalinguistic debates on the social and cultural meanings of these languages and offers opportunities for practices of 'vernacular norming'(cf. Johnstone and Baumgart 2004). This is an example for the interaction of several themes addressed in this volume.

The three chapters in this section examine the use and representation of minoritized languages in complex media ecologies and offer accounts of their fluid and often fragmented use there. The chapter by Máiréad Moriarty examines the impact of native language broadcasting on Irish and Basque students in terms of their language attitudes and reported language practices. Moriarty's analysis brings together the increasing linguistic heterogeneity in media discourse, the emergence of micro-level agents of language policy and planning, and the ideological nature of minority language media, which aim to "provide innovative contexts and practices" for minority language use (cf. also Moriarty and Pietikäinen 2011). Moriarty's results suggest that Basque and Irish students overwhelmingly regard native language television channels as "positive promoters" of the Irish and Basque language and identify certain media personalities as particularly influential promoters. However, Moriarty also argues that the impact of these channels on the community's language ideology crucially depends on the style of media programme. In the Irish case, performance genres and individual performers contribute to transforming the indexical values of Irish. Moriarty quotes evidence from online discussion boards to support the claim that Bishop's performance "triggered an ideological shift" by which "the Irish language gains a new indexical value of being cool".

In her chapter, Ana Deumert focuses on the web representation of indigenous African languages that lack mass literacy. The web presents a novel space of public visibility and written practice for these languages, yet not all web spaces are equally conductive to this. Deumert's comparison of Wikipedia and Facebook, two globally popular sites of participatory content, brings to the fore striking differences in terms of the genres and content that is contributed in isiXhosa and other African languages. The mere availability of Wikipedia articles in these languages says nothing about their content, which mostly consists of 'stubs' (i.e. short, incomplete articles) that are contributed by non-native speakers of the language. By contrast, Facebook pages devoted to isiXhosa are lively and dynamic, demanding full use of the language. Deumert explains this difference in terms of the types of knowledge and social interaction they invite. Wikipedia's "Western view of knowledge" turns out to inhibit the use of indigenous languages, but

Facebook's emphasis on digitally recontextualized social interaction makes room for elements of traditional knowledge, and genres of communicative ritual and verbal art. The chapter by Sari Pietikäinen focuses on the circulation of Sámi across Finnish media spaces. Drawing on the notion of rhizome and the framework of nexus analysis, Pietikäinen defines circulation as a "complex, rhizomatic sociolinguistic process". Even in the case of a small group of minoritized languages like Sámi, minority media spaces vary in terms of their target audiences, the cross-media spaces they operate in (e.g. combining a television programme with a website and social media pages), and the language practices and ideologies they endorse. Pietikäinen's analysis compares a "super fixed multilingual space" – a news television channel with Sámi-only language policy that tries "to police the boundaries by explicit norms and rules" – to a "strategically hybrid" space, i.e. a television comedy programme where Sámi is used together with Finnish and English in stylized performances of hybrid identities in a carnivalesque spirit.

In conclusion, Theme V examines a field of research that has been largely separate from the ones reviewed so far, and demonstrates how aspects of all five themes represented in this volume come together in practice. As far as minority language communities are concerned, the impact of media on language attitudes and use cannot be construed as 'copying' (cf. Trudgill 1986), thereby excluded from further theorizing. Having an impact on the minority community's language practices is an explicit aim of minority language media provision, and making a conscious decision to use the minoritized language is not an 'exceptional' case, as a traditional variationist view would assume. Likewise, the spread of new minority language vocabulary is not a peripheral aspect of media influence, but an important part of the intended revitalization process (cf. Moriarty, in this volume). We see in this research that "language change in minority language contexts is always [an] ideologically invested process" (Pietikäinen, in this volume). This suggests that language ideology processes ought to play a key role in the further study of mediatization and sociolinguistic change. Finally, this research demonstrates the importance of individual speakers as agents of sociolinguistic change, be it "diaspora elites" (Deumert) or performers whose mediatized language practices are widely recontextualized and responded to by audiences.

Acknowledgements

The conception of this volume originates in a thematic panel on "Interfaces between media, speech, and interaction" that was held at Sociolinguistics Symposium 17 in 2008. Most panel presenters contribute chapters to the volume. The volume's realization was facilitated by a research fellowship at the Freiburg Institute for Advanced Studies (FRIAS) from April to September 2012. I am indebted to Peter Auer, then director of the FRIAS School of Language & Literature, for his continuous support with this project. I also thank Florian Busch, postgraduate student in Hamburg, for editorial assistance in preparing the manuscript for publication.

I dedicate this volume to the sociolinguist and dear friend, Janet Spreckels (Heidelberg University of Education), who passed away too early in March 2014. Janet took part in the 2008 thematic panel, and her inspiring work on young people's media engagement lives on in this volume.

References

All weblinks last accessed and valid on 4 March 2013.

Agha, Asif 2003: The social life of cultural value. *Language and Communication* 23: 231–73.
Agha, Asif *2007: Language and social relations*. Cambridge: Cambridge University Press.
Agha, Asif 2011: Meet mediatization. *Language & Communication* 31 (3): 163–170.
Ammon, Ulrich 2005: Standard und Variation: Norm, Autorität, Legitimation. In: Ludwig Eichinger and Werner Kallmeyer (eds.), *Standardvariation: Wie viel Variation verträgt die deutsche Standardsprache?* 28–40. Berlin: de Gruyter.
Anderson, Benedict 2006: *Imagined communities: Reflections on the origin and spread of nationalism*. Revised edition. London/New York: Verso.
Andersson, Lars and Peter Trudgill 1990: *Bad language*. Oxford: Blackwell.
Androutsopoulos, Jannis 2001: 'From the streets to the screens and back again: On the mediated diffusion of variation patterns in contemporary German'. *LAUD Linguistic Agency*, A:522, University of Essen. URL: http://www.linse.uni-due.de/online-shop/details/261.html.
Androutsopoulos, Jannis 2005: „...und jetzt gehe ich chillen": Jugend- und Szenesprachen als Erneuerungsquellen des Standards. In: Ludwig Eichinger and Werner Kallmeyer (eds.), *Standardvariation: Wie viel Variation verträgt die deutsche Standardsprache?*171–206. Berlin: de Gruyter (IDS-Jahrbuch 2004).
Androutsopoulos, Jannis 2010a: The study of language and space in media discourse. In: Peter Auer and Jürgen E. Schmidt (eds.),*Language and space: An international handbook of linguistic variation. Volume I: Theory and methods*, 740–758. Berlin, New York: de Gruyter.
Androutsopoulos, Jannis 2010b: Ideologizing ethnolectal German. In: Sally Johnson and Tommaso M. Milani (eds.), *Language ideologies and media discourse*, 182–202. London: Continuum.
Androutsopoulos, Jannis 2011a: Language change and digital media: A review of conceptions and evidence. In: Tore Kristiansen and Nikolas Coupland (eds.), *Standard languages and language standards in a changing Europe*, 145–161. Oslo: Novus.
Androutsopoulos, Jannis 2011b: Die Erfindung des Ethnolekts. *Zeitschrift für Literaturwissenschaft und Linguistik* 164: 93–120.

Androutsopoulos, Jannis (ed.) 2012: *Language and society in cinematic discourse*. Special Issue, *Multilingua* 31 (2).

Androutsopoulos, Jannis 2013: Participatory culture and metalinguistic discourse: Performing and negotiating German dialects on YouTube. In: Deborah Tannen and Anna Marie Trester (eds.),*Discourse 2.0. Language and new media*, 47–71. Washington, DC: Georgetown University Press.

Auer, Peter 1997: Führt Dialektabbau zur Stärkung oder Schwächung der Standardvarietät? Zwei phonologische Fallstudien. In: Klaus J. Mattheier and Edgar Radtke (eds.), *Standardisierung und Destandardisierung europäischer Nationalsprachen*, 129–162. Frankfurt am Main: Peter Lang.

Auer, Peter 2013: Ethnische Marker im Deutschen zwischen Varietät und Stil. In: Arnulf Deppermann (ed.), *Das Deutsch der Migranten*, 9–40. Berlin/New York: de Gruyter.

Auer, Peter and Frans Hinskens 2005: The role of interpersonal accommodation in a theory of language change. In: Peter Auer, Frans Hinskens and Paul Kerswill (eds.), *Dialect change. Convergence and divergence in European languages*, 335–357. Cambridge: CUP.

Auer, Peter and Helmut Spiekermann 2011: Demotisation of the standard variety or de-standardisation? The changing status of German in late modernity (with special reference to southwestern Germany). In: Tore Kristiansen and Nikolas Coupland (eds.), *Standard languages and language standards in a changing Europe*, 161–176. Oslo: Novus Press.

Ayaß, Ruth and Cornelia Gerhardt (eds.) 2012: *The appropriation of media in everyday life. What people do with media*. London: Benjamins.

Bauman, Richard and Charles L. Briggs 1990: Poetics and performance as critical perspectives on language and social life. *Annual Review of Anthropology* 19: 59–88.

Beal, Joan C. 2009: Enregisterment, commodification and historical context: "Geordie" versus "Sheffieldish". *American Speech* 84 (2): 138–156.

Bell, Allan 1984: Language Style as audience design. *Language in Society* 13: 154–204.

Bell, Allan 1991: *Language of the news media*. Oxford: Blackwell.

Bell, Allan 2001: 'Bugger!' Media language, identity and post-modernity. *New Zealand Sociology* 16 (1):128–150.

Bell, Allan 2003: Poles apart: globalization and the development of news discourse across the twentieth century. In: Jean Aitchison and Diana M. Lewis (eds.), *New media language*, 7–17. London: Routledge.

Bell, Allan 2011: Leaving Home: De-europeanisation in a post-colonial variety ofbroadcast news language. In: Tore Kristiansen and Nikolas Coupland (eds.), *Standard languages and language standards in a changing Europe*, 177–198. Oslo: Novus.

Bell, Allan and Andy Gibson 2011: Staging language: An introduction to the sociolinguistics of performance. *Journal of Sociolinguistics* 15 (5): 555–572.

Benor, Sarah Bunin 2011: Jewish languages in the age of the Internet: an introduction. *Language & Communication* 31: 95–98.

Benor, Sarah Bunin and Tsvi Sadan (eds.) 2011: *Jewish languages in the age of the Internet*. Special Issue. *Language & Communication* 31 (2).

Birken-Silverman, Gabriele 2003: Mediale Genres im Kommunikationsstil einer Gruppe italienischer Migrantenjugendlicher. In: Stephan Habscheid and Ulla Fix (eds.), *Gruppenstile*, 247–270. Tübingen: Stauffenburg.

Blackledge, Adrian 2005: *Discourse and power in a multilingual world*. Amsterdam/ Philadelphia: Benjamins.

Blommaert, Jan (ed.) 1999: *Language ideological debates*. Berlin/New York: de Gruyter.

Blommaert, Jan 2005: In and out of class, codes and control: Globalisation, discourse and mobility. In: Mike Baynham and Anna De Fina (eds.), *Dislocations / Relocations: Narratives of displacement*, 128–141. Manchester: St. Jerome.

Blommaert, Jan 2007: Sociolinguistics and discourse analysis: Orders of indexicality and polycentricity. *Journal of Multicultural Discourses* 2 (2): 115–130.

Blommaert, Jan 2010: *The sociolinguistics of globalization*. Cambridge: Cambridge University Press.

Boberg, Charles 2000: Geolinguistic diffusion and the U.S.–Canada border. *Language Variation and Change* 12: 1–24.

Brandt, Wolfgang 2000: Sprache in Hörfunk und Fernsehen. In: Werner Besch, Anne Betten, Oskar Reichmann and Stefan Sonderegger (eds.), *Sprachgeschichte*, Vol. 2, 2159–2168. Berlin, New York: de Gruyter.

Branner, Rebecca 2002: Zitate aus der Medienwelt. *Muttersprache* 2002 (4): 337–359.

Bucholtz, Mary 2009: From Stance to Style: Gender, interaction, and indexicality in Mexican immigrant youth slang. In: Alexandra Jaffe (ed.), *Stance. Sociolinguistic perspectives*, 146–170. Oxford: Oxford University Press.

Buchstaller, Isabelle 2008: The *localization* of global linguistic variants. *English World-Wide* 29: 15–44.

Burger, Harald 2005: *Mediensprache*. Berlin/New York: de Gruyter.

Carvalho, Ana Maria 2004: I speak like the guys on TV: Palatalization and the urbanization of Uruguayan Portugese. *Language Variation and Change* 16: 127–151.

Chambers, Jack K. 1998: TV makes people sound the same. In: Laurie Bauer, Peter Trudgill (eds.), *Language myths*, 123–131. London: Penguin.

Chambers Jack K. 2003: *Sociolinguistic Theory*. 2nd ed. Oxford: Blackwell

Chambers, Jack K. 2005: Media power. Talk the talk? *Do You Speak American?* Online document. URL: http://www.pbs.org/speak/ahead/mediapower/media/

Clyne, Michael 1991: *Community languages: The Australian experience*. Cambridge: Cambridge University Press.

Cormack, Mike 2007: The Media and language maintenance. In: Mike Cormack and Niamh Hourigan (eds.), *Minority language media: Concepts, critiques and case studies*, 52–68. Clevedon: Multilingual Matters.

Cormack, Mike and Niamh Hourigan, (eds.) 2007: *Minority language media: Concepts, critiques and case studies*. Clevedon: Multilingual Matters.

Cotter, Colleen 2001: Raidióna Life: Innovations in the use of media for language revitalisation. *International Journal of the Sociology of Language* 140: 136–147.

Cotter, Colleen 2003: Prescription and practice: Motivations behind change in news discourse. *Journal of Historical Pragmatics* 4 (1): 45–74.

Coupland, Nikolas 2001: Dialect stylization in radio talk. *Language in Society* 30: 345–375.

Coupland, Nikolas 2007: *Style. Language variation and identity*. Cambridge: Cambridge University Press.

Coupland, Nikolas 2009a: Dialects, standards and social change. In: Marie Maegaard, Frans Gregersen, Pia Quist and Jens Normann Jørgensen (eds.), *Language attitudes, standardization and language change*, 27–48. Oslo: Novus.

Coupland, Nikolas 2009b: The mediated performance of vernaculars. *Journal of English Linguistics* 37 (3): 284–300.

Coupland, Nikolas (ed.) 2010: *The handbook of language and globalization*. Malden, MA: Wiley-Blackwell.

Coupland, Nikolas, Srikant Sarangi and Christopher N. Candlin (eds.) 2001: *Sociolinguistics and social theory.* London: Longman.

Crystal, David 2011: *Internet Linguistics.* London: Routledge.

Cutler, Cecilia 1999: Yorkville Crossing. White teens, hip hop, and African American English. *Journal of Sociolinguistics* 3 (4): 428–442.

De Houwer, Annick 2003: Language variation and local elements in family discourse. *Language Variation and Change* 15: 329–349.

Deppermann, Arnulf 2007: Playing with the voice of the other: Stylized Kanaksprak in conversations among German adolescents. In: Peter Auer (ed.), *Style and social identities: alternative approaches to linguistic heterogeneity,* 325–360. Berlin, New York: de Gruyter.

Deumert, Ana and Wim Vandenbussche 2003: Standard*languages: Taxonomies and histories.* In: Ana Deumert and Wim Vandenbussche (eds.), *Germanic standardizations: past to present,* 1–14. Amsterdam/Philadelphia: Benjamins.

Dirim, Inci and Peter Auer 2004: *Türkisch sprechen nicht nur die Türken. Über die Unschärfebeziehung zwischen Sprache und Ethnie in Deutschland.* Berlin/New York: de Gruyter.

Eckert, Penelope 2003: Elephants in the room. *Journal of Sociolinguistics* 7: 392–397.

Fairclough, Norman 1995: *Media Discourse.* London: Arnold.

Fairclough, Norman 1994: Conversationalization of public discourse and the authority of the consumer. In: Russell Keat, Nigel Whiteley and Nicholas Abercrombie (eds.), *The authority of the consumer,* 253–268. London: Routledge.

Fishman, Joshua A. (ed.) 1999: *Handbook of language and ethnic identity.* New York: Oxford University Press.

Fishman, Joshua A. (ed.) 2001: *Can threatened languages be saved? Reversing language shift revisited: A 21st century perspetive.* Clevedon: Multilingual Matters.

Gauntlett, David 1998: Ten things wrong with the 'effects model'. In: Roger Dickinson, Ramaswani Harindranath and Olga Linné (eds.), *Approaches to audiences – A reader,* 120–130. London: Arnold.

Giesecke, Michael 1992: *Sinnenwandel, Sprachwandel, Kulturwandel: Studien zur Vorgeschichte der Informationsgesellschaft.* Frankfurt am Main: Suhrkamp.

Gillespie, Marie 1995: *Television, ethnicity and cultural change.* London: Routledge.

Haarmann, Harald 2004: Abstand-Language – Ausbau-Language / Abstandsprache – Ausbausprache. In: Ulrich Ammon, Norbert Dittmar, Klaus J. Mattheier and Peter Trudgill (eds.), *Sociolinguistics. An international handbook of the science of language and society,* 2nd ed. Vol.1, 238–250. Berlin/New York: de Gruyter.

Hall, Stuart 1977: The Work of Representation. In: Stuart Hall (ed.), *Represenation: Cultural Representations and Signifying Practices,* 1–74. London: Sage.

Heller, Monica 2007: Bilingualism as ideology and practice. In: Monica Heller (ed.) *Bilingualism: a social approach,* 1–22. Palgrave Macmillan.

Herring, Susan C. 2003: Media and language change: Introduction. *Journal of Historical Pragmatics* 4 (1): 1–17.

Hewitt, Roger 1986: *White talk black talk. Inter-racial friendship and communication amongst adolescents.* Cambridge: CUP.

Hill, Jane 1995: Mock Spanish: A site for the indexical reproduction of racism in American English. URL: http://language-culture.binghamton.edu/symposia/2/part1/index.html.

Hjarvard, Stig 2004: The globalization of language: How the media contribute to the spread of English and the emergence of medialects. *Nordicom Review* 1–2: 75–97.

Hjarvard, Stig 2008: The mediatization of society. A theory of the media as agents of social and cultural change. *Nordicom Review* 29: 105–134.

Holly, Werner 1995: Language and television. In: Patrick Stevenson (ed.) *The German language and the real world*, 339–374. Oxford: Clarendon Press.

Holly, Werner and Ulrich Püschel 1993: Sprache und Fernsehen in der Bundesrepublik Deutschland. In: Bernd U. Biere and Helmut Henne (eds.), *Sprache in den Medien nach 1945*, 128–157. Tübingen: Niemeyer.

Holly, Werner, Ulrich Püschel and Jörg Bergmann (eds.) 2001: *Der sprechende Zuschauer: wie wir uns Fernsehen kommunikativ aneignen*. Wiesbaden: WestdeutscherVerlag.

Irvine, Judith T. and Susan Gal 2000: Language ideology and linguistic differentiation. In: Paul V. Kroskrity (ed.), *Regimes of language: Ideologies, polities, and identities*, 35–84. Santa Fe: School of American Research Press.

Jaffe, Alexandra 2007: Corsican on the airwaves: Media discourse, practice and audience in a context of minority language shift and revitalization. In: Sally Johnson and Astrid Ensslin (eds.), *Language in the Media*, 149–172. London: Continuum.

Jaffe, Alexandra 2009: Entextualization, mediatization and authentication: orthographic choice in media transcripts. *Text & Talk* 29 (5): 571–594.

Jaffe, Alexandra 2011: Sociolinguistic diversity in mainstream media: Authenticity, authority and processes of mediation and mediatization. *Journal of Language and Politics* 10 (4): 562–586.

Jensen, Klaus Bruhn 2002: *A handbook of media and communication research: qualitative and quantitative methodologies*. London: Routledge

Johnson, Sally and Tommaso M. Milani (eds.) 2010: *Language ideologies and media discourse*. London: Continuum.

Johnstone, Barbara 2004: Place, globalization, and linguistic variation. In: Carmen Fought (ed.), *Sociolinguistic variation: Critical reflections*, 65–83. Oxford: Oxford University Press.

Johnstone, Barbara 2009: Pittsburghese shirts: Commodification and the enregisterment of an urban dialect. *American Speech* 84 (2): 157–175.

Johnstone, Barbara 2010: Indexing the local. In: Nikolas Coupland (ed.), *The handbook of language and globalization*, 386–405. Malden, MA: Wiley-Blackwell.

Johnstone, Barbara 2011: Making Pittsburghese: Communication technology, expertise, and the discursive construction of a regional dialect. *Language & Communication* 31: 3–15.

Johnstone, Barbara, Jennifer Andrus and Andrew E. Danielson 2006: Mobility, indexicality, and the enregisterment of "Pittsburghese". *Journal of English Linguistics* 34: 77–104.

Johnstone, Barbara and Dan Baumgardt 2004: "Pittsburghese" online: Vernacular norming in conversation. *American Speech* 79: 115–145.

Keim, Inken 2003: Die Verwendung medialer Stilisierungen von Kanaksprak durch Migrantenjugendliche. *Kodikas/ Code. ArsSemiotica* 26: 1–2, 97–111.

Kristiansen, Tore 2001: Two standards: One for the media and one for the school. *Language Awareness* 10 (1): 9–24.

Kristiansen Tore and Nikolas Coupland (eds.) 2011: *Standard languages and language standards in a changing Europe standard language ideology in contemporary Europe*. Oslo: Novus.

Krotz, Friedrich 2007: *Mediatisierung. Fallstudien zum Wandel von Kommunikation*. Wiesbaden: VS.

Krotz, Friedrich 2009: Mediatization: A concept with which to grasp media and societal change. In: Knut Lundby (ed.), *Mediatization: Concept, changes, consequences*, 19–38. New York: Peter Lang.

Labov, William 2001: *Principles of linguistic change, Vol. 2 External factors*. Oxford: Blackwell.

Lameli, Alfred 2004: *Standard und Substandard. Regionalismen im diachronen Längsschnitt*. Stuttgart: Steiner.

Lameli, Alfred 2005: Standard und Regionalsprache – Konstanz und Wandel. In: Eckhard Eggers; Jürgen E. Schmidt; Dieter Stellmacher (eds.), *Moderne Dialekte – Neue Dialektologie*, 495–513. Stuttgart: Steiner.

Le Page, Robert B. and André Tabouret-Keller 1985: *Acts of identity: Creole-based approaches to language and ethnicity*. Cambridge: Cambridge University Press.

Leppänen, Sirpa and Arja Piirainen-Marsh 2009: Language policy in the making: an analysis of bilingual gaming activities. *Language Policy* 8 (3): 261–284.

Lexander, Kristin Vold 2011: Texting and African language literacy. *New Media & Society* 13 (3): 427–443.

Livingstone, Sonia 2009: *On the mediation of everything*. Journal of Communication 59 (1): 1–18.

Lundby, Knut 2009: Introduction: 'Mediatization' as key. In: Knut Lundby (ed.), *Mediatization: Concept, changes, consequences*, 1–18. New York: Peter Lang.

Lytra, Vally 2006: Mass media, music making and identities in an Athens primary school. In: Christa Dürscheid and Jürgen Spitzmüller (eds.), *Perspektiven der Jugendsprachforschung*, 261–280. Frankfurt am Main: Lang.

Milani, Tommaso M. 2010: What's in a name? Language ideology and social differentiation in a Swedish print-mediated debate. *Journal of Sociolinguistics* 14 (1) 2010: 116–142.

Milani, Tommaso M. and Sally Johnson 2010: Critical intersections: language ideologies and media discourse. In: Sally Johnson and Tommaso M. Milani (eds.), *Language ideologies and media discourse*, 3–14. London: Continuum.

Milroy, James and Lesley Milroy 1999: *Authority in language: Investigating language prescription and standardisation*. 3rd ed. London: Routledge

Milroy, Lesley 2008: Off the shelf or under the counter? On the social dynamics of sound changes. In: Christopher Cain and Geoffrey Russom (eds.), *Studies in the history of the English language 3*, 149–172. Berlin, New York: de Gruyter

Moriarty, Máiréad and Sari Pietikäinen 2011: Micro-level language-planning and grass-root initiatives: a case study of Irish language comedy and Inari Sámi rap. *Current Issues in Language Planning* 12 (3): 363–379.

Moring, Tom 2007: Functional completeness in minority language media. In: Mike Cormack and Niamh Hourigan (eds.), *Minority language media: Concepts, critiques and case studies*, 17–33. Clevedon: Multilingual Matters.

Muhr, Rudolf 2003: Language change via satellite: The influence of German television broadcasting on Austrian German. *Journal of Historical Pragmatics* 4 (1): 103–127.

Norris, Sigrid and Rodney H. Jones (eds.) 2005: *Discourse in action: introducing mediated discourse analysis*. London, New York: Routledge.

Ong, Walter J. 1982: *Orality and literacy. The technologizing of the word*. London/New York: Methuen.

Pappas, Panayiotis A. 2008: Stereotypes, variation and change: Understanding the change of coronal sonorants in a rural variety of Modern Greek. *Language Variation and Change* 20: 493–526.

Pennycook, Alastair 2007: *Global Englishes and transcultural flows*. London: Taylor and Francis.

Pujolar, Joan 2001: *Gender, heteroglossia and power: A sociolinguistic study of youth culture*. Berlin, New York: de Gruyter.

Rampton, Ben 1995: *Crossing. Language and ethnicity among adolescents*. London: Longman.

Rampton, Ben 1999: Deutsch in Inner London and the animation of an instructed foreign language. *Journal of Sociolinguistics* 3 (4): 480–504.

Reynolds, Mike and Giovanna Cascio 1999: It's short and it's spreading: The use of contracted forms in British newspapers: A change under way. In: Hans-Jürgen Diller (ed.), *English via various media*, 179–200. Heidelberg: Winter.

Schlobinski, Peter 1989: ‚Frau Meier hat Aids, Herr Tropfmann hat Herpes, was wollen Sie einsetzen?' Exemplarische Analyse eines Sprechstils. *Osnabrücker Beiträge zur Sprachtheorie* 41: 1–34.

Schmitz, Ulrich 2004: *Sprache in modernen Medien*. Berlin: E. Schmidt.

Schmitz, Ulrich 2005: Sprache und Massenkommunikation. In: Ulrich Ammon, Norbert Dittmar, Klaus J. Mattheier and Peter Trudgill (eds.), *Sociolinguistics*, Vol. 2, 1615–1628. Berlin: de Gruyter (HSK 3/2).

Schultz, Winfried 2004: Reconstructing mediatization as an analytical construct. *European Journal of Communication* 19 (1): 87–101.

Sebba, Mark 2007: *Spelling and society. The culture and politics of orthography around the world*. Cambridge: Cambridge University Press.

Shankar, Shalina 2004: Reel to real: Desi teens' linguistic engagement with Bollywood. *Pragmatics* 14 (2/3): 317–335.

Silverstein, Michael 2003: Indexical order and the dialectics of sociolinguistic life.*Language and Communication* 23: 193–229.

Spitulnik, Debra 1997: The social circulation of media discourse and the mediation of communities. In: Alessandro Duranti (ed.), *Linguistic anthropology. A reader*, 95–118. Oxford: Oxford University Press.

Spreckels, Janet 2006: *'Britneys, Fritten, Gangschta und wir': Identitätskonstitution in einer Mädchengruppe. Eine ethnographisch-gesprächsanalytische Untersuchung*. Frankfurt am Main: Peer Lang.

Squires, Lauren M. 2010: Enregistering internet language. *Language in Society* 39 (4): 457–92.

Squires, Lauren M. 2012: Whos punctuating what? Sociolinguistic variation in instant messaging. In: Alexandra Jaffe, Jannis Androutsopoulos, Mark Sebba and Sally Johnson (eds.), *Orthography as social action*, 289–323. Berlin/New York: Mouton de Gruyter.

Strätz, Esther 2011: *Sprachverwendung in der Chat-Kommunikation. Eine diachrone Untersuchung französischsprachiger Logfiles aus dem Internet Relay Chat*. Tübingen: Narr.

Stuart-Smith, Jane 2006: The influence of the media. In: Carmen Llamas, Louise Mullany and Peter Stockwell (eds.), *The Routledge companion to sociolinguistics*, 140–148. London: Routledge.

Stuart-Smith, Jane 2011: The view from the couch: changing perspectives on the role of the television in changing language ideologies and use. In: Tore Kristiansen and Nikolas Coupland (eds), *Standard languages and language standards in a changing Europe standard language ideology in contemporary Europe*, 223–239. Oslo: Novus.

Stuart-Smith, Jane 2012: English and the media: Television. In: Alexander Bergs and Laurel J. Brinton (eds), *Historical linguistics of English. An international handbook*, 1075–1088. Berlin, New York: Mouton de Gruyter.

Tagliamonte, Sali A. 2012: *Variationist sociolinguistics : change, observation, interpretation.* Malden, Mass.: Wiley-Blackwell.

Talbot, Mary 2007: *Media discourse: Representation and interaction.* Edinburgh: Edinburgh University Press.

Thurlow, Crispin 2006: From statistical panic to moral panic: The metadiscursive construction and popular exaggeration of new media language in the print media. *Journal of Computer Mediated Communication* 11(3). URL: http://jcmc.indiana.edu/vol11/issue3/thurlow.html.

Trudgill, Peter 1986: *Dialects in contact.* Oxford: Blackwell.

Trudgill, Peter 1988: Norwich Revisited: recent linguistic changes in an English urban dialect. *English World-Wide* 9 (1): 33–49.

Trudgill, Peter 1999: Norwich: endogenous and exogenous linguistic change. In: Paul Foulkes and Gerard J. Docherty (eds.), *Urban voices: Accent studies in the British isles*, 24–140. London: Arnold.

von Polenz, Peter 1999: *Deutsche Sprachgeschichte.* Vol. III. Berlin: de Gruyter.

Zilles, Ana M.S. 2005: The development of a new pronoun: The linguistic and social embedding of 'a gente' in Brazilian Portuguese. *Language Variation and Change* 17, 19–53.

Andreas Hepp
Mediatization.
A panorama of media and communication research

1 Introduction

The aim of this article is to outline the present status of mediatization research and its relevance for sociolinguistics. Such an undertaking is always selective as it is impossible to discuss a whole field of research in just a few pages. To reflect this problem, in the following I want to focus more on the main lines of discussion within mediatization research. For a deeper insight into detailed research results it is necessary to read the various publications quoted below. In a nutshell, the focus of this article is to give a certain "panorama" of the present status of mediatization research, the general approach and the promise it holds. However, using the term "panorama" also has further implications (cf. Hepp 2013a: 46–53): the mediatization approach gives us a "panorama" of how to integrate various detailed studies into a more general reflection on how media and communicative change is related to the transformation of our cultures and societies. With this general overview I hope to illustrate that mediatization research is also important for sociolinguistics, and that both would benefit from a deeper link.

To avoid any confusion about wording and translation (cf. for that Livingstone 2009: 3–5) it is necessary to say that also other terms than "mediatization" are used in media and communication research. For example, John B. Thompson (Thompson 1995: 46) wrote about the "mediazation of culture" when he analysed the role of media communication for the emergence of modernity. Others – especially within the German-speaking media and communication studies – prefer the term "medialization" (more about this below). However, as these terms are used to describe more or less the same phenomena, and as in the present international discussion "mediatization" has become somehow the standard, I will stick with "mediatization".

This said, I want to develop the following argumentation. First, I want to draft what I call a fundamental understanding of mediatization; that is a certain agreement on what mediatization means across the different traditions of mediatization research. Based on this I want to discuss – second – the development of mediatization research over the past decades. Here it is helpful to distinguish two traditions: the institutionalist and the social-constructivist. This helps to understand the different ways of doing mediatization research, while we have to bear in mind that there was always a certain overlap of these traditions and that recently both traditions have approached each other. This "combination" of both traditions is the core focus of the following section, in which I discuss the most recent aspects of mediatization research. All this leads to the conclusion, which is a statement linking mediatization research to sociolinguistic research more intensively.

2 A fundamental understanding of mediatization

While "mediatization" differs from the more general concept of "mediation", we nevertheless need both concepts as they designate different phenomena (cf. Couldry 2012: 134–137; Hepp 2013a: 31–38; Hjarvard 2012: 32–33). "Mediation" refers to the process of communication in general, that is how communication has to be understood as a process of mediating meaning construction. "Mediatization" is a category to describe change. In a certain sense we can link both concepts as follows: Mediatization reflects how the process of mediation has changed with the emergence of different kinds of media. This said, the concept of "mediation" describes a very fundamental moment of communication as symbolic interaction. In contrast to this, "mediatization" is much more specific in analysing the role of various media in the further process of socio-cultural change.

Fundamentally, the term "mediatization" does not refer to a single theory but to a more general approach of media and communication research. In this sense *mediatization is a concept used in order to analyse the interrelation between the change of media and communication on the one hand, and the change of culture and society on the other hand in a critical way*. In such a general orientation, the term mediatization implies quantitative as well as qualitative aspects. With regard to quantitative aspects, mediatization refers to the increasing temporal, spatial and social spread of media communication. That means that over time we have become more and more used to communicating via media in various contexts. With regard to qualitative aspects, mediatization refers to the role of the specificity of certain media within the process of sociocultural change. This means that it does "matter" which kind of media is used for which kind of communication. Some researchers understand this process of mediatization as a long-term process that has more or less been accompanying the whole history of humankind (Krotz 2009; Hepp 2013a: 46–54). Seen from such a perspective, human history is besides others a process of an intensifying and radicalising mediatization. In contrast to this, other researchers use the term of mediatization to describe the process of an increasing social and cultural relevance of the media since the emergence of so-called independent "mass media" (print, cinema, radio, television) (Hjarvard 2008; Strömbäck 2011).

In German-speaking countries as well as Scandinavia the term "mediatization" is partly used as a synonym of "medialization" (Asp 1990; Livingstone 2009: 4; Hjarvard and Finnemann 2010), especially within historical research and research on political communication. The primary argument for this is that the term "mediatization" already has a specific meaning within historical analyses, which is the suspension of the "imperial immediacy" in the German empire in Napoleonic times: A few territories were directly under the empire and therefore "immediated". The others were subordinated to a sovereign in-between (mainly a count). "Mediatization" in this context means that a territory that has been "immediated" became subordinated to a sovereign. Therefore, some media historians prefer the term "medialization" to avoid any misunderstanding.

Partly, there have been attempts to distinguish both terms in the sense that "mediatization" refers to the level of everyday media appropriation and/or the general communicative connectivity of present societies, whereas "medialization" refers to the level of institutionalized actors of the media or certain social fields and/or to what extent institutionalized ways of media representation have a certain influence in a society (cf. for example Steinmaurer 2003: 106–108). However, theses attempts were not successful, and within the international discourse the concept of "mediatization" became the core anchor (Lundby 2009b).

Within such a general frame we can distinguish two more concrete traditions of mediatization research, that is an institutionalist and a social-constructivist tradition (cf. Hepp 2013b). In the *institutionalist tradition*, media are understood more or less as independent social institutions with own sets of rules. Mediatization then refers to the adaption of different social fields or systems like, for example, politics or religion to these institutionalized rules. The latter are described as a "media logic" (Altheide and Snow 1979; Asp 1990), that is, in the widest sense of the word, institutionalized formats and forms of staging. This "media logic" on the one hand takes up non-mediatized forms of representation. On the other hand, non-media actors have to accommodate to this "media logic" if they want to be represented in the (mass) media or if they want to act successfully in a media culture and media society. Starting with such a preliminary understanding of "media logic", the concept became differentiated within that tradition, while the link to these original ideas remains.

The *social-constructivist tradition's* understanding of mediatization moves the role of various media as part of the process of the communicative construction of social and cultural reality into the foreground. Mediatization then refers to the process of a communicative construction of socio-cultural reality (Berger and Luckmann 1967; Knoblauch 2013) and the status of various media within this process is analysed (Hepp 2013a: 54–68). As a consequence, mediatization describes how certain processes of the communicative construction of reality become manifested in certain media and how, reversely, existing specifics of certain media have a contextualized "influence" on the process of the communicative construction of sociocultural reality.

In spite of these differences, both traditions of mediatization research – the institutionalist and the social-constructivist – share the argument that they reject an understanding of "mediatization research" as "effect research". This term refers to the original understanding of media influence; that is an understanding that is theorized as the "effect" of certain forms of media content (cf. for example Preiss et al. 2006). This understanding of media influence has been the subject of criticism for a long time. "Medium theory", for example, argued that the main "effect" of media is less via the communicated content but how certain kinds of media "change" our communication and perception (Meyrowitz 2009). Or the cultural studies approach can be understood as a general critique of any effect paradigm, emphasizing a "circle" of contested meaning production instead (Morley 1992: 45–58; Grossberg et al. 1998: 18–21).

In line with such a critique, the aim of mediatization research is – as already formulated – to investigate the interrelation between media communicative and socio-cultural change. These interrelations cannot be identified in an abstract way, but have to be analysed contextually and empirically. Therefore, mediatization as a concept is the starting point for various forms of empirical research, with a historical as well as a present orientation. For such a research, the concept of mediatization acts as a "panorama" (Latour 2007: 188; Hepp 2013s: 46–54) as it allows us to integrate different forms of grounded research into an overall view – or theory.

3 The development of mediatization research and theory[1]

Mediatization is not a new term of media and communication research but can be traced back to the first decades of the twentieth century and therefore to the beginning of so-called "mass communication research" (Averbeck-Lietz 2014). One example is Ernst Manheim (1933) in his post-doctoral thesis "The bearers of public opinion" (German: "*Die Träger der öffentlichen Meinung*"), which he had to withdraw because of the pressures in Nazi Germany. In this book he writes

---

1 The following is based on an argumentation developed originally in Hepp (2014).

about the "mediatization of direct human relationships" (German: "*Mediatisierung menschlicher Unmittelbarbeziehung*", 11). He uses this term in order to describe changes of social relations within modernity, changes that are marked by the so-called mass media. Jean Baudrillard (1976: 98) in "*L'échange symbolique et la mort*" (postmodern) described information as mediatized because there is no level of reality behind its mediation. Within his "Theory of Communicative Action" (German: "*Theorie des kommunikativen Handelns*", 1988a, 1988b), Jürgen Habermas uses the term mediatization to describe a sub process of the colonialization of the life world. However, he does not refer to communication media but to generalized symbolic media like power and money. In his edited volume "*Medier och kulturer*", Ulf Hannerz (1990) characterized the cultural influence of media as such (that is beyond their contents) on culture as mediatization. Or John B. Thompson writes in his book "Media and Modernity" (1995) about the "mediazation of culture", that is the increasingly irreversible mediation of culture by institutionalized mass media. These examples demonstrate that the term mediatization in its different variants is deeply related to social and cultural research as a whole. However, these general uses of the term do not offer any further theoretical consolidations.

The latter was achieved within the field of media and communication studies. Important reference points for this had been on the one hand the aforementioned "medium theory" in the tradition of Harold Innis, Marshall McLuhan and Joshua Meyrowitz (1995), on the other hand the "ecology of communication" by David Alheide and Robert Snow (Altheide and Snow 1979, Altheide and Snow 1988; Altheide 1995, 2013). The medium theory contributed the idea not only to focus on media contents but also to the influence of media in their materiality as a means of communication. While mediatization research rejects the very general and de-contextualising assumptions of medium theory, this fundamental insight of that approach is also an important reference point for mediatization research.

To understand the concept of mediatization more deeply, the ecology of communication as developed by Altheide and Snow has a higher relevance. Their point of departure was the condition of American mass communications research at the time, a practice whose focus was on media contents and their public influence. Altheide and Snow employed arguments drawn from symbolic interactionism, ethnomethodology and phenomenology to suggest that existing practice was poorly framed and directed, since "the role of media in our lives" (Altheide and Snow 1979: 7) was reduced to one among many variables affecting social processes. To understand the "role of media" they argued that it was necessary to ask how the media as a "form of communication" (1979: 9) transform our perception and our interpretation of the social. The conception of "media logic" is intended to capture this. Altheide and Snow establish, through a critical re-evaluation of classical sociological writings by Georg Simmel and Erving Goffman, that a "media logic" inheres not in media contents, but in the form of media communication. The latter should be understood as a "processual framework *through which* social action occurs" (Altheide and Snow 1979: 15, emphasis in original) – in this case, the social action of communication. This media logic as form is especially evident in the formats of mass communication, which Altheide and Snow treat as a connecting element in the entire process of the mediation of media communication – here there is a clear affinity with the work of Jesus Martín-Barbero (1993). Both authors retained this view of media logic in their later publications when dealing with the analysis of the forms and formats of mediation (see, for example, Altheide/Snow 1988; Altheide 2004). Altheide himself integrates this in a comprehensive theoretical approach of an "ecology of communication" (1995). His argument is that events as well as human action are altered by changes of information technologies and communication formats.

While Altheide and Snow themselves did not use the term mediatization but the more general concept of mediation, their arguments became an important reference point for developing the *institutionalist tradition* of mediatization research. Kent Asp (1990) was one of the first who related mediatization – or, as he wrote: "medialization" – to the assertion of a media logic. More concretely, he argues that for analysing the role of media in a society it is necessary to consider three "separate fields of influence" (Asp 1990: 48). This is, first, the field of the "market"; second the field of "ideology"; and third, the field of "*systems of norms* surrounding media production processes" (Asp 1990: 48). This third field – and here Asp explicitly refers to Altheide and Snow – can best be described as a field of "media logic". The latter is for him a "catch-all term" to summarize the dramaturgy, formats, routines and rationalities of the (mass) media. The matching to a "media logic" becomes the key of each (political) media coverage: "the extent to which the event 'fits' with media logic will decide whether or not the event will become news" (Asp 1990: 48).

In a certain sense, this idea is the initial spark of the institutionalist tradition of mediatization research, especially within political communication. This is dominated by the question of how various parts of culture and society (especially "politics") become orientated to a "media logic" (for an overview see Schrott 2009; Strömbäck 2011). Research within such a tradition had been done at various German-speaking universities, for example the University of Bielefeld (a.o. Weingart 1998), Düsseldorf (a.o. Vowe 2006), Greifswald (Donges 2008), Mainz (a.o. Kepplinger 2002) or Zurich (a.o. Imhof 2006). In further Europe we find these arguments for example at the University of Milano (Mazzoleni 2008), in Denmark at the University of Copenhagen (a.o. Hjarvard 2008) or in Sweden at the Mid Sweden University in Sundsvall (Strömbäck 2011). But also historical research on mediatization has a tendency to such an understanding of mediatization (see for example the writings by Stöber 2010; Wilke 2011). And beyond media and communication studies you can also find historical research that operates with such an understanding of mediatization (Bösch 2011).

However, it was especially Stig Hjarvard who condensed this discourse into an "institutional perspective" (Hjarvard 2008: 110). He makes two points. First of all, he is concerned with the analysis of the relationships between media as institutions and other social institutions. Secondly, and following on from this, he seeks to use the concept of mediatization to refer only to a particular form of the institutionalization of the media: "autonomous" social institutionalization, which he argues is the precondition for media institutions as such exerting an influence over other social institutions. For Europe, since the 1980s, he considers this condition to be given, as media (he includes alongside institutions of mass communication both mobile and Internet communication) became increasingly commercialized quite independently of "public steering" (Hjarvard 2008: 120). Only from this point can one speak meaningfully of "the mediatization of society [...] [as] the process whereby society to an increasing degree is submitted to, or becomes dependent on, the media and their logic" (Hjarvard 2008: 113). To give a practical example of this idea: if we think about a certain kind of medium like television, for example, this has a certain technology of representing images and sound, a technology one has to "meet" when communicating via television. Institutionally spoken, television is not only grounded in certain media organizations but also in certain formats and ways of representation that are linked to this kind of media. The main point here is that both ideas form a "logic" of television that we have to ground our communication on when we want to communicate via television.

The starting point of the *social-constructivist understanding of mediatization* is more symbolic interactionism and sociology of knowledge, but integrates also some fundamental considerations of medium theory. In a certain sense we can understand this approach as a resumption of the classical sociological reflections as we can find them in the work of Ernst Manheim (1933) (see above). Beside others, it was Friedrich Krotz who developed in his book "The mediatization of communicative action" (German: *"Die Mediatisierung des kommunikativen Handelns"*, 2001) an approach to mediatization that is more oriented towards a communication research based on practice theory and cultural studies. He understands mediatization – like individualization, commercialization and globalization – as a "meta process" of change, meaning as a comprehensive frame used to describe the change of culture and society in a theoretically informed way. In such a long-term perspective, the history of humankind can be described as a process "in whose progress more and more communication media became and become developed and used in various ways" (Krotz 2001: 33 [own translation]). However, it is crucial not to take the media as isolated phenomena but to reflect the change of communicative forms that goes hand in hand with media change: "in consequence more complex forms of mediatized communication have developed, and communication takes place more often, for longer, in more and more parts of life and in relation to more topics than media communication" (Krotz 2001: 33, originally emphasized [own translation]). This approach is linked with the argument that context-free definitions of mediatization cannot be appropriate. Therefore, we have to consider that we can distinguish various mediatization processes at different times and for different groups of people. All of them have to be described in a concrete way. The assumption of a coherent media logic is not helpful in such a perspective.

This complexity of mediatization is also emphasized by other academics, even when they position themselves between an institutionalist and social-constructivist understanding of mediatization. Winfried Schulz (2004) for example works out four different moments of mediatization in his much-noted article "Reconstructing Mediatization as an Analytical Concept". These are "extension", "substitution", "amalgamation" and "accommodation". "Extension" takes up the idea already proposed by Marshall McLuhan (McLuhan and Lapham 1994) within the framework of medium theory, discussed above, that the media are "extensions of man": that is, extensions of the possibilities of communicative action related to place, time and possible means of expression. Mediatization here means that the possibilities of human communicative action have increased with the passage of time. "Substitution" describes the fact that media have, wholly or in part, replaced social activities and social institutions. Schulz points to video and computer games which replace forms of face-to-face play. This is therefore a matter of how forms mediated by the media can displace non-media-mediated forms, this being a further moment of mediatization. "Amalgamation" describes the way in which action related to the media and action not so related become increasingly blurred and blended into one another. There are everyday examples of this that we can imagine, such as the combination of an activity unrelated to the media (driving a car) with one related to the media (listening to the radio); or using a mobile to arrange appointments while engaged in manual tasks at work. In this sense mediatization is a progressive process of amalgamation between media-related and non-media-related activities. Finally we come to "accommodation", and Schulz here uses the concept of media logic. He suggests that there is a tendency in different areas of society (politics, sport, and so forth) to become orientated to a "media logic", describing this primarily as a staging process effected by the use of television (Schulz 2004: 89). For Schulz, therefore, mediatization includes, but is not limited to the diffusion of a media logic. And additionally he defines media logic in a more narrow way than for example Stig Hjarvard does.

These arguments about the complexity and contradictoriness of mediatization are underscored by various empirical studies that focus less on the relation between mass media and politics than on the mediatization of other fields of culture and society. The interest here is especially the everyday media appropriation of the people in relation to their communicative practices. We can here for example refer to the research by André Jansson (2002) on the mediatization of consumption, Hubert Knoblauch's (2008) investigation of the mediatization of popular religion, Knut Lundby's (2011) analysis of the mediatization of faith in digital story telling, or my own research on the mediatization of communitization like diasporas or youth groups (Hepp et al. 2012; Hepp 2013a: 94–97; Hepp et al. 2014). We can take this research as an example to illustrate more in detail this approach to mediatization. Diasporas are communicatively constructed across a variety of media, beside traditional media of mass communication (television, print) increasingly digital media like email, the mobile phone or the social web. To understand this increasing mediatization of diaspora it is necessary to analyse the different media altogether. Doing this, one can demonstrate for example that with respect to the "identity orientation" of a migrant – being either "origin-oriented", "ethno-oriented" (to the diaspora) or "world-oriented" – the appropriation of the various media differs and therefore the communicative construction of his of her position within the diaspora. Following this, we cannot decipher a linear effect of one kind of media on what we call diaspora. But, if we analyse this complex "communicative figuration" (Hepp and Hasebrink 2013) altogether and compare it with earlier research on media and migration, it becomes evident that with an increasing mediatization of the diaspora the communicative articulation of this translocal and deterritorial communitization becomes more easily possible. At the same time, we can argue that the internal complexity of diasporas increases, beside others as this mediatization also supports moments of individualization. However, this is no easy effect but a "co-articulation".

The aim of research like this is to investigate the interrelation between media-communicative and socio-cultural change as part of the everyday communication practices and how the change of these practices is related to a changing communicative construction of reality. Under consideration in this kind of research are not only "classical" mass media but also the so-called "new" media of the internet and mobile communication. Increasingly, these kinds of studies have a tendency to focus on the whole "media environment", "media repertoire" or "communicative networking" of certain groups of people (cf. beside others Hasebrink/Domeyer 2012). These terms focus on different aspects: "media environment" is a concept to describe our whole surrounding of different media; the concept of "media repertoire" theorizes the individual selection of a person out of the possibility of different media; and using the term "communicative networking" we emphasize how (communicative) relations are built up with the use of different media. While these different terms consequently are necessary for describing different phenomena they all meet in the fundamental point that the present status of mediatization is marked by a "media manifold" (Couldry 2012), by "polymedia" (Madianou/Miller 2012) and "transmediality" (Evans 2011): if we want to understand the present mediatization, it seems to be necessary to grasp the entirety of different media in certain contexts instead of holding a single media view.

4 Combining the institutionalist and social-constructivist tradition

While the foregoing section emphasized the differences of the two traditions of mediatization research, the main argument at the beginning of this article was their shared fundamental position. As a reminder: We can say that both traditions share the argument that mediatization is a concept used to analyse the (longterm) interrelation between the change of media and communication on the one hand and culture and society on the other in a critical manner. This process of mediatization has two aspects; that is a quantitative and a qualitative one. Quantitatively, mediatization refers to the social, spacious and temporal spreading of technical communication media. Qualitatively, mediatization reflects the specificities of certain communication media. It is this qualitative point, where the difference of these two traditions comes in: the institutionalist tradition emphasizes with the assumption of a "media logic" the specificity of certain media as institutions – or maybe more concretely: as organizations. The social-constructivist tradition focuses rather on the specificity of media in the way that they alter communication as such.

However, and this is highly interesting, the discourse about mediatization has opened recently again in the sense that on the one hand exponents of the institutionalist tradition are re-opening the concept of media logic, and that on the other hand exponents of the social-constructivist tradition are emphasizing the necessity to also investigate the institutional dimension of mediatization. Stig Hjarvard, for example, defined mediatization in his latest book as "the process whereby culture and society to an increasing degree become dependent on the media and their logic" (Hjarvard 2013: 17). While the concept of media logic remains, it isn't in the core of this definition and is rather a "shorthand" of what he's interested in detail: "the various institutional, aesthetic, and technological modus operandi of the media, including the ways in which the media distribute material and symbolic resources, and operate with the help of formal and informal rules." (Hjarvard 2013: 17) Nick Couldry criticized in his latest book the concept of "media logic" because it unites a variety of "logics" under one "common 'logic'" (Couldry 2012: 135). On the other hand, he argues that the mediatization of politics "is arguably the clearest example of a sector where *something like* a 'media logic' is at work: in the day-to-day operations of policy generation, policy implementation and public deliberation." (Couldry 2012: 144). Therefore, an analysis of political organizations and their relation to various media that work like a "meta capital" across different social fields becomes necessary in order to be able to understand the mediatization of politics. Furthermore, Friedrich Krotz and myself argued in one recent publication that "we should describe the ways mediatization functions by what happens with communication, if individuals, institutions, and organizations use media, and if society and culture as a whole depend on specific media." (Krotz and Hepp 2013, 123 f.). By doing this, we tried to emphasize the necessity to reflect institutions and organizations also in a social-constructive perspective. We can understand arguments like these as an echo of something Knut Lundby reminded us already some years ago: "it is not viable to speak of an overall media logic; it is necessary to specify how various media capabilities are applied in various patterns of social interactions" (Lundby 2009a: 115). Maybe we can translate this statement by Knut Lundby as follows: recent research has demonstrated that the idea there would be an "overall media logic" is inappropriate; however we should not forget one core point of the institutionalist tradition, and that is to focus on the question of how processes of institutionalization change interaction and therefore also the communicative construction of our socio-cultural reality.

Two publications were an important stimulation for reaching this point of discourse. That is first the "address" written by Sonia Livingstone in 2008 as president of the International Communication Association (ICA), published in 2009. Her main argument within this publication is that the present media and communication change results in an increasing "mediation of everything". This is the main challenge for media and communication studies in a double sense: it is a challenge for the research agenda because the "mediation of everything" questions the idea that media as external institutions have an "effect" on other fields of culture and society. Therefore, we need new ways of research to analyse media communication critically. Second, it is a challenge for the discipline as it questions its well-defined area of research. If "everything is mediated" the borders of media and communication studies become blurred. Within such a frame, Sonia Livingstone discusses an integrative mediatization research as one possibility to handle these challenges.

The second publication that made this integrative move possible was the book "Mediatization: Concept, Changes, Consequences", edited by Knut Lundby

(Lundby 2009b). By bringing the various parts of the discussion about mediatization together, this book for the first time moved beyond the scope of former, well defined research traditions that also marked former handbook articles written about mediatization (cf. for example Mazzoleni 2008). Doing this, the book was an important impulse bringing the international discussion together and re-opening it. In this sense the above quoted argument by Knut Lundby can be understood as the core outcome of the volume's discussion in all.

As a result of this, it is not astonishing that the mediatization research has experienced dynamic progress during the last years. The core of this dynamic is that existing theoretical reflections on mediatization were taken as a base for empirical research to bring the "mediatization debate" (Couldry 2012: 134) forward. Recent research is becoming integrated into research networks and clusters. An early example for this move is the research network "Mediatized Stories. Mediation Perspectives on Digital Storytelling among Youth", funded by the Research Council of Norway 2006 to 2011 (for the results cf. Lundby 2008, 2014 and the issue 10 (3) of New Media & Society). Present examples are the "National Center of Competence in Research Democracy" at the University of Zurich with its research on the mediatization of politics (http://www.nccr-democracy.uzh. ch); the DFG funded priority research programme "Mediatized Worlds" that is coordinated at the ZeMKI, University of Bremen, and which focuses on the social world resp. life-world dimension of mediatization (http://www.mediatisiertewelten.de); or the research cluster "The Mediatization of Culture", which researches the relevance of digital media for the present cultural change at the University of Copenhagen (http://mediatization.ku.dk). And very recently, a research network of the Universities of Bremen and Hamburg was established to investigate the "communicative figurations" of mediatized cultures and societies (http://www. kommunikative-figurationen.de). Hand in hand with this we are confronted with an increasing international institutionalization of mediatization research. The most prominent example for this is the working group "Mediatization" (http:// www.mediatization.eu) within the European Communication Research and Education Association (ECREA). All this is reflected by a growing number of special issues of journals, for example with "Communications: European Journal for Communication Research" (2010, issue 35: 3), "Culture and Religion" (2011, issue 12: 2), "Empedocles: European Journal for the Philosophy of Communication" (2012, issue 3: 2) and "Communication Theory", the latter on "Conceptualising Mediatization" and being edited by Nick Couldry and myself (2013, issue 23: 3).

This said, future mediatization research has to handle at least four empirical and theoretical challenges. First of all, and based on the argument of the long-term process of mediatization, it becomes more necessary than ever before to integrate historical research more deeply into the research networks and clusters.

If mediatization research wants also to argue historically, it becomes necessary to develop a "historical mediatization research" that goes beyond the existing media history and is more concerned with the change of communication across the variety of changing media environments in total (cf. Averbeck-Lietz 2014). Second, the existing empirical foundation as well as theoretical orientation of mediatization research is very much oriented to the "West". Here there should be an "internationalization" (Thussu 2009) and "de-westernization" (Curran and Park 2000) of mediatization research, which means that there should be a shift of focus to regions as well as theoretical approaches beyond Europe or North America (Krotz 2014). Third, a challenge for empirical mediatization research that is occupied with present phenomena is to research "change" in a methodologically appropriate way. This means on the one hand to undertake long-term studies (*diachronous mediatization research*), and on the other hand to analyse certain turmoil situations in detail (*synchronous mediatization research*) (Hepp 2013b). For both forms of mediatization research it is necessary to develop the analytical instruments further. Fourth and finally, there is the huge challenge of integrating empirical studies on various mediatization phenomena into an overall theorising that won't become too abstract and won't lose its contextual sensitivity (Jensen 2013). However, exactly this is our main task when bearing the promises of mediatization research in mind. These four challenges demonstrate that the potential of mediatization research lies in a broad, (trans)culturally and (trans)nationally comparative research, that is historically informed and aimed at theory development.

5 Mediatization research and sociolinguistics

The arguments developed so far demonstrate that mediatization research is deeply rooted in media and communication studies. Here, the core focus is not the language as such but media communication. However, there are many links between mediatization research and the research agenda of sociolinguistics, especially if the latter is also interested in questions of "language in the media" or "media language". The core link is "communication". As outlined so far, the idea of present mediatization research is to investigate the change of media and communication in its interrelation with socio-cultural change by arguing that with media communicative change we are confronted with a change of the communicative construction of socio-cultural reality. Media and communication scholars focus at this point mainly on the "forms", "practices", "genres", "discourses", "contents", "actors", "technology" etc. of this changing communication as well as their institutional and organizational contexts. The interest is less on language itself. However, as we know from medium theory (cf. for example Ong 2002) this change of mediatization is also related to the change of language as such – at least in the long run. Just to name a historical and present example: the development of "standard languages" is deeply linked – beside other things – to mediatization as "standard languages" were built up first in orderly rooms and then by the printing press (beside other, non-media institutions; cf. Coupland and Kristiansen, in this volume). And recent developments in youth language cannot be understood beyond the mediatization of youth life in total (cf. Georgakopoulou and Lytra, in this volume).

At present, we do not have any deep cooperation between mediatization research and sociolinguistic research. Exemplarily, this can be proven by the fact that we find only rare references to sociolinguistics in mediatization research. A seldom early attempt to build a bridge from the side of mediatization research was a publication by Stig Hjarvard (2004) on the role of mediatization for the globalization of language. But also sociolinguists who use the term mediatization do this mainly without reflecting the knowledge of mediatization research (see *Androutsopoulos, in this volume*). In the journal "Language & Communication", for example, Asif Agha published recently an editorial article entitled "Meet Mediatization". In this article he argues that "mediatization is to speak of institutional practices that reflexively link processes of communication to processes of commoditization" (Agha 2011: 163). However, this understanding is developed without any references to mediatization research being undertaken by scholars of media and communication studies – and therefore Agha's definition is rather vague compared with the complexity of the mediatization approach discussed in this article so far. Another example might be Alexandra Jaffe. She recently defined mediatization a something that "refers to the organizational and orientational role performed by the media with respect to mutual perception, the allocation and adoption of diverse social roles, and human communication in general" (Jaffe 2011: 565, quoting Schmitz 2004 in Johnson and Ensslin 2007: 13). Again this is a rather narrow definition without any reference to the research within media and communication studies.

This said, a link between media and communication studies on the one side and sociolinguistics on the other side would be highly necessary for a productive discourse and adaption of this concept in sociolinguistics. Taking the best of both fields, it would become possible to discuss more detailed questions like, for example, the interrelation between mediatization and language change. And if we consider the most recent publications, there are very promising examples for that (cf. for example Dang-Anh et al. 2013). My hope with this article is that it opens such a discussion on how we can develop and deepen this collaboration.

In any case it would be an enormous stimulation – for mediatization research as well as for sociolinguistics.

References

Agha, Asif 2011: Meet mediatization. *Language & Communication* 31: 163–170.
Altheide, David L. 1995: *An Ecology of Communication: Cultural Formats of Control*. New Brunswick: AldineTransaction.
Altheide, David L. 2004: Media Logic and Political Communication. *Political Communication* 21: 293–296.
Altheide, David L. and Robert P. Snow 1979: *Media Logic*. Beverly Hills: Sage.
Altheide, David L. 2013: Media logic, social control and fear. *Communication Theory* 23 (3): 223–238.
Altheide, David L. and Robert P. Snow 1988: Toward a theory of mediation. In: James A, Anderson (ed.), *Communication Yearbook* 11, 194–223. Newbury Park: Sage.
Asp, Kent 1990: Medialization, media logic and mediarchy. *Nordicom Review* 11: 47–50.
Averbeck-Lietz, Stefanie 2014: Understanding mediatization in "first modernity": Sociological classics and their perspectives on mediated and mediatized societies. In: Knut Lundby (ed.): *Mediatization of communication*, in print. Berlin: de Gruyter.
Baudrillard, Jean 1976: *L'échange symbolique et la mort*. Paris: Gallimard.
Berger, Peter L. and Thomas Luckmann 1967: *The Social Construction of Reality: A Treatise in the Sociology of Knowledge*. London: Penguin.
Bösch, Frank 2011: *Mediengeschichte. Vom asiatischen Buchdruck zum Fernsehen*. Frankfurt a.M.: Campus.
Couldry, Nick 2012: *Media, Society, World: Social Theory and Digital Media Practice*. Cambridge, Oxford: Polity Press.
Couldry, Nick/Hepp, Andreas: 2013: Conceptualising mediatization: Contexts, traditions, arguments. *Communication Theory* 23 (3): 191–202.
Curran, James and Myung-Jin Park (eds.) 2000: *De-Westernizing Media Studies*. London/New York: Routledge.
Dang-Anh, Mark, Jessica Einspänner and Caja Thimm 2013: Mediatisierung und Medialität in Social Media: Das Diskurssystem „Twitter". In: Konstanze Marxand Monika Schwarz-Friesel (eds.), *Sprache und Kommunikation im technischen Zeitalter. Wieviel Internet (v)erträgt unsere Gesellschaft?*, 68–91 Berlin/Boston: de Gruyter.
Donges, Patrick 2008: *Medialisierung politischer Organisationen. Parteien in der Mediengesellschaft*. Wiesbaden: VS Verlag für Sozialwissenschaften.
Evans, Elizabeth 2011: *Transmedia Television: Audiences, New Media, and Daily Life*. London: Routledge.
Grossberg, Lawrence, Ellen Wartella, and D. Charleds Withney 1998: *MediaMaking. Mass Media in a Popular Culture*. London: Sage.
Habermas, Jürgen 1988a: *Theorie des kommunikativen Handelns. Bd. I. Handlungsrationalität und gesellschaftliche Rationalisierung*. Frankfurt a. M.: Suhrkamp Verlag.
Habermas, Jürgen 1988b: *Theorie des kommunikativen Handelns. Bd. II. Zur Kritik der funktionalistischen Vernunft*. Frankfurt a. M.: Suhrkamp Verlag.
Hannerz, Ulf (ed.) 1990: *Medier och kulturer*. Stockholm: Carlsson.

Hasebrink, Uwe and Hanna Domeyer 2012: Media repertoires as patterns of behaviour and as meaningful practices: A multimethod approach to media use in converging media environments. *Participations: Journal of Audience & Reception Studies* 9: 757–783.

Hepp, Andreas 2013a: *Cultures of Mediatization*. Cambridge: Polity Press.

Hepp, Andreas 2013b: The communicative figurations of mediatized worlds: Mediatization research in times of the 'mediation of everything'. *European Journal of Communication* 28(6): 615–629.

Hepp, Andreas, Cigdem Bozdag and Laura Suna 2012: Mediatized migrants: Media cultures and communicative networking in the diaspora. In: Leopoldina Fortunati, Raul Pertierra and Jane Vincent (eds.), *Migrations, Diaspora, and Information Technology in Global Societies*, 172–188. London: Routledge.

Hepp, Andreas, Matthias Berg and Cindy Roitsch 2014: Mediatized worlds of communitization: Young people as localists, centrists, multi-localists and pluralists. In: Andreas Hepp and Friedrich Krotz (eds.): *Mediatized Worlds: Culture and Society in a Media Age*, 174–203. London: Palgrave.

Hepp, Andreas and Uwe Hasebrink 2013: Translocal communicative figurations. In: Communicative Figurations | Working Papers, No 2 http://www.kommunikative-figurationen.de/fileadmin/redak_kofi/Arbeitspapiere/CoFi_EWP_No-2_Hepp_Hasebrink.pdf (16.5.2013).

Hjarvard, Stig 2004: The Globalization of language. How the media contribute to the spread of English and the emergence of medialects. *Nordicom Review* 1–2: 75–97.

Hjarvard, Stig 2008: The Mediatization of Society. A Theory of the Media as Agents of Social and Cultural Change. *Nordicom Review* 29: 105–134.

Hjarvard, Stig 2012: Doing the Right Thing. Media and Communication Studies in a Mediatized World. *Nordicom Review* 33: 27–34.

Hjarvard, Stig 2013: *The Mediatization of Culture and Society*. London: Routledge.

Hjarvard, Stig and Niels Ole Finnemann 2010: Medialisering. In: Soren Kolstrub, Gunhild Agger, Per Jauert and Kim Schroder (eds.), *Medie- et kommunikationsleksikon*, 311–312. Kopenhagen: Samdunfslitteratur.

Imhof, Kurt 2006: Mediengesellschaft und Medialisierung. *Medien & Kommunikationswissenschaft* 2: 5–29.

Jaffe, Alexandra 2011: Sociolinguistic diversity in mainstream media: Authenticity, authority and processes of mediation and mediatization. *Journal of Language and Politics* 10: 562–586.

Jansson, Andre 2002: The mediatization of consumption: Towards an analytical framework of image culture. *Journal of Consumer Culture* 2: 5–31.

Jensen, Klaus Bruhn 2013: Definitive and sensitizing conceptualizations of mediatization. *Communication Theory* 23 (3): 203–222.

Johnson, Sally and Astrid Ensslin 2007: Language in the media: Theory and practice. In: Sally Johnson and Astrid Ensslin (eds.), *Language in the Media. Representations, Identities, Ideologies*, 3–22. London: Continuum Press (Advances in Sociolinguistics).

Kepplinger, Hans Matthias 2002: Mediatization of Politics. Theory and Data. *Journal of Communication* 52: 972–986.

Knoblauch, Hubert 2008: Spirituality and popular religion in europe. *Social Compass* 55 (2): 140–153.

Knoblauch, Hubert 2013: Communicative constructivism and mediatization. *Communication Theory* 23 (3): 297–315.

Krotz, Friedrich: 2001 *Die Mediatisierung kommunikativen Handelns. Der Wandel von Alltag und sozialen Beziehungen, Kultur und Gesellschaft durch die Medien*. Opladen: Westdeutscher Verlag.

Krotz, Friedrich 2009: Mediatization: A concept with which to grasp media and societal change. In: Knut Lundby (ed.), *Mediatization: Concept, Changes, Consequences*, 19–38. New York: Peter Lang.

Krotz, Friedrich 2013: Introduction into the thematic issue „media and cultural change outside of Europe". *Communications* 38 (3): 245–249.

Krotz, Friedrich and Andreas Hepp 2013: A Concretization of mediatization: How mediatization works and why 'mediatized worlds' are a helpful concept for empirical mediatization research. *Empedocles. European Journal for the Philosophy of Communication* 3 (2): 119–134.

Latour, Bruno 2007: *Reassembling the Social: An Introduction to Actor-Network-Theory*. Oxford: Oxford University Press.

Livingstone, Sonia M. 2009: On the mediation of everything. *Journal of Communication* 59: 1–18.

Lundby, Knut (ed.) 2008: *Digital Storytelling, Mediatized Stories: Self-representations in New Media*. Berlin: Peter Lang.

Lundby, Knut 2009a: Media Logic: Looking for social interaction. In: Knut Lundby (ed.), *Mediatization: Concept, Changes, Consequences*, 101–119. New York: Peter Lang.

Lundby, Knut (ed.) 2009b: *Mediatization: Concept, Changes, Consequences*. New York: Peter Lang.

Lundby, Knut 2011: 'Mediatizing faith: Digital storytelling on the unspoken'. In: Michael Bailey and Guy Redden (eds.), *Mediating Faiths. Religion and Socio-Cultural Change in the Twenty-First Century*. Farnham: Ashgate,

Lundby, Knut (2014): Mediatized stories in mediatized worlds. In: Andreas Hepp and Friedrich Krotz (eds.): *Mediatized Worlds: Culture and Society in a Media Age*, 19–37. London: Palgrave.

Madianou, Mirca and Daniel Miller 2012: Polymedia: Towards a new theory of digital media in interpersonal communication. *International Journal of Cultural Studies*: 1–19.

Manheim, Ernst 1933: *Die Träger der öffentlichen Meinung. Studien zur Soziologie der Öffentlichkeit*. Brünn/Prag/Leipzig/Wien: Verlag Rudolf M. Rohrer.

Martín-Barbero, Jesús 1993: *Communication, Culture, and Hegemony: From the Media to Mediations*. London/Thousand Oaks/New Delhi: Sage.

Mazzoleni, Gianpietro 2008: Mediatization of society. In: Donsbach, Wolfgang (ed.), *The International Encyclopedia of Communication*, vol VII, 3052–3055. Oxford: Blackwell Publishing.

McLuhan, Marshall and Lewis H. Lapham 1994: *Understanding Media: The Extensions of Man*. Cambridge/London: MIT Press.

Meyrowitz, Joshua 1995: Medium theory. In: David Crowley and David Mitchell (eds.), *Communication Theory Today*, 50–77. Cambridge: Polity Press.

Meyrowitz, Joshua 2009: Medium theory: An alternative to the dominant paradigm of media effects. In:Robin L. Nabi and Mary Beth Oliver (eds.), *The Sage Handbook of Media Processes and Effects*, 517–530. Thousand Oaks, CA: Sage

Morley, David 1992: *Television Audiences and Cultural Studies*. London/New York: Routledge.

Ong, Walter J. 2002: *Orality and Literacy*. London: Routledge.

Preiss, Raymond W., Barbara Gayle, Nancy Burrell, Mike Allen and Jennings Bryant 2006: *Mass Media Effects Research: Advances Through Meta-analysis*. London: Routledge.

Schrott, Andrea 2009: Dimensions: catch-all label or technical term. In: Knut Lundby (ed.), *Mediatization: Concept, Changes, Consequences*, 41–61. New York: Peter Lang.

Schulz, Winfried 2004: Reconstructing mediatization as an Analytical concept. *European Journal of Communication* 19: 87–101.

Steinmaurer, Thomas 2003: Medien und gesellschaftlicher Wandel. Skizzen zu einem Modell. In: Markus Behmer, Friedrich Krotz, Rudolf Stöber, andCarsten Winter (eds.), *Medienentwicklung und gesellschaftlicher Wandel. Beiträge zu einer theoretischen und empirischen Herausforderung*, 103–119. Wiesbaden: Westdeutscher Verlag.

Stöber, Rudolf 2010: Medialisierung vor 1945. Wie tragfähig ist der Begriff als kommunikationshistorisches Konzept für Frühe Neuzeit und Moderne? In: Klaus Arnold, Christoph Classen, Susanne Kinnebrock, Edgar Lersch undHans-Ulrich Wagner (eds.), *Von der Politisierung der Medien zur Medialisierung des Politischen? Zum Verhältnis von Medien, Öffentlichkeiten und Politik im 20. Jahrhundert*, 77–94. Leipzig: Leipziger Universitätsverlag.

Strömbäck, Jesper 2011: Mediatization of politics. In: Erik P. Bucy and R-. Lance Holbert (eds.), *Sourcebook for Political Communication Research*, 367–382. London/New York: Routledge.

Thompson, John B. 1995: *The Media and Modernity. A Social Theory of the Media*. Cambridge: Cambridge University Press.

Thussu, Daya Kishan (ed.) 2009: *Internationalizing Media Studies*. London: Routledge.

Vowe, Gerhard 2006: Mediatisierung der Politik? Ein theoretischer Ansatz auf dem Prüfstand. *Publizistik* 51: 437–455.

Weingart, Peter 1998: Science and the media. *Research Policy* 27: 869–879.

Wilke, Jürgen 2011: *Von der frühen Zeitung zur Medialisierung. Gesammelte Studien II*. Bremen: edition lumière.

Nikolas Coupland
Sociolinguistic change, vernacularization and broadcast British media

1 Introduction

In this chapter I want to consider the merits and the actualization of two theo-retical concepts, sociolinguistic change and vernacularization[1]. Neither concept is new. Each of them has been invoked explicitly, but fitfully, in sociolinguistic theorizing; some of the value of each concept has been articulated in discussions of other, quite closely related, concepts. Mimicking the slogan used to advertise a well-known tablet computer, we might say that "we already know how to use these devices". Even so, I think it is true that the utility and importance of each of the concepts has yet to be clearly established. That is, and perhaps similarly to the position with the tablet computer, we might get better use out of the two concepts if we explore and become aware of their functionality and potential in more detail.

I want to suggest that different relevant sociolinguistic orientations to change have tended to be swamped by the concept of language change, and that there is value in distinguishing the concept of sociolinguistic change from the concept of language change. Sociolinguistic change, for example, can be construed as a broad set of language-implicating changes that are socially consequential, even though particular forms or "states" of a language may not themselves change as part of the process. When varieties *can* be shown to have moved through different states, there may or may not be socially significant implications. Sociolinguistic change needs to be theorized not only in relation to language change, but also in relation to social change, and this gives us the triad of change concepts whose inter-relationships I will discuss in the next section. In a following section I make the case that five main dimensions of change are implicated in what we should call sociolinguistic change.

In two further sections I come on to discuss the concept of vernacularization, prefaced by a commentary on the much better-established sociolinguistic notion of standardization. While standardization has been, we might say, a staple item in

---

[1] I am very grateful to Jannis Androutsopoulos and Tore Kristiansen for very helpful comments on an earlier version of this text. Deficiencies here are not theirs.

the theoretical repertoire of sociolinguistics, its countervailing concept, vernacularization, has been considered only rarely and rather thinly. I shall argue that standardization has been theoretically constrained by being construed mainly as a linguistic change, when accounts of standardization have shown it to be a socially transformative (and hence a sociolinguistic) change. My argument will then be that vernacularization should also be theorized as a dimension of sociolinguistic change. In a final section I provide some speculative comments on how it may be possible to discover and analyse vernacularization as a sociolinguistic change-in-progress in British broadcast media.

This cluster of theoretical issues has surfaced in the early stages of a pan-European project on Standard Language Ideologies in Contemporary Europe, "SLICE". In a recent edited volume (Kristiansen and Coupland 2011) Tore Kristiansen and I have compiled a series of "country reports" prepared by researchers in 15 European countries/ regions, overviewing broad sociolinguistic trajectories involving standard languages and ideologies of (de)standardization in the different sites over the last 50 or so years. These area reports are accompanied by several more theoretically-inclined chapters[2] whose remit to some extent overlaps with the remit of the present chapter, and indeed the remit of the present volume as a whole. Participants in the SLICE network share a commitment to developing research at the interface of media, linguistic usage, standard language ideology (SLI) and change. I hope that further critical discussion of sociolinguistic change and vernacularization will be helpful in these various endeavours, where a good deal of relevant empirical research remains to be done.

2 Language change, social change and sociolinguistic change

Language change has been modelled by linguists as change over time in language systems. Inspired and led by William Labov over several decades, language change is the most cohesively and extensively developed paradigm in sociolinguistics. Woolard (2008: 435) says that explaining language change has been "the original and central problem in the sociolinguistic project". But there has also been debate about the "social-ness" and "sociolinguistic-ness" of the language change paradigm.

In a landmark paper at the height of their empirical research into language change and social networking in Belfast, James Milroy and Lesley Milroy (1985a)

---

2 Those chapters are by Jannis Androutsopoulos; Peter Auer and Helmut Spiekerman; Allan Bell; Stefan Grondelaers, Roeland van Hout and Dirk Speelman; and Jane Stuart-Smith.

noted that there had been two different approaches to the study of linguistic change. One approach continued the long tradition of historical linguistics, aiming to expose rule-governed "possible" and "impossible" processes of linguistic change using idealized or reconstructed data. The other approach, which they associated with more modern quantitative sociolinguistics, was similarly committed to specifying changes from one state to another state of a linguistic variety, but also to specifying how linguistic changes move in predictable ways through speech communities. Milroy and Milroy's main aim in their paper was to show, on the basis of their Belfast research, how the social account of predictable linguistic change could be empirically strengthened by modelling the characteristics of social networks through which linguistic innovations can be transmitted.

Through their approach to social networks, Milroy and Milroy were clearly concerned to enrich the social account of language change research – to make it, we might say, "more sociolinguistic". In fact they made a conceptual distinction between "historical" and "sociolinguistic" approaches to change (1985a: 340–341), and explicitly included their own perspective within the second approach. Understanding the human and relational processes whereby linguistic innovations enter and permeate social networks is undoubtedly a sociolinguistic concern, although we should still interrogate the sense in which it is so. Labov has made similar distinctions as to the sociolinguistic-ness of different theoretical and methodological orientations to language change in his own research. In introducing his seminal three-volume series of books on language change, he said that his (2001) *Social Factors* volume "falls more properly within the domain of sociolinguistics" than his (1994) *Internal Factors* volume, because the later book deals with social group correlates of variation (Labov 1994: 2). What Milroy and Milroy labelled the "historical" perspective on language change is less overtly social, and in one sense less sociolinguistic, when it orients to processes and principles construed as working internally within linguistic systems. Labov also said that, in a broader sense, "all systematic studies of variation are sociolinguistic" if they seek to represent "the real process of linguistic change in the community" (1994: 2). The main objective of language change research is to discover principles guiding formal linguistic change through quantitative comparisons of situated speech data. It is the partly mysterious, partly discoverable properties of systemic change that have motivated the variationist paradigm.

There remains, however, an important regard in which variationist research, and even those approaches labelled "sociolinguistic" above, are not sociolinguistic: in its canonical form, variationism is not motivated to discover socially significant change, and it has no apparatus for gauging social impacts of change. Classic instances are patterns of directional phonological shift – "sound change", which Labov has described as "the major mechanism of linguistic change" (1994: 550).

It has often been said that variationist methodology forces a distinction between language and society in order to establish correlational relationships, and it subordinates the social to the linguistic. In its "sociolinguistic" mode it invokes social (distributional) data in order to model the nature of language change in particular community settings. It presupposes that the social order is a stable structure against which change in a language system becomes visible. Canonically, language change can be detected in apparent time, across generation groups within the same social class stratum of a designated speech community. Change, in this view, is decidedly linguistic and, in a particular sense, *not social* – there is a presumption of no change within the social order or in language-society relationships. The variationist method is challenged if we start to argue that the social structures through which innovative linguistic forms "move" are themselves mobile and unstable, if for example gender or class or age come to hold different values for successive generations in their relationships to language.

Observations of this sort have been made over several decades. I am rehearsing them here (see also Coupland 2007) simply to point to those aspects of change that canonical variationist sociolinguistics leaves untouched. Contemporary sociolinguistics is replete with very obviously socially-grounded perspectives on change, some of them specifically designed to enrich variationist accounts. For example, Woolard's (2008) paper (referred to above) explores the productive interface between linguistic anthropology and variationist sociolinguistics. She argues that, even when the main concern is with formal changes of state in language systems, there is value in bringing semiotic and ideological perspectives into play. She is able to review several major theoretical and empirical projects, by Peneleope Eckert, Judith Irvine and Susan Gal, Lesley Milroy, Michael Silverstein and others, that have explained linkages between language ideologies and language forms. She argues that "cultural conceptions of language structure and use inevitably shape and alter that structure" (Woolard 2008: 439).

However, the concept of sociolinguistic change, mooted in Coupland (2009), urges us to ask broader questions, where the interest is less in discovering structural change in language systems and more in discovering changing relationships between language and society and their instantiation at the level of practice. Sociolinguistic change research carries the specific presupposition that whatever we identify as language change happens in the context of social change, and that these dimensions need to be handled integratively. Sociolinguistic change research aspires to understand change that is both linguistic and social, as part of a socially constituted linguistics (Hymes 1974: 196, and see related discussions of linguistics and sociolinguistics in Rampton 2006). As I suggested earlier, the phrase "sociolinguistic change" and its cognates are already to some extent in circulation, for example in Gregory Guy's (1990) discussion of "the sociolinguistic types of change", in Suzanne Romaine's (1988) "sociolinguistic theory of language change", and in Jannis Androutsopoulos's (2011) discussion of change and digital media (which is an important source for later parts of the present chapter). Even so, and even though most sociolinguists are undoubtedly interested in the language/ social change interface, there has been no concerted discussion of what it means to construe change as being "sociolinguistic", and in my next section I hope to promote a discussion of this kind.

The long tradition of language change research sometimes imposes its priorities on sociolinguistic studies that are framed more open-endedly, and where social change is very much to the fore. In a comprehensive discussion, Hinskens, Auer and Kerswill (2005) review wide-ranging research into dialect change in Europe, centred on processes of dialect convergence and divergence. They comment on processes of dialect levelling and koineization, pidginization and creolization, and so on. They follow Labov in distinguishing between internal and social factors that promote or constrain dialect change, and very many social processes are considered, such as community isolation and contact, the role of borders, urbanization, national unification, social networking and demographic mobility. The social agenda of the reviewed research is therefore far more open than in classical variationism. Also, the implication is very much that social change is closely associated with specific sorts of linguistic change, the most obvious case perhaps being the linguistic correlates of demographic mobility and contact (Hinskens et al. 2005: 34–36). But the fundamental rationale for the research reviewed is defined in relation to language (or dialect) systems and their social distributions, with the presupposition that (changing) aspects of social structure act as independent variables impacting on language. As a result, the account of change is primarily focused on formal systems, heavily weighted towards the linguistic end of an implied language-society continuum. Very large socio-cultural themes are entertained in the review, but their impact is funnelled down into measurable details of potentially changing linguistic forms and patterns.

Metatheoretical and methodological concerns might explain these priorities. It may be that social change is considered to be too nebulous or too grand a theme for sociolinguistics. Social change has been modelled by social theorists, as well as in empirical sociology, as change over time in or across particular societies, or as change in social norms in a variety of respects. Social change is often summarized in process-nominals ending in "-ization" – globalization, civilization, individualization, commercialization, informalization, conversationalization, and so on, and not least mediatization (Androutsopoulos 2010a). The scale of social change implicated in such concepts is large, with very wide potential applicability. The changes in question are generally cultural while, at least within the variationist tradition, sociolinguistics has been more comfortable with social group/ demographic perspectives than with cultural frameworks. The changes implied in "-ization" nominals work on and through the "macro" social categories that fill out variationism's account of the social, and of course they operate across and beyond the bounded speech communities that were prioritized in that classical tradition. But social change clearly has its impact locally as well as globally. Glo-balization, for example, has been shown to be highly relevant – indeed point-edly so, through the concept of glocalization – to individuals, groups and local communities (Blommaert 2010; Chouliaraki and Fairclough 1999; Coupland 2010; Fairclough 2006; Pennycook 2007).

The concept of sociolinguistic change challenges us to explore the extent to which, and the ways in which, the historically evolving conditions of social life are carried in and experienced through language. It makes us wary of over-relying on a static demographic sociology, for example if we have reason to believe that social class is a shifting social formation (Coupland 2009, and see below) and a rather malleable social attribution (Rampton 2006; Snell 2010). It points us to language in use as a dimension of practice in which the social, and social change, are experienced and lived out. Research into sociolinguistic change is therefore not a matter of flirting with grandiose and abstract social-theoretical claims. In fact it is based in a commitment to avoid reductive social theorizing, and to ground interpretations of socio-cultural continuity and change in the empirical detail of language in use. In several cases, theorized social changes are clearly based in language and discourse, for example in that informalization and conver-sationalization imply a loosening of norms of "proper" social conduct in public, which will include "proper" ways of using language in specific settings (cf. Bell 2011). Some dimensions of social change are recognized to be focally linguistic/ discursive, e.g. the tendency towards synthetic personalization (Fairclough 1992) as a quality of social interaction in public that has emerged in Late Modernity. Mediatization (see Androutsopoulos, this issue, and below) is another social change based in new levels of reflexivity around language and meaning, and in new resources and norms for communicative exchange.

The concept of sociolinguistic change is therefore needed on several grounds. First, it challenges the dualism that underlies two traditions in the study of change (linguistic and social) and brings them together. It starts from the presumption that language and society need to be conceptualized as mutually constitutive pro-cesses, in the manner advocated many decades ago by Dell Hymes. Second, it can give us more perspective on the social value of language change within the lan-guage change paradigm itself. Many instances of canonical language change do have demonstrable social implications. To take just one example, Trudgill (2002: 29–32) makes the case that "dialect death" in Europe represents loss of valued cultural diversity on language-ecological grounds. But some changes over time in the distribution of formal features of speech are socially trivial, because no significant shift in language-society relations is entailed. Featural change in speech (including many sound changes) may simply perpetuate culturally understood indexical relations between speech and social structure from one generation to the next, if for example shifted vowel qualities and distributions continue to index the same social configurations in the same relationships that their precursors did. Where the ambition is primarily to demonstrate that a given "state of the variety" has changed, there is no motivation to distinguish between socially trivial and socially significant language changes. Third, the concept of sociolinguistic change opens a window on changing language-society relations that are *not* consequential on changes in linguistic forms and distributions. Although we might look for sociolinguistic change in the context of newly emergent linguistic resources and practices, sociolinguistic change can also be a matter of new values being attached to *un*changing language practices – language ideologies are, after all, likely to be less stable over time than the patterns of language use to which they relate. Fourth, sociolinguistic change provides a framework in which historical and epochal factors can be countenanced. What it means to be a speaker under changing social and cultural regimes (e.g. being a speaker of a minority language under post-nationalist conditions – Jaffe and Oliva 2013, Pietikäinen et al. forthcoming) comes into view, displacing the assumption that languages and varieties are autonomous systems that change state in essentially unchanging social matrices[3].

---

3 In a personal note Tore Kristiansen helpfully schematizes one of the oppositions I am discussing here in the following terms. In scenario (1) language changes, but sociolinguistic values (language-society relations) do not change. In scenario (2) sociolinguistic values change, but language does not change. My argument is indeed that scenario (1) can obtain in variationist accounts of language change, even though I agree with Kristiansen that we should look for value change as a possible motivation for language change. Scenario (2) only becomes researchable if we adopt the perspective of sociolinguistic change, although that perspective is also needed to explore a third schematic scenario where both values and language change. Kristiansen makes the further observation that "we do seem to have an instance of (1) in Denmark, in the sense that there are great changes in language usage (low/modern Copenhagen speech is overtaking high/conservative Copenhagen speech), while the ideological foundation remains intact (i. e. the language-society relation is still based on the belief that there is and should be a 'best language'). But we also seem to have an instance of (2), in the sense that a fundamental distinction between 'two ways of using language' (low/modern vs. high/conservative) is upheld, while there are great changes in the ideological sphere (the traditionally low accent is upgraded to 'best language', in particular in the perceptual dimension of 'dynamism' and in values linked to the media universe" (see also Kristiansen, this volume).

Many well-known types of change meet these criteria for sociolinguistic change, and one difficulty in using the concept of sociolinguistic change is that its remit is unlimited (whereas language change research submits itself to statistical criteria of significant difference). Obvious examples in the history of sociolinguistics include shifts from power-coded to more solidarity-coded T/V pronoun use in several European languages, shifts in gender-related forms of address and reference, planning-based initiatives to inculcate or exclude particular language codes in educational systems (where these have demonstrable impact), and so on. These are all instances of sociolinguistic change, at least to the extent that the changes in question are not merely formal and distributional and implicate changed language-society relations. The value in reconsidering these and other cases as instances of sociolinguistic change is precisely to press for analysis of why they are *not* merely matters of formal and distributional change. Below, I consider vernacularization as a candidate sociolinguistic change, in relation to standardization, which is of course a core concept in sociolinguistics. But I also want to reconsider standardization itself from the perspective of sociolinguistic (as opposed to linguistic) change. Vernacularization might then be generally viewed as a sociolinguistic counter-flow to standardization, in several different respects. Before coming onto those sections I try to consolidate my perspective on sociolinguistic change, and explore its relationship to media and mediatization.

3 Five dimensions of sociolinguistic change

As already implied in the previous section, five inter-linked dimensions need to be foregrounded in sociolinguistic change, as in Figure 1 (although this schema is inevitably parsimonious).

social norms		discursive practices
	media(tiza)tion	
cultural reflexivity		language ideologies

Figure 1: Five dimensions of sociolinguistic change

Each of the five dimensions in the figure is subject to change; indeed it seems reasonable to assume that sociolinguistic change is endemic in language-society relations, flooding through the simple model above, with dominant cultural currents (to use Ulf Hannerz's metaphor – Hannerz 1992) experiencing counter-currents in response to them. Sociolinguistic change is based in fluidity of this sort, which is unmarked relative to stability/ the absence of change. But it more particularly implies changing relations *among* the five different dimensions.

Three elements of the figure are very familiar sociolinguistic themes, and they need very little discussion here. Change over time in the formal makeup and distribution of speech styles (the classical concerns of the language change paradigm, as I have been arguing, above) is part, but only part, of the *discursive practices* dimension in the figure. A sociolinguistic change perspective needs to be alert to how speech itself enters into multiple relationships with other semiotic modes of action, so that "discourse" is a more appropriate designation than "language". Research into multimodal communication (e.g. Kress and van Leeuwen 2001) is based in the fact that meanings organized through linguistic text are qualified by and interact with meanings organized through other symbolic resources, most obviously visual symbolism. It has been argued that symbolic processes are becoming more multimodal over time, as technology develops and supports more complex audio-visual and visual-linguistic text exchanges, so that sociolinguistic change in Late Modernity is more likely to implicate cross-modal processes than previously.

An emphasis on "practice" (rather than "speech" or "sound") also broadens the analytic perspective by implying far more elaborate contextualization processes than those typically considered in language change research. For example, sociolinguistic change may involve widening or narrowing of stylistic and generic repertoires (repertoires of genres) linked to particular cultural value-systems, as in the case of the globalizing genre of "fun fearless female" magazine features in multi-national editions of *Cosmopolitan* (Machin and van Leeuwen 2007, 2010). In this instance we see a sociolinguistic change that is based in the global diffusion of a discourse genre, associated with specific ideologies of gender and individual female agency, which may have no specific implications of change at the level of linguistic forms and codes – *Cosmo*'s ideology can work through any given language. Agha's (2003, 2007) retheorizing of sociolinguistic indexicality, including his account of the enregisterment of Received Pronunciation (RP) in Britain (see below), explicitly recognizes this sort of dynamic movement in the widening or narrowing of the scope of what he calls "speech registers". In general, sociolinguistics is already quite active in researching the relationship between discursive practices and social change, and this dynamic was clearly foregrounded in Bourdieu's theory of practice (1977).

The interface between discursive practices and *language ideologies* (in Figure 1) is a rich seam of sociolinguistic change, as in the example of language-ideological changes relating to "properness" running ahead of or behind *social norms* (also in Figure 1) at the level of practice. Social norms have been a focal concern in sociolinguistics, certainly since Hymes proposed his SPEAKING mnemonic (N for norms) as a checklist of the main concerns of the ethnography of speaking (Hymes 1974). As we shall see below, standardization and vernacularization are trajectories of sociolinguistic change that are to a large extent contested and negotiated along the interfaces among ideologies, norms and practices. Variationist sociolinguists have sometimes been very explicit in arguing that shifting language ideologies are, in quite general terms, the "driving force" behind (classically conceived) language change (Kristiansen 2001, 2009). We therefore see arguments about whether, for example, interpersonal accommodation needs to be interpreted as an "automatic" rather than an identity-based, socio-psychologically motivated process (Trudgill 2008, and published responses to Trudgill in the same journal issue). But ideologies of language – culturally consolidated value-judgements on how language and discourse sit and should sit within more or less local social environments – are widely recognized to be responsive to, or ingrained in, social change, in relation to the politics of gender, social class, age, ethnicity, etc. Changes, for example, in the socio-economic circumstances of minorities, however defined, have been known for some time to impact on how ways of speaking are evaluated. Correspondingly, shifts in patterns of language use are often traceable to socio-economic aspirations (see, for example, Gal's classic study of code-choice in Oberwart – Gal 1979). Social norms – in the twin senses of what is socially normal and what is socially normative (Piippo 2012) – and the observable realities of discursive practices enter into complex relations with ideologies, and sociolinguistic change ripples along their multiple interfaces.

Cultural reflexivity and *media(tisa)tion* (in Figure 1) may be less familiar and more controversial dimensions of sociolinguistic change. In the study of change the most basic challenge is to establish when any specific change has occurred, how and from whose perspective, and how change comes to be acknowledged as such in a particular socio-cultural environment. Greg Urban has developed a helpful theoretical account of change in his discussion of "how culture moves through the world" (Urban 2001). He observes, anthropomorphically, that culture is a mixture of conservative and innovative tendencies – culture has both "inertial and accelerative properties" (2001: 32). In its "itchy" and "restless" aspect, a culture is desirous of change, although change can only come about when inertial tendencies are overcome, particularly through the involvement of "entrepreneurs" (not necessarily commercial agents) or metacultural brokers. Entrepreneurs, in Urban's schema, stimulate, evaluate and mediate cultural change. Social actors become aware of culture and of cultural change, but also of cultural continuity, precisely when a level of cultural reflexivity at a sufficient scale or representation is achieved. The very concept of culture, Urban argues, has to be negotiated at this "meta" level (cf. Jaworski, Coupland and Galasiński 2004), through iterative, reflexive, metacultural processes.

Urban's provocative account of cultural change spans both structural and agentive facets of culture, rather than simply opposing an overly structural conception of culture, and this is suggestive for our discussion of language change, social change and sociolinguistic change. He says that "structure (or system) is the result of a combination of the inertial and accelerative properties of culture" (2001: 32). We achieve a sense of a stable, structured culture, paradoxically, through "accelerative" initiatives – that is, through attempts to remake or to reinterpret cultural norms: "The world comes to appear as natural precisely because it conforms to an idea of the world – narrative linearization is in harmony with the textures of the lived world" (2001: 90). Urban identifies a "metaculture of tradition" whose workings consolidate a sense of cultural continuity. This opens up a perspective that could be valuable for language change research, in that the ubiquity of formal language change across the generations might not imply any meaningful cultural (or sociolinguistic) change. It might be the default process through which continuing sociolinguistic arrangements are perpetuated. For Urban, "a metaculture of modernity" underpins meaningful cultural change in Late Modernity, when metacultural activities make us aware of new normativities and of the distance between traditional and new arrangements. Metaculture surfaces as observable evaluative discourses about cultural forms and practices, which must include evaluations of language use itself, so that analyses of sociolinguistic change must be partly located at this "meta" level. Although it targets an extremely broad anthropological agenda, Urban's abstract theorizing of metaculture maps very well onto what I have so far attempted to characterize as sociolinguistic change. It is in metalinguistic and metacultural discourses (as one element of "discursive practices" in Figure 1) that we are likely to become aware of sociolinguistic change, particularly when those discourses focus in on sociolinguistic norms and ideological assessments of "what is meaningfully old" and "what is meaningfully new".

We might also follow Urban in his suggestion that metacultural discourses can be constitutive of change in their own right. As we will see below in relation to standardization and vernacularization, when new public discourses about language start to circulate within a culture, they have already begun to change the terms on which that culture engages with its sociolinguistic norms and practices. At the same time, indexically rich sociolinguistic performances also tend to articulate their metapragmatic and metacultural values, so reflexivity and practice (in Figure 1) need not be at all separate. Taking this line might therefore satisfy Woolard's concern (2008: 437) not to exclude the sociolinguistic analysis of language ideologies in discursive practice itself, and not to over-invest in "the construal of ideology solely or primarily as metalinguistic discourse".

As the fifth dimension of Figure 1, *media(tiza)tion* certainly includes the process of technological change, where the advent of new technologies both facilitates and demands new discursive literacies and practices. In the first place this is to say, quite simply, that we should expect many sorts of sociolinguistic change to arise in conjunction with new media technologies. Mediatization can be taken to refer to the historical process through which more and more aspects of social lives and socio-cultural understandings are achieved through technologically-mediated systems (Androutsopoulos, this volume; Livingstone 2009). On this definition, mediatization is a social change which creates new affordances for language use, including new patterns of self-presentation online and in new footings for mediated social interaction in new media. New media invite multimodal text construction and consumption, with implications for vernacularization (Busch 2006).

While media contexts and, more importantly, critical appreciation of processes of mediatization have been largely excluded from language change research, mass media are inevitably a powerful locus for sociolinguistic change. Variationists have argued that mass media do not and can not have a substantial direct influence on core aspects of spoken usage (Chambers 1995; Labov 2001: 228; Trudgill 2002: 149; see discussions in Coupland 2007: 184 ff., and especially Androutsopoulos, this volume, and Stuart-Smith 2011, this volume). Yet this formulation of cause and effect is remarkably stark and over-simplifies the relationship between social actors and mediational means. What we can say is that mediatization changes the terms of our social engagement with language, the more so as media resources, formats, representations and norms themselves change over time. Media are saturated with sociolinguistic indexicalities, in their representations of people, voices, situations and places. They continually reinvent indexical relations, positing new relations between ways of speaking and social ways of being. They are also saturated with (meta)discourses of indexicality, in the evaluative accounts of linguistic difference that they circulate and often trigger. Mediatization creates new patterns of public exposure to ways of speaking, new ways of embedding and disembedding voices into/ from social contexts, and new normativities for self-presentation and for social relations. Androutsopoulos (2010b) argues that technologically mediated discourse becomes a site of heteroglossic renegotiation, where the social meanings of sociolinguistic styles are displayed and potentially challenged.

The over-arching social change associated with mediatization is a heightening of sociolinguistic reflexivity. I suggest below that increasingly complex patterns of vocal display and enactment in mass media play a part in destabilizing and resisting standard language ideology in Britain. But it will also be important to explore the relationship between mediatization and more general processes of mediation. Mediation is central to sociolinguistic change in the sense that changing discourse practices have to be socially embedded into specific culturally meaningful frameworks (Scollon and Scollon 2004). Mediation therefore refers to a wide agenda of institutionalized and non-institutionalized framing and formatting processes which present themselves at particular historical and spatial junctures, constrained by particular ideological and normative forces. In any event, "the media" are not tangentially and debatably related to sociolinguistic change (which is what has generally been claimed to be the case in relation to language change); sociolinguistic change implies a renegotiation of mediational options.

4 Standardization as a sociolinguistic change

We can now move towards a discussion of vernacularization, but initially (in this section) through a short review of the sociolinguistics of standardization, which should be seen as dialectically linked to vernacularization. Standardization and vernacularization are opposing trajectories of sociolinguistic change, played out over considerable periods of time, but with new emphases and resonances in Late Modernity. Mass media have strong involvement in each of them.

Sociolinguistics has developed rich accounts of standardization, but there has been a tendency to model standardization under language change (as opposed to sociolinguistic change) assumptions. That is, standardization has often been described as featural change over time in the linguistic shape and prevalence of "prestige" varieties of speech or writing. Sociolinguistic research questions relating to standardness have correspondingly tended to be about "what is or is not standard" at a descriptive level, and about "who uses standard or nonstandard language", to what degree, where, etc.[4] The classical account of linguistic standardization (Haugen 1966) itself shows some aspects of this tendency, in its specification of four sub-processes: selection, codification, elaboration and acceptance. Deumert and Vandenbussche (2003: 9), who, incidentally, refer to standardization as a "sociolinguistic change", suggest that Haugen's model "is not exhaustive", and that "there remain a number of aspects of the standardiza-

---

4 Tore Kristiansen and I have recently overviewed sociolinguistic theorizing of standardization (Coupland and Kristiansen 2011: 20–26), from Haugen's foundational theory to other important, more recent, contributions by Auer, Cameron, Joseph, Lippi-Green, J. Milroy, L. Milroy, Pennycook and others, set against highly influential social-theoretic accounts of "civilization" and "distinction" by Norbert Elias (2000) and Pierre Bourdieu (2010). See also Coupland (2000) for a discussion of sociolinguists' reticence to approach "standard language" as an ideological rather than as a linguistic concept.

tion process which are not sufficiently covered". They point out that Haugen's model was ill-suited for the description of the motivations and the non-linguistic goals of the agents of standardization, and they point to Haugen's own awareness of this problem.

Much more has been at stake, of course, than how linguists should describe and locate "standard language" from one time-point to another or within particular communities, even if Haugen's four sub-processes have a somewhat innocent and apolitical air about them. It has been evident that the history of language standardization – a major narrative of European languages under modernity – has related to changing social ambitions and to social contestation, such as the drive towards unification around a common language in nation state-building, and the assertion of one particular social group's authority over others (see the "country reports" in Kristiansen and Coupland 2011). Standardization as a historical process has been a series of ideological initiatives to embed new social hierarchies and social norms, to validate nationalist discourses, and to normalize ways of mediating preferred linguistic varieties, and it is therefore a sociolinguistic change in the sense I have suggested above. Several sociolinguists have made the key observation that standardization (viewed as a historical, ideological process) is a more feasible and workable concept than "standard language" (as a variety), which is at best an idealization; it is ultimately futile to try to locate and describe a standard variety of a language. Cheshire and Milroy (1993: 3 ff.) see standardization as a drive towards uniformity; it is "the imposition of uniformity upon a class of objects" and "the suppression of variability". Milroy (2004: 162) writes that "the concept of standard is surprisingly underspecified and undertheorized". Yet sociolinguists have been generally at ease with "standard" and "nonstandard" as descriptive categories (see, for example, contributions to Bex and Watts 1999). In fact these have been primary concepts in variationist research, where "standard" varieties (and "standard" variants of sociolinguistic variables) have been assumed to "have social prestige", while "nonstandard" varieties and variants "are socially stigmatized".

Research in the language attitudes tradition, on the other hand, paints a more complex and nuanced picture of the social meanings of "standard and non-standard language", although it too has been complacent in defining varieties on these terms. In the British case, urban vernaculars (where "vernacular" is another under-theorized concept – see below) have been shown to have quite complex evaluative profiles, with their speakers downgraded on measures of perceived personal "competence" but sometimes upgraded on measures of "social attractiveness", and often with far more complex evaluative profiles in specific cases (Garrett 2010; Garrett, Coupland and Williams 2003). Both inside and outside language attitudes research, however, there has been rather little sociolinguistic effort to assess whether "standard language" and its associated ide-ologies are actually as cohesive and dominant as they are generally assumed to be, and how we should understand standardization as a sociolinguistic change. Descriptivist approaches have blunted sociolinguists' appreciation of standard-ization as a specific historical process tied to specific socio-cultural ambitions, which in fact may no longer be relevant in many settings.

Milroy (2004) makes the point that British and American conceptions of "standard English" have different historical and sociological bases, and that this has sometimes led to (in her view) unconvincing synchronic and diachronic anal-yses. Labov (1972) argued that rhotic speech emerged as a normatively prestigious feature of speech in New York City as a reaction against British norms that posi-tioned it as an "incorrect" and provincial speech feature in England. But Milroy, citing Bonfiglio (2002), puts the case that "in the early twentieth century, Amer-ican xenophobia became focused on the immigrant cities of the East Coast, with a concomitant loss of linguistic capital for their nonrhotic dialects". In this way, she argues, "standardization was a means of maintaining linguistic and racial purity [and] virtue and national vigor" (Milroy 2002: 163). Milroy notes that, under this ideological pressure, rhotic speech was adopted by East Coast USA radio networks in the 1930s and constructed as an element of the speech of the majority, but also as a speech feature *not* shared by African Americans and white Southerners. What is particularly interesting in this commentary is the argument that ideological values for ways of speaking are liable to shift over relatively short periods of time, also that ways of speaking can be reconfigured in relation not only to changing media norms but changing evaluative discourses. "Standard language" may not (or not always) be underpinned by coherent and self-evident social attributions of "prestige"; it can be shaped, inconclusively, in shifting and contested ideologies of language.

Agha's theoretical discussion of indexical processes (2007) is also fully compatible with a theory of sociolinguistic change, including its reflexive and metacultural dimensions. He is interested in "the emergence of a standard" and the consolidation of Received Pronunciation (RP) as, he suggests, a supralocal variety in Britain; Agha models the enregisterment of RP on these terms (2007: 203–232). He has little to say about ideological contests around RP, or about how RP may have already lost much of its ideological status as a "received" (norma-tively and consensually prestigious) speech style, although he does offer a brief commentary on public discussions of Estuary English. Nevertheless, he explains the sociolinguistic processes through which both enregisterment (and what we might call "re-" or "dis-enregisterment") are able to happen. Agha convincingly argues that cultural formations of all sorts "are dynamically altered by semiotic activities and practices" (2007: 78). Indexical values for ways of speaking enter more and more people's reflexive awareness over time, but transmission of this sort may also involve reanalysis or reconfiguration of "the sign phenomenon" in question (Agha 2007: 78). For Agha, normative standards for speech are therefore a particular kind of reflexive model (Agha 2007: 125) whose stability depends on a constant flow of confirmatory experiences by group members in discursive interactions. "Registers" in Agha's terms are always liable to experience "functional reanalysis", and he gives the example of "prestige" registers being taken up by "non-prestige" groups, possibly leading to hyperlectal distinctions being made within earlier prestige varieties by elites, who want to maintain their social superiority (Agha 2007: 158).

Agha also recognizes the role of mass media in relation to semiotic reanalysis, but he is careful not to claim that there is a directly causal relationship between mass media depictions of dialect and linguistic change:

> Contemporary mass media depictions are themselves the products of individuals caught up in larger historical processes; and the "uptake" of such messages by audiences involve processes of evaluative response that permit many degrees of freedom. I am concerned rather with the ways in which these representations expand the social domain of individuals acquainted with register stereotypes, and allow individuals, once aware of them, to respond to their characterological value in various ways, aligning their own self-images with them in some cases, transforming them in others through their own metasemiotic work. (Agha 2007: 202)

In this view, register expansion, when it occurs, is a matter of individuals' role alignment with a depicted (mediated) social meaning relation, and Agha suggests that public depictions "invite" realignment, generating a flow of social meaning that is ultimately "flexible, yet non-random" (Agha 2007: 203). Mass media depictions (such as RP historically becoming the default voice of BBC [British Broadcasting Corporation] newsreaders) "amplify the processes of which they are a part, e.g., by furnishing the same model of exemplary speech to very large audiences", thus "homogenizing the conditions for subsequent response behaviors and role alignments across a wide social domain" (Agha 2007: 225).

So language standardization may best be seen as a temporally and culturally specific prevailing of standard language ideology, a value structure in which a reified "standard language", in speech as well as writing (and which for many people includes RP), is considered authoritative and authentic (Coupland 2003) and in which "nonstandard" usage is discredited. Standardization is a sociolinguistic change which may, under some circumstances, facilitate language change among particular social groups. Whether standardization in Britain *did* generally occasion more use of "standard language" is actually disputed, for example by Stuart-Smith (2011). She points to the widespread view among sociolinguists that dialect variation in Britain was generally maintained through the (middle-to-late) decades of the twentieth century when standardization was, paradoxically, exerting its strongest influence[5]. Standardization certainly provided a focus for culturally reflexive discourses about correctness and properness of speech in heavily class-structured, pre- and post-World War II Britain. "Standard speech" in Britain was ideologized as a singular norm for "proper" speech and demeanour (Agha 2007: 240; Bourdieu 1991, 2010). In Agha's terms it was "amplified" by the BBC in the early years of its existence (see below). Linguists have played their part in consolidating "standard English" (as observed by Joseph 1987) through their repeated moves to describe it as an actual variety and by establishing it as a point of reference for the analysis of "nonstandard" speech features and styles. Standardization has been seen (teleologically, in the opinion of Deumert and Vandenbussche 2003) as a linear, continuing default process, perhaps along the lines of Elias's argument that the history of civilization can be analysed in incremental social changes towards a more refined and codified social order (Elias 2000; Coupland and Kristiansen 2011; Quilly and Loyal 2004), while the sociolinguistic literature has generally down-played the ideological contests in which it was engaged, which include specific contemporary forces lined up *against* standardization.

5 Vernacularization and destandardization

A good deal of social theory proposes, as a necessarily gross generalization, that linear models of social progress have lost their predictive power, just as state-building as a motivation for linguistic standardization in Europe (in Haugen's theory) has in many cases outlived its relevance. Pedersen (2009) explains how standardization and modernization were intertwined in the rise of bourgeois society (to different time-scales in different European national contexts), and this in itself implies the likelihood of its demise in Late Modernity. Late Modernity is often characterized by an unprecedented level of cultural complexity which generally loosens the predictive power of social structure and social histories

---

5 The assessment of whether there has been a general tendency to maintain versus eradicate dialect differences through levelling (for example in England) is, as Trudgill (2002) observes, difficult to make, partly because tendencies are visible at different linguistic levels. Trudgill says (2002: 149) that "the phonological systems of English show signs of diverging from one another" in a "normal pattern of linguistic change", although he is referring here to differences across national varieties among "native speakers". His more general thesis is that there has been massive "dedialectization" in many European countries, in respect of traditional dialects.

(Giddens 1991). Social class is a case in point, with the most extreme commentators arguing that class has become a "zombie category" in sociological analysis – a "figure" emptied of most of its meaning, circulating in the twilight, but to all intents and purposes dead (Beck and Beck-Gernsheim 2002).

Sociological survey research in Britain (some of which is reviewed in Coupland 2009) supports this claim to some extent, for example in finding that social class is nowadays a rather weak predictor of cultural tastes. The old British Establishment that supported a sharply hierarchical class structure is no longer in force, even though it is unquestionably true that social deprivation and inequality persist in Britain. The immediate question is whether "standard language" and "vernacular language" continue to coherently and decisively index higher and lower degrees of privilege and authority, and independent criteria of authenticity, in the way sociolinguists have assumed they do (or did), and how we should understand the role of media in (to put it simplistically) reversing standardization and promoting vernacularization. In the rest of this section I will comment on sociolinguistic research that has begun to make the argument that something like vernacularization is already in evidence, in Britain and elsewhere. But my main aim is to debate the criteria according to which vernacularization could be established to be a sociolinguistic change in progress.

Mugglestone's (1996) historical account of *Talking Proper* in Britain was the first extended attempt to draw attention to the historical unravelling of standard language ideology in Britain. As many others (including Agha) have done, Mugglestone's book takes as its main theme the hegemonic *rise* of RP as an elite norm, but in her last chapter she goes on to document what she calls "the rise of the regional" in British ways of speaking, from the 1960s onwards. Mugglestone's analysis implicitly refers to all five of the dimensions of sociolinguistic change summarized in Figure 1. RP in Britain, pre 1960, was ideologically bolstered by broadcast media, particularly TV and radio, in the early years of mass broadcasting. John Reith, first director general of the BBC, was metalinguistically explicit about the public service function of the BBC, part of which was to promote better standards of speech in Britain, with BBC TV announcers positioned as exemplary speakers. Mugglestone takes evaluative discourses as her evidence – public statements by influential people originally decrying regional vernaculars, then from 1960 starting to decry RP as a stuffy Establishment voice. Her argument is that reflexive commentaries on British ways of speaking changed, and that shifting ideologies of language started to undermine the authority and social normativity of RP.

We should note that Mugglestone is not making any claims about language change. It is well-known that, over the last 50 or so years, the phonological shape of what is considered to be RP has changed, even in the speech of its most exemplary speakers, including the (British) Queen (Agha 2007: 227; Harrington 2006; Harrington, Palethorpe and Watson 2000). The shape of, for example, vernacular Liverpool speech (which Mugglestone argues was a very salient case of a rising regional voice post-1960) may also have changed, perhaps through dialect levelling. But if Mugglestone's analysis is correct, the salient sociolinguistic change was a realignment of ideological values and social norms attaching to so-called "standard" and "urban British vernacular" varieties, linked to major social and ideological changes that shifted the balance between popular culture and Establishment values. Of course, phonological shift over time within the variety defined as RP (or its popular equivalent name) might have followed from some elite speakers' new preference to style themselves in less elite terms[6], and Mugglestone does offer some examples of public figures claiming that this was a familiar motivation.

The notion of destandardization has sometimes been applied to language change processes, for example in Hinskens et al.'s (2005) discussion of a possible European "dialect renaissance" from the 1970s. In Kristiansen's conception (discussed in Coupland and Kristiansen 2011), destandardization refers to an established "standard language" losing its authority as the singular "best" variety in a culture, in a process of value levelling and sociolinguistic democratization (and see Kerswill's 2001 discussion of meritocratic tendencies with RP). Kristiansen distinguishes destandardization from what (after Mattheier 1997) he calls "demotization", which is a process of change whereby respect for one particular "best" variety is transferred to a different variety, leaving a standard language ideology basically intact, but retargeted – and in the Danish case retargeted at "low Copenhagen" speech – see note 3). Bell (2011: 178) introduces the concept of "restandardization" as an alternative to demotization. Destandardization, then, is a hypothesized sociolinguistic change. On the other hand, demotization, which Kristiansen considers to be well-evidenced in Denmark, is a more marginal case, involving very little language-ideological change or socio-cultural consequences of any substance. For Kristiansen, destandardization is ethically desirable on egalitarian grounds, but not evidenced.

Vernacularization may in any case be a preferable concept, in order to focus on shifts towards a more positive valorization of vernacularity as well as a weaken-

---

6 Trudgill (2002: 178) notes that "People who are upwardly mobile or who come into the public eye may still in fact reduce the number of regional features in their accents... but they will no longer remove all such features. It is therefore undoubtedly true that many more people than was formerly the case can be heard in public situations, especially in the media, speaking with lower middle-class regional accents".

ing or restriction of standard language ideology. But it is important to emphasize the point (noted earlier) that language standardization is an ideological process that has never run to completion, also that standardization has always existed in a tension with vernacularization (not so named). "Vernacular" and "standard" are mutually defining concepts, although the general concept of vernacularity is in even more urgent need of clarification than its converse; it has never been securely defined in sociolinguistics since Labov's early claim (1972: 208) that "the vernacular" – in his determined and realist sense – should be recognized as the (psycholinguistically) least monitored, (structurally) most regular and (empirically) most important style of speech in a speech community[7].

Because vernacularity exists in mutual contradistinction to standardness, the same disadvantages of objectifying "vernaculars" ("vernacular varieties") as linguistic varieties surface as with "standards" ("standard varieties"). And if standardization is an ideological drive towards uniformity and (in Milroy and Milroy's terms) to suppress variation, then vernacularization should be defined as resistance to these movements; vernacularization is an ideological drive towards plurality and difference as they exist outside of the normatizing influences of standardization, although plurality in a descriptive sense might be just as impossible to evidence as uniformity. Bell (2011: 179) characterizes destandardization in very similar terms, invoking Bakhtin's (1981) distinction between centripetal and centrifugal ideological forces in relation to language variation. The etymology of (Latin) "vernus", referring to a slave who has gained some forms of autonomy is, as I have said elsewhere, suggestive in this regard (Coupland 2011: 595). Does vernacularization imply a struggle against containment? From a Bourdieu-inspired perspective, standardization can be construed as a funnelling and filtering process through which diverse cultural forms and practices are denied access into supposedly rarified cultural spaces defined by judgements of taste and propriety, and policed by authoritative discourses. Vernacularization is then a movement to reduce such filtering and blocking constraints, and to assert the value and legitimacy of diverse, culturally grounded forms and practices. In Figure 1's terms,

---

7 A recent use of the concept "vernacular" is Cheshire, Kerswill, Fox and Torgersen's (2011) paper on multicultural London English. The authors argue that the "vernacular base line" for many young London speakers has moved from one that was largely Cockney (or working-class London) in the 1980s to one that is largely multicultural today, even though they are regularly perceived to be speaking a "black" variety. While the (nominal) "vernacular" may be a useful short-hand in referring to a speech style that, according to descriptive criteria, is widely attested in a sample population, it risks foreclosing on contextual, ideological and perspectival issues. Is "the vernacular" not prone to contextual variation? Does (adjectival) "vernacular" imply low attributed status, and from whose perspectives?

vernacularization (or destandardization in Kristiansen's sense) as a sociolinguistic change will be most directly realized in the aspiration to allow previously "blocked" linguistic features, styles and genres to "pass the filter" into domains that have been the preserves of standardness. But it will also be reflected in changing norms and reflexive commentaries on usage; vernacular performances will be symbolically mediated into new contexts, and into popular consciousness. Through its state of tension with standardization, and like standardization itself, vernacularization will never fully run its course, and it will involve continuous evaluative renegotiations of where boundaries between adjudged "standards" and "vernaculars" lie.

Because vernacularity is inherently plural (there is never only one, uniform "vernacular") and based in an ideology of openness and accessibility, it is currently difficult to define its sociolinguistic frames of reference. Influenced by Labov's discussions of "the vernacular", "Black English Vernacular", and so on (Labov 1972, and see note 7), we may first think of dialect dimensions of vernacularity – the canonical conception of regionally and socially "nonstandard" speech, descriptively indexed by phonological, morpho-syntactic and lexical features. For the sake of simplicity, and because I am only aspiring to a preliminary account here, I shall restrict my comments on British media (in the next section) to this dialectal dimension of vernacularity and vernacularization. But in line with Elias and Bourdieu's theories of civilization and distinction, it is clear that many modes of social practice are evaluated and controlled in relation to norms of properness, taste, refinement, social desirability, etc. and their converses, including styles of personal demeanour, patterns of self-disclosure, modes of interpersonal address, politeness, tact and humour, and even the use/ non-use of particular languages. These and related dimensions of sociolinguistic performance are negotiated relative to local contextual norms, so it will not be possible to label particular features, utterances or styles "standard" or "vernacular" out of context. The touchstone will be how they are contextualized and reflexively evaluated, and vernacularization can only be established to be a sociolinguistic change relative to earlier normative constraints.

6 Vernacularization through broadcast British media: Research agenda

In this final section I explore the theoretical and methodological challenges that need to be overcome if we are to evidence vernacularization as a sociolinguistic change in progess. I limit my comments to British broadcast media, on the basis that (a) Britain is acknowledged to have been for some time a "standard language culture", (b) English in Britain is generally acknowledged to be a highly standardized language, (c) broadcast media in Britain, and the BBC in particular, have been intimately associated with linguistic standardization in the past (see references to Mugglestone and Agha, above, also the review in Bell 2011: 178 ff.), and (d) there have already been intimations (again in Mugglestone's research) that popular broadcast media are active in selectively resisting standard language ideology. I am not assuming that the BBC's historical role in connection with linguistic standardization has come to an abrupt end, or that SLI is no longer driving many representations and performances of spoken English in British broadcasting – I assume it is, albeit selectively and with some detectable, strong counter-currents.

If vernacularization is selective in relation to broadcast genres, then research initiatives will need to reflect this, for example in attending to specific genres on some principled basis[8]. News broadcasting has often been associated with SLI, and in fact Bell (2011: 178) argues that "broadcast news serves as the working definition of the standard language", largely by virtue of the positioning of exemplary speakers (Agha 2003) in the "news-reader" role. BBC news, particularly in its most prominently scheduled TV (BBC1 and BBC2 channels) and radio (Radio 4) news broadcasts, represents the broadcaster functioning in its "most serious" and "most authoritative" mode, and historically, this has provided the indexical basis for understanding broadcast RP. Contrastive real-time survey-type research in Britain would, we can safely assume, establish that the range of dialect styles featured in these news-reading slots has broadened over time, if only through the inclusion of some Welsh- and many Scottish-accented voices among the (short) list of senior news presenters[9].

Distributional evidence of this sort is of course relevant and would suggest the "unblocking of the filter of standardization" in one key broadcast domain. But such surveys are difficult to construct and to interpret. Welsh- and Scottish-accented English voices in Britain can be considered "vernacular" relative to RP, in the simple sense that they index regional provenance when RP is supposedly "regionless". However, another interpretation would be that the BBC is nowadays investing a slightly wider catchment of social personas with the authoritative role

---

8 The BBC currently recognizes that its programming spans ten main genres – "children's, comedy, drama, entertainment, factual, learning, music, news, religion & ethics, and sport" – several of them divided into sub-genres. See http://www.bbc.co.uk/tv/programmes/genres (this and other cited web pages were last consulted 2nd July 2013).

9 A list of current BBC news presenters is available at http://news.bbc.co.uk/aboutbbcnews/hi/profiles/default.stm?oo=463&askid=d21cf22f-53d0–49eb-876a-c9b36948e543–0-uk_gsb

once reserved for RP voices; it is standardizing them. The consequence would be a somewhat more inclusive conception of a broadcast "standard", and it might suggest a modest retreat from the ideological suppression of variability that constitutes standardization. But there would not be any evidence of positive valorizing of "vernaculars" *qua* vernaculars. There is also the particular consideration that Wales and Scotland can lay increasingly strong claims to degrees of national autonomy, and that some (definitely not all) of their accent varieties have been considered "standard", at least on their own cultural turf, by virtue of indexing preferred modes of national self-styling (see Garrett et al. 2003 for discussion of this issue in the Welsh case).

It would remain true that most class-linked British accents are deemed non-viable in "serious" news-presenting roles. A more productive focus might be on the wide range and large number of correspondent roles populated at the BBC (see the link at note 6), where "seriousness" and professional expertise are again prerequisites of the role but where accents are more variable and dialect indexicality seems to be increasingly less salient. In the dialect dimension, correspondents do not seem, nowadays, to have to perform professionalism through a fully-formed RP style, although there still appear to be restrictions on which dialect styles and features can fill out professional roles. Detailed stylistic analyses might reveal a pattern whereby key phonological markers of specific UK regions (e.g. "northern England" markers) have come to be considered compatible with professional demeanour. Correspondents are an interesting group because they are less pointedly positioned as performing "the voice of the BBC", and there may be semiotic utility, for them and for the broadcaster, in displaying a level of "vernacular groundedness", for example in the analysis of economic trends that impact on the general public.

Changing norms need to be established in dimensions of media design and recipiency, as well as in practice itself, so it will be necessary to supplement distributional surveys and stylistic analyses with attitudinal data of various sorts which can confirm associations between usages and value ascriptions. Media producers and performers necessarily have their own frameworks for appraising vocal "appropriateness" and audience appeal. Audiences are often motivated to engage in public and private metalinguistic appraisals of broadcast performers and performances, for example in the "complaint tradition" (consumers complaining about "standards" of English usage, as discussed by Milroy 2001; Milroy and Milroy 1985b). As I noted earlier, sociolinguistic research on standardization has mainly focussed on the forms and features of "standard" styles, and far less on the contextualization and social evaluation of styles. But attitudinal surveys (e.g. Coupland and Bishop 2007) have already picked up widening patterns of public acceptance and liking of some major British accent varieties that now have more currency in broadcasting, including more favourable orientations to Scottish (and to some extent Welsh) English varieties, as discussed above,

Back in the domain of practice, evidence of vernacularization is likely to be available when we look closely at the contextualization of dialect styles. SLI has not simply excluded vernacular styles from mass media contexts; it has required clear and consistent indexical relations to be matched with relevant vocal performances and performers (Androutsopoulos 2010a). Vernacularity, so to speak, has needed to know its place in mass media. Vernacular British accents were represented in early British TV, radio and film (Marriott 2002 deals with the particular case of a British war film), but audiences did not need to reflexively evaluate their meanings, which were evident in relevant characters' social roles – as aircraft mechanics, refuse collectors, music hall entertainers, or simply as "working class people". There tended to be normative congruence between voice and social role. A simple quantitative measure showing that, in some proportional calculation, contemporary British media display vernacular ways of speaking and identities more than they did previously (see Trudgill's observations in note 6) would not necessarily amount to evidence that new relations between language and society are being constructed. It might suggest a general shift in broadcasting priorities and genre representation away from public service functions towards popular entertainment (Thussu 2007), also towards more interactive and public-participation frameworks, and vernacularization in those senses. As in the case of news presenting, there are still relatively closed "no-go areas" for non-near-RP in the BBC, just as there are some relatively clear no-go areas for RP, such as in stand-up comedy, presenting for children or in DJing contemporary music (on BBC Radio 1). But dialect styles "not knowing their place" would be test cases for researching vernacularization; vernacularization can reside in the fracturing of traditional indexical relations.

There are many particular instances in contemporary British television and radio where vernacular voice not only features in a non-traditional media space (as in the BBC correspondents example, above) but where it plays productively against other semiotic aspects of persona projection. We see a rash of "celebrity experts", who are sometimes academics, generally not in direct employment by media corporations but commissioned to front prime-time series on "serious" themes, such as astronomy, environmental science, history or architecture. In several of these cases vernacular voice appears to have no conventional associations with place or class, but contributes to a composite styling of "the accessible and individualized expert" (cf. the suggestion of "vernacular groundedness", above). Mediatization is creating ever-more platforms for performance, and even the most durable media institutions need to help their performers and themselves compete for audience share. Semiotic constellations such as "the Glaswegian history expert" or "the Oldham astronomy expert" find coherence in an ideological system where commodification and individualization (cf. Bauman 2001; Beck and Beck-Gernsheim 2002) conspire to override more traditional meanings of class and authority.

When Mugglestone claimed that, for RP, the attribution "proper" was being supplanted by the attribution "posh", she implied that a formerly elite way of speaking that had been able to assert its own authoritative value from above was in the process of being re-ideologized as an unconvincing, overly self-regarding way of speaking, when seen from below. Perspectivizing language diversity "from below" may prove to be a generalisable quality of late-modern broadcasting in Britain. Mass media institutions appear to have new reservations about being seen to be "too posh", perhaps too uniformly so in specific programme formats or series. Outside of news and current affairs programming, in surprisingly diverse fields of public interest such as gardening, cookery, antiques collecting and nature watching, the BBC has kept faith with particular programme series which, for many viewers, came to define the Corporation's core values, with clear conservative and middle-class resonances. Recent years have seen moves to break up these mediated enclaves in semiotic terms, by introducing not only vernacular voices but non-elite perspectives.

Another manifestation of "from below" programming is visible in the stylization of RP performances, which quite overtly deconstruct older indexical relations between class and privilege (cf. Coupland 2007). With *Monty Python* as one of the earliest and most celebrated British instances, we have seen repeated incarnations of the "foolish posh" persona, not only in comedy itself but in a range of performers who deauthenticate the social meanings of their posh voices, self-consciously recontextualizing dialect "standardness" with projected uncertainties around their own seriousness, competence and commitment. There might prove to be two different versions: personas projected as being "posh but foolish", and personas projected as being "foolish because posh". These performances destabilize the traditional ideological value-structure of RP, at least in its more conservative styles, as "the voice of authority", where the general stylistic effect is self-parody. One instance is a frequently used voiceover announcer, most famous for his booming RP voice and his (prosodic and rhetorical) over-performance, who commonly introduces popular culture TV shows. Interestingly, he has a counterpart who performs hyper-dialectal Geordie (Newcastle) voiceovers and narration to similar shows (including a long-running reality game show). In these instances vocal stylization has clearly, once again, washed out traditional meanings of RP and vernacular voice. Dialectally very divergent styles have been disembedded from their sociolinguistic roots "in the community" and mediated into contexts where they have no clear-cut, independent indexical value, but contribute to unique semiotic confections of voice, image and demeanour.

If we stand back from these particular analytic possibilities and take in the widest spectrum of broadcast vocal indexicalities, we are confronted with an ever-more complex and diverse spread of forms and meanings. Globalization in its cultural dimension is a process of semiotic complexification and disembedding, and broadcast media provide platforms for these social actors to become reflexively aware of these expansive shifts. The sociolinguistics of style has focussed on how, in local instances, relatively coherent identities and stances can be reassembled from all this semiotic complexity. It has come to use the concept of "bricolage" (e.g. Bucholtz 2011; Coupland 2007; Eckert 2008; Stroud and Wee 2012), implying the possibility of constructing situated social meanings from complex, disjointed semiotic resources. But we should not forget that the fundamental sociolinguistic change here is towards increasing complexity in the context of increased reflexivity, and that broadcast media are deeply implicated in reflecting, exposing and indeed constructing that complexity. Sociolinguistically speaking, the "standard/vernacular" contrast was historically conceived in less complex, less mediatized and more socially structured circumstances (certainly in Britain). It is interesting to speculate that what I am calling vernacularization in this chapter may simply be an early stage of semiotic pluralization (because, as noted earlier, vernacularity is necessarily plural) preceding more radical shifts that might displace social class and "standardness" from their traditional positions defining Britain's most salient axis of sociolinguistic diversity.

References

Agha, Asif 2003: The social life of cultural value. *Language ad Communication* 23: 231–273.
Agha, Asif 2007: *Language and Social Relations*. Cambridge: Cambridge University Press.
Androutsopoulos, Jannis 2010a: The study of language and space in media discourse. In: P. Auer and J. E. Schmidt (eds.), *Language and Space* (Volume 1, *Theories and Methods*), 740–58. Berlin/New York: Walter de Gruyter.
Androutsopoulos, Jannis 2010b: Localizing the global on the participatory web. In: Nikolas Coupland (ed.), *Handbook of Language and Globalization*, 203–31. Malden, MA Oxford: Wiley-Blackwell.
Androutsopoulos, Jannis 2011: Language change and digital media: A review of conceptions and evidence. In: Tore Kristiansen and Nikolas Coupland (eds.), *Standard Languages and Language Standards in a Changing Europe*, 145–60. Oslo: Novus Press.
Bakhtin, Mikhail 1981: *The Dialogic Imagination* (ed. Michael Holquist). Austin: University of Texas Press.
Bauman, Z. 2001: *The Individualized Society*. Cambridge: Polity Press.

Beck, Ulrich and E. Beck-Gernsheim 2002: *Individualization: Institutionalized Individualism and its Social and Political Consequences*. London: Sage.

Bell, Allan 2011: Leaving home: De-europeanization in a post-colonial variety of broadcast news. In: Tore Kristianen and Nikolas Coupland (eds.), *Standard Languages and Language Standards in a Changing Europe*, 177–198. Oslo: Novus Press.

Bex, Tony and Richard Watts (eds.) 1999: *Standard English: The Widening Debate*. London: Routledge.

Blommaert, Jan 2010: *The Sociolinguistics of Globalization*. Cambridge: Cambridge University Press.

Bonfiglio, Thomas P. 2002: *Race and the Rise of Standard American*. Berlin and New York: Mouton de Gruyter.

Bourdieu, Pierre 1977: *Outline of a Theory of Practice*. Cambridge: Cambridge University Press.

Bourdieu, Pierre 1991: *Language and Symbolic Power*. Cambridge: Polity.

Bourdieu, Pierre 2010: *Distinction: A Social Critique of the Judgement of Taste*. London/New York: Routledge.

Bucholtz, Mary 2001: The whiteness of nerds: Superstandard English and racial markedness. *Journal of Linguistic Anthropology* 11: 84–100.

Busch, Brigitta 2006: Changing media spaces: The transformative power of heteroglossic practices. In: C. Mar-Molinero and P. Stevenson (eds.), *Language Ideologies, Policies and Practices: Language and the Future of Europe*, 206–19. Basingstoke: Palgrave Macmillan.

Chambers, J. K. 1995: *Sociolinguistic Theory*. Oxford UK/Cambridge USA: Blackwell.

Cheshire, Jenny, Paul Kerswill, Susan Fox and Eivind Torgersen 2011: Contact, the feature pool and the speech community: The emergence of Multicultural London English. *Journal of Sociolinguistics* 15, 2: 151–196.

Cheshire, Jenny and Lesley Milroy 1993: Syntactic variation in nonstandard dialects: Background issues. In: J. Milroy and L. Milroy (eds.), *Real English: The Grammar of English Dialects in the British Isles*, 3–33. London: Longman.

Chouliaraki, Lilie an Norman Fairclough: 1999: *Discourse in Late Modernity: Rethinking Critical Discourse Analysis*. Edinburgh: Edinburgh University Press.

Coupland, Nikolas 2000: Sociolinguistic prevarication over standard English. Review article: Review of Tony Bex and Richard J. Watts (eds.) (1999) *Standard English: The Widening Debate*. London and New York: Routledge. *Journal of Sociolinguistics* 4, 4: 630–642.

Coupland, Nikolas 2003: Sociolinguistic authenticities. *Journal of Sociolinguistics* 7, 3: 417–431.

Coupland, Nikolas 2007: *Style: Language, Variation and Identity*. Cambridge: Cambridge University Press.

Coupland, Nikolas 2009: Dialects, standards and social change. In: Marie Maegaard, Frans Gregersen, Pia Quist and Jens Normann Jørgensen (eds.), *Language Attitudes, Standardization and Language Change*, 27–50. Oslo: Novus.

Coupland, Nikolas (ed.) 2010: *Handbook of Language and Globalization*. Malden, MA/Oxford: Wiley-Blackwell.

Coupland, Nikolas 2011: Voice, place and genre in popular music performance. *Journal of Sociolinguistics* 15, 5: 573–602.

Coupland, Nikolas and Hywel Bishop 2007: Ideologised values for British accents. *Journal of Sociolinguistics* 11, 1: 74–103.

Coupland, Nikolas and Tore Kristiansen 2011: SLICE: Critical perspectives on language (de) standardisation. In: T. Kristiansen and N. Coupland (eds.), *Standard Languages and Language Standards in a Changing Europe*, 11–35. Oslo: Novus.

Deumert, Ana and Wim Vandenbussche (eds.). 2003: *Germanic Standardizations: Past to Present*. Amsterdam/Philadelphia: Benjamins. 1–14.

Eckert, Penelope 2008: Variation and the indexical field. *Journal of Sociolinguistics* 12, 4: 453–476.

Elias, Norbert 2000: *The Civilizing Process: Sociogenic and Psychogenic Investigations*. Malden, MA.: Blackwell Publishing.

Fairclough, Norman 1992: *Discourse and Social Change*. Cambridge: Polity Press.

Fairclough, Norman 1994: Conversationalisation of public discourse and the authority of the consumer. In: Russell Keat, Nigel Whitely and Nicholas Abercrombie (eds.), *The Authority of the Consumer*, 253–268. London: Routledge.

Fairclough, Norman 2006: *Language and Globalisation*. London: Routledge.

Garrett, Peter 2010: *Attitudes to Language*. Cambridge: Cambridge University Press.:

Garrett, Peter, Nikolas Coupland and Angie Williams 2003: *Investigating Language Attitudes: Social Meanings of Dialect, Ethnicity and Performance*. Cardiff: University of Wales Press.

Gal, Susan 1979: *Language Shift: Social Determinants of Linguistic Change in Bilingual Austria*. New York: Academic Press.

Giddens, Anthony 1991: *Modernity and Self-Identity: Self and Society in the Late Modern Age*. Cambridge: Polity.

Guy, Gregory 1990: The sociolinguistic types of change. *Diachronica* 7, 1: 47–67.

Hannerz, Ulf 1992: *Cultural Complexity: Studies in the Social Organization of Meaning*. New York: Columbia University Press.

Harrington, Jonathan 2006: An acoustic analysis of "happy-tensing" in the Queen's Christmas broadcasts. *Journal of Phonetics* 34: 439–457.

Harrington, Jonathan, Sallyanne Palethorpe and Catherine Watson 2000: Does the Queen speak the Queen's English? *Nature* 408 (December 21–28): 927–8.

Haugen, Einar 1966: Dialect, language, nation. *American Anthropologist* 68, 6: 922–935. (Extracted as Language standardization. In: Nikolas Coupland and Adam Jaworski (eds.) 1997, *Sociolinguistics: A Reader and Coursebook*. Basingstoke: Macmillan. 341–352.

Hinskens, Frans, Peter Auer and Paul Kerswill 2005: The study of dialect convergence and divergence: Conceptual and methodological considerations. In: P. Auer, F. Hinskens and P. Kerswill (eds.), *Dialect Change: Convergence and Divergence in European Languages*, 1–48. Cambridge: Cambridge University Press.

Hymes, Dell 1974: *Foundations in Sociolinguistics: An Ethnographic Approach*. Philadelphia: University of Pennsylvania Press.

Jaffe, Alexandra and Cedric Oliva 2013: Linguistic creativity in Corsican tourist context. In: Sari Pietikäinen and Helen Kelly-Holmes (eds.), *Mulilingualism and the Periphery*, 95–117. New York: Oxford University Press.

Jaworski, Adam, Nikolas Coupland and Darek Galasiński (eds.) 2004 : *Metalanguage: Social and Ideological Perspectives*. Berlin/New York: Mouton de Gruyter.

Joseph, John E. 1987: *Eloquence and Power: The Rise of Language Standards and Standard Languages*. London: Frances Pinter.

Kerswill, Paul 2001: Mobility, meritocracy and dialect levelling: The fading (and phasing) out of Received Pronunciation. In: P. Rajamäe and K. Vogelberg (eds.), *British Studies in the New Millennium: The Challenge of the Grassroots*, 45–58. Tartu: University of Tartu.

Kress, Gunther and Theo van Leeuwen 2001: *Multimodal Discourse: The Modes and Media of Contemporary Communication*. New York: Oxford University Press.

Kristiansen, Tore 2001: Two standards: One for the media and one for the school. *Language Awareness* 10, 1: 9–24.

Kristiansen, Tore 2009: The macro-social meanings of late-modern Danish accents. *Acta Linguistica Hafniensia* 41: 167–192.

Kristianen, Tore and Nikolas Coupland (eds.) 2011: *Standard Languages and Language Standards in a Changing Europe*. Oslo: Novus Press.

Labov, William 1972: *Sociolinguistic Patterns*. Philadelphia: University of Pennylvania Press.

Labov, William 1994: *Principles of Linguistic Change. Volume 1: Internal Factors*. Malden, MA and Oxford: Blackwell Publishers.

Labov, William 2001: *Principles of Linguistic Change. Volume 2: Social Factors*. Malden, MA/ Oxford: Blackwell Publishers.

Livingstone, Sonia 2009: On the mediation of everything. *Journal of Communication* 59, 1: 1–18.

Machin, David and Theo van Leeuwen 2007: *Global Media Discourse*. London: Routledge.

Machin, David and Theo van Leeuwen 2010: Global media and the regime of lifestyle. In: Nikolas Coupland (ed.), *Handbook of Language and Globalization*, 625–43. Malden, MA and Oxford: Wiley-Blackwell.

Marriott, Stephanie 2002: Dialect and dialectic in a British war film. *Journal of Sociolinguistics* 1, 2: 173–193.

Mattheier, K. J. 1997: Über Destandardisierung, Umstandardisierung und Standardisierung in modernen europäischen Standardsprachen. In: K. J. Mattheier and E. Radtke (eds.), *Standardisierung und Destandardisierung europäischer Nationalsprachen*, 1–9. Frankfurt a. M.: PeterLang.

Milroy, James 2001: Language ideologies and the consequences of standardization. *Journal of Sociolinguistics* 5, 4: 530–555.

Milroy, James and Lesley Milroy 1985a: Linguistic change, social network and speaker innovation. *Journal of Linguistics* 21: 339–384.

Milroy, James and Lesley Milroy 1985b: *Authority in Language: Investigating Language Prescription and Standardisation*. London/New York: Routledge and Kegan Paul.

Milroy, Lesley 2004: Language ideologies and linguistic change. In: C. Fought (ed.), *Socilinguistic Variation: Critical Reflections*. New York: Oxford University Press. 161–77.

Mugglestone, Lynda 1995: *Talking Proper: The Rise of Accent as Social Symbol*. Oxford: Clarendon Press.

Pedersen, Inge Lise 2009: The social embedding of standard language ideology through four hundred years of standardisation. In: M. Maegaard, F. Gregersen, P. Quist and J. N. Jørgensen (eds.), *Language Attitudes, Standardization and Language Change*, 51–68. Oslo: Novus.

Pennycook, Alastair 2007: *Global Englishes and Transcultural Flows*. London: Routledge.

Pietikäinen, Sari, Alexandra Jaffe, Hellen Kelly-Holmes and Nikolas Coupland (in preparation) : *Small Languages in New Circumstances*.

Piippo, Irina 2012: Viewing norms dialogically: An action-oriented approach to sociolinguistic metatheory. PhD Disertation, University of Helsinki.

Quilly, Stephen and Steven Loyal 2004: Towards a "central theory": The scope and relevance of the sociology of Norbert Elias. In: Steven Loyal and Stephen Quilley (eds.), *The Sociology of Norbert Elias*, 1–24. Cambridge: Cambridge University Press.

Rampton, Ben 2006: *Language in Late Modernity: Interaction in an Urban School.* Cambridge: Cambridge University Press.

Romaine, Suzanne 1988: Contributions from pidgin and creole studies to a sociolinguistic theory of language change. *International Journal of the Sociology of Language* 71: 59–66.

Scollon, Ron and Suzie Wong Scollon 2004: *Nexus Analysis: Discourse and the Emerging Internet.* London: Routledge.

Snell, Julia 2010: From sociolinguistic variation to socially strategic stylisation. *Journal of Sociolinguistics* 14, 5: 630–656.

Stroud, Christopher and Lionel Wee 2012: *Style, Identity and Literacy: English in Singapore.* Clevedon: Multilingual Matters.

Stuart-Smith, Jane 2011: The view from the couch: Changing perspectives on the role of television in changing language ideologies and use. In: T. Kristianen and N. Coupland (eds.), *Standard Languages and Language Standards in a Changing Europe,* 223–39. Oslo: Novus Press.

Thussu, Daia Kishan 2007: *News as Entertainment: The Global Rise of Infotainment.* Los Angeles: Sage.

Trudgill, Peter 2002: *Sociolinguistic Variation and Change.* Edinburgh: Edinburgh University Press.

Trudgill, Peter 2008: Colonial dialect contact in the history of European languages: On the irrelevance of identity to new-dialect formation. *Language in Society* 37, 2: 241–54.

Urban, Greg 2001: *Metaculture: How Culture Moves through the World.* Minneapolis: University of Minnesota Press.

Woolard, Kathryn 2008: Why *dat* now? Linguistic-anthropological contributions to the explanation of sociolingustic icons and change. *Journal of Sociolinguistics* 12, 4: 432–452.

Section II: **Media influence on language change**

Tore Kristiansen
Does mediated language influence immediate language?

1 Introduction

Language as such is 'mediated' in the sense that a formed substance is necessary to express linguistic meaning. In order to form the substance, we make use of technologies. We use 'physiological technologies' to form sound waves that make sense in spoken language, and gestures that make sense in signed language. We apply writing and printing technologies to a multitude of substances in forming 'strokes' to be made sense of in written language. While reminding us that 'mediation' is inherent to language in this fundamental sense, reference to the forming of substance – and thus the technological aspect of speaking, signing and writing – may also serve as an introductory reminder that 'language in use' always occurs (materializes) in context, and is inextricably tied up with the possibilities and limitations defined by contextual factors, of many kinds.

New technologies create new conditions and contexts for language use. Historically speaking, the reality of linguistic 'norm and variation' has undergone radical changes as the transmission/construction of meaning in society has gone from being only face-to-face (in purely oral cultures) to being mediated first by writing, then by broadcast media, and finally (for the time being) by internet-based social media – to mention the more conspicuous stages in the development of mediated language.

Notwithstanding the 'mediated' nature of language, as signalled above, a distinction between *immediate* language and *mediated* language – based on differences to do with context – will be central to the discussion in this chapter. *Immediate language* will be used to refer to language occurring in the context of face-to-face interaction, whereas *mediated language* will be reserved for language use based on some technology that 'liberates' the transmission/construction of meaning from the contextual constraints of face-to-face interaction. As speaking and signing are based on technologies that in themselves do not allow for communication beyond the context of face-to-face, ordinary everyday instances of speaking or signing are instances of immediate language. In contrast, as the technology of writing allows for (is created for) communication beyond the context of face-to-face, instances of written texts are instances of mediated language. Likewise, the language distributed by broadcast and internet technologies is mediated language, be it spoken, signed or written. The purpose of the chapter is to pursue the issue of *whether immediate language is influenced by mediated language* – and if so, to what extent, and in which ways.

While immediate language is subjected to conditions of micro-level (face-to-face) interaction, mediated language belongs at the macro-level of social life. The technologies of mass communication (writing and printing, broadcasting, the internet) are fundamental to the institutions that maintain the public spheres of modern society. Thus, mediated language is not just language that is 'liberated' from the constraints of here and now; mediated language is also language that is 'enmeshed' in the ideological structures of society at large. If we want to use particular terms for these two aspects of mediated language, *mediation* may be used for the introduction and existence of technologies that take linguistic communication beyond the context of face-to-face, while *mediatization* may be the more appropriate term for the repercussions on language from being invested in the fabric of the larger society. (For a general discussion of these terms, see Livingstone 2009.)

The mediation and mediatization aspects of mediated language relate differently to a distinction between *direct* and *indirect* influence which is central to the discussion in the chapter. In order to determine whether mediated language influence immediate language, we have to consider the possibility of both direct and indirect influence. Influence would be *direct* if it happens by *mediation* – i. e. by virtue of the introduction and existence of mass communication technologies as such. Influence would be *indirect* if it happens by *mediatization* – i. e. by virtue of language being invested in the power and value hierarchies which support and are supported by the technologies and institutions of mass media communication.

There is a long-standing tradition for controversy among linguists over the influence of writing, broadcast media, and more recently of internet-based social media on everyday language. Such influence is often trivialised if not totally denied. However, the linguistic approach to the issue tends to be limited to considerations of direct influence (mediation in the sense above), whereas the evaluative dimension of language use (and hence indirect influence through processes of mediatization) often falls outside of what linguistic scholars find appropriate to take into consideration. More surprisingly, the same kind of approach, and conclusion, is also subscribed to among variationist sociolinguistics. In particular concerning TV, this 'received view' has it that there is no influence from speech on TV on speech in everyday life. On the contrary, influence which leads to change is claimed to progress from immediate language to mediated language, possibly with some change in social evaluation (attitudes for short) in between: IMMEDIATE LANGUAGE → ATTITUDES → MEDIATED LANGUAGE.

In our work in Denmark, we have found and argued that ideology plays an important and even decisive role in language change, and we do believe that the media, not least television, has an influencing role in the process (Kristiansen 2001, 2009; Maegaard et al. 2013). The present chapter is an attempt to pursue this issue by comparing Denmark with Norway – thus comparing two countries which have developed very different standard–dialect constellations. Hopefully, the comparison will shed light on the reality of mediated language as a source of influence – and furthermore on the role of direct (mediation) vs. indirect (mediatization) influence – in processes of language change. Strongly expressed, the hypothesis for the comparison turns the commonly-suggested direction of influence around: MEDIATED LANGUAGE → ATTITUDES → IMMEDIATE LANGUAGE. The discussion will be limited to considering *speech* as an object to be influenced, and *writing* and *broadcast media* as sources of influence.[1]

2 Direct influence from writing on speech in Denmark?

When the Renaissance and the Reformation – the era of book printing and Bible translations – put the construction of national standards for writing (and reading!) on the agenda in many European countries, the speech heard in Copenhagen at the court and in academia was selected by the printers and pointed out by the early grammarians as the 'best language' to be used in writing. The issue as to whether the norm that was developed for writing and printing has had an impact on speech falls into two parts.

On the one hand, there is the question of the role of the norm for writing (in the sense of orthography) in relation to the spoken (Copenhagen) variety which it is claimed to represent. From the very beginning, the norm contained a number of features with a 'problematic' (not straightforward 'phonetic-writing') relationship to Copenhagen speech. Perhaps most noticeable in our context here is the use of the letters *b d g* to represent sounds that, through a general lenition of originally unvoiced stops after long vowels, by the 16th century had most likely been replaced by fricatives or even further lenitioned variants in Copenhagen as in Denmark more generally (most North Germanic varieties outside Denmark still have /p t

---

1 If other appropriate perspectives on the issue are left aside – such as the influence of mediation on signed language, and the influence of social media technology on immediate language – it is because such an extension would take us far beyond the scope of this article. For discussions on social media, see the chapters by Deumert, Georgakopoulou, Moriarty, Pietikäinen, and Squires and Irio in this volume.

k/). There is no general consensus in this matter, but it may well be that the gap between pronunciation and writing has played a role in sustaining a long-standing variation in speech and in motivating a return to less lenitioned and (arguably) more letter-like pronunciations. Words written with *d* (as in *hade*; cf. Norwegian *hate*; 'hate') are known to have been frequently pronounced with [j] in Copenhagen, but is in the modern standard consistently pronounced with an approximant [ð], called *det bløde d* 'the soft d'. Many words written with *b* (as in *håbe*; cf. Norwegian *håpe*; 'hope') vary stylistically in pronunciation between [w] and [b]. It is possible that these instances of variation and possible restoration in standard Danish pronunciation are to be seen as results of *direct* influence from writing – in the sense that (common representations of) 'letter pronunciations' are transferred directly to ordinary speech without any evaluative interference. However, social evaluation clearly appears to be part of the game when we consider that the persistent [b]-pronunciation in *-Vb(e)* words counts as the more formal option, while the disappeared [j]-pronunciation in *-Vd(e)* words used to be a Copenhagen working class stereotype. More importantly, it is beyond doubt that the many phonetic changes in Copenhagen speech over the last two hundred years in most cases have *distanced* the spoken form of words from their written form. The changes are testimonies to the insignificance of orthography's influence on people's phonetics, as strongly and convincingly argued by Brink and Lund (1975) in their monumental description of phonetic variation and change in Copenhagen speech from the first half of the nineteenth century into the post-Second World War decades.

On the other hand, there is the question of the role of the written norm in relation to all the other (non-Copenhagen) varieties. The fate of the traditional dialects in the same period testifies, again, to the insignificance of orthography's influence on people's everyday phonetics. Compulsory schooling was introduced in Denmark in 1814, and the school institution has ever since been the main instrument in the social elite's endeavours to institutionalize the written language as the medium of education and (national) culture. It has always been self-evident that the spoken corollary of the written language is Copenhagen upper-class speech, and that this spoken and written language, called *rigsdansk*, is the school's language, the target for teachers and pupils to strive for (Kristiansen 1990). All in vain. Pupils may have done what they could to talk 'properly' in the classroom, but in breaks between classes, they still spoke in the local dialect in 1960 (as is reported to have been the case in Hirtshals, a community in north-western Jutland which was thoroughly investigated with regard to both language use and language attitudes around 1980, at which time the children no longer used the local dialect during breaks; Hansen and Lund 1983).

It should be mentioned, though, that another type of candidate for direct influence from writing on speech is found in the western (Jutland and Funen based) version of *rigsdansk*. This variety, which is the common variety among young westerners today, differs from the eastern (Copenhagen based) version most prominently by virtue of intonation, i.e. features with no representation in writing, but also by virtue of a few phonological differences, including the pronunciation of the written endings *-ede* and *-et* (common conjugational and declinational morphemes). In the west, these endings are frequently pronounced with a dental stop instead of what is commonly known as *det bløde d* ('the soft d'), an approximant which is the 'standard' and predominant eastern pronunciation. Alien to these endings in the traditional dialects the western stop pronunciation is likely to have its roots in a pronunciation that was used when reading aloud; it was used for the letter *d* because the required 'soft d' was absent from the sound repertoire of the vast majority of the western traditional dialects. In spite of being the clearly most frequent of the very few segmental differences that separates the western and eastern versions of the standard, the awareness of it is low among both westerners and easterners. A reason why this difference goes largely unnoticed may be seen, arguably, in the fact that the *-et* ending (but hardly the *-ede* ending) can be heard with the stop pronunciation also among easterners – in situations where they wish to make their speech more 'distinct'. It seems to be a fairly common conception that the stop pronunciation is more distinct than 'the soft d' pronunciation – probably because the stop is conceived of as closer to the written form.

With a possible exception for the stop pronunciation in the *-ede* and *-et* endings – where little or no social evaluation seems to be involved (an assumption that needs to be tested in empirical research) – we can summarize that the medium of writing does not seem to have had much direct influence on immediate language use in Denmark, either standard or non-standard.

3 Direct influence from writing on speech in Norway?

At the time when book-printing and Bible-translations were among the first exponents of the historical processes to develop nation states and standard languages in Europe, Norway had been a part of the Danish kingdom for 200 years, and was to remain so for 200 years more. Ideologically, dialects in Norway were not conceived of as different from dialects in Denmark in terms of their relationship to the elite variety spoken in the power centre of the kingdom, in Copenhagen at the court and in academia.

The Danish written norm has had considerable influence on spoken language in Norway. Towards the end of the eighteenth century, the members of the Danish/ Norwegian upper class in some of the more important cities, Christiania (today's Oslo) in particular, had developed a standardized variety which was basically the written language with Norwegian phonology. Characteristic features included [p t k] for written *b d g*, as well as a stop consonant in the *-ede* and *-et* morphemes. And in accordance with written Danish (and Copenhagen speech), this upper class Oslo speech merged 'masculine' and 'feminine' and developed a two-gender system with definite 'common gender' forms ending in *-en* (*mannen* 'the man', *solen* 'the sun') and definite 'neuter' forms ending in *-et* (*huset* 'the house') – whereas Norwegian in general, except for the Bergen dialect, has three genders, with *-a* as the typical definite form of 'feminine' nouns in eastern varieties (*mannen* 'the man', *sola* 'the sun', *huset* 'the house').

It is possible to assume that inclusion of these new features were mainly a result of direct influence from the written language, in the sense that Norwegians must have ended definite feminine nouns in *-en* and not *-a* when reading aloud. Yet, as this difference has a long history as perhaps the best known social stereotype of Norwegian (*-en* is 'high', *-a* is 'low'), it is likely that social evaluation has influenced the use of the two forms, probably already in the initial developmental stages of the new Norwegian upper-class variety. Likewise, we may assume that Norwegians as a rule pronounced a stop in the *-ede* and *-et* endings when reading, simply because, like people in the western part of Denmark, they did not have the 'soft d' as part of their sound repertoire. However, unlike in Denmark today, the stop pronunciation was probably from the very beginning not only consciously recognized, but also evaluated as better than the Copenhagen pronunciation with 'soft d'.

In any case, there is no doubt that this Norwegian variety as a whole was generally recognized as highly influenced by the written language. In an article from 1832, the national liberation politician J.A. Hielm described it as "maybe rather a Danish dialect, modified in many aspects partly by the country's and region's older Norwegian dialect, partly by the book language or maybe inversely, the Norwegian original language in the same way modified by Danish".[2] There is also evidence that the variety's more transparent relationship to the written language added to the evaluative upgrading it earned from being the language of the urban upper class. For its closeness to writing, it could be considered the 'best language' in Denmark-Norway as a whole. An often quoted claim from the year 1779 by the Danish-born priest J.N. Wilse testifies to this: "The language spoken by people of

---

2 My translation of *maaske nærmest en Dansk Dialekt, modificeret i mange Dele deels ved Landets og Egnens ældre norske Dialekt, deels ved Bogsproget, eller maaskee omvendt, det norske Grundsprog paa samme Maade modificeret ved Dansk, og ved Bogsproget.*

distinction in Christiania is both the nicest in pronunciation and the closest to the main language which is used in writing .[3]"

Thus, when language became a high priority issue on the national liberation agenda around the middle of the nineteenth century, the creation of a Norwegian written language could be based either on what was referred to at the time as *dannet dagligtale* ('educated everyday speech') or on the Norwegian dialects as they were spoken by 'unspoiled' peasants. Both these roads to a Norwegian written standard were followed. The 'revolutionary' road was to discard the Danish-influenced variety spoken by the capital city upper-class, and instead construct the written norm on the basis of features that were shared by 'genuine' Norwegian dialects spoken by common people in the countryside. The 'reformist' road was to select the capital city upper-class variety as basis, not for creating a new written norm, but for making changes to the Danish written norm. Ideologically, this was possible because Norway was not fighting for its political independence against Denmark, but against Sweden (which had 'won' Norway in 1814 as an outcome of the Napoleonic wars). Linguistically, it posed no major challenges as the Norwegian *dannet dagligtale* had been developed on the basis of Danish writing. The most important aspect of the first Norwegianization of Danish orthography in 1907 (two years after full independence in 1905) was a fairly general change from *b d g* to *p t k* (in words like *håbe > håpe, gade > gate, kage > kake* 'hope, street, cake'); and the preterit ending *-ede* was replaced by *-et* (as in *kastede > kastet* 'trew').

Subsequently, a rather unique language situation developed in Norway. Since 1929, the outcome of the 'reformist' road has officially been called Bokmål ('Book language', or rather – somewhat self-contradictorily – 'Book speech'), and the 'revolutionary' road has officially been called Nynorsk (New Norwegian).[4] Because its orthography was construed as a (somewhat etymologizing) 'superstructure' that could unify the multitude of dialects, the Nynorsk written language was never conceived of as a medium for a particular spoken variety. Nobody speaks Nynorsk as their 'mother tongue'. People who write Nynorsk think of themselves as speakers of a dialect, not as speakers of Nynorsk. (One well-known slogan of the Nynorsk movement urged people in the 1970s to: *Tal dialekt*

---

3 My translation of *Det Sprog de fornemmere i Christiania tale, er baade det netteste i Udtale og nærmer sig meest til Hovedsproget som bruges i Skrift.*

4 It is decided locally which language is to be learned first by children in school, but from the 8th grade all Norwegians are taught to write in both languages, choosing one as their 'main language' and the other as their 'side language'. After peaking at nearly 40 per cent in 1939, the share of pupils who start school with Nynorsk fell drastically in the post-war decades, stabilizing at about 15 per cent in the 1970s.

og skriv nynorsk 'Speak dialect and write Nynorsk'). In contrast, it is not uncommon for people who use Bokmål in writing to think of themselves also as speakers of Bokmål. This may be seen as 'natural' and 'linguistically legitimate' in the case of those who are 'born into' the upper-class Oslo speech, which the Norwegianization of Danish spelling has been based on. It may still be 'natural,' but more as an ideological phenomenon with people whose speech might be argued to be linguistically 'better represented' in writing by Nynorsk than by Bokmål.

The important fact to point out in our perspective here is that none of the two Norwegian norms for writing seem to have had any direct influence on the way people talk. In spite of its very dominating position in the reality of writing (newspapers, books, etc.), written Bokmål seems neither to spearhead an advancement of traditional features of *dannet dagligtale* nor defend their previous position, as variationist studies show such features to be largely on the decline (as reported in Sandøy 1987: 252–253; Mæhlum et al. 2008: 155). As to Nynorsk, the language has developed no reality in speech at all except as a reading-aloud norm applied by some educated people in formal situations (broadcasted news presentations, university lectures, etc.).

4 Indirect influence from writing on speech in Denmark?

Communities with orthographies based on the phonetic principle are likely to develop ideologies about spelling as a guideline for proper speech. This holds true not only for languages with very simple letter-to-sound relationships (like Finnish, see Nuolijärvi and Vaattovaara 2011: 67), but more strikingly also for languages with a large gap between pronunciation and spelling. For English, Milroy and Milroy (1991: 66) mention that 'spelling-pronunciation' ideology succeeded in restoring initial [h] in words such as *herb, humour, humble, hotel*, which had remained [h]-less for many centuries in accordance with the French original. For Denmark, I established in a book-length study on how the 'norm and variation' issue is treated in schools (Kristiansen 1990) that the basic principle of spelling instruction is a request to 'speak distinctly in order to spell correctly'. The underlying assumption links the notion of 'distinct speech' to the written representation of words, and (re)produces the idea that there is a best way of speaking which is defined by writing. However, as the gap between pronunciation and spelling in Danish comes close to competing with this gap in English, the 'speak distinctly' principle is largely meaningless and has no effect as a pedagogical guideline to correct spelling. The same is true the other way round: as this kind of reference to a 'distinct' pronunciation most often will mean reference to a socially non-existing pronunciation, young people's immediate language is not influenced by the distinct-speech ideology in the sense that they begin to speak more 'spelling-like'. That is only half the story, however, as the distinct-speech ideology can be claimed to have a strong and negative effect on young people's linguistic self-image. The educational system as a whole produces a population which appears fairly united in the belief that they treat their language badly and speak it indistinctly. Public discourse is full of evidence to this effect. Danes are represented as particularly sloppy speakers who show little respect for their own language. Empirical studies indicate that Danes in general, and highly educated young Danes in particular, do indeed expose an extraordinarily low linguistic self-esteem. While the neighbouring Swedes strongly upgrade their own language in comparison with Danish, Danes agree with the Swedes and judge their own language to be less beautiful than Swedish (Kristiansen 2004).

The three Scandinavian languages have a common origin, and comparison with the neighbours is actually commonplace in the Danish complaints about their own slovenly ways with language. Because the Danish gap between 'sound and letter' results from a policy of keeping the orthography largely stable throughout centuries in spite of dramatic sound changes – sound changes which did not happen in Swedish and Norwegian – Danish is today far more similar to Swedish and Norwegian in writing than in speech. And since the relationship between pronunciation and spelling is simpler and more transparent in Swedish and Norwegian, there is little doubt that the Danes' possibility of seeing themselves in the Swedish and Norwegian mirror plays a decisive role in creating and sustaining their view of themselves as a bunch of mumblers – a nation that does not know how to treat its language with due respect by speaking distinctly. Reference to Swedish and Norwegian is actually a commonplace in this complaint tradition. Favourite examples are the lenition products, when the modern common Danish pronunciation of *sove, råbe, koge* ends in the same two-syllable /ɔuu/- diphthong in all three words, whereas Swedish and Norwegian pronunciations have consonants /v, p, k/ introducing the second syllable, corresponding to how the words are also written.

In brief, the mediating technology of writing does not influence immediate language directly, but by virtue of how the orthography is coded and maintained (i. e. 'words should have one fixed and stable form'), and by virtue of how the relationship between writing and speech is construed and taught in school (i. e. 'you need to speak distinctly in order to spell correctly'), a strong SLI (standard language ideology) dominates the Danish speech community. People have learned the lesson: 'The way we speak is not good enough; it is indistinct and does not live up to how it should be. There is a "best" language, the spoken counterpart of the written language, towards which we should all strive'. This ideology has beyond doubt been a driving force in the massive code shift which, from the 1960s onwards, has changed Denmark from a traditional dialect society to a highly standardized speech community.

5 Indirect influence from writing on speech in Norway?

In consequence of the 'reformist' and 'revolutionary' solutions to the language issue (see Section 3), Norway entered its era of full political independence in 1905 with two closely related written languages, which had been accorded equal status in a Parliamentary Act from 1885. Both camps, reformists and revolutionaries, had the same aim of contributing to building a 'normal' European nation state with a 'normal' standard language. Which road was the new state to support?

Throughout most of the twentieth century, the state pursued a policy of creating one written norm by allowing for a lot of variants in both existing norms which made them 'overlap', the idea being that subsequent progressive elision of non-overlapping forms would eventually result in only one written norm, of the rigid and stable kind that everyone else has. The principle, and the problems it caused, can be illustrated by the definite forms of (originally feminine) nouns where Nynorsk had -*i* in accordance with a number of western dialects, and Bokmål had -*en* corresponding to Danish standard and *dannet dagligtale* (*soli* vs. *solen* 'the sun'). In 1917, a reform introduced the optional variant -*a* (*sola*) in both orthographies in accordance with most eastern dialects. Subsequently, a reform in 1938 made the -*a* form obligatory in a lot of words in Bokmål, and upgraded the -*a* form to the 'main form' of the Nynorsk norm. The consequence was that the traditional social and cultural elite no longer saw the official language policy as a necessary element in the construction of the new Norwegian state, but rather saw it as a class-struggle effort by the social democrats in power. The explicit principle of the official policy stated that the two writing systems should be merged *på norsk folkemåls grund* 'on the basis of Norwegian common speech'. 'Educated speech' was no longer the basis of the Norwegianization project that created Bokmål. The -*a* form belonged to common people, including the working class of Oslo.

The upper-class reaction had to wait till after the war, but came in the 1950s in the form of strong 'anti-merger' campaigning, initiated and organized by the more conservative part of the 'reformist' camp. An increasing opposition prompted the state to retreat, and eventually the 'merger' politics was formally abandoned at the beginning of the twenty-first century. A whole century of 'language struggle', in which all parties involved aimed to create a 'normal' European state with a 'normal' standard language, ended in a situation unique to Norway:

two closely related official written norms, Nynorsk and Bokmål, both with an extensive system of variants which reflects dialectal differences.

Thus, the way in which the mediating technology of writing has been coded and maintained in Norway is very different from what we saw in the case of Denmark. Instead of writing a word in only one way, you can write a word in different ways. And – most importantly – these different ways are not pure spelling differences without any relation to speech: to start with, the option between Nynorsk and Bokmål is related to dialectal differences, and, in turn, the available options within Nynorsk and Bokmål do also reflect dialectal differences. When you teach and learn a writing system which reflects dialectal variation, you cannot avoid teaching and learning about dialectal variation and the relationship between speech and writing.[5] While it may be difficult for teachers and pupils to avoid reproducing SLI when they have to work with an orthography of the 'normal' Danish type, the 'abnormal' Norwegian system for writing has the opposite effect of vaccinating teachers and pupils against SLI and furthering 'a sense of linguistic diversity' which we may call 'dialect ideology' (DI).[6]

An understanding of the history and character of the Norwegian writing system and its role in developing DI instead of SLI is crucial to any attempt at explaining why present-day Norway is characterized not only by very vital traditional dialects, but by a dialectal diversity which is present and accepted as the normal state of affairs in all public domains: in schools, in media, and in Parliament.

---

5 It is actually forbidden by law for Norwegian teachers to correct the speech of their pupils. The duty is not for the pupils to appropriate a spoken standard, but for the teachers to adapt to the children's dialect. This principle was stipulated by a Parliamentary Act as far back as 1878, and at that time it was directed against the kind of speech corrections that were practised when children struggled with Danish or 'educated' pronunciation in reading-aloud exercises, but it has been restated several times since then and is still in force.

6 In his article on "The ideology of dialect in Switzerland", Richard J. Watts says in a footnote: "Peter Trudgill (personal communication) has pointed out to me that the situation in Norway may be compared to that in Switzerland with respect to the relationship between the dialects and the standard. Whether or not the notion of ideology of dialect can also be extended to cover the linguistic situation in Norway, however, must remain an open question for the moment" (Watts 1999: 99). If the question is still considered open, I think it is time for it to be closed.

6 Direct influence from broadcast media on speech?

The above account and comparison of Denmark and Norway indicates that writing has had limited direct influence on immediate language, while it has had much influence on language ideology – in ways that in turn have had important consequences for ordinary everyday language.

We now move on to look at whether similar or different conclusions are obtained when we ask: Does speech mediated by broadcast technology have an influence on people's immediate language? The traditional answer in variationist sociolinguistics is very clear, and has been persistently stressed and defended by leading figures of the discipline. The claim is that mediated language has no impact on immediate language. For someone's speech to be influenced, face-to-face interaction is necessary:

> The point about the TV set is that people, however much they watch and listen to it, do not talk to it (and even if they do, it cannot hear them!), with the result that no accommodation takes place. (Trudgill 1986: 40)

> [A]ll of the evidence (...) points to the conclusion that language is not systematically affected by the mass media, and is influenced primarily in face-to-face interaction with peers. (Labov (2001: 228)

There are many aspects to this issue, and few easy answers. I think one thing is clear: for a discussion to make sense, we need to be explicit about what we mean by what we are saying. To start with, what does it mean to point to *accommodation* (Trudgill) and *peers* (Labov) as characteristics of the kind of interaction where speech can be influenced? What happens in accommodation? Why peers? My own first associations go to the kind of 'social-psychological mechanisms' that take care of face-work and social identity construction. If that is a congenial understanding, relevant questions to the 'received view' position might address the underlying assumption that TV-watching does not in any way involve social identity work with a possible impact on watchers' use of language. (For questioning along this line, see Coupland 2007; Stuart-Smith 2011, and the chapter by Stuart-Smith and Ota in this volume). However, that line of questioning and reasoning is less pertinent if the influence on speech in face-to-face interaction is thought of not as 'social psychological mechanisms' but as 'automatic copying' dependent on frequency. To the extent that the variationist tradition builds on the 'automatic copying' understanding of influence (which seems to be increasingly the case with Labov and Trudgill; see discussion in Kristiansen 2011), the motivation for excluding the possibility of media influence becomes more unclear to me.

Another aspect we need to be clear and explicit about concerns the scope and extent of influence: 'what' and 'how much' is needed in order to talk of influence? There is no doubt, nor disagreement, that broadcast-usage of particular words or phrases, including particular pronunciations of these, may trigger temporary use in ordinary everyday speech. However, such instances of media influence will not qualify as direct in our sense, but as indirect. Social evaluation clearly plays a role in the life of 'fashionable ways with words'. This is not influence on usage or change in the sense of variationism. What variationists claim is that language is not *systematically* affected by mass media (see the quote from Labov above); the systems of sounds and grammar are left in peace. "There is no evidence for television or the other popular media disseminating or influencing sound changes or grammatical innovations", Chambers says, and sustains his point by referring to the quick and global spread of uptalk (i. e. high rising terminals, HRT):

> To date, uptalk is not a feature of any newsreader or weather analyst's speech on any natio-nal network anywhere in the world. More important, it is also not a regular, natural (unself-conscious) feature of any character's speech in sitcoms, soap operas, serials or interview shows anywhere in the world. Undoubtedly it will soon be, but that will only happen when television catches up with language change. Not vice versa. (Chambers 1998: 126)

A recent investigation in Denmark gives empirical support to the kind of under-standing and prediction that Chambers heralds here. Comparing real time changes in the pronunciation of short (a) in Danish Radio news reading with the real time development of a-fronting in the Copenhagen speech community, Thøgersen and Pharao (2013) established that the newsreader norm caught up with the community norm with a delay of some 20 years.

'[T]elevision catches up with language change, not vice versa' would be a reasonable statement to stress if someone claimed that innovative features of the 'regular, natural (unselfconscious)' kind that Chambers have in mind orig-inate with sitcom characters, not to speak of newsreaders, and then develop into language change (i. e. spread throughout the population). But has anybody ever claimed that? Chamber's position is more challenging in its other wording above. What does it mean that "[t]here is no evidence for television or the other popular media disseminating or influencing sound change or grammatical inno-vations"? If influence and dissemination are thought of as direct, as 'automatic copying', Chamber's claim is probably correct: there is no such evidence (and if direct influence does exist, without any intervention from 'social psychological mechanisms', evidence for it may in any case be difficult to obtain). However, Chamber's claim seems far more problematic to me if we take it as a denial that systematic aspects of everyday speech can be indirectly influenced by the value hierarchy which is reproduced – but also challenged and changed – by the many different ways with language in the many different formats and genres of modern broadcast media.

Furthermore, it seems to me that examples such as the two mentioned above do indicate that there is a *time and place* aspect to the influence issue that we need to be clear and explicit about. As an alternative to Chamber's model for world-wide diffusion of English innovations (like uptalk) without any media support, I find it reasonable to consider a model for Danish where innovations (like a-fronting) start and spread in a particular community (Copenhagen) before they with some delay in time appear and dominate in the media (because that community's speech dominates in the media, as it is the case with Copenhagen speech in Danish media). In that situation, the contention of a role for the media in the spread will apply first and foremost to 'other places' with the same media (the rest of Denmark). If an innovation in these 'other places' were found to parallel the media delay, it would constitute strong empirical support for the contention.

In the case of Danish a-fronting, it has been shown that communities across Denmark do indeed follow Copenhagen with some delay (Maegaard et al. 2013). But as the 'other places' lag behind in a non-uniform way, the distributional pattern found cannot result from direct media influence. (We must assume that direct influence from national broadcast media would yield the same result everywhere). The spread of a-fronting actually shows a gradual shift which indicates that the driving force is conditioned by either 'geographical distance' or 'population density', or both (so far the evidence does not allow us to decide). Thus, while the distributional pattern excludes direct media influence, it allows for two alternative explanations. On the one hand, it is compatible with the variationist tendency to rely on explanations in terms of 'automatic mechanisms' in face-to-face interaction. From this perspective, the spread of innovative features is explained by their frequency of occurrence as conditioned by factors such as geographical distance and population density. On the other hand, the distributional pattern found is also compatible with a view that holds that influence from broadcast language on everyday language is indirect and subjected to 'social psychological mechanisms' and ideological forces. I shall return to this issue in Section 7 below.

But first let me also suggest that we need to be more clear and explicit about whether we think of whole varieties (dialects) or individual variables when we talk of systematic change. One of the variationists' main arguments against any impact from the media is that *dialects live on*. Jane Stuart-Smith reports the argument as follows: "Sociolinguists working in the variationist paradigm on varieties of English in America and the UK have argued against a direct role for the broadcast media in systemic aspects of language change in direction of the standard, given the continued and documented diversity of non-standard dialects, particularly at the levels of phonology and morphosyntax (e.g. Milroy and Milroy 1985; Chambers 1998; Labov 2001): wholesale shifts do not appear to have taken place". Stuart-Smith goes on to say and document that "[t]his position contrasts strongly with that expressed by linguists and sociolinguists working outside English-speaking countries" (Stuart-Smith 2011: 224). Indeed, the dialects-live-on scenario is very far from Danish reality.

In brief, I think that a sensible discussion of the whole 'media influence' issue will have to begin by clarifying how the different positions understand 'influence', accompanied by explanations of how the defended understanding is compatible with the professed view of TV-watching versus face-to-face interaction in terms of potential for influence on speech. It may well be that the existing evidence at the level of variables does indeed testify to a limited impact from media speech on ordinary speech. However, to the extent that evidence about the relational strength between standard and dialects is accorded importance in the argument, I find it likely that the view on media influence would be less dismissive if the 'received view' had been developed in a less Anglo-world focused discipline.

7 Indirect influence from broadcast media on speech in Denmark?

In Denmark, dialect diversity is not being maintained; on the contrary, widespread and far-reaching levelling of regional dialects has characterized Danish society since the 1960s. Everywhere in the country, young Danes today speak 'standard Danish', i. e. a language which differs from Copenhagen speech almost exclusively in terms of prosodic features. There is plenty of evidence for this: Older people in the local communities know it from life experience, and it is documented by variationist studies from the 1970s onwards (see overviews in Pedersen 2003; Kristensen 2003).

In a search for possible explanations, we may look at what other societal changes gained momentum in the 1960s. What we find is a whole series of important changes which are more or less interlinked and can be grouped under the headline of *increased geographic and social mobility*: urbanisation of the population, physically as well as mentally (more and more people 'move to town', and 'the town moves to the countryside'); mobilization of the 'working force reserves' (a general political aim in the economically booming 1960s); inclusion of women in the labour market (the majority of women 'left the kitchen' relatively early in Denmark); institutionalization of childhood (linked to the preceding, most children begin spending their days in institutions from before they learn to talk);

increased demands on the labour force in terms of qualifications and flexibility (more people get more education; talk is of 'educational explosion' and 'life-long learning'). No doubt, all of these societal changes were necessary factors behind the general departure from local forms of language in favour of Copenhagen forms. However, in my understanding of what drives language change, such *objective* factors are not sufficient. The sufficient factors are of a *subjective* kind (Kristiansen, Garrett and Coupland 2005). What is important to stress, then, is that the Danish population by 1960 was thoroughly imbued with the belief that there is a 'best language' to be strived for and used in society's public domains (see Section 4). The population had not yet begun its massive desertion to Copenhagen speech, but it had been prepared. SLI was installed.

So, for the Copenhagenization of the Danish speech community to occur, the arrival of TV was probably not a necessary prerequisite. It is likely to have happened anyway. Nevertheless, it is far from unimportant that a new national public sphere developed from the 1960s onwards as the television apparatus became the main sitting room furniture in every home. The 'official' language ideology of the Danish Radio (the national broadcast cooperation which also includes the public TV station) is no different from the ideology which reigns in schools and in general public discourse. The language which Danish Radio (DR) employees are required to use is a 'conservative' version of the standard (i. e. traditionally high status Copenhagen speech). Some twenty years ago, the then general director of DR stood up in first line in the Establishment's battle against the increasing use of a 'modern' version of the standard (including many traditionally low status features of Copenhagen speech), by strongly and repeatedly requiring *klassisk rigsdansk* ('classical rigsdansk') on DR broadcast waves. In the present language policy guidelines, from 2009, the same requirement is euphemistically rephrased as the institution's obligation to "use a language that can be understood across cultural and social divisions". The overt stigmatizing of 'modern' features follows immediately in a statement which requires "orthographical and grammatical correct Danish with care for diction, pronunciation and vowel colours". As it is a corner stone of Danish SLI that 'conservative' phonetics is distinct and 'modern' phonetics is indistinct, nobody is in doubt about how to read this (regardless of the, strictly speaking, bewildering simultaneous reference to both written and spoken language). It does not become less clear as the guidelines go on to condemn "sloppy language use" and explicate it as "syllable cannibalism, wrong vowel colour and muddy consonants". Regarding dialects, the DR guidelines note that these are in danger of extinction in Denmark according to scholarly expertise, which is why DR intends to make dialects "a particular focus area" and will impel initiatives so that "the dialects can be heard on radio and TV, also in nation-wide transmissions and broad programme types".

The linguistic reality which can be heard on national DR channels is different. If traditional dialects are heard, it will usually be for comic effect. To some extent, presenters with traces of non-Copenhagen prosody are allowed access to news programmes, but only to the 'less serious' sections of weather forecast and sport. The discontinuance of the Copenhagen-based DR's monopoly situation in 1988, and the creation of the alternative TV2 with headquarters in Odense, did not change anything to this situation. More importantly in our context here, the 'modern' standard has been increasingly heard on prime time 'serious' TV programmes, after a start in the 1970s in programmes from the Children and Youth section of DR. At that time, the appearance of this language in children-and-youth-oriented programmes, both on radio and TV, was seen as a left-wing attack on the values of the Establishment – representatives of which in turn organized in different ways and very actively complained about how language and social values were undermined by the media. Arguably reduced both in frequency and strength, such complaints are still with us today, but the targets of criticism are not necessarily the same. Not much is heard about *det flade a* ('the flat a') nowadays, a feature that resulted from 'a-fronting' and a popular target of complaints in the 1970s, and certainly the most salient of the traditionally stigmatized features of 'low' Copenhagen. If 'the flat a' is not salient anymore, it seems reasonable to suggest that this is because the use of it has become mainstream news speech (as mentioned above).

Now what has happened at the level of language use is not only that the 'standard' language (Copenhagen speech) has spread to the whole country at the expense of the traditional local dialects; the variation within Copenhagen speech between 'conservative' and 'modern' is also spreading to the whole country. The empirical evidence confirms that the 'modern' variants are the more favoured ones among young people everywhere (overview and references in Maegaard et al. 2013). My argument is not that TV influenced people's speech directly, but that it did so indirectly by changing SLI in a way that is less likely to have happened in the same way, or to the same extent, without TV. The modern broadcast media do the best they can to construe 'informality', to break down the wall between the public and the private, etc. (Fairclough 1994 talks of 'conversationalization'), and the use of traditional capital-city 'low' features seems to be an important means to construe 'casual, relaxed, laid-back' ways with language. Thus, the media in general and TV in particular not only expose people to greater quantities of Copenhagen speech than before, and in that sense change the conditions for (at least passive) appropriation, they also make Copenhagen variation available in ways that might trigger the development of new representations and evaluations.

If we investigate this issue at the level of overt (consciously offered) attitudes, we find no trace of such an ideological development. When young people *do know*

Figure 1: Map showing the geographical location of the five LANCHART research sites for which SEE results are given in Figure 2, from east to west: Copenhagen, Næstved, Vissenbjerg, Odder, and Vinderup. The CON-SERVATIVE and MODERN Copenhagen voices used in the SEEs were the same in all five locations. The LOCAL voices used in Næstved were from Næstved, in Vissenbjerg from Odense, in Odder from Århus, and in Vinde-rup from Holstebro – a design which aimed to illuminate whether bigger cities across the country can aspire to the role as regional linguistic norm centres capable of competing with Copenhagen.

the attitudes-to-dialect purpose of the task they participate in, they perceive 'conservative' speech as *rigsdansk* and 'modern' speech as *københavnsk*, and (outside of Copenhagen) they downgrade *københavnsk* in relation to both *rigsdansk* and their own local dialect. That is, the reproduction of SLI lives on untouched as we know it from the traditional public sphere (where it is sustained in particular by the school institution).

However, if we investigate the issue at the level of covert (subconsciously offered) attitudes by designing and administering speaker evaluation experiments (SEE) so that the participants *do not know* the attitudes-to-dialect purpose of the task they participate in, we obtain a radically different evaluative pattern. The results for the sites studied in the LANCHART project (http://lanchart.hum. ku.dk/) are shown in Figure 2. First the distribution of these sites across the Danish geography is shown in Figure 1. The data was collected from 2005–2006.

Studies of this kind in Denmark since the late 1980s have consistently found that the evaluative ranking of varieties is turned upside down when the response condition changes from 'awareness' to 'non-awareness'. While assessment in the 'awareness' condition yields the ranking LOCAL > CONSERVATIVE > MODERN, assessment in the 'non-awareness' condition yields the ranking MODERN > CON-SERVATIVE > LOCAL, with the specification that MODERN does particularly well in the evaluative dimension of 'dynamism' (cf. scales 5–8 in Figure 2), while CON-SERVATIVE does as well or better in the evaluative dimension of 'superiority' (cf. scales 1–4 in Figure 2). (For a detailed presentation of these studies, see Kristiansen 2009). Arguably, the 'dynamic' values represent what it takes to be successful in the late-modern public sphere of broadcast media, while the 'superiority' values represent what it takes to be successful in the more traditional public

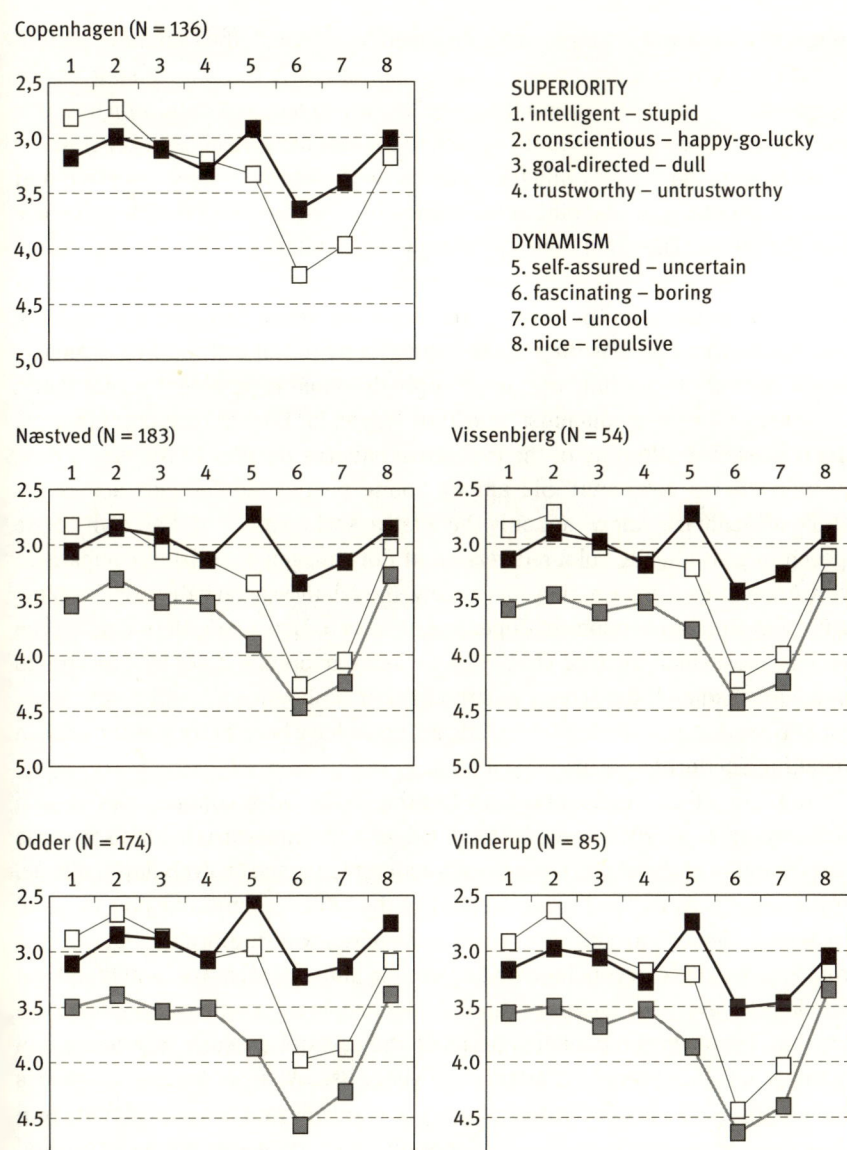

Figure 2: Results of SEEs in the five LANCHART communities (see Figure 1) showing subconscious evaluations of CONSERVATIVE (thin black curve), MODERN (thick black curve) and LOCAL (grey curve). (There were four voices representing each variety.) Entities on the X-axis are the eight measurement scales (personality traits) which – based on the evaluative patterns for CONSERVATIVE and MODERN – can be grouped into four 'superiority' scales (1–4) and four 'dynamism' scales (5–8). Values on the Y-axis are means on the seven-point measurement scales. A low value (high placement in the graphs) is a more positive evaluation (in the sense that *intelligent* is positive and *stupid* negative, etc.).

sphere of school and business. If the argument is accepted, the evaluative pattern as such is likely to represent a change in SLI, a newly developed 'split' in the representation of what 'the best language' is – an ideological 'split' which results from the addition of a new public sphere to societal life (Kristiansen 2001).

However, the 'split' evaluative pattern with regard to CONSERVATIVE and MODERN is not the main point of the argument in favour of a possible influence from the media. The main point is the copy-like similarity of the patterns. As we have seen, the persistence of dialect diversity is forwarded as a main argument against influence from the media. That argument must have as its underlying assumption that one is willing to see homogeneity (if not just reduced diversity) as evidence of media influence. If we apply the same logic here, I take it that a decisive role for the media must be acknowledged for Danish language ideology. The consistent uniformity of the evaluative patterns testifies to the very strong position of this new 'split' SLI among young people. Adolescents across the whole of Denmark 'know' not only the relative social values of their own LOCAL speech (a prosodically coloured version of Copenhagen speech) in comparison with Copenhagen speech, they also 'know' the relative social values of CONSERV-ATIVE and MODERN versions of Copenhagen speech. How on earth (including the western-most small town of Vinderup) does that happen – if not by exposure to broadcast media? If the school was the main installing instrument before 1960, our SEE results indicate that the broadcast media have been more instrumental in installing SLI during the last 50 years.

In Section 6 above, the delay in a-fronting in the 'other communities' (which in Maegaard et al. 2013 were Næstved, Odder and Vinderup), made us exclude the possibility of *direct* influence from broadcast language on everyday language. In the same way, as the lagging behind of the 'other communities' in terms of use has no ideological correspondence in the nationwide uniformity that emerges from Figure 2, we can conclude that a possible *indirect* influence from broadcast language on everyday language through ideology is no simple cause-effect rela-tionship. However, the Danish patterns do indicate quite clearly that changes in language ideology precede changes in language use. What we have established is that the three late-modern Danish accents that are relevant to social identity pro-cesses among young Danes in any community (i. e. CONSERVATIVE, MODERN, and LOCAL) are surrounded by the same covert evaluations all over Denmark, and that these evaluations correspond well to the general patterns of change in language use among young Danes. In itself, I see this as fairly convincing evidence that the national Danish broadcast media have a strong effect on language ideology, and that language ideology is a main driving force in language change.

Also notice that the Danish evidence can hardly be interpreted, in my view, as an indication of the SLI fortress beginning to crumble. It just flies its flag from another tower. The fundamental belief and message that there is a 'best language' to be strived for stands as strong as ever before.

8 Indirect influence from broadcast media on speech in Norway?

In contrast to Denmark, regional dialects are doing well in Norway. Nevertheless, the Norwegian case is no obvious support to the variationist claim that maintenance of dialect diversity contradicts media influence (see Section 6). In fact, I shall argue the opposite.

To start with, let us briefly return to the kind of objective factors which we referred to above in the case of Denmark under the heading of *increased geographical and social mobility* (Section 7). Based on such factors, it can be established that Norway and Denmark are very much alike (Kristiansen 1996). In consequence, if these factors were *sufficient* to explain changes in the use of everyday speech, the relative strength of dialects and standard(s) should have developed in parallel in Norway and Denmark. As this is clearly not the case, the sufficient factors must be sought for somewhere else. My contention is, as already signalled (Section 6), that we need to seek in the domain of subjectivities and ideologies. Hence, I shall focus on how the Norwegian broadcast media may have influenced the reality of everyday speech through their influence on the reality of beliefs and feelings about language.

In consequence of the longstanding 'language struggle' which resulted from the endeavours to create a Norwegian technology for writing (Section 5), the Norwegians entered the era of broadcasting, and became a nation of TV watchers like 'everywhere else' in the 1960–1970s, without the self-evident acceptance as 'everywhere else' of one particular speech variety as the 'natural' ruler of the broadcast waves. The notion of a spoken standard – whether such a thing exists and how to understand it – has always been highly controversial in Norway.[7] Without entering the discussion, it might be mentioned that arguments in favour of developing spoken standards – arguments which return with regularity on the agenda within the camps of both Nynorsk and Bokmål – receive little support, and often strong opposition.[8] It is not unusual, however, as mentioned before, for Bokmål writers

---

7 *Does Norway have a spoken standard language?* was the theme of a recent conference; contributions are published in Norsk Lingvistisk Tidsskrift 27 (1), 2009.
8 Young scholars from the budding discipline of sociolinguistics engaged in an important public debate of this kind in the early 1970s; see contributions collected in Wiggen 1973.

to think of themselves as Bokmål speakers (in contrast to Nynorsk writers who do not think of themselves as Nynorsk speakers).[9] In this sense, Bokmål may be said to have a reality as immediate language ('native' speech) for a part of the population. However, as Bokmål is a written norm which allows for free choice between alternative spellings that reflect dialectal and/or sociolectal differences in both phonology and grammar, the notion of a spoken Bokmål standard must be conceived of as wide (some would say fussy).

Now, what can a national broadcast cooperation do when there is no 'natural', commonly accepted pretender to the role as 'standard' radio and TV speech? The Norwegian national broadcasting cooperation, NRK, developed a set of guidelines which specified which appearance on the broadcast waves requires a spoken norm, and this spoken norm was defined as a reading-aloud norm for each of the two written norms. Sandøy (2011: 122) describes NRK policies as follows:

> Ever since NRK was established in 1933, it has been important for it to be loyal towards the language policy provided by the state (...). A consequence of this loyalty was that great tolerance was practised towards dialectal variation in pronunciation of the standard languages. As formulated in the 1996 version of the guidelines: 'Staff members can freely choose among the forms accepted in the norms for written language. NRK appreciates that staff members in their choices of forms and pronunciation give the standard a regional stamp'.

In this sense, Norway has spoken standards, and this conception of a spoken standard as a reading-aloud norm seems to be fairly common in Norway. Sandøy (2013: 126) talks of "*spoken standard languages* (SSL), corresponding to the reading style version of the two written standards Bokmål and Nynorsk (New Norwegian). In Norway, usage of SSL in this sense of 'reading style' has been quite normal in certain contexts. It is a way of speaking which typically preserves features of local accent or local phonology and thus 'reveals' the speakers' geographical origin".

Thus, regional variation is present in media speech not only because Nynorsk and Bokmål norms reflect different parts (western and eastern) of the dialectal landscape – the NRK guidelines require that 25 per cent of all broadcasted speech be in Nynorsk – but also because the norms and guidelines allow for use of 'standard with a regional stamp'. More importantly, maybe, the use of standard is required only for news reading and announcements; the use of dialects has been accepted and is on the increase in all other types of programmes. Sandøy (2011:

---

9 In a questionnaire study among close to 300 teachers, from different parts of Norway and from all levels of the educational system, 20.5 per cent answered Bokmål to the question *What do you call the kind of Norwegian you speak yourself?* One person (0.3 per cent) answered Nynorsk (Kristiansen 2008).

122) describes this development, which probably has its parallel only in German speaking Switzerland (see Burger 2005), as follows:

> Standard *contra* dialect turned out to be a hot-button issue. In more and more broadcasts journalists started using dialect. A considerable increase in dialect use was observed as early as the 1960s (Nesse 2007: 120). From the 1980s only news broadcasts and announcements were expected to be made in a standard language. In the 1990s the rules were relaxed one step further: only news headlines and announcements read from manuscripts were mandated to be in a standard language, and eventually, from 2010, even news may be read in dialect.

The national broadcast cooperation in Norway benefited from a monopoly situation which was discontinued at the same time as in Denmark, and the appearance of alternative radio and TV channels in the 1980–1990s did play, in contrast to in Denmark, an important role in strengthening the use of dialects in the new media universe. TV2, in particular, with headquarters in Bergen, was "a forerunner in the change of media style, and NRK had to play catch-up" (Sandøy 2011: 122).

The ways with language in the broadcast media have beyond doubt made a crucial contribution to strengthening 'dialect ideology' in the Norwegian population. This finds its expression in an increased use and acceptance of dialects also in other public domains, according to general impressions reported by Sandøy (2011: 123). As to explicit attitudes towards the use of dialects in the media, empirical studies do indeed show Norwegians to be very positive. In a representative telephone survey in 2002, a majority of some 80 per cent expressed a positive attitude towards use by employees of "everyday language in stead of standard language (i. e. Bokmål or Nynorsk)" in radio and TV transmissions (52.9 per cent claimed to be 'very positive', 27.6 per cent to be 'rather positive') (Kristiansen and Vikør 2006: 223). A representative web based questionnaire survey in 2009 showed a similar evaluative pattern in response to the statement that "it is OK for programme anchors in national radio and TV channels to speak dialect"; 49 per cent agreed 'completely', 28 per cent agreed 'somewhat' (http://www.sprakradet.no/nb-NO/Toppmeny/Aktuelt/Haldningsunder-soking-om-sprakbruk-i-NRK/).

9 Summary and conclusion

We have established that writing and printing seems to have had little or no *direct* influence on everyday speech, in either Denmark or Norway. We have argued, however, that the *indirect* influence has been important, as the technology of writing could be shown to have played very different roles in the domains of language ideology. The orthographies, and the use of them in school, created a strong SLI in DK, and a strong DI in Norway.

Thus, at the entrance to the new public sphere which was to be created from the 1960s onwards by the broadcast media, and TV in particular, the Norwegian situation was radically different from the Danish situation in terms of both language use and language ideology. In Denmark, the 'natural' consequence of the progressive expansion of the media universe was for the Danes to be exposed to a growing daily dose of Copenhagen speech. The 'natural' consequence in the Norwegian situation was for the country's dialectal diversity to be more frequently and broadly present in everyone's daily life than ever before. Furthermore, while the progressive 'informalization' of the media universe taught the Danes how CONSERVATIVE versus MODERN ways with Copenhagen speech are used and socially valued, Norwegians were accustomed to 'live with' a broad gamut of speech varieties as something 'natural' and unproblematic – and they learned not only to understand different dialects but also to accept or even appreciate dialect diversity.[10]

Peter Trudgill gave a speech a couple of years ago at the fiftieth anniversary of one of the language-struggling organizations in Norway. In a long and entertaining introduction, he made fun of the Norwegian 'writing situation' – and continued:

> Well, ladies and gentlemen, it is very easy to make fun of this situation, but as many of you know, I think it is a situation which is truly excellent. I know that you are aware of all the things that are wrong and inadequate and not as good as you would like in the Norwegian linguistic situation, but I urge you to compare with everywhere else. It may not be very good in Norway, but it's much worse everywhere else. [...] I want you to contrast the situation in Norway with the much much much much much worse situation everywhere else. [...] Norwegians for the most part feel free on the basis of equality to speak their regional dialects wherever and whenever they want. All right, you're immediately thinking it's not exactly like that. But that is the picture which is much much more true of this country than of any other country I know. [...] What I say to people outside Norway is that here in this country there is an enormous societal tolerance for linguistic diversity. Alright, you're aware of cases where it doesn't quite work like that. But believe me, compared to everywhere else, except for Switzerland and Luxembourg, that's true. An enormous tolerance in society for linguistic diversity and dialectal diversity. [...] So that's the contrast I'm holding up before you.

---

10 It is an interesting question whether an ideological restructuring is in progress with regard to the two versions of Bokmål, in Norway called the 'moderate' and 'radical' versions, corresponding to the ideological re-evaluation of the 'conservative' and 'modern' versions of Copenhagen speech in Denmark – and whether the broadcast media play a role in the process. The general impression is that the frequency of 'radical' Bokmål features is on the increase in news reading, but so far there is a lack of empirical evidence that can shed light on the ideological landscape.

Things aren't absolutely perfect in Norway, but they are pretty good compared to the other places I have been to. (Trudgill 2009)

We should stress that the Norwegians did not end in this (in my view also) positive situation by being particularly clever at 'language planning'[11], but because an 'abnormal' product resulted from a historical process with actors who all aimed at creating a 'normal' written language for Norwegian. On the assumption that rationality sides with diversity rather than unity in the domain of language, the Norwegian situation is a nice example of the 'cunning of reason' in history.

Trudgill speaks Norwegian and knows the Norwegian situation very well, and we will have a hard time finding his match when it comes to expertise on the linguistic situation in Europe in general. I have two reasons to quote him here. Firstly as a testimony to the correctness of the kind of 'dialect paradise' account I have given, because I know that it is often met with scepticism and distrust, not only in Denmark where I have lived and worked since 1974 after having grown up in Norway, but more generally, also by Norwegians themselves as repeatedly hinted at by Trudgill.

Secondly, and more importantly, I use the quote as a testimony to the claim that we need to be more explicit about our theoretical positions and their implications if our discussions about the influence of mediatization on everyday speech are to be meaningful. We are probably doomed to talk at cross purposes if we have different basic assumptions about, first, the nature of 'influence on speech' as either 'automatic' or 'social psychological' mechanisms, and, next, as change in terms of either 'variables' or 'varieties'. It must be differences in these, or other, basic assumptions that make Trudgill's views appear paradoxical to me. I am sure Trudgill understands the role of TV just as well as he understands the role of writing in the development of the "pretty good" Norwegian situation. Why recognize a role for writing and deny a role for TV? In my head there is no possible coexistence between Trudgill's account of the Norwegian situation and his claim to no influence from TV. I simply do not understand it.

My aim in this chapter has been to shed light on whether immediate language is influenced by mediated language. My approach has been to compare Denmark and Norway, with their very different standard–dialect constellations, and discuss the influence on speech in the two countries from technologies/ institutions of writing and broadcasting. The comparison results in an unconditional 'Yes, immediate language is influenced by mediated language'. Importantly, however, the influence is not direct, but indirect. *Mediation* in itself, understood

---

11 We may recall that Einar Haugen's foundational work in the discipline of 'language planning' deals with the Norwegian 'language struggle' (Haugen 1966).

as the introduction and existence of technologies that take linguistic communication beyond the context of face-to-face interaction, does not influence everyday language. It all depends on how mediation is realized, i. e. on *mediatization*, on how the relationship between immediate and mediated language is construed and administered in the society. Mediation, whether as writing or broadcasting, can be used (mediatized) either 'the Danish way' to create a strong SLI and moribund dialects, or it can be used (mediatized) 'the Norwegian way' to create a strong DI and vital dialects. Basically, the chapter illustrates what ought to be a banality: in themselves, technologies are politically innocent; the use of them is not.

References

Brink, Lars and Jørn Lund 1975: *Dansk rigsmål I, II. Lydudviklingen siden 1840 med særligt henblik på sociolekterne i København [Danish standard language I,II. The phonetic development since 1840 with regard to the sociolects of Copenhagen in particular].* København: Gyldendal.

Burger, Harald 2005: *Mediensprache.* Berlin/New York: de Gruyter.

Chambers, Jack 1998: TV makes people sound the same. In: Laurie Bauer and Peter Trudgill (eds.), *Language Myths*, 123–131. New York: Penguin.

Coupland, Nikolas 2007: *Style. Language Variation and Identity.* Cambridge: Cambridge University Press.

Fairclough, Norman 1994: Conversationalisation of public discourse and the authority of the consumer. In: R. Keat, N. Whitely and N. Abercrombie (eds.), *The Authority of the Consumer*, 253–268.London: Routledge.

Hansen, Elisabeth and Jørn Lund (eds.) 1983: *Skolen, Samfundet og Dialekten. 11 afhandlinger om elevers, læreres og forældres sprog og sprogsyn – belyst ud fra undersøgelser af forholdet mellem skole og dialekt i Hirtshals kommune [The School, the Society, and the Dialect. 11 theses on language and language view among pupils, teachers and parents – as illuminated by investigations of the relationship between school and dialect in Hirtshals commune].* Frederikshavn: Dafolo.

Haugen, Einar 1966: *Language Conflict and Language Planning: The Case of Modern Norwegian.* Cambridge, MA: Harvard University Press.

http://www.sprakradet.no/nb-NO/Toppmeny/Aktuelt/Haldningsundersoking-om-sprakbruk-i-NRK/

Kristensen, Kjeld 2003: Standard Danish, Copenhagen sociolects, and regional varieties in the 1900s. *International Journal of the Sociology of Language* 159: 29–43.

Kristiansen, Tore 1990: *Udtalenormering i skolen Skitse af en ideologisk bastion [Regimentation of pronunciation in school. Sketch of an ideological bastion].* Copenhagen: Gyldendal.

Kristiansen, Tore 1996: Det gode sprogsamfund: det norske eksempel [The good speech community: the Norwegian example]. *NyS* 21: 9–22.

Kristiansen, Tore 2001: Two standards: One for the media and one for the school. *Linguistic Awareness* 10(1): 9–24.

Kristiansen, Tore 2004: Sprogholdninger over Øresund [Language attitudes across Øresund] *Danske Talesprog* 5: 161–185.

Kristiansen, Tore 2008: Om forståelighed på tværs af dialekter og nabosprog – erfaringer, vurderinger og holdninger blandt norske lærere [On intelligibility across dialects and neighbouring languages – experiences, evaluations and attitudes among Norwegian teachers]. In: Atle Næss and Thomas Egan (eds.), *Vandringer i ordenes landskap: Et festskrift til Lars Anders Kulbrandstad på 60-årsdagen* [Strolls in the landscape of words: A festschrift for Lars Anders Kulbrandstad at his 60th anniversary], 43–65. Vallset: Oplandske Bokforlag.

Kristiansen, Tore 2009: The macro-level social meanings of late-modern Danish accents. *Acta Linguistica Hafniensia* 41: 167–192.

Kristiansen, Tore, Peter Garrett and Nikolas Coupland 2005: Introducing subjectivities in language variation and change. *Acta Linguistica Hafniensia* 37: 9–35.

Kristiansen, Tore and Lars Vikør (eds.) 2006: *Nordiske språkhaldningar. Ei meiningsmåling [Nordic language attitudes. A survey study]*. Oslo: Novus Forlag.

Labov, William 2001: *Principles of Linguistic Change, Vol. 2: Social Factors*. Oxford: Blackwell.

Livingstone, Sonia 2009: On the mediation of everything: ICA presidential address 2008. *Journal of communication* 59(1): 1–18.

Maegaard, Marie, Torben Juel Jensen, Tore Kristiansen and Jens Normann Jørgensen 2013: Diffusion of language change: Accommodation to a moving target. *Journal of Sociolinguistics* 17(1): 3–36.

Milroy, Lesley and James Milroy 1991: *Authority in Language. Investigating language prescription & standardisation*. London: Routledge.

Mæhlum, Brit, Gunnstein Akselberg, Unn Røyneland and Helge Sandøy 2008: *Språkmøte. Innføring i sosiolingvistikk [Meeting in language. Introduction to sociolinguistics]*. Oslo: Cappelen Akademisk Forlag.

Nuolijärvi, Pirkko and Johanna Vaattovaara 2011: De-standardisation in progress in Finnish society? In: Tore Kristiansen and Nikolas Coupland (eds.), *Standard Languages and Language Standards in a Changing Europe*, 67–74. Oslo: Novus Press.

Pedersen, Inge Lise 2003: Traditional dialects of Danish and the de-dialectalization 1900–2000. *International Journal of the Sociology of Language* 159: 9–28.

Sandøy, Helge 1987: *Norsk dialektkunnskap [Norwegian dialectology]*. Oslo: Novus Forlag.

Sandøy, Helge 2011: Language culture in Norway: A tradition of questioning standard language norms. In: Tore Kristiansen and Nikolas Coupland (eds.), *Standard Languages and Language Standards in a Changing Europe*, 119–126. Oslo: Novus Press.

Sandøy, Helge 2013: Driving forces – in the Norwegian perspective. In: Tore Kristiansen and Stefan Grondelaers (eds.), *Language (de)standardisation in Late Modern Europe: Experimental Studies*, 125–151. Oslo: Novus Press.

Stuart-Smith, Jane 2011: The view from the couch: Changing perspectives on the role of television in changing language ideologies and use. In: Tore Kristiansen and Nikolas Coupland (eds.), *Standard Languages and Language Standards in a Changing Europe*, 223–239. Oslo: Novus Press.

Thøgersen, Jacob and Nicolai Pharao 2013: Changing pronunciation but stable social evaluation? *University of Pennsylvania Working Papers in Linguistics* 19(2): 191–201.

Trudgill, Peter 1986: *Dialects in Contact*. Oxford: Blackwell.

Trudgill, Peter 2009: Samnorskprosjektet – suksess eller fiasko? Foredrag holdt på LSS-jubilæumsseminaret i Litteraturhuset i Oslo [The Samnorsk project – success or failure? Talk given at the LSS anniversary seminar in Litteraturhuset in Oslo]. *Språklig Samling* 4: 5–10.

Watts, Richard J. 1999: The ideology of dialect in Switzerland. In: Jan Blommaert (ed.), *Language Ideological Debates*, 67–103. Berlin/New York: Mouton de Gruyter.

Wiggen, Geir (ed.) 1973: *Ny målstrid. Ei samling artikler og innlegg om språk, samfunn og ideologi [New language struggle. A collection of articles and contributions on language, society and ideology]*. Oslo: Novus.

Jane Stuart-Smith and Ichiro Ota

Media models, 'the shelf', and stylistic variation in East and West. Rethinking the influence of the media on language variation and change

1 Introduction

This paper discusses the influence of the broadcast media within a particular branch of sociolinguistics, variationist sociolinguistics (e.g. Labov 1972, 2001; Tagliamonte 2012). We present an overview of the debate that watching TV or listening to the radio have a long-term structural impact on spoken language. We note that the position taken is affected by the sociolinguistic context of the academic researchers. The dominant discussion of media influence on language variation and change tends to assume simultaneous, widespread shifts would be provoked (e.g. Chambers 1998); that some features might be adopted and others ignored is puzzling (e.g. Trudgill 1986); but the primacy of interaction as the locus of variation and change is regarded as the main obstacle (Labov 2001). At the same time, variationist sociolinguistics is now being enriched by 'third wave' approaches (e.g. Eckert 2012), which emphasize the importance of the social meaning carried by linguistic variation, and with that, the potential for the media to offer new meanings, and/or new resources for speakers to exploit for their own stylistic purposes (cf. Coupland 2007). Moreover, not all structural changes seem to be transmitted by regular interaction, some look as if they have been "taken right off the shelf" (Eckert 2003: 395).

Here we consider instances of sound change in progress in two very different sociolinguistic contexts, from the East – the southernmost city in Japan, Kagoshima, and the West – the large post-industrial city of Glasgow, UK. In so doing, we also explore the extent to which the broadcast media might constitute "the shelf", or perhaps better "some shelves", offering linguistic resources for the speaker/viewer to appropriate and/or enhance, even at the level of structural linguistic change. The emerging theme from our chapter is that despite substantial differences in language and sociolinguistic context, these ongoing sound changes associated with the broadcast media in Japanese and in Scottish English show some strong underlying similarities, particularly with respect to style and social meaning. We begin by laying out briefly the theoretical context, first with a brief survey of the debate about media influence on language (Section 2), then perspectives on media influence on social behaviours from mass communications studies (Section 3), and we outline predictions for possible media impact on sociolinguistic systems from these two bodies of research in Section 4. We then present results from the two case studies, Kagoshima Japanese in Sections 5 and 6 and Glaswegian English in Section 7. The final section 8 draws together key results and theoretical predictions to make a series of common observations about the influence of the media on speech. Variationist sociolinguistics emerges as a powerful tool for identifying instances of structural variation and change where the media may be an accelerating factor, but even more so if we can both investigate stylistic variation beyond the vernacular, and embrace the theoretical insights of the third wave – that linguistic variation carries social meaning – since this seems to be at the heart of any linguistic change which is linked with the media.

2 Language variation and change and the influence of the media

Social interaction entails linguistic variation; speakers make tiny adjustments at all levels of language as they interact (Coupland et al. 1991). Over time some of this intra-, and then interpersonal, variability becomes community change (Trudgill 1986), though the exact mechanisms remain unclear (e.g. Auer and Hinskens 2005). One of the main achievements of variationist sociolinguistics has been to establish tools and theoretical principles with which to describe and account for these processes (e.g. Labov 1972). Linguistic variation which is associated with change in progress is structured, constrained by linguistic and social factors, and sensitive to shifts in speech style (Labov 1972; 2001; Tagliamonte 2012).

Whilst the processes engendering linguistic shifts primarily occur in spoken interaction (Labov 2001), and are reflected secondarily in writing, the advent of accessible print media, such as the printed book and then journals and newspapers, has had some impact both on structural change, and importantly on the ideologies surrounding spoken varieties which can also facilitate change (e.g. Smith 1991). Experiencing spoken language without the possibility of social interaction arguably began with the public broadcasting of films with sound,[1] but personal experience privately and in the home (Holly et al. 2001), began with the first radio broadcasts and then with television. Personal ownership of television sets shows

---

[1] The early phonograph recordings of dialect narratives played in salons in early twentieth century America discussed by Baumann 2011 may have been amongst the very first opportunities.

the classic S-curve of a diffusing innovation across the second half of the twentieth century (Bushman and Huesmann 2001).

The impact of the broadcast media, and especially television, on spoken language is more difficult to identify. This is at least partly because its main propagation overlapped with periods of major social and economic change during and after the Second World War, in particular increased geographical mobility, widespread changes in education, and processes of both urbanization and counter-urbanization (cf. Milroy 2001), which are known to have had substantial impact on traditional dialects. In the following sections, we summarize the discussion of the possible influence of the media into three "positions", which in turn depend on the sociolinguistic context of linguistic researchers and the kinds of language change involved.[2]

2.1 Position A: The broadcast media promote language standardization

Many linguists working on languages of different genetic/linguistic heritage assume that exposure to the broadcast media has had, and continues to have, an impact on structural linguistic changes leading to standardization (e.g. Mase 1981; Lameli 2004). The changes are usually larger shifts from traditional dialects towards standard varieties, especially after the Second World War, which are also motivated by other major demographic factors such as education and enhanced mobility. Such changes often entail a shift from one dialect to another by bidialectal speakers who become increasingly monodialectal (cf. Trudgill 1986), and then subsequent leveling to the structures of the remaining leveled dialects (e.g. Kagoshima Japanese, Section 5).

Whilst there has undoubtedly been substantial structural standardization in such dialects, there is very little direct evidence to support these assertions, if only because it is very difficult to disentangle the inferred effects of exposure on the broadcast media from those which were also influential, as for example in Japan, where standardization and dedialectalization occurred alongside (a) the post-war national implementation of a common education system using Standard Japanese, (b) substantially increased migration for work and leisure, and (c) widespread access to Standard Japanese in the broadcast media.

The few variationist studies on standardization and the media have produced inconclusive results. Naro (1981) found a significant correlation between self-re-

---

2 For the interaction between spoken language and written "new" and/or social media, see e.g. Tagliamonte (2012).

ported exposure to soap operas and using a standard morpho-syntactic feature in Brazilian Portuguese. He argued that speakers were trying to emulate not only the linguistic, but also the social-cultural, sophistication represented by these shows. Naro and Scherre (1996) found a similar result, though their media variable is difficult to interpret. Carvahlo (2004), on the other hand, also looking at South American Portuguese, but in a Uruguayan border town, did not find statistical correlations with a phonological change in progress, increased palatalization, and exposure to the same Brazilian soap operas, even though her informants themselves thought that they were trying to "talk like the guys on TV". Saladino's (1990) study of a South Italian dialect also did not find statistical support for the influence of exposure to standard Italian in the media.

Contexts of dialect standardization seem to share a sociolinguistic context in that the varieties undergoing shift often experience lower social prestige than the standard varieties represented in the media, towards which structural shifts are progressing. The changes are not simply language changes, they represent aspects of the linguistic system which are closely associated with particular bundles of social and ideological meaning. The standard varieties are usually highly enregistered (Agha 2003), and the dialectal differences are usually well above the level of conscious awareness.

There is no consensus about the possible mechanisms of media influence in shifts of this kind. Some assume behavioural responses as a result of increased exposure to standard varieties experienced in the media (e.g. Yokoyama and Sanada 2010), others envisage quite fluid relationships between community and media, alongside other social and demographic factors promulgating the changes (Brandt 2000); and still others suggest that such shifting is within the conscious control of speakers who use the broadcast media as desirable models for copying (e.g. Trudgill 1986). Interestingly, one of the popular ideologies surrounding such changes is that the broadcast media must be involved, even if this cannot be established (e.g. Carvalho 2004).

2.2 Position B: The broadcast media do not affect systemic linguistic change

By contrast some sociolinguists working mainly on English have rejected the influence of the broadcast media on standardization, as well as on systemic language change in general (e.g. Labov 2001: 228). The main arguments against media influence are based on different kinds of evidence (see also Sayers 2014).

First, despite popular beliefs that the broadcast media would lead to a widespread standardization of regional dialects, sociolinguistic studies on varieties of English, have shown, and continue to show, that regional dialects are not rapidly converging to the standard, and that there is vigorous maintenance of local dialect diversity (e.g. Milroy and Milroy 1985; Labov 2001).[3]

Second, children do not seem able to acquire their first language and/or primary grammatical or phonological contrasts solely from exposure to pre-recorded language presented by film or TV (Chambers 1998; Kuhl et al. 2003). Empirical evidence for first language acquisition from television appears to be largely restricted to lexical items, as shown for example, by the research on *Sesame Street* (e.g. Rice et al. 1990). The mechanisms of learning about language from audio-visual media appear somewhat different from face-to-face interaction (Kuhl 2010; Stuart-Smith et al. 2011).

Third, media models may not provide sufficient instances of changes in progress (Chambers 1998; Labov 2001: 385; Dion and Poplack 2007); the sociolinguistic constraints between media and community language may be different, making it difficult to assume "strong transfer" (e.g. Buchstaller and D'Arcy 2009) or regular learning from the media (cf. Dion and Poplack 2007); and media language is more likely to lag than lead in changes (Labov 2001: 385; though see Tagliamonte and Roberts 2005). The difficulty of pinpointing specific representations of variation in the media as potential stimuli for language changes is further complicated by the fact that media language may be adapted for particular audiences (Milroy and Milroy 1985: 29–31 after Bell 1984). There is a complex reciprocal relationship between media representations of linguistic variation and actual community norms (Tagliamonte and Roberts 2005; cf. Coupland 2009; Section 7.4).

Fourth, the invocation of media influence to explain only some changes, like the spread of linguistic innovations (see 2.3 below), seems *ad hoc* (Trudgill 1988: 44), and potentially difficult, especially alongside long term observations of geographical diffusion (Trudgill e.g. 1986: 40; cf. Kerswill 2003).

Fifth, diffusion of innovations research, which is relevant to linguistic change, establishes two generalizations. Interpersonal channels are relatively more important at the persuasion stage of the diffusion process, whereas mass media channels are more instrumental at the knowledge stage (Milroy and Milroy 1985:30, after Rogers, now 2003: 205). Second, at the level of particular individuals ("opinion leaders") who play a role in diffusing innovations to the population, far more influence is assigned to personal contacts than the mass media (Labov 2001: 356, after Katz and Lazarsfeld 1955).

---

3 It is difficult to know to what extent, if at all, this conclusion relates to the fact that many traditional dialects of English have already shown substantial levelling and may not be analogous to the sharp post-war bidialectalism of e.g. Japan and/or many European languages.

This last argument also brings us back to the main underlying reason for rejecting the mass media, namely the indisputable assumption that the mechanisms for language change must be located primarily in the complex processes of personal interaction when people talk with each other in their daily lives (Trudgill 1986; Chambers 1998; Labov 2001; 2010).

This leaves the broadcast media with a restricted role for directly affecting language change. They are thought to be involved in the spread of lexical items, idioms, and catchphrases (e.g. Trudgill 1986; cf. Charkova 2007; Rice et al. 1990) – linguistic features at a particular linguistic level which also seems to exist at a higher level of conscious awareness. Change to core features of grammar in conjunction with the broadcast media are also regarded as resulting from conscious imitation of media models, for example where there is a decision to adopt a standard variety which may be linguistically distinct from a local dialect (see 2.1. above).

These views implicitly seem to assume that the media should cause a strong behavioural response on language. The lack of evidence for the "wholesale transfer of form and function" of media language into community language (Buchstaller 2008), seems to have led to a complete rejection of media influence. And the core and correct assumption that language change happens in social interaction has been taken to entail no role for the media at all. This particular discourse around the influence of the media on language implies strong separation of factors, either social interaction, or powerful media (cf. Brandt 2000). Demarcations are inherent in terms of language acquisition, levels of language and of consciousness, restricting media influence from structural linguistic change below the level of consciousness. At the same time, exposure to the media might shift attitudes, and indirectly sometimes promote change (e.g. Milroy and Milroy 1985; Trudgill 1988).

It is not difficult to reject such "strong" views of media influence on language change because they are obviously wrong: watching TV clearly does not lead to people all sounding the same (Chambers 1998). Even where traditional dialects are being abandoned, speakers are not cloning the repertoires of newsreaders; some features are shifting but many remain locally distinctive. Rather, the circumstantial evidence points to something more subtle and less well defined. Most of the time language variation and change progresses within speakers and communities "undisturbed", but sometimes, some elements, or sets of elements seem to become linked to the media, either without comment, or emerging in popular discourse. Standardization involving (some) linguistic shifts to highly enregistered features is one instance of structural linguistic change which may be linked to the media (Position A). We consider now the other exception, Position C, the rapid diffusion of linguistic elements, which appear to be on the one hand tightly connected to bundles of local social meaning, but on the other, apparently easily lifted off the media "shelf".

2.3 Position C: The media may be involved in some "off the shelf" changes

The turn of the 21st century is popularly associated with astonishingly swift shifts in technology and accompanying social behaviours. This period has also witnessed some notable instances of rapidly diffusing linguistic change (Tagliamonte 2012), often called "off the shelf" changes (Milroy 2007). One of the most well-documented changes has been the explosive expansion of the quotative *be like* across varieties of English (e.g. Tagliamonte ibid; Buchstaller and D'Arcy 2009; Sayers 2014). Other examples include the consonantal changes, such as TH-fronting and L-vocalization, associated with London English, diffusing through British English (e.g. Kerswill 2003), or – from a non English context – the rapid spread of the phrasal tone, with no pitch fall but just a rise at the end, for the negative particle *nai* (in e.g. *kawai-ku nai?* 'It's cute, isn't it?') across Japanese dialects, thought to have started in Tokyo metropolitan area (Tanaka 2010).

Changes of this kind typically show rapid diffusion across very large geographical (and sometimes cultural) distances involving linguistic varieties which may be different from each other in many other respects. In some cases they are also overtly associated with particular styles or groups, such as *be like* with "Valley Girl"/ "California", which may also have contributed to their accelerated take-off (Tagliamonte and D'Arcy 2007, after Labov 2001). These characteristics, and in particular the geographical distances involved and the special role of social meaning in these changes, pose an interesting challenge for sociolinguistic theory. Eckert's reflection (2003: 395) provided part of the basis for Milroy's (2007) subsequent typology of language changes into "under the counter" and "off the shelf": "We need to ask ourselves what kind of changes require the kind of repeated exposure that social interaction gives, and what kinds can be taken right off the shelf."

The many voices and representations offered by the broadcast media provide one (or more) of the possible "shelves" where such resources might exist. Coupland (2007: 172, 184–187) points out how language use in the media can offer new social meanings for existing linguistic features, including the stylistic elevation of individual celebrities, such as Tess Daley's idiolect of Northern English on *Strictly Come Dancing*, thus (re)contextualizing linguistic variation (Coupland 2009). He also discusses the extent to which strict divisions between media language and community language are becoming blurred as linguistic styles are produced and reproduced (cf. Tagliamonte and Roberts 2005's analysis of intensifiers in

Friends), and importantly how some stylistic variation within the community "increasingly [has] the feel of mediated discourse" (2007: 185). For example, quotative *be like* affords particular speakers (often girls and women) particular narrative strategies such as increased focus on the self and expression of inner thought (Tagliamonte and D'Arcy 2004), which in turn enable these speakers to "do more performative utterance, including putting fabricated/reconstructed "thoughts" and emotional expressive tokens into their speaking" (Coupland 2007: 186). Theoretically, these ideas depend on reflexive notions of style and speaker agency (e.g. Eckert and Rickford 2003). They also presume interesting intersections between stylized representations of language in the media and linguistic styling in the community, and potential overlaps between indexical fields of social meaning (Eckert 2008). Moreover, the notion of the broadcast media as "shelves" making available stylistic resources for speakers' own personal interactional needs, is consistent with the theory of "bricolage" (e.g. Eckert 2008), that speakers actively construct sociolinguistic personae using the resources available to them.

These links between stylistic variation, social meaning, and the media potentially acting as a shelf, connects the two exceptions to regular linguistic change solely through face-to-face interaction, language standardization (Position A) and rapid linguistic diffusion (Position C), albeit at a rather abstract level. This becomes clear when we consider evidence from two such sociolinguistic contexts, in Japan and in Scotland (Sections 5–7 below). However, first we need to consider the possible mechanisms that might be involved. How might people take things off the media shelf? Do they "take" them? Can they resist what's on the shelf? And why is the link between linguistic variation and social meaning so important? In the following section we review media influence from the broader perspective of theories of mass communication.

3 What is media influence? The view from mass communication studies

3.1 From "media effects" to "active audiences"

The possible impact of the broadcast media on social behaviours has been researched for nearly a century within the interconnecting fields which together make up mass communication studies (e.g. McQuail 2010). Early research on the media until the 1960s formed the basis for the media effects paradigm. This assumed a "powerful media" characterized as a transmission model, with a source sending a message (stimulus) to a receiver resulting in inevitable behavioural effects; the image of a hypodermic needle injecting material into the waiting masses was commonly referred to (McQuail 2010). Systematic investigation of the one-step model, e.g. the Payne Fund studies of the 1930s looking at the impact of film on children, or the electoral campaign research of the 1940s and 50s, failed to find direct evidence, and led to the two-step model, which interposed interpersonal communication between Opinion Leaders, who might be directly affected by the media, and the community (Katz and Lazerfeld 1955; cf. Labov 2001). There was a general restriction to the notion of "limited effects", summarized by Klapper (1960: 8): "Mass communication ordinarily does not serve as a necessary and sufficient cause of audience effects, but rather functions among and through a nexus of mediating factors and influences". Subsequent research concentrated on the "uses and gratifications" of media use, as well as "mediated effects", assuming more complex models which allow for audience response and processing within their social and cultural context.

The 1970s saw the development of different approaches which shared an emphasis on qualitative methodologies using deep analysis of the potential meaning of media messages (see e.g. Curran 1996). Particularly influential has been the 'cultural studies/interpretative' approach, which assumes that the impact of television lies in the interpretation of numerous potential meanings of the media message by the audience. The primary role of the audience is emphasized by Stuart Hall in his seminal paper (1980) on 'encoding/decoding', which discusses the production and reception of media meanings. Despite the theoretical divisions between the two paradigms, there is a clear desire for their integration (e.g. Gunter 2000: 9).

3.2 Evidence for media influence on social behavior, cognition, and individuals

Much research into the largely unplanned effects of the broadcast media on behaviour has focussed on antisocial effects, such as aggression and violence. While few would deny any impact, verdicts range from the categorical (e.g. Strasburger 1995: 13) to the cautious (e.g. Gunter and McAleer 1997: 116). Reviews of actual studies show complex results (e.g. Strasburger 1995; Gunter 2000), though there is longitudinal correlational evidence for reported exposure to media violence and reported aggressive behaviour (e.g. Lefkowitz et al. 1972). Experiments have demonstrated short-term triggering of aggressive behaviours after watching a stimulus film, though these were less direct imitation than responses embedded within existing patterns of behaviour (e.g. the classic study of Bandura et al. 1963). Other experimental evidence shows that people may respond to television as if what is presented is real, for example, size and physical movement of people on film, responses to negative (emotional) content (Reeves and Nass 1996). At the same time, the key findings of this work are that viewers' existing socialization appears to be central to any possible influence, and, as Bushman and Huesmann (2001: 233–234) state: "The theme ... is *not* that media violence is *the* cause of aggression and violence in our society, or even that it is the *most* important cause. The theme is that accumulating research evidence has revealed that media violence is *one* factor that contributes significantly to aggression and violence in our society [their emphasis]".

Early research on media effects on cognition was preoccupied with attitudinal change. However, evidence for media-induced attitudinal change was difficult to find (Gunter 2000: 195). Work which considered planned effects of media persuasion, e.g. campaigning (Klapper 1960: 15–16), mainly observed reinforcement of currently-held attitudes or constancy of opinion; attitudinal change was rare. This led to the introduction of interpersonal relationships as a key factor in persuasive change (Katz and Lazarsfeld 1955). Other research on cognition has considered "the degree to which the different media have come to interpose themselves between ourselves and any experience of the world beyond our immediate personal environment" (McQuail 2010: 64), e.g. the work on "cultivation" effects by Gerbner and colleagues. Content analysis demonstrated that the television consistently portrayed a more violent world than the real world. Comparison of survey data of television exposure with that of perceptions of social reality showed that heavy viewers were more likely to show television bias in their perceptions of the frequency of real violence, their own involvement with violence, and greater fearfulness.

Work in the "active audience" paradigm has deepened our understanding of cognitive impact in terms of individual responses to media texts. Viewers are active decoders who may select from the material offered, as in e.g. Morley's classic *Nationwide* study (1980), where certain groups took the dominant meanings from the current affairs programme, others took oppositional meanings, and yet others "refused to read it at all". Note however, that the audience may not always be able to resist; see especially the work of the Glasgow Media Group on the impact of news and popular violent film (e.g. Philo 1999, 2008).

It has also been long recognized (Reeves and Nass 1996) that the media can offer vicarious personal interaction on the one hand, and act as a tool for facilitating social intercourse on the other (Klapper 1960: 176). Viewers can show differing degrees of involvement with media figures, who may "serve as something akin to a screen community with whom the viewer regularly talks and interacts ... as an extended kin grouping" (Noble 1975 on children's involvement in McQuail 2010: 406).

The mass media are included as one of the possible two channels in the modeling of the diffusion of innovations (the other is interpersonal), see 2.2. above;

mass media are more important at the knowledge stage of diffusion. However there are differences according to individual adopters, with different types innovating at different rates. When considered according to "adopter category", media channels are relatively more important for "earlier adopters" and "innovators", for whom the mass media message can be enough to move them over the mental threshold to adoption (Rogers 2003). What this means is that, as we might expect, inherent likeliness to innovate, as well as personality traits (cf. Yu 2011) constrain influence at the level of the individual. Rogers (2003) also emphasizes the extent to which congruence of an innovation with existing beliefs is important for the successful adoption of an innovation by a community.

3.3 Modeling media influence

How media influence might come about is framed differently within the two paradigms but shares the core assumption that the viewer's own experience of the world plays a central role. Within media effects, explanations have ranged from "social learning" theory (e.g. Bandura et al. 1963), to activation and/or associated triggering of stored routines by media stimuli (Berkowitz 1984), extended in Bargh et al.'s (e.g. 1996) "perception-action" theory of implicit priming, low-level automatic responses which are constrained by situational relevance. Cognitive psychological approaches couch influence in terms of "schema" theory, for example, Gunter (2000: 233) explains:

> "viewers use multiple cognitive schemas when interpreting TV programmes. In order to make sense of a programme, viewers must find connections between the media text and their own inner world ... When interpreting a TV programme, viewers spontaneously use a whole set of cognitive schemas to serve as interpretative frames of reference."

Similarly Reeves and Nass (1996: 252) conclude their review of studies which emphasize the Media Equation ("media = real life") by stating: "Ultimately, it's the pictures in our heads that matter, not the ones on the screens".

Within the "active audiences" paradigm, Hall (1980) provides a starting point for theorizing media influence. Hall argues that meaning is negotiated by the viewer within the context of their local, socially and culturally situated experience of the world. When considering the decoding of televisual signs he makes two key points. First he notes that processing televisual signs is "habitual and naturalized", i. e. we are extremely used to doing it and we feel as if we are perceiving something real, even when the object (e.g. a television drama) is only a two-dimensional representation, without any physical presence (it isn't real). Second, decoding is most effective when there is a "fundamental alignment and reciprocity" between what is represented and the viewer's own experience of that sign.

Interestingly, irrespective of paradigm, what seems to be important is not what the media does to the viewer, but rather what the viewer does with the media, and especially what the viewer brings to each media experience. We now return to the implications of these findings and models for sociolinguistic theory.

4 Extrapolating models of media influence to sociolinguistics

What can sociolinguists learn from this which is relevant to language variation and change? We consider first some general points, and then focus on the notion of the media as a "shelf"/ "some shelves" for particular sociolinguistic variation.

4.1 General implications

The broadcast media do seem to influence social behaviours, but crucially this is not by overriding existing social norms. We also probably should not expect media language simply to replace community language norms, nor is this evidenced (Labov 2001).

Exposure to media content is not securely linked to shifts in behaviour, rather what seems important is attention to media content through heightened psychological or emotional engagement (Gunter 2000). Sociolinguistic research suggests that mere exposure to other dialects via the broadcast media does not seem to have appreciable effects on local dialects, as far as we are aware (Labov 2001). But programmes and/or characters which are the subject of strong psychological engagement, and so which are relevant to speaker/viewers' own social experiences, might be sociolinguistically relevant too.

The viewer's existing experience and socialization is fundamental in constraining any observable behavioural influence. We should expect the viewer's linguistic system to exert even stronger constraints, especially given the continual loops of speech production and perception which are active during live interaction with someone who is physically present (Kuhl 2010; Pickering and Garrod 2013; Redcay et al 2010). We predict that speakers will parse TV programs through the filter of their being active members of actual speech communities. Just as linguistic variants transmitted between speakers in dialect contact are incorporated into existing dialects and assigned local social meanings (congruent or not with their former ones) (e.g. Trudgill 1986), the constraints on any possible structural shifts after engaging with a media dialect may be far greater, since the viewer's own stored real-world language experience is the only vehicle for parsing media language at all (cf. Buchstaller and D'Arcy's 2009 emphasis on the importance of local constraints in negotiating the spread of *be like*).

Similarly, elicited imitation of media behaviours is always mediated through individuals' existing behavioural patterns. The same is likely to apply to language (see e.g. Mitterer and Ernestus 2008). At the broader level of discourse, and the more general parsing of media texts, "communicative appropriation" (*Kommunikative (Fernseh)aneignung*) developed by Holly and colleagues (e.g. Holly et al. 2001), drawing on audience reception theory (e.g. Morley 1980), accounts for the range of linguistic and communicative activities that take place during and after watching television. On the one hand, appropriation refers to what happens linguistically as speaker/viewers make sense of television, on the other, to the observed integration of chunks of media language into speakers' subsequent discourse, which always serve purposes of the particular interaction (e.g. Branner 2002; Androustopoulos 2001).

4.2 The broadcast media as a stylistic "shelf" for language variation

How could these observations relate to the notion of the media acting as a "shelf"? We make some suggestions below.

Although both sociolinguistic and media academic discourse describe processes of styling and appropriation in terms of what speakers are "doing", this does not presume volition or conscious awareness on the part of speakers. Explicit awareness of sociolinguistic behaviour of the self (and even that of others) is not easily linked to actual behaviour, or supposed motivating factors (Kristiansen 2009; Bargh et al. 1996). It also seems to be constrained by linguistic level (some aspects are more accessible, e.g. lexis, than others, e.g. morpho-syntax, phonology). This seems to apply as much to linguistic variation that is associated with the broadcast media as with any other kind of social factor. People might think that "off the shelf" changes are the result of speaker-viewers voluntarily adopting features from the TV, but the actual mechanisms involve numerous factors and are much more complex, even if engaging with a favourite programme is involved (see Section 7). Moreover, whilst media language usage probably does affect speakers' awareness of linguistic varieties and variation (Milroy and Milroy 1985), and indeed is integrally involved in the development of ideologies about linguistic variants (Agha 2003), it is still very unclear how media influence on attitudinal and/or ideological shifts relate to actual changes in linguistic usage (cf. Trudgill 1988; Stuart-Smith 2006).

Complexity must be assumed for any process of "taking", "adapting" or "borrowing" linguistic elements from the media, as Androutsopoulos (2001: 24) notes: "the notion of *appropriation* stresses the fact that recipients are not just imitating media fragments, but they may creatively modify them and use them for their own purposes" [my emphasis]. The German reflexive verb *sich aneignen* 'to take for oneself, make one's own' reflects this more clearly than the English term. The point here is that the interactional needs of particular speakers in particular contexts determine how appropriated chunks of media language may surface in talk, and the shared meanings accessible to interlocutors may not be similarly accessible to the analyst. Notions of direct imitation or mimesis are not easily helpful for pinpointing the processes underlying appropriation of media language (Branner 2002).

Following on from this, closer inspection of cases of linguistic diffusion does not provide easy support for direct lifting from the media. Buchstaller and D'Arcy (2009) argue for the notion of "weak transfer" for the global spread of *be like* at least partly because of the lack of congruence in sociolinguistic constraints in three different international varieties of English. While knowledge of the surface form and some "apparently universal constraints" might be facilitated by mass media, they propose that "other perhaps "high context" information, such as social meaning and the constraints on tense/temporal reference, which may be a function of narrative structure, is created in and through the local routinization of forms in the respective local variety" (Buchstaller and D'Arcy 2009: 322). In other words, any conceptualization of "off the shelf" changes (Milroy 2007) probably needs to be redefined as changes which *look* as if they have been taken right off the shelf. The similarity across locales may be rather superficial (cf. Dion and Poplack 2007; Section 7). This raises further questions about exactly how such transmission, and/or "transformation under transfer" might take place, and more fundamentally, what it is that we think we are modeling when we talk about media "influence".

However, the core characteristic about "off the shelf" changes, whether or not they are linked with the broadcast media (Milroy 2007 points out that rapid linguistic diffusion associated with celebrity is not limited to the 20th century), is rather that such changes constitute particular sites of coincidence between linguistic variation and social meaning. With or without speakers' awareness, these features appear to offer stylistic opportunities, linking meaning making at the micro level of interaction with the macro level of broader, supra-local language ideologies. In some senses this could be a description of the kind of classic indexicality captured in, for example, theories of stance-taking and linguistic variation (e.g. Kiesling 2009). But as Coupland (2007) recognizes, "off the shelf" features may also permit elements of performance, allowing speakers special stylistic license to mediate their speech even between each other.

We explore these suggestions by looking at data from two variationist studies, from two very different sociolinguistic contexts, for two phonological features. We begin with phrasal tone in Kagoshima Japanese.

5 Hearing features "on the shelf"? Phrasal pitch in Kagoshima Japanese and Tokyo Japanese media models

5.1 Accent and tone in Kagoshima Japanese

Kagoshima Japanese is a notoriously incomprehensible dialect of Japanese, which is also known for having a particular tonal "melody" which distinguishes it from Standard Japanese. While Standard Japanese has numbers of moras and several patterns of lexical accent, Kagoshima Japanese has two types of "melody", Tone A and Tone B. In Standard Japanese word accent is lexically specified such that a word is either "accented", and so has a pitch fall, e.g. NA.mi.da, 'tear', or is "unaccented" and has no pitch fall, e.g. hi.ga.shi, 'east'. The base tone of Standard Japanese is High tone (H). In Kagoshima Japanese, the accentual patterns are also specified for each word, but the base tone is Low.

Since the base tone is Low (L), lexical accent in Kagoshima Japanese is indicated by a High tone that appears among Low tone units, e.g. na.mi.DA, 'tear', or hi.GA.shi 'east'. This leads to a fundamental difference in the alignment of the tones in the two dialects, such that e.g. *namida-ga* 'tear-NOM' has the tone sequence HLLL in Standard Japanese, but LLLH in Kagoshima Japanese. As a result native speakers of Kagoshima dialect feel that the pitch-rise in a prosodic word (e.g. a compound of a noun and a case-marking particle) is the most distinctive phonological feature of their dialect.

5.2 Kagoshima – sociolinguistic context

Kagoshima prefecture is located in the southernmost part of Japan (see Figure 1 Ota and Takano, this volume). Kagoshima City is the centre of politics, economics, and culture in Southern Kyushu with a population of over 600,000 in 2011. Probably because of its geographical location and relative delays in establishing social infrastructures for transportation and communication after WWII, Kagoshima has been an area with lower geographical mobility, and consequently far less dialect contact, than other remote metropolitan areas such as Hokkaido's capital Sapporo. "Satsuma", the old name of Kagoshima, is well-known for the young *samurais'* great works during the Meiji Restoration.

Most regional dialects of Japanese have been affected by Standard Japanese, and the shifts can be illustrated as a continuum from "traditional" to "near-standard" one. For Kagoshima Japanese we hypothesize three (or possibly four) stages of shift (Figure 1).

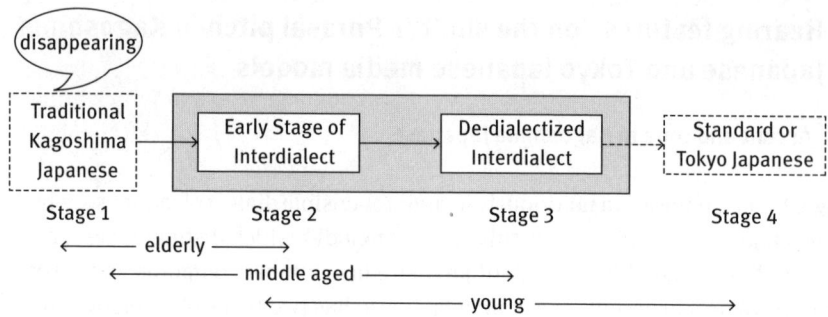

Figure 1: Language shift in Kagoshima Japanese

Traditional Kagoshima Japanese is still the main repertoire for elderly people and people in rural areas, but is declining and rarely heard in younger or urban dwellers. Early Stage of Interdialect is created by interference from Standard Japanese through education and dialect contact. Almost all lexical and grammatical items have been replaced by standard forms, making it more generally comprehensible than traditional dialect, but the traditional two-melody-type accentual system is still well preserved. More de-dialectized Interdialect is the latest stage of language shift which still preserves dialect features. In most respects it is like Standard Japanese but there are still some instances of dialect phonology, such as accentuation. This seems to have become a default repertoire for younger speakers since around 2000. This highly standardized form of Kagoshima Japanese is less stigmatized than the other two varieties, but still has less overt prestige than the national standard. Standard Japanese is theoretically the final stage of the shift, though our results show that Standard Japanese spoken in Kagoshima has a local accent with respect to that spoken elsewhere, e.g. Tokyo.

The range of linguistic repertoires which speakers can use is indicated by the width of horizontal arrows for each generation. Formality does not work here as a norm for choosing linguistic elements, as the more de-dialectalized Interdialect is the default speech repertoire for the younger generation even if their interlocutors have good command of Kagoshima dialect. Standard Japanese is confined to certain formal situations, such as a job interview. Although the register is quite limited, bidialectalism is well established for young Kagoshima speakers.

However, their excellent command of Standard Japanese is limited to the use of the appropriate accentuation placement. Our phonetic analysis (5.4.) shows how the phonetic implementation of these accents still shows some phonetic differences in Standard Japanese when spoken in Kagoshima.

Local language ideologies towards the dialect continuum are complex. The older generation tends to be proud of their historical memories and have strong emotional attachment to the local culture. At the same time, the community still holds some ideas which originated in the *samurai* society, such as feudalism and male chauvinism. Not surprisingly, local (and younger) people have negative and ambivalent feelings towards the dialect. There is much affection for traditional Kagoshima dialect, which is regarded as a useful tool to express "true" feelings, but at the same time it is also stigmatized as "inferior" due to associations of rusticity, lack of sophistication, and incomprehensibility (Ota 2009).

5.3 The media and phrasal pitch change in Japanese (Study 1)

Traditional lexical and grammatical features have almost disappeared from many regional dialects (Ota and Takano this volume). As a result the younger generation speak forms of interdialect, and also have a very good command of Standard Japanese (Sibata 1998). At the same time, despite different local dialects, the auditory impression of regional forms of Standard Japanese is that they are very much alike: especially phrasal pitch contours produced by young people show remarkably similar "flat" pitch patterning.

Takano and Ota (2007) hypothesized that this auditory resemblance was related to Standard Tokyo Japanese mediated by television or other audio-visual media (e.g. videos).[4] They carried out two production experiments in two remote areas, Hokkaido in the north and Kagoshima in the south. In the first, participants were asked to read sentences composed of a sequence of accented (i. e. with pitch fall) words in Standard Japanese. Pitch transitions were examined at several points in the sentences (see Ota and Takano, this volume). The results showed a close resemblance of (flatter) pitch patterning in young speakers from the two cities geographically located at opposite ends of Japan.[5]

---

4 Video contents became available to ordinary people around the mid 1980s with a rapid increase of video rental shops.
5 Speakers from Sapporo were also in the sample, but they behaved like older dialect speakers. Takano and Ota (this volume) speculate that this is because of an imbalance in gender.

These findings are difficult to explain solely in terms of dialect contact, since it is difficult to assume that people living in such remote areas have regular contact with each other. This led Takano and Ota to speculate that the broadcast media could be an additional factor in the rapid (i. e. within several decades) and seemingly nation-wide homogenization of phrasal pitch patterning. Specifically, Standard Japanese represented in media seemed to be a possible candidate, and so a second experiment was designed. Young participants from Hokkaido and Kagoshima read 3 news passages (each of them is about 20 seconds) previously broadcast on the NHK TV news show, and their phrasal pitch patterns were compared with those of the original TV announcer. The results showed striking similarities in the patterning of the pitch contour between speakers and the TV newsreader.

Clearly there is ongoing language change which is leading to a nationwide homogenization of phrasal pitch patterning in regional forms of Standard Japanese. It is likely that several factors are driving this change, including some degree of dialect contact, as well as Standard Japanese used in state education since the 1950s. But at the same time, the results of both experiments, and in particular, the use of "non-natural" speech tasks (reading sentences and news scripts) to elicit Standard Japanese, show an interesting intersection between speech style and pitch patterning. When required to manipulate speech style in order to perform these tasks, speakers from different areas converged on very similar phrasal pitch contours, with each other and with the broadcast media. This suggests that using less natural speech elicitation tasks may offer a special window onto speakers' mental representations, both of what they are storing (but usually not accessing), and also of what they are witnessing, i. e. what is on the "media shelf". Whether they use this particular "shelf" as a resource for everyday interaction is another matter; these young speakers are unlikely to appropriate linguistic elements from the styles of state news broadcasters. But given the right task, they are able to demonstrate access to the patterns which characterize this news reading style.

5.4 The media and Prosodic Subordination in Japanese (Study 2)

The results of Study 1 suggest that speakers' styles can be constructed by referring to linguistic resources drawn from the media. Ota et al. (2012) carried out a second study which considered the speech of college students (19–24 years) in three distinct areas of Japan, Sapporo (Hokkaido), Fukuoka (Northern Kyushu), and Kagoshima (Southern Kyushu), in two different (non-natural) speech styles (see Table 1). Tokyo Japanese was also included to examine the extent to which regional varieties were patterning like Standard Japanese. Participants were asked to read out target sentences and to play roles in scripted conversations. The recordings were made in their own dialects (so e.g. Interdialect Kagoshima Japanese) and Standard Japanese. Tokyo speakers did the tasks in Standard Japanese. Only Standard Japanese results are discussed here.

	Sapporo	Fukuoka	Kagoshima	Tokyo	Total
Male	4	5	6	10	25
Female	7	6	6	9	28
Total	11	11	12	19	53

Table 1: Participants (college students) in Study 2 according to gender and region

For this study, the analysis of phrasal pitch patterning was better specified to consider a prosodic tone unit called the "multiword accentual phrase (MAP)" consisting of two prosodic words (Igarashi 2014). Flattening of phrasal pitch is expressed in terms of Prosodic Subordination, whereby the pitch rise in the second prosodic word of the MAP is suppressed, making the whole MAP sound like one tonal "unit", and resulting in an audibly flatter overall phrasal pitch contour. Ota et al. (2012) quantified the degree of Prosodic Subordination by calculating a measure of "pitch valley", as shown in Figure 2 (greater Prosodic Subordination is observed in smaller pitch valley values). The study considered four combinations of MAP but we give only the overall results here.

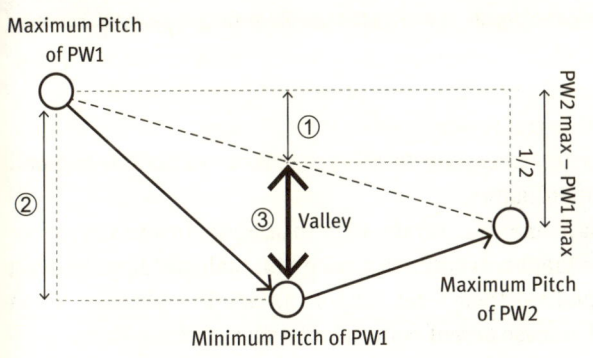

Maximum Pitch of PW1

① Valley

② ③ Valley

Minimum Pitch of PW1

Maximum Pitch of PW2

PW2 max − PW1 max

1/2

Figure 2: Schematic diagram of the calculation of the "pitch valley" measure. PW = Prosodic Word

① (PW2 max − PW1 max) / 2 + ② PW1 max − PW2 min = ③ Valley

Given the homogenization of pitch patterns found in Study 1, and the knowledge that greater Prosodic Subordination (and so flatter phrasal pitch contours) is a feature of the Standard Japanese spoken in Tokyo, Ota et al. (2012) hypothesized that the magnitude of Prosodic Subordination of Standard Japanese produced across the three remote regions (Sapporo, Fukuoka, and Kagoshima) would be similar to each other, and also to that of Tokyo (and so Standard) Japanese, subject to speech style and gender.

Results for overall pitch valley are shown in Figure 3. The first observation we can make is that, as expected, Tokyo speakers show the lowest pitch valley values, though there is an interaction of style and gender, such that scripted conversations show more Prosodic Subordination than read sentences, but women show more pitch flattening in read sentences.

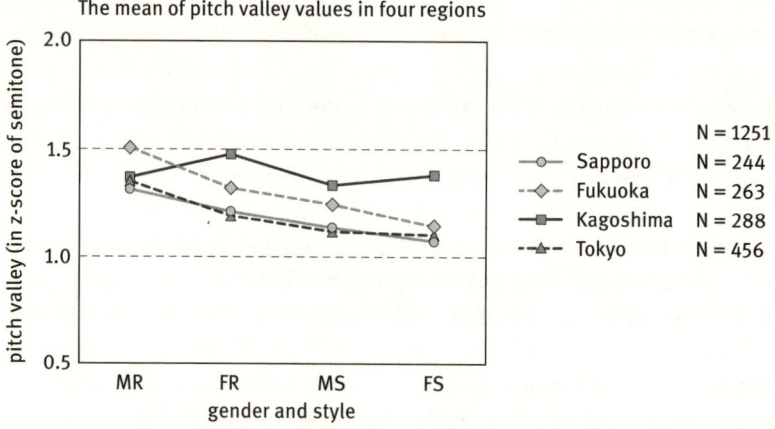

Figure 3: Average values of pitch valley in Standard Japanese for all four MAP conditions spoken by college students in four regions of Japan, according to style (R=reading, S=scripted conversation) and gender (M=male, F=female)

There are three main findings for region:

(1) Sapporo coincides almost exactly with Tokyo in terms of both degree and patterning of Prosodic Subordination.

(2) Fukuoka shows the same style/gender pattern as Sapporo and Tokyo, but with less Prosodic Subordination overall, particularly in male speakers reading the sentences, who maintained their local Fukuoka phonetic realization when producing the Standard Japanese accent pattern for this task.

(3) Kagoshima generally shows much less Prosodic Subordination than the other two remote dialects, and than Tokyo. It also shows a different pattern according to gender and style. Female Kagoshima speakers use less Prosodic Subordination than all other dialects in both speech styles. Kagoshima men also show more local phonetic realizations than Sapporo and Tokyo, though their

pitch valley measures are more like the Fukuoka men in the scripted conversations, and even less so in read sentences.

At first sight, these results look rather different from those of Study 1. This is partly because Study 2 included more combinations of word accent; examination of specific patterns, for example "accented+accented" shows almost complete convergence across dialects for both speech styles for female speakers. We consider the general pattern for each dialect in turn. Sapporo dialect has clearly converged with that of Tokyo, which may relate partly to dialect contact (post-war settlers came from Tokyo), but also to other factors such as education, and probably also the media (given the remote location and low opportunities for direct contact). Speakers of Fukuoka Japanese, with its own regional dialect, shows some evidence of Prosodic Subordination, especially in the scripted conversations, though Fukuoka male speakers seem to find it more difficult to approximate Standard Japanese in read sentences, maintaining some local phonetic realizations.

The speakers who are most different are from Kagoshima: like all the other dialect speakers, they have mastered the Standard Japanese phonological word accent correctly, but their phonetic realization is different. Interestingly, if compared with older speakers, there is apparent-time evidence for pitch flattening in progress. But local phonetic realization constrains the pitch contours. The men look as if they converge in the sentence reading task, but whilst their pitch valley measures are statistically the same as Tokyo and Sapporo, their pitch patterns sound rather unusual, as if they are hypercorrecting – they are trying, but failing to approximate Standard Japanese. In the scripted conversations, their higher pitch valleys result from phonetic transfer from their usual Kagoshima Interdialect realizations.

The female speakers seem to be doing something different, which relates both to local prestige norms, and also to the media, but in an unexpected way. In Kagoshima dialect, extensive pitch excursions are typical of glamorous elegant femininity. Here the Kagoshima women show – with respect to older women – some Prosodic Subordination in the read sentences, but they also retain some local pitch excursions indexing "elegant local lady". In the scripted conversations, something else is happening: Kagoshima women used extended pitch contours which sounded like those of voice actors in *anime* cartoons. We think that playing a role in a drama in Standard Japanese resulted in a task which was as "unnatural" as reading sentences. Recall that using Standard Japanese is still restricted to specific domains in Kagoshima; trying to approximate the phonetic implementation of Standard Japanese typical of a conversation may still beyond their stylistic manipulation. As a result, the task forced them to access a language model from "elsewhere".

Producing Standard Japanese usually makes Kagoshima speakers refer to a model which gives normative examples of Standard Japanese, such as TV news broadcasting. *Anime* language may have been the most familiar and easily accessible example of Standard Japanese to play out the scripted drama. The language of *anime* and dubbing characters is well known for its stereotypical prosodic features such as wider pitch range, clear division of intonational phrase by grammatical structure, and exaggerated pitch patterns in emotional expression. Strong psychological engagement with *anime* and *anime* characters may lead to stronger stored traces in memory, and hence resources for activation when necessary. We noted above that shift to standard dialects is often linked to orientation to media models.

These data suggest that young Kagoshima speakers are still hearing (and storing) voices from the media "shelf", even long after they have become competent bidialectals. Aspects of these voices may also be accessible when they need to style themselves for a task of this kind (playing a role in a scripted conversation requires the participant to perform, even if that role is him or herself).That this is restricted to the female speakers also suggests an interesting sociolinguistic coincidence between media and the local, in terms of phonetic realization, since extended pitch is a prestigious feature of local Kagoshima dialect/Interdialect, but only for women. Thus even in a context of language standardization, where "authoritative" media genres such as news broadcasting might be assumed to exert most influence, a closer look at phonological, and especially phonetic, patterning reveals that the locus of influence is viewers and their stylistic context. Viewers engage, store and activate media features from the appropriate media "shelves", i. e. appropriate to their stylistic context and then usage. We explore this in terms of variation and social meaning, in Eckert's (2008) framework of the "indexical field" below.

6 Indexical fields and social meaning of pitch patterning in Japanese

Eckert (2008) proposes the notion of the "indexical field" as: "[a] constellation of ideologically-related meanings, any one of which can be activated in the situated use of the variable. The field is fluid, and each new activation has the potential to change the field by building on ideological connections." Figure 4 illustrates how Japanese pitch patterning and its social meanings are interrelated in two indexical fields. Sapporo, Fukuoka, and Tokyo, which have the same Standard Japanese type tone structure, with a High tone base (Shibatani 1990), share the same large indexical field. Since Kagoshima's tone structure is based on L tone,

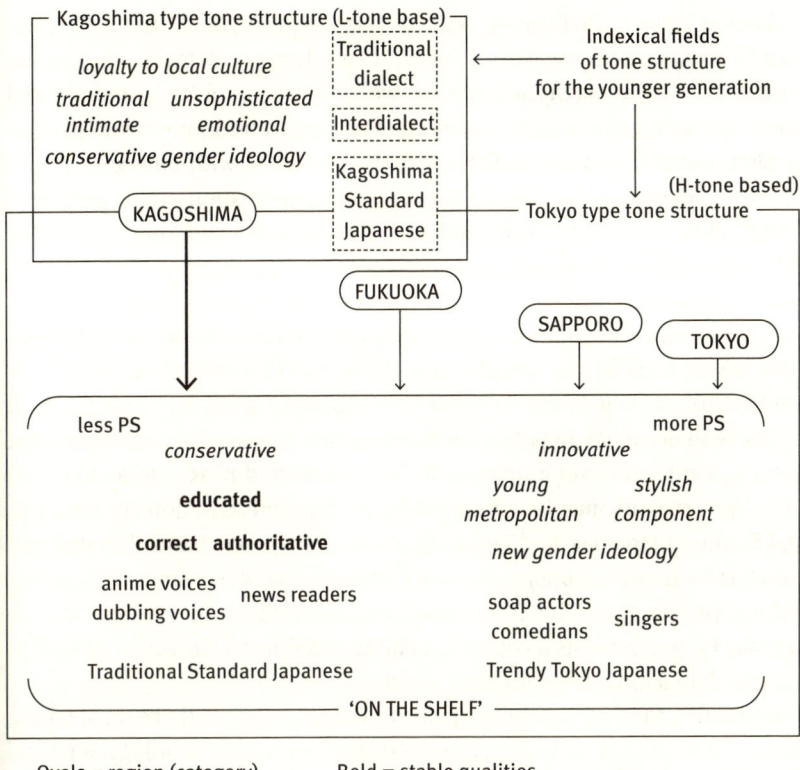

Figure 4: Tone structures for Standard Japanese and Kagoshima Japanese and their indexical fields

it forms a different indexical field. In addition, young Kagoshima people are bidialectal, and partly share the indexical field of the Standard Japanese tone type. The dotted boxes indicate typical variants of pitch patterning. In the indexical field for Kagoshima tone structure, there are three variants, Traditional Dialect, Interdialect, and the Kagoshima-accented Standard Japanese. In Standard Japanese we identify two, Traditional Standard Japanese and Trendy Tokyo Japanese.[6]

Social meanings ascribed to pitch patterning are stable and emergent. Meanings in bold are more stable: Traditional Standard Japanese is usually recognized

---

[6] In fact, Fukuoka has another dialectal tone structure, called 'tonal plateau' (Ota, Nikaido and Takano 2010), which should be included for a more comprehensive understanding of social meaning of pitch patterning.

everywhere in Japan as "educated" and "correct", and so Traditional tone structure can be used to help speakers position themselves in interaction to express epistemic stance (e.g. Johnstone 2009), as well as conservativism. The italicized meanings are emergent, which may be less diffused and more localized. The flatter pitch variant, with a smaller valley, is associated with emergent meanings. It often appears in the speech of the younger generation and is perceived as "young" (Takano and Ota 2007). But it is also associated with other emergent, related meanings, for social life in a metropolitan area, such as "innovative", "stylish", "competent", etc.

We can surmise that young people in Sapporo and Fukuoka might style themselves by taking stances in a situation like the scripted conversation, where they needed to construct a persona for the role (as opposed to the more neutral task of reading sentences). We hypothesize that for these speakers, actual occasional experience of prosodic subordination in stance-taking during interaction with young Tokyo speakers may be enhanced by media representations of both traditional Standard Japanese and Trendy Japanese. On the one hand, Trendy Japanese models such as soap operas, variety and music shows enhance their actual experience. On the other, the Traditional Japanese variants in e.g. news broadcasting may help to serve as a contrast, helping to delineate the social meanings of flatter pitch in a local sociolinguistic context.

The situation for the Kagoshima speakers, living on the southern tip of Japan, is different. They are able to use the Standard Japanese tonal phonology, but their access to the social meanings for this indexical field (and even the feature itself) for its phonetic realizations is probably restricted largely to the media. Their sociolinguistic reference point for producing Standard Japanese is usually the more conservative Traditional Standard Japanese tone type shown in e.g. news broadcasting, but, as the results for the scripted conversation show, if necessary they are able to access both the realization and the social meanings of the tone structure shown in *anime*. At the same time, important local social meanings are carried by Kagoshima phonetic realization of tone, and this may also help preserve a greater pitch valley, and so much less Prosodic Subordination overall.

The Kagoshima example in particular relates to a specific context of strongly enregistered local and standard, alongside some core linguistic structural differences. Trudgill (e.g. 1986) suggested that speakers in this kind of situation may orient to standard varieties in the media (see also Carvahlo 2004). But it is far from clear that these Kagoshima speakers are trying to do this. Using Standard Japanese phonology is a part of their repertoire, to which they can shift as they need, e.g. if talking to Standard Japanese speakers for specific purposes in a formal discussion, as part of their day-to-day processes of persona construction. But in so doing they do not lose their connections with Kagoshima *phonetically*. Maintaining local phonetic realizations (itself contingent on their continued ability to drift into Interdialect), reflects the importance of the local sociolinguistic context with its indexical array of meanings for these speakers, probably because Kagoshima is so far from metropolitan Tokyo in so many ways.

The nature of the media model that speakers have in mind is also interesting. *anime* characters are cartoons voiced by actors, as opposed to films of actors. They are very clearly not "real". The Kagoshima data show that for these speakers construction of a sociolinguistic persona can include aspects which relate not to a *real* figure, but rather may have some features of a stereotypical character appearing in *anime*.[7] Recent research on interaction with computers and avatars shows that self-identification with non-real "social agents" is quite usual (Reeves and Nass 1996; Staum-Casasanto et al. 2010). What is important, though, is the congruence of local linguistic patterning with that of the media model – those (female) Kagoshima speakers who already use pitch excursion with a specific social meaning are also those who appropriate the more extended pitch typical of *anime*.

7 Taking features "right off the shelf"? Rapid consonant change in Glasgow and "Mockney" media models

7.1 Rapid consonant diffusion in the UK and media influence

The context of the Glasgow study is the widespread homogenization of the consonant systems of British urban accents which showed a sharp acceleration in the 1990s (Foulkes and Docherty 1999), especially through the diffusion of a set of consonant features associated with London English, including TH-fronting ([f] for /θ/ in e.g. *think*), DH-fronting ([v] for /dh/ in e.g. *brother*), and L-vocalization (using a high back (un)rounded vowel for coda /l/ in e.g. *milk*). While these features seem to have been spreading northwards from the South East, mainly from city to city (Kerswill 2003), there have been observed instances in more remote locations since the early 1980s (e.g. Trudgill 1988; Macafee 1983). The detailed contribution of the changes in each variety vary, but overall, the result are leading

---

7 Azuma (2009), a Japanese critic on Japanese contemporary culture (especially on *otaku* culture), develops a very similar discussion on the current situation of novels in Japan. Citing other critics' comments, he points out how in the postmodern world, realism in novels for young people can be constructed on worlds which include those previously depicted in *manga* and *anime*.

to a homogenization of the consonant system away from RP and/or Standard Southern British English (Foulkes and Docherty 1999).

The idea that the media, and specifically television programmes representing vernacular London ("Cockney") accents might somehow be responsible for the rapid diffusion of these features arose primarily because of the profile of the speakers using them most, non-mobile working-class adolescents. This posed a challenge for the "change-by-accommodation" model of language change (Auer and Hinskens 2005) formulated by Trudgill (1986) which presumes face-to-face interaction as the conduit for linguistic diffusion. Trudgill was puzzled by the distribution of the innovations in his Norwich data, and discussed the possibility that, alongside less obvious forms of dialect contact, positive attitudes towards programmes such as the popular London-based TV crime drama, *Minder,* might indirectly facilitate their spread (e.g. 1988). Exposure to the media, and in particular TV programmes aimed at young people, was also suggested as partly promoting these features as "youth norms" (e.g. Williams and Kerswill 1999); and certainly TH-fronting is enregistered as an inherent part of "yoof culture". But despite speculation, there was no evidence that the influence of the media was really involved in these changes, nor many elsewhere.

7.2 Glasgow – sociolinguistic context

Although Edinburgh is the political capital of Scotland, Glasgow's seafaring and industrial history resulted in it being by far the larger city, receiving large influxes of migrants from the Highlands and Ireland and overseas. The population of Glasgow is now stable at around 600,000, but the entire conurbation is closer to 1.5 million, and this after half a century of planned counter-urbanization. The Central Belt of Scotland is a long way from England. Glasgow is 160 km to Carlisle, the closest English city, and 720 km from London. Culturally and even politically it is distinct from England, with a different legal, education, and health system. There is overt awareness of Scottish versus English identities, which are often articulated in terms of linguistic differences, and acutely at the Scottish English border.

Linguistically, Glaswegian is described as a sociolinguistic continuum ranging from Scottish Standard English spoken by middle-class speakers to the now fairly leveled continuation of West Central Scots in Glaswegian vernacular, spoken by working-class speakers, and generally regarded as "slang" (e.g. Macafee 1983). Scottish Standard English is evaluated fairly uniformly as overtly prestigious (in education and the professions), but at the same time, Glasgow dialect has strong covert prestige, with stereotypical associations with hard-work ing, straight-talking, shipyard workers, so that hypercorrection in both directions is very common.

The phonology of Glaswegian vernacular is different from that of English English dialects in several respects, and even from Scottish Standard English, with distinctive vowels and lexical incidence (e.g. Stuart-Smith 2004). Whilst T-glottalling has been attested in the city since the turn of the 19th century, features like TH-fronting are unexpected in this dialect. They also have to compete with vigorous local non-standard variants, for example, [h] for /θ/, as in *I [h]ink*. This means that unlike other urban accents, where a single non-standard variant [f] alternates with standard [θ], in Glaswegian, supralocal [f] alternates with local [h], giving two non-standard variants (Stuart-Smith and Timmins 2007).

The first published observation of the "London" features in Glasgow was in passing by Macafee in (1983), though Seamus Simpson (pc) remembers a few instances during National Service in the 1950s. The innovations seem to have traveled up to Scotland through the increased mobility of WWII, and probably began transmitting gradually from generation to generation by regular incrementation (Labov 2007). They took off during the late 1980s or early 1990s, since by 1997, TH-fronting and L-vocalization were well established in working-class adolescent speech, though with a thoroughly "local" evaluation, and firmly embedded in an otherwise Glaswegian phonology (these speakers do *not* sound like Londoners, nor do they want to; Stuart-Smith et al. 2007). The first indication of any form of conscious awareness was an article in 2001 in the Edinburgh newspaper, *The Scotsman*, entitled "In need of speech ferapy" on urban youngsters, though in fact L-vocalization seems to be more available for comment (MacFarlane and Stuart-Smith 2012). The press, especially the local Scottish media, assumed that the changes were taking place because of media influence (e.g. "Glesca' drowns in the English Estuary'), but it was unclear that London-based programmes would even be watched by Glaswegian teenagers, let alone be able to exert any kind of influence over their speech production.

The Glasgow Media Project ran from 2002–5 and combined variationist sociolinguistic methods with those of media effects research to investigate the possible influence of media representations of London dialects (Media-Cockney) on Glaswegian vernacular, and to examine the evidence for imitating media language and short-term shifting induced by watching television. We worked with 36 adolescents aged 10–15 over two years, and 12 adults, all born and raised in Maryhill, a city district with high rates of social and economic deprivation. The project analysed a range of phonological variables, consonantal and vocalic, as well as substantial demographic and social data, including self-reported exposure and engagement with the broadcast media. We discuss selected results below (for details, see Stuart-Smith 2006; Stuart-Smith 2011; Stuart-Smith et al. 2013).

7.3 Consonant change and media influence in Glasgow

The phonetic analysis confirmed both apparent and real-time increases in TH-fronting, DH-fronting and L-vocalization, but no apparent-time change for the vowels (/a ɪ ʉ/). All variables were subjected to a large-scale multi-factorial regression analysis, which considered the relative contribution of a number of social factors within, and then across, a series of categories, such as dialect contact, language attitudes, social practices, exposure and engagement with the media, and so on. The main findings were:

- linguistic factors showed very strong effects, suggesting that the innovations have become strongly embedded in Glasgow dialect, which is consistent with regular transmission over some time (as in fact is suggested by their known history)
- social practices were the strongest extralinguistic factor, specifically our informants rejecting school uniforms for Glasgow street style in hair and dress
- strong psychological engagement with either the programme and/or the characters in Cockney soap opera, *EastEnders*, showed the next strongest positive effects
- contact with family and friends in England showed some positive effects

So the changes traveled north and gradually started percolating through the community, but at some point became attached to particular local social meanings, particularly class-based ideologies of being not being like their "posh" neighbours, which helped them take off (cf. Tagliamonte and D'Arcy 2007 after Labov 2001), probably during the early 1980s when they became noticeable (cf. Eckert 2008; Macafee 1983). Our study shows that twenty years later, the changes have become well-embedded and are being accelerated by their links with particular local social practices, continued dripfeeding from diffusion via dialect contact, and (somehow) by engaging with a particular London-based TV soap opera and its characters.

We also found that TV emerged as an accelerating factor in these changes alone, but not for vowel variation: TV influence does not lead to blanket shifts. It is also striking that the significant TV variables were engagement with, as opposed to exposure to, a drama: simply watching the TV, or it being on because others are watching it, is not related to these changes (Gunter 2000). And in terms of mechanism, the various imitation tasks showed that our informants could tell that (media-)Cockney was different, but they were not clear how, nor could they reliably imitate the features that are changing. Unlike e.g. Carvalho's (2004) findings, there was also no evidence of any desire to emulate this accent or these features. One boy even said: "it's alright but I wouldnae want to speak like it but". Our informants are not taking the features off the media shelf in any conscious way (cf. Buchstaller and D'Arcy 2009).

Further information about the possible mechanism of TV influence in these changes emerges from three aspects of the results. The first is the importance of the speaker/viewers' sociolinguistic system. It is not surprising that the vowels show no links with *EastEnders*. Media-Cockney vowel variants are incongruent in terms of phonological system, phonetic realization, and social meaning: for example, Cockney [a] is most similar to the speech of refined old ladies in the most middle-class area of Glasgow. There are more points of congruence for the consonant innovations (see below). This suggests that TV influence does not entail imposing "external" features onto viewers' systems, but rather that viewers' existing sociolinguistic knowledge acts primarily as a filter.

The second changes "viewers" to "viewer", for the statistical modeling showed a surprising result. There are no correlations between media preferences and social practices, and these variables could be entered together into the regressions. This means that we cannot assume that media influence is indirect via shared social practices, that our kids hang out together, watch TV together, and share linguistic practices – which we might expect (and which might in fact be so with other groups, such as young adults sharing flats who might watch TV together). Our younger adolescents, who don't report watching TV with friends, show individual patterns of TV preferences; in turn, TV influence on these particular features appears to work at the level of individual social cognition. The third relates to the overall pattern of changes for Glasgow dialect, which is not in fact homogenization; TV is not making people sound "the same" (Chambers 1998). In Glasgow it is quite the opposite, ongoing supralocal innovations are becoming established alongside vigorous local variants, leading to a richer array of features. Perhaps over the very long term homogenization will take place, but in the short term we find enhanced diversity.

7.4 Media models and community norms: From Mockney to Jockney?

An important aspect of the role of TV in these changes is understanding better what speaker/viewers are actually offered by media representations of Cockney ("Mockney"). A key strand of the project was a detailed phonetic analysis of the speech of the characters of the London-based TV programmes that our informants reported watching. Most popular – and also linked statistically – was the working-class Cockney soap drama, *EastEnders*. First broadcast in 1985, *East-Enders* became a sociological phenomenon within a few years (e.g. Buckingham

1987), and at the time of the data collection was being broadcast four times a week, attracting an audience of almost a third of the UK population. We analyzed vowels and consonants from a week's worth of episodes broadcast towards the end of our data collection period, concentrating on those characters who were mentioned by our informants, and who were also carrying the main storylines.

As expected, the vowels of media-Cockney are very different from those of Glaswegian, phonologically and phonetically. The three consonant innovations now found in Glasgow dialect were also evident in *EastEnders*. Taking TH-fronting as a representative example, there were three main findings when compared with Glaswegian, and also London English (Stuart-Smith et al. 2013):

1. Glaswegian adolescents use proportionately much more [f] than is found in *EastEnders* characters, who in turn show far less TH-fronting than London English.
2. TH-fronting is used more by male characters than female ones, but Glaswegian shows no evidence of gendered distribution in the innovations.
3. The linguistic constraints (position in word) for [f] in *EastEnders* generally follow those of Southern English, though this does not extend to male characters, who unusually show more [f] in word-initial position. But these are different from the constraints shown by [f] in Glaswegian, whose distribution is affected by that of local [h].

This comparison of media-Cockney and Glasgow dialect has some interesting implications. It is clear that strong engagement with the programme and its characters has not resulted in any kind of wholesale imposition of features, form and function (cf. Buchstaller and D'Arcy 2009). Like Dion and Poplack (2007), we also cannot assume that the consonant innovations in Glasgow result from any kind of usual language acquisition process with the TV as the primary input.

Rather we find that there are some instances of these features in (some) characters in *EastEnders*. We also find these features with their own local social and linguistic patterning in Glaswegian speakers, and particularly in those with strong psychological engagement with the drama. To uncover the possible mechanisms linking these findings, we looked more closely at how the features function in the speech of characters and in the drama itself. For whilst we tend to talk about media influence in terms of discrete blocks of media-represented information somehow affecting discrete blocks of speech – which is the implication from, e.g. comparing average percentages of variant usage – this is not how the speaker/viewer actually experiences the language of the media. Viewers may well end up with aggregated averages of experienced tokens, but what may be just as important is how these are experienced in the micro-context of each interactional move between characters as the drama unfolds, and especially how that might relate to real-world experience of interaction for the viewer.

We carried out a functional analysis of the consonant features in *EastEnders,* according to location, interlocutor, and emotional and/or dramatic speech act. Illustrating our findings with TH-fronting, [f] was more commonly used when

- characters were talking to each other in the Queen Vic, the local pub
- characters were talking only to one other character, as opposed to in larger groups
- and when the other character is a friend, then a family member (as opposed to partners or rivals)
- and when the content of the turn was: carefully emphasized, worried or sad, laughing or joking, and confused or nervous.

In terms of direct indexing of speaker groups or types, the media-Cockney consonant features belong to an accent which our informants told us was certainly different from their own, and for some, clearly English as opposed to Scottish. Their portrayal in *EastEnders* is linked particularly to working-class men with difficult and sometimes rough lifestyles, which is also accessible to some of our informants.[8] But we note that Glaswegian does not show a gendered distribution of any of the consonant innovations, so we cannot assume direct links with particular groups is necessarily meaningful for these features for these speakers.

Perhaps more interesting are the indexicalities which can be inferred from usage of the features throughout the drama. We see that TH-fronting is used more between pairs of friends chatting together in the pub, and for a range of interactional moves between them, for speech which is carefully emphasized, and/ or which helps convey some troubled emotional states, but also for joking. We know from communication with the makers of the program at an early state in the research that there are no dialect coaches, and that actors use their own resources to convey their characters. Our analysis suggests that the consonant features provide some of the resources to fulfill some of the stances taken by some actors in order to convey their roles as the drama unfolds.

The indexical fields for these features as portrayed in *EastEnders* may relate to those of actual London English. They involve a degree of stylization, if only because it is possible to identify specific points in the drama at which they are employed. But we can infer arrays of social meanings relating to some speak-

---

8 Our individual informants also did not always share perceptions of direct indexing of groups. For example, a couple thought that the accent was 'posh', which is not expected for a working-class accent.

er-types (tough working-class man; typical Cockney), to some interactional contexts (with a friend in a pub), and to some stances (emphatic; troubled emotions; joking). *EastEnders* then can be seen to act as one particular media shelf which offers some resources, either features, or probably more likely, features *and* associated social meanings (Coupland 2009) – at different levels of enregisterment. In the following section we explore how this might link to speech in the real world of a Glaswegian adolescent.

7.5 Style, stance and media "influence"

As in the Japanese studies, the Glasgow results also showed some interesting patterns according to speech style. Speech was recorded from speakers under two conditions, conversations of up to 40 minutes between self-selected, same-sex pairs of speakers without the fieldworker present, and a read wordlist of around 200 words, with the fieldworker present. The Media Project (2003) used exactly the same method as the earlier corpus collected in 1997, with the same fieldworker, and mainly the same school. We had expected that the wordlists would elicit carefully monitored speech, and this was found in middle-class, and some older working-class speakers. But the young working-class adolescents showed almost the opposite behaviour. They rattled through the list, sometimes laughing and/or commenting on items, and shifting to a style which involved using more non-standard realizations of all phonemes, though Scots lexical-phonological variants, such as *hink* for *think* or *oot* for *out* were avoided. It was clear that reading out the wordlist for the recording provided a stylistic opportunity for these speakers to perform their speech as "ours" – and non-standard – in relation to the persona of the University fieldworker (Stuart-Smith et al. 2007; see Coupland 2007). In so doing they took a particular stance to the task, and to the fieldworker, and this entailed particular shifts in their linguistic repertoire.

In both studies, the supralocal variants for the three consonant variables were used far more frequently in the read wordlists than the conversations. This was particularly marked for DH-fronting, which in the 1997 corpus was only found in wordlists, and in 2003, was found in wordlists and sporadically in spontaneous speech. For both TH-fronting and DH-fronting, it was clear that [f] and [v] respectively occurred in contexts where either the local non-standard variant was blocked by standard orthography (e.g. in Scots forms which take [h]), or where there was no local non-standard variant, e.g. [v] for /dh/ occurred most in word-final position, whereas local [ɾ] for /dh/ can only occur intervocalically. The new supralocal variants seemed to be functioning as *the* non-standard option.

The statistical analysis showed correlations with TV for both speech styles for TH and L, and DH only in wordlists (there was insufficient data for conversations), but the models had better explanation of variance for read speech. This is presumably because the many additional variables that constrain variation in spontaneous conversational speech, such as prosodic, discourse and pragmatic factors, were not included in the regressions. But it may also be because this speech style itself particularly motivated the use of the innovative variants.

This assumption is supported by a different variable, derhoticization of postvocalic /r/, which showed a similar stylistic pattern, but which has a rather different trajectory of change. Derhoticization is a vernacular change from below which has been reported since the turn of the 20th century, and which has no apparent links with English English non-rhotic speech (Lawson et al. 2011, Stuart-Smith et al. 2014). Derhoticization showed a split result in the regression analysis: in spontaneous speech, the variable patterned like the vowel variables, showing only linguistic factors as significant; in wordlists, derhoticization patterned like the consonant innovations, and was linked also with extra-linguistic factors, especially anti-school social practices and strong psychological engagement with *EastEnders*, amongst others (though not dialect contact). This result is interesting because derhoticization has never been linked with the English media, and direct contact with non-rhotic varieties of English appears to have no influence. But here we find that indirect contact with representations of non-rhotic London English is linked with using more non-rhotic variants, but only in read speech.

Somewhat akin to the Japanese role-play task, the Glasgow results show that the less natural speech style of reading out a wordlist gave our informants a stylistic opportunity to perform, and when this happened something interesting happened linguistically. Without the wordlists, DH-fronting would have been absent from the 97 corpus, and sporadic in that of 2003. This stylistic variation shows us that certain features of Glaswegian are socially special. When our informants shift to the stance of performing "their" repertoire, the consonant innovations appear or proliferate, and these are statistically linked with engaging with *EastEnders*, and so with dramatic, stylized representations of London English, even for a sound change whose final outcome is similar to English English, but which has been progressing as a system-internal change.

The links between style-shifting, the increased use of the diffusing features, and media engagement, help provide a starting point for understanding media influence on speech. The features which are changing, and which are linked with the media, are not just phonologically particular, they also carry particular social meanings which relate to specific interactional moves at specific moments. This is reminiscent of the exploitation of larger linguistic chunks which are known to originate in the broadcast media. Rampton (1995) observed that his London adolescents' use of appropriated media language occurred at liminal moments in their discourse, points which acted as thresholds from one part of the discourse to the next. Branner (2002) made a similar observation for her German teenagers. Media-appropriated material of larger linguistic chunks seems to surface at particular points in the discourse, allowing the speaker to perform specific interactional moves. In the case of the Glaswegian changes, we have no evidence that the phonetic variants have somehow "leaked" from words or catchphrases appropriated from *EastEnders*, in fact, our informants talk very little about TV, and use very few American or Scottish-English items in this way.

The connections probably lie in how speaker/viewers decode media representations of speech (see Section 3). We have already claimed that speakers parse media speech through the filter of their own experience as active members of actual speech communities. The wealth of circumstantial evidence indicating little impact of media influence on community norms, as well as the specific evidence from the Glasgow study, suggests that filtering entails rejection (or lack of or poor storage, or rapid decay) of the majority of media language, even if this is experienced with high engagement. But these results suggest that Hall's notion of the efficacy of decoding in terms of "fundamental alignment and reciprocity" of representation and experience may occasionally pertain, but that this must hold in terms of both linguistic structure *and* social meaning.

We suggest that in this case the opportunity for such alignment and reciprocity was provided both by existence of the variants within Glaswegian vernacular, albeit peripherally – and with linguistic constraints determined by the local dialect – and by the existence of some shared or overlapping social meanings, particularly in terms of their use for making particular interactional moves. Media influence of media-Cockney on Glaswegian vernacular translates into highly-engaged viewers parsing *EastEnders* through their filter of being Glasgow dialect speakers, but with a few features which already carry some kind of special social meaning, being enhanced because of the overlapping of their actual indexical field of use with that of the stylized indexical field presented by the characters as the drama unfolds before them. We suggested above (7.4) that these may relate to particular ways of negotiating friendship. In other words, we suggest that the intersection in social meaning that these features can convey in local interaction for these speakers' own purposes with that shown at a stylized level in drama is the key to understanding why media influence might affect some features and not others (Macaulay 2005). Speakers unwittingly use the media shelf to enhance or perhaps validate existing socially-meaningful linguistic resources.

8 Emerging themes on speech in the community and speech on the (media) "shelf": Perspectives from East and West

Only certain accent features are linked with the media, but most are not.

In Glasgow there is only evidence for variants of /θ/ /dh/ and /l/ (and coda /r/ in read speech) being correlated with engaging with *EastEnders*. The vowels show no links at all. In Japanese only certain suprasegmental features are linked, specifically the implementation of pitch for lexical word accent. We find that the phonological structure of Standard Japanese word accent seems to be well mastered in Kagoshima as well as the other remote accents, but the phonetic realization of pitch is local. If television offers models for these speakers, it is mainly the phonological structure which seems to be affected, enhancing existing knowledge provided through education, and possibly some dialect contact. In both varieties only very specific aspects of the sound system are linked with the broadcast media. There is, as predicted, no evidence for blanket shifts or imposition of features as a result of media influence. Nor is there evidence for any kind of conscious imitation or orientation towards media models, even in the Japanese data where the media provide pretty much the only possible models for the Kagoshima speakers.

The accent features which are linked with the media are also features that show particular kinds of social meaning.

Flattening of phrasal pitch in Standard Japanese has special associations of being young and trendy. At the same time, more modulation in pitch patterning in Kagoshima indicates both being a local to Kagoshima, and with even greater excursions, being a glamorous local lady. The feature which is changing in remote dialects is one which carries both local and supralocal social meanings. Neither these nor their precise phonetic realizations are necessarily the same, but the shifted phonetic realizations together with supralocal meanings can extend the local indexical field in useful ways for young Kagoshima speakers. Similarly, the four consonant variables whose changes are linked with TV in Glasgow, also have local variants with local social meanings: all four could co-occur in a style cluster for a "straight-talking, tough Glasgow guy". The Southern English innovations have supralocal meanings of "cool", "non-posh", "urban" youth. We have seen how the new variants extend the non-standard stylistic repertoire for Glaswegian adolescents, providing new resources which are at once local (cool, urban, us = here in this particular part of the city as opposed to the posh neighbours) and supralocal (identified by analysts, but not overtly recognized as such by speakers). In both cases, engaging with the media enables existing socially-meaning phonetic resources to be extended, suggesting that, as predicted, the viewer's existing sociolinguistic experience is primary in constraining media influence. In both, local identities are linked with supralocal identities such that speakers can be local, but not too local. This looks like bricolage at the fine phonetic level (cf. Eckert 2008).

The accent features linked with the media are more apparent in speech styles which in turn entail particular kinds of performance.

The Japanese data consisted only of less natural speech elicitation tasks, read sentences, a read passage, and a scripted conversation for a role play. Kagoshima speakers, who usually use Interdialect to different degrees, had to produce Standard Japanese in order to complete the tasks. They could manage to get the phonology right, and some aspects of the pitch realization, showing some Prosodic Subordination. Study 1, with the restricted accent combination, showed complete convergence of dialect speakers with the newsreader. Study 2 showed convergence in the expected "accented+accented" context, and pitch flattening in others. But the scripted conversations were difficult, so the Kagoshima women turned to the highly stylized pitch patterns of media *anime* for their model. The general change in Japanese towards flattening of phrasal pitch is foreshadowed in these elicited speech tasks from the Kagoshima sample.

The Glaswegians read out their wordlists taking a clear stance towards the task and the person and role of the fieldworker. In so doing they produced more instances of the innovative variants in the wordlists, and these – and even der-hoticization, which is a long-term vernacular change – were statistically linked with engaging with *EastEnders*. In both cases, the features are sensitive to style such that they emerge in tasks to elicit speech which were unusual for the speakers. They are, as it were, within the possible stylistic repertoire, but for specific purposes. Again, changes which are now clearly underway, were more apparent in less natural elicited speech, indeed DH-fronting was so restricted at the early stages of the change that it was only observed in wordlists in 1997. For both, the links with the media are only visible through these style shifts.

The use of these variants in these particular stylistic moments provides a bridge between the appropriation of media fragments in discourse, observed and discussed in the interactional sociolinguistic literature (e.g. Rampton 1985; Holly et al. 2001; Androutsopoulos 2001). We noted above that such appropriation often takes place at "liminal" or "liminoid" points in the talk, at boundaries. It may be that these speech elicitation tasks functioned in a similar way, being at the edge of our speakers' usual stylistic behavior. It is extremely interesting that engaging in peripheral stylistic performing facilitates the exploitation of variation which is stored and/or enhanced from engaging with the media.

Stylistic variation in these accent features seems to relate to stylistic and stylized variation presented by media models of different kinds.

Kagoshima Japanese speakers need to use media models as a source of additional information for the implementation of phrasal pitch in Standard Japanese. But these models are themselves instances of particular registers. Reading the news in any language entails specific linguistic features, compromising a speech style, and sometimes stylization (e.g. in English hyperarticulation of plosives is very common). The voice actors of *anime* cartoons are producing not only Standard Tokyo Japanese, but – like the voices for most cartoons – clearly using stylized features, including exaggerated pitch patterns. Our functional analysis of the use of innovative variants in media-Cockney showed how the representation of engaging dramatic personae for *EastEnders* also entails stylization; TH-fronting occurs more at specific points in the drama.

In both cases, the features which are changing, and which are subject to stylistic shifts within the dialect, are also those which are stylized to a greater or lesser extent in the media representation. It looks as if the overlap of indexical fields between the real world experience of the speaker/hearer and that of the represented media world, is either at the edge of speaker's possible stylistic repertoire, or in very specific areas. For the Glaswegians, the performance of localness together with the stance of being "us" versus being (posh) "you" seems to be within the range of these speakers, and in fact can be heard in overt displays of street talk by adolescents. For the Japanese, speaking Standard Japanese is very restricted, and the styles elicited in the Studies may not in fact be used – but clearly the resources are there, should they be needed. We wonder whether they may enable speakers to mediate their own talk even between each other.

We also see how supralocal features are entering the local systems through peripheral/unusual speech styles before percolating more widely. In this respect, these changes look typical of changes "from above", apparent in hypercorrection in closely monitored speech tasks (Labov 1972). The difference is that the prestige of these features is not connected with the standard in terms of authority, correctness, and elite. These are popular prestige norms, whose supralocal attraction is shared, but not even necessarily available for report by the local dialect speakers themselves.

Speakers are not aware that they use these accent features, or that their "source" might be the broadcast media.

In some cases of rapid diffusion, speakers are able to comment on possible media sources for a feature. For example, *be like* seems to be accessible to English speakers, native and non-native, as a feature with a specific location (America, California) and represented in the media. In neither case here were the speakers aware that they used the accent features which are changing, nor did they know (or indicate that they knew), that the changes might somehow be "from the media". In Glasgow, adolescents who feel that their linguistic variation – local and supralocal – is thoroughly local, appear to be completely unaware either that the supralocal features do occur elsewhere (in real or mediated varieties), or that they share some social meanings. Japanese speakers across Japan recognize flatter phrasal pitch as sounding "young" (Takano and Ota 2007), but there is no evidence that Kagoshima speakers know that they are participating in this change, or that they are witnessing it daily on TV.

There may be a good reason for this: we know that in both cases, the initiation and ongoing transmission of these sound changes was/is the result of other social factors. It seems likely that both changes arrived through dialect contact, and are being topped up by less overt forms of contact. But at the same time, they are being propelled forward by participation in local social practices (we know this for Glasgow, and suspect it for Kagoshima, given the apparent-time increase). Education is another key factor for the Japanese change; whereas orientation against education is more important in Glasgow. Whatever the detail, the key point is the same. As predicted, the media is identified as an additional accelerating factor in changes which are already in progress (cf. Brandt 2000).

9 Concluding remarks

Our survey of these two different phonological changes in two very different contexts, coincides in an important respect. The influence of the media on speech, as far as it can be inferred from these studies, depends fundamentally on the speaker/ viewers and their own position in negotiating local social meaning through linguistic variation. Speakers parse the broadcast media through their local dialect systems, and if shifts take place which are linked with the media, the features in the community are limited, are sensitive to stylistic variation and carry particular kinds of social meaning. The same features in the media are also limited, occur in particular styles or stylized forms of varieties, and carry certain social meanings which may not be the same as the local, but which can extend the local speaker's indexical field in useful ways for their own interactional moves. We suggest that enhancement of the local occurs when there is congruence linguistically and socially, i. e. that there is some overlap of indexical fields but crucially that the linguistic element to which the field pertains also overlaps in some way.

Two other conclusions can also be drawn. Whilst the majority of sociolinguistic research on media and language is carried out within an interactional framework (Gumperz 1982), it is clear that variationist sociolinguistics is a powerful tool for identifying instances where the media may be involved in language change. At the same time, it is also clear that "third wave" approaches need to be embraced, at least theoretically. We need to harness the power of variationist sociolinguistics with the theoretical insight that social meaning is core for speakers, especially because special kinds of social meaning afforded by variation seems to be at the heart of any change linked to the media.

Finally, the Japanese study especially, but also the Glasgow study, show the importance of manipulating stylistic variation for understanding language change in conjunction with the media. We need to feel confident about eliciting speech which we know not to be the vernacular, and to explore more and different "less natural" speech styles. This is particularly because media representations usually show styled or stylized language, which in turn is variation which exists at the "edge" of stylistic variation for language in the community. Not only are changes associated with the media special in terms of social meaning, they also seem to inhabit the blurry zone between media language and mediated language that Coupland (2007) opens up at the very end of his book. So to return to Eckert's (2003: 395) analogy, media shelves may present potentially useful resources for speaker/viewers, but only if they can implicitly recognize them.

References

Agha, Asif 2003: The Social Life of Cultural Value. *Language and Communication.* 23: 231–73.

Androutsopoulos, Jannis 2001: From the streets to the screens and back again: On the mediated diffusion of ethnolectal patterns in contemporary German. *Series A: General and Theoretical Papers*. Essen: University of Essen.

Auer, Peter and Frans Hinskens 2005: The role of interpersonal accommodation in a theory of language change. In: Peter Auer, Frans Hinskens and Paul Kerswill (eds.), *Dialect Change: Convergence and Divergence in European Languages*, 335–357. Cambridge: Cambridge University Press.

Ayass, Ruth and Cornelia Gerhardt 2012: *The Appropriation of Media in Everyday Life*. Amsterdam: Benjamins.

Azuma, Hiroki 2009: *Otaku: Japan's Database Animals*. Translated by Jonathan E. Abel and Shion Kono. Minneapolis: University of Minnesota Press.

Babel, Molly 2012: Evidence for phonetic and social selectivity in spontaneous phonetic imitation. *Journal of Phonetics* 40: 177–189.

Bandura, Albert, Dorothea Ross and Sheila Ross 1963: Imitation of film-mediated aggressive models. *Journal of Abnormal and Social Psychology.* 66: 3–11.

Bargh, John, Mark Chen and Lara Burrows 1996: Automaticity of social behavior: Direct effects of trait construct and stereotype activation on action. *Journal of Personality and Social Psychology.* 71: 230–244.

Bauman, Richard 1992: Performance. In: Richard Bauman (ed.), *Folklore, Cultural Performances, and Popular Entertainments*, 41–9. New York/Oxford: Oxford University Press.

Baumann, Richard 2011: "Better than any monument": Envisioning Museums of the Spoken Word. *Museum Anthropology Review* 5: 1–13.

Berkowitz, Leonard: 1984: Some effects of thoughts on anti- and prosocial influences of media events: A cognitive-neoassociation analysis. *Psychological Bulletin* 95: 410–27.

Brandt, Wolfgang 2000: Sprache in Hörfunk und Fernsehen. In: Werner Besch, Werner, Anne Betten, Oscar Reichman, and Stefan Sonderegger (eds.), *Sprachgeschichte: Ein Handbuch zur Geschichte der deutschen Sprache und ihrer Erforschung*. 2nd edn. Vol II, 2159–2168. Berlin/New York: Mouton de Gruyter.

Branner, Rebecca 2002: Zitate aus der Medienwelt: Zu form und Funktion von Werbezitaten in natürlichen Gesprächen. *Muttersprache* 4: 337–59.

Bucholtz, Mary 2009: From stance to style: gender. interaction. and indexicality in Mexican immigrant youth slang. In: Alexandra Jaffe (ed.), *Sociolinguistic Perspectives on Stance*, 146–70. New York: Oxford University Press.

Buchstaller, Isabelle 2008: The localization of global linguistic variants. *English World-Wide* 29: 15–44.

Buchstaller, Isabelle and Alex D'Arcy 2009: Localised globalisation: A multi-local. multivariate investigation of quotative *be like*. *Journal of Sociolinguistics* 13: 291–331.

Buckingham, David 1987: *Public secrets: EastEnders & its audience*. London: BFI.

Bushman, Brad and L. Rowell Huesmann 2001: Effects of televised violence on aggression. In: Dorothy Singer and Jerome Singers (eds.), *Handbook of Children and the Media*. 223–54. Thousand Oaks CA: Sage. 223–54.

Carvalho, Ana Maria 2004: I speak like the guys on TV: Palatalization and the urbanization of Uruguayan Portuguese. *Language, Variation and Change* 16: 127–51.

Chambers, Jack 1998: TV makes people sound the same. In: Laurie Bauer and Peter Trudgill (eds.), *Language Myths*, 123–31. New York: Penguin.

Charkova, Krassimira 2007: A language without borders: English slang and Bulgarian learners of English. *Language Learning* 57: 369–416.

Coupland, Nikolas 2007: *Style: Language variation and identity*. Cambridge: Cambridge University Press.

Coupland, Nikolas 2009: Dialects, standards and social change. In: Marie Maegaard, Frans Gregersen, Pia Quist and Jens Norman Jorgensen (eds.), *Language attitudes, standardization and language change,* 27–49. Novus Forlag: Oslo.

Curran, James 1996: The new revisionism in Mass Communications research: A reappraisal. In: James Curran, David Morley and Valerie Walkerdine (eds.), *Cultural Studies and Communications*, 256–278. London: Arnold.

Dion, Natalie and Shana Poplack 2007: Linguistic mythbusting: The role of the media in diffusing change. Paper presented at NWAV36. University of Pennsylvania. Philadelphia. PA.

Eckert, Penelope 2003: Elephants in the room. *Journal of Sociolinguistics* 7: 392–397.

Eckert, Penelope 2008: Variation and the indexical field. *Journal of Sociolinguistics* 12: 453–476.

Eckert, Penelope 2012: Three waves of variation study: The emergence of meaning in the study of variation. *Annual Review of Anthropology* 41: 87–100.

Eckert Penelope and John Rickford 2003: *Style and Sociolinguistic Variation*. Cambridge: Cambridge University Press.

Foulkes, Paul and Gerard Docherty (eds.) 1999: *Urban Voices: variation and change in British accents*. London: Edward Arnold.

Gunter, Barrie 2000: *Media research methods: Measuring audiences, reactions and impact*. London: Sage.

Gunter, Barrie and Jill McAleer 1997: Children and Television. (2nd edition). London: Routledge.

Hall, Stuart 1980: Encoding/decoding. In: *Culture, Media, Language: Working Papers on Cultural Studies. 1972–79*, 128–38. Birmingham: Hutchinson with the Centre for Contemporary Cultural Studies.

Harris, Richard 2004: *A Cognitive Psychology of Mass Communication*. Fourth Edition. Mahwah, NJ: Lawrence Erlbaum.

Holly, Werner, Ulrich Püschel and Jörg Bergmann (eds.) 2001: *Der sprechende Zuschauer*. Wiesbaden: WV.

Igarashi, Yosuke 2014: Typology of intonational phrasing in Japanese dialects. In: Sun-Ah Jun (ed.) *Prosodic Typology*, the second volume, 464–492, New York: Oxford University Press.

Katz, Elihu and Paul Lazarsfeld 1955: *Personal Influence: The part played by people in the flow of mass communications*. Glencoe, Il: Free Press.

Kerswill, Paul 2003: Models of linguistic change and diffusion: new evidence from dialect levelling in British English. In: David Britain and Jenny Cheshire (eds.), *Social Dialectology. In honour of Peter Trudgill*, 223–43. Amsterdam: Benjamins.

Kiesling, Scott 2009: Style as stance: Stance as the explanation for patterns of sociolinguistic variation. In: Alexandra Jaffe (ed.) *Sociolinguistic Perspectives on Stance*. New York: OUP.

Klapper, Joseph Thomas 1960: *The effects of mass communication*. Glencoe: Free Press.

Kristiansen, Tore 2009: The macro-level social meanings of late-modern Danish accents. *Acta Linguistica Hafniensia* 41: 167–192.

Kuhl, Patricia 2010: Brain mechanisms in early language acquisition. *Neuron* 67: 713–775.

Kuhl, Patricia, Feng-Ming Tsao and Huei-Mei Liu 2003: Foreign-language experience in infancy: Effects of short-term exposure and social interaction on phonetic learning. *Proceedings of the National Academy of Sciences* 100 (15): 9096–9101.

Labov, William 1972: *Sociolinguistic patterns*. Oxford: Blackwell.

Labov, William 2001: *Principles of Linguistic Change: II Social Factors*. Oxford: Blackwell.

Labov, William 2007: Transmission and diffusion. *Language* 83: 344–87.

Lameli, Alfred 2004: Dynamik im oberen Substandard. In: Hermann Scheuringer and Stephan Gaisbauer (eds), *Tagungsberichte der 8. Bayerisch-osterreichischen Dialektologentagung*, 197–208. (Schriften zur Literatur und Sprache in Oberösterreich, 8) Linz: Adalbert-Stifter-Institut des Landes Oberösterreich.

Lawson, Robert 2011: Patterns of Linguistic Variation among Glaswegian Adolescent Males. *Journal of Sociolinguistics* 15: 226–255.

Lefkowitz, Monroe, Leonard Eron, Leopold Walder and L. Rowell Huesmann 1972: Television violence and children aggression: A follow-up study. In: George Comstock and Eli Rubinstein (eds*), Television and social behavior. Volume 3: Television and adolescent aggressiveness*, 35–135. Rockville: National Institute of Mental Health.

Macafee, Caroline 1983: *Varieties of English around the world: Glasgow*. Amsterdam: Benjamin.

Macaulay, Ronald 1977: *Language, Social Class and Education: A Glasgow Study*. Edinburgh: Edinburgh University Press.

Mase, Yoshio 1981: Gengokeisei ni oyobosu terebi oyobi toshi no genngo no eikyoo [The influence of TV language and urban dialect on language acquisition]. *Kokugogaku [Studies in the Japanese language]* 125; 1–19. Kokugo gakkai [The Society for the Study of Japanese Language].

MacFarlane, Andrew and Stuart-Smith, Jane 2012: 'One of them sounds sort of Glasgow Uni-ish': Social judgements and fine phonetic variation in Glasgow. *Lingua*. 122: 764–78.

McQuail, Dennis 2010: *McQuail's Mass Communication Theory*. Sixth Edition. London: Sage.

Meyerhoff, Miriam and Nancy Niedzielski 2003: The globalisation of vernacular variation. *Journal of Sociolinguistics* 7: 534–555.

Milroy, Lesley 2007: Off the shelf or over the counter? On the social dynamics of sound changes. In: Christopher Cain and Geoffrey Russom (eds.), *Studies in the History of the English Language*. Vol. 3, 149–172. Berlin/New York: Mouton de Gruyter.

Milroy, James and Lesley Milroy 1985: *Authority in Language: Investigating language prescription and standardization*. London: Routledge.

Mitterer, Holge and Miriam Ernestus 2008: The link between speech perception and production is phonological and abstract: Evidence from the shadowing task. *Cognition* 109: 168–173.

Moriarty, Máiréad 2009: Normalising language through television: the case of the Irish language television channel, TG4. *Journal of Multicultural Discourses* 4: 137–49.

Morley, David 1980: *The Nationwide Audience*. London: British Film Institute Television Monograph.

Naro, Anthony 1981: The social and structural dimensions of syntactic changes. *Lingua*. 57: 63–98.

Naro, Anthony and Maria Marta Pereira Scherre 1996: Contact with media and linguistic variation. In: Jennifer Arnold, Renee Blake and Brad Davidson (eds), *Sociolinguistic variation: Data, theory and analysis*. 223–28. *(Selected papers from NWAV 23)*. Stanford, CA: Center for the Study of Language and Information (CSLI) Publications.

Ota, Ichiro 2009: Kyushu ni okeru gengo no kiki to hanashite no ishiki [Linguistic unstability and linguistic attitude in Kyushu]. *Language*, 38(7), 32-39, Tokyo: Taishukan Shoten.

Ota, Ichiro, Hitoshi Nikaido and Shoji Takano 2010: Variability of phrasal tone in Fukuoka Japanese. Barry Heselwood and Clive Upton (eds.) *Proceedings of Methods XIII: Papers from the Thirteenth International Conference on Methods in Dialectology, 2008*, 362–371, Frankfurt a. M.: Peter Lang.

Ota, Ichiro, Shoji Takano, Hitoshi Nikaido, Akira Utsugi and Yashiyuki Asahi 2012: Sociolinguistic variation in the pitch movement of Japanese dialects. Poster presentation at NWAV-Asia Pacific 2, 2 August 2012, National Institute for Japanese Language and Linguistics (NINJAL), Japan.

Pardo, Jennifer, Rachel Gibbons, Alexandra Suppes and Robert Krauss 2012: Phonetic convergence in college roommates. *Journal of Phonetics*. 40: 190–197.

Philo, Greg 1999: Children and film/video/TV violence. In: Greg Philo (ed.), *Message received: Glasgow Media Group research 1993–1998*, 35–53. London: Longman.

Philo, Greg 2008: Debates on the active audience: A comparison of the Birmingham and Glasgow approaches. *Journalism Studies* 9: 535–544.

Pickering, Martin and Simon Garrod 2013: An integrated theory of language production and comprehension. *Brain and Behavioural Sciences* 36: 329–347.

Preston, Dennis 1992: "Talking black, talking white": A study in variety imitation. In: Joan Hall, Nick Doane and Dick Ringler (eds.), *Old English and New*, 327–355. New York: Garland.

Preston, Dennis (ed.) 1999: *Handbook of Perceptual Dialectology*. Amsterdam: Benjamins.

Rampton, Ben 1995: *Crossing: Language and ethnicity among adolescents*. Harlow: Longman.
Redcay, Elizabeth, David Dodell-Feder, Mark Pearrow, Penelope Mavros, Mario Kleiner, John Gabrieli and Rebecca Saxe 2010: Live face-to-face interaction during fMRI: A new tool for social cognitive neuroscience. *NeuroImage* 50: 1639–1647.
Reeves, Byron and Clifford Nass 1996: *The Media Equation: How People Treat Computers, Television, and New Media like Real People and Places*. Cambridge: Cambridge University Press.
Rice, Mabel, Aletha Huston, Rosemarie Truglio and John Wright 1990: Words from "Sesame Street": Learning vocabulary while viewing. *Developmental Psychology* 26: 421–428.
Rindal, Ulrikke 2010: Constructing identity with L2: Pronunciation and attitudes among Norwegian learners of English. *Journal of Sociolinguistics* 14: 240–261.
Rogers, Everett 2003: *Diffusion of innovations*. Fifth edition. New York: Free Press.
Saladino, Rosa 1990: Language shift in standard Italian and dialect: A case study. *Language Variation and Change* 2: 57–70.
Sayers, Dave 2014: The mediated innovation model: A framework for researching media influence in language change. *Journal of Sociolinguistics*. 18: 185–212.
Shibatani, Masayoshi 1990: *The languages of Japan*. Cambridge, U.K.: Cambridge University Press.
Sibata, Takesi 1998: *Takesi Sibata: Sociolinguistics in Japanese contexts*. (English version of his 1978a work with a preface by the editors.) Edited by Tetsuya Kunihiro, Fumio Inoue, and Daniel Long. Berlin/New York: Mouton de Gruyter.
Smith, Jeremy 1991: *An Historical Study of English*. London: Taylor and Francis.
Strasburger, Victor 1995: *Adolescents and the media: Medical and psychological impact*. London: Sage.
Stuart-Smith, Jane 1999: Glasgow: Accent and voice quality. In: Paul Foulkes and Gerard Doherty (eds.), *Urban voices: Accent studies in the British Isles*, 201–222. Edward Arnold.
Stuart-Smith, Jane 2003: The phonology of Modern Urban Scots. In: John Corbett, Derrick McClure and Jane Stuart-Smith (eds.), *The Edinburgh companion to Scots*, 110–37. Edinburgh: Edinburgh University Press.
Stuart-Smith, Jane 2004: The Phonology of Scottish English. In: Clive Upton (ed.) *Varieties of English: Vol. 1: Phonology*, 47–67. Berlin/New York: Mouton de Gruyter.
Stuart-Smith, Jane 2006: The influence of media on language. In: Carmen Llamas, Peter Stockwell and Louise Mullany (eds.), *The Routledge Companion to Sociolinguistics*, 140–148. London: Routledge.
Stuart-Smith, Jane 2011: The view from the couch: changing perspectives on the role of the television in changing language ideologies and use. In: Tore Kristiansen and Nikolas Coupland (eds.), *Standard Languages and Language Standards in a Changing Europe*, 223–239. Oslo: Novus.
Stuart-Smith, Jane 2012: English and the Media: Television. In: Anton Berg and Laurel Brinton (eds.), *Historical Linguistics of English*, 1075–1088. Berlin: de Gruyter.
Stuart-Smith, Jane and Claire Timmins 2007: "Tell her to shut her moof": The role of the lexicon in TH-fronting in Glaswegian. In: Graham Caie, Carole Hough and Irene Wotherspoon (eds.), *The Power of Words*, 171–178. Amsterdam: Rodopi.
Stuart-Smith, Jane and Claire Timmins 2010: The role of the individual in language variation and change. In: Carmen Llamas and Dominic Watt (eds.), *Language and Identities*, 39–54. Edinburgh: Edinburgh University Press.

Stuart-Smith, Jane, Claire Timmins and Fiona Tweedie 2006: Conservation and innovation in a traditional dialect: L-vocalization in Glaswegian. *English World Wide* 27: 71–87.

Stuart-Smith, Jane, Claire Timmins and Fiona Tweedie 2007: "Talkin Jockney?": Accent change in Glaswegian. *Journal of Sociolinguistics* 11: 221–261.

Stuart-Smith, Jane, Claire Timmins, Gwilym Pryce and Barrie Gunter 2013: Television is also a factor in language change: Evidence from an urban dialect. *Language* 89: 1–36.

Stuart-Smith, Jane, Eleanor Lawson and James Scobbie 2014: Derhoticization in Scottish English: lessons we can learn from sociophonetic data. In: Chiara Celata and Silvia Calmai (eds.), *Advances in Sociophonetics*, 57–94. Amsterdam: Benjamins.

Stuart-Smith, Jane, Rachel Smith, Tamara Rathcke, Francesco Li Santi and Sophie Holmes 2011: Responding to accents after experiencing interactive or mediated speech. *Proceedings of the 17th International Congress of Phonetic Sciences (ICPhS)*, Hong Kong.1914–1917.

Stuart-Smith, Jane, Timmins, Claire, Gwilym Pryce and Barrie Gunter in preparation: *Mediating the local: The role of television for a changing urban vernacular*. Oxford: Oxford University Press.

Tagliamonte, Sali 2012: *Variationist Sociolinguistics: Change, observation, interpretation*. Oxford: Wiley-Blackwell.

Tagliamonte, Sali and Alex D' Arcy 2007: Frequency and variation in the community grammar: Tracking a new change through the generations. *Language Variation and Change* 19: 199–217.

Tagliamonte, Sali and Chris Roberts 2005: So weird; so cool; so innovative: The use of intensifiers in the television series *Friends*. *American Speech* 80: 280–300.

Takano, Shoji and Ichiro Ota 2007: *A sociophonetic study of the levelling of sentence pitch among younger speakers of Japanese: register, perception and social meanings*. Final Report, 16520284, Japan Ministry of Education, Culture, Sports, Science and Technology.

Tanaka, Yukari 2010: *Shutoken ni okeru gengo dootai no kenkyuu [A Study of Lingutistic Ddynamism in Tokyo Metropokitan Area]*. Tokyo: Kazama Shoin.

Torrance, Karen 2002: *Language attitudes and language change in Glaswegian Speech*. MPhil Dissertation. Department of English Language. University of Glasgow.

Trudgill, Peter 1986: *Dialects in Contact*. Oxford: Blackwell.

Trudgill, Peter 1988: Norwich revisited: Recent linguistic changes in an English urban dialect. *English World-Wide* 9: 33–49.

Wells, John 1982: *Accents of English*. Cambridge: Cambridge University Press.

Williams, Ann and Paul Kerswill 1999: Dialect Levelling: Change and Continuity in Milton Keynes Reading and Hull. In: Paul Foulkes and Gerard Docherty (eds.), *Urban Voices: Accent Studies in the British Isles*, 141–162. London: Arnold.

Yokoyama, Shoichi and Haruko Sanada 2010: Gengo no shoogai shuutoku moderu ni yoru kyootsuugoka yosoku [Predictions of dialect standardisation by the "Life-long Assimilation of Language Change" model], *Nihongo no kenkyuu [Studies in the Japanese Language]\i0, 6(2)*, 31–45. Nihongo Gakkai (The Society for Japanese Linguistics).

Ichiro Ota and Shoji Takano
The media influence on language change in Japanese sociolinguistic contexts

1 Introduction

In this article, we will consider the influence of media on the language change that has taken place in most of the regional dialects of Japanese within the past several decades. We will critically review the results of previous studies (Section 2), demonstrate our research results which afford the possibility of a media impact on language (Section 3 and 4), and put forward a suggestion for further research in the future (Section 5). By the word 'media', we mainly have in mind those that have audio and visual (moving) images such as television or video content. We will start our discussion with what makes us believe that our language is under the influence of media in Japanese sociolinguistic contexts. Figure 1 shows the regions (in boxes) and the research sites that will be mentioned in the article, and we encourage readers to refer to this map for the locations when needed.

1.1 Standard Japanese, television Japanese, and the media

It is frequently said, perhaps everywhere that has television, that TV makes people sound the same (Chambers 1998) or that TV weakens regional dialects. Similar ideas about language change are generally shared in Japan as well, such as: "children these days only speak Standard Japanese and don't speak our dialects because of TV." Such comments indicate that regional dialects have been losing their linguistic characteristics and increasing in homogeneity *under the influence of media language falling from the sky*. In fact, we should note that there are two aspects to these comments. One is about the language change of regional dialects toward the standard variety, and the other is on a nationwide diffusion of televised language features.

The former type of language change, called *hyoojunngo-ka* or 'standardization,' represents a huge, nationwide levelling of dialects toward the standard variety.[1] There are two notions about 'the standard variety'" of Japanese. First,

---

[1] This 'standardization' does not denote a historical process like the emergence of Standard

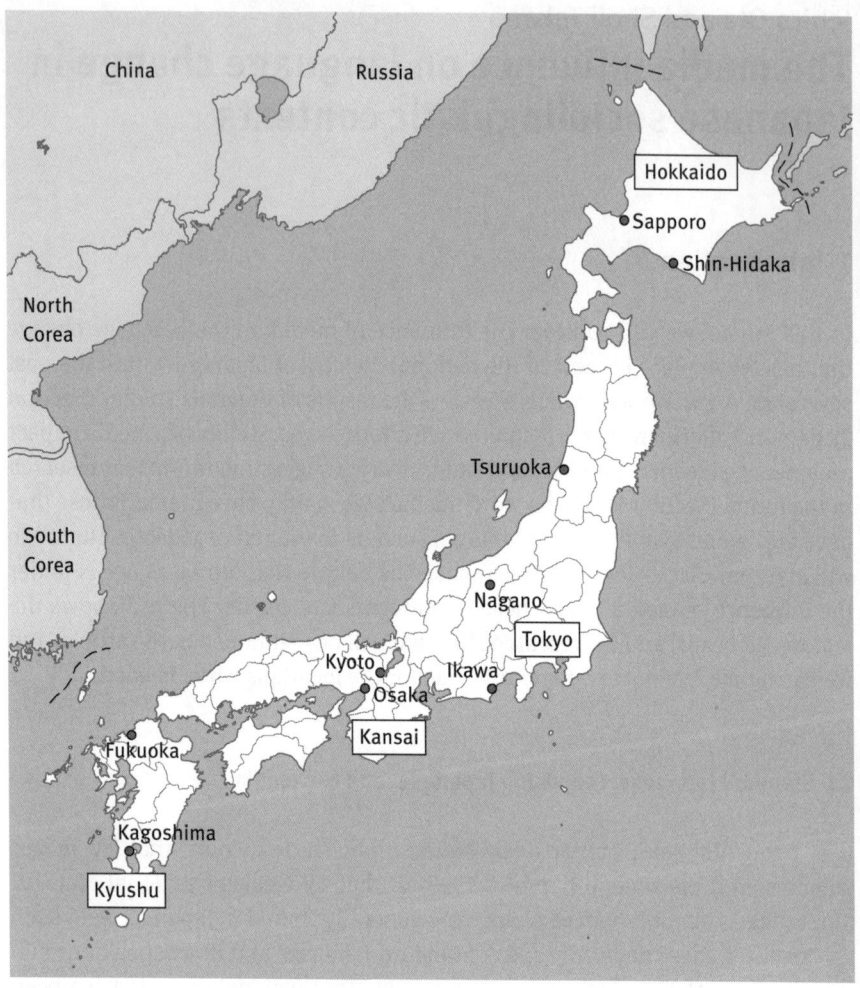

Figure 1: Map of Japan and the research sites.

the notion of *hyoojungo*, or Standard Japanese, which was officially established in 1916, based on the language of well-educated people in Tokyo. Second, there is a new notion, *kyootsuugo* or Common Japanese, which replaced Standard Japanese after the Second World War. This is a less prescriptive version of Standard

Japanese but rather the fact that dialects of different regions have become de-dialectized and are acquiring uniformity. We appreciate Jannis Androutsopoulos's helpful comment on this.

Japanese with an emphasis on comprehensibility among speakers with different regional backgrounds. Precisely speaking, they are different, but their distinction is not always clear; people have only vague normative ideas about them.

The standard variety is an essential linguistic device for a nation to establish the foundation of communication among people with linguistic diversity. In order to build up the regime of a modern nation, the concept of the standard variety (i. e. Standard Japanese) was first introduced into school education in Japan in the early 1900s (Lee 1996), but its impact was not significant enough to cause large transformations of dialects—the effect of education was slow and very limited (cf. Sibata 1958).[2] However, during the post-war period, from the 1950s to the 1970s, there was a rapid diffusion of the linguistic features, grammar and lexical items in particular, of the standard variety into most regional dialects. Consequently, bi-dialectalism – the co-existence of a 'standardized', or de-dialectized, regional variety and the standard variety – has emerged. This diffusion of the standard variety is generally regarded as a result of the influence of TV, because its rate and geographical range are far beyond those of face-to-face interaction.

Another type of nationwide diffusion is the rapid spread of linguistic features that are used particularly on TV. Hereinafter, we call these features Television Japanese (or TV Japanese). TV Japanese can be observed at all levels of the linguistic system, such as pitch-accent patterns (e.g. a new type of lexical accent for *kuma*, or 'bear', illustrated in Section 3), flat pitch pattern for foreign words indexing a particular meaning (e.g. 'specialist'; Inoue 1998), lexical or grammatical items (e.g. adopting dialectal features of socially dominant areas like Kansai, the area that includes Kyoto and Osaka), and intonation features (e.g. a rapid spread of *tobihane*, or "hopping", intonation in negative interrogatives in Tanaka 2010). These may be originally local features, but once they are picked up by the mass media their rate of diffusion is extraordinarily fast. For example, the hopping intonation, which was originally used in the Tokyo area in the early 1990s (Tanaka 2010), started appearing 'on air' around the late 1990s or early 2000s, and it took only a few years for young people in Kagoshima (almost 1,400 kilometres away from Tokyo) to start using this feature. These are clearly 'off-the-shelf' types of changes (Eckert 2008; Milroy 2007), and, when they are linguistically salient, people are well conscious that they are adopted from TV (cf. Trudgill 1986).

---

2 Sibata's (1958) report gives us an intriguing example of how poor a command of the Standard Japanese that primary school pupils had in a rural area of Kagoshima in the mid-1950s, which is the time before the advent of TV. He describes their standard variety as 'dried,' – i. e. there is no liveliness in it.

1.2 Is the media impact a sociolinguistic myth in Japan?

These nationwide linguistic changes took place after the arrival and during the proliferation of TV at an extraordinary speed, so most people simply ascribe these changes to this broadcasting media. The period of the rapid proliferation of TV also coincides with the large scale social change after the Second World War. TV broadcasting in Japan started in 1953, and TV ownership began to increase explosively around 1960, reaching the highest percentage in 1970 (see Fig. 2). During this period, the establishment of the new social system was almost completed, and the economy had fully recovered from the damage of the war, which made people much more geographically mobile for business, commuting, migration, etc. As a consequence, these changes of social conditions helped to promote dialect contact (Trudgill 1986).

Despite these changes, Takesi Sibata, who founded the study of Japanese sociolinguistics and left a massive amount of insightful achievements, argued (1978a, 1998) that dialect contact is the major reason for standardization of regional dialects. Although the broadcasting media – TV and radio – could present *real*, or animate, examples of the speech of the standard variety, Sibata hesitated to approve of the influence of media on standardization.[3]

Sibata's reluctance probably comes from the results of research studies conducted by the National Institute for Japanese Language (NIJL), the predecessor of the National Institute of Japanese Language and Linguistics (NINJAL), in 1950 and 1971. The research groups could not find a clear correlation between the use of the standard forms and the time spent watching TV, as claimed by Western sociolinguists (cf. Chambers 1998).

However, there are quite a few scholars who assume the influence of TV on language. For example, Kuno (1999: 63), a Japanese dialectologist, makes the following comment about the influence of TV on young people.

> They [i.e. young people] live their lives under the strong influence of the standard variety from the time of their birth because the standard variety is available to them everywhere *through TV or any other media* and in everyday interaction.
>
> (Our translation and emphasis)

---

3 According to Takehiro Shioda (personal communication), an academic researcher at the NHK Broadcasting Culture Research Institute, Sibata himself seemed to believe in the media influence on standardization at least to some extent. Although he could not give a decisive comment on the impact of media because the researches of the former NINJAL focused just on people's *command* of the standard variety, not on their comprehension ability (Sibata 1978b), he seemed to be sure that media language is somewhat relevant to language change.

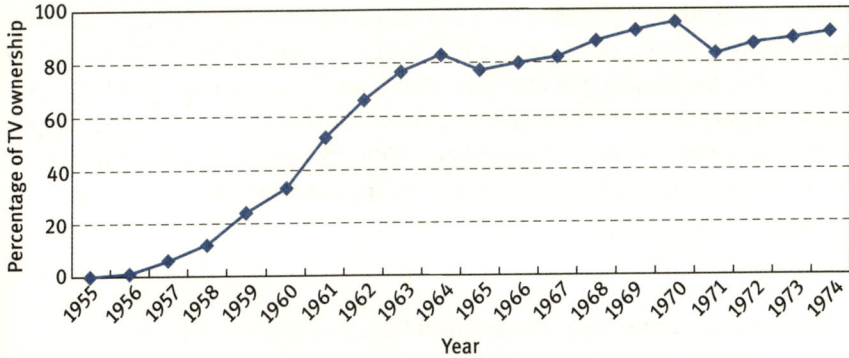

Figure 2: The spread of television in Japanese households (Ono 1993: 57)

Here, he makes a special mention of TV, implying that TV is one of the key factors of standardization. Similar views have been tacitly accepted among Japanese dialectologists and are prevalent in the literatures on language standardization and language change. But this kind of view is generally presented merely as an assumption or premise, and hardly any effort has been made to establish a further, reliable confirmation. Therefore, the impact of the media on Japanese dialects is still an open sociolinguistic question.

Actually, there are some linguistic reports that mention the impact of media (Mase 1981, 1996; National Institute for Japanese Language 1953, 1974, 2007; Ono 1993; see Section 2). Although they are not as theoretically and methodologically elaborated as the Glasgow Media Project (Stuart-Smith 2011, 2012; Stuart-Smith et al. 2013), they are suggestive enough to assure us that the media *is* closely related to language change in some way. Thus, we will review the results of these studies in the following section and see what can be said about the media impact on Japanese language.

2 Evidence from survey results: The apparent-time paradigm and the real-time paradigm

Surveys of language change are generally categorized into two types: apparent-time studies and real-time studies. The former provides a whole picture of the linguistic condition of a speech community with a synchronic perspective. In the latter paradigm, we can follow what *really* happened to the language with a comparison between the present and the past. Theoretically, they are not opposed but rather complementary to each other, and if we had research results in both paradigms they could give us the best illustration of how our language has been influenced by the media. Here we will review some prior studies done by three authors, Mase (1981, 1996), Ono (1993), and NIJL (1953, 1974, 2007). While the most examples that we will cite from Mase's and Ono's reports (in 2.1) are presented mainly in the apparent-time paradigm, the reports of NIJL provide empirical evidence in the real-time paradigm. With the evidence of these reports, it would be not unreasonable to claim that the broadcasting media can be an influential factor on language of a local community.

2.1 Surveys of Yoshio Mase and Yoneichi Ono

2.1.1 Accentual change surveys of Mase (1981, 1996)

Mase (1981, 1996) is the only report so far that has directly addressed the theme of TV's influence on Japanese language. He tried to show the evidence of its influence not only by following the course of standardization of lexical accents in the apparent-time paradigm, but also by referring to the result of his own previous research done at the same site with a real-time perspective. His report, which is based on the research in 1978 and 1979, does not use any concept of contemporary sociolinguistics in the West, but he develops a careful and elaborated discussion comparable with that of current variation theory.

2.1.2 The pitch-accent system of Japanese dialects

Before going into the details, it would be helpful to introduce the basics of the pitch-accent system of Japanese. According to Shibatani (1990), in the Japanese accentual system, the arrangement of tones for a word is lexically specified. For example, two-mora words with the same phonemic sets can be distinguished by their tone structures.

> ame (LH) 'candy'
> ame (HL) 'rain'
> (Shibatani 1990: 177)

There are some types of accentual systems in Japanese dialects. One is the Tokyo type, which has n (the number of tone units) $+ 1$ patterns and one basic tone melody, H (or high) tone; for a word with three tone units, it has four patterns, with the high tone as its basic tone, as shown in Table 1.

Except for the last one, the other three patterns have an 'accent', or a pitch fall, within the accent domain, consisting, for example, of a noun and a case-marking particle. These types are called *accented*. On the other hand, if there is no pitch

Pattern	Word (+ case-marking particle)	Tone	Meaning
Initial fall	*karasu(-ga)*	HLL(+L)	crow (-NOM)
Mid fall	*kokoro(-ga)*	LHL(+L)	mind (-NOM)
End fall	*otoko(-ga)*	LHH(+L)	man (-NOM)
No Fall (or Flat)	*sakura(-ga)*	LHH(+H)	cherry (-NOM)

Table 1. Accent patterns of Tokyo Japanese for three-mora words

fall, as in ki.TSU.NE (LHH) ('fox') or with a pitch rise at the final tone unit, as in ki.tsu.NE (LLH) in some dialects, the type is called *unaccented*.

The Keihan accent, mainly spoken in the Osaka and Kyoto areas, also has *n + 1* patterns, but there are two basic tone melodies, one beginning with the H (high) tone and the other with the L (low) tone. All words can be divided into 'accented' or 'unaccented' in the Tokyo- and Kansai-type systems.

In addition, there is another type of dialect with no distinction of tone arrangement. This is called the accentless type dialect, which is mainly found in northern Kanto, southern Tohoku, and Kyushu. People with this accent type are generally not very sensitive to accentual differences. We will see this type of dialect in Section 2.1.4.

2.1.3 Standardization of a Tokyo type accent area, Odagiri, Nagano

Mase (1981) assumes that, on the condition that people grow up with TV by the end of the linguistically critical period, it would be possible that the language from TV could be more influential than other varieties available to them. His reasoning is based on the cause-and-effect logic that is generally employed in the theoretical model in the variation theory, although he merely reports the research outcomes without any variationist-type statistical confirmation. However, the results are convincing enough to provide evidence that TV language has had an influence on standardization of dialects in his research areas, Odagiri and Sakurae-cho in Nagano (this section), and Ikawa in Shizuoka (2.1.4).

First, we will look at the results of the studies performed at two sites of Nagano City. Odagiri used to be a small village, but now it is a suburban area of the city. The research there was carried out in 1978. The other research site is Sakurae-cho, an inner-city area, and its research was carried out in 1979. These two areas had the Tokyo-type accentual system, but the accentual patterns for lexical items were not always identical (see Table 2). Since Mase had done studies in both areas once before in 1961, he chose them again to see whether his argument in the 1961 research, which appeared in his 1965 paper, was still valid by employing the real-time paradigm.

The participants' responses were elicited by a word-reading task only, and they were classified on the basis of their accent patterns.[4] Figures 3 and 4 show the scores of Common Japanese and TV Japanese, which demonstrate how the accentual change progressed in the apparent-time paradigm. As a whole, younger groups achieved higher scores for both varieties. In particular, there are big leaps of the scores for both areas in the groups born between 1946–1957 and after 1958. They are exactly the groups who have grown up with TV during the period of first language acquisition. Therefore, it is conceivable that they were able to access the language broadcasted on TV as a source of linguistic input.

Mase (1981) assumed that there were the three potential factors which would impact heavily on a child's acquisition of lexical accent: the local dialect, the prestigious dialect of a neighbouring city, and TV language. Among them, he hypothesized that the media language was more influential than a prestigious dialect of a neighbouring area (and probably their own local dialect as well). His conclusion in the 1965 study was that the standardization of accent observed among the younger generation of Odagiri was imported from its urban (i. e. socially prestigious) area, Sakurae-cho. This means that the language of the urban area functions as the key factor for language change (standardization in this case) in surrounding areas. However, Mase surmised that, considering the quick spread of TV in the 1960s, as shown in Fig. 2, TV could be a more powerful promoting force of language change.

Word	Accent Patterns	JuniorHigh Students in Odagiri (%)		JuniorHigh Students in Sakurae-cho (%)	
		1978	1961	1978	1961
awa-ga **'bubble-NOM'**	LH + L (older pattern in Odagiri)	96.5	33.3	78.1	11.4
	HL+ L	3.5	66.7	21.9	88.6

Table 2: Accentual change of junior-high students in two residential areas of Nagano (Mase 1981)

---

4 There is no detailed description of the research method in Mase (1981), but one of his former students, Yasue Nakato, kindly informed us about it. The source of the information is Mase himself (Nakato, personal communication).

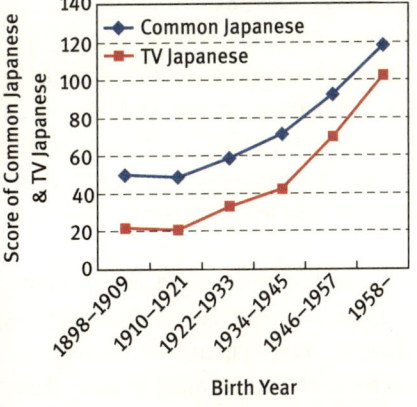
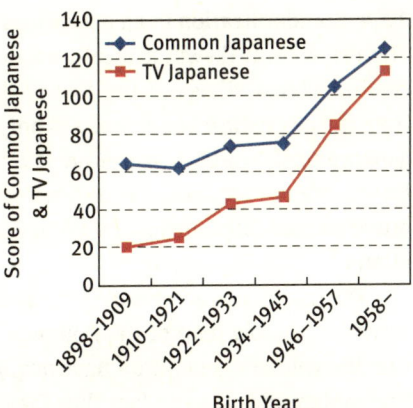

Figure 3: The Common Japanese and TV Japanese scores for Odagiri in 1978 (the full score is 182) (Mase 1996: 17)

Figure 4: The Common Japanese and TV Japanese scores for Sakurae-cho in 1979 (the full score is 182) (Mase 1996: 17)

He compared the degree of standardization of lexical accent in these two areas. If the language of the urban area is still influential as a desirable model of language change for surrounding areas, as Mase (1965) concluded, Sakurae-cho, the urban area, should be ahead of Odagiri in its scores for the standard or Common Japanese accents. However, the 1981 result showed that, with respect to junior high students' adoption of the Common Japanese accents, Odagiri *was* ahead in some lexical items. For example, as shown in Table 2, the accent pattern of *awa-ga* 'bubble-NOM' in Odagiri used to be a.WA + ga (LH+L, 33.3 % in 1961). Considering the fact that this is the very pattern that 100 % in 1961 and 75 % in 1978 of the older generation produced, this accent not only is identical with Common Japanese, but it was also once the local pattern. However, the youngest generation (the primary and secondary school pupils) in 1961 seemed to move toward the local prestigious type, A.wa + ga (HL+L, 66.7 %), which was the pattern of Sakurae-cho. The year of 1961 is in the pre-TV age. The standard forms of lexical accents were unlikely to be available for people living in a rural area, so that younger people seem to have been attracted to the prestigious, or perhaps stylish, urban accent. About 20 years later, the younger generation of the 1978 research came back to the LH + L pattern (96.5 %) which was likely to be frequently heard on TV broadcast as an accent pattern of the standard variety. On the other hand, the percentage of Sakurae-cho is behind (88.6 %). Therefore, this result indicates that TV language became more influential than a neighbouring prestigious dialect in the late 1970s. This will be the presumptive evidence to support our claim for media influence on language change.

2.1.4 Standardization in an accentless area, Ikawa, Shizuoka

The research in Ikawa, a rural area of Shizuoka City, was done in 1980. It is a small, isolated village at the foot of the Southern Japanese Alps. The distance from the city centre of Shizuoka is only about 55 kilometres, but, considering its geographical location, surrounded by mountains and with insufficient public transportation services, it is difficult to imagine that people would have had frequent interactions outside the village that could have led to dialect contact situations.

The traditional accentual system of the Ikawa dialect was the accentless type. However, the big leap of the Common Japanese score in Figure 5 demonstrates that the younger generation have acquired the Common Japanese type of accentual system, despite the fact that they scarcely had contact outside the village. The people born around 1960 could have had a TV set in their households since or shortly after their birth, which leads us to presume that they may well have been under the influence of TV during the period of their language acquisition.

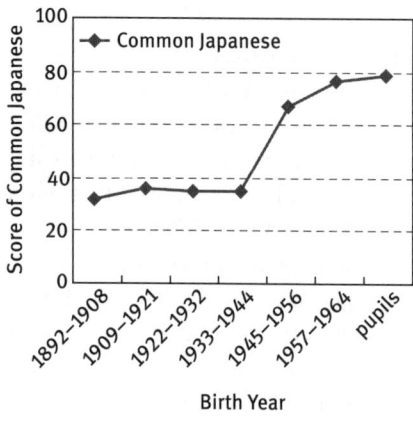

Figure 5: The Common Japanese score for Ikawa in 1980 (the full score is 96) (Mase 1996: 19)

There is no doubt that dialect contact in interaction is one of the major forces of language change. However, Mase turns down this possibility for the case of Ikawa because the Common Japanese score of the older (pre-TV) generation is much smaller, even if they had experiences of living in other places. In spite of the fact that they had had more chances of dialect contact than the younger generation, this group had not acquired the Common Japanese accents properly. In addition, the Common Japanese scores of the younger generation, including pupils with fewer experiences of living outside of the village, are higher than those of other surrounding areas with the Tokyo-type (i. e. the same as Common Japanese) accent system (Mase 1981: 16). Therefore, it would be reasonable to regard media language as the most likely driving force behind this language change. Mase

(1996) calls for more comprehensive, interdisciplinary research on the relationship between language change and the media, but we have not yet seen such a report here in Japan.

2.1.5 Standardization of lexical accent in Sapporo, Hokkaido

Ono (1993) investigated the standardization of Sapporo Japanese based on random sampling of 128 inhabitants from eight age cohorts. All of his data were derived from the tasks of reading aloud a number of carefully constructed sentences as well as a few longer passages. Although this is a study in progress, Ono (1993) discusses synchronic variation in accentual patterns of nouns across generations.

The accentual patterns of Hokkaido (Sapporo) Japanese belong to the Tokyo type. Two-mora nouns, which have been a common focus of prior studies, can be classified into the five types (in conjunction with tones aligned to the immediately following case-marking particles such as the nominal -*ga*) shown in Table 3.

	Type I	Type II	Type III	Type IV	Type V
Tokyo	LH + H	*LH + L*	LH + L	*HL + L*	*HL + L*
Hokkaido	LH + H	*LH + H*	LH + L	$HL^N + L, LH^W + L$	$HL^N + L, LH^W + L$

Table 3. Comparisons between Tokyo and Hokkaido Japanese accentual patterns (two-mora nouns)

The table indicates the tonal discrepancies (italicized) between Tokyo and Hokkaido Japanese in Types II (e.g. *kami-ga* 'paper-NOM'), IV and V accentual patterns. Types IV and V accent patterns in Hokkaido Japanese are not constrained systematically by the typology of nouns per se but by the kinds of vowels in the second mora: if it is narrow vowels (i, u), the accent pattern is identical to the Tokyo type, $HL^N + L$ (e.g. *hashi-ga* 'chopsticks-NOM'), and if it is open vowels (a, e, o), it follows the different pattern, $LH^W + L$ (e.g., *sora-ga* 'sky-NOM').

Figure 6 demonstrates that the generation of speakers who were born during the period 1951–1960 began to shift drastically toward the Common Japanese accent patterns with respect to all of these three accent types, and this trend increased steadily with the succeeding generations.

Ono (1993) argues for the linguistic effects of television as a potential cause of this large-scale standardization of Hokkaido Japanese. As we can infer from Fig. 6, the generation of speakers with rapid standardization (born 1951–1960) comprise a sociolinguistically distinct group, which significantly differs from the preceding generations in terms of their exposure to language varieties through television. This generation of speakers grew up virtually with the new, 'exciting'

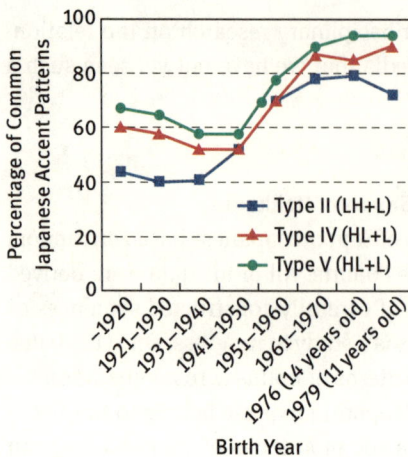

Figure 6: Generational variability in accentual patterns of two-mora nouns

arrival of television sets in their households, and no matter where they lived it was possible to receive Common Japanese as part of the linguistic input on which their language acquisition was based.

2.2 Standardization in the real time paradigm: NIJL (1953, 1974, 2007)

2.2.1 The Tsuruoka survey

The National Institute of Japanese Language and Linguistics (NINJAL) and its predecessor The National Institute for Japanese Language (NIJL) have carried out consecutive surveys to gain an overview of standardization in a local community. The research site is Tsuruoka City, Yamagata Prefecture, about 450 km north of Tokyo. Tsuruoka is a typical local city in the Tohoku Region (the north-eastern part of Japan) with a population of about 135,000 in 2012. The Tohoku Region is well known for its heavily accented, or stigmatized, dialect called *zuuzuu-ben* (zûzû dialect) (Sibata 1998).

The first survey started in 1950, and since then, three follow-up surveys have been carried out approximately every 20 years, in 1971, 1991, and 2011.[5] This is a carefully designed and large-scale social-survey-type study. The informants consist of random samples chosen from the residential register for a cross-sectional study (e.g. 577 in 1950, 457 in 1971, 405 in 1991), and panel samples for

---

5 The 2011 report had not yet been published at the time of writing this article.

a longitudinal study (e.g. 107 in 1971, and 53 in 1991).[6] Although Tsuruoka has become bigger with some administrative consolidations since 1924, the samples were selected from almost the same residential areas. There is no other survey comparable to this one with a real-time perspective.

The linguistic aspects investigated are phonological segments, lexical accent, grammar, and lexical items, and the data were collected through interviews with a questionnaire. The information on the informants collected in the 1991 survey included demography; residential history; birthplaces of participant, spouse, and parents; communication beyond Tsuruoka; exposure to mass media; and language attitude. Since this study tried to take a general picture of language change in a local community, the media influence is just one of their interests. But the results are suggestive enough for us to argue about the interaction of media and language.

The research results show us the stages in the movement toward Common Japanese that the local variety has followed. In the preface to the second survey report, NIJL (1974) suggested that potential factors for the standardization were mobility, education, and the mass media (especially TV). Interestingly, it was less than 20 years from the first TV broadcast that the researchers assumed TV to be a crucial force of language change. Probably this assumption was made, based on their observations of linguistic situations in local communities. They must have witnessed rapid and drastic changes toward Common Japanese taking place in most regional dialects. It is true that greater mobility and higher educational standards could have played important roles, but the diffusion of Common Japanese was so quick that, even though language change could be caused by the interaction of linguistic and social factors, the researchers could not help suspecting a powerful factor that had not existed in 1950, i. e. television.

2.2.2 The relationship between phonological change in Tsuruoka and the media

From here, we will focus on the phonological change taking place in segmental phonemes and lexical accent, and we will consider how TV is involved in standardization. The rate of standardization is not the same for all linguistic items, yet the more recent the birth year and/or the survey time, the more Common Japanese forms we find.

---

6 The 1991 survey also includes 261 samples from the 1971 survey as the second group of panel samples.

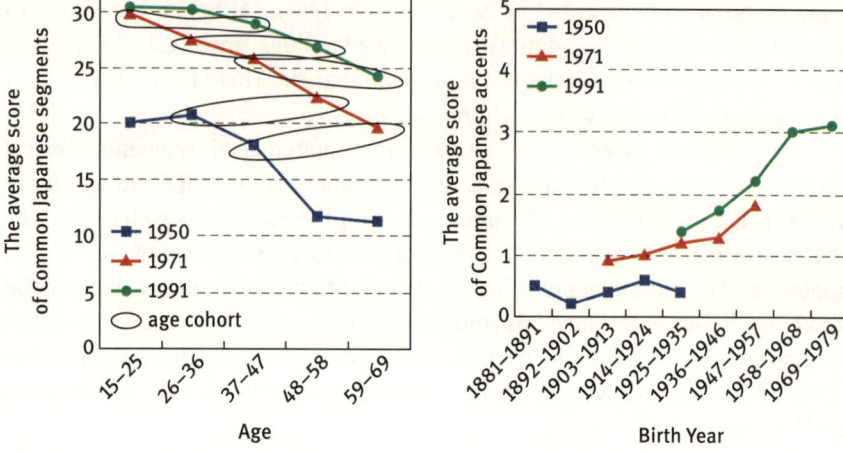

Figure 7: Correlation between Common Japanese score of phonological segments and age in Tsuruoka surveys (NIJL 2007: 23)

Figure 8: Correlation between Common Japanese score of lexical accents and age cohort in Tsuruoka surveys (NIJL 2007: 23).

Figure 7 shows the Common Japanese scores of phonological segments described in terms of age. The scores displayed on the vertical dimension are the average number of the Common Japanese forms that each age group produced at the different survey times. The maximum score is 31.[7] As we expected above, the most recent (i. e. 1991) survey achieved the best scores for each age group, the second-most recent one (i. e. 1974) comes next, and the 1950 one last. However, each age cohort, designated by a circle in the figure, achieved almost the same scores of Common Japanese even at the different survey times.[8] For example, the score of the 26–36 age group in the 1950 survey is 20.8, and they achieved 22.3 in 1971. This indicates that the linguistic command for phonological segments, once acquired, will hardly change for a lifetime, and that for acquisition of segmental phonemes, linguistic inputs before the linguistically critical period are most

---

7 In order to collect phonetic realization of segmental phonemes, picture description tasks were employed for 25 out of 31 items, and answering an interviewer's questions for the rest. The tokens of lexical accents were obtained by picture description task only.

8 In Fig. 7, the score of 15–25 age group of the 1950 survey is irregularly low. Although they are the pre-TV generation, they achieved 25.7 in 1971, 20 years after the first survey. During these 20 years, they improved their linguistic ability as bilinguals. This is because they obtained linguistic input which allowed them to acquire the standard variety even after the linguistically critical period. In other words, by means of the arrival and spread of TV.

crucial. Therefore, the gaps in score among these three surveys are regarded as a reflection of linguistic situations at the time of each survey. We presume that the linguistic situation of the 1950 survey did not offer sufficient linguistic inputs for a better command of Common Japanese, but that of 1971 and 1991 did so success-fully. This happened presumably because the linguistic situations were altered by the change of social condition.

Then, what caused the change of the linguistic situation for language acquisi-tion? As mentioned above, NIJL (1974) refers to three possible factors for language change: (1) increasing occasions for dialect contact due to the growth of mobil-ity, (2) higher standards of education, and (3) rapid development of mass media. Actually, the percentage of young people in Tsuruoka who went on to further edu-cation after secondary education rose remarkably from 34.3 per cent in 1950 to 78.2 per cent in 1971. The chances for dialect contact had also increased consider-ably because of the development of communications technology (e.g. the spread of telephones) and improved transportation. However, the greatest change that happened in the first 20 years (between 1950 and 1971) was the emergence of a new media, television. By the end of March 1972, 94.9 per cent of the households in Tsuruoka owned a television. It is true that the other two factors contributed to the diffusion of Common Japanese accent, but NIJL (1974: 111) argues that TV had the biggest influence on the change of dialect. Their discussion was rather impressionistic and did not present any specific evidence as might be found in a correlational analysis, but it is not easy to reject their view if we admit from our own experience that TV is a potential (and the most probable) factor in altering our 'real' language usage (cf. Stuart-Smith and Ota in this volume).

Another result would constitute better evidence for the influence of TV. Figure 8 shows the Common Japanese score of lexical accent that each cohort achieved in the three surveys. The maximum score for this linguistic item is 5. Interestingly, the scores differ at each interval, which contradicts the results shown in Fig. 7. These score gaps are bigger than those of segmental phonemes, which indicates that the informants could have been acquiring a better command of Common Japanese for lexical accent even after the linguistically critical period. This is pre-sumably because the linguistic situation can be changed along with social con-ditions, and a new situation offers a new set of linguistic inputs for local people.

Therefore, the gaps in Fig. 8 should be considered a consequence of some social changes. Yokoyama and Sanada (2010) presume that the most conceiv-able change of social condition between 1950 and 1971 that is related to language acquisition is the spread of TV. There is also a gap of scores between 1971 and 1991, but it is smaller, probably because the impact of TV language may have been reduced since TV was no longer a 'new' technology.

2.3 What do these surveys tell us?

To summarize this section, it would be better once again to think about the meaning of the media impact on standardization of regional dialects in Japanese sociolinguistic contexts. When we say "standardization of dialect", it usually includes two different aspects of standardization. One is the systematic change of dialect toward the standard variety, or Common Japanese. The other is the development of an individual speaker's command of the standard variety. The term 'standardization' refers to the former in general contexts, but it seems that most surveys in Japan have investigated the latter, if we interpret carefully the quality of survey responses and what the responses reflect. In most of the surveys conducted thus far with dialectological interests, the speech data have been collected by elicitation through quizzes or describing pictures in an interview setting. The quality of the responses is rather different from that of the spontaneous speech data collected in a sociolinguistic interview, which represents the language actually used by speakers in discourse (cf. Labov 1984).

Hence, the results of standardization surveys should not be considered as the actual use of the standard variety (or Common Japanese) but rather as the projection of the individual's command of it, which coexists with that of the regional variety in his or her linguistic system as a bi-dialectal speaker (cf. NIJL 2007). The impact of the media on dialects does not simply lead to a systematic change of the language of both the individual and the community. The better command of Common Japanese that individuals have, the more linguistic resources are available to them for styling or stylizing (cf. Coupland 2007). Also, we should insist once again that, no matter which theoretical positions in Section 2 of Stuart-Smith and Ota (in this volume) you take, it is an obvious fact that the rapid development of the command of Common Japanese *coincides* with the spread of TV.

3 Similarity beyond geographical distance: De-standardization in lexical accent and sentential pitch trajectory

Thus far, we have discussed the potential effects of the media, especially given the proliferation of television sets in Japanese households, on first-language acquisition and the resulting large-scale standardization of local dialects towards Common Japanese. In contrast, the present section discusses the coexistence of linguistic variation and change in the opposite direction (i. e., 'de-standardization' or the formation of new dialects), which is commonly observed in the speech of younger generations all over the country. As explained earlier (1.1), TV Japanese has not only exposed the TV generations (those who were born roughly after the

950s) to Common Japanese input but also has contributed to the transmission of innovative features that do not necessarily correspond with 'standard' Common Japanese. In the following sections, we empirically demonstrate, by focusing particularly on lexical accents and sentential pitch, that those innovative features are transmitted by younger speakers of different dialects around the country as 'supra-local' variables.

3.1 Emergence of a de-standardized version of lexical accent

Linguistic innovations toward de-standardization by the younger generations have been well-known as the formation of *shin-hoogen* ('new dialect') in Japanese sociolinguistic contexts. Inoue (1983), for example, claims that the emergence of new dialects is characteristic of both initial and intermediate stages of language change (i. e. standardization in this context). Referring specifically to the role of television, Inoue further pointed out that the nationwide transmission of TV Japanese had progressed because the casual style of speech that people are constantly exposed to on TV programmes is more approachable than standard Japanese, which is associated with formality and literacy.

Figures 9 and 10, which present examples of diffusion of a de-standardized accent from past studies (Mase 1981; Ono 1993), provide empirical evidence for the nationwide transmission of an identical, innovative TV Japanese accent for the word *kuma* ('bear') in Odagiri (see Section 2.1.3.) and Sapporo (Hokkaido) (see Fig. 1, the map of Japan).

Despite geographical distance and the lack of direct mutual contact, the lexical accent ku.MA (LH) for *kuma* ('bear'), which was the Common Japanese type accent, has been replaced by a non-standard, innovative TV Japanese accent pattern, KU.ma (HL) both in Odagiri and Sapporo. The innovation in Odagiri (Fig. 9) started in the group born during the period 1947–1957, and the TV accent exceeded at the youngest group born after 1958. Similar to this pattern of change in Odagiri, the generation of Sapporo Japanese speakers who grew up with television (1958–1969) initiated the replacement of the Common Japanese accent (LH) by the TV Japanese accent (HL) (Fig. 10). In these geographically distant places, where it is very unlikely that inhabitants will have direct mutual contact, the course of standardization of the local dialects (towards Common Japanese) has been drastically altered in an identical fashion since the propagation of television in the context of children's first-language acquisition.

Another robust piece of empirical evidence can be obtained from NIJL's (2007) Tsuruoka dialect survey (Fig. 11), which also shows how a newer TV-type accent for *channeru* ('[TV] channel') replaces an older one, along with the quick

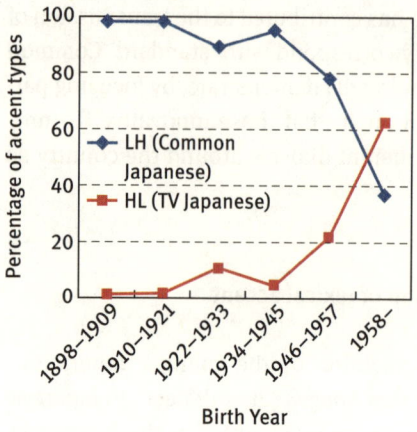

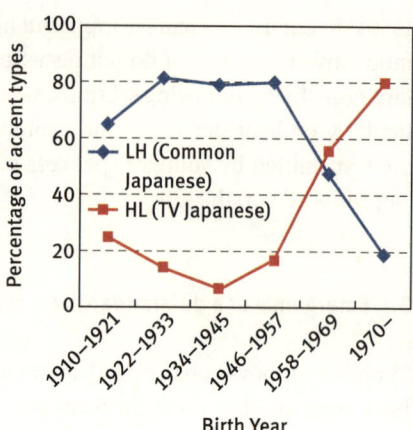

Figure 9: Replacement of *kuma* ('bear') in Odagiri with the non-standard TV accent (Mase 1981: 12)

Figure 10: Replacement *kuma* ('bear') in Sapporo with the non-standard TV accent (Ono 1993).

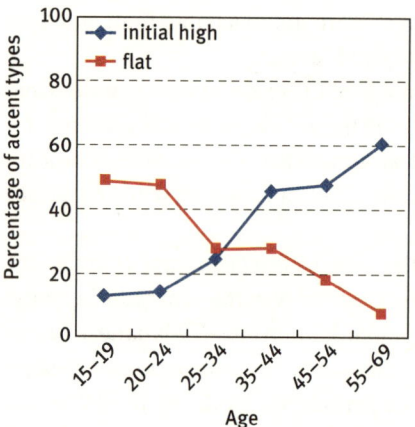

Figure 11: Systematic correlation between speakers' birth year and the accent for the word *channeru* ('channel') in the Tsuruoka surveys (NIJL 2007: 141)

spread of TV starting from around 1960. The initial high accent pattern has been replaced by the flat accent pattern. Both are considered to be Common Japanese in the fourth edition of the NHK accent dictionary published in 1998, but the flat one, which is usually heard on TV, is diffusing among younger people. The lines intersect at the 25–34 cohort – people born between 1957 and 1966, who are the first cohort surrounded by the TV accent during their period of language acquisition. For the cohorts born after 1966, the score of the flat accent greatly exceeds the other.

These results clearly indicate that TV Japanese exerted 'supra-local' effects on first-language acquisition of children regardless of where they were born or grew up. The impact of the audio-visual media such as TV and video content on language seems relatively smaller these days because many regional dialects have already been levelled out and have increased the homogeneity of their linguistic features. However, it is true that the media are still one of the powerful factors in the sense that they are constantly changing linguistic situations by introducing new linguistic materials as inputs for language acquisition. Of particular significance are the facts that the media allow those new materials to be adopted simultaneously by the younger generations all over the country without direct communicative contact and that these uniformitarian innovations (i. e. de-standardization) coexist with large-scale standardization of local dialects in Japan.[9] The following section presents further empirical evidence for this uniformitarian impact of the media, focusing on sentential prosody.

3.2 Sentential pitch levelling as a supra-local innovation and its social meanings

More than three decades ago, Sibata (1978a) first pointed out that pitch in Japanese had increasingly been levelled in the speech of younger generations. Sibata restricts his observations to the speech of younger people in Tokyo, while suggesting the necessity to look into other local dialects for further confirmation of this potential linguistic change. It is certainly an intriguing question: Is the levelling of sentential pitch simply a localized phenomenon specific to Tokyo, or is it a nationwide linguistic change-in-progress observed in the speech of the younger generations throughout the country?

---

9 The linguistic effects of television are also evident in the 'supra-local' adaptation of Kansai (western Japan) dialect features by the younger generations. In the volume Jinnouchi and Tomosada (2005), which investigates the current state of reception of Kansai dialects in various regions of Japan, a number of chapters (e.g. covering Okinawa, Hiroshima, Okayama, Tokyo, and Sapporo) point out that television is responsible for younger speakers' adoption of Kansai dialects in each local community. All of the chapters, though without any scientific evidence, share an interpretation of social meanings of Kansai dialects associated with the popular culture of Kansai-style comedies. Comedians from Kansai are not expected to shift their dialects to Common Japanese (and if they do so, they usually sound strange!). Their rigorous use of Kansai dialects contributes to their effectiveness in making people laugh, and is well-accepted by young people all over Japan.

In this section, we illustrate the levelling of sentential pitch (F0) as another example of a supra-local (i. e. de-standardizing) innovation, which we hypothesize results from the uniformitarian force of the media operating on the TV generations. A series of our studies show that pitch contours in the speech of the younger generations in Japan have become (at least stylistically) similar on a nationwide scale, despite large discrepancies in the accentual systems of different dialects and the scarcity of speakers' direct mutual contacts (Takano and Ota 2005, 2007; Ota and Takano 2007, 2008a,b,c; Ota et al., 2012).

For our fieldwork sites, we chose two dialect regions at opposite ends of Japan (Hokkaido and Kagoshima) that differ typologically from each other in accentual systems (Hirayama 1960) and that can also be assumed to lack direct mutual contact (see Figure 1). Data on Hokkaido dialects, which are generally divided into two subgroups (i. e. inland and coastal), were collected in two places, the city of Sapporo (inland) and the rural town of Shin-Hidaka on the south coast of Hokkaido (coastal). Kagoshima dialect data were collected in the city of Kagoshima.

Given the general fact that descriptions of prosody are stylistically deprived in past studies, we aimed to examine this variable as demonstrated in multiple registers derived from three specific speech-production tasks: (1) reading aloud artificial sentences in isolation, (2) news passage reading, and (3) spontaneously describing a cartoon story. They were considered to differ in the continuum of context of use, with Task (3) at the most naturalistic end. In the succeeding sections, we will discuss the findings mainly from the first two tasks (i. e. sentences and news passages read aloud), based on our recent re-analyses of the data.[10]

As illustrated in Section 2.1.2., Japanese is a pitch-accent language. Each word is specified as either accented (*yuu-kaku*) or unaccented (*mu-kaku*), although there is a great deal of dialectal variation. As the stimuli, we constructed five artificial, de-contextualized sentences that consisted only of accented words. For example, a sentence */Do'ryoku/ /shite'mo/ /i'mi ga/ /na'i/* ('It is meaningless to make efforts') consists of four accented accentual phrases (AP hereinafter),[11] and each AP contains one accented word. We constructed several sets of five 4-AP sentences like this and asked each participant to read them aloud.

---

10 This process has been supported by the NINJAL Collaborative Research Project (organized by Yoshiyuki Asahi), "A construction of a typological theory on linguistic change and variation based on dialect contact phenomena." The third task focuses on age-related variability in 'de-accentuation' or de-phrasing of accentual phrases in a more naturalistic context for speech production. Our re-analyses of the data are underway, and the results will soon be presented.

11 An AP is demarcated by /x'x/, where 'x' indicates the location of a lexical accent.

Table 4 shows the demographic information on the participants and the number of tokens (i. e. number of sentences read aloud) analyzed for each of the speaker groups. Note that our data do not include the older generation of Kagoshima-dialect speakers. In the course of our fieldwork, we decided not to take into consideration older Kagoshima speakers for our region/age comparisons because even in the read-aloud task their sentential pitch contours were far too distinct to be comparable with the remaining groups. Each participant read a set of five different de-contextualized sentences.[12] The Hokkaido participants in particular read each sentence at least twice, and we decided to include all of the readings as tokens for analysis.

Speaker Groups	No. of Speakers	No. of Tokens
Sapporo Young (20 to 23 years of age)	16 (1 males, 15 females)	149
Sapporo Old (51 to 77)	10 (10 females)	105
Shin-Hidaka Young (14 to 21)	10 (7 males, 3 females)	98
Shin-Hidaka Old (57 to 77)	15 (6 males, 9 females)	166
Kagoshima Young (19 to 20)	7 (2 males, 5 females)	35

Table 4. Participants in the task of reading de-contextualized sentences, and the number of tokens analysed

To measure degrees of magnitude of pitch (F0) movement, we focused on five aspects of movement (Fig. 12): Shift 1 [S1: the first AP peak to its bottom], Shift 2 [S2: the first AP bottom to the second AP peak], Shift 3 [S3: the second AP peak to its bottom], Shift 4 [S4: the second AP bottom to the third AP peak] and Shift 5 [S5: the first AP bottom to the second AP bottom] (Fig. 12). Shift 5 in particular is meant to measure the degree of pitch declination.

Measurements of pitch values (i. e. Hz) were executed at 0.01-s intervals automatically by PitchWorks for PC (Scicon RandD Inc in Beverly Hills, CA). We converted those raw Hz to z-scores for normalization, and then we manually identified each of the following scores: first AP peak, first AP bottom, second AP peak, second AP bottom, and third AP peak. Finally, we calculated the difference between two scores (e.g. AP1 peak – AP1 bottom for Shift 1) as an index for each of the above-mentioned shifts in pitch (Shifts 1 through 5; see Table 5).

---

12 It was not necessarily the case that all of the participants read the identical set of de-contextualized sentences because we modified a few of the stimuli sentences in the course of our fieldwork.

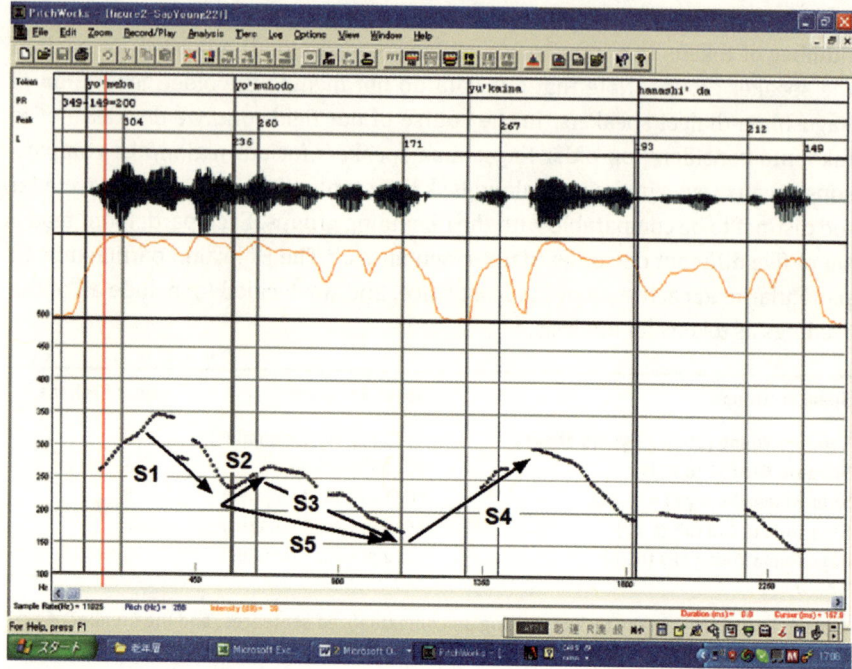

Figure 12: Measuring pitch movement with one of the stimuli (/Yo'meba/(AP1) /yo'muhodo/ (AP2) /yu'kaina/(AP3) /hanashi' da/(AP4)) read by a 22-year-old Sapporo woman[13]

Speaker Groups	Shift 1	Shift 2	Shift 3	Shift 4	Shift 5
Sapporo Young	−1.71	0.61	−1.43	1.39	−0.82
Sapporo Old	−1.88	0.91	−1.48	1.88	−0.57
Shin-Hidaka Young	−0.93	0.30	−0.90	0.95	−0.59
Shin-Hidaka Old	−1.68	0.90	−1.49	1.85	−0.59
Kagoshima Young	−0.94	0.36	−0.76	0.70	−0.39

Table 5. Pitch movement indices (based on z-scores) across five age/region groups (read-aloud sentences)

It is evident in Table 5 and its schematic representation (Fig. 13) that the two younger groups (Shin-Hidaka and Kagoshima) show almost identical patterns of pitch movement, as do the two older groups (Sapporo and Shin-Hidaka, marked

---

13 Our identification of each AP peak is based on an actual trajectory of pitch regardless of the perceptual alignment of pitch accent, usually with a vowel.

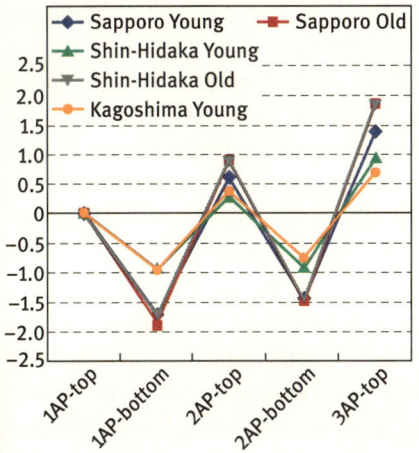

Figure 13: Schematic representation of pitch shifts across five age/region groups (read-aloud sentences).

by dotted lines), which creates two homogeneous age groups. The younger group shows relatively 'levelled' realizations of pitch as compared with the older group, which shows greater degrees of rise and fall in pitch contours. The pattern of Sapporo younger speakers is rather similar to that of the older groups, but it is still consistent with smaller indices of rise and fall than those of the older groups.

Of particular significance are the facts that the younger participants from Hokkaido and Kagoshima speak in almost identical pitch contours despite the infrequency of their mutual contact as well as large differences in their accentual systems.

A series of statistical analyses[14] confirmed significant differences between the two age groups of Hokkaido with respect to all the points of measurement.[15] Among the three younger groups, no statistically significant differences were found between the Shin-Hidaka and Kagoshima groups for any of the indices, but the Sapporo younger group significantly differed from both Shin-Hidaka and Kagoshima in Shift 1 (S –1.71, SH –0.93, K –0.94) and Shift 5 (S –0.82, SH –0.59,

---

14 Due to the lack of data in the Kagoshima older group, statistical analyses were conducted through two steps: firstly to test the differences between the four region/age groups only from Hokkaido (Sapporo Younger, Sapporo Older, Shin-Hidaka Younger, Shin-Hidaka Older), and secondly to test the differences among the three younger groups (Sapporo, Shin-Hidaka, Kagoshima).

15 ANOVA (region x age x gender, p < 0.05) was used, and it revealed the following age-group differences: S1- young –1.40/old –1.76; S2- young 0.49/old 0.90; S3- young –1.22/old –1.49; S4- young 1.23/old 1.86; S5- young –0.73/old –0.58.

K –0.39), and from Shin-Hidaka alone in Shift 2 (S 0.61, SH 0.30).[16] Statistical analyses also demonstrated that regardless of their region or age cohorts, women consistently show greater degrees of shifts in pitch than men. This particular finding may suggest that Sapporo younger speakers' deviations from the other two younger groups are due to the skewed composition of gender in the data (i. e. 15 females and 1 male).

Declination of pitch (Shift 5 in Table 5) is also found to be statistically signifi-cant between the two age groups in Hokkaido, as reflected in the younger speak-ers having a steeper declination (–0.73) than that of the older speakers (–0.58). However, the three younger groups (Sapporo, Shin-Hidaka, and Kagoshima) are found not to be homogeneous. Similar to the patterns of pitch shifts discussed above, the Sapporo younger group demonstrates a greater degree of declination (–0.82), to a statistically significant extent, than the remaining groups, Shin-Hi-daka (–0.59) and Kagoshima (–0.39). Here again, it is confirmed that women's values for Shift 5 (declination) are consistently larger than those of men regard-less of the region/age groupings, and thus it might also be the case that Sapporo younger speakers' divergent behaviour stems from the skewed sampling in rela-tion to gender.

Moreover, our recent investigation of variable formation of accentual phrases in Japanese (Ota et al. 2012) involved two additional research sites: Fukuoka (northern Kyushu) and Tokyo (as well as Sapporo and Kagoshima) (see Figure 1, the map of Japan). As compared with older counterparts,[17] greater degrees of what we call "prosodic subordination"[18] have been consistently found in the speech of younger speakers living all over the country, regardless of the speech production tasks (isolated sentence reading, performing roles in scripted conver-sations). These results further confirmed more 'levelled' realizations of pitch as nationwide innovations prevalent among the younger generations.

Based on past studies and our own investigation, we are insistent that pitch levelling carries particular social meanings among younger people in Japan. Sibata (1995: 178–187), for example, argue that among younger speakers of Tokyo, the levelling of lexical accents "is explosively diffusing as an 'ingroup code', which conveys the images of being 'novel', 'youthful', and 'metropolitan'". Fur-

---

16 ANOVA (region x gender, p < 0.05) was used.
17 These older groups include only the speakers from Fukuoka and Sapporo.
18 Given multiple sentences produced by the tasks of reading aloud and performing in scripted conversations, the degree of prosodic subordination was based on the depth of a pitch valley between the first and second APs. The shallower the pitch valley is, the greater are the degrees of prosodic subordination that are identified, which implies that pitch contours are more levelled (as far as the initial part of the utterance in question is concerned).

thermore, Sibata conjectures that the levelling of intonation or "an overall pitch of speaking" initiated the levelling of lexical accents (pp. 185–186), along with youngsters' general preference for "non-prominence". This can be interpreted to mean that the levelling of sentential pitch has helped the levelling of lexical accents to act as a reinforcer.[19]

Ota and Takano (2007) conducted an experiment to examine the social meanings of levelled pitch, adapting the matched-guise format. The experiment included 156 college students (Sapporo 77, Kagoshima 79), who were asked to guess the speaker's age from hearing read-aloud sentences that contained the pairs of sentences—one of the pair being in its original, 'levelled' pitch and the other being a synthesized version with greater degrees of pitch shifts (although both were produced by the same speakers). The judges tended to perceive the speakers with a synthesized version with more dynamic pitch contours to be older than the originals. This is to say that levelled pitch struck the listeners as 'youthfulness' of the speaker. Part of Sibata's above-mentioned insights into social meanings has been confirmed empirically.

Although we lack substantial direct evidence at this point, we are tempted to interpret this innovation as linguistically exemplifying younger speakers' positive attitudes toward the youth culture or indexicalizing of their youth identity. Moreover, if it can be assumed, as Sibata (1995) claims, that this particular innovation originates in Tokyo, the media are a very likely vehicle for delivering such social meanings as 'novelty' or 'metropolitanism' associated with the city to younger speakers around the country, regardless of their dialectal origins and the scarcity of direct communicative interactions.

4 Stylized performance based on the media models

As mentioned in 2.3., dialectological surveys on Japanese standardization have focused primarily on the development of command of the standard variety within individual speakers. In such a methodological tradition of sociolinguistic research in Japan, the media, especially television, have been given special operational meanings. In a number of past studies that primarily use questionnaire-based

---

19 The levelling of lexical accents or 'de-accentuation' among younger speakers in Japan is another common example of supra-local linguistic innovations running counter to the large-scale standardization of Japanese dialects. This particular innovation has been reported in a number of previous studies that deal with standardization of different local dialects, including Hokkaido and Tokyo (e.g., Sibata 1959; Nomoto 1960; Haga 1961; NIJL 1965; Inoue 1981; NIJL 1997).

elicitation techniques in interview settings, 'television' represents the domain of social lives that requires the speaker's most formal, standardized style of speech. Researchers often took advantage of 'television' to elicit formal-style speech from their informants, asking them: "How would you say it [a variant in question] if you had a chance to say it appearing on television?" (e.g. Hokkaido Hoogen Kenkyuu-kai 1978; Inoue 1983). Informants who had a better command of Common Japanese were expected to be able to 'perform' their formal-style speech with the word 'television' as the situational cue.

Such prescribed effects of television as a virtual sociolinguistic domain are attested to in the varying Japanese uses of prosody. Sugitou (1983), for example, analyses regional variation in lexical accents from a passage-reading task in a laboratory setting and points out that the researcher's overt instructions to college students (informants) engaged in the task seem to heavily affect how words are accented. An instruction such as "read as if you were a television announcer" significantly contributes to their production of standard Japanese accents as compared with the spontaneous reading of an identical passage in their native dialects. Although it was quite unlikely that the participants had had any chance to talk on TV before or were actually announcers, they succeeded in stylizing their linguistic performance toward the Common Japanese (or Standard Japanese) that is considered appropriate to the social domain.

As part of our research project (Section 3.2), we examined pitch variability in younger speakers' news readings in terms of similarity or dissimilarity to language employed in the media. We asked the participants to read the following excerpt of a news passage from an evening news program on NHK (March 28, 2002).[20] Most participants were newly recruited (see Table 6).

(*kono choo'sa wa*) /*otona'shiku mi'eteita kodomo ga*/ (IU1)[21]
this   survey TOP   obedient   look   child   SUB[22]

/*totsuzen boo'ryoku o huruida'su to itta*/ (IU2)
suddenly   violence OBJ do-begin PAT   say

/*saikin no kodomo'tachi no*
recent GEN   children   GEN

mondai koo'doo no ha'ikei o saguroo' to/ (IU3) ....
problem behaviour GEN background OBJ investigate   PAT

---

20 NHK is the semi-governmental broadcasting company located in Tokyo.
21 The phrase at the beginning, *kono choo'sa wa*, was often pronounced as a separate intonation phrase by the subjects. Therefore, it was disregarded in the analysis.
22 OBJ = Object Case Marker; PAT = Postpositional Particle; GEN = Genitive Case Marker.

Translation:
'This survey aims to investigate the background to the recent problematic issue of children who appear mild-mannered, then suddenly start to exhibit violent behaviour.'

Speaker Groups	No. of Speakers	No. of Tokens
Sapporo Young (20 to 23 years of age)	10 (5 males, 5 females)	20
Shin-Hidaka Young (17 to 29)	10 (5 males, 5 females)	18
Kagoshima Young (19 to 20)	11 (5 males, 6 females)	22

Table 6. Participants in the task of news-passage reading, and the number of tokens analysed

We first identified a single intonation unit (IU hereinafter) based primarily on the Japanese ToBI system for prosodic transcriptions (Venditti 2005), and then we broke down the passage into segments as the units of analysis. We determined the beginning of a brand new IU based on Break Index 3 (i. e. the intonation phrase boundary), the largest juncture typically accompanied by pitch reset, pause, and final syllable lengthening.[23] Consequently, the passage shown above as an example was divided into three IUs.

Based on the identical procedures in our analyses of pitch levelling discussed above (Section 3.2.), Figures 14–16 compare pitch shifts between the three younger groups and the NHK newscaster who actually read the passage on the air.

The homogeneity of the three younger groups is found to be robust in this production task, and the patterns of pitch shifts are very similar to that of the NHK newscaster. Our statistical analyses indicate no significant differences among the three younger groups, except for the Sapporo younger speakers' high values in 2AP-top in IU2 (Sapporo 1.48, vs. Kagoshima 0.89, cf., Shin-Hidaka 1.20) and in IU3 (Sapporo 1.40 vs. S-Hidaka 0.76, Kagoshima 0.68).[24] While it is quite unlikely that these younger speakers actually heard this particular news broadcast on television, the supra-regional similarity indicates that people have acquired the competence of stylizing their linguistic performance following the mental models

---

23 Other criteria for determining an intonation unit come from Cruttenden's notion of 'intonation group boundaries' (1986: 37) and Chafe's discourse notion of 'intonation unit' (1993: 57). In the former, a unit is based on an identification of such markers as pause, anacrusis, final syllable lengthening, and pitch level change, whereas the latter includes a wider repertoire including such devices as both pre- and post-pauses, acceleration/deceleration in syllable duration, overall pitch declination, and voice quality (e.g. creaky voice at the end).

24 Comparisons between two age groups indicate a statistically significant difference only in Shift 1 in IU2: older group –1.26, younger group –0.81. This result means that it is likely that the older speakers' linguistic performance is also subject to the media models.

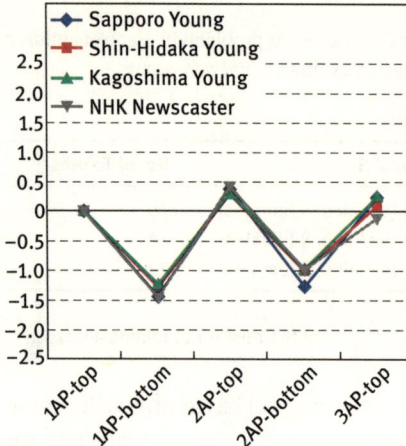

Figure 14: IU1: /otona'shiku/ /mi'eteita/ / kodomo ga/

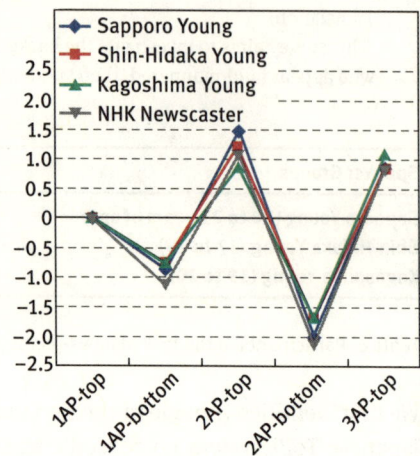

Figure 15: IU2: /totsuzen/ /boo'ryoku o/ / huruida'su to itta/

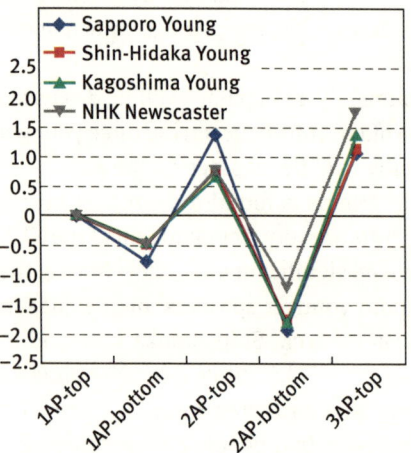

Figure 16: IU3: /saikin no/ /kodomo'tachi no/ /mondai koo'doo no/ (/haikei o/ /saguroo' to/)

provided by the media. Being exposed equally to a news-reading register in their daily lives, the speakers seem to somewhat 'know' or have acquired information about how to enunciate news in 'proper' pitch contours, regardless of their dialectal origins.

5 Discussion and conclusion

It is an extremely difficult task to establish the cause-and-effect relationships between the media and linguistic change in Japanese sociolinguistic contexts, primarily because the appearance of TV, the most pervasive medium, coincides temporally with the post-Second World War modernization of the society, when a number of social changes (e.g. the rise in educational standards, social and geographical mobility) 'standardized' how people talked and what they knew about their language. Unique to Japanese sociolinguistic contexts, however, the effects of the media (especially television) have been tacitly acknowledged as a social factor promoting language standardization without rigorous scientific investigation. Nevertheless, we tried to justify this perspective mainly by assembling 'indirect' evidence from past influential work.

To address the other side of the coin of standardization of local dialects in Japan, we also shed light on linguistic innovations running counter to standardization ('de-standardization') carried out typically by the younger generations all over the country. As rather 'direct' empirical evidence, we demonstrated that the way of transmission of non-Common, innovative TV Japanese variants is supra-local in its nature. The variants spread not through direct human contact (i. e. dialect contact) but through exposure to such media as television, which are equally available all over the country.

We then infer, though without substantial evidence, that this supra-local spread of non-standard, innovative features is attributed to the youth cultural norms or the youth identity shared by younger people in the society. After finding no systematic correlation between the hours of exposure to television and the adaptation of innovative variants among individuals, Mase (1996), for example, suggested the importance of individual personality for adopting the features of TV language. The pupils at Odagiri Junior High School were divided in terms of the TV Japanese score into three groups, the more TV Japanese group, the less TV Japanese group, and the middle group. Mase found that in the more TV Japanese group there were more people with higher scores in active and positive personality. This indicates that TV cannot change language by itself. The change needs to be caused by speakers when they want something more than what they have. It is vital for future research to pursue more qualitative investigations into the speakers' 'identity work' in local communities and its relationships with the adaptation of language use available in the media.

Finally, we also illustrated that the effects of the media sometimes surface in the speaker's conscious, stylistic manipulations of linguistic performance based on his or her mental models. In Japanese sociolinguistic contexts in particular, 'television' is a special public space. It has had a special status as the trigger for the ultimate formal speech. This finding implies that the media language has had a uniformitarian impact on Japanese language socialization without any regional discrepancies and that language use in the media, at least in Japan, could be regarded as an integral part of speakers' competence—or at least their knowledge about the language. We suggest that future researchers should not consider the vernacular as the only resource for investigating linguistic change and variation but rather should develop versatile perspectives on speakers' stylized performance and its social meanings, to which we are sure the media contribute significantly.

References

Chafe, Wallace L. 1993: Prosodic and functional units of language. In: J. A. Edwards and M. D. Lampert (eds.), *Talking data*, 33–43. Hillsdale, NJ: Lawrence Erlbaum.

Chambers, J.K. (Jack) 1998: TV makes people sound the same. In: Laurie Bauer and Peter Trudgill (eds.), *Language Myths*, 123–131. London: Penguin Books.

Coupland, Nikolas 2007: *Style: Language variation and identity*. Cambridge, U.K.: Cambridge University Press.

Cruttenden, Alan 1986: *Intonation*. Cambridge, U.K.: Cambridge University Press.

Eckert, Penelope 2008: Variation and the indexical field. *Journal of sociolinguistics*. 12: 453–476.

Haga, Yasushi 1961: Hougen no jittai to kyoutsuugo-ka no mondai: Hokkaido [The reality of dialects and problems with standardisation: the case of Hokkaido]. In: Y. Endo et al. (eds.), *Hougen-gaku kouza [Lectures on Dialectology]* 2; 100–126. Tokyo: Tokyo-do Shuppan.

Hirayama, Teruo 1960: *Zenkoku akusento jiten [Regional accent dictionary]*. Tokyo: Tokyo-do Shuppan.

Hokkaido Hoogen Kenkyuu-kai (ed.) 1978: *Kyootsuugo-ka no Jittai [The current state of standardisation]*. Hokkaido Hoogen Kenkyuu-kai Soosho [The Serial Report of Dialectological Circle of Hokkaido] No. 1.

Inoue, Fumio 1981: Hokkaido nai no hoogen-sa [Regional differences within Hokkaido dialect]. In: Hokkaido Hougen Kenkyuu-kai (ed.), *Igarashi Saburo Sensei Koki Kinen Shukuga Ronbun-shuu [Collection of Papers for the Seventieth Birthday of Professor Igarashi Saburo]*, 72–83. Hokkaido Hougen Kenkyuu-kai [Dialectological Circle of Hokkaido].

Inoue, Fumio (ed.) 1983: *Shin-hoogen to Kotoba no Midare ni Kansuru Shakaigengogaku-teki Kenkyuu [A sociolinguistic study of new dialects and language deterioration]*. Project report. Kagaku Kenkyuu-hi Hojokin (Soogoo Kenkyuu (A)) [Grant-in-Aid for Scientific Research (KAKENHI) (A)].

Inoue, Fumio 1998: *Nihongo watching [Watching the sociolinguistic trends of Japanese]*. Tokyo: Iwanami Shoten.

Jinnouchi, Masataka, and Kenji Tomosada (eds.) 2005: *Kansai Hoogen no Hirogari to Komyuni-keeshon no Yukue [The spread of Kansai dialects and the state of communication in the future]*. Osaka: Izumi Shoin.

Kuno, Makoto 1999: Wakamono wa kyootsuugo ni jishin ga nai [Young people are not confident in their command of the Common Japanese]. In: Kazuyuki Sato and Masato Yoneda (eds.),

Doonaru nihon no kotoba [What is going to happen to Japanese language?], 60–64. Tokyo: Taishukan Shoten.

Labov, William 1984: Field methods of the Project on Linguistic Change and Variation. In J. Baugh and J. Sherzer (eds.), *Language in use*, 28–53. Englewood Cliffs, NJ: Prentice Hall.

Labov, William 2001: *Principles of language change: Vol. 2, Social factors*. Oxford, U.K.: Blackwell.

Lee, Yeonsuk 1996: *Kokugo to yuu shisoo ["Kokugo" (the national language) as an ideology]*. Tokyo: Iwanami Shoten.

Mase, Yoshio 1965: Akusento henka no yooin [Factors of accentual change]. *Todai ronkyuu* 5; 54–61. Tokyo Metropolitan University.

Mase, Yoshio 1981: Gengokeisei ni oyobosu terebi oyobi toshi no genngo no eikyoo [The influence of TV language and urban dialect on language acquisition]. *Kokugogaku [Studies in the Japanese language]* 125; 1–19. Kokugo gakkai [The Society for the Study of Japanese Language].

Mase, Yoshio 1996: Terebi to chiikigo no henyoo [TV and the transformation of regional varieties]. *Nihongogaku [The Japanese Linguistics]* 15(10); 13–27. Tokyo: Meiji Shoin.

Milroy, Lesley 2007: Off the shelf or under the counter? On the social dynamics of sound change. In: Christopher M. Cain and Geoffrey Russom (eds.), *Studies in the history of the English language 3: Managing chaos, strategies for identifying change in English*, 149–171. Berlin/New York: Mouton de Gruyter.

National Institute for Japanese Language 1953: *Chiikishakai no gengoseikatsu: Tsuruoka ni okeru jittaichoosa [The language life in a local community: A fact-finding survey]*. Tokyo: Shuuei Shuppan.

National Institute for Japanese Language 1965: *Kyootsuu-go-ka no katei [The processes of standardization]*. NIJL Research Report 27.

National Institute for Japanese Language 1974: *Chiikishakai no gengoseikatsu: Tsuruoka ni okeru 20-nen mae tono hikaku [The language life in a local community: A real-time comparison with 20 years ago]*. Tokyo: Shuuei Shuppan.

National Institute for Japanese Language (1997): *Hokkaido ni okeru Kyoutsuugo-ka toGengo Seikatsu no Jittai [Change toward a common language and the reality of lives of dialect speakers]*. Research Report, Kokuritsu Kokugo Kenkyuu-sho.

National Institute for Japanese Language (ed.) 2007: *Chiikishakai no gengoseikatsu: Tsuruoka ni okeru 20-nen kankaku no keizokuchoosa [The language life in a local community: The results of three serial surveys in Tsuruoka every 20 years]*. Tokyo: NINJAL.

Nomoto, Kikuo 1960: Hokkaido-hoogen no akusento [Accents of Hokkaido dialects]. *Keiryoo Kokugogaku [Mathematical Linguistics]* 15; 10–16. Keiryoo Kokugo gakkai [The Mathematical Linguistic Society of Japan].

Ono, Yoneichi 1993: *Sapporo-shi hoogen taninzuu choosa shiryoo ni tsuite* [On data from a survey of Sapporo Japanese]. In: M. Kato (ed.), *Higashi Nihon no Onsei [Speech of Eastern Japan]*. Monbushoo Juuten Ryooiki Kenkyuu [Grant-in-Aid for Scientific Research on Priority Areas] (No. 04207102) Project Report, 51–86.

Ota, Ichiro and Shoji Takano 2007: Shakai onsei gaku-teki heni o toraeru tameno onsei chooshu jikken ni kansuru koosatsu [A reflection on the methodological problems of auditory experiment for sociophonetic variation]. *Cultural Science Reports* 66; 23–42. Kagoshima University.

Ota, Ichiro and Shoji Takano 2008a: Ebyousha tasuku ni miru onchou heni no kousatsu [Notes on pitch variation observed in picture description task]. *Cultural Science Report* 67; 1–13. Kagoshima University.

Ota, Ichiro and Shoji Takano 2008b: Onchou ga shimesu mono: Akusento-ku no dephrasing to recomposing [What pitch variability indicates: Accentual dephrasing and recomposing]. *Cultural Science Reports* 68; 27–38. Kagoshima University.

Ota, Ichiro and Shoji Takano 2008c: Onchou-men no gengo henka ni kansuru onchou choushu jikken to ebyousha tasuku no kekka kara no kousatsu [A study of pitch change based on the data from speech perception experiments and the picture description task] *Proceedings of the 21st Meeting of the Japanese Association of Sociolinguistic Sciences*, 336–339.

Ota, Ichiro, Shoji Takano, Hitoshi Nikaido, Akira Utsugi and Yashiyuki Asahi 2012: Sociolinguistic variation in the pitch movement of Japanese dialects. Poster presentation at NWAV-Asia Pacific 2, NINJAL, Japan.

Shibatani, Masayoshi 1990: *The languages of Japan*. Cambridge, U.K.: Cambridge University Press.

Sibata, Takesi 1958: *Nihon no hoogen [The dialects in Japan]*. Tokyo: Iwanami Shoten.

Sibata, Takeshi 1959: Hokkaido ni umareta kyoutsuu-go [A common language born in Hokkaido]. *Gengo Seikatsu [Language Life]* 90; 26–37. Tokyo: Chikuma Shobo.

Sibata, Takesi 1978a: *Shakai-gengogaku no kadai [Issues in sociolinguistics]*. Tokyo: Sanseido.

Sibata, Takesi 1978b: *Hoogen no sekai [The world of dialects]*. Tokyo: Heibon-sha.

Sibata, Takesi 1995: *Nihongo wa omoshiroi [The Japanese language is interesting]*. Tokyo: Iwanami Shoten.

Sibata, Takesi 1998: *Takesi Sibata: Sociolinguistics in Japanese contexts*. (English version of his 1978a work with a preface by the editors.) Edited by Tetsuya Kunihiro, Fumio Inoue and Daniel Long. Berlin/New York: Mouton de Gruyter.

Stuart-Smith, Jane 2011: The view from the couch: Changing perspectives on the role of the television in changing language ideologies and use. In: Tore Kristiansen and Nikolas Coupland (eds.), *Standard languages and language standards in a changing Europe*, 223–239, Oslo: Novus.

Stuart-Smith, Jane 2012: English and the media: Television. In: A. Berg and L. Brinton (eds.), *Historical linguistics of English HSK* 34(1): 1075–1088. Berlin/New York: Mouton de Gruyter.

Stuart-Smith, Jane, Gwilym Pryce, Claire Timmins and Barrie Gunter: 2013: Television can also be a factor in language change: Evidence from an urban dialect. *Language* 89(3), 1–36.

Sugitou, Miyoko 1983: Akusento no "yure" ["Variability" in accents]. *Nihongogaku [The Japanese Linguistics]* 8(3); 15–26. Tokyo: Meiji Shoin.

Takano, Shoji and Ichiro Ota 2005: Nihongo onsei ni okeru picchi heitanka genshou no shikouteki kenkyuu: Heni rironteki kanten kara [A preliminary study of Japanese pitch leveling from a perspective of variation theory]. *Proceedings of the 16th Meeting of the Japanese Association of Sociolinguistic Sciences*, 220–223.

Takano, Shoji and Ichiro Ota 2007: *A sociolinguistic study of pitch leveling in Japanese based on data from the Hokkaido and Kagoshima dialects*. The Project Report for Grant-in-Aid for Scientific Research [C-1] (No. 16520284) .

Tanaka, Yukari 2010: *Shutoken ni okeru gengodootai no kenkyuu [A study of dynamics of language in the Tokyo metropolitan area]*. Tokyo: Kasama Shoin.

Trudgill, Peter 1986: *Dialect in contact*. Oxford, U.K.: Blackwell.

Venditti, Jennifer J. 2005: The J_ToBI model of Japanese intonation. In: S-A. Jun (ed.), *Prosodic typology: The phonology of intonation and phrasing*, 172–200. Oxford, U.K.: Oxford University Press.

Yokoyama, Shoichi and Haruko Sanada 2010: Gengo no shoogai shuutoku moderu ni yoru kyootsuugoka yosoku [Predictions of dialect standardisation by the "Life-long Assimilation of Language Change" model], *Nihongo no kenkyuu [Studies in the Japanese Language]*, 6(2), 31–45. Nihongo Gakkai [The Society for Japanese Linguistics].

Isabelle Buchstaller
Commentary: Television and language use. What do we mean by influence and how do we detect it?

Section 2 starts off on an old romantic theme, the idea that mediation is fundamental to all language use in the sense that – irrespectively of the medium of communication – we always need to transfer the language of thought into symbols (see i. e. Schlegel 1927). As Kristiansen points out, these days we simply have a larger repertoire of technologies at our avail in order to communicate concepts, ideas, thoughts and opinions: In addition to the use of our speech organs for creating interactive spoken language and strokes or keys for writing script, we have created a range of mediated forms of language use. [1] And while the development of language mediation is an evolutionary process from oral communication to writing to broadcast media and, finally, and most recently, to internet-based social media, it is important to bear in mind that all forms of language mediation face limitations; those of the modern media are simply different in kind.

With the exception of Kristiansen's contribution, which also considers the influence of writing on interactive spoken language, the main focus of section 2 is the influence of television on language change. Three aspects merit particular attention when reading these articles: Why focus on TV? What is affected by TV? What do we mean by influence? I will comment briefly on these questions.

1 Why focus on TV?

In the age of social media, the investigation of the influence of television on language use might seem positively anachronistic. But there are very good reasons why linguists should explore the possible impact of TV on the language of interactive and day-to-day communication. One is its early occurrence: Ota and Takano report that TV ownership in Japan exploded in the 1960s and became almost ubiquitous during the 1970s (a parallel development has been described for the United States and most western European countries, see Ofcom 2010, www.tvhis-

---

1 The influence of sign language TV programmes on signed languages is not discussed in this volume and seems to be severely under-researched (see however, Elton 2010 and Woll 1994).

tory.tv). This time-depth allows for longitudinal diachronic studies on the impact of television, starting in the generation prior to the mass take-up of broadcast TV and extending to two subsequent generations that have grown up with increasing TV presence in their lives.

Potentially even more important than the diachronic time depth of TV exposure is the crucial and as of yet unresolved issue of its impact on younger people's lives. The Kaiser Foundation reports that in 2009, US American 8–18 year olds spent approximately 4 hours 30 minutes per day watching television (live, on demand and on the internet), which is more time than any other leisure activity). A study by the Nielsen Foundation (2009) suggests that children in other English-speaking countries, such as Ireland and South Africa, have even longer viewing times. Ota and Takano make a powerful point about the ubiquity of TV language before critical age and its unknown influence on the language acquisition process. Indeed, while there is ample evidence that children cannot acquire language *solely* from television (see Kuhl 2010 inter alia), we know that TV has the potential to diffuse (knowledge about) linguistic variants as well as attitudes and ideologies towards these forms and their users. By providing access to stereotyped personae and stances associated with the use of certain linguistic features, broadcast television impacts upon young speakers' metalinguistic awareness and might even affect their systemic language use, especially if such cognitive bundles of forms and perceptions are encountered early and persistently. Childhood TV engagement and its role in shaping young speakers' viewership provides an important backdrop for the two contributions that focus on adolescent speakers (Ota and Tanako, Stuart-Smith and Ota). If these age brackets appropriate linguistic material from the media – and the chapters provide good evidence that this might be the case – we will need to find out to what extent early media engagement and indeed childhood recruitment of stylistic resources might have a preparatory or softening effect towards the later adoption of media-based linguistic matter.

2 What is affected by TV?

The lion's share of feature-based sociolinguistic inquiry into the relationship between the media and language use revolves around two key areas of interest: (i) the diffusion of standard forms and varieties via the media as well as (ii) the nationwide (or indeed global) dissemination of linguistic features found in media language.

In terms of the former, Stuart-Smith and Ota point out we have to differentiate between the spread of the standard language resulting in bidialectalism (i. e. the additive development of individual speakers' command of the standard variety), and movement towards a standard or supralocal variety at the expense of dialectal diversity. For Japan, Ota and Takano (p. 171) report a "nationwide levelling of dialects towards the standard variety". But the jury is still out on the question whether the development is additive or suppletive since (especially older) research seems to rely on surveys that test speakers' ability to produce standard forms without investigating their continued use of the dialect in more natural and spontaneous registers. Indeed, Ota and Takano's more recent research reveals the continued use of some local forms, especially in geographically more remote areas. In the UK, the consonantal systems in many varieties have increasingly undergone levelling since the 1980s/90s, leading to a large scale homogenization of speakers' phonemic repertoire. However, as Stuart-Smith and Ota report, local outcomes in terms of linguistic constraints and social indexicalities suggest that there is not complete homogenization (yet?). Indeed, Kristiansen's contribution beautifully illustrates the social relativity regarding the role of the media in the standardization process by detailing the close relationship between the portrayal of (non-)standard varieties on television and hegemonic societal standard language ideologies. Comparing Denmark and Norway he convincingly argues that the media bolsters and indeed plays a defining part in shaping dominant beliefs about normative language use, resulting in inverse effects in the two neighbouring countries: the Norwegian media substantiate a language ideology that embraces and celebrates dialectal diversity, giving air space to local dialects and eschewing standardization even in formal (i. e. newsreader) registers. In Denmark, the opposite effect holds, and the promulgation of the variety associated with educated Kopenhagen speakers in more and more media contexts parallels or indeed supports its mushrooming in face-to-face registers.

The supralocal spread of innovative linguistic features has been reported in countries such as England (glottalization, th-fronting), Japan (pitch track changes, prosodic subordination), but also across larger linguistic communities (HRT and new quotatives in the English speaking world, palatalization in Southern American Portuguese, etc.). The question is if and, if yes, to what extent the spread of these features is mediated by the old and new media. Stuart-Smith and Ota's and Ota and Tanako's contributions attribute a conducive role to the media in the dissemination of such non-standard features. Note however that, at first glance, this process seems to proceed differently in Japan and the English-speaking world, giving rise to vastly dissimilar outcomes. In Japan, Ota and Takano (p. 173) report the "rapid spread of linguistic features that are used particularly in TV". They describe this process as "uniformitarian" (p. 189), a relatively homogenous development, whereby speakers simultaneously adopt innovative materials (such as prosodic subordination and innovative pitch contours) without interpersonal contact. Especially the levelled pitch seems to be taken up across the country in non-continguous communities with the same social constraints (young, female) as well as attitudinal load attached to them.

This is interesting, since it is exactly these aspects of social meaning that have not transferred well for other well-known spreading features, such as the globally available quotative *be like*, which reveals locally idiosyncratic patterns in every locale investigated (Buchstaller and D'Arcy 2006). Indeed, also the phonetic variables reported on in Stuart-Smith and Ota are constrained in fundamentally different ways in Glasgow than in southern varieties of British English. Thus, close examination of the linguistic and social parameters that govern geographically spreading features in different English-speaking communities seems to suggest that the reception and adoption of such linguistic innovations is fundamentally localized to the respective community of speakers. And so, in the past few years, sociolinguists in the English-speaking world (see Eckert 2003; Milroy 2007) have adopted the concepts of "off the shelf" (i. e. easy to pick up wholesale, such as lexical innovations) and "under the counter" (i. e. tricky to access and potentially altered along the way, presumably (morpho)syntactic and phonetic features?). Unfortunately, to date, we lack even the most fundamental grasp of how changes at different levels of linguistic modularity can be classified into these mercantile metaphors. Empirical studies will reveal to what extent linguistic innovations at higher or lower levels of linguistic structure and different degrees of saliency lend themselves to mediation (of social or linguistic constraints, entire or transformed) by broadcast television or indeed by other types of media.

Furthermore, we need to differentiate, as Stuart-Smith and Ota rightly do, between what speakers can get from these media shelves and what they choose to take: What types of information about language can possibly be picked up by speakers when watching and how do they engage with this TV material? What types of language change seem to be taken from the media shelf with their social and functional boots on and which changes seem to involve a much more active engagement with local meaning production? Indeed, research has shown that even in cases where the media provides a seemingly accessible shelf, speakers engage with the material in locally idiosyncratic ways (Buchstaller and D'Arcy 2009; Buchstaller 2014). And so, when Stuart Smith and Ota (in this volume) probed deeper into the supralocal Japanese pitch changes, they found a localized pattern in the social information young speakers store about these spreading features (youthful, metropolitan vs. educated, correct and authoritative). What is more, young female speakers in the remote town of Kagoshima incorporated the production of pitch patterns into the local social meanings of femininity and elegance, resulting in a fundamentally different uptake of country-wide available pitch movements. We thus find a very similar situation to Glashow, where young non-mobile working class speakers have similarly incorporated supralocally available material into their local linguistic system, social practices and meaning making processes. These findings demonstrate that even in cases of superficially simple transfer, speakers are actively engaged in adopting and adapting the material they recruit from media shelves. Linguistic variants found on TV are mediated once again: through the individual's personal choices, existing local experiences and linguistic habitus.

3 What do we mean by influence and how do we detect it?

Different research traditions have conceptualized and therefore ideologized the impact of the media on language use differentially. These range from the tacit assumption that TV influences dialects (and therefore the acceptance of much more circumstantial evidence) in Japan and Germany over more evidence-driven approaches amongst southern American researchers, where the correlation between exposure or engagement with TV and linguistic production tends to be accepted as evidence given social and attitudinal motives to assimilate (see Naro and Scherre 1996; Cavalho 2004) to the widespread rejection of the role of TV on systemic language change amongst (earlier) Anglo-American sociolinguists. More recently, however, increasing consolidation of findings and cross-fertilization beyond individual sub-disciplines and research groups (of which the present volume is a magnificent example) have kick-started a discussion about what type of evidence (and how much of it) is needed to be considered suggestive for media effects on language use (see Kristiansen, Stuart-Smith and Ota). This question is vitally important since it also forces us to ask which methodologies are best suited to collect such evidence.

There is no question that it is extremely difficult if not downright impossible to establish a direct causal relationship between the media and linguistic change. The large-scale social changes industrialized societies have undergone since the Second World War make teasing out the effect of TV on language change impossible. And so, media research generally considers the view that media consumption can be directly correlated to social behaviour as antiquated. What, then counts as evidence for the effect of TV on interactive language use and how do we procure such evidence?

Kristiansen (p. 115) suggests that indirect TV influence changes standard language ideology in a way that is "less likely to have happened in the same way, or to the same extent, without TV". What I take this to mean is that mediation or mediatization, similarly to other -isms, is, paraphrasing Urry (2003), not new or distinctive in kind but distinctive in its rapidity and geographical remit. Hence, following Kristiansen, we might theorize that the process whereby speakers appropriate innovative elements in order to do interactional and interpersonal work along roughly similar lines (but nevertheless fundamentally shaped by local social and ideological constraints) would not have happened with such speed across non-consecutive geographical areas without the media.

What this basically means is that way in which the media make available information about linguistic resources (variants, features, ways of talking, intonation contours etc.) is unprecedented in its accessibility, reaching audiences across vast areas of space simultaneously and offering shelves of stylistic opportunities that are linked to media personalities, situated stances and indexicalities. Speakers across the linguistic community (or even beyond, see for example the recent Gangham style-mania that swept the globe) can appropriate such linguistic materials for different aims, be it to index media registers, to style themselves or others or to create differentiation of various kinds.

Note, however, that this uptake is not a blanket one: All three articles report that stylistic opportunities are taken up unequally, depending on the type of speaker and on their stance towards the material, the media persona(e) associated with them or the media shelves themselves. Hence, as Ota and Takano point out "TV cannot change language by itself. The change needs to be caused by speakers when they want something more than what they have" (p. 199). What we need, thus, is more information about the speakers who pick up linguistic resources from the media. Apart from their viewing history, an important conducive factor seems to be indirect TV influence changes standard language ideology in a way that is speakers' involvement with the media characters who exploit such features (Stuart-Smith and Ota). Mase's research (1996) also suggests that personality traits play a role in whether speakers can be moved over the adoption threshold, with active and positive personalities adopting features of TV language more readily. Are these speakers the early adopters that Rogers (2003) has identified in the diffusion of changes more generally (and which Labov has confirmed for language change)? Are they the "gregarious individuals" Denis' (2001) identified in the incipient stages of innovations? More work needs to be done before we know whether we can generalize Mase's and Ota and Takano's findings.

Finally, the appropriated material has to relate in meaningful ways to the local social, situational and ideological contexts of speaking. Stuart-Smith and Ota appeal to Hall's (1980) notions of alignment and reciprocity, linking meaning at the micro level of interaction with macro levels of representation and ideologies to explain the uptake of mediated features. This reminds me of Hill's (1995) concept of dual indexicality: The mediated material is so attractive because it can simultaneously index relevant aspects of the source (and with it the indexical field of the media outlets and personae with which they are associated) but it can also index stances, social meanings etc. in the very local context in which it is used. As such, the study of media influence on language use benefits from the incorporation of third wave models, which appeal to speaker agency in the creation of styles and personae, including identity projection or social indexicality theory. And so, the picking up of features from the media shelf can be conceptualized as a conscious act of stylization, an act of bricolage (Hebdige 1979), where speakers appropriate material according to mental models acquired from the media and incorporate it into locally relevant categories and indexicalities. Unsurprisingly, perhaps, the stylistic manipulation of mediated features is frequently found in performed sequences, when speakers use them as creative resources to construct alternative worlds or enact real, virtual or media-based personae, a finding that interacts well with non-representational, interactional and theatrical approaches to language (see i. e. Hymes 1975 concept of "breakthrough into performance"). Indeed, while the empirical study of the impact of TV on language is deeply steeped in the research traditions of the branches of linguistics and the countries in which they are conducted, it is noticeable that empirical methodologies that collect less natural styles of speech (role play, minimal pair tasks, etc.) are the ones that tend to allow informants to draw on material that is stylistically linked with media representation and performance. As Stuart-Smith and Ota point out, such experimental methods can afford a window into speakers' mental representations, both in terms of what they are storing but also what they are witnessing, i. e. what is on the media shelf.

It is, however, notoriously difficult to determine which fragments are the speakers' own words and which aspects of linguistic production reference other speakers, stances or media representations. Put another way: Where does the representation of mediated material begin and where does it end? Which resources have been picked up directly from the media (first?) and which ones have been acquired 2nd or 3rd hand? These are thorny questions that have plagued researchers in linguistics and stylistics for eons.[2] Note, for example, Goffman's (1981) contention that speech is always parasitic on prior material, a lamination of recycled chunks and other people's voices resulting in an intertextual mosaic of second-hand resources (see also Bakhtin's 1986 notion of "polyvoicedness"). The interactive and intertextual nature of speaker performance thus blurs the distinction between mediation via the media and mediation via other, often interpersonal, channels – or indeed via both.

---

2 The question to which extent speakers' performance consists of 2nd hand material, prefabricated ideas or 'common goods' has been topicalised in Flaubert's 'Dictionnaire des idées reçues' (1912) and its fictional counterpart 'Bouvard et Pécuchet' (1881).

What this effectively means is that processes of language change which involve the media are immensely complex, contingent not only on the role of broadcast television but also on the type of consumer, their participation in online activity and their interpersonal interactions in the real and virtual world. This is especially the case since onscreen activity works in tandem with TV consumption in providing media shelves for innovative linguistic forms (Madden et al. 2013, The Kaiser Foundation). Importantly, these online communities provide the support of stylistic (including linguistic) practices via shared involvement in virtual networks (see Paolillo 2001; Maybaum 2013). To date, however, our knowledge of how engagement with media figures compares to online or indeed face-to-face communities is still very sketchy. In future research, the role of online/onscreen communities merits a more explicit place in our models of media influence on language use.

To come back to Stuart-Smith and Ota's question (p. 140) what "we are modelling when we talk about media 'influence'", I would argue that we are stipulating speakers' "repeating, recycling and recontextualizing media discourse" (Spitulnik 1997:98) as one more shelf, together with material from other shelves. Looking at media 'influence' in this way, broadcast television is just one more repository of stylistic resources from which speakers can choose to draw when using language creatively, while simultaneously availing themselves of a multitude of other sources such as writing, interactional language use or other, newer and older media. What distinguishes the media shelf, apart from its relative novelty and increasing multifacedness, is its pervasiveness, making resources available to vast numbers of speakers simultaneously.

References

Bakhtin, Mikhail M. 1986: *Speech Genres and Other Late Essays*, edited by Caryl Emerson and Michael Holquist, translated by Vern W. McGee. Austin, TX: University of Texas Press.

Buchstaller, Isabelle and Alexandra D'Arcy 2009: Localised globalization: A multi-local, multi-variate investigation of *be like*. *Journal of Sociolinguistics* 13: 291–331.

Buchstaller, Isabelle 2014: *Quotation: New Trends and Sociolinguistic Implications*. Malden/Oxford: Wiley Blackwell.

Carvalho, Ana Maria 2004: I speak like the guys on TV: Palatalization and the urbanization of Uruguayan Portuguese. *Language Variation and Change* 16: 127–151.

Denis, Derek 2011: Innovators and innovation: Tracking the innovators of *and stuff* in York English. *University of Pennsylvania Working Papers in Linguistics* 17(2), accessed 17. August 2013.

Eckert, Penelope 2003: Elephants in the Room. *Journal of Sociolinguistics*, 7(3): 392–397.

Elton, F. 2010: Changing the way we sign: An analysis of the signing style used by translators in the Queen's Christmas Speech since the 1980s. Birkbeck College, University of London.

Flaubert, Gustave 1912: *Dictionnaire des Idées Reçues*. Paris: Louis Conard.

Flaubert, Gustave 1881: *Bouvard et Pécuchet*. Paris: Alphonse Lemerre.

Goffmann Erving 1981: *Forms of Talk*. Oxford: Blackwell.

Hall, Stuart 1980: Encoding/decoding. In Stuart Hall, Dorothy Hobson, Andrew Lowe and Paul Willis (eds.), *Culture. Media. Language: Working Papers on Cultural Studies*, 128–138. Birmingham: Routledge with the Center for Contemporary Cultural Studies, University of Birmingham.

Hebdige, Dick 1979: *Subculture: The Meaning of Style*. London: Methuen.

Hill, Jane 1995: Mock Spanish: A site for the indexical reproduction of racism in American English. *Language & Culture, Symposium 2*, http://language-culture.binghamton.edu/symposia/2/part1/, accessed 17.August 2013.

Hymes, Dell 1975: Breakthrough into performance. In: Dan Ben-Amos and Kenneth Goldstein (eds.), *Folklore: Performance and Communication*, 11–74. The Hague: Mouton.

The Henry J. Kaiser Family Foundation 2011: Generation M2 media in the lives of 8- to 18-year-olds. http://www.kff.org/entmedia/upload/8010.pdf, accessed February 22, 2012.

Kuhl, Patricia 2010: Brain mechanisms in early language acquisition. *Neuron* 67: 713–775.

Madden, Mary, Amanda Lehnhart, Sandra Cortesi, Urs Gasser, Maeve Duggan, Aaron Smith and Meredith Beaton 2013: Teens, social media and privacy. Pew Research Centre Report. Harvard: The Berkman Center for Internet and Society, Harvard University.

Mase, Yoshio 1996: Terebi to chiikigo no henyoo (TV and the transformation of regional varieties). *Nihongogaku (The Japanese Linguistics)* 15(10): 13–27.

Maybaum, Rebecca 2013: "Good morning tweethearts!": The diffusion of a lexical innovation in Twitter. *Newcastle Working Papers in* Linguistics 19: Selected Papers from Sociolinguistics Summer School 4, http://www.ncl.ac.uk/linguistics/assets/documents/7.Maybaum_NWPL.pdf, accessed 26. August 2013.

Milroy, Lesley 2007: Off the shelf or under the counter? On the social dynamics of sound changes. In: Christopher Cain and Geoffrey Russom (eds.), *Studies in the History of the English Language III: Managing Chaos; Strategies for Identifying Change in English*, 149–172. Berlin/New York: Mouton de Gruyter.

Naro, Anthony and Maria Marta Perreira Scherre 1996: Contact with media and linguistic variation. In: Jennifer Arnold, Renée Blake, Brad Davidson, Scott Schwenter, and Julie Solomon (eds.), *Sociolinguistic Variation: Data, Theory and Analysis. Selected Papers from NWAV 23 at Stanford*, 223–228. Stanford: CSLI Publications..

The Nielsen Foundation 2009: How teens use media: A Nielsen Report on the myths and realities of teen media trends'. At http://blog.nielsen.com/nielsenwire/reports /nielsen_howteensusemedia_june09.pdf, accessed 1. August 2012.

Ofcom Communications Market Report: 2010: www.ofcom.org.uk, accessed 26. August 2013

Paolillo, John: 2001: Language variation on Internet Relay Chat: A social network approach. *Journal of Sociolinguistics* 5: 180–213.

Rogers, Everett 2003: *Diffusion of Innovations*. New York: Free Press.

von Schlegel, August Wilhelm: 1827: Indische Bibliothek, Volume 2. E. Webb.

Spitulnik, Debra 1997: The Social circulation of media discourse and the mediation of communities. In: Alessandro Duranti (ed.), *Linguistic Anthropology: A Reader,* 95–118. Oxford: Oxford University Press.

Urry, John 2003: *Global Complexity*. Cambridge, U.K.: Polity Press.

Woll, B. 1994: The influence of television on the deaf community in Britain. In: Inger Ahlgren, Britta Bergman and Mary Brennan (eds.), *Perspectives on Sign Language Use: Papers from the Fifth International Symposium on Sign Language Research*, 293–301. Durham: The International Sign Linguistics Association.

Section III: **Media engagement in interactional practice**

Alexandra Georgakopoulou

'Girlpower or girl (in) trouble?' Identities and discourses in the (new) media engagements of adolescents' school-based interaction

1 Introduction

In media consumption studies, there has been little empirical work on how media products permeate everyday life beyond the context of immediate audience-text encounter (Bird 2003; Moores 2000). In similar vein, sociolinguistic studies have only recently begun to document ordinary people's media engagements in a variety of everyday contexts, beyond the point of initial (however, active) consumption. A case in point is studies of media appropriations and references within classroom interaction that have stressed their performative roles, as activities that develop in parallel with the formal instruction and present various interactional affordances (e.g. Rampton 2006). In this increasingly important line of inquiry, there is still much scope for exploring how media engagements, particularly those related to new technologies, as a phenomenon with increasing resonance in people's daily lives, impact on their identities and social relations. Having as its starting point that online and offline experiences are enmeshed in daily life, and that their inter-relationships should become an object of investigation (see Georgakopoulou 2013a), this chapter focuses on the discursive (re) constructions of media engagements in the interactions of students in a London comprehensive school.

Using data from two female students, the analysis focuses on two discursive instances of media engagements that were found to raise issues of normative behaviour and to therefore be crucial for the positioning of self and other: a) talk about media engagements that interactionally make relevant issues of knowledge, access to, recognition and approval (or lack of) one another's media engagements and b) stories about new media engagements (I call these breaking news). Using small stories research and positioning analysis (e.g. Georgakopoulou 2007, 2008; Bamberg and Georgakopoulou 2008) as an apparatus for looking into discursive constructions of self and other, I will show that both types of media engagements routinely accomplish and map with the participants' positions in peer-groups and their –mainly gendered- identities. In particular, I will identify two distinct positionings in the case of each of the two girls and examine what kinds of self-projects are engendered, necessitated or constrained for each of them. I will argue for the resonance of these positionings with two widely circulating and in many ways contradictory discourses about young women: the discourse of girlpower and the 'can' do girl on the one hand and the discourse of girls at risk and in trouble on the other. I will claim that 'girlpower' and 'girls at risk' co-articulate with discourses about new media as arenas for opportunities for social networking and self-enhancement on the one hand and as sites of danger and victimization on the other.

2 Data and methods

The data for this chapter come from the study of a London comprehensive school entitled Urban Classroom Culture and Interaction (UCCI, 2005–2008), part of the ESRC Programme in Identities & Social Action (www.identities.org.uk).[1] The project involved two phases of data collection following nine students from year nine and into year ten. The school in question was attended approximately by 1000 students with a diverse population with South Asian and African-Caribbean ethnicities forming the two largest groups. The aim of the project was to study, through a focus on interactional data, what kinds of identities the students constructed for themselves and others in their daily lives at school. Following up on previous studies of London schools (Rampton 2006), we were particularly interested in how the students' discursively constructed knowledge in, familiarity and engagement with new media impinged on their identities at school. Key-questions in this respect were:
- How do participants locally do and report new media engagements (henceforth NMEs)?
- What do they see as a 'critical incident', 'key-episode', how & why?
- How do they account for and reflect on such practices? With what kinds of orientations to which discourses?

The different data-sets consisted of:
- A filed diary with ethnographic observations;
- 180 hours of radio-mic recordings of interactions in class and in the playground from 9 focal students (5 female, 4 male, 13+ years old when the

---

1 The project team comprised Ben Rampton (Director), Roxy Harris, Alexandra Georgakopoulou, Constant Leung, Caroline Dover and Lauren Small.

project started) who were from a range of ethnicities and varied greatly in their academic performances;

- 10 hours of research interviews with the focal students;
- playback sessions with the focal students with selected key-excerpts from the radio-mic data;
- supplementary documentation covering Year 9–10 demographics and school performance, staff and parent handbooks, lesson handouts, etc.;
- a Teachers' project with focus group interviews, questionnaires and playback sessions.

2.1 A practice-based approach to (new) media engagements and identities

The above methods of data collection allowed us to follow a practice-based approach to language and identities according to which language performs actions in specific environments and is part of other social practices, shaping and being shaped by them (e.g. Agha 2007; Briggs 1998; Hanks 1996). There is recurrence and systematicity in such actions including regularity of occurrence (iterativity) in the various semiotic choices involved. Capturing this iterativity is both an analytical aim and a principle built into data collection. It is essential, for instance, to access data that allow the analyst to capture not only what is going on in local interactions but also what the participants' socio-spatial orientations are: who does what and how in different environments and over time. It is also important to tap into the tellers' meta-representations and reflections on their communication practices. The method of *linguistic ethnography* is particularly well suited to this (for a discussion, see Rampton 2007). As I will show below, this facilitates the inquiry into if and how local interactions resonate with widely circulating discourses: what is it that the participants invoke as relevant for them, where does this derive from and what possible contestations accompany such enactments?

In previous work (2007), I developed a heuristic for a practice-based discourse analysis, which charts the inter-animations of three separable but interrelated layers: *ways of telling-sites-tellers*. The heuristic was developed within the framework of small stories research (Georgakopoulou 2007, 2008; Bamberg 2006), an epistemological paradigm for the analysis of narrative and identities, but it is applicable to all discourse activities. Ways of telling refer to the communicative how: the socioculturally shaped and more or less conventionalized semiotic and in particular verbal choices of a particular discourse activity. The stories' aboutness, the types of events and experience they narrate, is important in this respect. The relations of a current telling with previous and anticipated tellings are also significant. Above all though, ways of telling capture the sequential features of an activity and, to do so, they draw significantly on conversation analytic modes (e.g. Jefferson 1978). Sequentiality includes how discourse activities are methodically introduced into and exited from conversations, what types of action, telling roles and rights they raise for the interlocutors, what modes of co-construction and interactional management between interlocutors are to be found in them.

Sites refer to the social spaces in which activities take place and capture the conglomerate of situational context factors ranging from physical (e.g. seating) arrangements to mediational tools that the participants may employ. Recent research in sociolinguistics has demonstrated the importance of physical, lived and practiced space for language and social interaction (e.g. Blommaert, Collins & Slembrouck 2005). The specific emplacement of activities can shape the semiotic resources employed for their accomplishments and equally, discourse activities can constitute a place as an arena for specific social practices. Places come with specific affordances or constraints as well as with normative expectations and valuation scales of what languages, genres, discourse activities etc., are appropriate, how and by whom (idem). In the case of stories, the concept of sites has allowed me to tap into the significance of social spaces not just for the here-and-now of the storytelling activities but also for the taleworlds invoked in the participants' stories.

Finally, with the notion of tellers, I have paid attention to the participants of a communicative activity as complex entities, as actors with social identities, as here-and-now communicators with particular in situ roles of participation (cf. *discourse identities*, Zimmerman 1998), as characters in tales (cf. Bamberg's model of positioning) and, last but not least, as individuals with specific biographies and self-projects.[2] Self-projects consist in the ways in which tellers see themselves over time through the stories they tell.

Following multi-scalar conceptualizations of context (Blommaert & Rampton 2011), I accept that there is durability, contingency and indexicality involved in all three layers above. Meaning making is not just a matter of the here-and-now, the

---

2 In Bamberg's terms (1997), the interaction between the tellers as characters in tales and as here-and-now communicators holds the key to what tellers signal as more or less stable and consistent aspects of themselves beyond the current storytelling situation; in other words, what their ethos of self and their 'consistent' biographical identities are (Johnstone 2009). As I discuss in detail elsewhere (Georgakopoulou 2013b), the triptych of ways of telling-sites-tellers productively builds on these three levels of positioning but extends them a) with the addition of the layer of sites and the ethnographically grounded understandings of who people are in specific contexts and b) with a multi-method approach that ensures access to the participants' moments of reflexivity on themselves and their stories.

intersubjectivity of the moment, but also of 'resources, expectations and experiences that originate in, circulate through and are destined for networks and processes that can be very different in their reach and duration' (idem: 9). The provenance of such resources can be signaled in more or less implicit and indirect (*indexical*, Silverstein 1985) ways. These assumptions inform the ways in which the analysis forges links between semiotic choices in local contexts and larger social identities. The assumption is that it is impossible to capture the whole of a teller's social identities. Instead, the iterativity of specific ways of telling (in this case, media engagements) in specific sites can serve as a window into what specific facets of a teller's self are presented as relatively foregrounded, durable, subject to negotiation and so on. As we will see below, the above heuristic will form a key-apparatus for the fine grain analysis of media engagements in the data and their relationship with positioning self and other.

3 (New) Media engagements-in-interaction

3.1 A survey

Peer-talk in the classroom is a broad category that content-wise includes all talk that is not 'on-task', the main task at hand being the lesson underway. Our analysis showed that of the many different things that peer-talk could have been about, a substantial part of it was about (new) media engagements. Such engagements ranged from actual uses of technologies (e.g. having the mobile phone on in class, even if officially this was not allowed) to performative enactments (e.g. singing, 'imitating' characters from TV series) and to interactional re-workings of engagements, e.g. stories about MSN interactions as well as to meta-talk: e.g. what new music video participants liked or not and why. Media engagements thus proved to be a major aspect of the students' lived experience outside of the classroom and by extension of their talk about it in the classroom.[3] By way of illustration, below is a snapshot of Nadia, a focal student, talk in class (in a lesson of Design Technology):

Min 2:   Sings Mariah Carey (*We belong together*)
Min 6:   Tells story about a text that Jerome has sent her
Min 8:   Sings line from film Miss Congeniality

---

3 As I have shown elsewhere (2011), this engagement permeated classrooms as an unmarked state of play rather than momentarily (re)defining arrangements within them. I have also discussed (idem) what its implications are for the management of the school day and the relations between teachers and students.

Min 9:   Hums same Mariah Carey song
Min 11: Tells story about communication with Jerome (again) on MSN
Min 15: Performatively enacts Danone yoghurt advertisement jingle
Min 16: Sings another line from Mariah Carey song (*who am I gonna lean on?*)
Min 17: Tells story about IM screen names

Media engagements (henceforth MEs) such as the above by and large did not relate to or complement the curriculum or the formal instruction of the moment.[4] Having established the pervasiveness of MEs in the classrooms, the first step we took towards their closer analysis was to conduct a survey that would draw out any differences amongst individuals. We examined the first 8 hours of the radio-mic recordings of 5 of our focal istudents (3 female, 2 male) in the two phases of the project (2005 and 2006; $8 \times 5 \times 2 = 80$ hrs). We identified 531 episodes[5] in which they audibly used, referred to or performed music, TV, mobiles, mp3s, PSPs, PCs, internet, electronic games, magazines, newspaper, fashion, body-care, 'recreational food' and sport. These were annotated on protocols, which recorded main participants, location, +/– physical use of (new) media object, topic, mode of performance, +/– links to classroom activity, and other relevant specifics. The survey showed that MEs averaged out at 7 an hour, but, as we can see in Table 1 below, there were differences between individuals.

3.2 Ways of telling media engagements

On the basis of the above quantitative results, I conducted a fine grain analysis of the two (female) students, (who we call) Nadia and Habibah, who produced the largest number of MEs. This involved looking into the ways of telling of MEs, which in the first instance involved their embeddedness in the surrounding talk, in particular if they were topically relevant in relation to a preceding topic or indeed the classroom instruction. I also analyzed their interactional management, namely their initiation and uptake (e.g. who initiated what and how and who responded and in what ways). As Table 2 below shows, Nadia and Habibah present significant differences in the interactional management of their MEs. Nadia not only initiates more MEs than Habibah but also, once launched into the

---

4 There were only nine episodes in 80 hours where students themselves volunteered a link between the curriculum and their MEs.
5 An episode was defined as a sequence of talk introducing and often sustaining a (new) media cultural theme, bounded by periods of talk and activity devoted to other matters. As silent media engagements (e.g. reading text-messages) might well be undetected in our radio-mic recordings, the total figure could be greater.

INFORMANT	MEs feature as a TOPIC	MEs are PERFORMED (humming, singing & mimicry)	Personal (rather than curriculum directed) use of HARDWARE/SOFTWARE	TOTAL
Nadia (f; Armenian/ African mixed race)	122	91	24	237
Habibah (f; Pakistani descent)	63	59	0	122
Husain (m; Pakistani descent)	42	12	9	63
Otis (m; African Caribbean descent, born in Jamaica)	61	5	19	85
Sairah (f.; Kurdish refugee from Iraq)	16	8	0	24
TOTAL	304	175	52	531

Table 1: Number of episodes recorded inside & outside class during 16 hrs per informant[6]

(New) media engagements are ...	Nadia (132 engagements)	Habibah (82 engagements)
... initiated by the informant	92% (121)	71%* (58)
... taken up by other participants (e.g. positively assessed, elaborated, sang along with)	93% (123)	28% (23)
... built up into stories	30% (40)	16% (13)
... topically linked to prior talk	91% (120)	5% (4)
Involvement in positive assessment sequences (e.g 'I love this song')	66% (29/44)	29% (12/42)
Involvement in negative assessment sequences (e.g. 'that's horrible')	34% (15/44)	71% (30/42)

* a lot of Habibah's initiations involved eliciting e.g. some singing from others

Table 2: Comparison of Nadia and Habibah's interactional practices around MEs in Phase 1

conversation, her MEs are largely taken up by her interlocutors and become part of the interaction. Nadia's MEs are also by and large topically linked to prior peer-talk while Habibah's aren't. As we will see below, this difference is linked with

---

6 Table reproduced from the end-of-term project report (Rampton et al 2008).

what genres of MEs the two participants tend to produce, including the number and type of stories. Nadia also serves as an assessor of other people's MEs on the basis of e.g. quality of performance (e.g. songs), good knowledge of the sources, competent uses of new media, etc. Her own contributions tend to be positively assessed, while Habibah's clearly aren't.

Let us illustrate some of these key-differences between Nadia and Habibah's MEs.

1) Participants: H(abibah), L(ily). Drama lesson has begun but the two girls are standing outside the classroom door (which is half open) despite the teacher repeatedly urging them to go in.

1 H:	d' you like *(.)* d' you like Mariah Carey's new song? um how // does it-
2. L:	// where's the light for he:re?
3. H:	//B-
4. L:	//there's darkness=
5. H:	Beau – something
6.	((teacher talking in background))
7. H:	oi
8. L:	(chewing gum)
9. H:	(there)
10. L:	//chewing gum
11. H:	oi? How does Mariah Carey's new song go?
12. L:	I don't know j- uh
13. H:	((sings)) *we belong together (.)* we belong together
14. L:	I like Gwen Stefani's new one (.) B.A.N.A N=
15 H & L:	=Banana's!
16 H:	yeah ((sings)) *cos I ain't no hollaback girl I ain't no hollaback girl*

((further down))

34 H:	how does Mariah Carey's new song go?
35 L:	(1) what abou::t//
36 H:	// I <u>love</u> that song (.) but I forgot how it //goes
37 L:	// ((sings another song)) *I steady trying to find my motive (.) motive //why I do what I done*
38 H:	//no I don't like to sing that locked up
39 L:	//*freedom aint gettin' not closer*
40 H:	//if Lonely (.) Lonely (.) I'll sing Lonely=
41 L:	=*closer no matter how far I go my car is stolen* ((laughing)) *stolen*
42 H:	((laughs))
43 L:	*so registration* ((banging noise))

((further down))

245 H: ((sings)) *I wish you were her // to sleep in your t-shirt*
246 L: // Miss (   ) cut her hair
247 H: *then we make love I sleep in your t-shirt*
248 L: I want- I wanna buy that song man=
249 H: =*Wake up in your t*-shirt *hm hm hm hm hm hm hm*
250 L: is it a white t-shirt with red on it?
251 H: I don't know=
252 L: =the actual t-shirt *(.)* cos I seen the video innit?
253 H: no there's no video to it
254 L: yeah (.) there is (.) there is?
255 H: t-shirt?
256 L: yea:h *(.)* there's videos to every song you spa:stic
257 H: yea:h (.) but it's not out yet
258 L: yeah
259 H: don't lie?
260 L: I seen it on (MTV Base   )
261 H: t-shirt?
262 L: yeah?
263 H: don't lie? oh my God I have to see that

Instances of singing or humming, more than other reworkings of MEs, tend to be non-topically relevant and more divorced from surrounding activity (people can e.g. hum to themselves). It is therefore no accident that Habibah emerged in our survey as the participant who sang more than anybody else. This is related to the fact that Habibah's MEs tended to be non-topically relevant: a song can be introduced in conversational *medias res*, without any apparent links with the preceding activity. But it is also the uptake of her MEs that is significantly reduced compared to Nadia. In the example above, Habibah's attempts to get Lily to sing her favourite song are not taken up; in Jefferson's terms, they are 'sequentially deleted' (1978). This failed elicitation along with the repeated display of lack of knowledge (*how does it go?*, lines 1,11, 34) by Habibah is a common feature in her interactional management of MEs. In contrast, Lily's initiation of two songs (l. 14, 37) is taken up by Habibah. When Habibah manages to elicit Habibah's positive assessment for her song initiation (lines 245–249), she, again, displays lack of knowledge about the video of that song. Lily's epistemic proclamation (*'there's videos to every song'*, l. 256) followed by her characterization of Habibah as *'you spastic'* (256) is also typical. Habibah is frequently cast by her friends and classmates as being 'clueless' regarding (new) media. Her lack of knowledge of specific sources frequently attracts negative assessments of this sort.

The excerpt is also illustrative of how Habibah's MEs generated some kind of trouble both interactionally, i. e. for Habibah as a here-and-now interlocutor, and as a character in stories (see 3.3 below). Trouble is a continuum concept (e.g. see Wetherell 1998) and can certainly vary in its intensity. The interactional clues of trouble are normally hesitations, self-repairs and delayed responses, which show the participants' awareness of some kind of breach of normative expectations. In this case, I employ the term trouble to refer to any more or less momentary and drastic interactional departures from normative expectations about behaviour in relation to MEs. Participants routinely display surprise or other (reflexive) orientations to the unexpectedness and markedness of such instances, flagging up gaps between what is expected and what is done.

2) Participants: N(adia), H(abibah) and S(henice). Period: Textiles.

Habibah complains about her sister stealing her MSN password. Subsequently, Habibah brags about hacking into Dylan's MSN account and "making his life hell" to which she is heavily criticized by both Nadia and Shenice for 'cussing people'.

1. N: Why (.) why was she on your MSN a:nyway?

2. H:　She knows my password (.) innit (.) I have to change my password (2) bitch=

3 N: =　You're pissed you know

4 H:　She's a bitch! She changed my screen name everything (.) she changed everything=

5 N: =　I know.

6 H:　She chats bare shit to //(　　　)

7 N:　//She goes 'ha ha (.) I changed her (Habibah's') screen name'. I goes to her (.) Habiba's not

8　　　gonna be <u>happy!</u>

9 H:　((laughs))

10 Sh: Why don't you just change your password?

11 H:　Yeah I'm gonna do that today //innit (.) I don't even have a phone (.) fuckin' hell=

12 N:　=How come?

13 H:　Not allowed (.) ((repeating parents words)) >I'm too young I'm not responsible<

14 N:　(10) how does your boyfriend contact you?=

15 H:　=Oh online innit (.) um chat to them online or like when my dad's not home ((hurried tone))

16　　　'quickly phone my house' ((laughs))

Habibah was much more involved in trouble instances than Nadia both in interactional terms and in the emplotted references to MEs which invariably reported trouble (some kind of abuse of technologies by others or herself, see 3.3. below). We can see both of these kinds of trouble in the above excerpt. Here, I will discuss lines 10–16, one of the many instances where Habibah talks about her lack of access to certain technologies. Habibah is not allowed access to a mobile phone by her father who is elsewhere described by her as 'messed up' for policing her mediated interactions (e.g. on MSN). The delayed response by Nadia (10 secs, l. 4) to Habibah's evaluative reference to her lack of a mobile phone (l. 11) suggests how marked not having a phone is for Nadia. Notably, her daily life and that of her peer-group are new media-saturated.

One of the most important indicators of Nadia's key-leading role in the arena of media engagements is her interactions with the teachers.[7] There are very few instances when the teachers step into peer-talk in order to police it. In tune with this, there are also few cases when the teachers attempt to join in, thus momentarily switching from their official roles as teachers and in effect bystanders of the peer-talk to more informal and symmetrical roles as fellow interlocutors or 'peers' with the students. As the examples below show, in these cases, Nadia tended to display resistance: this was done by her correcting or negatively assessing the teachers' contributions, thus turning the tables on the officially dictated formal instruction arrangements which place the teacher in the role of assessor and the students in the role of the assessed.

3) Participants: Nadia, Shenice, Basheera, Mr Vaston. The girls discuss the group 'Destiny's Child' and their teacher, Mr Vaston, joins in the conversation.

1 B:	((Hums tune to Destiny's Child, 'Lose My Breath'))
2 N:	I hate that song (.) I love to dance to it (.) but I hate the song!
3 B:	Yeah I know (.) but it's – the video's heavy though (put it out)
4 Mr V:	are you two talking about Destiny's Child?
5 B:	yeah.
6 Mr V:	no::: Nelly is the best
7 B:	(don't) you //like them?
8 N:	//Kelly
9 Mr V:	Nel//ly
10 N:	//there's no Nelly (in it)
11 B:	((in sing-song voice)) Kelly ((laughs))

We can see how Nadia corrects Mr Vaston's erroneous reference to one of the singers in Destiny's Child as Nelly. Basheera clearly has the chance to do so (l. 7), but she does not. In similar vein, in the excerpt below, it is again Nadia who takes the teacher on, in the whole class discussion, about his reference to the London radio station Kiss.

4) Participants: N(adia), L(aura) and Mr T(urner)

1 Mr T:	Failing that we can just say (.) hey lets listen to (1) whatever radio stations you listen to (.)
2	Kiss one hundred ((100))

---

7 Although Nadia was the informant most frequently involved in media engagements episodes (c. 15 episodes per hour), she was seldom challenged or reprimanded by teachers, and she was also the highest school-achiever among our informants.

3 N: OH GOD! who listens to Kiss↑
4 Mr T: I don't
5 N: Good (.) it's rubbish ((sings)) *Kiss one hundred*
((inaudible multiple speakers))
6 Mr T: no listen (   ) this morning I was listening to Heart one ou six two ((106.2))
7 N: ((sings)) *Heart one ou six point two*
((further down))
14 Mr T: cos when it came through (.) no cos when it came through I was the same age as
         you Husain
15 H:?   (a:h you're lying)
16 Mr T: The very first song that they did was you're the one that I want=
17 N: ((sings)) *you're the one that I want (.) you are the one the one ooh ooh ooh honey*
18 Mr T: (they played all the songs   ) they did boogie oogie oogie (.) d' you
         know that
19   one?
20 N: How does it go? HOW DOES IT GO?
21 Mr T: ((sings)) *get down boogie oogie oogie*
22 N: OH GOD ple:ase stop↓
23 Mr T: (   ) I had big big frilly hair

Nadia here too enacts a gate-keeping role by negatively assessing the teacher's media engagement in unmitigated terms (l. 5) and eliciting a performative enactment of a song from the teacher, only to assess it negatively (l. 22). The teacher's subsequent reference to his '*big, frilly hair*' (23) in the past can be taken as a display of (past) qualities of being trendy, an attempt to produce his past credentials and participation in the popular culture which in the current context seems to be monopolized by Nadia (primarily) and the other students.[8]

Nadia does this sort of gatekeeping of MEs vis-à-vis her classmates too, both in the peer conversations and in the interviews. In the excerpt below, she employs a knowingly cryptic reference while talking about UK celebrities Jordan and Jodie Marsh: 'smart ones will get that joke' (l. 17). The term 'smart' is recurrent in association with media engagements. 'Smart' and its opposite 'stupid' are frequently employed to refer to (in)competence and knowledge (or not) in the area of MEs.

5) Playback interview with N(adia), Sh(enice) and L(aura)

1 I: So why do you think people want to be famous?=
2 N: like Jordan and Jodie Marsh? I don't give them any ratings at all!=
3 Sh: =ne//ver

<hr>

8 Elsewhere, Nadia suggests that she listened to Kiss when she was three and calls a friend who confesses listening to Kiss 'sissy'. Shenice who frequently acts as a teller-aide for Nadia, also suggests in the playback interview, that 'white people no offense would listen to Kiss'.

4 L: // mm-mm
5 N: they're famous because //they have
6 L: did you see her wedding ring?
7 N: who?
8 L: //Jordan
9 Sh: //no I didn't see it
10 L: that was lovely=
11 N: =oh she wore that little mini thing innit (.) urgh:: ((tuts))
12 Sh: she DI:D?
13 N: yeah (.) she wore that little dress with the little-
14 L: ((laughing)) d'you know how much Peter Andre was crying oh my-
15 Sh: why?
16 N: cos he always thought (.) he always thought (.) s-he was gonna get married
17   to the mysterious girl under the waterfall ((giggles)) (.) smart ones will get that joke.

To sum up so far, Nadia in her MEs emerges as somebody who engages in productive referencing. She is an initiator, an assessor and a recipient of positive assessments. Her MEs are taken up. She displays recognition, competence, and knowledge. It is worth noting here that throughout the interactional data, Nadia displays a propensity for: creatively reworking stock phrases and one liners from films and TV series; stylizing media references and being asked by other participants to produce performative enactments of e.g. characters from films, etc. She is also never caught not-knowing in the very frequent quizzes in the local context about who sings what, who appears in which video, etc. In contrast, Habibah tends to be non-productive in her MEs. She is an elicitor rather than an initiator and when she initiates, her referencing is non-topically relevant nor is it taken up. She negatively self-assesses and is negatively assessed for her MEs. She displays non-recognition, lack of knowledge & access and her MEs frequently generate interactional trouble and/or report some kind of trouble in stories.

I have shown elsewhere (2011) that more than an illicit, side activity, MEs in peer-talk seem to have developed, in Bourdieu's terms, in a social field that carries a lot of symbolic capital for the participants (1986: 176ff) and that tends to resist regulation or appropriation from the teachers. On that basis, their common discursive re-working in the classroom becomes an activity in which participation or lack of it has real implications for their roles within the peer-group. Rather than being egalitarian, social fields are arenas for the struggle over resources. From this point of view, we can assume that the above differences between Nadia and Habibah get drawn into their peer-group roles and relations but are also important constituents of their self-projects. Below, I will show how this is the case.

3.3 Small stories of new media engagements: Routines and transgressions

A significant number of both Nadia's and Habibah's NMEs were in the form of small stories: 45 % in Nadia's case and 37 % in Habibah's. These stories were mostly reports of recent mediated interactions (e.g., on MSN, on myspace) of the participants with boys they were interested in. In fact, Nadia told on average 12 such stories per period. I have called such stories *breaking news* and defined them as stories of very recent ('yesterday') and/or still happening ('just now') events that routinely lead to the need for further narrative making with frequent *updates* on the evolving events and/or *projections* (stories of events to take place in the near future). Stories have been focal in the study of identities and have been widely held as a unique mode of communication for constructing self (e.g. for an overview see chapter 6 in De Fina and Georgakopoulou 2011). Several studies have demonstrated how the telling of stories can afford numerous opportunities for interactionally positioning self and other in multiple scenarios that are revealing of how the tellers perceive themselves and others and what they deem as in/ appropriate behaviour and action (e.g. Bamberg & Georgakopoulou 2008; Schiffrin 1996). Such positionings are to be found in, among others, the narrators as characters in their tales, in what stories are told and how. In the data at hand, the stories' plot shows the importance of new media as arenas for reportable experiences and relational work in the participants' daily lives. As characters in tales, Habibah and Nadia present largely opposing positionings: Habibah frequently reports trouble in her stories of NMEs , as we will see below. Nadia on the other hand emerges as somebody who participates actively in new media sites and develops a web of sociabilites: she is the one who is 'contacted' (texted, called, asked to chat on MSN, etc.) as opposed to being 'blanked'. The following example is typical of this.

6) Participants: N(adia), S(henice). Period 1, Design Technology

1. N: Oh how can yesterday yeah
2.   I was like who is my boo WHO is my boo
3.   (   ) (canine) d-dum
4.   Andy (.) d-dum
5.   Jack (.) d-dum
6.   All of them yeah
7. S: Mm
8. S: [your face you're like]
    ((further down))
9. N: Today yeah (2) I put them all in a conversation together and I wrote hi
10.   everyone started writing hi innit?
11.   yeah (.) and all you see is

12.	>I'm your boo I'm your boo I'm your boo I'm your boo< I'm your boo
13.	in all different kinda writing though (.)
14.	like (.) >capitals not capitals some capitals not capitals< get me
15.	and it was so: funny (.) I was like ((laughs))
16. S:	Ra boy
17. N:	Urgh man Nee keeps saying that I'm his future wifey
18. S:	That's disgusting
19. N:	No it isn't
20. S:	[Who's Knee?]
21. N:	Knee as in Knee cap?
22. S:	[Yeah (.) who's that?]
23. N:	[One boy that lives in] Hampstead
24. S:	[( )]
25. N:	[He's funny]No: he usually-
26.	I'll tell him to come see me in Kilburn star
27.	Yeah (.) he's always in Kilburn
28.	Yeah he's like (.) look at this picture of my beautiful (.) future wifey
29.	And he show- (.) he put a picture of me >and I was like< (1)
30.	are you mad a- you have seen me ri:ght?
31.	he's like yea:h >I was like< (.)
32.	Where does the beautiful come into it? ((giggles))
33.	He's like [oo:::::::::h]
34. S:	[Don't say that] Nadia
35. N:	Just agree with me!
36. S:	No:
37. N:	Just AGREE!=
38. S:	=Okay (.) fine
39. N:	Tha:nk you.

As we can see, in her mediated interactions, Nadia assumes and is ascribed a variety of positive online roles and attributes (e.g. beautiful, Excerpt 7, line 28) that are nonetheless not divorced from her everyday offline roles and relationships. For instance, the use of the kinship term 'future wifey' (Excerpt 7, line 28) is suggestive of a developing relationship between the male character and Nadia, as our ethnography attested to. Furthermore, Nadia is frequently seen and talked about as 'beautiful' by her friends and interlocutors, but as in the story above, this is put in the mouths of other characters in Nadia's tales and echoed by her interlocutors in the here-and-now of the storytelling situation. As studies have shown (for a discussion see Georgakopoulou 2007), inserting positive attributes about the teller in the taleworld can be an effective means for positive self-presentation in the here-and-now.

Participation in new media sites and ability to operate in them was highly valued by all the different social networks in the school, as our ethnography attested to. In the girls' peer groups such participation was intimately linked with notions of popularity.[9] Two-thirds of Nadia's breaking news stories reported social networking that brings self-enhancement but 75% of Habibah's stories reported *transgressions*, such as incidents of improprieties in relation to the use of new media (e.g. hacking, stealing people's account details, etc.). For the two girls, new media sites operated to different degrees as arenas filled with opportunities for socialization particularly in terms of hetero-sociality, but also as worlds that pose risk to personal well being and safety and that can bring 'trouble' in their personal lives.

If we go back to excerpt 2 about Habibah's sister stealing her MSN password, we can see how stories of trouble are frequently accompanied by negative attributes about the characters in the taleworld. Habibah's sister's reported transgression attracts negative evaluations from Habibah ('she's a bitch' line 4, 'she chats bare shit', line 6). The interlocutors collude in such assessments but at the same time, their feedback is typical of the interactional drafting of such stories, as I will discuss below. For instance, Shenice's suggestion that Habibah change her password (line 10) puts the onus on Habibah to protect herself from this and other possible transgressions. Similarly, as I have already argued, Habibah's admission that she does not own a mobile phone (line 11) because 'she is not allowed one' (line 13) is received as a marked and dispreferred response (Pomerantz 1984), as the significantly long pause of 10 seconds by Nadia in line 14 suggests. Nadia's and Shenice's feedback to Habibah's transgression lead to the realization that the main mode of communication between Habibah and her boyfriend is online, which makes the impact of her sister stealing her MSN account even more severe in Habibah's everyday life.

How participants deal with the transgressive behaviour directed at them tends to be the main talking point generated during the telling of such stories. The collaborative formulations and assessments of the events make relevant notions of personal accountability, knowledge and competence in new media, as arenas where the onus is on the teller to manage and avoid any inappropriate behaviour directed against them: little contestation or feedback is provided on the actual inappropriateness of the events and actions reported. Instead, it is the agentive courses of action that the teller ought to have undertaken that were discussed, as can see in and debated. This applies to Nadia's transgressions too. The excerpt below is from a story about Nadia's face-pic having been stolen and put

---

9 Our data pre-date Twitter and the Facebook explosion but the notions of new media popularity that we found to be operative in our study are readily compatible with the concepts of followership and the high number of friends on Facebook as indicators of networking esteem.

on various sites without her permission.[10] Miranda's contribution is typical of the feedback that this and other transgressions tend to receive.

7) Participants: M(iranda), N(adia)

> 55 M(iranda): Don't trust anyone (with)
> 56 N(adia): I don't trust (.) I don't send my pictures to <u>no one</u> (.) only my // bredrins
> 57 M: / /So how did he get it (.) he's / /( )
> 58 N: / / Cos he STOLE it
> 59 M: ((inaudible))
> 60 N: yeah it was my display picture (.) and he stole it> copy and pasted it everywhere< and put it=
> 61 M: = No no (.) the stealer programme ain't you got that? I have that=
> 62 N: =no but I can still take you lots' picture (.) you don't need // no pro-
> 63 M: / /How?
> 64 N: Just (.) click screen innit
> 65 M: Is it a // nice one?

We can see here how the onus is placed on Nadia protecting herself. But Nadia constructs expertise in technologies by counter-acting Miranda's suggestion that she use a specific programme for protection (l. 62, 64). In contrast, Habibah in excerpt 2 seemed to be unable to act upon the feedback provided to her due to lack of access to a mobile phone. As I will show below, Nadia and Habibah also differ in how they reflect on their stories of transgressions.

3.4 Ways of telling and sites as windows into the tellers of media engagements

3.4.1 Situated identities

NMEs connect with sites in two ways: one pertains to the tales, that is, the world of the stories about NMEs, and the other pertains to the here and now. Within the tale, new media sites, as we have seen, provide the productive settings of plots and create the characters' social worlds. This is where the tellers present both themselves as characters and other characters in the dual capacity of agentive and epistemic selves (cf. Bruner 1990): as individuals who undertake more or less appropriate actions that in turn shape and are shaped by their feelings, thoughts and beliefs. As studies of storytelling have demonstrated (Georgakopoulou 1997; Schiffrin 1996), there are many meaningful associations to be made between how tellers present themselves in their stories and how they wish to be perceived in

---

10 For the full storytelling event and a detailed discussion of it see Georgakopoulou 2013a).

the here-and-now of their telling. Within the telling situation, MEs shape the classroom site as a polycentric space (Blommaert, Collins and Slembrouck 2005), where peer-talk occupies a very important position alongside whole class instruction. One useful heuristic for analytically tapping into the interconnections between ways of telling and sites comes from Zimmerman's (1998) mapping of local interactional identities onto larger social identities. In his terms, *discourse identities,* which encompass the local participation roles in a given interaction, coalesce with specific *situated identities.* These link the local activity with the affordances or constraints of a specific social setting (e.g. an institution, p.94). From this point of view, the expectation in the data would be that the participants' situated identities would be in the form of an 'identity set', that is, teacher-student, with different permutations, e.g. a good student, a bad student, a disciplined student, etc., coming into play in a particular situation. Nonetheless, as we have seen, the students' discourse identities are shaped by media engagements, which make other situated identities relevant in the multi-space of the classroom. These situated identities include that of a friend, a member of a peer-group and a popular and new media culture user, consumer, connoisseur. These identities, as we saw, also pertain to the tellers as characters in their stories. In Zimmerman's terms (1998), situated identities propose to interlocutors how they should understand the relevance of a given exchange and what kinds of things they should expect in the ensuing discussion (89). They also provide a glimpse of which 'transportable' identities, that is, identities that the speakers *bring along* with them to any interaction (e.g. gender, age, ethnicity) but not necessarily *bring about,* may be relevant in a given exchange.

If we apply the above to Nadia's and Habibah's differences in their discourse and situated identities around MEs, we can note how they link to their profiles and positions in the peer-group prestige hierarchy (cf. Georgakopoulou 2008). Through our ethnography, Nadia emerged as the leading figure in the popular girls' group in the class. This popularity was multi-faceted and included aspects that the participants audibly oriented to or were in a position to reflect on in interviews, such as her looks[11], the way she wore her uniform[12], her taste in music, her 'smart' uses of new media, the fact that she was 'liked' by boys. We can speculate about the importance of other factors, e.g. the fact that her family allowed exten-

---

11 Mixed-race looks both for boys and for girls appeared to be the most aspired to in the school under study.
12 Nadia wore trousers and she pulled them very low in her waist, which was clearly the 'cool' way of wearing the school uniform.

sive access to new media (MSN/internet/mobiles) or that she had an older brother in the same school and could socialize with older kids and be protected by them. In contrast, Habibah maintained rather fraught relationships in a relatively isolated and ethnically insulated girls' group, which comprised girls of Indian or Pakistani origin.[13] Their family environments imposed many constraints, including not allowing any relationships with boys and, as we saw above, restricting access to new technologies. Habibah's lack in popularity was profoundly shaped by the fact that, as we saw above, she was a follower rather than a leader in popular and media culture, with tastes that were sometimes mocked. Habibah struggled with the categorisations 'fat' and 'ugly'; and was generally unsuccessful with boys, despite strenuously seeking their attention. A factor that may have inadvertently made Habibah's daily life at school trickier and contributed to her lack of socializing was that she was academically weak and frequently disciplined by teachers.

3.4.2 Reflections

As I have suggested, one aspect of our multi-method approach involved capturing orientations to normative expectations in moments of participants' reflexivity both in local interactions and in situations in which they are asked to produce their own commentary on their communication practices. What was notable in such moments was that the individual's ability to handle new media competently and knowledgeably so as to avoid and manage any breachings of norms emerged as highly valued. Exactly as in the interactional management of media engagements in the classroom data, a premium was placed on the individual being able to act in a 'smart' way in new media so as to maximize opportunities for socialization while at the same time managing trouble and transgressions. Nadia's and Habibah's interviews both attest to this in different ways. As we have seen, even in the case of transgressions, Nadia presents herself as somebody who ultimately manages trouble and who forms a strategy for dealing with comparable situations in the future. This is done in the actual tellings of the stories with Nadia's attempts to formulate generic scenarios out of the individual events. But it is also done in reflexive environments that are temporally removed from the events and their telling. When asked to listen again to their stories of new media engagements and reflect on them, Nadia positioned herself as somebody who had formed a strategy for dealing with comparable situations in the future. Con-

---

13 Ethnically-inflected discriminatory terms, such as 'freshie' and 'Paki' were frequently employed against Habibah and her friends by other students.

sider Nadia's response to the story about her face-pic having been stolen, when played back to her by Lauren, the fieldworker, in the playback interview session:

9) Playback interview session with Nadia

```
1    L(auren): alright I'll just play the next one (.) and I've got some questions for you ok?
2          So this is just the next bit ((extract played))
3    N(adia): seriously (.) I sound like a man
4    L:   but how do people get your pictures then?
5    N:   O:h (.) they're my friends (.) I send it to them.
6    L:   Okay//
7    N:   But //only p- I don't sent my picture to just anyone  (5 seconds)
8    L:   Okay if you go on websites and stuff (.) do you put your pictures// on
9    N:   I put my picture on one of my friend's website (.) and then bare people stole it (0.5)
10   L:   Okay.
11   N:   And like some girl was claiming she was me (.) an – cos someone goes to me oh
12        (.) one of my friends said to me (.) this girl's saying she's you and I was like
13        WHAT? and then this boy added me (.) and I didn't know who he was
14   L:   right=
15   N:   =and he goes (.) is that you in the picture (.) and I said yeah
16   L:   mhmmm
17   N:   and this is him (.) why are you lying for (.) cos that's my firiend Sherelle (.)
18        I said WHAT? I SAID DON'T CHAT RUBBISH (.) she was like yeah
19        he goes yea:h that's her innit? but then – and then he goes (.) here's her email
20        if you wanna talk to her (.) I looked at the email and I already knew who she was
21   L:   Oh (.) // okay
22   N:   // So I was like (.) why is this girl beggin it for (.)and then she got boyed off funny
          though                                                     min 8.33
((further down)) min 16.45
188  L:   okay let me ask you a bit more about face pic and stuff then (.) because we are
189       talking about what you do (.) or how you know people are who they say they are
190       so if you find out someone's using false information (.) what do you do about
191       that?
192  N:   you boy them off (.) you make them cry (.) and then you >block and delete
193       them< and say don't ever talk – chat to me again
194  L:   so how do you go – how do you do that then?
195  N:   what? boy them off?
196  L:   yeah
197  N:   cuss them down
198  L:   okay
```

We can see above how between Nadia's first telling of the events and her reflections on it, Nadia has formulated a generic scenario for dealing with comparable transgressions that involves 'blocking and deleting', 'boying off' and 'cussing down' culprits. The recurrence and idiomaticity of the lexical choices for the recommended course of action attests to a level of crystallization in it. The generic course of action also seems to suggest that Nadia has attempted to manage risk in new media environments. This is in line with other reflexive choices of Nadia regarding transgressions where she positions herself as somebody who can move from having been exposed to risk to re-claiming agency in navigating that risk. In contrast to this, in her playback interview, Habibah displays uncertainty and lack of familiarity with new media in general and appropriate conduct in them in particular. She is also positioned by her friends who are being co-interviewed as lacking in 'smart' behaviour in new media sites.

10) Playback interview session with H(abibah), L(ily) and M(assuda)

```
1   I(interviewer): Ok so how do people get your MSN addresses and //stuff like that?
2   H:   //oh I put mine on Hi-Five=
3   L:   =what's Hi five?
4   H:   it's like – um this uh (.) thing yeah? you can upload pictures and meet new people
         there
5   I:   ok so how did you get on that?
6   M:   //I sent (.) I sent her
7   H:   //(I want um)
8   L:   I just went on the // website
9   M:   // cos I'm on it but I'm not an idiot (.) and I don't put my email address on it but SHE
         does=
10  L:   =Peter does
11  M:   =(Peter) some people do //because it's SAD
12  H:   //some people NO they're not sad (.) they want to meet new people and I- I
13       met bare people yea:h?
```

In the above excerpt, the interviewer seeks Habibah's reflections on stories of transgression involving people stealing her personal details online, as we saw in excerpt 2. When Habibah is selected by the interviewer as the recipient of the question of how she got on Hi-Five (line 5), Massuda self-selects to respond by saying that it was she who sent Habibah the details (line 6). Habibah's friends frequently claim introducing Habibah into new media sites. In line 9, Massuda sets up an explicit contrast between her own 'smart' behaviour (I'm not stupid) on Hi-Five and Habibah's ('but she does'). Picking up on Lilly's mitigation of this criticism of Habibah (line 10) and Masuda's upholding of it (line 11), Habibah goes on to diffuse her own responsibility for incompetent use of new media by talking in third parties terms (some people NO they're not sad (.) they want to meet new people, line 12). When she moves away from this generic discourse to first person narration (line 13, I met bare people), she shifts emphasis from her own accountability to the people who conduct themselves in inappropriate ways using the evaluative attribution 'bare', which we discussed above. This positioning of remaining the victim is very different to Nadia's agentive positioning of developing strategies for managing transgressions, which we saw above.

3.4.3 Positionings of girlpower and girl (in) trouble

What sorts of transportable identities do the above positionings make –more or less indirectly- relevant? Nadia and Habibah operate in MEs as girls of a specific age and with specific regulations from adults, be their parents or teachers, interacting with boys, getting in trouble with boys etc., and so to suggest that gender (in its co-articulations with other identities, such as ethnicity and age) is relevant in these cases seems to me to be a rather uncontroversial statement to make. What is more notable however is that Nadia's and Habibah's gendered engagements with the media, particularly the new media, present distinct resonances with discourses about new femininities and meanings that converge around them in a variety of public and policy domains (e.g. the press, schools, parents). Cultural studies analysts who have proposed new femininities as characteristic of the '90s and beyond in the UK contemporary life (e.g. Harris 2004; McRobbie 2007) have claimed that they have marked a shift from earlier (e.g. in the 70s) positionings of young women as invisible and peripheral in the youth culture towards the emergence of young women in the spheres of leisure, consumption practices and employment as agentive, pleasure-seeking individuals who find their place and voice in the new world order, take their destiny in their hands and assert their presence in the new times. This new category of young womanhood is associated with capacity, success, attainment, enjoyment, fun and entitlement. The terms which are often employed to refer to these changing modes of femininity are indicative of a changed engagement with the social world not just on the part of (young) women but also on the part of feminist scholarship: new femininities (McRobbie 1991), 'can do girl' (Harris 2004), 'third wave feminism', 'post-feminism'. These changes have been closely associated in the literature with late modernity and the explosion in the '90s of rave/club culture, young women's magazine readership, fashion, girl bands such as the Spice Girls, etc. (see Hollands 1995).

Two largely competing discourses have been claimed to describe best the lived experience of contemporary young women (in the Anglo-American world), that of 'girlpower' and of 'girls at risk' (Aapola et al 2005; Harris 2004). Girlpower epitomizes the 'can do girl' culture and the new femininities as described above, suggesting to young women that they can get what they want and do what they want. 'Girls at risk' on the other hand articulates a set of moral and social concerns in relation to young women such as teenage pregnancy and sexually transmitted diseases, drug taking, involvement in crime, and more recently, risks from the use of new media. The two discourses are by no means completely separable or unrelated: As Gonick (2006) suggests, moral panics focusing on out-of-control girls can be seen as expressions of anxiety concerning the changing position of young women in society. Furthermore, girlpower and girl at risk should not be seen as orthogonal. Instead, they can be assumed to co-exist and be inhabited by the same woman in the same interaction, etc. (Kehily 2008). As Kehily puts it, 'we can see them as subject positions available across a range of social sites' and intersecting with class-based and other identities (62). Their intermingling is increasingly being documented in studies that see new media as environments for 'taking risky opportunities' (Livingstone 2008) for young people, young women in particular.

Another note of caveat has to do with a considerable backlash regarding new femininities. Feminist scholarship has increasingly been alive to the realization that the girlpower representations may also regulate and oppress women and the earlier over-celebration of the pleasures of the can do girl have been giving way to a more balanced view of what tensions or pains may be involved for young women (e.g. Kehily 2008; McRobbie 2007). Within popular culture and (new) media in particular, there is evidence of a continued objectification of young women and their bodies at times co-opted by a neo-liberal and girl-powered pressure for girls to self-disclose, to present themselves in public and digital arenas as confident, 'sexy' and 'available' (e.g. Dobson 2012; Gill 2007).

With all the above qualifications in mind, the discourses of girlpower and girls at risk are readily identifiable in the MEs of Nadia and Habibah, with girlpower and the 'can do' girl being more prevalent in Nadia's case and with the risk and trouble elements being more pronounced in Habibah's positionings, as I showed above. Nadia in particular, as we saw, seems to be able to move from a positioning of having exposed herself to risk to a positioning of re-claiming agency in navigating that risk. We also saw how we can identify elements of these discourses in the interactional management of NMEs and the values of the local social network.

The convergence of new femininities with the active consumption of NMEs that emerges in the data is an under-researched configuration. As Kearney (2013) remarks, even though the digital revolution has been part of young women's active participation in the changing late modern landscape, it remains "a considerably understudied component of contemporary female youth culture" (p. 4). There are however two notable observations in the scarce research that both connect with the findings of this study and make the need for further studies imperative. The first is that empowerment discourse features have very frequently accompanied media education programmes for girls (e.g. for American girls in the late 1990s). These have combined with an emphasis on how girls can protect protecting themselves from media representations that will affect their self-esteem (idem: 124).

The other observation concerns the (earlier) association of new technologies with stereotypical notions of masculine identities which cast the girls as technically ignorant (idem). In this respect, the emphasis of the local social networks in this study on competent and smart NMEs can be seen as closely associated with the counter-discourses of new girlhood that have departed from some of the core stereotypes of feminine identities (e.g. technical ignorance). The findings of this study also connect with another growing line of inquiry. The internet was initially seen as a transformative space for the performance of femininity, within a liberal and girl-powered milieu. There is a move away however from such celebratory views towards more measured and empirically grounded studies of the pressures and constraints that the participation and self-representation of girls in digital media may be posing (e.g. Dobson 2012). This study can advance our understanding of this with its focus on how girls' NMEs, can impact on their everyday, offline, positionings and roles within their friendship groups.

4 Concluding remarks

Having as its starting point the increasing importance of MEs in the daily lives of adolescents, this chapter has focused on the interactional (re)constructions of MEs in the school-based interactions of students in a London comprehensive school. Our initial finding that MEs, in particular NMEs, permeated classrooms, was further substantiated by a survey of the focal students. On its basis, a fine-grain analysis was conducted for the MEs of two female focal participants. The analysis drew on the heuristic of ways of telling-sites-tellers, developed as part of small stories research, as a practice-based paradigm for social interaction and identities analysis. Two interactional instances of MEs were found to be salient: a) talk that interactionally make relevant issues of knowledge, access to, recognition and approval or lack of one another's MEs and b) small stories about NMEs. Nadia and Habibah were found to differ significantly with respect to the ways of telling both these instances of MEs. Nadia's MEs were interactionally ratified and positively assessed while she too appeared to take on assessing positions vis-à-vis her interlocutors' MEs. Her stories positioned Nadia as a prolific and knowledgeable user of new media. In contrast, Habibah's MEs foregrounded her lack of competence in uses and familiarity with sources and her experiences of trouble. They also tended not to be taken up so as to create topics of relevance within local interactions. I argued that media-related situated identities were paramount in the classrooms and at the expense of officially designated identities such as that of a student. As a result, positive positionings around media-related identities carried a lot of symbolic capital for the participants. Such positionings involved the tellers actively participating in and telling stories about new media environments, about how they cater to their relational enhancement in them, and about how they manage risk and trouble. The joint construction of breaking news stories in particular involved shaping norms and expectations about (im)propriety in such environments. Concepts of regulation, risk and trouble around NMEs were focal considerations in the peer groups of the particular school. The positioning of an empowered, knowledgeable and competent self in relation to new media environments was highly valued. As I showed, for Nadia, MEs entailed a predominantly empowering discourse about self that stressed networking and enhanced sociability, while in Habibah's case, regulation featured prominently, with much more emphasis on lack of access, risk and prohibition. In this respect, both girls' media-related positionings appeared to be resonant with the socio-cultural context of young women's new femininities and the freedom but also the constraints and the dilemmas that they are associated with. In this respect, the differences between the two girls should not be over-stressed. Rather than serving as dichotomous choices for Nadia and Habibah and their friendship groups, girl-power and risk and trouble are implicated in the stories and interactional management of NMEs in varying ways and to varying degrees, resulting in contingent, more or less affiliations with one or the other.

The above findings provide evidence for how knowledge, expertise and forms of participation associated with instances of MEs are inextricable parts of individuals' identities. MEs prove to serve as major structuring forces in peer-group interactions, shaping the individuals' distinct sense of self within these arenas that includes their sense of heterosociability, their ethical scenarios about how to display oneself and their social relations inside and outside of school.

Further studies can usefully draw on this study's methodology and build on and extend the remit of its findings by exploring (new) media engagements as a site for individual struggle or self-enhancement, posing specific challenges or providing opportunities to individuals for aligning with specific micro-cultures, for finding a voice or having their voice stifled, for making certain voices more hearable and more widely available than others (see Shuman 2005). There is also scope for exploring what kinds of new communication practices in individual students and in their peer groups are more or less directly associated with MEs, in particular with social media engagements[14] which have exploded, since the empirical work for this study was conducted.

---

14 As Boyd remarks with reference to the popularity of social networking sites among adolescents, they provide 'teens with a space to work out identity and status, make sense of cultural clues, and negotiate public life' (2007: 18).

References

Aapola, S., M. Gonick and A. Harris 2005: *Young femininity, girlhood, power and social change*. Basingstoke: Palgrave.

Agha, A. 2007: *Language and social relations*. Cambridge: Cambridge University Press.

Bamberg, M. 1997: Positioning between structure and performance. *Journal of Narrative and Life History 7*, 1–4: 335–342.

Bamberg, M. 2006: Stories: big or small? Why do we care? *Narrative Inquiry* 16: 147–155.

Bamberg, M. and A. Georgakopoulou.: 2008: Small stories as a new perspective in narrative and identity analysis. *Text & Talk* 28: 377–396.

Bird, E. 2003: *The Audience In Everyday Life: Living In A Media World*. New York: Routledge.

Blommaert, J., J. Collins and S. Slembrouck 2005: *Polycentricity* and interactional regimes in "global neighborhoods". *Ethnography* 6: 205–235.

Blommaert, J. and B. Rampton 2011: Language and superdiversity: A position paper. *Working Papers in Urban Language and Literacies* 70. At www.kcl.ac.uk/ldc (Last accessed: 30/06/2012).

Bourdieu, P. 1986: The forms of capital. In: J. G. Richardson., *Handbook of Theory and Research for the Sociology of Capital*, 241–258. New York: Greenwood Press.

Briggs, C. 1998: Notes on a 'confession': On the construction of gender, sexuality, and violence in an infanticide case. *Pragmatics* 7: 519–546.

Boyd, D. 2007: Why youth (heart) social network sites: the role of networked publics in teenage social life. In: D. Buckingham (ed.), *MacArthur Foundation Series on Digital Learning – Youth, Identity, and Digital Media Volume*, 119–142. Cambridge, MA: MIT Press.

Bruner, J. 1990: *Acts of meaning*. Cambridge, MA: Harvard University Press.

De Fina, A. A. and Georgakopoulou 2011: *Analyzing Narrative: Discourse and Sociolinguistic Perspectives*. Cambridge: Cambridge University Press.

Dobson, A. S. 2012: Unpacking performative shamelessness and viewer dismissal in Australian young women's social network site self-representations: protective shields for young women in the online post-feminist context? *Paper presented to the Conference on Girls and Digital Culture, King's College London, 13–14 September 2012*.

Georgakopoulou, A. 1997: *Narrative performances. A study of Modern Greek storytelling*. Amsterdam/Philadelphia: John Benjamins.

Georgakopoulou, A. 2007: *Small stories, interaction and identities*. Amsterdam/Philadelphia: John Benjamins.

Georgakopoulou, A. 2008: 'On MSN with buff boys' Self- and other-identity claims in the context of small stories. *Journal of Sociolinguistics* 12: 597–626.

Georgakopoulou, A. 2011: Teachers, students and ways of telling in classroom sites: A case of out of (work)place identities. In: J. Angouri and M. Marra (eds.), *Constructing identities at work*, 155–178. London: Palgrave.

Georgakopoulou, A. 2013a: Narrative analysis and CMC. In: S. Herring, D. Stein and T. Virtanen (eds.), *Handbook of the Pragmatics of CMC*, 695–716. Berlin/Boston: Mouton de Gruyter.

Georgakopoulou, A. 2013b: Storytelling on the go: Breaking news stories as a travelling narrative genre. In: M. Hatavara, L.-C. Hydén and M. Hyvärinen (eds.), *The Travelling Concepts of Narrative*, 201–224. Amsterdam/Philadelphia: John Benjamins.

Gill, R. 2007: *Gender and the media*. Cambridge: Polity Press.

Gonick, M. 2006: Between 'girl power' and 'reviving Ophelia': constituting the neoliberal subject. *National Association of Women's Studies Journal* 18: 1–23.

Hanks, W. 1996: *Language and communicative practices*. Boulder, CO: Westview Press.

Harris, A. 2004: *Future girl*. London: Routledge.

Hollands, R. 1995: *Friday night, Saturday night: youth cultural identification in the post industrial city*. Newcastle upon Tyne: The University of Newcastle upon Tyne.

Jefferson, G. 1978: Sequential aspects of storytelling in conversation. In: J. Schenkein (ed.), *Studies in the organisation of conversational interaction*, 219–249. New York: Academic Press.

Johnstone, B. 2009: Stance, style, and the linguistic individual. In: A. Jaffe (ed.), *Stance. Sociolinguistic perspectives*, 29–52. Oxford: Oxford University Press.

Kearney, M.C. 2013: *Girls make media*. Abingdon/New York: Routledge.

Kehily, M.J. 2008: Taking centre stage? Girlhood and the contradictions of femininity across three generations. *Girlhood Studies* 1: 51–71.

Livingstone, S. 2008: Taking risky opportunities in youthful content creation: teenagers use of social networking sites for intimacy, privacy and self-expression. *New Media & Society* 10(3): 393–411.

McRobbie, A. 1991: *Feminism and youth culture: From Jackie to just seventeen*. London: McMillan.

McRobbie, A. 2007: *Post-feminist disorders? Culture, gender and social change*. London: Sage.

Moores, S. 2000: *Media and everyday life in modern society*. Edinburgh: Edinburgh University Press.

Pomerantz, A. 1984: Agreeing and disagreeing with assessments: Some features of preferred/dispreferred turn shapes. In: J. M. Atkinson and J. Heritage (eds.), *Structures of Social Action*, 57–101. Cambridge: Cambridge University Press.

Rampton, B. 2006: *Language in Late Modernity. Interaction in an Urban School*. Cambridge: Cambridge University Press.

Rampton, B. 2007: Linguistic ethnography & the study of identities. Writing Papers in Urban Languages & Literacies. Paper 43. Available: www.kcl.ac.uk/schools/sspp/education/research/groups/llg/wpull41.html (last accessed 30/06/2012).

Rampton, B., R. Harris, A. Georgakopoulou, C. Leung, L. Small, and C. Dover 2008: Urban classroom culture and interaction: End-of-project report. *Working Papers in Urban Language & Literacies. Paper 53*. Available: www.kcl.ac.uk/schools/sspp/education/research/groups/llg/wpull41.html (last accessed 30/06/2012).

Schiffrin, D. 1996: Narrative as self-portrait: sociolinguistic constructions of identity. *Language in Society* 25: 167–203.

Shuman, A. 2005: Other People's Stories: Entitlement Claims and the Critique of Empathy. Urbana: University of Illinois Press.

Silverstein, M. 1985: Language and the culture of gender: at the intersection of structure, usage, and ideology. In: E. Mertz and R. Parmentier (eds.), *Semiotic Mediation: Sociocultural and Psychological Perspectives*, 219–259. Orlando: Academic Press.

Wetherell, M. 1998: Positioning and interepretative repertoires: conversation analysis and interpretative respertoires in dialogue. *Discourse & Society* 9: 387–412.

Zimmerman, D. H. 1998: Identity, context and interaction. In: A. Antaki and S. Widdicombe (eds.), *Identities in Talk*, 87–106. London: Sage.

Transcription conventions:

//	the point in a turn where the utterance of the next speaker begins to overlap
=	two utterances closely connected without a noticeable overlap
( )	speech that can't be deciphered
(text)	analyst's guess at speech that's hard to decipher
(( ))	stage directions
(.)	micro-pause, not timed
(1.)	approximate length of a pause in seconds
____	emphasized speech
> <	faster than normal speech
:::	extended speech
?	Question
↑ ↓	Rising Falling Intonation

Vally Lytra
Multilingualism, multimodality and media engagement in classroom talk and action[1]

1 Introduction

Significant linguistic, cultural, societal and demographic changes have taken place in the last two decades as a result of globalization, transnational population movements and the spread of new technologies. They have urged researchers to interrogate how these changes have re-shaped communicative practices in different kinds of sociolinguistic spaces, in different semiotic modes, media and genres. In this book chapter, I examine the intersection of multilingualism, multimodality and media engagement in classroom talk and action in a Turkish complementary school in North London. Complementary schools, which are also known as community or supplementary schools in the UK, have been set up by particular cultural, linguistic or religious communities to teach the community language, culture and history to the younger, mainly British-born generation. Turkish complementary schools in particular were established in London principally from the early 1980s onwards to maintain and develop Turkish language and culture for the offspring of the increasingly diverse Turkish-speaking communities.[2] The latter have been formed as part of consecutive transnational migration flows of Turkish-speaking Cypriot Turks, Turks and Kurds from Turkey and Turkish-speaking people who have migrated to the UK from other predominantly EU countries.

1 The financial assistance of the Economic and Social Research Council, UK for the project "Investigating Multilingualism in Complementary Schools in Four Communities" upon which this book chapter draws its data is duly acknowledged. Many thanks to Angela Creese, Adrian Blackledge, Arvind Bhatt, Shehila Hamid, Li Wei and Chao-Jung Wu, and in particular to Dilek Yağcıoğlu-Ali and Taşkın Baraç for insightful discussions during and after the completion of the research project. Earlier versions of this chapter were presented at Sociolinguistics Symposium 17 in Amsterdam (3–5/04/2008), the AILA Language and Migration Network, University of Southampton (2–3/06/2008) and the SWELL seminar at the University of Bern (12/03/2010). I am grateful to Jannis Androutsopoulos and the other participants of the seminar "Mediatisation and Sociolinguistic Change" (FRIAS 19–20/07/2012) for their constructive feedback. All shortcomings are of course mine.
2 The term "Turkish-speaking communities" is a collective term commonly employed in the UK literature to describe Turkish-speaking Cypriot-Turkish, mainland Turkish and Kurdish people living in Britain (Issa 2005; Mehmet-Ali 2001; Creese et al. 2008; Lytra 2011).

I take a case-study approach, focusing on one particular child, Baran, a 10-year old Londoner of Turkish heritage, as he interacts with his classmates and teacher during Turkish language and literacy lessons. In particular, I focus on his private communicative practices with his classmates sitting in close proximity in the margins of classroom talk and action. These involve the initiation and participation in spontaneous talk about popular culture, in particular hip-hop, as well as listening to, evaluating and sharing rap music through their mobile phones. I juxtapose Baran's spontaneous media engagement with his participation in a planned teacher-led literacy activity around the singing and dancing of a Turkish folk song for the celebration of Mother's Day. Drawing on field notes, interactional and interview data and still photography, I ask the following questions: (1) what kind of linguistic and other semiotic resources and artifacts does Baran draw upon in the impromptu private peer talk and the planned, teacher-led literacy activity around music and songs? (2) how does Baran's selection, combination and transformation of his linguistic and other semiotic resources shape and is shaped by the obstacles and opportunities of the institutional context of the Turkish complementary school classroom? (3) what can the empirical focus on these different activities around music and song in this educational site reveal about linguistic and cultural change at the interactional and individual levels and in the context of the community? To examine the intersection of multilingualism, multimodality and media engagement during Turkish lessons, I draw on recent research on multilingualism that situates linguistic practices in their social, cultural, historical and political contexts and views language users as social actors who draw on their linguistic and other semiotic resources in more or less strategic ways as they pursue their interactional goals (Blackledge and Creese 2010; Heller 2007; Martin-Jones, Blackledge and Creese 2012). My analysis is also informed by the work of Goodwin (2000) who has sought to incorporate a multimodal perspective in the investigation of situated interaction, focusing on the role of material artefacts in structuring talk and action.

In the next sections, I first present key concepts for the examination of multilingualism, multimodality and media engagement in the complementary school classroom setting, followed by a brief description of the methods. Then, I move on to the context of the research, namely the Turkish-speaking communities and their schools in London. Through the examination of Baran's talk and action, I explore the ways he draws on, combines and transforms different sets of linguistic and other semiotic resources, cultural content, musical traditions and genres in private peer and public pupil-teacher interactions and I reflect on the relationship between language, media engagement and linguistic and cultural change at the interactional, individual and community levels.

2 Multilingualism, multimodality and media engagement

Pennycook (2010) argues that in the age of global flows and networks we need to consider that "language may be undergoing such forms of transition as to require new ways of conceptualization in terms of local activities, resources and practices" (: 86). Indeed, recent research on multilingualism has sought to destabilize the notion of languages as whole, bounded systems arguing for an understanding of language "as a set of resources which circulate in unequal ways in social networks and discursive spaces, and whose meaning and values are socially constructed within the constraints of social organizational processes, under specific historical conditions" (Heller 2007: 2). This conceptualization of language shifts the analytical lens away from the ideological association of a 'single' language and nationhood defined by a priori claims to a focus on speakers as social actors and agents and their communicative resources. It echoes Blommaert's position (2010) that in order to investigate the new and complex multilingual realities "we need to develop an awareness that it is not necessarily the language you speak, but how you speak it, when you can speak it, and to whom that matters. It is a matter of voice, not of language" (Blommaert 2010: 196).

Moreover, this conceptualization of language captures its heteroglossic nature, which encompasses "(a) the simultaneous use of different kinds of forms or signs, and (b) the tensions and conflicts among those signs, based on the sociohistorical associations they carry with them" (Bailey 2007: 257). In this respect, the concept of heteroglossia includes both monolingual and multilingual forms and foregrounds the way social actors distinguish, understand and interpret the indexical meanings of linguistic forms. Rather than being fixed, these meanings are "shifting, subjective and negotiated" (Bailey 2007: 258). In the context of the present book chapter, this analytical shift allows us to examine the relationship between Baran's linguistic resources and interactional practices and the institutional and historical processes in which they are located; the configuration of linguistic and cultural repertoires privileged by Turkish school and the teacher, as exemplified in the choice of the traditional folk song as curriculum for the celebration of Mother's Day and those available to Baran through his media consumption and production. Moreover, a focus on Baran's situated practices urges us to pay attention not only to the use of diverse linguistic resources but also to the multiple communicative modes (e.g. text, images, sound, visual design), or "the multimodal embedding of linguistic data" (Androutsopoulos 2010: 212).

In line with this analytical focus, recent research in multilingualism has also turned to the highly multimodal nature of communication. Multimodality is seen as "communication in the widest sense, including gesture, oral, performance, artistic, linguistic, digital, electronic, graphic and artefact-related" (Pahl and

Rowsell 2006: 6). Although language is seen as a central mode of communication, it is examined in relation to other modes (e.g. image, writing, speech, moving image, action, artifacts). As Kress et al (2005) postulate taking a multimodal approach can provide "a fuller, richer and more accurate sense of what language is, and what it is not" (: 2). They further argue that

> where before there was a common sense about the capacities of language, which left the potentials of what language can do in many ways implicit and unexamined, now, looking at language in the context of other means of meaning making gives the possibility of a much sharper, more precise, and more nuanced understanding both of the (different) potentials of speech and of writing, and of their limitations" (Kress et al 2005: 2).

By situating Baran's linguistic resources within a wider communicational landscape, we can investigate how these interact with visual, kinaesthetic and artifact related resources and examine relations between modes, texts and languages.

To this end, I draw on the work of Goodwin (2000) who considers how talk is juxtaposed with other modes and mutually elaborate each other. In his own research of the unfolding of a dispute between three young girls of Mexican and Central American heritage, he illustrates how the girls deploy multilingual talk along with a range of other resources, such as gestures, bodily displays and gaze. Moreover, he shows how the hopscotch grid in the playground functions as a semiotic structure in the build environment, which provides the organizational frame against which the girls' game unfolds. Similar to the hopscotch grid in Goodwin's study, I attend to the ways that the mobile phone provides the material and semiotic structure organizing Baran's talk and action, the participation frameworks and encompassing activities, such as listening to rap songs and sharing music files with the songs in question. At the same time, I take into account the distinct affordances offered by mobile phones to shape interaction. Listening to rap songs and sharing music files via mobiles phones during the lesson, for instance, transcends constraints of time and space, collapsing binary distinctions, such as inside and outside classroom spaces, leisure and lesson. Moreover, mobile phones as technologies of mediation impose particular media constraints on their users (e.g. in terms of the visual design) but also allow for user agency in co-constructing among peers a personalized, semiotically-rich media environment (e.g. making strategic and situated decisions about accepting, rejecting, and compiling lists of favourite rap tunes).

Language-focused research on media engagement has started to explore the role of new media in meaning-making and identity construction in the lives of immigrant youth. For example, in their study of teenage immigrants from the former Soviet Union to Israel, Elias and Lemish (2009) examined the ways young people use the internet as a "safe" resource to construct hybrid, diasporic identities drawing on multiple cultural words and experiences as they transition into a new society (: 548). This focus resonates with McLean's (2010) case study of a Caribbean American adolescent's digital practices (instant messaging and social networking via Facebook and MySpace). The author illustrates how the digital world the young woman inhabits has been transformed into a "virtual 'home'" where she can adapt to the US while staying connected to the Caribbean (McLean 2010: 13). In this context, her multilingual resources (standard and vernacular forms of English) can co-exist and her Trinidadian accent and use of slang can be considered as valued cultural and linguistic resources rather than be positioned as deficit.

Studies on mobile phones as technologies of mediation with an analytical focus on language, discourse and literacy have received moderate attention (see, for instance, Spilioti 2011 on text messaging; Nishimura 2011 on mobile storytelling). Although not focusing on the intersection of youth and immigration, this line of research is relevant for the present book chapter in two ways: it moves away from "medium-related" to more ethnographically driven "user-related" perspectives (cf. Androutsopoulos 2010). Moreover, it attends to "the inherent multimodality and cultural embeddedness of the[se] different ways of (inter)acting with/through new media" (Thurlow and Mroczek 2011: xxxii).

3 Methodology

The data for this book chapter come from a research project, which explored multilingualism and identity performances in complementary schools in four ethno-linguistic minority communities in the UK (ESRC, RES-000-23-1180). The research project took an ethnographically informed case study approach, foregrounding the voices and experiences of the different actors (children, parents, teachers and school administrators) learning and communicating in Bengali schools in Birmingham, Chinese (Cantonese and Mandarin) schools in Manchester, Gujarati schools in Leicester and Turkish schools in London (Creese et al 2008a). For the purpose of this chapter, I use data from the Turkish case study only.

The research project builds on existing work on collaborative and team ethnography, which has illustrated the importance of doing ethnography in teams by bringing together a range of complementary voices and perspectives but also possible challenging interpretations in order to best represent the research participants (Conteh, Gregory, Kearney and Mor 2005; Creese et al 2008b). Researchers were paired with one researcher being bilingual in English and the community language in each site. In the Turkish case study in particular, there were three researchers, as the second researcher had to withdraw from the study for family reasons and a third researcher was recruited towards the end of the study. The three researchers who collaborated in the Turkish case study had different linguistic and cultural backgrounds, performed different subject positionings and developed different relationships with the research participants. The author is bilingual (in Greek and English) and has a good knowledge of Turkish language and culture. Prior to the research project, she had worked with and researched Turkish-speaking children in Greece. The other two researchers were bilingual in Turkish and English. The first researcher had experience teaching Turkish-speaking young people at University level in Cyprus and the second researcher had significant teaching experience in Turkish complementary schools and with Turkish-speaking children in London state secondary schools.

For the Turkish case study, the researchers collaborated with two schools located in different parts of London; one in the east and the other in the west. In both schools, we observed a range of settings, including classrooms, break-times, school assemblies and other formal school-sponsored events (e.g. national celebrations) once a week. After four weeks of close observations, we selected four key participant children; one of the children was Baran. From the beginning of the fieldwork, Baran came across as an engaged and enthusiastic learner, which was the reason he was selected to take part in the research project. After consulting with his teacher and his mother, it was agreed that he would wear a clip-on microphone to digitally record his interactions during Turkish literacy classes, in the break-times and during school assemblies over a period of six weeks. During this period, we interviewed Baran, his mother and teacher along with the other focal children, their mothers, teachers and members of the schools' managing committees. Throughout the 10-week fieldwork, the researchers also video-recorded parts of literacy classes, school assemblies and celebrations and collected documentary data relating to each school's policy, planning and curriculum and photographs. Informed consent was solicited prior to and throughout the data collection. In this book chapter, I draw on field notes, interviews, digital recordings and still photography collected during different phases of the research project.

4 The context of the study: Turkish-speaking communities and their schools in London

The diversity of Turkish-speaking communities has been well documented (e.g. Küçükcan 1999; Issa 2005; Mehmet-Ali 2001). The Turkish-speaking communities in the UK are comprised of Cypriot-Turks, Turks and Kurds from mainland Turkey and more recently Turkish-speaking peoples who have immigrated to the UK via other European Union countries. It is estimated that Turkish-speaking peoples in the UK are around 180,000–200,000. The largest concentration is in the Greater London area, although pockets can be found in major cities around the UK (e.g. Birmingham, Manchester and Edinburgh). Migration flows from Cyprus to the UK occurred in the aftermath of World War II and the Turkish invasion in 1974 (officially known in Turkey as the Cyprus Peace Operation) triggered by inter-communal violence and economic hardship on the island. Immigration from Turkey to the UK started in the 1970s as part of supplying manual labour to post-WWII European markets. It was accelerated during the 1980s and 1990s with Turkish-speaking peoples increasingly settling to the UK via other European Union countries (e.g. Germany, France, the Netherlands and Greece). Kurds with roots in Turkey immigrated to the UK from the late 1980s mainly as asylum seekers due to on-going conflict in South-East Turkey. Besides the diversity evident in their composition and migration trajectories, there are further divisions within the Turkish-speaking communities along the lines of language, social class, economic activity, educational background and achievement, religious and political affiliation.

The two schools in this research project were founded in the late 80s. "East London Turkish School" attracted children and families living mainly in North, North-East and East London where Turkish-speaking communities have traditionally settled and continue to live. At the time of the fieldwork it had about 250 registered pupils. Most of the children were of Cypriot-Turkish background, although there were some children whose families came from mainland Turkey or had moved to Cyprus as settlers. "West London Turkish School" had a larger catchment area with children coming from West and North-West London and its environs. At the time of the fieldwork there were about 110 registered children. The majority of the children's families were from mainland Turkey, although almost half of the children had a parent who was not Turkish.

At the time of the fieldwork, Baran and his younger brother had been pupils at the "East London Turkish School" for four years. Every Saturday morning from 10.30 am until 13.30 pm Baran attended the Turkish intermediate class for 9–13 year olds taught by Hasan Bey, a trained primary school teacher with a primary maths specialization on a 5-year appointment by the Turkish Ministry of Education to teach in Turkish schools in London.

5 Results

5.1 Baran's linguistic repertoire and everyday media engagement

Baran was born in London and was 12 years old when he participated in the research project. In his interview, which he asked to be carried out in English, Baran spoke at length about his language practices and attitudes towards his developing multilingual skills. He explains that "when I talk to my brother I mostly talk English" because that "is how we get along". With his friends he uses English too, but with adults he uses Turkish because "they know English a bit but they won't understand coz I think they won't be able to follow me because I'd talk fast and coz they know more Turkish". When prompted by the researcher, he elaborates further on his language choices and code-switching practices:

Excerpt 1

Researcher: How do you adjust your Turkish, I mean what are the adjustments you make in your Turkish?
Baran: I just ... I ... I don't use proper words and I just sometimes use slang words
Researcher: With .. with adults or with your friends?
Baran: Mostly with my friends. When I just was saying a slang word and that. With my friends I speak like a bit of Turkish and a bit of English there. I mostly in a sentence I mostly speak English but maybe one word would be in Turkish.

(interview with Baran, June 2006)

Baran is able to talk at length about the linguistic resources he uses and how he strategically employs them depending on context and participation in his everyday life. He also describes how he moves seamlessly between languages when speaking with his Turkish friends: "I'll say 'come play .. come play football', I say 'gel futbol oynayalim' ... I may put one word in the sentence so like half of the sentence would be in Turkish", a language practice he seems to consider as unmarked and "natural". Baran's treatment of his multilingualism as ordinary is complemented by his pride in his multilingual skills, particularly vis-à-vis his English-speaking friends in his mainstream school "who speak one main language".

During his interview, Baran also provides a wealth of information about his regular media consumption and production practices. He reports watching mostly Turkish satellite TV, particularly police detective series, and some English TV and DVDs. He also serfs the internet, plays on his PlayStation, texts and talks on the mobile with his friends from school and reads PlayStation 2 magazines and football books- all in English. At the same time, he explains that he uses new technologies to stay in touch with family in Turkey and improve his Turkish. He adds that he uses MSN and texts his cousins and uncles in Turkey because "I have to speak with them Turkish" and that he checks out Turkish internet sites: "I sometimes go like ... Turkish Airlines and read some news so that I could get my Turkish even better". Baran's musical tastes are informed by popular culture, particularly Turkish pop represented by singers such as Tarkan and Kenan Doğulu. Both singers' reputations have transcended the boarders of Turkey and have attracted an international audience. Moreover, he mentions listening to rap artists in English, like Eminem. At home, he is exposed to a larger range of Turkish musical traditions and genres as his mother reports listening to classical Turkish music, Turkish folk and pop music. As documented in other studies of immigrant youth's media engagement, Baran's media practices, preferences and dispositions reveal a sustained orientation towards both the country he was born and lives in and his parents' country of origin emphasizing the interconnectedness of his practices and life experiences across physical and virtual spaces (D'Haenens, Koeman and Saeys 2007; McLean 2010; Elias and Lemish 2009).

5.2 Teaching and learning in Turkish school

Recent research in complementary school classrooms has demonstrated the importance of these educational, linguistic, cultural and social spaces for transmitting aspects of the community language, culture and history to the younger predominantly British-born generation (e.g. Blackledge and Creese 2010; Creese et al 2009; Li Wei and Wu 2010; see also studies in Creese and Martin 2006; Lytra and Martin 2010). At the same time, it has shown that complementary schools function as agents of standardization privileging the teaching and learning of the standard form of the community language and transmitting norms regarding what counts as correct language use and authentic cultural expression (e.g. Blackledge and Creese 2010; Li Wei 2011; Lytra 2011).

Turkish complementary schools, which are of interest to us here, sought to reproduce aspects of Turkish national culture and identity mediated through the transmission of standard Turkish. Standard Turkish enjoys high symbolic, social and economic capital in Turkey and the diaspora, including the members of the Turkish-speaking communities in London. It is highly valued as the language of education, or as the "correct" form of Turkish (Issa 2005). In Turkish complementary schools, parents and teachers routinely referred to standard Turkish as "temiz Türkçe" <clean/proper Turkish> (Lytra and Baraç 2008; Lytra 2012a). Moreover, language and literacy teaching incorporated the extensive use of stories, folk takes and songs as curriculum (Lytra 2011). These pedagogic practices emerged in what appeared to be a conventional teacher-fronted and controlled classroom interactional order, which exhibited the following features: teachers made use of the I-R-F sequence, the traditional pattern of classroom talk where the teacher initiates, the pupils respond and then the teacher provides feedback; teachers made extensive use of vocabulary building and grammar substitution drills, dictation exercises and the (silent) reading of texts followed by a set of reading comprehension questions checking meaning (Lytra and Baraç 2009; Lytra et al 2010). These pedagogic practices intended to give teachers a good deal of control over the regulation of participation rights and curriculum content.

While these pedagogic practices were salient, it is important to acknowledge that pupils did not docilely submit to teacher authority: pupils often made contributions that did not fit the official agenda, or they retreated to private pupil talk and engaged with their mobile phones. In the next section, I shift my attention to Baran's private peer talk and examine the discursive spaces he and his classmates co-constructed beyond the boundaries of the canonical classroom talk and action.

5.3 "I'm always on mobile innit": Baran's media engagement in Turkish class

While actively participating in the lesson by seeking to clarify the meaning of unknown words or volunteering to read aloud a text, Baran initiated and participated in both extended and fleeting interactions with his male classmates about hip-hop artists as well as listened to, evaluated and shared their songs via their mobile phones. Similar to other formal institutional contexts, the use of mobile phones during the lesson was explicitly sanctioned. We observed the teacher repeatedly warn the pupils: "telefonları kaldırın" <put your phones away>. Nevertheless, these warnings did not hinder the boys' on-going media engagement. The latter was triggered and sustained by their mobile phones stowed away in a school bag casually lying on the desk but within easy reach or kept in their hand or pockets throughout the duration of the lesson. The mobile phones helped them stay connected, or as Axelsson (2010: 35) maintains, remain in a state of "perpetual contact" with their peers, transforming the classroom environment both physically and socially.

Baran's Turkish class took place in a typical mainstream primary school classroom. Desks were aligned in rows facing the teacher and the whiteboard. Mobile phones allowed Baran and his classmates to communicate across classroom space, take part in a range of peer interactions (e.g. evaluating shared songs, comparing features of mobile phones, listening to rap lyrics) and ultimately bring aspects of digital technologies and popular culture into the classroom. In other words, mobile phones provided the material structure with which the boys

Figure 1: Baran listening to music on his mobile phone

Figure 2: Metin showing Cem a particular feature on his mobile phone

interacted and made choices (e.g. they listened to music, sent and received text and sound). Moreover, they offered a complex set of semiotic resources, such as music, text, sound, visual design, in addition to linguistic resources, which Baran and his classmates drew upon as they negotiated the unfolding activity. Image 1 has captured Baran, who seems to be listening to music on his mobile phone.

Baran's bodily display indicates his orientation towards the mobile phone and the activity he seems to be clandestinely engaged in while the teacher is correcting the vocabulary exercise with the whole class: rather than facing the white board, he has turned his body sideways away from the teacher. He has tilted his head to the left and is clasping the mobile phone with his hand. His postural orientation indicates his intense engagement with the mobile phone without, however seeming to completely disassociate himself from the on-going classroom activity. The next image 2 illustrates Metin showing Cem a particular feature on his mobile phone. On this occasion, the lesson seems to have been temporarily put on hold while Hasan Bey is doing the rounds, checking and marking the work sheets at the children's desks.

The boys' engagement is not only expressed through talk mediated by text and visual design on the screen of the mobile phone but also through their embodied orientation to the activity: Metin has turned his body sideways away from his desk towards Cem while Cem is leaning forwards towards Metin. The boys' gaze is fixed on the screen. Through the use of different semiotic modalities (i.e. talk, body posture and gaze), the two boys are co-constructing a two-party participation framework and a shared orientation towards the development of the activity being accomplished. In this respect, both images illustrate the centrality of the mobile phone as "material structure in the surround [...] which can provide semiotic structure without which the constitution of particular kinds of action being invoked through talk would be impossible" (Goodwin 2000: 1492). They also foreground the way the boys capitalize on the medium-specific affordances of mobile phones as personalized, portable and information-rich artifacts to mediate their social interaction in the classroom space.

The following digitally recorded excerpt takes place at the beginning of the lesson. Hasan Bey has handed out a text and has asked the pupils to read it silently and then answer the reading comprehension questions. Baran and Metin are sitting next to each other. Galip is sitting behind them. The children are settling down and about to begin working on the assigned reading task. Baran inquires whether anyone has the song "When I'm Gone" by hip hop artist Eminem (line 1), while another boy seems to be listening to a song on his mobile phone.

Excerpt 2³

1	Baran:	Who got 'When I'm Gone'? Who got song?
2	A boy:	Can you hear this? … You can man!
3	Another boy:	*Telefonları kaldırın beyler!* <Put away your telephones people!>
4	Hasan Bey:	*Telefonları kaldırın, iki haftanız kaldı* <Put away your telephones!
5		You've got two weeks left (before the end of the school year)>
		(Faint music can be heard in the background)
6	Baran:	Who got good song like Eminem? My friend … you got … (inaudible)
7	Galip:	I've got another 60 (songs), not I've got another 63 (songs) aye, got 8 got another 60, … Tom and Jerry Lewis (inaudible)?
9	Baran:	What's that?
10	Galip:	I … Tom and Jerry Lewis.
11	Baran:	Wooow woooow what's Tom and Jerry Lewis?
12	Galip:	You know Tom and Jerry. Have you heard, have seen, have you
13		watched Tom and Jerry?
14	Baran:	yeah, hahaha
15	Galip:	Have you see.. have you seen when it starts the beat?
16	Baran:	yeah.
17	Galip:	yeah, but it's really…
18	Baran:	turn that
19	Galip:	you know it goes … ddttdddtttddtt (hums the tune)…
20	Baran:	turn that.. xx *mi vermiş?* <has he given xx?>
21	Galip:	who … is that ?
		(Hasan Bey can be heard taking the register while Galip resumes humming the tune)
22	Metin:	I'm doing my work.
23	Baran:	*dersimizi iyi, iyi yapalım cocuklar!* <Let's nicely do our work
24		nicely nicely children!>

(digital recording 10/06/2006)

---

3 Transcription conventions: English translation: <…>; researcher's comments: (…)

The boy's warning to put away the mobile phones is repeated by Hasan Bey who reminds the children that they only have a couple of weeks of classes left until the end of the school year (lines 4–5). However, the teacher's warning to focus on the lesson seems to go unheeded as Baran inquires once more if anyone has a "good song" like a song by Eminem to share with him (line 6). Galip responds that he has many songs stored on his mobile phone (about 60–63 songs) and then he and Baran embark on a discussion of a particular tune from the cartoon "Tom and Jerry". It is worth noting that similar fleeting popular culture references were triggered by and embedded in the boys' media engagement activities in other interactional moments. Such references generated a web of intertextual relations that could, for instance, be traced back to an original tune, as in the case of the reference to the "Tom and Jerry" cartoon (see also Georgakopoulou this volume). The boys' discussion of "Tom and Jerry" is brought to a close as Hasan Bey takes the register and the children seem to be reorienting back to the assigned task: Metin announces (presumably to the other boys) that he is now doing his work (line 22) to which Baran responds by parodying the voice of the teacher in Turkish "let's do our work nicely nicely children!" Baran's remark is produced in a loud, declarative voice in standard Turkish as he seems to be addressing it to both Metin and the rest of class. This is in contrast to the preceding private pupil-pupil talk about songs and tunes, which was soft-spoken and almost exclusively in vernacular English.

Goffman's concept of "frames" is a useful analytic tool to examine how Baran and his classmates oscillate between the assigned task and media engagement during the lesson. Frames are viewed as dynamic mechanisms through which participants structure their social and personal experiences in order to make sense of what is going on in a given interaction (1974: 10–11). Participants deploy clusters of contextualization cues, which function as framing devices and signal how to interpret utterances, movement, or gestures (: ibid). As the excerpt above illustrates, contextualization cues may include different sets of linguistic resources and voices as well as the use of prosody, gestures and the manipulation of artifacts. Through the use of these clusters of cues, Baran and his classmates delineate different activities (e.g. talk about hip hop artists and their songs stored on their mobile phones juxtaposed with talk about the reading comprehension task).

In the next digitally recorded episode that takes place shortly after the previous one, we observe how Baran dips in and out of different frames. The examination of the sequential and interactional production of frames allow us to explore further how Baran listens to, comments on and shares music via his mobile phone with his peers against the backdrop of whole-class pedagogic practices and routines occupying the official classroom floor, notably reading silently and writing the answers to the reading comprehension questions. Hasan Bey is still making the rounds from desk to desk addressing clarification questions and checking homework. Baran calls for the teacher's attention in Turkish (lines 1–2), but the teacher seems to be occupied with another pupil. While waiting for his turn, Baran switches back to English and demands urgently that Galip sends him a song by 50 Cent he seems to have been listening to (line 3).

Excerpt 3

1	Baran	*oğretmenim!* <teacher> (wining like a toddler) *oyyetmenim!*
2		<teacherrr!>
		(Hasan Bey can be heard in the background, explaining sth to another pupil)
3	Baran	send me that 50 Cent thingy! Send me that now! Send me that now!
4	Galip	(inaudible)
5	Baran	I work that
6	Galip	I think 50 Cent is out of control
7	Baran	let me hear it
8	Galip	listen to this
		(Baran and Galip are listening to the song)
9	Baran	send me that now
10	Galip	I already have done
11	Baran	what song is that? Is that "Seventh of the Sin"? Say you send? Hey
12		what's the matter? What's your format? It's made from (inaudible)
13	Boy	let me hear it! Let me hear it!
14	Baran	what's the fucking Turkish swear word for "you cunt"? I'll bang you
15		over you fucking fat cunt! Come then. Come then. You're coming up
16		now? You're off (inaudible). The week before I asked him to come up
17		.... just to ring it here when there's no teacher, when there's no teacher
19		and he says no
18	Hasan Bey	(to Baran) *kapanr mısın?* <can you turn it off?>

(digital recording 10/06/2006)

After listening to the song together on Galip's mobile phone, Baran insists that Galip sends him the song by 50 Cent they just listened to (line 9). When Galip explains that he has already done so (line 10), Baran asks the title of the song and inquires about the format in which Galip sent the song (lines 11–12). This is followed by a tirade of threats and insults (lines 14–16) presumably directed at Galip or at one of the other boys. In fact, Baran further elaborates by way of an example where upon the culprit refused to ring Baran on his mobile phone when the teacher was absent (lines 16–17). The interaction is brought to a close when Hasan Bey comes over to Baran and asks him to put his mobile phone away.

Baran is not only immersed in American popular culture but also follows closely the Turkish diasporic hip-hop scene. Indeed, Ceza <Punishment> was one of the most influential Turkish rappers. Originally from Turkey, he had made his singing career in Germany. While Hasan Bey is still checking the children's homework, Baran and Metin who seem to have swiftly completed the reading comprehension questions, continue undeterred to exchange rap songs. In the next excerpt, Metin sends Baran one of Ceza's songs:

Excerpt 4

1	Metin	(to Baran) accept it (the Turkish rap song)
2	Baran	what?
3	Metin	accept it
4	Baran	I did
		(rap song can be heard in the background)
5	Baran	(inaudible) swear if you understand Turkish (inaudible) swear ...
6		it's quite good yeah

(digital recording 10/06/2006)

As Baran is listening to Ceza's rap he challenges Metin about his understanding of the Turkish rap lyrics and evaluates the said song as "quite good" (lines 5–6). A few turns later, Baran resumes his evaluation of Turkish rap lyrics this time comparing the lyrics of Ceza to the African-American rapper 50 Cent, enthusiastically commenting that they all swear the same way: "you listen to your rap like 50 Cent when he swears yeah it's exactly like in Turkish".

As the three digital recorded excerpts showed, Baran and his peers continuously collected, exchanged, stored, deleted and updated their music files on their mobile phones and evaluated the rap tunes they listened to. Their media engagement reflected their personal music and aesthetic preferences, popular culture interests as well as their peer concerns for sociability and being "always on mobile". In so doing, Baran drew on and combined different sets of linguistic and other semiotic resources: standard and vernacular forms of English and Turkish, popular cultural forms, slang, insults, mock threats of physical abuse, medium-specific vocabulary. His spontaneous private talk collaborated his self-reports that he speaks mostly in English with his peers intermingled with slang words and some words in Turkish, frequently swear words and other terms of abuse.

In the next section, I discuss what happens when Hasan Bey brings in the traditional Turkish folk song "Annemize" <to our mothers> for the celebration of Mother's Day and plays it on the tape-recorder and when pupils are given more space to express themselves in the main classroom floor.

5.4 "Annemize": Singing for Mother's Day

As our participant observations revealed, Baran was attentive to the teacher and keen to learn. Whilst actively engaged in listening to rap tunes and sharing songs via his mobile phone, he was not opposed to the main business of the classroom: he completed the assigned work swiftly and effortlessly and self-selected to read aloud the reading comprehension texts or correct the grammar and vocabulary tasks on the white board. His high competence in standard Turkish placed him as one of the top pupils in a class with children who had a wide range of linguistic abilities and preferences in standard and vernacular forms of Turkish. His commitment to learning and improving his Turkish literacy can also be gleaned at in his interview. Baran acknowledges the significance of attending Turkish school in order to "improve [his] writing" and elaborates that "in Turkish the alphabet is so much different than in English. So they're like two types of [i] one without a dot and one with a dot and I keep on mixing them up". At the same time, Baran seemed critical of what he was taught and the way he was taught in Turkish school. When asked how teaching could be improved, he suggested to:

> do different stuff instead of giving us sheets. Cos most of the time teacher gives us sheets. Two pieces of sheet, one that writes a poem and other paper got the questions and we always do [that], he don't give us like, writing tests, we just speak, we write it, we don't do that much.

During our 10-week fieldwork in Hasan Bey's class, we observed the teacher followed a more or less regimented curriculum and a set of established pedagogic routines and practices. Nevertheless, in the context of these pedagogic practices Hasan Bey initiated a limited range of literacy activities that provided discursive spaces for the pupils' self-expression in the main classroom floor (Lytra 2011). One such occasion was the introduction of the Turkish folk song "Annezmize" <To our mothers> as curriculum. The song chosen by Hasan Bey belongs to a completely different genre from the hip-hop tunes Baran and his peers listened to, shared and evaluated. It was a traditional folk song of the "türkü" genre celebrating the theme of motherhood; hence, it was deemed culturally authenic material for classroom use in general and the celebration of Mother's Day in particular. It was not clear to us how well known this particular song was to the children but, as I show, they immediately recognized the rhythm and beat of the "türkü".

Hasan Bey introduces the song by playing it once on the tape-recorder and then explaining to the pupils that he will dictate the lyrics and that the pupils will write them down. As the next digitally recorded excerpt indicates, while Hasan Bey is dictating the lyrics, Baran and Galip send, accept or reject hip-hop tunes via their mobile phones.

Excerpt 5

1	Hasan Bey	*ben söyleyeceğim siz yazın* <I'll dicᴛate and you'll write down>
2	Baran	*tahtaya yazabılır mısın? Benim iyi yazım yok* <can you write it on the
3		board? I'm not good at writing>
4	Hasan Bey	*söylediklerimi yazamıyor musunuz?* <can't you write down what I'm
5		saying?>
6	Baran	why is my phone on?
7	Hasan Bey	*başlık yazın annenize başlık .. evet yazıyoruz .. yazıyoruz annenize*
8		*bu şarkıyı ben söylecem siz yazıyorsunuz* <write the title for your
9		mother the title .. yes we are writing .. we are writing for your mother
10		I will tell you the lyrics and you will write them
11	Baran	exactly you dickhead .. no I'm not I don't mind
12	Hasan Bey	(he dictates) *güneşin alası çok* <the sun has many colours>
13	Baran	I rejected it .. *yemin et* <swear to God>
14	Galip	*yemin ediyorum Kuran carpsin* <I swear to God, swear on the
15		Qur'an>
16	Baran	*yemin et* <swear to God>
17	Galip	*yemin ederim* <I swear to God>
18	Baran	no say *yemin ederim*. Say *yemin ederim*. *Kuran carpsin* <No say I
19		swear to God say I swear to God swear on the Qur'an>
20	Galip	I swear to all my life
21	Baran	no rejected I don't want that Indian song man
22	Galip	it ain't Indian
23	Hasan Bey	*her evin çilesi çok* <every house has many problems>

(digital recording 10/06/2006)

The teacher plays one stanza at a time. He dictates the lyrics line by line in a very slow pace allowing ample time for the pupils to write them down. At the end of each stanza, he stops the tape-recorder. He summarizes the key points and moral message, explains unknown words and comments on the beauty of the lyrics with noticeably limited pupil uptake. From the onset of the dictation and throughout its duration, it appears that Baran is attending to two simultaneous frames: on the one hand, the institutionally-oriented frame of the dictation task directed and controlled by the teacher (lines 2–3) and on the other hand the peer-oriented frame he co-constructs with Galip as they continue to share and evaluate songs via their mobile phones (lines 11–22). Hasan Bey's heavily scripted teacher-talk is contrasted to Baran's "on-line" moment-to-moment interaction with Galip mediated via their mobile phones. They two boys draw on elements from a range of linguistic sources: standard and vernacular forms of English and Turkish and Islamic expressions, as they appear to be locked into a dispute over a song Baran seems to have rejected because he considers it an Indian song.

When the dictation task is completed, Hasan Bey plays the song once again and suggests that the pupils sing along and dance. Baran takes up enthusiastically the teacher's suggestion, dancing and urging his classmates to participate too:

Excerpt 6

1	Hasan Bey	*Dinliyorsunuz. Sizde söyleyin dans yapabılırsınız* <you are listening.
2		You can sing along too you can dance>
		(music is heard)
3	Baran	*hadi* <let's do it>
4	Galip	hey dance Turkish style .. Turkish style ... *düğün* (giggles) <wedding
5		ceremony>
6	Baran	*hadi halay çekelim* <let's do line dancing> .. *halay çekelim lan* <line
7		dancing man> .. do you know how to *halay çek* <line dance>? *Hadi*
8		*halay çekelim lan* <let's do line dancing>. Whoever is doing it with
9		me? *Halay çekelim* <line dancing>.. hey just come, just come, just
10		come man .. fuck you .. it's gonna be joke.
		(Baran combines movement from traditional dances and more contemporary
		Turkish music and dance genres)
11	Baran	Hey hey I know how to do it .. aahh my penis ..
		(Music stops. Hasan Bey is trying to get the students into groups so that they
		can perform the song)
12	Baran	wait shush I'm gonna sing.. *evet* <yes>
		(music is resumed)
13	Hasan Bey	*söylüyoruz* <we are singing>
14	Baran	wait Galip let's sing <Baran is singing along>

(digital recording 10/06/2006)

There is a stark contrast between the content, rhyme and beat of the hip-hop tunes Baran and his peers have been listening to and the "türkü" the teacher plays during the lesson. While hip-hop reflects the aesthetic preferences of Baran and his peers, the "türkü" seems to reflect those of their teachers and parents' generations. This contrast is encapsulated in Baran's assessment of the song in the form of a jibe to Metin, as the children are singing along: "Metin annesi bu şarkıyı söyler .. Metin annesi" <Metin's mother would sing this song .. Metin's mother>. Nevertheless, the ease with which Baran and his peers join in the singing indicates a strong familiarity with this music genre. Indeed, Baran and Galip's rendition of the song points to the combination of different aesthetic preferances: movements from traditional folk dance and the "halay" – a dance commonly performed at weddings and other community celebrations – are creatively mixed with gestures from more contemporary Turkish dance genres (lines 4–11). In this respect, the traditional folk song "becomes the springboard for an ad hoc multisemiotic performance" (Lytra 2011: 32), with strong jocular overtones (e.g. swearing and even ridicule of the singing and dancing activity, lines 10–11).

In this singing and dancing activity, the boundaries between institutional and peer-oriented frames seem to be blurred. As the two frames are brought together, a discursive space in the main classroom floor is opened where pupils can weave in a range of different linguistic and other semiotic resources. This temporary reframing of the teacher-initiated and controlled activity into a somewhat more pupil-orchestrated one allows for a momentary renegotiation of the interactional order and pupil agency. Nevertheless, there are limitations to how far Baran and his peers' exuberance and their transformation of the song is accepted by the teacher. Clearly, Hasan Bey's ensuing disciplinary action to send out some of the more boisterous boys, including Baran, and his threats to report them to the school principle and inform their parents reveals that the teacher interprets their transformation of the song as an act of subversion.

6 Discussion and conclusion

In this chapter, I investigated the intersection of multilingualism, multimodality and media engagement in the talk and action of a 10-year old boy, Baran, as he interacted with his peers and teacher in a London Turkish complementary school. I showed how Baran flexibly combined features from standard and vernacular forms of English and Turkish, terms of jocular abuse and Islamic expressions with the manipulation of prosody, body posture, gaze and gesture in his impromptu private talk with his peers mediated through the use of the mobile phone. Drawing on his knowledge and expertise in popular culture, particularly hip-hop music, he listened to, exchanged and evaluated songs by Eminem, 50 Cent and Ceza in the margins of the main classroom floor while simultaneously engaging actively with the lesson (e.g. seeking to clarify the meaning of new words, volunteering to read aloud or come to the whiteboard to correct a vocabulary task).

His media engagement revealed the situated, intentional and participant-oriented deployment of his linguistic and other semiotic resources (cf. McLean 2010; also Georgakopoulou, this volume). It also highlighted the role of the mobile phone in occasioning talk and action. Similar to the hopscotch grid in Goodwin's study (2000: 1505), the mobile phone "provide[d] crucial frameworks for the building of action that could not exist without it", for instance, sending, accepting or rejecting tunes and clandestinely listening to them during the lesson. In addition to facilitating interaction and functioning as a medium for peer connectivity, it functioned as a tool for self-expression. In particular, the mobile phone opened possibilities for constructing and supporting particular forms of media-centric "expert" identities. Drawing on Ito et al. (2008: 20), I suggest that besides building social relations and negotiating peer hierarchies, Baran's media engagement with and through mobile phones pointed to "the beginning of a more media-centric form of engagement". In addition to listening and sharing rap tunes, the boys "experimented with the possibilities and limitations of mobile technology", by hacking into each other's mobile and exploring the different applications on their phones, as they sought to showcase and develop their knowledge of mobile digital devices (Ito et al 2008: 20; see also Lytra 2012b).

The data analysis also brought into sharp focus the obstacles and opportunities of the institutional setting. Although using mobile phones was officially banned and offenders were constantly reminded to put their mobile phones away, it appeared that unofficially Hasan Bey seemed to allow these activities to co-exist along side the different teacher-initiated literacy activities as long as they remained more or less concealed and took place in the periphery of the main classroom talk and activity. This particular classroom settlement meant that the rap tunes Baran and his classmates so avidly listened to on their mobile phones were never assimilated in the curriculum. The boys' on-going, low-key media engagement mediated via their mobile phones remained as Maybin (2007) has eloquently put it very much "under the desk".[4] The lack of tuning into children's digital and popular cultural literacies is not unique to Turkish schools. Rather it reflects dominant pedagogic practices and discourses in mainstream schools too. Herein lies a paradox, which Millard (2006) aptly captures as follows: "children are becoming multimodally [and I would add and digitally] literate whilst their schools' more explicit practices remain stubbornly print-bound" (: 234). To this end, Millard has put forth developing a "literacy of fusion" which draws on children's out-of school literacies, including digital and popular cultural literacies, to support school-based learning (Millard 2006: 234). In a similar vein, González, Moll and Amanti (2005), Sánchez (2007) and others working with immigrant children have advocated the importance of developing pedagogies that use and valorize the full range of children's linguistic, cultural, multimodal, embodied and transnational resources and experiences. Clearly, the incorporation of Baran and his peers' Turkish rap tunes as transnational "funds of knowledge" (González, Moll and Amanti 2005) into the lesson in the future calls for a rethinking of what counts as correct language use and authentic cultural expression for Turkish schools and their teachers.

The empirical focus on these different activities around music and song provided a lens for the examination of linguistic and cultural change at the inter-

---

4 By literacies "under the desk" Maybin (2006) refers to "a range of unofficial literacy activities which appeared to be clearly 'off-task' in terms of institutional norms" (: 519).

actional, individual and community levels. The teacher-initiated and planned literacy activity around music and song opened up a discursive space in the main classroom floor where Baran weaved in a range of semiotic resources, music preferences and genres, as he attempted to transform the traditional folk song "Annemize" <to our mothers> by combining movements from Turkish line-dancing and more contemporary dance forms. By mixing traditional and contemporary Turkish song and dance he sought to create an alternative hybrid genre and redefine the classroom interactional order. As a result, in the singing and dancing activity that followed the dictation, the boundaries between institutional and peer-oriented frames seemed to blur, as Baran engaged in a multi-semiotic expressive performance in the main classroom floor. His heteroglossic performance temporarily disrupted the canonical classroom interactional order and brought to the fore the tensions between the teaching of language and culture as representing a particular national, territorial entity and culture as lived experience in a transnational cosmopolitan setting.

Baran's consumption and production of different musical and dance genres (e.g. hip-hop, traditional folk music) and their creative transformation into an alternative hybrid form pointed to a process of forging a new route "as opposed to the choice of either resisted assimilation or the search for 'tradition' and 'authenticity'" (Sharma 1996: 40). His media engagement revealed an understanding of Turkish language and culture as every day lived experience (Baraç 2009; Blackledge and Creese 2010; Lytra 2011). Unlike the dominant conceptualization of language and culture in heritage education as "something one holds onto to vaguely as one's remembrances" (García 2005: 601), for Baran, Turkish language and culture was seen "as something that is used in the present or that can be projected in the future" (García 2005: 601). Baran's understanding of language and culture pointed to broader tensions between many members of the older generation of teachers, parents and community members and the younger generation of mainly British-born youth. The former regarded that one of the main aims of Turkish school was to provide an anchoring, to keep the younger generation connected with Turkey and Cyprus through the transmission of standard Turkish, authentic cultural narratives and identities. Baran did not reject this aim of Turkish school. Rather, he embraced it showing an active interest in improving his Turkish and participating in the lesson. Simultaneously, through the weaving of monolingual and multilingual forms and other semiotic resources and artifacts Baran put forth a more flexible, urbane response than that proposed by many members of his teachers and parents' generation (Blackledge and Creese 2010; Lytra 2011). As Baraç (2009) has argued, "such musical remixes can be seen as an attempt to mediate between the expectations of their parents and the community school both of which promote Turkish music, folk-culture and those of mainstream British peer culture" (: 49). Baran's response draws on the dynamic coexistence of old and new, the "türkü" and hip-hop, standard and vernacular forms of Turkish and English. It points to what Pennycook (2007), Sarkar and Low (2012) and others have referred to as the "ordinariness" of linguistic diversity and multilingualism: "difference and diversity, multilingualism and hybridity are not rare and exotic conditions to be sought out and celebrated but the quotidian ordinariness of everyday life" (Pennycook 2007: 95).

References

Androutsopoulos, Jannis 2010: Localising the global on the participatory web: Vernacular spectacles as local responses to global media flows. In: Nicholas Coupland (ed.), Handbook of Language and Globalization, 203–231. Oxford: Wiley-Blackwell.

Axelsson, Ann-Sophie 2010: Perpetual and personal: Swedish young adults and their use of mobile phones. New Media & Society. 12(1): 35–54.

Bailey, Benjamin 2007: Heteroglossia and boundaries. In: Monica Heller (ed.), Bilingualism: A Social Approach, 257–274. Basingstoke: Palgrave/Macmillan

Baraç, Taşkin 2009: Language use and emerging ethnicities among London born youth of Turkish descent. Unpublished MA thesis. King's College London.

Blackledge, Adrian and Angela Creese 2010: Multilingualism. A Critical Perspective. London: Continuum.

Blommaert, Jan 2010: The Sociolinguistics of Globalization. Cambridge: Cambridge University Press.

Creese, Angela and Peter Martin 2006: Interaction in complementary school contexts: Developing identities of choice: An introduction. Language and Education 20 (1): 1–4.

Creese, Angela, Taşkin Baraç, Adrian Blackledge, Arvind Bhatt, Shahela Hamid, Li Wei, Vally Lytra, Peter Martin, Chao-Jung Wu and Dilek Yağcıoğlu-Ali 2008a: Investigating Multilingualism in Complementary Schools in Four Communities, End-of-project report, available online at www.esrcsocietytoday.ac.uk/esrcinfocentre/viewawardpage.aspx?awardnumber=RES-000-023-1180.

Creese, Angela, Arvind Bhatt, Nirmala Bhojani and Peter Martin 2008b: Fieldnotes in team ethnography: Researching complementary schools. Journal of Qualitative Research 8, 223–242.

Creese Angela, Wu, Chao-Jung and Adrian Blackledge 2009: Folk stories and social identification in multilingual classrooms. Linguistics and Education 20(4): 350–365.

Conteh, Jean, Eve Gregory, Chris Kearney and Aura Mor 2005: On Writing Educational Ethnographies: The Art of Collusion. Stoke-on-Trent, UK: Trentham.

García, Ofelia 2005: Positioning heritage languages in the United States The Modern Language Journal 89(4): 601–605.

D' Haenens, Leen, Joyce Koeman and Frieda Saeys 2007: Digital citizenship among ethnic minority youths in the Netherlands and Flanders New Media & Society 9(2): 278–299.

Elias, Nelly and Dafna Lemish 2009: Spinning the web of identity: The roles of the internet in the lives of immigrant adolescents. New Media & Society 11(4):533–551.

Goodwin, Charles 2000: Action and embodiment within situated human interaction. *Journal of Pragmatics* 32: 1489–1522.

Goffman, Erving 1974: *Frame Analysis: An essay on the Organisation of Experience*. New York: Harper & Row.

González, Norma, Luis C. Moll and Cathy Amanti 2005: *Funds of Knowledge: Theorizing Practice in Households, Communities and Classrooms*. Mahwah, NJ: Erlbaum Associates.

Heller, Monica 2007: Bilingualism as Ideology and Practice. In: Monica Heller (ed.), *Bilingualism: A Social Approach*, 1–22. Basingstoke: Palgrave/Macmillan.

Issa, Tözün 2005: *Talking Turkey: The Language, Culture and Identity of Turkish Speaking Children in Britain*. Stoke-on-Trent: Trentham.

Kress, Gunther, Carrey Jewitt, Jill Bourne, Anton Franks, John Hardcastle, Ken Jones, and Euan Reid 2005: *English in Urban Classrooms: Multimodal Perspectives on Teaching and Learning*. London: Routledge/Falmer.

Ito, Mizuko, Heather Horst, Matteo,Bittanti, Danah Boyd, Becky Herr-Stephenson, Patricia G. Lange, C.J. Pascoe and Laura Robinson 2008: Living and Learning with New Media: Summary Findings from the Digital Youth Project. The John D. and Catherine T. MacArthur Foundation. http://digitalyouth.ischool.berkeley.edu/report

Küçükcan, Talip 1999: *Politics of Ethnicity, Identity and Religion: Turkish Muslims in Britain*. Aldershot: Ashgate.

Li Wei2011: Multilinguality, multimodality, and multicompetence: code- and mode switching by minority ethnic children in complementary schools. *The Modern Language Journal* 95(3):370–383.

Li Wei and Chao-Jung Wu 2010: Literacy and socialisational teaching in Chinese complementary schools. In: Vally Lytra and Peter Martin (eds.), *Sites of Multilingualism. Complementary Schools in Britain Today*, 33–44. Stoke-on-Trent: Trentham.

Lytra, Vally 2011: Negotiating language, culture and pupil agency in complementary school classrooms. *Linguistics and Education* 22(1):23–26.

Lytra, Vally 2012a: Discursive constructions of language and identity: Parents' perspectives in London Turkish complementary schools. *Journal of Multilingual and Multicultural Development* 33(1):85–100.

Lytra, Vally 2012b: Multilingualism and multimodality. In: Marilyn Martin-Jones, Adrian Blackledge and Angela Creese (eds.), *The Routledge Handbook of Multilingualism*, 521–537. Abingdon: Routledge.

Lytra, Vally and Taşkin Baraç 2009: Multilingual practices and identity negotiations among Turkish-speaking young people in a diasporic context. In: Anna-Brita Stedström and Annette Jørgensen (eds.), *Youngspeak in a Multilingual Perspective*, 55–78. Amsterdam: Benjamins.

Lytra, Vally and Peter Martin (eds.) 2010: *Sites of Multilingualism. Complementary Schools in Britain Today*. Stoke-on-Trent: Trentham.

Lytra, Vally, Peter Martin, Taşkin Baraç and Arvind Bhatt 2010: Investigating the intersection of multilingualism and multimodality in Turkish and Gujarati literacy classes". In: Vally Lytra and Peter Martin (eds.), *Sites of Multilingualism Complementary Schools in Britain Today*, 19–31. Stoke-on-Trent: Trentham.

Maybin, Janet 2007: Literacy under and over the desk: Oppositions and heterogeneity. *Language and Education* 21(6): 515–530.

Martin-Jones, Marilyn, Adrian Blackledge and Angela Creese 2012: Introduction: A sociolinguistics of multilingualism. In: Marilyn Martin-Jones, Adrian Blackledge and Angela Creese (eds.), *The Routledge Handbook of Multilingualism*, 1–26. Abingdon: Routledge.

McLean, Cheryl 2011: : A space called home: An immigrant adolescent's digital literacy practices. *Journal of Adolescent and Adult Literacy* 54(1): 13–22.

Mehmet-Ali, Aydin 2001: *Turkish-Speaking Communities and Education: No Delight*. London: Fatal Publications.

Millard, Elaine 2006: Transformative pedagogy: Teachers creating a literacy of fusion. In: Kate Pahl and Jennifer Rowsell (eds.), *Travel Notes from the New Literacy Studies*, 234–253. Clevedon: Multilingual Matters.

Nishimura, Yukiko 2011: Japanese *Keitai* novels and ideologies of literacy. In: Crispin Thurlow and Kristine Mroczek (eds.), *Digital Discourse. Language in the New Media*, 86–109. Oxford: Oxford University Press.

Pennycook, Alistair 2007: *Global Englishes and Transcultural Flows*. London: Routledge.

Pennycook, Alistair 2010: *Language as Social Practice*. London: Routledge.

Pahl, Kate and Jennifer Rowsell (2006): Introduction. In: Kate Pahl and Jennifer Rowsell (eds.), *Travel Notes from the New Literacy Studies. Instances of Practice*, 1–15. Clevedon: Multilingual Matters.

Sánchez, Patricia 2007: Cultural authenticity and transnational Latina youth: Constructing a meta-narrative across boarders. *Linguistics and Education* 18: 258–282.

Sarkar, Mela and Bronwen Low 2012: Multilingualism and popular culture. In: Marilyn Martin-Jones, Adrian Blackledge and Angela Creese (eds.), *The Routledge Handbook of Multilingualism*, 403–418. Abingdon: Routledge.

Sharma, Sanjay 1996: Noisy Asians or Asian noise? In: Sanjay Sharma, John Hutnyk and Ash Sharma (eds.), *Disorienting Rhythms: The Politics of the new Asian Dance Music*, 32–57. London: Zed Books.

Spilioti, Tereza 2011: Beyond genre: Closings and relational work in text-messaging. In: Crispin Thurlow and Kristine Mroczek (eds.), *Digital Discourse. Language in the New Media*, 69–85. Oxford: Oxford University Press.

Thurlow, Cripsin and Kristine Mroczek (eds.) 2011: *Digital Discourse. Language in the New Media*. Oxford: Oxford University Press.

Ben Rampton
Commentary: 'Agents' or 'participation'. Sociolinguistic frameworks for the study of media engagement

New media are increasingly influential in schools, and this is often unconnected to the curriculum.[1] But how does this actually affect the texture of everyday life? This is a question addressed by the two chapters in this section, by Vally Lytra and Alexandra Georgakopoulou.

Their answers are partly shaped by differences in focus and scope. Lytra builds a macro-sociolinguistic sketch of complementary schools and Turkish speakers in the UK, and shows popular cultural media engagement (PCME) impacting on the reproduction of traditional ethnic culture, an issue that Georgakopoulou only mentions in passing. Georgakopoulou, on the other hand, draws on field-work that involved 100 field-site visits over two years (rather than ten visits over three months),[2] studies two students with very different peer profiles (rather than one), and provides a detailed account of the links between PCME and positioning within peer-group hierarchies. But their accounts also incline towards two rather different perspectives on everyday communication, each with a substantial pedigree. In what follows, I shall try to bring out this difference, simplifying but hopefully not wholly misrepresenting the approach in each chapter in the interests of a wider argument. After that, I will offer an assessment of the implications for our understanding of PCME.

The first perspective emphasizes the agency of speakers. It emerged in sociolinguistics as a reaction to structuralism, which, according to Giles and Smith 1979, "cast the role of the normal speakers as a kind of 'sociolinguistic automaton'", treating "speech behaviour as ... a blob of clay moulded by situational constraints" (pp.46, 64). In contrast, agent-focused sociolinguistics offers an

> understanding of language ... which ... is rather different from the established theories of structuralism, and could be characterized as *flexible* and *fragmentary* .... [S]peakers... use their speech in a remarkably sensitive way to locate themselves and the situation of speaking in a multi-dimensional space, whilst at the same time conveying the message contai-

---

1 See Rampton et al. 2008 and Harris and Rampton 2010a: 256–257.
2 See Rampton et al. 2008: 6.

ned in the 'meaning' of their sentences ... In other words, every utterance may be seen as an *act of identity* by its speaker (Hudson 1980: 231, 233)

The second perspective acknowledges agency, but the capacity to control and influence what happens is no longer centred in the speaker. Instead, it is dispersed among the participants, artefacts, circumstances and histories that make up the communicative situation. This view often draws on ethnomethodology and conversation analysis, and it is a way of seeing that analysts often develop and practise in micro-analytic data sessions. McDermott characterizes it as a "move away from a linguistics of speakers towards a linguistics of participation" (1988: 61), and within this frame,

> [a]rticulateness and inarticulateness are not the properties of persons or their utterances; they are the properties of situations that arrange for the differential availability of words and ways of appreciating words across persons in a community (1988: 61)

Moerman (1988) plays up the difference. He recognizes that social scientists no longer see actors as 'social dopes' (or sociolinguistic automata) – they "honor social actors as intelligent beings":

> But the actors they construct are... omnipotent creatures with ravenous appetites. A constant calculator ..., this imagined actor chooses among preformed alternatives in a stripped down world ... The social dope ... has been replaced by a cardsharp, by a free-wheeling cultural entrepreneur. (1988: 56)

Instead, he invokes conversation analysis, also citing Bourdieu:

> Conversation analysis constructs a different actor: a 'virtuoso' (Bourdieu 1977: 79) for whom '[t]he schemes of thought and expression he has acquired are the basis for the intentionless invention of regulated improvisation'; an actor who thinks, if that is the word for it, on his feet. Those feet, in turn, are planted on some craft in a wind-buffeted sea .... If social analysis must construct a person, it is more apt to imagine him as a surfer whose practiced body moves unthinkingly with wave, wind, and board ... Such an actor, with 'No thinker behind the thoughts; no doer behind the deeds', better captures the agent of actual interactive events. (1988: 67)

Although the alignment certainly isn't absolute, Lytra's paper often leans towards the 'linguistics of speakers'. It thematizes Baran as someone who agentively "draws on, combines and transforms different sets of linguistic and other semiotic resources" (p. 246), focuses on his "situated, intentional and participant-oriented deployment of... resources", and sees the mobile phone "as a tool for self-expression" (p. 263). In line with this, the classifications in Lytra's interactional data description involve illocutionary speech acts, an approach to analysis that is frequently characterized as speaker-centred (e.g. 'warn', 'evaluate', 'summarize', 'explains', 'ridicule').

Georgakopoulou leans more to 'the linguistics of participation'. In this account, identities emerge interactively, and the analysis integrates what individuals say and do with how their actions and utterances are treated by recipients. So Nadia, for example, is characterized as an "an initiator, an assessor and a recipient of positive assessments" (p. 229), as someone who "assumes and is ascribed... positive online roles" (p. 231). In a similar vein, the quantitative comparison of Nadia and Habiba in Table 2 focuses on *relational* practices, which are necessarily based on the analysis of sequences of turns ("initiated by informant" [an analytic assessment that entails scrutiny of the preceding talk]; "taken up by other participants"; "topically linked"; "involved in positive assessment sequence"). And instead of simply being the embodied individuals who can each be heard producing different turns in the field recordings, selves are "discursive constructions" (p. 217), with the "self-projects" that participants engage in being "engendered, necessitated or constrained" interactively.

So there are discernible differences in how these two papers approach interaction. The first dwells on the named and embodied individual, who is seen as skilfully mobilising resources in accordance with the needs and options s/he perceives in the situation. The second prioritizes interactional activity itself, which it treats as a dialectic of moves in which embodied persons position and get positioned by one another, to the extent that it becomes hard to "know the dancer from the dance" (McDermott 1988: 44, following Yeats 1928). Although I certainly don't manage it in all of my own work, I think there are at least three reasons why the second approach produces a fuller picture of popular cultural media engagement.

First, as conversation analysts have amply demonstrated in their attention to sequences of turns rather than to single utterances, researchers can often get a better understanding of the interactional significance of any given act if they also consider the response that it elicits. So, for example, Lytra sees Baran's fusion of different musical and dance genres as 'creative', but it is easy for an action's novelty to the outside analyst to mislead him/her into thinking that it is an innovation for the local participants as well (Sapir 1949: 504; Becker 1995: 229; Rampton 2010). This mixing of genres is in fact treated as a negative disruption in the teacher's (eventual) response, so Lytra's positive characterization looks somewhat controversial and calls for a clearer warrant in the reaction of the other local interactants.

Second, both projects are operating in sites where the boundary between research and practical intervention is often very permeable (schools), and they offer different perspectives on the responsibility for what transpires in the environments they study. With its emphasis on agency and its traceable links to "a psychology of intelligence and skills" (McDermott 1988:61), speaker-centred analysis loads a lot of responsibility for what happens onto the individual, and there is a risk that in the educational uptake of research, findings are used to blame individuals for the weak positions where they find themselves. In contrast, the linguistics of participation connects with "a psychology of concerted arrangements for information dispersal" (*ibid*) (distributed cognition), and activity-centred analysis sees states and actions as being jointly produced by the participants and the situations in which they come together. This leads to findings that are harder to assimiliate within the individualising ideologies that dominate education, and indeed Varenne and McDermott argue that "to respect the individual, politically and morally, one must analytically cast one's eyes away" (1998: 155), turning instead to the task of "document[ing] carefully the social conditions in which [individuals] must always express themselves" (1998: 145). There are no issues of victim-blaming in Lytra's paper because it centres on a person who is generally well-rated in the environment she studies, but it is worth asking how an agent-centred linguistics would handle the comparison of high and low performing students that Georgakopoulou engages in, and what its portrait of an informant like Habibah would look like. If speaker-centred analysis is driven by emancipatory political principles, there is pressure to produce character portraits that are positive, even heroic, and cases like Habibah's present a challenge.

Third, analysis centred on interaction is better at bringing out the ordinariness of the practices in focus. Lytra closes her paper with a quotation from Pennycook:

> difference and diversity, multilingualism and hybridity are not rare and exotic conditions to be sought out and celebrated but the quotidian ordinariness of everyday life. (2007: 95)

This is absolutely right, but it points to a tension that is central to ethnography and consists of a dialectic between the theories, debates, issues and formulations that engage researchers on their home turf in the academy on the one hand – for example, "difference and diversity, multilingualism and hybridity" – and on the other, the perspectives and priorities of the people in ordinary life whom they study. It is very difficult to balance these two sets of concerns, but there is a vital buffer to analytic invasion of the ordinary in the attention that activity-centred analysis gives to sequences and the way that acts are received in endless cycles of act and response/act and response (adjacency). This is made very clear in the Goodwin paper cited by Lytra:[3]

---

3 Goodwin's approach is very much activity- rather than speaker-centred: "any participation

the analyst cannot simply take an inventory of all semiotic resources in a setting that could potentially be brought into play, and use this inventory as a frame to describe a relevant context ... [N]ot all possible and relevant resources are in play at any particular moment ... To describe the context we have to track in detail the temporal unfolding of the interaction, while attending to what the participants themselves are constituting for each other as the phenomena to be taken into account for the organization of the action of the moment. (Goodwin 2000: 1504)

Tuning to the perspectives operating in the practices being studied is widely recognized as a way of making space for the mundane, and we have already referred to it. But once this commitment and approach are in place, it is not at all straightforward mobilising the apparatus of scholarship so that its relationship with the ordinary becomes really productive. At this point of our discussion, it is worth looking more closely at the crafting in Georgakopoulou's chapter, which mainly engages with two literatures – linguistics/discourse analysis and feminist cultural studies. It is worth taking each in turn.

Early on, Georgakopoulou draws a distinction between 'ways of telling', 'sites' and 'tellers', and behind this lies a massive apparatus of scholarship in linguistics, narrative, conversation and discourse analysis, much of it focused on structures and systems. But the chapter's overall interest is in meaning-making and communicative action, and the underlying assumption is that these emerge in a complex and contingent interplay between participant understanding and a potentially huge range of semiotic systems, covering phonetics, grammar, turn-taking, narrative structure and much more. Knowing exactly what the options and conventions within a given system are at any one moment is vital, but it is impossible to take a particular atomistic, sub-systemic selection and extrapolate directly to its communicative significance – this can only be done in relation to the larger semiotic ensemble (including of course the dynamics of adjacency). In this context, Georgakopoulou's 'ways of telling', 'sites' and 'tellers' can be seen as 'mid-level' integrative concepts that bring together a lot of the same semiotic systems but focus our analytic gaze on broadly distinguishable aspects of the communicative process. The hope is that these broader, more encompassing/multi-semiotic foci will facilitate the production of analytic claims that can actually illuminate participants' lived experience and connect with their own accounts of it. And yes, as the analysis proceeds, Georgakopoulou shows that indeed they do help us to see different patterns in how her informants' engage with popular cultural

---

framework is an ongoing contingent accomplishment, something not under the control of a single party (who can at best make proposals about the structure of participation that should be operative at any moment), but rather something that has to be continuously achieved through public displays of orientation within ongoing processes of interaction" (2000: 1500).

media. Throughout the chapter, Georgakopoulou uses the term 'heuristic', positioning the scholarly literature as a source of 'sensitising' concepts "suggest[ing] directions along which to look" rather than 'definitive' constructs "provid[ing] prescriptions of what to see" (Blumer 1969: 148). Handled deftly like this, the linguistics literature becomes a valuable resource for ethnography, offering a rich and empirically robust collection of frameworks and procedures for exploring the details of social life, extending ethnography into intricate zones of culture and society that might otherwise be missed.

The literature in feminist cultural studies operates differently, and rather than functioning at the chapter's analytic core, it provides an answer to the ever-pressing 'so what?' question. Georgakopoulou makes it clear that this literature wasn't her starting baseline when she says that linguistic ethnography allows her to enquire "*if* and *how* local interactions resonate with widely circulating discourses" (p. 219; emphases added). And in terms of the actual history of the analysis itself, it sounds as though the contradictory discourses about 'girl power' and 'girls at risk' moved into focus when, as often happens in ethnography, the analyst asked herself: 'what are the questions to which these data provide some answers?' (reversing the orthodox sequence of enquiry). But once the connection is made, the analysis offers a powerful but nuanced description of how deeply these big themes permeate the girls' PCMEs. In a process of re-perspectivization, the two discourses and the tensions between them are brought 'down to earth', so we can see how they are routinely handled by people they refer to and affect. Here we can see that they're inescapable but also ordinary and mostly liveable, and if we follow these girls through the scenes in which these discourses become salient, we can start to document a plurality of tactics and stances it would be hard to predict from afar. So, for example, in addition to being weakened by discourses of risk in the ways that Georgakopoulou discusses, Habibah also participated in interactions where heterosexual risk was associated with intense sociability and excitement (Harris and Rampton 2010b).

So there are two scholarly literatures that are vital to Georgakopoulou's chapter, but neither is allowed to dominate. Linguistics may be pervasive, but rather than prescribing what must be looked at when, where, and how, it is treated as a sensitising heuristic, while cultural studies only enters as an interlocutor in the later stages of the analytic process. This leaves space for the discovery and description of patterns in local practice, and although she dwells more on some than others, Georgakopoulou gradually builds up a cumulative picture of the part that PCME plays in processes and systems of different duration, scope and social reach – moment-to-moment interaction, reiterated ways of telling, reflective narratives, cross-situational self-projects, peer-group roles, school achievement, pupil-teacher and parent-child relations. Different aspects of PCME play a part in processes at many levels of cultural organization, and these layers often interact in contingent ways that have to be investigated empirically.[4]

This makes it impossible to *predict* whether and how processes and phenomena identified outside the field, in the academy or in public discourse, actually link with the ways that people interact together in particular activities in particular settings (i.e. whether and how notions like hybridity are or aren't part of the "quotidian ordinariness of everyday life"). It also presents a major challenge for projects committed to the empirical analysis of 'intersectionality', which start with the analytic/academic identification of multiplicity in X or Y – multiple identities, multilingualism, multi-media and/or multi-modality – and then look for the ways in which these interact together in everyday settings. The risk for intersectional analysis is that the conceptual entities identified at the start will mutate or disappear as one's analytic gaze moves through the multi-layered processes coming together in any social field, and it may well turn out that one can only hold onto the initial terms if one's willing to disregard the ecologies in which signs, categories and actions gain meaning. Yes, it is vital to link the great debates to detailed analyses of the everyday, but Georgakopoulou's chapter shows us how to do this. Know the literatures and let them suggest directions, but don't revere them, and when it comes to analysis, keep them mostly backstage (sorting the props, walk-on parts etc). Work inductively with the complex moving ensembles of practice, moving backwards and forwards between the layered processes operating in the social field you're looking at. And only then turn to see whether, how and how far it's possible to translate the emerging portrait of cultural organization into terms that engage with the wider debates.

References

Becker, Alton 1995: *Beyond Translation: Essays towards a Modern Philology.* Ann Arbor: University of Michigan Press.
Blommaert, Jan 2013: *Ethnography, Superdiversity and Linguistic Landscapes: Chronicles of Complexity.* Bristol: Multilingual Matters.
Blumer, Herbert 1969: *Symbolic Interactionism.* Berkeley: University of California Press.
Bourdieu, Pierre 1977: *Outline of a Theory of Practice.* Cambridge: Cambridge University Press.
Giles, Howard and Philip Smith 1979: Accommodation theory: Optimal levels of convergence. In: Howard Giles and Robert St Clair (eds.), *Language and Social Psychology,* 45–65. Oxford: Blackwell.

---

4 See Rampton 2006: Ch. 3.8 on multileveled analysis of PCME and Blommaert 2013: Ch. 1 on sociolinguistic complexity.

Goodwin, Charles 2000: Action and embodiment within situated human interaction. *Journal of Pragmatics* 32: 1489–1522.
Harris, Roxy and Ben Rampton 2010a: Change in urban classroom culture and interaction. In: Karen Littleton and Christine Howe (eds.), *Educational Dialogues: Understanding and Promoting Productive Interaction*, 240–264. London: Routledge.
Harris, Roxy and Ben Rampton 2010b: Ethnicities without guarantees: An empirical approach. In: Margaret Wetherell (ed.), *Identity in the 21st Century: New Trends in Changing Times*, 95–119. Basingstoke: Palgrave Macmillan.
Hudson, Richard 1980: *Sociolinguistics*. Cambridge: Cambridge University Press.
McDermott, Ray. 1988. Inarticulateness. In: Deborah Tannen (ed.), *Linguistics in Context: Connecting Observation and Understanding*, 37–68. New Jersey: Ablex.
Moerman, Michael 1988: *Talking Culture: Ethnography & Conversation Analysis*. Philadelphia: University of Pennsylvania Press.
Pennycook, Alastair 2007: *Global Englishes and Transcultural Flows*. London: Routledge.
Rampton, Ben 2006: *Language in Language Modernity: Interaction in an Urban School*. Cambridge: Cambridge University Press.
Rampton, Ben 2010: An everyday poetics of class and ethnicity in stylization and crossing. *Working Papers in Urban Language & Literacies* 59. King's College London. www.kcl. ac.uk/innovation/groups/ldc/publications/workingpapers/download.aspx
Rampton, Ben, Roxy Harris, Alexandra Georgakopoulou, Constant Leung, Lauren Small and Caroline Dover 2008: *Urban Classroom Culture and Interaction: End-of-Project Report Working Papers in Urban Language & Literacies* 53. King's College London. www.kcl. ac.uk/innovation/groups/ldc/publications/workingpapers/download.aspx
Sapir, Edward 1949: *Edward Sapir: Selected Writings in Language, Culture and Personality*. (ed. David Mandelbaum) Berkeley: University of California Press
Varenne, Herve and Ray McDermott 1998: *Successful Failure*. Colorado: Westview Press.
Yeats, William Butler [1928] 1950: Among school children. In: *The Collected Poems of W. B. Yeats*, 242–245. Basingstoke: Macmillan.

Section IV: **Change in mass-mediatized and digitally mediated language**

Ulrich Schmitz

Semiotic economy, growth of mass media discourse, and change of written language through multimodal techniques.

The case of newspapers (printed and online) and web services

1 Introduction: What is at issue?

First of all, this article provides a short overview over the relationship between communication technology and language history (Section 2). Subsequently, Sections 3 to 5 draw on examples from printed and online mass media to demonstrate how technological developments lead to highly extensive and complex communication and messages. This goes beyond many of the forms produced by semiotic economy (maximal communicative efficiency) in the past – especially beyond traditional conventions of monomodal (purely written) texts, which, through textual coherence and grammatical (formal) cohesion, are geared to wholeness to convey sense.

In order to exploit the heterogeneous bulk of information that is medially communicated every day, a modular and multimodal architecture beyond the linear and often monomodal boundaries of traditional orality and writtenness develops in printed and online mass medial communication. The usual hierarchical structures were (and still are) aimed at a comprehensive, bottom-up style of perception from smaller parts to the bigger whole. Instead, in recent decades the growing mass of information is presented unitized to facilitate a selective, top-down style of navigation from visually-presented shop windows to single pieces of information.

For this purpose, smaller elements are presented for random selection and combination on all scales (full message, edition or homepage, topic category, piece, article, paragraph, sentence, word group). In this environment designed for fast usage, texts and their constituents – in comparison to conventional writtenness – become shorter and more fragmented. They are designed for selective perception (zapping) rather than for holistic reading. Grammar organizes smaller elements, is of less structural relevance than graphic design and consequently abandons grammatical marking more and more in favour of analytic or isolating constructions.

In this paper, these characteristic developments will be discussed and illustrated by typical examples. Section 3 analyzes texts and text types of printed newspapers, Section 4 those of online newspapers and Section 5 of the World Wide Web. The tendencies described above increasingly become visible step by step. Section 6 provides a summary and outlook.

2 Communication technology and language history

Throughout history, the world's population has grown. Increasingly complex societies were created and the communication between human beings intensified; as part of the division of labour, social relations and individual roles diversified. Social exchange accordingly became more demanding, and the purposes, types and contents of messages became increasingly diverse. Due to innovative transport techniques, great distances could be travelled more securely, more easily and more often. Step by step, new communication techniques were invented,[1] which enabled communication beyond the original limitations of face-to-face situations. By means of writing, indirect communication relatively independent from time and space has been possible for about 6,000 years.[2] Written (and also illustrated) documents can be copied any number of times – by means of woodblock printing from around 1,100 years ago and letterpress printing from around 500 years ago.

Not only communicative potential but also cultural opportunities in general are enormously extended by written communication.[3] As is generally known, writing changes language: every alphabetized person has a relationship to writing, oral communication differs from written communication concerning form and content, norms of lexical accurateness and formal correctness become more important and apply to larger spheres of communication, a literary and a standard language develop, varieties are diversified, complex (also comparative) linguistics arise. Letterpress printing and consequently compulsory education democratized writing. At the same time writtenness is regarded as more reliable and more prestigious than orality – entailing consequences for oral cultures and dialects. All these trends and developments have been thoroughly researched.[4]

---

1 Cf. e.g. Leroi-Gourhan 1993; Ong 1982.
2 According to Ehlich (1983: 32) in a „zerdehnten Sprechsituation" (stretched communication situation).
3 Cf. e.g. Ong 1982.
4 Cf. e.g. Dürscheid 2012: 23–62; Füssel 1999; Giesecke 2006; Ludwig 2005; Mattheier 2000; von Polenz 1991–1999.

After lettering and letterpress printing, first the telephone and audiovisual mass media and then computers caused the third big revolution in the history of communication as they have been used as universal semiotic machines by huge parts of the population for about thirty years. Now even orality and non-written modes (pictures, sound, film) have been engineered – first with different devices and finally with a single digital platform. Many dimensions of original (face-to-face) communication, which could not be simulated by written means only, can now be technically implemented and transported independently from space and time (as well synchronously as quasi-synchronously[5]). Engineered communication is becoming more multimodal – to variable extents according to the form of communication.[6] Although writing is gaining additional functions (e.g. in SMS, chats and link labels), it is losing its culturally and eminently respectable position of monopoly. The brunt of information is not necessarily born by writing. Thus texts in audiovisual and digital media are often only parts of multimodal communication. They do not have to comply with norms of internal wholeness, closeness, coherence and comprehensibility (and standardized formal correctness and cohesion) in the way these are enforced by autonomous scripturality due to its modal limitations.

Moreover, computer-based hypertechnique allows for unlimited connections of all modes (orality, scripturality, picture, sound, film etc.) and of all desired documents and parts of documents. Consequently, the conventional ideal of full and self-contained written texts is largely invalid. According to the communicative function the most different kinds of text types, text-picture-combinations[7], fragments, hybrids and other arrangements can be created and selectively used ad hoc from case to case.

Since computer communication tends to engineer all dimensions of the original face-to-face communication, the media-historical limitations of engineered communication are abolished. The integration of the communication partners into a more or less common situation can be created or at least simulated by the means of multimodal characters. The degree of temporal stretching[8] can be manipulated to any extent, even to the point of total abolition as in simultaneous online communication. Spatial distances are hardly experienced as such. The more qualities of direct communication can be adopted by engineered communi-

---

5 Cf. Dürscheid 2003.
6 Cf. e.g. Baron 2008; Bucher 2010; Kress and Van Leeuwen 2001; Kress 2010; Thurlow and Mroczek (eds.) 2011.
7 For a complete systematics cf. Wetzchewald 2012.
8 'Zerdehnung', cf. above n. 2.

cation, the more successfully it becomes a normal part of everyday communication. Today, most people in most parts of the world are used to a highly complex and simultaneous interplay of all kinds of engineered and direct communication. Linguistic forms and customs accordingly become more diverse.

The consequences for the system of language(s) that might result from media-based language use can only be determined in the long run and retrospectively. First of all, the fundamental architecture (grammar, syntax, core lexicon) of languages only changes more or less in the long run. Secondly, not only media-historical conditions affect language change, but also the increasing complexity of societies and the inner economy of language.[9] Semiotic economy plays an important role in the question of how to convey as much information as possible as appropriately and efficiently. Depending on technical conditions, each communication medium provides its own terms to accomplish this task.

In general, the media intensify, accelerate and differentiate language use. More people communicate more often, faster and in more manifold ways: interactively by phone and smartphone, SMS, e-mail, social media, web services etc., as well as more or less unidirectionally by old and new mass media. The usual rules adjust to these changes. There are no norms independent from their use; consequently they change with every use. According to Saussure, 'every symbol only exists because it is thrown into circulation', and it changes its identity in every moment.[10] Thus rules and signs will change by the degree to which the circulation is accelerating and changing. Media accelerate and differentiate the circulation of characters and therefore the alteration of the ways of use, rules, norms, lexicon and grammar. The more the circulation is medially engineered, the bigger the impact of medial conditions on everyone's language use.

Already visible today are (i) new forms of communication and linguistic varieties, (ii) an intense contact between the varieties and entire languages (at the moment in particular with the dominant American English) and corresponding hybrid forms in syntax and lexicon, (iii) the distribution of information to interacting modes (oral and written language, visual design, picture, sound) as well as (iv), according to the growing quantity of information, the increasing unitized division into small parts in magazine-like forms which is geared to a precise and selective usage. There is extensive research on the first three issues.[11] In the fol-

---

9 Cf. e.g. Cherubim 1975; Jones and Esch 2002; Mattheier 1998; Miller 2010; resp. Roelcke 2002.
10 "ein jedes Symbol existiert nur, *weil es* in die Zirkulation hineingeworfen ist" (Saussure 1997: 107).
11 Cf. e.g., to name only a few, Aitchison and Lewis 2003; Androutsopoulos 2006; Crystal 2011; Johnson and Ensslin 2007; Rowe and Wyss (eds.) 2009.

lowing Sections 3 to 5, however, particularly the last point – as related to the third – will be closely considered and illustrated with characteristic examples from mass media: printed newspapers (Section 3), online newspapers (Section 4), and web services (Section 5).

3 Texts in printed newspapers

How many texts does a daily newspaper contain? Let us take the *Rheinische Post* on Pentecost (26 May) 2012 for example, a German regional daily newspaper that has a run of over 430,000 copies (Fig. 1). On workdays it consists of four parts (A = politics and culture, B = business, sports etc., C = Dusseldorf, D = local section), on weekends there is an additional quadripartite magazine (M) printed on the same paper, also in the same six-column format (35 × 51.2 cm) as well as an inserted two-sided advertisement (W).

Figure 1: *Rheinische Post*, 26 May 2012, front page (detail)

Obviously, we are not confronted with pure writtenness, but with blends of alphanumeric, iconic and graphic elements. At first glance, therefore, it seems not so easy to isolate different 'texts': Where does one end, where does the next begin?

Page	Topic category	Texts	incl. Ads	Page	Topic category	Texts	incl. Ads
A1	– [front page]	22	1	C1	*Landeshauptstadt D'dorf*	12	2
A2	*Stimme des Westens*	12	0	C2	*Düsseldorf*	7	1
A3	*Land & Leute*	7	1	C3	*Düsseldorf*	8	2
A4	*Politik*	8	1	C4&5	– [advertisement]	1	1
A5	*Politik*	4	1	C6	*Düsseldorf*	10	4
A6	*Politik*	5	1	C7	*Düsseldorfer Kultur*	6	1
A7	*Kultur*	3	1	C8	*Düsseldorf*	10	1
A8	*Kultur*	9	1	∑ C		54	12
∑ A		70	7	D1	*Ratingen Heiligenhaus*	15	4
B1	*Wirtschaft*	14	0	D2	*Ratingen*	22	15
B2	*Wirtschaft*	11	0	D3	*Heiligenhaus*	11	2
B3	*Wirtschaft*	4	1	D4	*Ratingen*	6	1
B4	*Wirtschaft*	15	0	D5	*Ratinger Kultur*	10	3
B5	*Sport*	13	0	D6	*Düsseldorfer Sport*	9	0
B6	*Sport*	7	0	D7	*Düsseldorfer Sport*	8	1
B7	*Sport*	4	1	D8	*Events & Termine*	26	20
B8	*Fernsehen*	5	0	D9	– [advertisements]	44	44
B9	*Fernsehen*	5	0	D10	– [family announce- ments]	19	19
B10	*Fernsehen*	2	0				
B11	*Tierwelt*	57	56	D11	– [family announce- ments]	12	12
B12	*Marktplatz*	144	144				
B13	*Marktplatz*	154	154	D12	– [obituaries]	11	11
B14	*Marktplatz*	95	95	D13	– [obituaries]	13	13
B15	*Wissen/Roman*	8	0	D14	– [obituaries]	10	10
B16	*Gesellschaft*	15	0	D15	– [obituaries & ads]	24	23
∑ B		553	451	D16	– [advertisement]	1	1
				∑ D		241	179
				∑A-D		918	649

Once you accept signs other than letters as parts of texts and the visual design as a criterion for defining the units, however, the problem is easy to solve. We understand *text* as 'a limited number of linguistic signs which is coherent in itself and as a whole indicates a recognizable communicative function'.[12] We do not insist on full sentences: we allow for formally discontinuous messages (e.g. charts) and see information boxes, photos, diagrams and other graphic elements as parts of their respective text unit if they affiliate thematically and communicatively.

---

12 "eine begrenzte Folge von sprachlichen Zeichen, die in sich kohärent ist und die als Ganzes eine erkennbare kommunikative Funktion signalisiert" (Brinker 2010: 17).

Page	Topic category	Texte	incl. Ads	Page	Topic category	Texte	incl. Ads
M1	*das magazin am samstag*	4	0	M22	*Ehewünsche &*	129	129
M2&3	*Leben*	7	0		*Bekanntschaften*		
M4	*Leben*	6	0	M23	*Auto & Mobil*	7	1
M5	*Leben*	7	0	M24	*Auto & Mobil*	78	75
M6	*Spass mit Kruschel*	11	0	M25	*Auto & Mobil*	10	5
M7	*Reise & Welt*	6	1	M26	*Auto & Mobil*	194	194
M8	*Reise & Welt*	14	10	M27	*Auto & Mobil*	203	203
M9	*Reise & Welt*	6	1	M28	*Auto & Mobil*	5	2
M10	*Reise & Welt*	14	10	M29	*Immobilien & Geld*	8	1
M11	*Reise & Welt*	2	1	M30	*Immobilien & Geld*	150	150
M12	*Reise & Welt*	5	3	M31	*Immobilien & Geld*	94	94
M13	*Reise & Welt*	8	5	M32	*Immobilien & Geld*	48	48
M14	*Reise & Welt*	101	101	M33	*Immobilien & Geld*	116	116
M15	*Beruf & Karriere*	10	1	M34	*Immobilien & Geld*	117	117
M16	*Beruf & Karriere*	58	58	M35	*Immobilien & Geld*	52	52
M17	*Beruf & Karriere*	27	27	M36	*Immobilien & Geld*	142	142
M18	*Beruf & Karriere*	70	70	∑ M		1808	1716
M19	*Beruf & Karriere*	20	20	W1	– [advertisement]	1	1
M20	*Beruf & Karriere*	13	13	W2	– [advertisement]	1	1
M21	*Beruf & Karriere*	66	66				
				∑total		2728	2367

Table 1: Contents of the *Rheinische Post*, 26 May 2012
(German language headline of each page in italics)

Concerning the limitation, the graphic presentation (lines, blank areas) will be our reference point in cases of doubt. The single text units can be identified quite objectively in this way (independent from individual opinions).[13]

In this way we count (see Table 1) 918 texts on the 48 pages of the main sections A–D, 269 editorial texts and 649 advertisements. The 36-page weekend supplement M contains 1,808 texts: 92 editorial texts and 1,716 adverts. Including the inserted advert the reader therefore receives 2728 texts, thereof 361 editorial texts and 2367 ads, for the price of € 1.50.

---

13 Competing notions of text (cf. Adamzik 2004: 38–41; Klemm 2002) are therefore irrelevant. Cases of doubt were dealt with in the following way: (1) The advert for an airline spreads over two areas within the weather forecast on page A2. The weather forecast and the ad are counted as one text each. (2) The ten exchange tables on p. B4 could possibly be divided into smaller units. (3) The TV programmes on p. B8–10 counted as one text could be counted as much smaller units (e.g. according to channel). (4) The 61st episode of the serialised novel on p. B15 is classified as one text although it is just a part of a much longer text.

Figure 2: Wetter (*Rheinische Post*, 26 May 2012, p. 1)

At first, let us take a look at the editorial texts. The longest text in the main section (and the one covering the largest area as well) can be found on page A6. It covers two-thirds of the page (including photo and chart) and is about the illegal landing of an amateur pilot on the Red Square in Moscow 25 years ago. The longest article in the magazine fills four-thirds of the pages M2 and M3, mainly with 27 labelled photos and two commented ground plans, and presents "Neue Ideen für den Balkon" ('New ideas for your balcony'). The shortest and smallest text is the "Wetter" ('Weather') on the front page: "Heute. Es herrscht verbreitet und durchweg sonniges Wetter." ('Today. There is widespread and sunny weather throughout.') including sun-pictograms for "morning" and "evening" and a "13" in a blue and a "26" in a red circle, which can commonly be understood as the daily minimum and maximum (Fig. 2).

The most extensive advert covers the double page C4–5. It advertises an equestrian sports fair using four pictures, a sitemap, an info box and a report which appears to be journalistic. In contrast, the shortest classified advert only comprises 17 characters naming a web address: "www.boconcept.de".

This already gives an insight to the enormous spectrum of topics and text types which occur in a German daily newspaper. Text types are, again according to Brinker, 'conventionally valid patterns for complex speech acts and can be described as typical combinations of contextual (situative) communicative-functional and structural (grammatical and thematic) characteristics'.[14] Typically journalistic text types can be found in the editorial sections: news, reports, long and short versions of weather forecasts, commentaries (ironic and non-ironic), concert and also CD reviews, interpretations of paintings, quotes of the day, press

---

14 „*konventionell geltende Muster* für komplexe sprachliche Handlungen und lassen sich als jeweils typische Verbindungen von kontextuellen (situativen), kommunikativ-funktionalen und strukturellen (grammatischen und thematischen) Merkmalen beschreiben." (Brinker 2010:125)

reviews, the masthead, info boxes, the "Number of the Day", sport results ("Sport in Zahlen"), team line-ups, exchange tables, counselling of all kinds (financial advice, advice for cat owners, "Entspannt reisen mit Enkelkind" ("Relaxed travelling with your grandchildren"), travel reports, travel tips, automotive tests, science-based factual information ("Drei Zeichen für schlechte Wasserqualität" = "Three signs of poor water quality"), simply presented general knowledge (the meaning and significance of Pentecost), the TV programme, information on current events, traffic reports, emergency services, recipes, cartoons and comic strips, jokes, Sudoku and other puzzles, serialized novels, and the "Question of the Day" (including an invitation to vote online and the result of the previous day).[15] Amongst the adverts are product and image advertisements, information on current events, calls for donations, information about doctors' offices, marriage announcements, lonely hearts ads, obituaries, cryptic personal messages[16] and other classified ads of all kinds (services, building, real estate, cars, arts, leisure, hobby, contacts etc.).[17]

The sheer quantity (nearly 32 texts per page; without the magazine 19 texts per page) shows that the prototypical text (a coherent sequence of interdependent sentences with a descriptive, narrative or argumentative intention) is very prominent but relatively rare. Furthermore, a look through the newspaper reveals that smaller text types, fragmentary, elliptic and discontinuous texts, accompanying paratexts, info charts, pictures and other graphic means play a central role. The entire newspaper turns out to be a conventionally sorted collection of the most different pieces of information; it is geared at efficient navigation through the extensive offer and fast legibility of the single units. These units are organized in a modular rather than in a linear way: similar to pictures they can be perceived top down (from the overall whole to the finer detail). The architecture of

---

15 Lüger (1995:77–151) identifies five groups of text types in the press, (a) contact-oriented, (b) focused on information (message, hard news, soft news, report, feature, presentation of problem), (c) focused on opinion (commentary, ironic commentary, review, interview), (d) inviting and (e) instructing texts (operations instructions, advice). All of these occur but the range is even wider. The styles of speech of the several text types seem to be quite homogenous within the *Rheinische Post*, not necessarily, however, within all daily newspapers or even different press products, as Lüger (1995:152; cf. 11983:103) believed thirty years ago.

16 E.g. „Endlich kapiert/ M und M und M und O und P/ Mit Absicht auf die falsche Fährte fehlgeführt./ Verstanden, da gehöre ich nicht zu,/ es reicht!" (p. D10) In English: „Finally got it / M & M & M & O & P/ Set on the wrong track intentionally./ I understand, that's not my cup of tea,/ I've had it!"

17 E.g. coloured on 4.5 × 4 cm: „Millionär (42/180/78) vergibt *3-Zimmer-Wohnung kostenfrei* an attraktive Muse, b.m.B." [plus box number]. In English: „Millionaire (42/180/78) awards *3-room apartment for free* to attractive muse, p.s.p." [please send picture].

the respective visual communication area draws the attention from the whole to smaller units such as the headline or heading, pictures, labels, info charts, continuous texts with crossheadings and other graphic elements. Columns, crossheadings and other graphic means often structure longer texts as a selectively usable collection of more or less autarkic modules. A lot of information is presented in short texts, pictures, charts and other elliptic info boxes. Accompanying pictures and charts take pressure off the text, shorten and fragment it and make it more elliptic – compared to traditional text entities (cf. Figure 2).

Such more or less discontinuous, disintegrated texts and text collections (even if monomodal) in mass media have been described earlier.[18] They feature a magazine-like architecture, consisting of clusters and aggregations of fragments not to be read in full, but selectively. The history of media reception is a long journey from full-text reading to selective reading.[19] The producers react by dividing their products and texts into smaller and smaller units, so that zapping and fragmentation increasingly drive each other to extremes. Multimodality pushes this development even further.

Traditional full texts have a more or less hierarchically ordered structure of meaning within their linear sequence of written characters. From the particular units (e.g. words) the reader therefore needs to deduce the respective more complex entity (e.g. sentences) bit by bit (bottom up). Mapping these hierarchies onto linear sequences lies in the responsibility of grammar. The flatter (more compartmentalized) these hierarchies are, the less grammar is needed, the simpler it can be. The German sample text (above and in Fig. 2) „Heute Es herrscht verbreitet und durchweg sonniges Wetter." separates the time-deictic adverb „Heute" (as well as the surrounding written elements "Wetter", "morgens", "nachmittags", "13" and "26") from the main clause without interpunction and highlights it typographically as an independent unit of meaning. Only seven words are left for the main clause; of these only the verb and the adjective are grammatically marked ("t" for 3rd pers. sg. pres.; "es" for nom. sg. masc.). Subject and predicate ("es herrscht", corresponding to English "there is"), which often carry the main meaning or denotation of sentences, are semantically empty; one could easily abandon them. They merely have the old-fashioned purpose of at least recalling grammatical integrity. Seen from a traditional point of view the actually shorter version "Heute herrscht verbreitet und durchweg sonniges Wetter." would have

---

18 Püschel 1992, 1997; Schmitz 1996a; Weingarten 1997. For online news: Althaus and Tewksbury 2002; Brodde-Lange and Verhein-Jarren 2001; Kang and Choi 1999; Lewis 2003.
19 „Von der Ganzlektüre zur selektiven Lektüre" (Jakobs and Püschel 1998: 165). For earlier times cf. Hrbek 1995: 277.

been more sensible. However, this would have been too much of the anatomy of a coherent text for the purpose of visual, selective and quick perception instead of a linear bottom-up perception.

Thus, in multimodal communication there is a division of labour between grammar and design.[20] Once you present a complex variety of pieces of information on one page it is visual design which organizes their architecture as well as the first steps of reception and understanding. The smaller these pieces are and the deeper they are embedded in multimodal environment, the less grammar is necessary to organize the verbal parts. Very often, shorter texts are designed in a discontinuous way, e.g. as lists or fragments, or they come as series of ellipses or single words, even in combination with icons and other pictures. Some types of texts, e.g. exchange tables (page B4) and crosswords (page D15), can do completely without grammar as they comply with their own text-type specific rules.

Figure 3: First edition of the *Rheinische Post*, 2 March 1946, front page[21]

20 Cf. Schmitz 2010: 403–406, 2011. For "design and arrangements", Kress 2010: 132–158.

21 <www.rp-online.de/niederrhein-nord/kleve/nachrichten/schueler-lesen-zeitung-jetzt-an-melden-fuer-das-fruehjahrs-projekt-1.1047697> (1 June 2012).

Let us compare the 2012 edition discussed so far with the first edition of the *Rheinische Post*, dating 2 March 1946 (Figure 3).[22] Both issues place ten editorial texts (no advertisements) on the upper half of the front page (cf. Figures. 1 and 3). The older issue, in black and white, appeared at a time when there was no TV in Germany and computers could not be perceived of. Except for a small photo it only presents longer texts with headings in relatively small font size. The 2012 issue, in contrast, comes in an elaborate, multicoloured layout, with one large and four small pictures, rich typography and a comparatively large amount of white space, which serves to visually delineate the various elements. The first edition looks more like a textbook set in columns, whereas the recent one is rather reminiscent of a chequered pin board (or even a modern computer screen). To put it briefly: back then, plenty of text was formulated for careful reading in a simple five-column presentation, whereas today, 66 years later, most effort is invested into visual presentation and complex design for quick reference – reading versus browsing.[23]

This is reflected in the number of words. Within the same area, the *Rheinische Post* places 1,324 words in 1946, but only 325 in 2012. That is slightly less than a quarter (24.5 per cent). Hence, the older texts are much longer on average. They have larger coherent units of meaning as well as a more complex syntax and morphology (not to be traced in detail here). Texts consisting of one or two sentences only, as they often appear in 2012, were barely conceivable in 1946. Today, on the other hand, most texts do not work autonomously as they did before, but as part of nested units of information built of text, graphic elements and design.

On the whole and from a historical perspective, traditional monomodal (only written) full texts evolve into magazine-like compilations of different information units: headings, headlines, subheadings, short core messages (lead or teaser), main texts with crossheadings, photos with or without accompanying texts, info charts with and without keys, other graphic content (e.g. pictograms, arrows, logos) as well as graphic design elements (e.g. colour, different font sizes, bold print, lines, blank areas). Five tendencies go hand in hand: (1) The quantity and diversity of information increases – in part to cater for heterogeneous public interest. (2) The share of autonomously coherent main texts becomes smaller. (3) Main texts become shorter. (4) The share of paratexts[24], i. e. side texts, which accompany the main text in an inviting, describing, orientating, commenting or subsidiary way, becomes bigger. (5) The number of non-written components increases.

---

22 For going further back in newspaper history cf. e.g. Püschel 1991.
23 For text design in newspapers, Bucher 1996, 2001.
24 Detailed (but only for books) Genette 1997.

4 Texts in online newspapers

Let us now turn to online newspapers. How many texts do they contain?

The online edition of the *Rheinische Post* <*www.rp-online.de*> as of 29 May 2012 will serve as our example. It is actually not possible to count the pieces of one single 'edition' since there are no temporal or spatial limitations. Numerous hyperlinks lead to various pieces which are updated during the day, as well as to older information offers and to interactive information services; for some of these the desk is not responsible. This virtual three-dimensionality is continuously in progress; on this very day more than half of the offers on the first hierarchical level has been replaced or fundamentally altered after eight hours.

In order to draw a comparison we will confine ourselves to the page <*www. rp-online.de*>as it appears when accessed at 2 pm, without clicking on the integrated links (as though there was just a single scrollable screen without any content lying 'behind' hyperlinks) (see Figure 4).

We will disregard the paratextual tabs at the top and bottom of the entire site and only take into consideration the rest: a scrollable area of the length of four A4 formats which has three to four columns (framed by sometimes rhythmically changing adverts at the top and the right side). This equals five-thirds of a page of the print edition. Within this area we find 77 texts[25], optically and thematically clearly delimited information units[26], whereof seven are adverts. Converted to the area of one page of the printed newspaper, there would be 46 texts on a page. This is almost two and a half times more than the main part of the printed newspaper (without the "Magazine," to be fair). This shows that the pieces of information (the pictures as well as the written texts) are considerably smaller. In order to facilitate the most efficient orientation for the users, a very conservative layout has been chosen: the site appears to be a notice board with strictly right-angled boxes to enable fast and selective perception. Most pieces of information include a thematic allocation in an elliptically phrased heading in red font (e.g. "Gewalt-verbrechen in Bottrop"; in English: "Violent crime in Bottrop") and a headline in black font (e.g. "Erschossener Motorradfahrer ein Bandido?" = "Shot motorcyclist – a *Bandido*?"); the two constitute the core of the message. Bigger parts additionally contain a short continuous text (mostly totalling one to three main clauses) as well as a picture (predominantly left-hand side next to the continuous text); the text is connected to a longer article lying 'behind', which can be accessed over

---

25 In comparison to 28 texts in the first five-thirds of the print edition, including an advert.
26 Six in the first quarter, 16 in the second, 29 in the third and 26 in the fourth. The news ticker in the first quarter is counted as one text.

Figure 4: *www.rp-online.de*, 29 May 2012 at 2 pm (upper quarter)

the link "mehr" (= "more"). Moreover, several videos and photo galleries as well as various services (e.g. "Stauwarner", "Spiele"; = "Traffic Report", "Games") are offered.

We can find twelve types of texts, eight of which appear in printed newspapers in a modified form, i. e. hard news, soft news, weather forecast, commentaries, reports, advice, film reviews, and adverts, as well as four online-specific ones: a news ticker, short-text links to service packages (e.g. "Arztsuche" = "Search for doctors"), videos, and photo galleries (on all kinds of issues). For comparison: 15 text types appear on the first five-thirds of the first pages of the printed edition, including hard news, soft news, the weather forecast, a commentary and an advert (but no report, advice or film review). In addition, there is a background story, ironic commentary, quote of the day, person of the day, personality, press review, masthead and cartoon and finally – with a similar function as the headline links and teasers online – a topic overview and teasers. The online edition features 52 fifty-two photos and 22 link pictograms, the printed edition only ten photos. Whereas the range of text types in the printed edition is broader than in the online edition, a lot more and smaller information units and also illustrations are available online.

Thus we cannot find a single conventional full text whose coherence is produced solely through written means. The longest text sequence occurs in the first report, which also comprises the only big photo (top left corner in Fig. 4). In addition to the red and black headline, it contains four simple main clauses and the hyperlink labelled with "mehr" ("more"). These four sentences fully correspond to the conventions of traditional hard news in print media. All the other news and other information units are (in some cases considerably) shorter, are accompanied by smaller pictures and heavily diverge from traditional conventions of text types the further we scroll down the page. Very often we only find thematic allocations plus headlines as the designation of a link for further details (e.g. "Studie der Bundesagentur für Arbeit / Weniger Befristungen für junge Menschen" = "Report by the Federal Employment Agency / Less temporary contracts for young people"; see Figure 5).

Figure 5: *www.rp-online.de,* 29 May 2012 at 2 pm
(Detail from the upper part of the second quarter)

In a smaller quantity (especially at the top of the site), teaser-like beginnings of longer texts can be found, which are continued when clicking on the link; to a larger extent (especially at the bottom of the page) there are only paratexts, i. e. titles of categories, headlines, the link "mehr", and similar link labels or pictograms. An inverted ratio of text and paratext can be found in comparison to the print edition. Only a small part of the texts is reminiscent of conventional full texts; the larger share consists of topic labels and text fragments.

Similar observations can be made for most online newspapers. There are two reasons for this. First of all, front pages of online newspapers only show a compact cross-section of the entire range of contents. In contrast to the use of printed newspapers the average user will not exploit large parts of the entire offer (e.g. more than a fifth). In this sense the front page must not be understood as a (more or less systematic) table of contents, but as a window (for arousing interest and) for facilitating a fast choice. Secondly, online newspapers do not aim at providing a more or less complete or seemingly representative picture of the most important current events. They rather present an extensive spectrum of fragments from discourses of all kinds (current events, entertainment, everyday life issues, services) that make use of the interactive and multimodal opportunities of the World Wide Web, which is impossible for printed newspapers. Online newspapers are not geared towards reading longer or shorter texts; they focus on facilitating the selective, isolated and fast use of a very heterogeneous range of information in order to provide orientation in everyday life. The objective therefore is multiplicity, not necessarily coherence.

From a historical perspective, online newspapers intensify the five tendencies identified for printed newspapers in part three: (1) The quantity and diversity increase further to satisfy even more heterogeneous public demands. (2) In order to provide orientation within the abundance of offers, the share of autonomously coherent main texts (at least on the front page is reduced. (3) For the same reason, the remaining main texts become even shorter. (4) The majority of the front page consists of paratexts and visual characters (e.g. pictograms). Predominantly they only serve as labels for links and make further information accessible. These characters are of varying types and can contain longer coherent texts on further hierarchy levels. (5) The number of non-written components increases further. Multimodality becomes more complex: apart from single photos, charts and pictograms (as in printed newspapers) there are extensive photo galleries, animations, videos and audio files.

5 Texts on the World Wide Web

In this chapter, we will see how the five tendencies just described are taken to extremes in avant-garde parts of the web, so much so that the traditional concept of text no longer applies and definitely loses its value. In web services, there is not just one sender (person, group, or institution) that produces messages to be read by recipients. Instead, automatic mono- or multimodal information systems are used by people to interactively give and select information and produce messages. For this purpose, the (wo)man-machine interface on the screen must be designed as efficiently as possible in order to meet all needs of semiotic economy: information has to be presented as unerring, fast, and easy to grasp. Traditional writtenness does not achieve these aims. This is why the output of web services is (1) potentially infinite and extremely varied, (2) does not usually contain autonomously coherent texts, (3 and 4) but short language fragments (mainly paratexts) only, combined with and surrounded by visual characters, (5) and embedded in rich multimodal landscapes.

Let us have a closer look at the web. Because, even if we take all texts into consideration that have ever been published on *rp-online.de*, this only amounts to a tiny fraction of the information in the World Wide Web. But how many texts and text types does the World Wide Web contain? In 1998 there were 26 million 'pages' (usually comprising several texts and other data), in 2000 there were one billion, in the middle of 2008 one trillion. [27] At this point people quit counting – because the number changes within seconds and also because it is not relevant.[28] The web comprises a bulk of the most different information, which is infinitely extensible in all digitizable modes, provided by a literally uncountable number of institutions and persons. On account of the illustration we will confine ourselves to some of the services offered by *Google*.

Apart from the prominent search engines for texts and pictures, there are searchable maps, satellite pictures and photographed streets including additional information and services of all kinds (Google *Maps, Earth, Street View*), Google *Books* provides access to millions of books, *Scholar* to scientific documents, *Translate* translates entered texts into over 60 languages, *Blogger* creates blogs, *Talk* enables voice over IP etc. Briefly said: all imaginable text types, types

---

27 A thousand billion, this means over 148 pages per individual (based on a population of over 6.7 billion according to <www.pdwb.de/nd02.htm> on 1 June 2012).
28 "„Strictly speaking, the number of pages out there is infinite" <http://googleblog.blogspot.de/2008/07/we-knew-web-was-big.html> 1 June 2012; from there, the above mentioned numbers of 'pages' were taken.

of pictures and text-picture combinations as well as other mono-, bi- and multi-modal kinds of documents and information occur. Global attempts of counting or classifying them are pointless. Many contain the most varied texts and paratexts; very often in diverse mixtures with other modes (e.g. pictures, films, sounds), or they refer to them. Others facilitate the production of these texts (written, oral or multimodal), and yet others the editing and processing of texts (e.g. translating). All we can state is that everything that can possibly be communicated via technical means can actually be found on the web: fully coherent traditional types of texts, all sorts of discontinuous texts, lists, fragments, bi- and multimodal semiotic compositions, songs, films, videos, written and spoken dialogues, texts, writing and (semiotic) work in progress etc., often with language contributing only one part of the meaning of the messages.

Thus, the traditional prototypical notion of text (as a self-contained, coherent written document dealing with one particular subject) dissolves completely. More precisely: Our conventional idea of prototypical text types, although not entirely obsolete, is guided by bygone times. This applies to all common linguistic notions of text. Traditional prototypical texts – such as letters, minutes, school essays, nonfiction books, novels, papers in humanities, etc. – are meant to feature inner wholeness and coherence: They are supposed to pursue a topic and/or an aim according to a certain inner logic in a formally correct way so that a more or less complex but cohesive, full sense emerges. It is generally expected that authors will not hand over such a text until it is completely formulated in written form and is labelled finished and completed. (Even if this of course does not determine the way the reader handles it.)

This ideal is due to the technical limitations of pure (monomodal) written-ness. Everything that is supposed to be communicated needs to be expressed situation-independently in written form. The focus on a single mode of expression (writing) enforces inner wholeness and has given rise to most text types; hence this was and still is an enormous cultural achievement. The advantages are obvious und will persist within the evolution of communication. Many older text types not only are present in older forms of communication, they continue to exist in new communication forms as well. The World Wide Web is full of these kinds of traditional texts. However, you will not find them on the first hierarchical levels but in deeper layers after several clicks. Even then, in many or most cases long coherent texts on the web (such as books, long descriptions, work reports etc.) will not be read completely from the first to the last line. Rather, people use long electronic texts in short extracts – for research, focussing on particular details, just browsing or for a targeted search, often zapping between several documents. And, perhaps most of the newly composed messages on the web are not of the traditional types but rather text-picture or other multimodal combinations, fragments, and interactive works in progress: they appear in a state of semiotic flux.

Everything that is technically possible is brought into being, and multimodal forms of communication broaden the traditional range. This is already apparent in the earlier history of communication but, in an amazing variety of manifestations, is carried to extremes on the web. In contrast to the absolute amount, the relative amount of conventional monomodally-written monologic texts decreases because of text-picture conglomerations (such as in Figure 4), audiovisual documents (e.g. on *Youtube*), virtual worlds (e.g. *Second Life*) and interactive ways of communication (e.g. on *Facebook*). Written texts rarely remain autonomous: with increasing frequency they appear as components of bi- or multimodal communication and often they are only comprehensible in dynamic multimodal relationships. As a result, written passages tend to become shorter, more fragmented, more transitory and easier to modify interactively.

Many written passages are not independent and isolated, in fact they are, along with (audio)visual messages, produced and used semi-automatically for specific purposes as stages in communicative processes. The frequently used Google Services are not the only examples but very characteristic for this. The directions in Fig. 6 could also, with some (rather needless because uneconomical) effort, be verbalized in seven or eight sentences as a traditional full text, but then they would not be easy to use. The dynamic multimodal version is distinctly more efficient and thus more common.

Figure 6: http://maps.google.de (13 June 2012)

This example, like many others, cannot do without the written part, yet none of the written passages carries meaning standing on its own. Fig. 6 shows the key moment in a sequence of interactive man-machine communication (which could easily be continued, extended and varied). In the larger area on the right-hand side of the screen we see an aerial shot (enriched with cartographic information), which is – with a well-conceived and communicatively efficient design – filled, overlaid and accompanied by many single words, letters, characters and pictograms of all kinds and function. The smaller blank area to left of this also contains various written characters of this kind. However, in this case they are not placed on a picture as a background, and they would possibly be understood without the picture in the right to which they refer (partly explicitly, partly implicitly) deictically. Do these characters on the left-hand side therefore amount to a text? At least it is structured in lines and can largely be read from the upper left to the bottom right. This visual design (areal units, pictograms, colour, bold print), however, leads to a selective perception of single parts. Moreover: from the viewpoint of traditional writtenness we cannot find a single full sentence, but rather ellipses, fragments, abbreviations and digits. With respect to grammar, only the plural (and once the simple past) is marked, nothing else.

Three kinds of illocutionary acts occur: assertives ('this is it', 'it is called ...'), directives from the machine to the user ("Nach Westen Richtung Constantin-straße starten" = "Start west towards Constantine Road") and inversely directives (as link labels), which are used for controlling the machine ("Route berechnen" = "Get directions") – the latter being computives as a new type of speech acts, which is not used to interact with people but to control computers by semiotic means (Schmitz 1996b). This, of course, is miles away from classic notions of 'text' and even of 'human communication'. Even leaving out of account such computives, conventional written texts are not familiar with this kind of heterogeneous mixture, particularly with the 'dialogic' exchange of the role of the 'sender' and the 'recipient'; obviously, these passages are also not based on an oral dialogue.

What can be identified here as text or as paratext – or as picture and para-picture? There is no deciding, because all kinds of signs build up the message together – in a way which enables users to pick from the offered collection of pictures, signs and characters and choose what seems relevant for them. (This initially was the purpose of the presented set of signs.) Thus there is no good reason for labelling the written elements in this multimodal communication as 'text' or 'texts'; because without a picture and without visual design they are neither coherent nor cohesive. They rather make reasonable sense in a multimodal context and even here only as a result (or partial result) of a bigger interaction, i. e. a semi-automatic act of seeking and giving information. Grice's cooperative principles (1975: 45–46) are not accomplished within one autonomous text (as in a written minute), but in correspondence with other visual characters and within a communicative act. Malinowski (1930: 306–307) would say: within a "context of situation". Admittedly the situational context does not spring from an original act, in which participants interact physically, but, with its schematic structures, is simulated automatically in man-machine interaction. The products of this kind of communication are not usual static texts for left-to-right reading, but transient semiotic constructs designed for quick use and consumption, and, in contrast to conventional full texts, not meant to survive a brief moment.

Hence it is not useful to count texts on the web. However, it is possible to identify 'conventionally valid patterns for complex speech acts' – or rather communication acts –which can be described 'as typical combinations of contextual (situative) communicative-functional and structural (grammatical and thematic) characteristics' (which has not been done yet). According to Brinkers (2010: 125) generally accepted definition these would be text types – or let us rather call them message types and, as the case may be, message production types. Consequently, we should broaden the notion of text past pure writtenness (and if necessary orality). Alternatively, one could introduce new terms such as 'piece of communication', 'text-picture type', 'multimodal kind of interaction', etc. Science has neither been able to conceptualize this medially induced language change nor to empirically measure its extent. This applies to all multimodal relationships and appearances as well as to techniques of verbalization in a narrower sense.

If one accepts this argument, the appearance of what we are used to call text has changed during the course of time, and mainly by technical developments. Multimodality, although "the normal state of human communication" (Kress 2010: 1), cannot be simulated by writing. To the extent that non-verbal modes of communication can be reproduced with technical means, media communication is becoming multimodal. How far you want to stretch the notion of text depends upon caprice and usefulness. For printed media such as newspapers, as they only work with static visual signs (cf. Section 3 above), the classic definition seems to suffice more or less – at least as long as the different units are separated by visual means (such as blank areas). For web services, however, 'text' is too narrow a word to denote all the multimodal and interactive forms of communication. Online newspapers (Section 4) are something in between. We may be excited to see where further technical developments and social needs will lead us in future.

6 Summary and outlook

Following aspects may be observed: (1) The media intensify, multiply and accelerate communication. (2) This also expedites language change and makes it more complex. (3) A medially supported multiplicity of discourses, with an increased level of communication and the wealth of information on the one hand, and the increase of societal complexity due to economic factors on the other, have a reinforcing effect on one another. (4) An acceleration of the social traffic of this extent enhances the receptiveness of individuals and groups, but they also come up against their limits and are overstrained. (5) As a consequence, the interplay between semiotic economy and the exuberant growth of the media discourse intensifies language change. (6) Messages do not necessarily become shorter, but are increasingly divided into small sections. Mass-media products tend to be in magazine format; dialogical forms of communication tend to include faster changes. (7) Due to technical development, more 'natural' communication channels and modes can be mechanized perfectly (to appear authentic) and can be integrated into a single communication device. (8) This is how 'real' and 'virtual' worlds are interweaved; similar to the relation between 'reality' and linguistic 'acquisition' that we are familiar with. (9) Thus the borders between speech, writing, non-verbal sounds and static and moving pictures, originating in technical limitations, are overcome. At first merely technically but consequently also semiotically – in favour of medially imparted multimodal sign complexes which have been, until now, only known from non-mechanized ('life-world') communication.

(10) A bulk of complex semiotic formats, multimodal texts (communication and interaction spaces, sound sequences) and semiotic types (types of texts and picture combinations etc.) is developed in this way in different forms of communication, according to societal opportunities and needs. (11) Older forms persist in parallel (as long as they fulfil their functions), adjust to newer forms to greater or lesser extent (in order to survive the evolution of communication) or they become obsolete and disappear (if they fall into disuse). (12) Tempo, density, complexity, fragmentation and multimodality are followed by hybrid forms: old borders disappear; previously separated forms are blended; the formerly unexpected becomes possible. (13) When viewed up close, it may seem overwhelming (at least for seniors). However, this is part of the traditional logic of communication and media history: an increasing interplay between an augmentation of complexity and semiotic economy. (14) Communication becomes faster and more frequent, more varied and fragmented, more selective and ephemeral. (15) Language adjusts to the fact that forms, ways and devices of technical and natural communication are becoming more manifold. Conventional boundaries between natural and technical communication, as well as between mass medial and interactive communication, dissolve. Non-oral communication is closely connected to everyday actions, as has been the case with oral communication until now. New linguistic varieties arise. Inner multilingualism diversifies. Complex amounts of

information are unitized into smaller parts. Common ideas of wholeness resolve themselves or become obsolete. Units of meaning are unitized and offered for any desired selection and sequence. Verbal elements become parts of multimodal messages. They are mainly organized by visual design in order to be perceived as efficiently as possible. The verbal passages become smaller, shorter and more elliptic; the language becomes analytic rather than synthetic. (16) Instead of spending a lot of time on composing and reading conventional full texts, we handle modularly constructed multimodal messages more often, faster, more selectively and briefly. Here, language occurs mainly by bits, to the extent that grammar assigns its structuring function more and more to visual design. In this way, huge amounts of information can be handled fast and efficiently.

References

Adamzik, Kirsten 2004: *Textlinguistik. Eine einführende Darstellung*. Tübingen: Niemeyer.
Aitchison, Jean/ and Diana M. Lewis (eds.) 2003: *New media language*. London/New York: Routledge.
Althaus, Scott L. and David Tewksbury 2002: Agenda setting and the „new" news: Patterns of issue importance among readers of the paper and online versions of the *New York Times*. In: *Communication Research* 29: 180–207.
Androutsopoulos, Jannis (ed.) 2006: *Sociolinguistics and computer-mediated communication*. Theme Issue, *Journal of Sociolinguistics*, 10.4.
Baron, Naomi S. 2008: *Always on. Language in an online and mobile world*. New York/ Oxford: Oxford University Press.
Brinker, Klaus 2010: *Linguistische Textanalyse. Eine Einführung in Grundbegriffe und Methoden* [1985]. 5th ed. Berlin: Erich Schmidt.
Brodde-Lange, Kirsten and Annette Verhein-Jarren 2001: News im Netz. Sprache in Online-Medien am Beispiel von Nachrichtentexten. In: Dieter Möhn, DieterRoß and Marita Tjarks-Sobhani (eds.), *Mediensprache und Medienlinguistik*. Festschrift für Jörg Hennig, 339–352. Frankfurt a.M. et al.: Peter Lang.
Bucher, Hans-Jürgen 1996: Textdesign – Zaubermittel der Verständlichkeit? Die Tageszeitung auf dem Weg zum interaktiven Medium. In: Ernest W. B. Hess-Lüttich, Werner Holly and Ulrich Püschel (eds.), *Textstrukturen im Medienwandel*, 31–59. Frankfurt/M.: Peter Lang.
Bucher, Hans-Jürgen 2001: *Texten und Textdesign*. Wiesbaden: Westdeutscher Verlag.
Bucher, Hans-Jürgen 2010: Multimodalität – eine Universalie des Medienwandels. Problemstellungen und Theorien der Multimodalitätsforschung. In: Hans-Jürgen Bucher, Thomas Gloning and Kathrin Lehnen (eds.), *Neue Medien – neue Formate. Ausdifferenzierung und Konvergenz in der Medienkommunikation*, 41–79. Frankfurt a.M./ New York: Campus.
Cherubim, Dieter (ed.) 1975: *Sprachwandel. Reader zur diachronischen Sprachwissenschaft*. Berlin/New York: de Gruyter.
Crystal, David 2011: *Internet linguistics. A Student Guide*. London/New York: Routledge.

Dürscheid, Christa 2003: Medienkommunikation im Kontinuum von Mündlichkeit und Schrift-
lichkeit. Theoretische und empirische Probleme. *Zeitschrift für Angewandte Linguistik*, No.
38: 37–56.
Dürscheid, Christa 2012: *Einführung in die Schriftlinguistik*. Göttingen: Vandenhoeck &
Ruprecht (UTB).
Ehlich, Konrad 1983: Text und sprachliches Handeln. Die Entstehung von Texten aus dem
Bedürfnis nach Überlieferung. In: Aleida Assmann, Jan Assmann and Christof Hardmeier
(eds.), *Schrift und Gedächtnis. Beiträge zur Archäologie der literarischen Kommunikation*,
24–43. München: Fink.
Füssel, Stephan 1999: *Gutenberg und seine Wirkung*. Frankfurt a. M./Leipzig: Insel.
Genette, Gérard 1997: *Paratexts. Thresholds of interpretation*. Cambridge: Cambridge University
Press [1st ed. in French 1987].
Giesecke, Michael 2006: *Der Buchdruck in der frühen Neuzeit. Eine historische Fallstudie über
die Durchsetzung neuer Informations- und Kommunikationstechnologien* [1991]. 4th ed.
Frankfurt a.m.: Suhrkamp.
Grice, H. Paul 1975: Logic and conversation. In: Peter Cole, Peter and Jerry L. Morgan (eds.),
Syntax and semantics. Vol. 3: Speech Acts, 41–58. New York/ London: Academic Press.
Hrbek, Anja 1995: *Vier Jahrhunderte Zeitungsgeschichte in Oberitalien. Text-, sprach- und
allgemeingeschichtliche Entwicklungen in der „Gazzetta di Mantova" und vergleichbaren
Zeitungen*. Tübingen: Niemeyer.
Jakobs, Eva-Maria and Ulrich Püschel 1998: Von der Druckstraße auf den Datenhighway. In:
Heidrun Kämper and Hartmut Schmidt (eds.), *Das 20. Jahrhundert. Sprachgeschichte –
Zeitgeschichte*. Institut für deutsche Sprache, Jahrbuch 1997, 163–187. Berlin/New York:
de Gruyter.
Johnson, Sally A.and Astrid Ensslin (eds.) 2007: *Language in the media. Representations,
identities, ideologies*. London/New York: Continuum.
Jones, Mari C. and Edith Esch (eds.) 2002: *Language change. The interplay of internal, external
and extra-linguistic factors*. Berlin/New York: Mouton de Gruyter.
Kang, Naewon and Junho H. Choi 1999: Structural implications of the crossposting network of
international news in cyberspace. *Communication Research* 26: 454–481.
Klemm, Michael 2002: Ausgangspunkte: Jedem seinen Textbegriff? Textdefinitionen im
Vergleich. In: Ulla Fix, Kirsten Adamzik, Gerd Antos and Michael Klemm (eds.), *Brauchen
wir einen neuen Textbegriff? Antworten auf eine Preisfrage*, 17–29. Frankfurt a.M.: Peter
Lang.
Kress, Gunther 2010: *Multimodality. A social semiotic approach to contemporary
communication*. London New York: Routledge.
Kress, Gunther and Theo Van Leeuwen 2001: *Multimodal discourse. The modes and media of
contemporary communication*. London: Hodder Arnold.
Leroi-Gourhan. André 1993: *Gesture and speech*. Cambridge, Mass. etc.: MIT Press [1st ed. in
French 1964/65].
Lewis, Diana M. 2003: Online news. A new genre? In: Jean Aitchison, and Diana M. Lewis (eds.),
New media language, 95–104. London/New York: Routledge.
Ludwig, Otto 2005: *Geschichte des Schreibens*. Vol. 1: Von der Antike zum Buchdruck. Berlin
New York: de Gruyter.
Lüger, Heinz-Helmut 1995: *Pressesprache* [1983]. 2th ed. Tübingen: Niemeyer.
Malinowski, Bronislaw 1930: The problem of meaning in primitive languages. In: C[harles]
K.Ogden and I[vor] A[rmstrong] Richards (eds.), *The meaning of meaning. A study of the*

influence of language upon thought and of the science of symbolism, 296–336. [1st ed. 1923]. London: Harcourt, Brace & Company.

Mattheier, Klaus J. 1998: Allgemeine Aspekte einer Theorie des Sprachwandels. In: Werner Besch, Anne Betten, Oskar Reichmann and Stefan Sonderegger (eds.), *Sprachgeschichte. Ein Handbuch zur Geschichte der deutschen Sprache und ihrer Erforschung*. 1. Teilband (HSK 2.1)), 824–836. Berlin/New York: de Gruyter.

Mattheier, Klaus J. 2000: Die Herausbildung neuzeitlicher Schriftsprachen. In: Werner Besch, Anne Betten, Oskar Reichmann and Stefan Sonderegger (eds.), *Sprachgeschichte. Ein Handbuch zur Geschichte der deutschen Sprache und ihrer Erforschung*. 2. Teilband (HSK 2.2, 1085–1107. Berlin/New York: de Gruyter.

Miller, D. Gary 2010: *Language change and linguistic theory*. 2 vols. Oxford etc.: Oxford University Press.

Ong, Walter J. 1982: *Orality and literacy. The technologizing of the word*. London/New York: Methuen.

von Polenz, Peter 1991–1999: *Deutsche Sprachgeschichte vom Spätmittelalter bis zur Gegenwart*. 3 vols. [vol. 1: 2nd ed. 2000]. Berlin/New York: de Gruyter.

Püschel, Ulrich 1991: Journalistische Textsorten im 19. Jahrhundert. In: Rainer Wimmer (ed.), *Das 19. Jahrhundert. Sprachgeschichtliche Wurzeln des heutigen Deutsch*. Institut für deutsche Sprache, Jahrbuch 1990, 428–447. Berlin/New York: de Gruyter.

Püschel, Ulrich 1992: Von der Pyramide zum Cluster. Textsorten und Textsortenmischung in Fernsehnachrichten. In: Ernest W. B. Hess-Lüttich (ed.), *Medienkultur – Kulturkonflikt. Massenmedien in der interkulturellen und internationalen Kommunikation*, 233–258. Opladen: Westdeutscher Verlag.

Püschel, Ulrich 1997: „Puzzle-Texte" – Bemerkungen zum Textbegriff. In: Gerd Antos and Heike Tietz (eds.), *Die Zukunft der Textlinguistik. Traditionen, Transformationen, Trends*, 27–41. Tübingen: Niemeyer.

Roelcke, Thorsten 2002: *Kommunikative Effizienz. Eine Modellskizze*. Heidelberg: C. Winter.

Rowe, Charley and Eva L. Wyss (eds.) 2009): *Language and new media. Linguistic, cultural, and technological evolutions*. Cresskill, NJ: Hampton Press.

Saussure, Ferdinand de 1997: *Linguistik und Semiologie. Notizen aus dem Nachlaß. Texte, Briefe und Dokumente*. (Ed. Johannes Fehr.) Frankfurt a.M.: Suhrkamp.

Schmitz, Ulrich 1996a: ZAP und Sinn. Fragmentarische Textkonstitution durch überfordernde Medienrezeption. In: Ernest W. B. Hess-Lüttich, Werner Holly, and Ulrich Püschel (eds.), *Textstrukturen im Medienwandel*, 11–29. Frankfurt a.M.: Peter Lang.

Schmitz, Ulrich 1996b: Zur Sprache im Internet. Skizze einiger Eigenschaften und Probleme. In: Rainer Fabian (ed.), *media paradise. Die multimediale Zukunft von Kindern und Jugendlichen*, 89–105. Oldenburg: bis. [Digital version: <www.linse.uni-due.de/publikationenliste/articles/zur-sprache-im-internet-skizze-einiger-eigenschaften-und-probleme.html>].

Schmitz, Ulrich 2010: Schrift an Bild im World Wide Web. Articulirte Pixel und die schweifende Unbestimmtheit des Vorstellens. In: Arnulf Deppermann and Angelika Linke (eds.), *Sprache intermedial. Stimme und Schrift, Bild und Ton*. Jahrbuch des Instituts für Deutsche Sprache 2009, 383–418. Berlin/New York: de Gruyter.

Schmitz, Ulrich 2011: Blickfang und Mitteilung. Zur Arbeitsteilung von Design und Grammatik in der Werbekommunikation. *Zeitschrift für Angewandte Linguistik*, No. 54: 79–109.

Thurlow, Crispin and Kristine Mroczek (eds.) 2011: *Digital discourse: language in the new media*. Oxford/New York: Oxford University Press.

Weingarten, Rüdiger1997: Textstrukturen in neuen Medien: Clusterung und Aggregation. In: Rüdiger Weingarten (ed.), *Sprachwandel durch Computer*, 215–237. Opladen: Westdeutscher Verlag.

Wetzchewald, Marcus 2012: *Junktoren zwischen Text und Bild – dargestellt anhand der Unternehmenskommunikation im Internet*. Duisburg: Universitätsverlag Rhein-Ruhr.

Martin Luginbühl
Genre profiles and genre change. The case of TV news

1 Introduction

There is a broad consensus in genre studies from the "new rhetoric" as well in the "Textlinguistik" tradition of German linguistics that genre change is linked to social change.[1] Despite the fact that this relation between genre change and social change is pretty complex, changes on the micro level of genre styles are quite often related directly (and sometimes rather recklessly) to the macro level of national or even global cultures.[2] In TV news studies, genre styles of single TV news shows are often conveyed as characteristics of an entire national TV news style or even as characteristics of a national populace; sometimes the characteristics of (mostly American) TV news shows are generalized globally insinuating a homogeneous global TV news culture.

The main argument of this article is the assumption that we gain a better understanding of genre change in its relation to social change if we look at an analytic meso-level between the style of single genres on a micro-level and social change on a macro-level and that we can do so by analysing and comparing what I call "genre profiles". The concept of genre profiles does not neglect the necessity for an in-depth look at genre style (on the contrary it relies on it), but it makes visible the contouring of an entire genre 'network'. This again lets us understand the significance of single genres within them and lets us thus get an interpretation basis and

---

1 I am aware of the differences between the concept of "genre" and "Textsorte" – as well of the differences between the various "schools" that study genre (cf. Bhatia 2004: 10) and differences between various conceptualizations of "Textsorte" (cf. Adamzik 2004: 31–48). But as new works in all those fields see genres or Textsorten as social action, I will conflate the different concepts here and translate "Textsorte" as 'genre'.
2 By style I do not only mean different formulaic aspects like rhetoric figures. I understand style as a socially relevant way of realizing a communicative action (Sandig 2006). So next to rhetoric figures all forms are relevant that can and have to be shaped and thus have the potential to carry meaning by differentiation: Next to lexis and grammar also aspects of content, news narratives, communicative functions and situations created by the genres, materiality and other generic aspects are relevant. In addition, given the multimodality of TV news, I also take into consideration the design of images, colours, proportions etc.

an understanding of their social value. Compared to the analysis of a single genre, changes in genre profiles are a meso-level phenomenon, have a broader empirical base and can contextualize changes of single genres.

Looking for example at the style of newsreader and anchor items (i. e. stories read from a newsreader or an anchor on camera[3]) from the Swiss *Tagesschau* from different decades and looking at them *only* would give the impression of quite an extraordinary genre stability. Neglecting the content details, the wording of a newsreader item from 1968 could also be realized in an anchor item from today and vice versa. These wordings stage a maximum of distance to the audience and a maximum of detachment (cf. Luginbühl 2009, 2011) by using the inverted pyramid style[4] as well as formal language and by abstaining from emotional or evaluating phrasings. This again could be related to a journalistic culture with a low market orientation, as it is not at all oriented towards an audience involvement (and this could be overgeneralized as a feature of European TV news of public broadcast stations or as a consequence of a general detachment of Swiss people and so on).

But if we look at the entire genre profiles (cf. section 4), we get quite a different picture: The items read by a newsreader or an anchor dropped from a share of more than 20 per cent of the show's duration in 1968 to less than 4 per cent in 2005. This is not yet genre death – but it is a very clear sign that the significance of these genres changed. This again can be related to the meaning of this form mentioned before: To stage a detached proclamation of an absolute truth. A look at the genre profiles will show that these two genres have been replaced by (partly new developing) genres with another meaning of the genre form. Like this a social change in the editorial staff regarding crucial norms and values of journalistic culture (a phenomenon on the macro level) can be made evident and plausible by an analysis of genre profiles (meso level) which again is rooted in an analysis of single genre's style (micro level).

Changes in genre profiles can be related to changes of other context factors (like e.g. changes in media technology, media systems, but also changes in language use of other communities etc.). But above all these changes can be related

---

3 A newsreader restricts himself (there were only men in the Swiss "Tagesschau" and the "CBS Evening News") to reading news from a sheet of paper in a very distanced and formal manner, only rarely looking into the camera. If a newsreader leads-in a story at all, he summarizes the most important facts of the event. An anchor is more of a host, addressing the audience directly, leading it through the show, interviewing correspondents and experts etc.

4 The inverted pyramid style is a metaphor for a style of structuring information in a news text, with the most important information (Who?, What?, When?, Where?, Why?, How?) first, then moving on to less important details and finally to more general or background information.

to the people using those genres. In order to avoid overgeneralizations, I will use the term "community" here (instead of "nation" or "society"). In my understanding, a community is a group of individuals thinking of themselves as being part of a social category (cf. Tajfel and Turner 1986). This understanding includes communities on very different levels, like social groups interacting which each other on a daily basis (like the staff of a TV news show), they can be ethnic groups, societies of a nation, translocal groups etc. An individual is part of several communities.

I will first elaborate an understanding of genres as cultural artifacts, playing a pivotal role in social change as a crucial mean for adjusting and establishing common norms and values in a community. I will argue that genre change, especially change of genre forms, and cultural change are interdependent (section 2). I will then develop a methodological framework for the analysis of genre profiles (section 3). In the next section the results of the comparative genre profile analysis of the American *CBS Evening News* and the Swiss *Tagesschau* are presented along the three analytical perspectives of genre profiles (section 4). Finally, I will discuss the results, relating them to changes in journalistic cultures (section 5).[5]

2 Genre change and social change

As mentioned before, changes in the language use of mass media genres are related to a lot of different context factors – other media genres, i. e. the generic context being one of them (cf. Devitt 2004: 91). Several scholars (like Straßner 2001; Muckenhaupt 2000: 41; Mould 1984; Barkin 2003: 28; Schwitalla 1993) have pointed out that TV news genres relied in their first years on genres of movie theatre newsreels and radio news shows. The Swiss *Tagesschau* for instance consisted entirely of film items (i. e. news footage with an off-voice commenting) in the beginning. This replication of established genres in the first phase of new media seems to be the usual case in genre history (Eckkrammer 2011; Raible 2006; Devitt 2004). These replicated genres then start being varied, which can lead to the emergence of new genres, once a variation becomes stable and is regarded as (and often labeled as) a new genre (Eckkrammer 2011: 194).

Of course these variations of the replicated genres are partly enabled by the new possibilities that the new medium offers. But genre changes are always related to new functions a genre is thought to fulfill within a community. Barnhurst and Nerone (2001) analyse the history of newspaper, and they show how

---

5 For a more detailled discussion see Luginbühl (2014).

the form of news "includes the way the medium imagines itself to be and to act. In its physical arrangement, structure, and format, a newspaper reiterates an ideal of itself" (Barnhurst and Nerone 2001: 3). In their analysis they illustrate how changes in cultural configurations can be related to changes in newspaper genres. And they reject rightly what they call "technological determinism" (Barnhurst and Nerone 2001: 8), namely the idea of technological changes as driving force behind genre change; a force that is often assumed in mass media genre studies. A look at TV news shows supports that view of Barnhurst and Nerone: not all technological innovations have been applied right away (the Swiss *Tagesschau* e.g. could have shown correspondents on scene already in the 1960s, but it started doing so only in the late 1970s); other technological innovations only perfected already realized practices (the teleprompter, for example, perfected the gaze into the camera of the *CBS* anchors, previously enabled by text boards invisible for the audience).

Of course there are other factors next to generic contexts and technological changes that can have an influence on genre change in TV shows, like media system, media market, target audience, political system, national (or: local / international) orientation of the show, etc. (cf. Luginbühl 2010; Hauser and Luginbühl 2012). It may be impossible to identify the impact of the single factors, but I want to focus on two aspects that seem crucial to me regarding genre change: the meaning of the forms and the norms and values of a community using certain genres.

Although genre change can be influenced by many different factors, these factors usually do not have a direct influence on genres. It is the *perception and interpretation* of these factors by the people using a genre that decides whether a genre changes, remains unchanged or falls into desuetude. I therefore see genre change primarily related to new or changing communicative needs. But it is important to see that the meaning of a genre can change due to changes of the genre context, even if the form and function of this genre do not seem to change; language use is not only influenced by external context factors, it is a context factor on its own, influencing genre style, genre choice etc. Language therefore does not only change *in* media (because of changing technologies, media systems or markets), it also changes *through* media. This is especially true for mass media. Journalistic communities using and creating genres may be small, but their social impact can be huge. The journalist's language use is influenced by and designed with regard to the language of the audience, at the same time it can serve as a model, influencing for example the way we speak and think about politics, wars, economics, etc., but also influencing our expectations of a trustworthy representation of reality.

I will focus in my analysis on genre forms, which are not simply a carrier of information, but which have a meaning of their own – working perhaps on a more subtle, but maybe therefore in an underestimated, not less powerful way.

Genres have for a long time been considered as textual attributes, an approach that looks at genre form in isolation of its context. Mittell called it the "'textualist assumption'" (Mittell 2004: 172), Devitt (2009: 28) speaks of "formalism". With that assumption came the conceptualization of genres as constituting themselves as a category through common features. But like all categories genres are no intrinsic, "natural" categories, as the works of new genre theory or newer studies of the German "Textlinguistik" point out, they are "social action" (Miller 1984) constituted by discursive practices of human communities, i. e. social practices within a certain culture. As such they rely on, respond to and can also shape social and communicative needs. Once established (e.g. by acquiring a common name, cf. Miller and Shepherd 2004; Eckkrammer 2010: 58), genres do have common traits, which nevertheless can be on very different levels like different aspects of form, content or reader/audience effect. It is at this point that they seem to be stable and "natural" entities.

But genres never are fully stable. As they are realized within a situated activity, as they have to adjust to cultural, situational and individual needs, they have to be flexible to a certain degree. On the other hand genres have to be stable in order to remain recognizable and thus facilitate communication by providing a reliable pattern for fulfilling a communicative need. Genres, as Devitt (2004: 116) puts it, "balance flexibility and stability", and understanding them as form *only* means neglecting their basis in social, communicative processes. Genres thus facilitate interaction by suggesting conventional and tested, yet flexible patterns of behavior. At the same time communicative genres also *construct* recurring communicative situations, and given their binding character they structure verbal interaction and thus structure the way social reality is constructed.[6] Genre studies within the tradition of "new rhetorics" as well as the "Textlinguistik" tradition emphasize this social dimension of genres. Bhatia, Flowerdew, and Johnes (2008), to quote just one example, consider the "use [of texts, M.L.] in social contexts" as a "common commitment" (Bhatia, Flowerdew and Johnes 2008: 3) of different approaches to genre, especially the "multiperspective genre analysis" (Bhatia, Flowerdew and Johnes 2008: 14).

In my analysis I will focus on the cultural context of genres, i. e. a dynamic formation of norms and values of a group that influence (and as we will see are influenced by) genres and genre change. This cultural view is important regarding the interpretation of genre profiles. Discourse communities (be they small like

---

6 Giddens (1984: 25) called that the "duality of structure"; genres can thus be regarded as "social systems [that M.L.] are both medium and outcome of the practices they recursively organize" (Giddens 1984: 25).

the community of practice consisting of the staff of a TV news show or big like an entire nation) have to sustain and negotiate their values and norms, their world view (which does not have to be homogeneous, but can be conflicting).[7] In order to do so they have to balance their norms and values (Linke 2011), which can be perceived in cultural artifacts and are thus related to the symbolic dimension of human action (cf. Goodenough 1957/64; Geertz 1973; Barth 1989). In this understanding of culture, all symbolic action, such as the use of genres, always serve – among other things, of course – the communitarization (and therefore the differentiation) by expressing norms and values, for example in genre choice and genre form. This aspect of expressing is important, as it means that norms and values have to be indicated in a perceivable manner – and this means in a manner that is somehow semiotically *materialized* in the cultural artifact. The semiosis – and that means the genre *form* – is thus crucial for cultural processes, as these processes are realized within and at the same time subject to its conditions. Genres as semiotic entities serve communities to negotiate, i. e. establish, stabilize or change their common norms and values. Against the backdrop of these collective norms and values, habitualized and conventionalized forms of language use – genres – emerge (cf. Linke 2011). Culture thus can be transmitted and changed in and through communicative exchanges, whereas this process of negotiating relies inevitably on semiotic processes, genres playing a crucial role in it.

Focusing on genre choice and genre style, I will turn my attention to the form of communication, as it is the changing (or sometimes stable) genre style as well as the changing genre profiles that are a collective product and thus most suitable for indicating norms and values. This is especially true for TV news shows (and other mass media genres), where similar contents are presented in quite different forms – changing between shows, nations, languages and phases (cf. Luginbühl 2010). While the content and the main function ("to inform") are comparable, differences in form can be interpreted culturalistically.

The realization of genres as an establishment of collectively acknowledged patterns of language use is always based on stylistic choices, which are not mandatory and therefore could have been made differently; sometimes we can even choose between different genres. What often seems to be – in retrospect – a "logical" consequence of contextual factors are, in fact, stylistic (and therefore generic) decisions, which offer to realize a meaning exceeding the propositional

---

7 Like genre, culture has for a long time been conceptualized as a static, homogeneous, often nationally defined set of norms and values (cf. Tylor 1871, but already Herder [1772] 1985). This conceptualization changed during the second half of the 20th century towards an understanding of culture as entities of heterogeneous norms and values of different discourse communities.

content of utterances as "an aspect of substance on a higher level" (Miller 1984: 160) or a form of "secondary significance" (Linke 2011: 30, my translation). The unemotional, inverted pyramid style of the newsreader and anchor items offers for example to realize the impression of detachment, distance and the seemingly unmediated depiction of an absolute, unquestionable truth (instead, for example, closeness to the audience and an almost live reporting of an always developing news story). This again means that (changing) features of genres can be regarded as cultural "positionings", as genres are collective phenomena and style is "meaning made visible" (Fix 2011: 72, my translation). We even have to take into account the possibility that language use can change before the corresponding changes in interpretations and goals become conscious to the language users (cf. Linke 2011).

It is important to note that in this view the genre form is not at all only a carrier, but that it is meaningful and plays an important role in this process of negotiation, which is only possible if norms and values are displayed on a perceivable and thus semiotic level. Common norms and values emerge like this in a process of joint semiotic action (Linke 2009). This importance of form is also acknowledged and emphasized in newer publications of the new genre studies (cf. Devitt 2009).

3 Genre profiles

Next to the cultural and situational context, also *generic contexts* have to be considered for an adequate understanding of genre and especially of genre change: genres are in systematic relationships to other genres. Several concepts have been introduced to grasp this "inter-genre-ality" (Devitt 2009: 44) of genre. Devitt (1991: 339) speaks of "genre sets" consisting of genres produced by a particular professional group, Bazerman (1994: 97) of the more comprehensive "genre systems" referring to interrelated genres interacting in specific settings, Bhatia (2004) speaks of "genre colonies" (Bhatia 2004: 29) consisting of genres with similar function, and on a more abstract level of "disciplinary genres" consisting of all genres of a particular disciplinary or professional domain (Bhatia 2004: 54–55).

In the German "Textlinguistik" concepts like 'genre intertextuality' ("Textsorten-Intertextualität", Klein 2000) or 'genre networks' ("Textsortennetze" Adamzik 2001, 2004: 94–106) have been established to describe functional, situational, formal and topical relations between genres (cf. Hauser 2012; Adamzik 2011; Janich 2008). Adamzik (2011) firstly distinguishes 'genre fields' ("Textsortenfelder", consisting of topical or functional similar and thus interchangeable genres) and based on Fairclough (2003) 'genre chains' ("Textsortenketten", consisting of ordered genres constituting an expectable chain) and secondly integrates fields and chains into 'genre networks' as a more adequate model for genre relations within an interaction system.

All these concepts are based on the observation that genres exist neither individually nor independently. They are linked to other genres that precede or follow them, for example in a production process or within a "super- or macro-genre" like a TV news show (i. e. "a constellation of individually recognized genres", Bhatia 2004: 57), they are linked to genres with a similar function, which occur in similar situations or which treat the same topic and so on. This means that the significance and value of a genre also depends on the genre system of a community; a system that can be related to the sociological concept of the 'communicative budget of a society' ("kommunikativer Haushalt einer Gesellschaft") by Luckmann (1988), focusing the interdependency of genres.

This interdependency is not only observable in a synchronic view, but also in a diachronic perspective: the emergence or change of genres is linked to their generic context (Devitt 2004: 92–101; Gansel 2011; Eckkrammer 2011). If we agree that genres are typified actions for the realization of communicative actions, then the emergence of new genres or the change of existing genres has to be related to situational and/or cultural changes of the community realizing these genres. New situations (or more precisely as new situations *interpreted* situations) or new norms and values of a community lead to needs that the existing genres cannot fulfill – which is dependent on the actual genre context. And if genres emerge or change, the entire generic context changes, as the significance and value of a single genre depends on this context.

As genres are collectively established, passed on or changed, also genre networks are culturally coined. And if we understand genres and genre networks as key sites for cultural negotiations, then the analysis of genre can grant access to cultural and social change. As mentioned above, the change of single genres over time has been described in many studies, and in some of them (like Bazerman 1994; Bendel 1998; Campbell and Jamieson 1990; Berkenkotter and Huckin 1995; Berkenkotter and Luginbühl 2014; Fleskes 1996; Nickl 2000; Warnke 1996; Yates 1989) the link to social change has been made. What nevertheless remains unsatisfying is the lack of an intermediate analytical level between the micro-level of single genres and the macro-level of the culture of a community (cf. Adamzik 2010: 31). While based on a qualitative analysis of single genres, genre profiles deliver the contour of entire super-genres in an empirically comprehensible manner; changes (or stability) of such contours again can be more plausibly related to social change, as genre profiles analyse a much bigger section of genre activity of the community in question than the analysis of a single genre would.

With the framework of "genre profiles" I suggest an intermediate analytical level for the description and analysis of changes in genre networks. The concept of "genre profiles" is not directly concerned with the stylistic formation of a genre at a given time within a certain community, but with the contour of genres within a super-genre like a TV news show. The analysis will show in which dominant forms reality and reporting have been and are represented and which changes can be observed and if there really is an 'Americanization' of the Swiss *Tagess-chau*, as it is often said about European TV news shows (Blum 2006; Genz et al. 2001; Thussu 2003).

This outline is analysed under three perspectives: the choice of the genres realized ("genre *repertoire*"), the relative amount they are realized ("genre *fre-quency*") and the way they build genre chains ("genre *networks*").

Genre repertoire

As recurring situations usually do not demand for one single genre, we cannot only make a stylistic choice within one genre, but we can also make a choice on the level of genre itself. It is thus important to look at the question of which genres are realized by a certain community (which could be an entire society) at a given time. The term "repertoire" has been introduced by Bakhtin (1986: 60) and then borrowed by Orlikowski and Yates (1994) and Devitt (2004), who defines it as a "set of genres that a group owns, acting through which a group achieves all of its purposes, not just those connected to a particular activity" (Devitt 2004: 57).

If we look at super-genres, we can look at the repertoires within these super-genres, and we can trace the rise of a genre ("genre genesis") in a diachronic perspective as well as "genre death" within a super-genre. As mentioned above, the genre "newsreader item" or "anchor item" have not been realized in the Swiss *Tagesschau* first format of the 1950s. The following change in genre repertoire in the 1960s can be related to a whole new self-concept of the show with the introduction of a newsreader, seemingly proclaiming an absolute truth.

Genre frequency

Within a genre profile, it is not only important to identify the genres realized, but also to know something about the quantitative occurrence of a genre. Of course, frequency does not equal importance, but the quantitative significance is important when it comes to changes within a genre profile without a change in the genre repertoire. A frequent genre can become rather insignificant long before its "death" (that's why a look at genre repertoire is not enough) and it can be replaced by another genre (be it a new one or just a more frequently used one).

Frequency can be counted by number of tokens or by their expansion (length in space or time). It might depend on the kind of genre profile to be analysed whether the frequency of tokens or their expansion, i. e. their share will allow more insights in the quantitative occurrence. In the case of TV news it seems more adequate to measure frequency in terms of expansion, as this delivers a more appropriate view on the overall appearance of a show. Again the "newsreader item" and the "anchor item" in the Swiss *Tagesschau* can serve as prime examples: after its emergence in the 1960, it stayed a key genre with a share between 17 and 21 per cent, falling under 10 per cent after 1980 and disappearing in the week analysed of 1999, but re-emerging in the new show's format of 2005 (3.8 per cent share). It will be important to see by which genre it has been replaced and to think about its re-emergence.

Genre networks

Generic contexts not only are coined by genre repertoires and genre frequencies, but also by intertextual relations between these genres. As mentioned above, these relations can be found on the formal, functional and/or content level, and they can be observed in a diachronic as well as in a synchronic or typological perspective (cf. Luginbühl et al. 2002: 19–25). A lead-in for example is intertextually related synchronically to other stories on the same issue (content), to lead-ins in the same and in other TV news shows (formal) and to the story that it announces (functional). These relations can also be analysed in a diachronic perspective. Regarding genre profiles all usual and regular relations are relevant, especially those within the genre repertoire at stake. It makes for example a difference regarding audience orientation if there is a lead-in by an anchor introducing every major story (which is the case in the *CBS Evening News*) or if the stories are just strung together without a person in a news studio (which was the case in the 1950s *Tagesschau*). In my analysis I will focus on "genre linkings" as conventionalized genre chains within the TV news shows.

Figure 1 tries to illustrate very rudimentarily the intermediate level of genre profiles, indicating the increasing level of abstractness by the three levels. In and through the use of genres norms and values are established, passed on and changed; at the same time existing norms and values shape genres. A genre profile as an analytical concept is in between; it is based on observations of single genres, but combines a look at all genres within a certain array (like a super genre) and thus allows an empirical well-grounded interpretation of the cultural meaning and significance of genres. Culture can be related to the norms and values of a very small group of people (the editorial staff of a TV news show, a family, a school class) up to an entire society (cf. the concept of the "communicative budget of a society"); in both cases the norms and values can be heterogeneous, conflicting and dynamic.

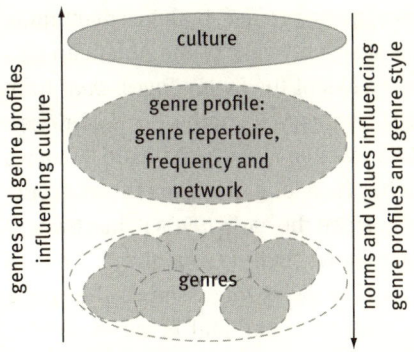

Figure 1: Genre profiles as intermediate level between genres and culture

Defining genre profiles as a combined view of genre repertoires, frequencies and networks, there is an analytical framework looking at genres from three different angles, but always on an intermediate level. And in each angle it is also about making choices. These choices are not on the level of a single genre style, but concern stylistic phenomena on an intermediate level between genres and the communicative budget of a community. The following analysis will show how the genre profiles of the two shows compared changed in very different ways. The significance of these changes, so I would argue, only comes to full light when genre profiles are taken into consideration, next to the change of single genre styles. We will see that the changes of the *CBS Evening News* are less dramatic and all tend into the same direction (closeness to the audience, immediacy in reporting, authenticity through journalists on scene of the event). In the Swiss *Tagesschau*, the changes in genre profiles indicate several changes in the "news culture": from a predominantly entertaining show in the 1950s to a detached declaration of a static truth in the 1960s and the 1970s (authenticity through distance), turning to more closeness to the audience and reporting on scene since the 1980s – but with a slight return to more traditional ways of reporting in the newest format since 2005. All these phases come with a specific genre profile.

4 Genre profiles in TV news shows

The analytical framework of genre profiles is now applied and discussed in the context of the super-genre of TV news. The analysis will be restricted to the broadcast genres in the shows themselves, neglecting genres relevant during production. Focusing on the published genres the analysis turns to the genres relevant for the audience.

My corpus allows a contrastive analysis of genre profiles, both in a diachronic and a synchronic way. The corpus consists of seven weeks of the American *CBS Evening News* from 1968 to 2005 and eight weeks of the Swiss *Tagesschau* from 1958 to 2005 (there is no archive for the *CBS Evening News* of the 1950s editions), with one to two weeks per decade.[8] The *CBS Evening News* is the main TV news show of the commercial TV network *CBS*. It has for a long time been the most successful US-American TV network news show, since the early 1990s it has been in the third place of the three big network news shows (behind *ABC* and *NCB*), with a share of nearly six million people each day.[9] The Swiss *Tagesschau* is the public TV station's main TV news show. As there is no other national TV news show in German, it is the most successful TV news show in Switzerland; but besides that it is one of the most successful shows of the public Swiss TV station since the 1970s, with about one million people watching daily, which equals to a market share of more than 60 per cent. Both shows claim to report the most important events of the last 24 hours in a balanced, objective way. They both are aired during prime time and last about 20 minutes.

This corpus design allows comparisons on different levels. We can see how the two shows design comparable communicative tasks differently with regard to genres, and we can examine differences between the shows as well as between different phases of the two shows. These comparisons again facilitate the recognition of highly conventionalized forms of reporting as culturally coined artifacts – which is not self-evident, as these conventions are so familiar that their forms often seem to be "natural", the only ones possible.

Although genres are not stable and as they can bend, split up and mix (Bhatia 2004: 73), the analysis of genre repertoires and genre frequencies has to define single genres as selectively and accurately as possible. In most of the cases TV news genres cannot be discerned by their content (a TV news story can report on any event) and only in some cases by their function as the genres often have the same function. A functionally based genre would be the lead-ins, which nevertheless fulfill different other functions (cf. Luginbühl 2009). I thus discerned the genres in a first step based on features of the modes used and the communicative situation established, referring to the ethno-categories of the journalists mentioned in the shows themselves or in journalism handbooks.

Based on criteria like "combination of news footage and language yes or no", "dialogue or monologue", "narrator on, off or partially on", "narrator as animator

---

8 For more details cf. Luginbühl (2014).
9 Cf. Pew Project for Excellence in Journalism 2011, <http://stateofthemedia.org/2012/network-news-the-pace-of-change-accelerates/network-by-the-numbers/> [28 January 2013]

or identified as author", "narrator within a studio or in the news field" I distinguish the following genres:

- *Opening credits, closing credits* (genres demarcating TV news shows from the preceding and following shows; usually footage containing some kind of globe and the show's logo, fading to the newsroom)
- *Headlines* (genres with news footage and the anchor speaking off camera at the beginning of the show, introducing the main stories)
- *Greeting, good-bye* (genres with the anchor on camera, addressed directly to the audience at the beginning and the end of the show)
- *Programme notice, programme preview, story preview* (genres with the anchor on camera, announcing an upcoming programme: the next show of the evening [programme notice], a story in the next edition of the TV news show [programme preview], a story in the same edition of the show [story preview])
- *Lead-in, lead-out* (genres with the anchor on camera, introducing a news story, sometimes completing it by latest developments or some additional information; often with a over-the-shoulder graphic illustrating the news story)
- *Anchor item* (story read by the anchor on camera; often with a over-the-shoulder graphic illustrating the news story)
- *Newsreader item* (story read by a newsreader; a person who first and foremost reads news, and does so in a very formal, detached way)
- *Anchor voice-over* (montage of anchor item, fading to news footage with anchor speaking off camera, i. e. "voice-over")
- *Film item* (news footage with voice-over by anchor or newsreader)
- *Package* (story produced and told by a correspondent, usually containing news footage, parts of interviews or statements, footage of correspondent on scene)
- *Statement* (sound-bite of a person on camera, not belonging to the editorial staff)
- *Interview* (interview with another journalist or with a person not belonging to the editorial staff, usually interviewer and interviewee on camera)
- *Stand up* (story told by a correspondent on camera and on scene, no news footage)
- *Commentary* (commentary by a member of the editorial staff on camera, in the news studio)
- *On screen item* (written text, no news footage, no spoken text)
- *Special cases* (not fitting one of the above characterizations; usually individual cases)

This methodology is a compromise, allowing an overview of genre profiles, but at the cost of a detailed consideration of genre variation. But as mentioned above, the analysis of genre profiles is not an alternative for qualitative stylistic analysis, but a complement. Nevertheless, unclear cases (like sporadic hybrids) have been counted as "special cases". And in the analysis I will focus on overall trends over decades, not on the precise percentages in the single weeks. Comparing TV news shows, different "formats" can be distinguished regarding their genre profiles; they differ regarding their central and peripheral genres and regarding the way they usually are combined.

Genre repertoires

Table 1 shows the genres realized in at least one of the two shows since 1958 (*Tagesschau*) or 1968 (*CBS Evening News*) and 2005 (the table only includes the English genre names). In the following, I will subsume opening and closing credits, headlines, greeting and goodbye as well as programme notice, programme preview and story preview as "news presentation" genres.

Looking at these repertoires, two observations are striking:

– Both shows realize more or less the same genres, and there are only a few; the genre repertoires are quite narrow. This comes as no surprise: TV news stories have to be produced daily within short time, so the reliance on a few established patterns becomes crucial. The genres realized aim on the one hand at the contact to and orientation for the audience (like greetings, previews or headlines), and to the reporting of events on the other (like anchor items or packages). It is nevertheless interesting to see that there are certain genres that are not realized in either show. This is the case for dialogical genres without clear role allocation, e.g. between studio guests, as they can be found in Japanese TV news shows (cf. Gatzen 2001). These kind of dialogical genres are – compared to the interview – less controllable, which contradicts the image the shows analysed here are trying to communicate, which reveal a core value: to provide a controlled view of the world's events, allowing for chaos and conflict in the news field, but never in the studio.

– There are just a few genres that are realized in only one of the two shows. I will focus on newscaster items and stand ups, as the others (story preview, on screen items) only play a marginal role. In the *CBS Evening News* all stories are told by identified and visible persons, namely the anchor or a correspondent. Both of them seem very trustworthy: the anchor is not only very familiar to the audience, but he or she also uses quite familiar language and is visually "brought close" to the audience by using close shots. The correspondents are often familiar as well and seem trustworthy as they are shown to be on the scene of the reported event, thus acting as eyewitnesses of these events.

	CBS Evening News	Tagesschau	
Opening Credits, Closing Credits	✓	✓	
Headlines	✓	✓	
Greeting, Goodbye	✓	✓	
Programme Notice	✓	✓	News presentation genres
Programme Preview	✓	✓	
Story Preview	✓	Ø	
Lead-In, Lead-Out	✓	✓	
Anchor Item	✓	✓	
Newscaster Item	Ø[9]	✓	
Anchor Voice-Over	✓	✓	
Film Item	✓	✓	
Package	✓	✓	
Statement	✓	✓	
Interview	✓	✓	
Stand Up	✓	✓	
Commentary	✓	Ø[10]	
On Screen Item	✓	Ø	
Special cases	✓	✓	

Table 1: Genre repertoires of the "CBS Evening News" and the "Tagesschau"

This kind of reporting is brought to an extreme in the "stand up", a story entirely consisting of a correspondent on scene, speaking into the camera – a genre not realized in the *Tagesschau*. The "newscaster items", not realized in the *CBS Evening News*, are on the other hand something like the opposite: they are stories read by a very reserved and distanced newsreader, usually reading from a sheet of paper appearing like a "reading machine" (Ballstaedt 1980: 227, my translation). While the genre repertoires are quite similar, we can see slight tendencies regarding central values: trustworthiness through closeness versus trustworthiness through distance. And we also can see that at least certain genres are related to certain ways of reporting, or put differently to certain journalistic cultures of reporting.

---

10 There were newscaster items in a show of 7 April 1949, archived at the Paley Center for Media, Los Angeles and New York, signature T82:0129.

11 There are commentaries in the *Tagesschau*, but only on very seldom occasions and there are no instances in my corpus.

Genre frequencies

The question of cultural change (or stability) only becomes relevant if we look at genre frequencies (and thus changes in genre repertoires, but also in genre significances). Again: frequency does not equal importance. The greetings at the beginning of TV news shows usually are short, but they are very important regarding the staged relationship to the audience and the entire framing of the show (cf. Luginbühl 2009). But as mentioned above, genres usually come with a certain way of reporting, of addressing the audience, of staging authenticity and of evaluating the reported events. That is why changes in genre frequencies are an important indicator of cultural change. A long-term change in frequency is, as we will see, a reliable indicator of cultural change – even more so if we agree that culture not only shapes genres, but also is shaped by them.

Table 2 shows the genre frequency of the Swiss *Tagesschau* from 1968 to 2005, indicating the combined duration of the genres realized in the corresponding week in relation to the show's duration. Opening and closing credits and the year 1958 are not included, as the show then consisted only of film items, strung together without any news presentation (like the newsreels in movie theatres at that time did).

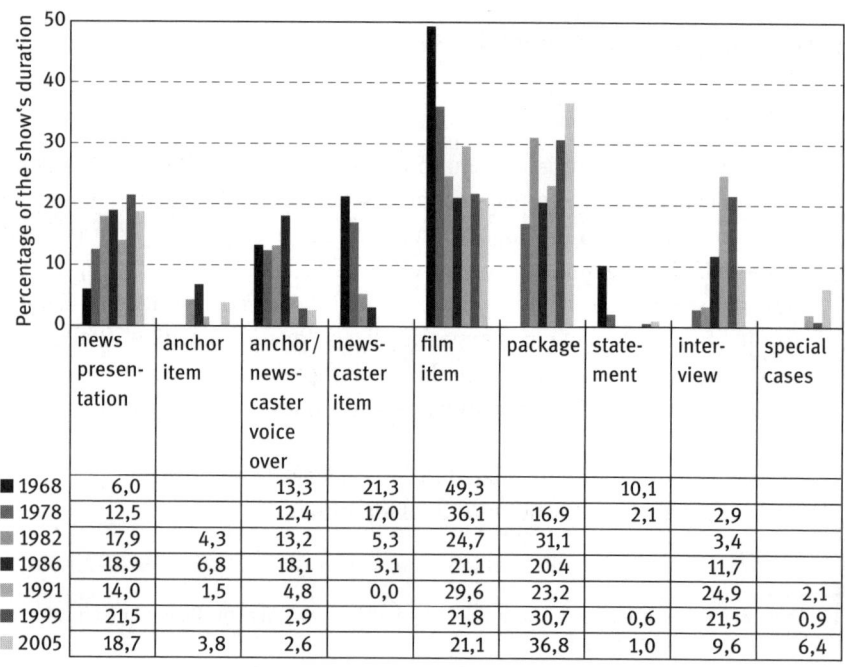

	news presen- tation	anchor item	anchor/ news- caster voice over	news- caster item	film item	package	state- ment	inter- view	special cases
■ 1968	6,0		13,3	21,3	49,3		10,1		
■ 1978	12,5		12,4	17,0	36,1	16,9	2,1	2,9	
■ 1982	17,9	4,3	13,2	5,3	24,7	31,1		3,4	
■ 1986	18,9	6,8	18,1	3,1	21,1	20,4		11,7	
■ 1991	14,0	1,5	4,8	0,0	29,6	23,2		24,9	2,1
■ 1999	21,5		2,9		21,8	30,7	0,6	21,5	0,9
■ 2005	18,7	3,8	2,6		21,1	36,8	1,0	9,6	6,4

Table 2: Genre frequency of the "Tagesschau" 1968–2005

As table 2 shows, the genre frequencies changed a lot during the last six decades. It also shows – most importantly – that the genre frequencies do not change in a random manner, but that there are quite obvious trends regarding the most important genres.

The frequency of news presentation genres increased from 0 per cent (in 1958, not in table 2) to about 20 per cent. This is first evidence that the orientation towards the audience changed. And it is an example for a form evolving from culturally peripheral to pivotal (cf. Posner 1991: 56).

Looking at the frequencies of the other genres we not only can see some trends, we can also see that the genres are internally linked, they are in a *commercium* (cf. Aschenberg 2002: 167), a commerce: some of them expand or emerge newly-made at the cost of certain (not all!) others, which become peripheral or even disappear. The rise of the packages (from 0 per cent to more than 35 per cent) is not at the cost of all, but just of some other genres, especially film items, newscaster items (which disappeared entirely), statements and anchor/newscaster voice-overs (which become more or less insignificant). Other genres gained in significance during that time as well (like all news presenting genres, but also like interviews until the mid-1990s).

The emergence and rise of the package in the Swiss *Tagesschau* replacing the main share of the film item is part of a paradigm shift. As indicated above, packages (like stand ups) are related to a certain kind of objectivity and prototypically to a certain way of storytelling. In the film items, facts are declared in a distanced, seemingly unchangeable way by an invisible, anonymous news reader, an almost unremarkable camera work and no obvious perspective of a reporting individual. As the film items of the 1960s and 1970s as well as the newscaster items stress a detached, neutral declaration of information, there seems to be a static and absolute truth "out there" "independent of the existence of any perceiver" (Hanitzsch 2007: 376). This kind of reporting can be labeled as totalitarian objectivism; it stages the impression of depicting an unmediated replication of reality. Its market orientation is low, as it comes without dramatic storytelling or emotions; we could speak of an orientation towards citizens (cf. Hanitzsch 2007).[12]

Packages on the other hand promote a different way of reporting: packages tend to mark their medial representation as something always selectively influenced by professional, but individual interpretation, and they do so by showing and naming an individual report, by more clearly showing that the package is a crafted product and by emphasizing the temporary status of the information

---

12 There were a lot of humourous and entertaining film items in the 1950s; nevertheless the kind of objectivity realized there remains the same.

given; reporting seems to be a never-ending process of investigation. In addition, packages usually tell a news story in a more or less dramatic and emotional way. This relates to a different kind of objectivism: truth is relative and dynamic, it is conceptualized as something fluid. And of course there is an entirely different relation to the audience in a film item with an anonymous, invisible newsreader and a package with a familiar correspondent on camera. We could call this subjectivist objectivity and market orientation towards consumers (cf. Hanitzsch 2007).

A combined look at genre frequency and genre style delivers an empirically tested way to see the dynamics of packages and film items; it can be complemented by a look at other genres (like the rising share of news presentation, also promoting a more intense relation to the audience).

Table 3 shows the genre frequency of the *CBS Evening News*, where entirely different genre profiles are realized.

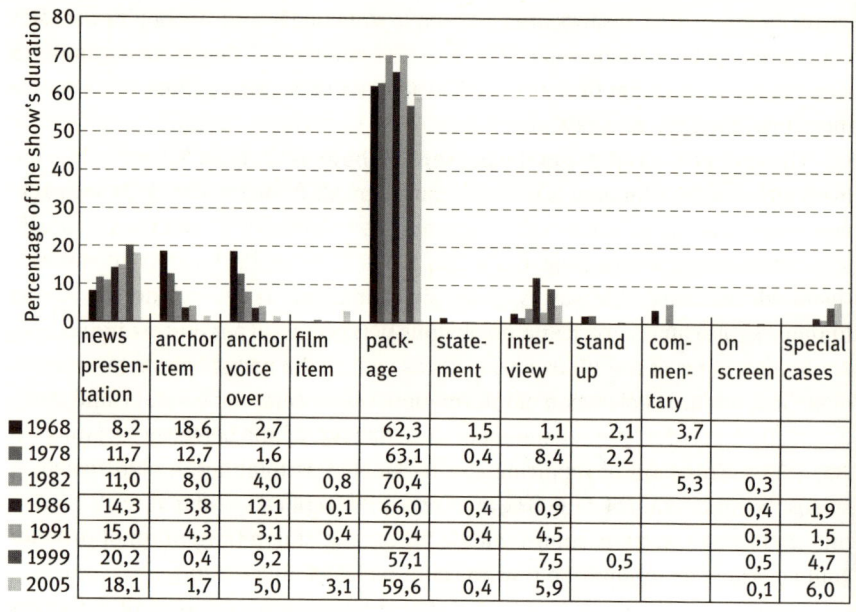

	news presentation	anchor item	anchor voice over	film item	package	statement	interview	stand up	commentary	on screen	special cases
1968	8,2	18,6	2,7		62,3	1,5	1,1	2,1	3,7		
1978	11,7	12,7	1,6		63,1	0,4	8,4	2,2			
1982	11,0	8,0	4,0	0,8	70,4				5,3	0,3	
1986	14,3	3,8	12,1	0,1	66,0	0,4	0,9			0,4	1,9
1991	15,0	4,3	3,1	0,4	70,4	0,4	4,5			0,3	1,5
1999	20,2	0,4	9,2		57,1		7,5	0,5		0,5	4,7
2005	18,1	1,7	5,0	3,1	59,6	0,4	5,9			0,1	6,0

Table 3: Genre frequency of the "CBS Evening News" 1968–2005

The genre frequencies in the *CBS Evening News* are much more stable compared to the *Tagesschau*. And since the 1960s the package is the dominant genre, adding up to 60–70 per cent of the show's duration. The changes that can be observed are nevertheless interesting: like in the Swiss *Tagesschau* the news presenting genres doubled their frequency while anchor items dropped from almost 20 per cent to less than 2 per cent. Also here we can observe that genres are internally linked:

In weeks, where the share of packages is slightly smaller, this is mostly due to presentation genres, anchor voice-overs and interviews.

It is important to see these charts in comparison, because like this we can see its characteristics in a bigger context. Comparing only TV news shows from public TV stations of European countries or of US American network news would probably not let us recognize the specific features – which not seldom leads to overgeneralizations in TV news studies, assuming that there is a stable and globalized TV news show genre profile.

It becomes obvious that the genre profiles with respect to their frequencies evolve very differently, the *Tagesschau* profile being much more changing than the *CBS Evening News* profile. While in the latter the package with an identified, usually visible journalist on scene is at the center of reporting, in the *Tagesschau* genres with anonymous authors prevail in the 1960s and 1970s; in the film item even the animator remains anonymous in all but his voice. This has changed since the 1980s, where news presentation genres and packages gain significance. Looking at these relations within the genre repertoires we can see how genres are no isolated phenomena. This can serve as an argument that changes in genre profiles are connected to an additional meaning of the genre form – if we assume that reporting on facts of an event could be realized in always the same forms. And this again means that also stability in genre profiles is connected to the meaning of form.

Genre linkings:
In the case of TV news, the genres are never strung together incidentally, but they are organized on different levels. Be it, that they are strung together in a "news block" because they belong to the same genre (e.g. a "news block" of film items about foreign news), be it, that they treat the same topic and realize different functions regarding the coverage of this topic (like summary in a lead-in, details in a package, reactions in a film item and evaluation in a commentary), be it, that there is a conventionalized syntagmatic order (also containing dependent genres) which could be looked at as "genre linking". Looking at these orders, I distinguish conventionalized orders (*"sequential clusters"*, like lead-in – package – interview with correspondent) and half-conventionalized orders (*"serial clusters"*, like anchor item – lead-in – package – anchor item – anchor item – anchor voice-over – lead out) (for the term "cluster" cf. Püschel 1992). Also by looking at such clusters and their changes we can learn something about genre profiles and the culture they are based upon and which they establish.

Sequential clusters (as conventionalized orders) are an important intermediate dimension regarding genre networks. TV news shows increasingly organize the regular coverage in a sequentialized way, a phenomenon that could be described as "sequentialization" of genres within the super-genre of TV news shows. In the *CBS Evening News* the order "lead-in – package" is already sequentialized in the 1960s: there are no packages without lead-ins, which makes the anchor appear to be an all-knowing mediator of news. In the show of 1949 the film items were broadcast without lead-ins.

In the Swiss *Tagesschau* film items were for a long time the crucial genre. But they were not sequentialized until the 1980s; until then most film items were broadcast without any lead-in. Similar to the newsreader item, where truth is announced in a distanced way, the not-sequentialized film items contribute to this impression of delivering (or "showing") an unmediated truth. In the 1990s both shows sequentialized the cluster "lead-in – package – interview with correspondent". Here several changes converge that occurred in both shows: the correspondents appear as experts in the interviews (instead of reporters) and the coverage is conversationalized (cf. Fairclough 1995) to a certain degree (instead of a monologue in a stand-up at the end of a package). Over all, this sequentialization also stands for a *segmentation* of the news coverage. Instead of covering an event in one genre (e.g. a film item) there is a tendency towards pair sequences (lead-in – film item/package) and to multipart sequential clusters. These changes are related to a changing orientation to the audience (more explicit structure of coverage), a changing role of the journalists (from reporter to expert) and a "dialogized" coverage.

Only in cases of extended coverage sequential clusters are replaced by half-conventionalized serial clusters. These are usually based upon sequential clusters, but reduplicate some elements or entire sequential clusters. The serial clusters of the 1960s and 1970s have in both shows been structured according to the inverted pyramid. In a newsreader item or an anchor item the most important facts about the event are given, then they are elaborated in a package (with lead-in) and in further newsreader/anchor items, they are contextualized with newsreader/anchor voice-overs or other packages about reactions or consequences and finally they are evaluated in a commentary. These serial clusters can be discontinuous, placing the commentary or a funny kicker about the topic at the end of a show.

Since the mid-1980s (*CBS*) and the early 1990s (*Tagesschau*) other kinds of content structures can also be found in serial clusters. There still is a summarizing lead-in at the beginning, but the content of the following genres does not follow the inverted pyramid style, but reports the event from different angles (e.g. packages from war correspondents stationed in different places), giving the impression of an all-embracing, and yet multiperspective and thus balanced coverage. With this content structure comes an explicit organization of clusters through the anchors of the show, establishing the news studio as "deictic zero point of enunciation" (Montgomery 2007: 40).

5 Conclusion

The two compared TV news shows share more or less the same genre repertoires, but they make different use of these repertoires. As the single genres have different forms of reporting, their forms have different meanings. Some of them stage objectivity by pretending to report without a certain perspective and from a detached point of view, delivering the impression of reporting an absolute, unmediated truth. Others have a visible narrator on scene, who is close to the event and delivers the current state of investigation, which could change any time. A look at the different genres under these aspects does not show real fundamental changes (some Swiss film items of the 1950s being the only exception).[13] But a look at the "genre profiles" shows important differences between the two shows and in the case of the *Tagesschau* far-reaching changes within this show.

In the Swiss *Tagesschau*, a fundamental change can be observed in the early 1980s. In the 1960s and 1970s genres were realized, that are well suited to present the news in a detached and proclaiming way. The genre profile started to change with new formats introduced after 1980. With these new formats introducing an anchor (instead of a newsreader) came the rise of packages and of news presentation genres – the package making more personal and more investigative reporting easy, as the correspondents deliver the current state of a never-ending process of investigation, her- or himself investigating on scene; the news presentation by an anchor as an optimal genre for "parasocial" communication, realizing patterns of private face-to-face communication in the publicly accessible sphere. At the same time, film items and anchor items become less important, while the newscaster item disappeared altogether. Nevertheless: the change is not unidirectional, as there were very entertaining film items in the 1950s and a re-emergence of the anchor item in the newest format of 2005. What we can observe is kind of a wave-movement, which makes the label "Americanization" too simple. We also can see that a look at genre profiles always has to be complemented by a look at genre style change.

The genre profiles of the *CBS Evening News* are much more stable: packages have been and are the pivotal genre, but the share of news presenting genres

---

13 There are changes regarding other aspects though, like the fastening pace of the genres or the use of more informal style.

(above all lead-ins) has also grown over time. The journalistic culture seems to be more stable here; a look at changes of single genre styles shows the intensification of certain aspects (like live-reporting, being on scene etc.), but no fundamental changes besides the change of the correspondents from reporters to experts and the dialogization of news reporting.

Regarding genre linkings, a growing sequentialization can be observed. While the packages of the *CBS Evening News* have conventionally be linked to lead-ins already in the 1960s, the *Tagesschau* film items have often been broadcast without lead-in – according to the mentioned totalitarian objectivity. In the 1990s, both showed sequentialized chains that include a dialogization of the reporting as well as a change in the journalists' roles, changing from reporters to experts. In addition, a trend towards a multiperspective, fragmented news coverage can be observed, which has intensified the conceptualization of truth as something fluid (subjectivist objectivity).

A combined view of the meaning of genre form and genre profiles allows an empirical, well tested cultural analysis of the genres and generic contexts. Changing repertoires and changing frequencies as well as some changes in genre networks allow us to see the "big picture" of genre change, hinting at trends in cultural change.

In order to avoid overgeneralizations, I suggest – at least in a first step – an analysis in terms of journalistic culture. Comparing the roles of the *Tagesschau* and the *CBS Evening News* journalists we can see a diminishing difference in objectivity and market orientation (both core values of journalistic cultures, cf. Hanitzsch 2007) that is centered around the packages and the anchors as hosts. While the *CBS Evening News* realizes subjectivist objectivity and a consumer-oriented market orientation from the very beginning (and intensifying over time), the *Tagesschau* started with a totalitarian objectivity and a consumer-oriented market orientation in the 1950s, changing to a citizen-oriented market orientation in the 1960s and 1970s; then changing slowly (but not entirely!) to a more subjectivist objectivity and a more consumer-oriented market orientation since the 1980s. The newest format, though, allows some more traces of a citizen-oriented market orientation to re-emerge.

The changes observed are all based in genre style, in the meaning of genre form, but they also influence the genre profiles of the super-genres. And as genre profiles change, the significance and value of single genres change – given their changing status in the respective profile. Thus we can see that genre profiles are influenced by cultural norms and values of an editorial staff (which again depends on the interpretation of a very complex set of influencing factors), and at the same time genre profiles are one of these influencing factors, establishing cultural norms and values.

Genre profiles are thus on an intermediate level between the micro-level of genre style and the macro-level of culture, allowing to relate the two levels. The analysis of genre profiles allows the positioning of single texts in the context of parallel textualizations and it lets us recognize different stages of genre network contours. The notion of genre profiles allows the provision of empirical evidence for the significance of genres within super-genres and changes in genre profiles can be related to changes of the non-linguistic context (e.g. changes in the media system, media market or technical equipment) or to cultural change which prefigures itself in language use – or which is realized in it.

References

Adamzik, Kirsten 2001: Grundfragen einer kontrastiven Textologie. In: Kirsten Adamzik (ed.), *Kontrastive Textologie. Untersuchungen am Beispiel deutscher und französischer Sprach- und Literaturwissenschaft*, 13–48. Tübingen: Narr.

Adamzik, Kirsten 2004: *Textlinguistik. Eine einführende Darstellung*. Tübingen: Niemeyer.

Adamzik, Kirsten 2010: Texte im Kulturvergleich. Überlegungen zum Problemfeld in Zeiten von Globalisierung und gesellschaftlicher Parzellierung. In: Martin Luginbühl and Stefan Hauser (eds.), *MedienTextKultur. Linguistische Beiträge zur kontrastiven Medienanalyse*, 17–41. Landau: Verlag Empirische Pädagogik.

Adamzik, Kirsten 2011: Textsortennetze. In: Stephan Habscheid (ed.), *Textsorten, Handlungsmuster, Oberflächen. Linguistische Typologien der Kommunikation*, 367–386. Berlin/New York: de Gruyter.

Aschenberg, Heidi 2002: Historische Textsortenlinguistik – Beobachtungen und Gedanken. In: Martina Drescher (ed.), *Textsorten im romanischen Sprachvergleich*, 153–170. Tübingen: Stauffenburg.

Bakhtin, Michail M. 1986: The Problem of Speech Genres. In: Caryl Emerson and Michael Holquist (eds.), *Speech Genres & Other Late Essays*. Trans. Vern W. McGee, 60–102. Austin: University of Texas Press.

Ballstaedt, Steffen Peter 1980: Nachrichtensprache und Verstehen. In: Helmut Kreuzer (ed.), *Fernsehforschung und Fernsehkritik*, 226–241. Göttingen: Vandenhoeck & Ruprecht.

Barkin, Steve M. 2003: *American Television News. The Media Marketplace and the Public Interest*. Armonk, N.Y.: M. E. Sharpe.

Barnhurst, Kevin G. and John C. Nerone 2001: *The form of news. A history*. New York: Guilford.

Barth, Fredrik 1989: Analysis of culture in complex societies. *Ethnos* 54(3–4): 120–142.

Bazerman, Charles 1994: Systems of genres and the enhancement of social intentions. In: Aviva Freedman and Peter Medway (eds.), *Genre and New Rhetoric*, 79–101. London: Tayler & Francis.

Bendel, Sylvia 1998: *Werbeanzeigen von 1622–1798. Entstehung und Entwicklung einer Textsorte*. Tübingen: Niemeyer.

Berkenkotter, Carol and T.N. Huckin 1995: *Genre Knowledge in Disciplinary Communication – Cognition/Culture/Power*. Hillsdale, NJ: Lawrence Erlbaum Ass.

Berkenkotter, Carol and Martin Luginbühl 2014: Producing genres: Pattern variation and genre development. To appear in: Eva-Maria Jakobs and Daniel Perrin (eds.) (= Handbooks of

Applied Linguistics 10). pp. 285–304., *Handbook of Writing and Text Production*. Berlin/ Boston: Mouton de Gruyter.

Bhatia, Vijay K. 2004: *Worlds of written discourse. A genre-based view*. (Advances in applied linguistics). London/New York: continuum.

Bhatia, Vijay K., John Flowerdew, and Rodney H. Jones 2008: Approaches to discourse analysis. In: Vijay K. Bhatia, John Flowerdew and Rodney H. Jones (eds.), *Advances in Discourse Studies*, 1–17. London: Routledge.

Blum, Roger 2006: Mediensysteme gehorchen der Politik. Ein Weltatlas nach medienpolitischen Kriterien. *Neue Zürcher Zeitung* 27. Oktober 2006. http://www.nzz. ch/2006/10/27/em/articleDOOQB.html [31.1.2013].

Campbell, Karlyn Kohrs and Kathleen Hall Jamieson 1990: *Deeds Done in Words. Presidential Rhetoric and the Genres of Governance*. Chicago: University of Chicago Press.

Devitt, Amy J. 1991: Intertextuality in tax accounting: Generic, referential, and functional. In: Charles Bazerman and James G. Paradis (eds.), *Textual dynamics of the professions*, 336–380. Madison, WI: University of Wisconsin Press.

Devitt, Amy J. 2004: *Writing Genres*. Carbondale: Southern Illinois University Press.

Devitt, Amy J. 2009: Re-fusing form in genre study. In: Janet Giltrow, Janet and Dieter Stein (eds.), *Genres in the Internet*, 27–47. Amsterdam: Benjamins.

Eckkrammer, Eva Martha 2010: Kontrastive Medientextologie und die historische Dimension. Eine theoretisch-methodische Auslotung. In: Martin Luginbühl and Stefan Hauser (eds.), *MedienTextKultur. Linguistische Beiträge zur kontrastiven Medienanalyse*, 43–65. Landau: Verlag Empirische Pädagogik.

Eckkrammer, Eva Martha 2011: Diachrone Medienanalyse. Zur Analyse multimodaler Vertextungsstrategien in historischer Sicht. In: Hartmut Stöckl and Jan Georg Schneider (eds.), *Medientheorien und Multimodalität. Ein TV-Werbespot – Sieben methodische Beschreibungsansätze*, 190–215. Köln: Halem.

Fairclough, Norman 1995: *Media Discourse*. London etc.: Arnold.

Fairclough, Norman 2003: *Analysing Discourse. Textual Analysis for Social Research*. London: Routledge.

Fix, Ulla 2011: Fraktale Narration. Eine semiotisch-textstilistische Analyse. In: Jan Georg Schneider and Hartmut Stöckl (eds.), *Medientheorien und Multimodalität. Ein TV-Werbespot – Sieben methodische Beschreibungsansätze*, 70–87. Köln: Halem.

Fleskes, Gabriele 1996 : *Untersuchungen zur Textsortengeschichte im 19. Jahrhundert. Am Beispiel der ersten deutschen Eisenbahnen*. Tübingen: Niemeyer.

Gansel, Christina 2011: *Textsortenlinguistik*. Stuttgart: Vandenhoeck & Ruprecht.

Gatzen, Barbara 2001: *Fernsehnachrichten in Japan: Inszenierungsstrategien im interkulturellem Vergleich mit Deutschland*. Tübingen: Narr.

Geertz, Clifford 1973: Thick Description: Toward an Interpretive Theory of Culture. In: Clifford Geertz (ed.), *The Interpretation of Cultures: Selected Essays*, 3–30. New York: Basic Books.

Genz, Andreas, Klaus Schönbach and Holli A. Semetko 2001: "Amerikanisierung"? Politik in den Fernsehnachrichten während der Bundestagswahlkämpfe 1990–1998. In: Hans-Dieter Klingemann and Max Kaase (eds.), *Wahlen und Wähler. Analysen aus Anlass der Bundestagswahl 1998*, 401–413. Wiesbaden: Westdeutscher Verlag.

Giddens, Anthony 1984: *The Constitution of Society*. Berkeley: University of California Press.

Goodenough, Ward H. 1957/64: Cultural Anthropology and Linguistics. In: Dell H. Hymes (ed.), *Language in Culture and Society. A Reader in Linguistics and Anthropology*, 36–40. New York: Harper & Row.

Hanitzsch, Thomas 2007: Deconstructing Journalism Culture: Towards a universal theory. *Communication Theory* 17/4: 367–385.

Hauser, Stefan 2012: Textsortennetze im Wandel. Aspekte einer Archäologie der Pressekommunikation. In: Christian Grösslinger, Gudrun Held and Hartmut Stöckl (eds.), *Pressetextsorten jenseits der ‚News'*, 181–196. Frankfurt a. M.: Peter Lang.

Hauser, Stefan and Martin Luginbühl 2012: What defines news culture? Insights from multifactorial parallel text analysis. In: Stefan Hauser and Martin Luginbühl (eds.), *Contrastive Media Analysis. Approaches to linguistc and cultural aspects of mass media communication*, 201–218. Amsterdam: Benjamins.

Herder, Johann Gottfried [1772] 1985: *Ueber die neuere deutsche Literatur. Fragmente.* Im Auftrag der Nationalen Forschungs- und Gedenkstätten der klassischen deutschen Literatur in Weimar, ed. by Regine Otto. Berlin/Weimar: Aufbau-Verlag.

Janich, Nina 2008: Intertextualität und Text(sorten)vernetzung. In: Nina Janich (ed.), *Textlinguistik. 15 Einführungen*, 177–196. Tübingen: Narr.

Klein, Josef: 2000: Intertextualität, Geltungsmodus, Texthandlungsmuster: Drei vernachlässigte Kategorien der Textsortenforschung – exemplifiziert an politischen und medialen Textsorten. In: Kirsten Adamzik (ed.), *Textsorten, Reflexionen und Analysen*, 31–44. (Textsorten 1) Tübingen: Stauffenburg.

Linke, Angelika 2009: Stil und Kultur. In: Ulla Fix, Andreas Gardt and Joachim Knape (eds.), *Rhetorik und Stilistik*, 1131–1144. Berlin/New York: de Gruyter.

Linke, Angelika 2011: Signifikante Muster – Perspektiven einer kulturanalytischen Linguistik. In: Elisabeth Wåghäll Nivre, Brigitte Kaute, Bo Andersson, Barbro Landén and Dessislava Stoeva-Holm (eds.), *Begegnungen. Das VIII. Nordisch-Baltische Germanistentreffen in Sigtuna vom 11. bis zum 13. 6. 2009*, 23–44. Stockholm: Acta Universitatis Stockholmiensis.

Luckmann, Thomas 1988: Kommunikative Gattungen im kommunikativen „Haushalt" einer Gesellschaft. In: Gisela Smolka-Koerdt, Peter M. Spangenberg and Dagmar Tillmann-Bartylla (eds.), *Der Ursprung von Literatur. Medien, Rollen, Kommunikationssituationen zwischen 1450 und 1650*, 279–288. München: Fink.

Luginbühl, Martin 2009: Disclosing and announcing, interpreting and entertaining. A comparative study on the history of TV news presentation in an American and a European national TV news show. In: Charley Rowe and Eva L. Wyss (eds.), *Language and New Media: Linguistic, Cultural, and Technological Evolutions*, 245–281. Cresskill, NJ: Hampton Press.

Luginbühl, Martin 2010: Sind Textsorten national geprägt? Nachrichtensendungen im Vergleich. In: Martin Luginbühl and Stefan Hauser (eds.), *MedienTextKultur. Linguistische Beiträge zur kontrastiven Medienanalyse*, 179–207. Landau: Verlag Empirische Pädagogik.

Luginbühl, Martin 2011: Closeness and distance. The changing relationship to the audience in the American TV news show "CBS Evening News" and the Swiss "Tagesschau". In: Karin Aijmer (ed.), *Contrastive Pragmatics*, 123–142. Philadelphia/Amsterdam: Benjamins.

Luginbühl, Martin 2014: *Medienkultur und Medienlinguistik. Textsortengeschichte(n) der amerikanischen „CBS Evening News" und der Schweizer Tagesschau* (Sprache in Kommunikation und Medien 4). Bern: Peter Lang.

Luginbühl, Martin, Thomas Baumberger, Kathrine Schwab and Harald Burger 2002: *Medientexte zwischen Autor und Publikum. Eine Studie zur Intertextualität in Presse, Radio und Fernsehen.* Zürich: Seismo.

Miller, Carolyn R. 1984: Genre as social action. *Quarterly Journal of Speech* 70: 151–167.

Miller, Carolyn R. and Dawn Shepherd 2009: Questions for genre theory from the blogosphere. In: Janet Giltrow and Dieter Stein (eds.), *Genres in the Internet*, 263–290. Amsterdam: Benjamins.

Mittell, Jason 2004: A cultural approach to television genre theory. In: Robert C. Allen and Annette Hill (eds.), *The television studies reader*, 171–181. London/New York: Routledge.

Montgomery, Martin 2007: *The discourse of broadcast news. A linguistic approach*. London: Routledge.

Mould, David H. 1984: Historical Trends in the Criticism of the News reel and Television News, 1930–1955. *Journal of Popular Film & Television* 12/3: 118–126.

Muckenhaupt, Manfred 2000: *Fernsehnachrichten gestern und heute*. Tübingen: Narr.

Nickl, Markus 2000: *Gebrauchsanleitungen. Ein Beitrag zur Textsortengeschichte seit 1950*. Tübingen: Narr.

Orlikowski, Wanda J. and JoAnne Yates 1994: Genre Repertoire: The Structuring of Communicative Practices in Organizations. *Administrative Science Quarterly* 39: 541–574.

Posner, Roland 1991: Kultur als Zeichensystem. Zur semiotischen Explikation kulturwissen-schaftlicher Grundbegriffe. In: Aleida Assmann and Dietrich Harth (eds.), *Kultur als Lebenswelt und Monument*, 37–74. Frankfurt a. M.: Fischer.

Raible, Wolfgang 2006: *Medien-Kulturgeschichte. Mediatisierung als Grundlage unserer kulturellen Entwicklung*. Heidelberg: Winter.

Sandig, Barbara 2006: *Textstilistik des Deutschen*. Berlin/New York: de Gruyter.

Schwitalla, Johannes 1993: Textsortenwandel in den Medien nach 1945 in der Bundesrepublik Deutschland. Ein Überblick. In: Bernd Ulrich Biere and Helmut Henne (eds.), *Sprache in den Medien nach 1945*, 1–29. Tübingen: Niemeyer.

Straßner, Erich 2001: Von der Korrespondenz zum Hypertext. Zeitungssprache im Wandel. In: Ulrich Breuer and Jarmo Korhonen (eds.), *Mediensprache – Medienkritik*, 87–102. Frankfurt a. M. etc.: Peter Lang.

Tajfel, Henri and John C. Turner 1986: The social identity theory of inter-group behavior. In: Stephen Worchel and William G. Austin (eds.), *Psychology of Intergroup Relations*, 7–24. Chicago: Nelson-Hall.

Thussu, Daya Kishan 2003: Live TV and bloodless deaths: War, infotainment and 24/7 news. In: Daya Kishan Thussu and Des Freedman (eds.), *War and the media: reporting conflict 24/7*, 117–132. London/Thousand Oaks CA: Sage.

Tylor, Edward Burnett 1871: *Primitive Culture. Research into the Development of Mythologie, Philosophy, Religion, Language, Art and Custom*. London: Murray.

Warnke, Ingo 1996: Historische Dimensionen pragmatischer Textorganisation – Analytische Konzeption und empirische Untersuchung am Beispiel der Intertextualität in spätmittel-alterlichen Reichslandfrieden. In: Susanne Michaelis and Doris Tophinke (eds.), *Texte – Konstitution, Verarbeitung, Typik*, 131–148. München/Newcastle: Lincom Europa.

Yates, JoAnne 1989: *Control Through Communication. The Rise of System in American Management*. Baltimore: Johns Hopkins University Press.

Lauren Squires and Josh Iorio
Tweets in the news.
Legitimizing medium, standardizing form

1 Introduction

The number and variety of digital communication technologies have increased rapidly over the past two decades. Accordingly, language users have adapted their linguistic practices to the affordances of different communication formats. These changing formats of computer-mediated language breed an ever-changing sociolinguistic context, in which established media institutions must confront new technologies and the language that is mediated through these technologies. Sociolinguistic change engenders tension between new sites of linguistic mediation (such as Twitter) and existing sites of both mediation and mediatization (such as newspapers). This chapter examines the tensions between "new" text-based digital media and "old" text-based mass media that represent them, where a major tension pertains to the vernacularity of new media forms of communication versus the heavily-enforced language standards of print and broadcast mass media (Jaffe 2009; Cotter 2010b; Squires 2011). How are "new" media texts recontextualized within "old" ones, and what does this intertextuality suggest about the effects of new media on language ideologies, standardization, and legitimization of language?

Our chapter considers "tweets" — the instantly broadcast text updates on the microblogging platform Twitter (http://www.twitter.com) — as "source texts" for journalistic work, incorporated by journalists into "news texts" (Van Hout et al. 2011). We label the text of tweets that is incorporated into journalistic texts "reported tweets." We look at mainstream news outlets' practice of using tweets as quotable information sources, focusing on the changing valuation of both the medium of Twitter and the language used within it, specifically nonstandard orthographic lexical items. To do this, we explore from several angles the trajectory of tweets in the mainstream U.S. media since Twitter's inception in 2006, examining change in the quantity of reported tweets, the context of reported tweets, and the linguistic and orthographic character of reported tweets. We show that while the medium of Twitter and practice of tweeting have been legitimized, the trend in representing linguistic practice within the medium has been one predominantly of standardization, with the vernacularity of the medium more commonly erased, rather than highlighted, over time.

2 Background

2.1 Twitter in the news media

A primary area of sociolinguistic change brought about by new media pertains not to the linguistic system itself, but rather to issues of practice, style, and genre. Androutsopoulos (2011: 153) identifies a key change in "the elaboration of vernacular writing" — casual, unedited written language in increasingly more spaces. The presence of new media has fostered sociocultural scenarios wherein "more people write, people write more, and unregimented writing goes public" (Androutsopoulos 2011: 154). In the sense of being unregulated, new media spaces are fundamentally vernacular spaces for language, and their proliferation could be argued to effect a vernacularization of language in the public sphere (Coupland, this volume). At the same time that new media platforms offer users vernacular interaction, they offer journalists a greater supply of "quotables." Through the publicization facilitated by the Web, more vernacular texts become more readily available for detachment, recontextualization, and circulation. Journalists' uptake of texts from "microblogging" services such as Twitter embodies the intertextual dynamic of vernacular texts being recontextualized within more-standard texts.

Through Twitter, users broadcast typed messages that are limited to 140 characters (including punctuation marks, letters, and spaces; publicizing links to photographs or other Websites is also common practice). The character limit for these "tweets" is the service's defining techno-linguistic constraint, distinguishing it from the interactions available on most blogs, message boards, or social network sites. Twitter differs from other modes of text-based information exchange, such as text messaging (which also has character limits), in that it is fundamentally public. By default, tweets are viewable by anyone on the Web and even appear in Web search engine results. Though users can choose to restrict their tweets to be seen only by those who follow them, the central idea behind Twitter is to make short text messages publicly available. Twitter thus is emblematic of Androutsopoulos' (2011) description of new media as increasing the quantity of *unregimented* language in *public*. Through Twitter, this unregimented language is also immediately entextualized (Bauman and Briggs 1990) as a short, cohering unit, automatically bounded and available for quotation and circulation. As Georgakopoulou (forthcoming) puts it, "[s]mall is portable"–tweets are ready-made for re-use in other texts, such as news reports.

Mainstream news media represent key sites of tension between vernacular and institutionalized discourse. When journalists quote a tweet and recontextualize it within a news story, "[p]ublic vernacular writing is ... intertwined with professionally crafted, institutionally framed language" (Androutsopoulos 2011: 154). A tweet used as a news source is decontextualized from its native vernacular medium and recontextualized in an institutional medium. These processes of de- and re-contextualization (Bauman and Briggs 1990; Georgakopoulou, forthcoming) are suffused with both journalistic ideologies (Van Hout et al. 2011; Cotter 2010b) and linguistic ideologies (Spitulnik 1997; Jaworski 2007; Coupland 2009; Jaffe 2009; Squires 2011). That is, metalinguistic representations of tweets reflect ideologies within the field of journalism – a field of "language workers" (Thurlow and Bell 2009) – about both appropriate news sources and appropriate language.

From the standpoint of journalistic practice, using tweets as source texts indicates a belief in both the veracity and the newsworthiness of the tweet's content. According to Van Hout et al. (2011), the identification of appropriate, reliable sources is a central element of news production. Further, Van Hout et al. argue that the process of selecting quotes, deciding "who gets to speak on what," constitutes "the enactment of social power through authorship and representation" (Van Hout et al. 2011: 1877). Historically, the reliance on "official" and "elite" sources has been a cornerstone of news practice (Van Hout et al. 2011; Cotter 2010b). But the mass availability of tweets from notable public figures has the potential to disrupt the historical reliance on institutionally-sanctioned sources. Information that previously could only be obtained by personal interview or press conference is now freely available directly from celebrities, athletes, and politicians and other public officials, via their personal Twitter or Facebook feeds (for analyses of celebrity use of Twitter and the creation of celebrity through Twitter, see Page 2012a, 2012b). Such information is not only easily accessible, but additionally carries a sense of being authentic and "unfiltered" (see Georgakapoulou, forthcoming; Page 2012b).

The reported tweet in the following excerpt about American singer Kelly Clarkson exemplifies the accessibility of celebrities' tweets, and also the potential for tweets themselves to become news sources:

(1) Singer Kelly Clarkson scrambled Thursday to beat back a fire storm unleashed when a day earlier she tweeted her endorsement of Republican Ron Paul for president [of the United States of America].

The first-season "American Idol" champion wrote, "I love Ron Paul. I liked him a lot during the last Republican nomination and no one gave him a chance. If he wins the nomination for the Republican party in 2012 he's got my vote. Too bad he probably won't."

(Tatko-Peterson 2011)

Clarkson's tweet—which could be read as simply an expression of personal senti-ment—is taken to represent an official political "endorsement," although she did not frame it formally in that way. Reported tweets thus suggest the news media's willingness to view Twitter as a legitimate medium from which to draw news, which seems to indicate a shift in journalistic ideology towards the reliance on non-institutional sources for newsworthy information. The shift is simultane-ously one of what Gershon (2010: 389) calls "media ideology" – the "beliefs, atti-tudes, and strategies about a single medium".

2.2 Vernacularity and authenticity in Twitter quotations

As much as journalistic sourcing decisions are about *who* gets to be quoted, and what communicative practices produce legitimate quotations, those decisions must also be about how quoted sources get to *sound* — that is, which linguistic styles are permissible *ways of speaking* to the public. Here, journalistic, media, and linguistic ideologies intersect. Even when it is used by public figures with "official" or "institutional" roles, Twitter remains a vernacular site of social prac-tice. And its vernacularity likely contributes to the appeal of public figures' tweets to both the public and journalists, for vernacularity is often perceived as a marker of authenticity (Jaffe 2009; Coupland 2009; Cotter 2010a; Page, 2012b).

Though there is little work to date that documents the general linguistic practices of Twitter users, Zappavigna (2012: 20) argues that tweets "typically contain non-standard orthography." Those working in text processing fields have also found challenges in applying traditional programs to the analysis of Twitter because of its nonstandard qualities (Puniyani et al. 2010). Additionally, the language of Twitter stereotypically consists of features commonly attributed to language in new media more generally. The comic in Figure 1 exemplifies the stereotypical uses of abbreviation, initialism, and nonstandard punctuation, in addition to Twitter-specific features such as hashtags and "retweets" (the re-broadcasting of another user's tweet; boyd et al. 2010, Zappavigna 2012).

The humorous profile of Twitter language used in Figure 1 looks similar to the stereotypical nonstandard portrayals of new media language more generally found in the mainstream news media (Thurlow 2006; Thurlow and Bell 2009; Squires 2010). However, at least one study suggests that such abbreviated lan-guage is perceived as normative on Twitter. Russ (2012) performed a social judg-ment experiment that exposed social media users to screenshots of Facebook and Twitter updates, then collected their impressions of the authors on multiple social dimensions. Updates were written either with abbreviated, nonstandard spellings, or non-abbreviated, standard spellings. Participants rated authors

Figure 1: "The Twitter bird in real life," by Agent-X Comics (http://www.agent-x.com. au/comic/the-twitter-bird-in-real-life/). The comic parodies Twitter (visually referencing Twitter's logo, a blue bird "tweeting") by showing stereotypical abbreviated language and other Twitter-specific features

in the abbreviated condition as younger, less intelligent, and less formal than in the non-abbreviated condition. However, the non-abbreviated Twitter posts were rated as less "tech-savvy" than either abbreviated Twitter posts or Facebook posts. Russ's data indicate that abbreviation is one "norm" on Twitter, with non-abbreviated language being perceived as coming from a less experienced user—perhaps abbreviated style is also a component of authenticity on Twitter.

At the same time, "non-standard grammar/punctuation" has been reported to render tweets less credible (Morris et al. 2012). Thus, some vernacular features occurring in Twitter may be what Paolillo (2001: 181) has called "'standard,' yet non-legitimized." That is, they are standard within a particular community, but not standard (hence not legitimized) outside of that community. Paolillo (2001: 209) asks, "What is the power center that confers legitimacy to particular linguistic forms?" While mainstream news media have a relatively clear "power center," this is not the case for spaces such as Twitter, and so norms that differ from those of the mainstream media are likely to emerge.

Because of its decentralized and unregulated nature, Twitter's overall linguistic practice likely also reflects multiple vernaculars, which may not be perceived by all as equally authentic. For instance, vernacular written features can be grounded in offline language associated with particular cultural ways of speaking, or in natively textual language that has emerged from online communities. Vernaculars can emerge from "speech communities" or from "text communities." The originating mode of a particular vernacular may play some role in how it is viewed in terms of its authenticity. In online, text-based contexts such as Twitter, while textual vernacularity may be perceived as authentic, it may also be perceived as "exotic" or "revolutionary" by the news media, who generally frame textual vernacularity as "inherently contrary and detrimental to more established modes of language and, by implication, the moral order," as argued by Thurlow (2006: 688).

Further, Thurlow's work demonstrates that a range of linguistic ideologies about the vernacular character of computer-mediated language use assume that nonstandard forms are entirely "non-strategic" rather than stylistically meaningful. This idea comes from the media's apparent belief that in CMC, nonstandard forms have supplanted standard forms entirely (Thurlow 2006; Squires 2010), rather than nonstandard and standard forms coexisting. However, vernacular forms in CMC (as in spoken language) are often "strategic," in that they perform self-presentational identity work and carry stylistic meanings (Paolillo 2001; Tagliamonte and Denis 2008; Iorio 2010; Hinrichs 2012; Squires 2012).

Vernacular forms in tweets, then, may be strategic on the part of their users, but they potentially bring their written form into conflict with the journalistic practices of mainstream news media, which privilege regimented standard language (Cotter 2010a). Standard English orthography is highly standardized, and its ongoing re-standardization occurs partly through English print publications like newspapers and magazines (Sebba, 2007; Cotter 2010b; Zelizer 1995; see also Moschonas, this volume). In Sebba's (2007: 43–47; Table 2.1) terms, news media texts constitute institution-based "texts for publication," and so their orthographic/linguistic usage is heavily regulated. Twitter, by contrast, constitutes a form of noninstitutional "electronic media" which, at least to some degree, presumes a "self" or "in-group" readership. Tweets thus exist within a far less regulated space of orthographic/linguistic practice; they have no clear "power center" to metalinguistically enforce language norms.

In the case of what we are calling "reported tweets," due to tweets' unregulated status, there is rich heteroglossic potential between the vernacular linguistic form of a tweet and the heavily standardized linguistic form of a media story that quotes it. For instance, in example (2), the nonstandard features (indicated in bold) contained within the reported tweet contrasts with the highly standardized form of the encapsulating journalistic narrative.

(2) [Jason] Trawick announced Friday on "Access Hollywood" that he and [Britney] Spears are engaged. The two have been dating since 2009. Spears hinted at the big news with a tweet Friday morning that read, "**OMG**. Last night Jason surprised me with the one gift I've been waiting for. **Can't** wait to show you! **SO SO SO** excited**!!!!**"

(Pioneer Press 2011; emphases ours)

In this example, the reported tweets contain vernacular features based on both spoken (e.g. the intensifying repetition of "so" in "SO SO SO"; subject omission in the final sentence beginning "Can't") and written (e.g. "OMG"; multiplicity of exclamation marks "!!!!") norms. These features are situated within the standard context of the surrounding text.

The juxtaposition of vernacular features in tweets with the "conservative, prescriptive, and mainstream" (Cotter 2010b: 189; Cotter, this volume) language of journalists provides for a discursive context where the linguistic values of two communities (i. e. Twitter users and journalists) can potentially come into conflict. We thus might expect journalists, because of their linguistic values, to be somewhat hesitant to consider vernacular new media platforms like Twitter to be fit as direct news sources.

Cotter (2010a: 1897) found that journalists sometimes intentionally quote nonstandard language in order to "capture 'authenticity' or set up the role of [the speaker as a] language authority," which indicates that in some cases, there may be room in the journalistic ideology for the vernacular. If journalists seek to represent tweets as authentic, either as authentically originating from Twitter or authentically representative of the original author's style, might journalists intentionally select tweets with more vernacular features, effecting a type of vernacularization of the news media more generally (Coupland, this volume)? On this note, Cotter (2010b) writes:

> Quotes, given the importance placed on their authenticity, are not subject to the stylistic constraints that govern news stories. Yet quotes are not verbatim depositions or transcripts: reporters are taught to be selective in which elements of an utterance to use as a quote. This of course raises important linguistic questions for journalists which have socially meaningful implications: When does a reporter 'clean up' the grammar of an interviewee? (150)

Zelizer (1995) quotes journalism style guides' directives to journalists to correct items like nonstandard grammar or speech-specific linguistic shortenings (e.g., *gonna*). The expected vernacular character of tweets would seem patently at odds with the imperative that journalists use and maintain the established standards of written English. Thus, in addition to examining patterns of journalists' incorporation of tweets as new sources over time, we ask what the linguistic character is of the reported tweets, and whether any increase in reported tweets over time has entailed an increase in vernacular written features occurring in the standard language context of the news.

3 Research Questions

The issues highlighted above point towards a general question about sociolinguistic behavior in the face of sociolinguistic change: how do institutional media respond to new vernacular forms of interpersonal media and the language used in them? As new media platforms become established as sites of public information broadcast by individuals, and particularly as they become utilized for persona management by public figures (such as politicians, celebrities, athletes, and organizations), they enter the realm of "quotables." The relevance of Twitter as a news *topic* has risen steadily (and rapidly) since its inception in 2006 (Arceneaux and Schmitz Weiss 2010); thus, the use of Twitter as a news *source* provides a case study for examining mass media's negotiation of new media texts.

Our analyses speak to three distinct but related research questions: Has the quantity of reported tweets increased since Twitter's inception? Has the nature of reported tweets' contextualization – including the types of stories they appear in and how they are metalinguistically introduced within a story – changed? And has the presence of nonstandard, vernacular linguistic features in reported tweets increased or decreased over time?

The discussion to follow explores the treatment of reported tweets in the mainstream media from a phenomenological level to the level of the lexical item. Since reportage in different domains may display different trajectories, we chose to compare reportage between two domains of mass media: entertainment (ENT) and sports (SPT). These domains are well-suited for an investigation into quoting practices because they are personality-focused domains of culture, being driven largely by events surrounding individual celebrities and athletes; we would expect to find utilization of individuals' Twitter feeds to enrich stories in these domains. Additionally, the two domains have been shown to be less formal linguistically than other news genres (Reynolds and Cascio 1999), which we believe might increase our chances of identifying quoting practices surrounding nonstandard orthography in particular.

4 Analyses and Discussion

4.1 Changes in quantity: Trajectory of reported tweets from 2006–2011

The first step in our analysis is to determine whether reported tweets are becoming more common in mainstream reportage. In order to examine the change in quantity of reported tweets over time in the two domains, we leveraged the search capabilities of LexisNexis, an international newspaper and newswire database, to identify all cases where the term "tweeted" appeared in the sports and entertainment sections of mainstream U.S. newspapers and newswires from 2006 through 2011. The search was limited to U.S. national publications (e.g., *New York Times*), major U.S. regional publications (e.g., *Pittsburgh Post-Gazette*), and the U.S. national lines from international newswires (e.g., Associated Press).

Our goal with this approach was to quickly describe the quantitative trajectory of tweets from Twitter's inception through the writing of this chapter in order to determine whether tweets have become more "quotable" over time. For each successful search return, we identified the case (or cases) of "tweeted" in the article and determined whether the search term referred to a reported Twitter update or some other use of "tweeted" that was not associated with Twitter. When we identified patterns in the use of "tweeted" that did not refer to Twitter updates, we used Boolean operators to tailor the search strings to return more relevant results (e.g. SEARCH tweeted NOT bird). In this way, we were able to focus our search to return only those cases of "tweeted" that referred to reported Twitter updates. We tallied the total number of returns for "tweeted" per news article and organized the resulting dataset to reflect a month-by-month account.

Our results using this method show that the first case of a quoted "tweet" in the sports domain occurred in February 2009 in the *Chicago Sun Times,* and for the entertainment domain in March 2009 at the Associated Press Online. The initial emergence of tweets as a quotable source of reportage in the two domains thus seems to have occurred at roughly the same time. Since Twitter debuted in July 2006, it took approximately 2.5 years for the mainstream media to recognize the quotable value of "tweeting." While it is unclear whether there was a particular event that triggered the emergence of reported "tweeting" in the mainstream media, the fact that they emerged simultaneously in two domains suggests that this may be the case, considering the 2.5 year lag between when tweets were available to be quoted and when they first emerged as quoted (see also Arceneaux and Schmitz Weiss (2010), on high-profile public events precipitating news coverage of Twitter).

Although reference to "tweeted" material emerged around the same time in both domains, their rate of quotation is different, which provides the first piece of evidence that we may expect to find differences in how tweets are recontextualized in the two domains. Figure 2 shows the trajectory of the number of quoted tweets in news articles from 2006 through 2011. The solid lines represent the trajectory of the collected data, while the dashed lines represent the linearly regressed trend of the dataset. In Figure 2, the number of reported tweets for both domains increases over the data collection period, which echoes the time-course of the media's growing interest in Twitter in general (identified for an earlier time period by Arceneaux and Schmitz Weiss 2010). However, by comparing the slopes of the regression lines, we observe that the rate of increase for the sports domain is 5.1 times greater than the rate for the entertainment domain. Based on this difference, our analysis indicates that tweets are playing a more substantial role in the sports reportage compared to the entertainment reportage.

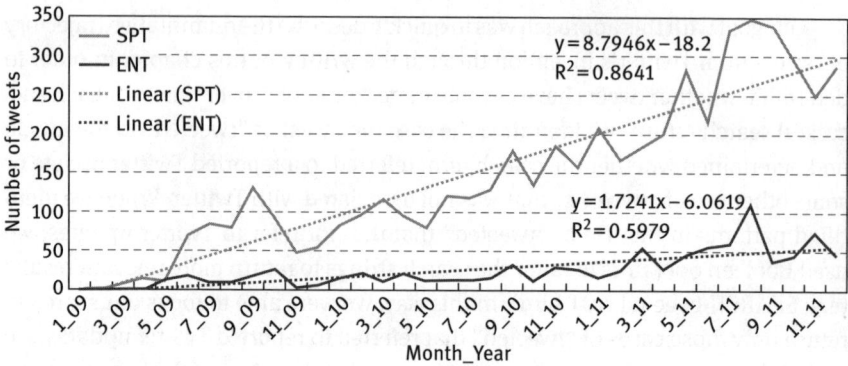

Figure 2: Search returns in LexisNexis for "tweeted" (January 2009 – December 2011)

From the linear regressions in Figure 2, we can also determine that the variability in the number of tweets differs between the datasets for the two domains, indicated by an R^2 value of 0.86 for SPT and 0.60 for ENT. The difference between these R^2 values suggests that the increase in reported tweets is more constant (and consistent) for ENT compared to SPT. So while we observe a more rapid (and erratic) increase in the number of reported tweets in mainstream sports news, we observe a more gradual (and systematic) increase for entertainment news. These differences suggest that the two domains value tweets differently, and so we would expect to observe differences also in how they frame the tweets for their readership.

4.2 Changes in context: Recontextualizing reported tweets

In this section, we explore two questions as they relate to the time period of 2009–2011: 1) What types of stories do reported tweets appear in, and 2) Are reported tweets introduced differently from other types of reported material? These questions focus on whether mainstream news views the use of reported tweets as becoming more normalized in practice or whether reported tweets are seen as novel and exotic.

To answer the first question, we again used LexisNexis to identify cases of reported tweets that occurred in stories that were explicitly metadiscursive — that is, stories that were in some way or another about Twitter itself. We expected that over time, tweets would become more likely to be reported in stories without a focus on Twitter, but that in earlier years, reported tweets may have most likely been used as a source of reportage when Twitter *was the story*. In LexisNexis, we conducted a search of headlines for stories that contained reported tweets (using the keyword "tweeted") noting whether the headlines for these stories contained

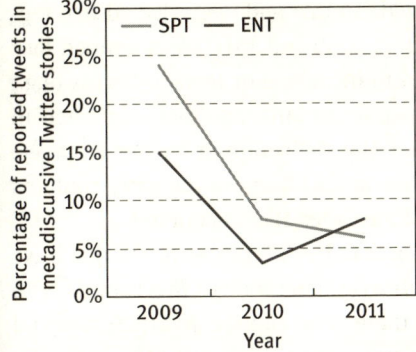

Figure 3: Diachronic change in overt reference to Twitter in headlines

reference to Twitter. Thus, the resulting dataset is comprised of articles that are explicitly framed as being about Twitter and that contain reported tweets. We tallied the total number of these "metadiscursive Twitter stories" by year and domain and then compared these values to the total number of news articles that contained reported tweets.

The results are presented in Figure 3. They show an aggregate decrease in the percentage of metadiscursive Twitter stories after an initial peak in 2009, although the decrease for the sports domain is more pronounced (18 % change from 2009–2011) than for the entertainment domain (7 % change). At the same time as reported tweets become more common in mainstream media contexts, then, their role also seems to become one of broader interest. That is, tweets cease being incorporated as frequently into explicitly metadiscursive contexts, and more frequently are used as quote sources for a broader range of stories. Figure 3 suggests a rapid shift from the purpose of reported tweets being incorporated in their earliest mentions (in 2009) to their purpose thereafter. In the earlier contexts, reported tweets were often incorporated as evidence of Twitter phenomena under analysis by a story; they quickly became a source of reportable content available for more general purposes.

While the overall trajectory of the metadiscursive Twitter stories decreases over time for both domains, the patterns of decrease differ. The percentage of stories decreases consistently in the sports domain, but the percentage troughs in 2010 for the entertainment domain. This difference suggests that the two domains are at different stages of normalizing their relationship with the reported tweets, or that the journalistic practice of using tweets as sources in the two domains is still being negotiated.

To further explore how reported tweets are metadiscursively framed, we adopt a more micro-analytical approach to investigate how, within given news stories, reported tweets are recontextualized. To this end, we selected five representative stories each in both domains from 2009 and 2011. We examined four features of these stories: 1) the verbs used to introduce or refer to tweets (e.g., *wrote; said; tweeted*), 2) the verbs used to refer to language that originated in other modes of communication, 3) whether any stylization of Twitter language occurs in the body of the article or headline, and 4) whether the story contains commentary about the formal properties of the tweet(s) being quoted.

Among the 20 stories, there do not appear to be differences in the quotative markers used to refer to the reported tweets over time, though this sample is so limited that we are hesitant to claim that there is no change. In all 20 sampled stories, quotes that are retrieved from Twitter are metalinguistically treated as distinct from quotes retrieved by other means — from a written statement, an oral interview, a text message, or another source. In most stories, the Twitter quotes themselves were referred to as having been "tweeted" by the speaker, though other formulations of past-tense verbs were occasionally also used; Table 1 shows these results.

As can be seen from data for quoted tweets in the table, even when the verb used is not "tweet," it is typically (85% of the time) made explicit that Twitter was the medium of origin for the quote. While quotes originating on Twitter are all highlighted as such, other quotes in the surrounding stories are signaled as coming from spoken language or, when specified, a written statement (Table 1, Other Quoted Material). This suggests that while quotes from other sources tend to be assumed to have come from either oral interaction or written statements (on behalf of athletes, organizations, or celebrities), tweets are specified as a distinct type of source.

Another aspect of the metadiscursive context of reported tweets concerns whether the news article metalinguistically highlights a tweets' orthographic form — either by explicit comment, or by stylization of tweets as a genre accompanying the reported tweet. In this small sample, the sports domain had one instance of this highlighting in 2009 and one in 2011; the entertainment domain had two in 2009. Here are the two cases of stylization from the 2009 entertainment stories:

(3)   "Notice my hand in the back. It's pouring a bottle of water!!!" she Tweeted. "C'mon guys! Do
      you think I would really pee in the entry way to the Abbey in broad DAYLIGHT!!!" Uh, NO!!!
      And don't waste all your 140 characters on exclamation points!!!!!!

(Walker, 2009)

(4)   STOP BEING MEAN TO JESSICA SIMPSON! STOP IT RIGHT NOW!!:

(McMullen, 2009)

Quoted Tweets		Other Quoted Material	
Introductory phrase	**#**	**Introductory phrase**	**#**
tweeted	21	said	30
used Twitter/the site to...	3	says	4
posted on Twitter	1	added	3
said in a tweet that read	1	tells	3
judging from one of his recent tweets...	1	according to	1
... with posts such as this:	1	joked	1
from the Inquirer's own @Jeff_McLane	1	said in a statement	1
got into a virtual Twitter argument	1	said in a teleconference	1
offers witty tweets	1	quoted as saying	1
writing to his ... followers	1	warned	1
tweeted ... among them [the tweets]:	1		
SUBTOTAL (explicit reference to Twitter)	**33**		
wrote	2		
responded	1		
said	1		
was the message from	1		
none	1		
SUBTOTAL (no explicit reference to Twitter)	**6**		
TOTAL	**39**	**TOTAL**	**46**
% introduced with explicit reference to Twitter 85%			

Table 1: Comparison of introductory phrases used to introduce reported tweets vs. other types of reported material

In (3), the television star Jaime Pressly's tweet is quoted, then the author responds to her tweet in a style that parodies her Twitter usage including multiple exclamation marks and capital letters. Similarly, in (4) (same publication), the multiple exclamation mark appears to allude to the use of multiple exclamation marks in Twitter (though Jessica Simpson's quoted tweet doesn't contain them; note also that here the capital letters are part of the headline style of this section of the publication).

In the sports stories, (5) below shows not stylization, but rather overt commentary that serves as an apology for Shaquille O'Neal's Twitter style, which includes several nonstandard features. This story appeared in 2009.

(5) Just leavn lebrons party, i have no voice, can u hear this, ...C i told u, no voice, lol.

> You'll have to forgive Phoenix Suns center Shaquille O'Neal for the shorthand and funky
> punctuation in this message, which he posted on Twitter during All-Star weekend. Abbrevi-
> ations of all sorts are the norm on Twitter, where users have a maximum of 140 characters
> to let people know what's up. (Slezak 2009)

This story was about Twitter use by athletes, and explicitly comments on what was seen as typical language for tweets, using terms like "funky punctuation," "shorthand," and "abbreviations." O'Neal's quoted tweet that introduces the article is an exemplar of these features, providing an emblematic representation of tweets *as nonstandard* for this story about athletes' use of Twitter.

Commentary about tweets' orthographic form continues in 2011; one of our selected stories provides a good example of the media's continued separation of tweeting from other communicative practices. The headline reads: "They said (or tweeted) it," and the story consists of simply a list of quotes, which the paper describes as "[a] sampling of Twitter posts (pardon the misspellings), quotes and text messages from current and former players about Jay Cutler" (Atlanta Journal-Constitution 2011). Such a description sets up tweets as a meaningfully separate discursive category from these other formats; they are not referred to as "quotes," which we assume refers to spoken language; and they are different from "text messages." It is furthermore notable that the article explicitly frames tweets as the *only* one of these forms of speech subject to some kind of nonstandard practice ("misspellings"). Among the quoted material in this particular story, we identified only one case that we would consider a "misspelling": <how> for *who*. There are four instances where standard orthography would call for apostrophes, and two instances of <u> for *you*. It is unclear to which of these features the term "misspellings" is meant to be applied by the article's introduction; "misspelling" implies that the usage is non-strategic, an accident, a mistake. While apostrophe omission could rightly be seen as non-strategic, we would argue strongly that <u> is strategically deployed as part of one's style in CMC (as in Shaquille O'Neal's tweet above). Yet this report treats any deviation from standard as accidental "misspellings," suggesting a continued concern on the part of the print media with the nonstandard language in Twitter, even as it accepts Twitter as a source of information.

Indeed, the perceived vernacularity of tweets may have inhibited earlier uptake of tweets by journalists. The early tendency for reported tweets to occur in metadiscursive stories resonates with research by Arceneaux and Schmitz Weiss (2010), who found that stories about Twitter from 2006–2009 shared a primary focus of explaining the medium itself. Two components of this explanation were the *brevity* and *speed* that presumably constrain Twitter users when they create their posts. That these properties were focused on by the media shows an awareness (or, perhaps, fabrication) of Twitter as encompassing a unique genre of communication, and their notion that Twitter's format directly constrains one's textual practice. As Arceneaux and Schmitz Weiss put it (2010: 1268): "For some writers, the extreme brevity of posts was a drawback, as the format encourages the kind of cryptic, condensed language associated with text messaging in general." Arceneaux and Schmitz Weiss do not explore the language ideologies that may have been evident in these media mentions, but we suggest that a media ideology that Twitter posts bear nonstandard language similar to that of text messaging may have prevented more early uptake of tweets by journalists.

From our analysis of the recontextualization of reported tweets, we discovered that although the stories are becoming less explicitly focused on the origin of reported tweets on Twitter, the fact that tweets are different from other sources of traditional quotation remains salient in how the tweets are framed within the stories at the phrasal (and lexical) level. Our analysis of how tweets are framed suggests that the tweets themselves may be becoming legitimized by mainstream media, in that the novelty of the medium is decreasing. The next section asks whether the same pattern of legitimization occurs for the linguistic forms prevalent in tweets.

4.3 Changes in character: The linguistic and orthographic profile of reported tweets

The final component of our analysis focuses on the linguistic form of reported tweets, specifically in change over time of the representation of nonstandard orthography. We collected the text of tweets (or portions of tweets) that were quoted in mainstream media articles. For this analysis, in addition to major U.S. print newspapers and lifestyle/entertainment magazines, we searched mainstream online news sources (e.g. Entertainment and Sports Programming Network – *ESPN.com*; Thirty-Mile Zone – *TMZ.com;* Sports Illustrated – *SI.com*). Using the search field on each website or the search capabilities of LexisNexis for the newspapers and magazines, we searched for the terms "tweeted" and "a tweet." Once we located the reported tweet in the article, we copied the quoted tweet and metadata about it, including its source and date of publication, into a database for analysis. Through this method we developed a diachronically organized corpus of reported tweets in both the entertainment and sports domains.

A Python[1] script was developed that tagged each lexical item in the reported tweets based on membership in three categories:

---

1 Python is an open source, general purpose, high-level programming language, see http://

CM: features perceived to be emblematic of computer-mediated communication or the internet (e.g., *LOL* or *afk*)

PS: lexical items including phonetic and prosodic spellings (e.g., *sooooo* or *hawt*)

TY: typographical errors (e.g., keystroke errors such as *gaint*, word boundary errors such as *alot*, and apostrophe omission such as in *dont*)

Our typology was an adaptation of the typology developed by Androutsopoulos (2000: 520–522) for offline media texts and refined based on the context of Twitter updates and the results from a pilot study of athletes' use of Twitter and mainstream sports reportage's quotation of their tweets (Iorio and Squires 2011). Our alterations to the Androutsopoulos typology consisted of conflating the types he proposed into high-level categories that reflected vernacular orthography based in speech communities, (i. e., PS), and those that are enregistered as being emblematic of online written discourse or emerging from text communities (i. e., CM; see Squires 2010). Although they are based in communities whose members interact through different modalities, we consider both PS and CM to be strategic spellings in that they reflect self-presentational identity work. Although features like PS and CM may be viewed as more or less strategic on the part of Twitter users, TY may be seen as non-strategic or simply "mistaken."

In order to assign each lexical item in the corpus to the appropriate nonstandard type, the Python script compared each item to items in a CM, PS, TY and standard spelling (ST) wordlist. The ST wordlist was based on the 12dicts Wordlists (Beale 2007), which contains about 75,000 correlated common word entries from 12 dictionaries of Standard American English that vary widely by publisher, style, completeness and depth. The CM, PS, and TY wordlists were developed by the authors and tailored to the corpora by using the tagger to identify all lexical items not present in the ST wordlist. After tagging all ST items in the tweets, the tagger returned all untagged (or nonstandard) items. These items were assigned to the appropriate wordlist (either CM, PS, or TY) and the process was repeated until no untagged items were identified. The script ignored punctuation except in the case of apostrophes. Since apostrophes are typically word-internal, we considered them a part of the lexical item. For standard uses of apostrophes (e.g. to indicate possession or in contractions), the lexical item was tagged as ST. The script also identified lexical items that could be assigned to two types (e.g. ambiguity between a standard abbreviation "im," short for "instant messenger," and "im," a contraction with a missing apostrophe, which we categorized under TY). These cases were manually reviewed and assigned to the appropriate category. Once the tagging process was completed, we computationally extracted the total

---

www.python.org/ for more information.

number of lexical items by type from the entertainment and sports corpora and organized these data by year for comparison.

Our corpora contain 1,451 tweets composed of 19,449 lexical items in the entertainment and sports domains. The top ten highest-ranked items by type based on the number of times they occur in each corpus appears in Table 2. The rankings in Table 2 highlight a number of interesting facts about the two corpora that provide context for the analysis to follow.

	ST (N = 18,715)				CM (N = 401)				PS (N = 244)				TY (N = 89)			
Rank	SPT	#	ENT	#	SPT	#	ENT	#	SPT	#	ENT	#	SPT	#	ENT	#
1	the	406	the	318	u	53	u	43	soo[2]	35	soo	70	im	12	im	6
2	to	351	i	294	2	27	2	16	yall	8	yall	8	dont	6	didnt	2
3	i	266	to	210	n	21	4	12	aggh	3	yay	3	briefley	2	dont	2
4	a	245	a	208	lol	15	lol	11	cuz	3	dat	2				
5	and	182	and	172	4	13	w	10	jus	3	haha	2				
6	for	154	my	142	b	12	1	9	yess	3	mmm	2				
7	my	144	of	130	ur	8	r	8	bouta	2	neffew	2				
8	is	124	in	125	r	7	:)	6	dat	2	bumbed	2				
9	me	122	is	105	thx	7	ur	6	feelin	2						
10	in	118	for	90	lmao	6	n	5	goin	2						

Table 2: Highest ranked lexical items by type and domain

First, the highest ranked items across all types are identical (e.g. "the", "u", "soo", and "im" for both SPT and ENT), and the subsequently ranked items are remarkably similar. More specifically, we would expect *function words* (words with grammatical function but little semantic content), to be the highest ranked items for any corpus of English. Since the function words appear as the 10 highest ranked standard items, we can infer that the tagging script operated as intended.

Second, *alphanumeric replacements* (e.g. "2" for "two" and "u" for "you") (Iorio 2010) or *grapheme substitutions* (e.g. "thx" for "thanks") (Androutsopoulos 2000) are highly ranked in both corpora, in addition to abbreviations (e.g. "lol") that are emblematic of online written discourse. *Colloquial spellings* (Androutsopoulos 2000) like "yall" and "dat" appeared in both corpora under

---

2 Prosodic spellings where an arbitrary number of graphemes were added to a word to elongate the vowel were conflated in our dataset, e.g. "soo" was counted as the same form as "sooo" and "soooo".

the PS type, with the *prosodic spelling* (Androutsopoulos 2000) "soo" occurring as the highest ranked PS item for both corpora. There were very few cases of TY that overlapped between the two corpora, although a pattern emerged in that the most common TY items contained missing apostrophes.[3]

Our general conclusion about the rankings is that, from lexical and orthographic standpoints, the profiles of both corpora are comparable. There is little difference between the two corpora in terms of the nonstandard spellings that appear, which suggests that any difference in frequency between the domains can be attributed to differences in the ideologies of the domains about vernacular features rather than differences in the vernacular nonstandard character between the two domains. Further, all of these most-common nonstandard items are within what Sebba (2007: 32–34) calls the "zone of social meaning": close enough to standard orthography to be recognizable, but deviant enough to be recognizable as such. Since both the sports and entertainment populations' reported tweets contain similar linguistic resources, our analysis can focus on differences between how these items are represented in the two domains, rather than on differences between the orthographic styles of athletes and entertainment personalities.

To examine the linguistic/orthographic profile of tweets as reported by these domains over time, we performed a lexical analysis of the ENT and SPT corpora. The overall corpus statistics are presented in Tables 3 and 4. To reflect the rate of diachronic change described in Figure 2, we balanced the two corpora such that we collected twice as many tweets from 2010 as we did from 2009 and twice as many from 2011 as we did from 2010. Also, it was difficult to retrieve stories from the Web with reported tweets the further back in time we searched.

	2009	2010	2011	Total
ENT	103	195	428	726
SPT	100	196	429	725
total	203	391	857	1451

Table 3: Total number of tweets per domain

	2009	2010	2011	total
ENT	1554	2326	5213	9093
SPT	1471	3206	5679	10356
total	3025	5532	10892	19449

Table 4: Total number of lexical items per domain

---

3 Although the use or omission of apostrophes has been analyzed as constituting part of one's sociolinguistic style in media like instant messaging (see Squires 2012), we categorize it here along with TY under the assumption that the news media view this type of nonstandardism as a non-strategic "mistake" rather than intentional, stylistic spelling (as we discussed above).

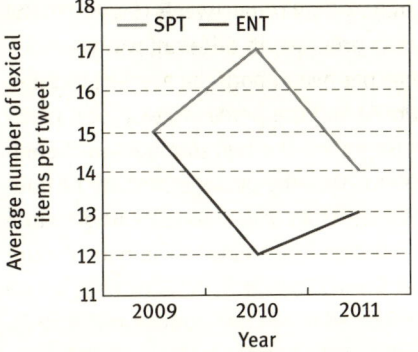

Figure 4: Average number of lexical items per tweet

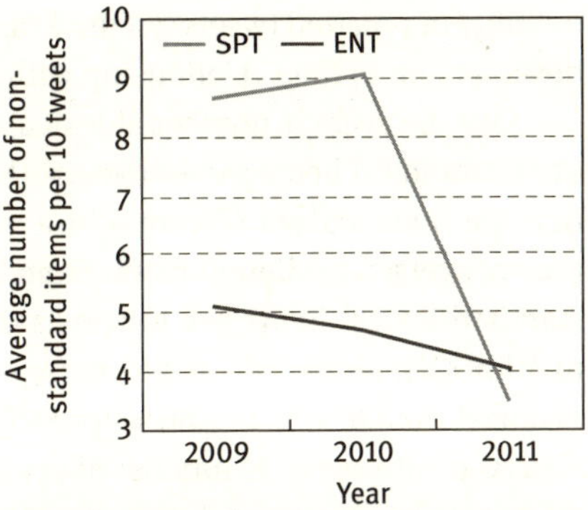

Figure 5: Average number of nonstandard items per 10 tweets

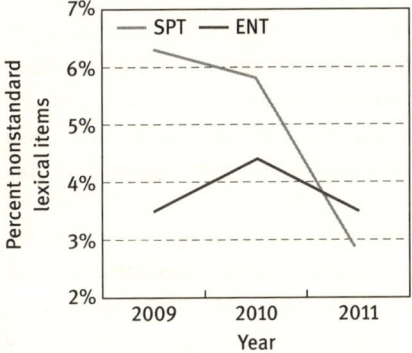

Figure 6: Percent nonstandard items (number of nonstandard items / total number of items)

When we examine the lexical composition of the two corpora more closely, we observe differences between the two domains in terms of the average number of total lexical items per tweet (Figure 4), the average number of nonstandard lexical items (Figure 5), and the percentage of nonstandard items (Figure 6).

In Figure 4, for both domains, the average number of lexical items per tweet in 2009 is 15 and decreases to 14 for SPT and 13 for ENT by 2011. While a change in the average by 1 or 2 over 3 years is hardly surprising, the course in which the change occurred was unexpected. While the overall trajectory of the average number of lexical items per tweet is negative for both SPT and ENT (i. e. the reported tweets are becoming shorter over time), the patterns for the two domains diverge in 2010: SPT *increases* from 15 items to 17 items on average while ENT *decreases* from 15 items to 12 items. This divergence provides further evidence that, although the two domains are moving in the same direction in terms of the quantity of reported tweets (Figure 2) and in how they frame tweets (Figure 3), the development of their relationship with tweets proceeds in different ways.

Like the average number of lexical items per tweet, both the average number of nonstandard items per 10 tweets[4] (Figure 5) and the percentage of total items that are nonstandard (Figure 6) are converging for the two domains, although they converge at different rates. From 2009 to 2012, the average number of nonstandard lexical items per 10 tweets decreased from 9 to 4 for SPT and from 5 to 4 for ENT. Similarly, the percentage of nonstandard items in the two corpora changed from 6.30 % to 2.80 % for SPT and from 3.50 % to 3.49 % for ENT. As we observed with the total number of tweets reported in the two domains (Figure 2), these patterns have correlated trajectories (i. e. either both positive or both negative) but proceed at different rates. For SPT, the diachronic change occurs rapidly in the quantity of reported tweets, the average number of nonstandard items, and the percentage of the corpus that is nonstandard. For ENT, the changes in the same direction are much more subtle.

While we have already seen differences in the two news domains, we have yet to examine whether different types of nonstandardisms (TY v. CM v. PS) are also treated differently. We turn now to an analysis of patterns between the two domains in how they treat different types of nonstandard spellings and how this treatment changes over time.

Table 5 presents the percentage of nonstandard items (total number of NS items divided by the total number of items) by type for the two domains over time. Figure 7 represents these data graphically. A number of interesting findings emerge that demonstrate how the different nonstandard types pattern differently in the two domains.

	ENT-CM	SPT-CM	ENT-PS	SPT-PS	ENT-TY	SPT-TY
2009	1.32 %	2.82 %	1.32 %	1.77 %	0.69 %	1.11 %
2010	1.90 %	3.28 %	1.41 %	1.37 %	0.50 %	0.66 %
2011	1.82 %	1.36 %	1.21 %	0.88 %	0.17 %	0.30 %

Table 5: Percentage of NS items by type in two domains (January 2009- December 2011)

---

4 We present the average number of NS items per 10 tweets rather than per tweet because the averaged values are all less than one, and tweets can only be conceptualized as whole number entities.

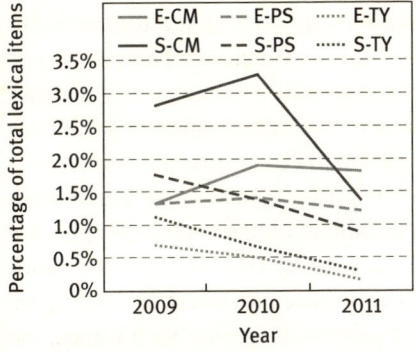

Figure 7: Percentage of NS items by type in two domains (January 2009 – December 2011)

For both domains, as we have noted above for nonstandard spellings in general (Figure 6), the general trajectory of the nonstandard spellings is negative for most of the types. The exception to this generalization is for CM forms in ENT, which *increases* slightly from 1.32% in 2009 to 1.82% in 2011 with a peak at 1.90% in 2010. During the same time span, CM *decreased* for SPT from 2.82% in 2009 to 1.36% in 2011. Similarly, the percentage of PS forms for ENT remains relatively stable throughout the study period (from 1.32% to 1.21%) while it decreases for SPT (from 1.77% to 0.88%). The presence of CM and PS in reported tweets for SPT decreases over time, while they either remain constant or increase over time for ENT. This suggests that the two domains are treating the two types of nonstandardisms differently.

The trajectory for TY is negative for both domains and proceeds at about the same rate. We argue that the TY type represents nonstandardisms perceived as non-strategic spellings; that is, spellings that are the result of mistaken typing, rather than stylistic habit. Our results suggest that this distinction is recognized by the media as well, since typos have been nearly eliminated from reportage since 2009, whereas other forms have not. The negative trajectory for both domains suggests a number of possible interpretations: 1) that both SPT and ENT are actively editing typos out of the reported tweets, 2) that athletes and entertainment personalities are using fewer typos, perhaps because they understand that their tweets may be quoted, and/or 3) that media producers are choosing tweets that do not contain typographical errors. Of all three types, the trajectory for TY is the most consistent between the two domains as they approach 0 in 2011, showing that both ENT and SPT are treating TY differently from the other types and similarly to each other. This indicates that the mainstream media in both domains value to different degrees the inclusion of the other types of nonstandard spellings — which we consider strategic, in contrast to TY — in their reportage.

The two most illuminating patterns in the comparison of strategic nonstandard types between the two domains are: 1) sports tweets are becoming more standard on a whole to a greater extent than those in the entertainment coverage, and 2) the features associated with computer-mediated communication have decreased in the sports coverage but increased in the entertainment coverage.

One possible explanation as to why the sports tweets are becoming more standard pertains to the institutional context in which athletes and celebrities are tweeting. Athletes represent the organizations for which they work, while celebrities represent themselves. Given this difference, athletes are bound by the policies of sports teams, owners, and leagues, while celebrities are not; for instance, the National Football League (NFL) has strict policies regimenting when players are allowed to tweet, and fines violators. Thus, athletes are scrutinized for what they post to Twitter, when they post, and how often they post, as is demonstrated by the following ESPN headlines (the relevant sports leagues are noted in parentheses):

(6) "Cleveland Indians' Chris Perez fined $750 for 'reckless' tweet" – April 20, 2012 (Major League Baseball) (Associated Press 2012)

(7) "Twitter poses fine line for players" – March 19th, 2012 (National Collegiate Athletic Association College Football) (Adelson 2012)

(8) "Helio Castroneves fined $30,000, given probation for Twitter comment" – September 27, 2011 (IndyCar Racing) (Associated Press 2011)

(9) "NFL fines Chad Ochocinco $25K for in-game tweets" – August 24th, 2010 (National Football League) (ESPN.com News Services 2010)

To contextualize the monetary penalty given by the NFL to Chad Ochocinco in Example 8, note that the NFL also fined James Harrison $5,000 for an illegal hit on another player ("NFL fines James Harrison $5,000 for slamming Vince Young" – September 22, 2010) (Associated Press, 2010). That is, a player was fined five times as much money for tweeting during a game than for illegally and dangerously playing the game!

The U.S. professional sports leagues and teams (i. e. the athletes' employers) are still trying to understand the role that Twitter plays in their sport. Teams and leagues are highly involved in public image management, which was, until athletes began to use Twitter, largely within their control. Thus, the players are made to be sensitive to not only the timing of their tweets and the content, but potentially also their form. Consequently, tweets in the sports domains may be becoming more standard because of the fact that athletes are forced (in some cases with steep monetary consequences) to carefully consider their tweets. No such institutionally regulative apparatus exists for celebrity culture at large; in the entertainment domain, non-athlete celebrities are largely responsible for their own public image and have the relative freedom to tweet what and how they want (though their tweets are, increasingly, under public scrutiny).

While this line of reasoning can explain why the two domains exhibit different levels of tweet standardization, it does not explain why strategic spellings associated with computer-mediated communication are *increasing* in the entertainment domain. We suggest that this difference emerges from the differing perceptions of personae likely to be quoted in sports versus entertainment news, and thus that the sociocultural context of the news itself is important in interpreting the patterns in the news' treatment of new media language. Thurlow (2006) and Squires (2010) have written about the sociolinguistic indexicalities of the forms we have categorized as CM (Sebba 2007 and contributions in Jaffe et al. 2012 explore the social meanings of orthographic variability more generally). Both argue that these forms are enregistered—construed as features that belong to CMC. In addition, these forms are often indexically linked with young people, with an assumption that young people are the primary users of CMC and the concomitant orthographic forms, and with females, with stereotypes about teen girls' language practices being easily accessible in contemporary media (Jones and Schieffelin 2009).

U.S. popular culture is also somewhat youth-centric, and celebrity culture itself is associated with "trendy" language practices. Celebrities are, in public discourse, perceived as language innovators, with their patterns specifically perceived as linked to young girls (see Chan 2011 for an example). Therefore, whereas celebrity popular culture might welcome nonstandardisms on Twitter perceived as "trendy," this same acceptance of "linguistic fashion" may not be operable within athletic culture. Thus, we suggest that the indexical fields for CM and PS features differ, aligning with the sociocultural perceptions of entertainment and sports culture respectively. CM features do not decrease for the entertainment domain because for celebrities, these features signal authenticity and "realness"; for athletes, they may be, along with other nonstandard features, more connected to perceived professional insubordination.

The differing levels and rates of change in the representation of strategic (CM and PS) vs. non-strategic (TY) spellings in the corpora implies that the language ideologies underlying the media's reportage acknowledge a distinction between certain nonstandard spellings as a vehicle for the orthographic expression of personae, and other nonstandard spellings as a perhaps simpler reflection of carelessness. These sets of features may be differently enregistered, perceived as carrying different social meanings (Agha 2003; Johnstone and Kiesling 2008; Squires 2010).

A generally striking feature in our data is the minimal extent to which nonstandard lexical items were found in the corpora of reported tweets at all — in the two corpora combined, nonstandard lexical items comprise just 4.38 % of total lexical items, or approximately one nonstandard item per every two tweets. These numbers resonate with previous findings about nonstandard features in computer-mediated communication that found nonstandard features to be a much less prominent part of CMC exchanges than is often reported by the media (Baron 2004; Tagliamonte and Denis 2008; Squires 2010). In this sense, the proportion of nonstandard items in the reported tweets may be in line with the proportion of nonstandard items in language originating in CMC (though we can't make direct comparisons). At any rate, the total proportion of lexical items containing nonstandard features remains low from 2009 to 2011; the media are not presenting quoted tweets as vastly nonstandard.

In sum, the findings from the analysis of nonstandard types in both domains suggest that a process of standardization is occurring more actively (and more rapidly) for sports news compared to entertainment news, as evidenced in a decrease in the percentage of strategic nonstandard spelling types for SPT and an increase or no change in the percentage of strategic nonstandard spelling types for ENT. More specifically, strategic spellings in both domains are represented differently. CM forms are increasing for ENT and decreasing for SPT. PS forms are remaining stable for ENT and decreasing for SPT. The difference in how the two domains represent different types of strategic nonstandard spellings suggests that they assign different values (or meanings) to the two types. While the representation of nonstandardisms in the SPT and ENT corpora differs by type and rate of change for the strategic spellings, both domains have represented non-strategic spellings in similar ways over time, as evidenced in the consistent decrease in the percentage of TY in both corpora.

5 Conclusions

Our findings show that in the time since Twitter has been available to users, its status within the public discourse of the mainstream media has changed— undoubtedly, it continues to change as the site and its use evolve. As an online platform for exchanging short, predominantly verbal and text-based messages, Twitter makes available a medium for informal written interaction, with the resultant texts accessible to the public. This publicity makes it possible for newsworthy people — such as celebrities, professional athletes, and politicians — to broadcast reports and thoughts, which become directly accessible to mass media sources for detachment, recontextualization, and (re-)circulation. Our analysis shows that the media's treatment of language generated on Twitter changed in its first five years of existence in the following general ways: tweets became more frequent as quoted material within mainstream media; the metadiscursive novelty of Twitter and tweets decreased rapidly; and reported tweets became slightly more linguistically standard.

Taken as a case study for mediatization and sociolinguistic change, we can summarize our findings in terms of changes in both media ideologies and language ideologies, with the assumption that journalists' practices are part of larger societal norms, and indeed work to set those norms. Figure 8 illustrates a schematic timeline involving three time points and the news media's representations of Twitter as a medium, on the one hand, and as a site for language use, on the other. The first time point represents Twitter's earliest days of existence; in this time, few sources were quoting or mentioning tweets, indicating perceptions of Twitter as a fundamentally personal medium (the status of language used on Twitter is likewise implied to be personal).

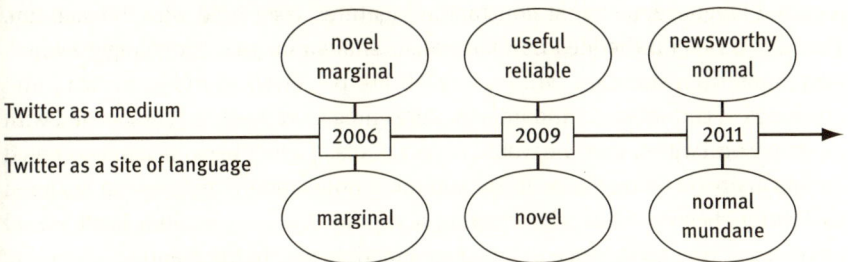

Figure 8: News media's representation of Twitter and language in tweets over time

As the number of tweets circulated by mass media increased in 2009, Twitter was also being brought to the fore of public discourses due to several current events, including terrorist attacks in Mumbai (2008), a US Airways Flight Crash (2009), and post-election protests in Iran (2009) (Arceneaux and Schmitz Weiss 2010). Our data confirm that 2009 marks the beginning of serious media consideration of Twitter as a source for reliable material; this date coincides, then, with its seeming relevance as a cultural practice.

Along with the continual increase of reported tweets through 2011, the percentage of reported tweets that appeared in metadiscursive Twitter stories decreased rapidly. By 2011, the vernacular medium of Twitter seems fully normalized as a site of newsworthy information.

In terms of Twitter as a site of vernacular linguistic practice, however, the trajectory of change is somewhat different. We observed that as tweets became more commonplace in the reportage, CMC features decreased in the sports domain but increased in the entertainment domain. The decrease of CMC features in the sports domain is likely partly due to the fact that in the earlier years, more tweets were included in stories as explicit examples of tweeting as an activity for sports players (and fans); in that time, CMC features such as *lol* would have provided an emblematic symbol of tweets' authenticity, and contributing to its represented novelty. However, as the medium became more of a go-to source for finding quotes from these athletes, CMC features became more dispreferred. Rather than indicating a changing indexicality for these features, we suggest that the enregisterment (Agha 2003; Johnstone and Kiesling 2008; Squires 2010) of the features as new media-specific remained constant. Rather, what changed was the impetus for including tweets: from illustration of novelty to legitimized news source. The representation of more-standard language in tweets is thus part of the project of the news media's legitimization of this new media site as a credible news source. This is corroborated by the lesser inclusion of both phonetic spellings and typos, as well.

We had anticipated that as Twitter became more accepted as a source for reported language, so might nonstandard features associated with the medium. This was based on the idea that journalists share a language ideology in which deviations from standard written English are perceived to index sociocultural attributes. If certain nonstandardisms were enregistered as being associated with language on Twitter, then we would expect that as Twitter became more accepted among mainstream media, so too would those nonstandard features enregistered as Twitter-specific. Thus, the growing acceptance of the medium itself would entail a growing acceptance of language practices within the medium, including the nonstandard.

Contrary to expectation, the number of nonstandard lexical items decreased for both domains, but much more dramatically for sports than for entertainment reportage. Thus, rather than the growth of new media pushing highly regulated spaces of discourse to relax their standards (or conceptions of what is "standard"), representations of new media converge in their treatment of the form and the medium: they increasingly appropriate discursive resources from the medium (tweets) to suit their needs, but at the same time, they frame these resources as distinctive media of communication. This does not, however, entail a growing acceptance of nonstandard linguistic practice native to the medium; rather, the language of tweets is represented as being in closer alignment with the language of the standard news media itself. Thus, while the vernacular medium of Twitter is legitimized over time, vernacular language does not follow.

Our questions about the process of quoting tweets in the news media were driven by an underlying assumption that journalists may wrestle with questions of both technological and linguistic change because of their unique positions as language guardians, and concomitant ideologies that value linguistic conservatism and standardization (Cotter 2010b). We wondered whether public figures' use of public, informal communicative media like Twitter has presented a motivator for changing those ideologies, a pressure towards an acceptance of new technological sites for "legitimate" but informal language use, and thus towards an acceptance of orthographic deviations from standard English — if not in the journalists' own writing, at least in the language they deem worthy of reproducing. We found that the opposite was true: while tweets were being incorporated more often, and framed as less novel, they were also becoming more standard in form.

The data leave us with the following implication: tweets have in a general sense been legitimized as a news source, with quote-worthy language; however, this has not implied that nonstandard written features common to Twitter messages have equally been legitimized. In fact, while tweets have taken a more prominent role in news coverage, this has not been accompanied by increasing acceptance of vernacular language practices "native" to tweets. Instead, the representations of language in reported tweets overall have moved toward alignment with the standard, regulated language that surrounds them in a news context.

References

Adelson, Andrea 2012: Twitter poses fine line for players. BIG EAST BLOG. *ESPN.com*. 19 March 2012. http://espn.go.com/blog/bigeast/post/_/id/31280/ accessed 15 May 2012.

Agha, Asif 2003: The social life of cultural value. *Language and Communication* 23: 231–273.

Androutsopoulos, Jannis 2000: Non-standard spellings in media texts: the case of German fanzines. *Journal of Sociolinguistics* 4(4): 514–533.

Androutsopoulos, Jannis 2011: Language change and digital media: A review of conceptions and evidence. In: Kristiansen Tore and Nikolas Coupland (eds.), *Standard languages and language standards in a changing Europe*, 145–161. Oslo: Novus.

Arceneaux, Noah and Amy Schmitz Weiss 2010: Seems stupid until you try it: press coverage of Twitter, 2006–9. *New Media & Society* 12(8): 1262–1279.

Associated Press 2010: NFL fines James Harrison $5,000. NFL. *ESPN.com*. 22 September 2010. http://sports.espn.go.com/nfl/news/story?id=5605435 accessed 15 May 2012.

Associated Press 2011: Tweets cost Helio Castroneves $30K. MORE SPORTS. *ESPN.com*. 27 September 2011. http://espn.go.com/racing/indycar/story/_/id/7027963/ accessed 15 May 2012.

Associated Press 2012: Chris Perez fined $750 for tweet. MLB. *ESPN.com*. 20 April 2012. http://espn.go.com/mlb/story/_/id/7836385/ accessed 15 May 2012.

Atlanta Journal Constitution 2011: They said (or tweeted) it. *Atlanta Journal Constitution*. SPORTS. 25 January 2011.

Baron, Naomi S. 2004: See you online: gender issues in college student use of instant messaging. *Journal of Language and Social Psychology* 23: 397–423.

Bauman, Richard and Charles L. Briggs 1990: Poetics and performance as critical perspectives on language and social life. *Annual Review of Anthropology* 19: 59–88.

Beale, Alan 2007: *12dicts Wordlists*. http://wordlist.sourceforge.net/12dicts-readme-r5.html accessed 29 April 2012.

boyd, danah, Scott Golder and Gilad Lotan 2010: Tweet, tweet, retweet: Conversational aspects of retweeting on Twitter, *Proceedings of the 2010 43rd Hawaii International Conference on System Sciences*, pp. 1–10. Available from: ACM Digital Library. [29 March 2013].

Chan, Amanda 2011: Vocal fry and young women: Are they trying to sound like Ke$ha and Britney? *The Huffington Post*, 15 December 2011. http://www.huffingtonpost.com /2011/12/15/ vocal -fry-raspy- voice-speech- trend-pattern-young-women_n_1151293.html accessed 24 May 2012.

Coupland, Nikolas. 2009 : The mediated performance of vernaculars. *Journal of English Linguistics 37(3)*:284–300.

Cotter, Colleen 2010a: Diversity awareness and the role of language in cultural representations in news stories. *Journal of Pragmatics* 43: 1890–1899.

Cotter, Colleen 2010b: *News talk: Investigating the language of journalism*. Cambridge: Cambridge University Press.

ESPN.com News Services 2010: Chad Ochocinco fined $25K. NFL. *ESPN.com*. 25 August 2010. http://sports.espn.go.com/nfl/trainingcamp10/news/story?id=5493157 accessed 15 May 2012.

Georgakopoulou, Alexandra forthcoming: Narrative/life of the moment: From telling a story to taking a narrative stance. In Brian Schiff (ed.), *Life and Narrative*. Oxford: Oxford University Press.

Gershon, Ilana 2010: Breaking up is hard to do: Media switching and media ideologies. *Journal of Linguistic Anthropology* 20(2): 289–405.

Hinrichs, Lars 2012: How to spell the vernacular: a multivariate study of Jamaican e-mails and blogs. In: Alexandra Jaffe, Jannis Androutsopoulos, Mark Sebba and Sally Johnson (eds.), *Orthography as Social Action: Scripts, Spelling, Identity and Power*, 325–358. Berlin/ Boston: Mouton de Gruyter.

Iorio, Josh 2010: Explaining Orthographic Variation in a Virtual Community: Linguistic, Social, and Contextual Factors. Austin, TX: University of Texas at Austin Ph.D. Dissertation.

Iorio, Josh and Lauren Squires 2011: Neva tweet b 4 da gms: Legitimizing non-standard orthography through mainstream sports reportage. Paper presented at Georgetown University Roundtable on Linguistics (Discourse 2.0: Language and New Media), March 10–13, Georgetown University, Washington, DC.

Jaffe, Alexandra 2009: Entextualization, mediatization and authentication: orthographic choice in media transcripts. *Text & Talk* 29(5): 571–594.

Jaffe, Alexandra, Jannis Androutsopoulos, Mark Sebba and Sally Johnson (eds.): 2012: *Orthography as Social Action: Scripts, Spelling, Identity and Power*. Berlin/Boston: Mouton de Gruyter.

Jaworski, Adam 2007: Language in the media: Authenticity and othering. In: Sally Johnson and Astrid Ensslin (eds.), *Language in the Media: Identity, Representation, Ideology*, 271–280. London: Continuum.

Johnstone, Barbara and Scott F. Kiesling 2008: Indexicality and experience: Exploring the meanings of /aw/ monophthongization in Pittsburgh. *Journal of Sociolinguistics* 12: 5–33.

Jones, Graham and Bambi B. Schieffelin 2009: Enquoting Voices, Accomplishing Talk: Uses of *Be + Like* in Instant Messaging. *Language & Communication* 29(1): 77–113.

McMullen, Randy 2009: People: Flight attendant sues Oprah Winfrey over airplane sex allegations. *Contra Costa Times*. 12 October 2009. NEWS.

Morris, Meredith Ringel, Scott Counts, Asta Roseway, Aaron Hoff and Julia Schwarz 2012: *Tweeting is Believing? Understanding Microblog Credibility Perceptions*. CSCW'12. February 11–15, Seattle, Washington, USA.

Page, Ruth E. 2012a: The linguistics of self-branding and micro-celebrity in Twitter: The role of hashtags. *Discourse & Communication* 6: 181–201.

Page, Ruth E. 2012b: *Stories and social media: Identities and interaction*.New York: Routledge.

Paolillo, John 2001: Language variation on Internet Relay Chat: A social network approach. *Journal of Sociolinguistics* 5(2): 180–213.

Pioneer Press 2011: Britney Spears is engaged. *St. Paul Pioneer Press*. Entertainment. 15 December 2011.

Puniyani, Kriti, Jacob Eisenstein, Shay Cohen and Eric P. Xing 2010: Social links from latent topics in microblogs. *Proceedings of the NAACL HLT 2010 Workshop on Computational Linguistics in a World of Social Media*, 19–20. Los Angeles, California.

Reynolds, Mike and Giovanna Cascio 1999: It's short and it's spreading: the use of contracted forms in British newspapers: a change under way. In: Erwin Otto, Hans-Jürgen Diller, and Gerd Stratmann (eds.), *English via Various Media*, 179–200. Heidelberg: Winter.

Russ, Brice 2012: *Social meaning in social media: Perceptual judgments of orthographic variation on Facebook and Twitter*. Unpublished talk, Department of Linguistics, The Ohio State University, May 11.

Sebba, Mark 2007: *Spelling and Society*. Cambridge: Cambridge University Press.

Slezak, Carol 2009: @jock_twitter; Star athletes are connecting with fans like never before using Twitter, with the appeal being its personal touch. SPORTS. *Chicago Sun Times*. 22 February 2009.:

Spitulnik, Debra 1997: The social circulation of media discourse and the mediation of communities. *Journal of Linguistic Anthropology* 6: 161–187.

Squires, Lauren 2010: Enregistering internet language. *Language in Society* 39(4): 457–492.

Squires, Lauren 2011: Voicing "sexy text": Heteroglossia and erasure in TV news broadcast representations of Detroit's text message scandal. In: Crispin Thurlow and Kristine Mozcrek (eds.), *Digital Discourse: Language in the New Media*, 3–25. Oxford: Oxford University Press.

Squires, Lauren 2012: Whos punctuating what? Sociolinguistic variation in instant messaging. In: Alexandra Jaffe, Jannis Androutsopoulos, Mark Sebba and Sally Johnson (eds.), *Orthography as Social Action: Scripts, Spelling, Identity and Power*, 289–324. Berlin/ Boston: Mouton de Gruyter.

Tagliamonte, Sali A. and Derek Denis 2008: Linguistic ruin? LOL! Instant messaging and teen language. *American Speech* 83(1): 3–34.

Tatko-Peterson, Ann 2011: People: Kelly Clarkson assailed on Twitter after endorsing Ron Paul. *San Jose Mercury News* (California). Breaking; News; Entertainment; Gossip. 29 December 2011.

Thurlow, Crispin 2006: From statistical panic to moral panic: The metadiscursive construction and popular exaggeration of new media language in the print media. *Journal of Computer-Mediated Communication* 11.

Thurlow, Crispin and Katherine Bell: 2009: Against technologization: Young people's new media discourse as creative cultural practice. *Journal of Computer-Mediated Communication* 14: 1038–1049.

Van Hout, Tom., Henk Pander Maat and Wim de Preter 2011: Writing from news sources: The case of Apple TV. *Journal of Pragmatics* 43: 1876–1889.

Walker, Vicki 2009: Brad Pitt says he's not running for mayor of New Orleans. BREAKING. *Contra Costa Times*. 13 August 2009.

Zappavigna, Michele 2012: *Discourse of Twitter and Social Media: How We Use Language to Create Affiliation on the Web*. London: Continuum.

Zelizer, Barbie 1995: Text, talk, and journalistic quoting practices. *The Communication Review* 1(1): 33–51.

Jürgen Spitzmüller
Commentary: Mediality, mediatization and sociolinguistic change

The three chapters in this section deal with aspects of change on the level of genres. Although all three chapters (at least mainly) focus on genres of news reporting, they do so in quite different ways. Ulrich Schmitz' chapter describes some rather fundamental changes in the way texts are composed and structured (primarily) by example of newspaper and online news genres. He suggests that textual genres in general, and in particular news reporting genres (and consequently the consumption of news), are subject to grave transformation processes in the wake of media evolution. Martin Luginbühl looks at the changes of functional interrelations between sub-genres of the "super-genre" TV news. Rather than general media change, he is interested in structural change within this particular "super-genre", primarily as far as selection, linking and balancing of functional parts within news shows is concerned (in Saussurean terms, we could say he is concerned with the changing "values" of [sub-]genres within a "super-genre"). Lauren Squires and Josh Iorio, finally, focus on how a genre is entextualized within, and thus inter-generically linked to, another genre and how such entextualization changes over time and with the growing social establishment of the embedded genre. Rather than with the question what "makes" up a (super-) genre, these two authors therefore deal with the question of how different genres relate and link to each other, and how these links are subject to sociolinguistic change.

The differences, however, do not only concern the scope of the analysis. When reading these three chapters, asking how they relate to this section's theme "change in media language and media discourse" as well as towards each other, I was struck by the conceptual differences more than by what connects the chapters. In my comment, I will thus start with these conceptual differences. This is certainly not to say that the three chapters do not have any connections. On the contrary. All authors obviously share the fundamental idea that sociolinguistic change manifests itself in change of communicative patterns and routines. Therefore, they regard this level of routines and patterns – the generic level – as a key to the understanding of sociolinguistic change, as a strong link between social actors and the media. The different ways of depicting this connection in the three chapters, however, strikes me as most interesting, since it brings to the fore some issues which, even if they are well-known and long-discussed, still seem to be dissensual and crucial in socio and media linguistics.

In a second step, I will (fully aware that this complicates the picture even more) propose yet another perspective, which is not really missing from these chapters, but is perhaps not as clearly developed as it could be. I will propose, as a complement to media and mediatization, the concept of mediality and try to show with regard to the chapters focused here, why I think this complement is useful for the analysis of mediatization and sociolinguistic change.

1 'Media' – 'mediality' – 'mediatization'

It is a truism that medium and media are notoriously weak and ambiguous, but also heatedly discussed concepts in media studies (see Androutsopoulos, in this volume). Due to its "complicated etymology" ("verwickelte Begriffsgeschichte"; Mersch 2009: 12), *medium* may well mean quite different things in different texts, depending on the disciplinary or scholarly tradition these texts are located in. This also becomes apparent in the three chapters. Whereas Schmitz primarily understands media as technical tools that provide specific possibilities for communication (which is a quite common notion especially in German media linguistics; see Habscheid 2000 for a survey), Luginbühl as well as Squires and Iorio regard the media primarily as social institutions consisting of more or less powerful groups of actors (such as journalists). This is a concept originating in cultural studies (cf. Hepp, in this volume), which is becoming increasingly popular in linguistics (cf. Androutsopoulos, in this volume; Johnson and Ensslin 2007).

As far as language and sociolinguistic change are concerned, these different notions result in fundamentally different assumptions about the causes of change. From Schmitz' point of view, media themselves 'cause' language change (or change of language use, for that matter) due to the changing forms of communication they allow for ("the media intensify, accelerate and differentiate language use"). Luginbühl as well as Squires and Iorio, on the other hand, highlight that media are driven by social agents, people who use media and make sense by means of media. In this view, it is not so much the language that is controlled by the media. Rather, the media (and through them, language) are controlled by social actors and institutions. Thus, these chapters (explicitly at least Luginbühl's, likewise Androutsopoulos, in this volume) reject "the idea of technological changes as driving force behind genre change" (Luginbühl, in this volume), or the "technological determinism", as this idea is somewhat disparagingly termed (Androutsopoulos 2006: 421; Luginbühl, in this volume). Instead, they put forward the idea that strong institutions ("journalistic communities" which "may be small, but their social impact can be huge", as Luginbühl has it) drive forward media, genre and language change.

Furthermore, the notion of media as tools that 'enable' or 'ease' communication is connected with the idea that media should provide, and media/language change tends towards, "maximal communicative efficiency" (Schmitz, in this volume; also cf. Schmitz' basic concept of "semiotic economy"). A 'good tool' is an 'efficient tool', after all. Moreover, this idea is perfectly in line with the transportational model of communication/mediation which often underlies conceptions of media as tools (cf. Schneider 2006). The notion of media as institutions, on the other hand, seems to be connected with the idea that media serve the interests and express the ideology of the institutional actors, an idea which still bears the media- and socially critical heritage from the context it was developed in, although the critical impetus is not made very explicit in these chapters. In any case, both concepts have many implications, which become manifest in the way the respective chapters depict media, mediatization and media/language change, in other words: each of these concepts highlights and hides different aspects of media.

In addition to the discussed concepts, however, Squires and Iorio as well as Luginbühl scratch a third notion of medium when they draw on Gershon's (2010: 389) concept of "media ideology" (Squires and Iorio) and on Barnhurst's and Nerone's (2001: 3) idea of "medial self-imagination" (Luginbühl), respectively. Both notions are in line with what Hepp (in this volume) calls the "social-constructivist tradition" of mediatization research. They put into focus a concept which indeed should be considered next to the central concepts discussed in this volume (media and mediatization), namely *mediality*. Mediality is a term which has become increasingly popular in German media theory (cf. Scheider 2008). It transfers the well-known distinction between text and textuality to the level of media, in the sense that it focuses on the (perceived) conditions of something which is considered 'a medium' just as textuality focuses on the "textual conditions", i. e. the perceived conditions of something which is considered 'a text' (see McGann 1991). Mediality, thus, is an interpretive phenomenon which, as it were, is to be found in they eyes of the beholders, i. e. which puts the recipients of mediated communication to the fore. Mediality is connected to *mediality expectations*, what recipients think 'is' a medium, what recipients think a particular medium can 'accomplish' (the "function a genre is thought to fulfil within a community"; Luginbühl, in this volume), what people think a form of mediation 'tells' about the message or the messenger. It also is connected to *mediality perceptions*, i. e. the way in which, and the degree to which, recipients perceive something as being 'mediated' (what Bolter and Grusin 1999: 19 call the "immediacy-hypermediacy-continuum"). Furthermore, mediality is connected to *mediality ascriptions*, the values, features, abilities and limitations social actors ascribe to something they perceive as being a particular 'medium' (these ascriptions are, as it were, what Gershon calls "media ideologies").

Medium, mediality and mediatization are closely interconnected, but they describe different things nonetheless. A 'medium', from an interpretive point of view, is something to which 'mediality' is ascribed, and the mediality (i. e. the expectations, perceptions and ascriptions of particular social actors) determines whether and how a 'medium' is delimitated from and/or connected with other 'media'. From this perspective, it is well possible that technology plays the main role and indeed 'determines' media use, if technology is perceived as the main factor by the media recipients (i. e. is discursively central). However, it might as well be possible that institutions play the main role and 'determine' media use, if institutions (or specific groups of actors) are perceived as the main factor by the media recipients.

If we look at media history (and the history of media studies, for that matter), we can clearly observe how media are conceived differently in different times. The crucial question is, why this is the case. One possible answer is: because we observe (discursive) changes in mediality (cf. Spitzmüller 2013: 29–58 for an elaboration of this argument). As far as mediatization is concerned, it can be argued that mediatization – if conceived as "the proliferation of media communication in all areas of social life and the central role of media in socio-cultural change" (Androutsopoulos, in this volume) – relies on mediality, the degree to which and the way how this "proliferation of media communication" is actually perceived and evaluated by specific social actors. Drawing on Agha's (2005) most seminal concept, we can also say that mediality describes the way in which media and the process of mediatization are culturally 'enregistered' (see Section V) and thus socially or discursively 'visible'. In other words: sociolinguistic change may entail a change of perceived media conditions – a change of mediality.

2 Cui bono?

What do we gain with yet another level of analysis? In the following, I intend to exemplify the usefulness of the proposed concept with regard to the three chapters in question. Nota bene, my comments here are to be read as complementary thoughts, which do not aim to challenge the argumentation of the chapters. On the contrary. Just as the three chapters complement each other through their different perspectives on the subject (and their different conception of the subject), my comments suggest how a more systematic interpretive perspective could broaden the picture (just as the instrumental and institutional notions of media described above complement and broaden the picture drawn by an interpretive analysis). Since this is a comment and not a full chapter of its own, I crave the reader's indulgence for the highly indicative character of the following.

Schmitz highlights the grand trends in his chapter: the trend towards 'efficiency' or 'economy', the trend towards 'fragmentation', the trend "from full-text reading to selective reading" and so on. As always when such long lines are drawn, we are obliged to ask: can things really be described in such general terms? There is no doubt that the structure of newspapers has changed significantly; there is plenty of evidence for this (see Barnhurst and Nerone 2001; for German newspapers see e.g. Bucher 1998). Also, it is well likely that the internet has brought new forms of text into attention. However, from an interpretive point of view, the stress is on attention. As historical sociolinguistics begins to reveal, the 'typical' forms of text we used to compare the 'new media texts' to were never the only forms of texts (see e.g. Elspaß 2005). Likewise, the 'new' forms often highlighted in computer-mediated communication analyses are not the only (and probably not even the most frequent) forms of texts in the new media, where a lot of 'traditional' communication is going on. However, as much as specific forms of text seem to be more salient in 'traditional' communication (and thus shaped our notion of text), other forms seem to be more salient in 'new' media, and the latter are usually those forms which seem to deviate from 'traditional' texts (cf. Squires 2010: 462–463). So it is maybe not so much (or at least not only) the media that change here, but mediality: the expectation that particular media consist of particular forms of communication, and that 'new' media should entail 'new' forms of communication (cf. Squires 2010: 462). Mediality expectations entail textuality expectations. The question, 'what is a text?', as discussed by Schmitz, implies the question of what social actors consider to be 'a text' (at a given time). Hence, from an interpretive point of view, the question is not so much whether text boundaries dissolve, but rather, whether textuality (and thus: mediality) expectations change. The same applies to 'efficiency'. Is efficiency really a communicative-historical constant, or is it rather a discursive construct that shapes the mediality expectations of particular ('econo-centric') societies?

What has been said for texts also applies to genres. How are genres conceived, delimitated, linked, ordered and evaluated by social actors themselves? Which mediality expectations do social actors have with regard to particular genres? Luginbühl suggests that the "unemotional, inverted pyramid style of the newsreader" is perceived as an "unmediated depiction of an absolute, unquestionable truth". However, to whom does this apply, and how do we know that? Furthermore: do social actors conceive the thing which is called 'super-genre' by Luginbühl as a coherent entity? Do they conceive what the author separates as 'genres' (e.g. an "opening credit") as single entities? How do they relate the various parts of a TV news show in terms of weight, order, interrelations? In other words: do "genre profiles" exist outside the media linguist's head, and if so, do they look the same? If we perceive genres as functional social constructs and ethno-categories (as Luginbühl does), what does this mean for genre profiles? These questions are clearly scratched in Luginbühl's chapter, but they are not answered (and probably cannot be answered easily). In any case, the mediality on the level of genre relations seems to be a challenging task for sociolinguistic media(tization) research.

This becomes most apparent in Squire and Iorio's chapter. This chapter deals with "reported" tweets, and it is clear that "reported" tweets are not the same as "tweeted" tweets. Since the authors did not (as far as I can see) compare the "reported" tweets with their "tweeted" counterparts (or even check if they really exist), their chapter actually cannot (and obviously also does not want to) make any statement about Twitter communication, but only about the representation of Twitter communication in newspapers (and furthermore, due to the method of corpus compilation, only about the subset which is explicitly framed by a particular *verbum dicendi*). Now, what characterizes reported tweets on the level of mediality? Most notably a mediality tension, or polymediality, if you like it more Bakhtinean. Reported tweets are entextualized entities which are part of an intergeneric relation that contrasts – via the "intertextual gap" (Briggs and Bauman 1992: 149) – the mediality expectations displayed towards the matrix and the embedded genre, i. e. towards news reports on the one hand and towards tweets on the other. With this idea in mind, we could pose further questions: is the observed trend towards standardization related to a change in mediality expectations? And if so, on which level? Do the expectations towards tweeting change, or the expectations towards reporting tweets, or both? In other words: do Squires and Iorio, to re-use Bolters and Grusins (1999: 19) terms, observe a decreasing hypermediality (i. e. medial salience) of Twitter quotes? And if so, why is that? Does it conform to a decreasing hypermediality of tweets? A decreasing perception (and/or construction) of the "genre gap" by the journalists? Or both? And if hypermediality decreases (and 'immediacy' therefore raises), what about the reported tweets that are not framed by a verbum dicendi and therefore not detectable by the authors' method? Isn't it important to include those in order to complete the picture of how tweets are "perceived" as a medium – to get hold of their mediality?

I do not know the answer to any of these questions. However it strikes me that the instructive thoughts about mediatization and sociolinguistic change provided by the three chapters in this section could be productively complemented by a sharper focus on the change of media perceptions and the question of how the change of these perceptions relates to the change of media and language use.

References

Agha, Asif 2005: Voice, Footing, Enregisterment. *Journal of Linguistic Anthropology* 15/1: 38–59.

Androutsopoulos, Jannis 2006: Introduction: Sociolinguistics and computer-mediated communication. *Journal of Sociolinguistics* 10/4: 419–138.

Barnhurst, Kevin G. and John C. Nerone 2001: The Form of News. A History. New York/London: Guilford.

Bolter, Jay David and Richard Arthur Grusin 1999: Remediation. Understanding New Media. Cambridge, MA/London: MIT Press.

Briggs, Charles L. and Richard Bauman 1992: Genre, Intertextuality, and Social Power. *Journal of Linguistic Anthropology* 2/2: 131–172.

Bucher, Hans-Jürgen 1998: Vom Textdesign zum Hypertext. Gedruckte und elektronische Zeitungen als nicht-lineare Medien. In: Werner Holly and Bernd Ulrich Biere (eds.): *Medien im Wandel*. Opladen: Westdeutscher Verlag: 63–102.

Elspaß, Stephan 2005: *Sprachgeschichte von unten. Untersuchungen zum geschriebenen Alltagsdeutsch im 19. Jahrhundert*. Tübingen: Niemeyer.

Gershon, Ilana 2010: Breaking up is hard to do: Media switching and media ideologies. *Journal of Linguistic Anthropology* 20/2: 289–405.

Habscheid, Stephan 2000: 'Medium' in der Pragmatik. Eine kritische Bestandsaufnahme. *Deutsche Sprache* 28/2: 126–143.

Johnson, Sally and Astrid Ensslin 2007: Language in the Media: Theory and Practice. In: Sally Johnson and Astrid Ensslin (eds.): *Language in the Media. Representations, Identities, Ideologies*: 3–22. London: Continuum Press.

McGann, Jerome J. 1991: *The Textual Condition*. Princeton: Princeton University Press.

Mersch, Dieter 2009: *Medientheorien zur Einführung*. 2nd ed. Hamburg: Junius.

Schneider, Jan Georg 2006: Gibt es nichtmediale Kommunikation? *Zeitschrift für Angewandte Linguistik* 44: 71–90.

Schneider, Jan Georg 2008: *Spielräume der Medialität. Linguistische Gegenstandskonstitution aus medientheoretischer und pragmatischer Perspektive*. Berlin/New York: de Gruyter.

Spitzmüller, Jürgen 2013: *Graphische Variation als soziale Praxis. Eine soziolinguistische Theorie skripturaler 'Sichtbarkeit'*. Berlin/Boston: De Gruyter.

Squires, Lauren 2010: Enregistering internet language. *Language in Society* 39: 457–492.

Section V: **Enregisterment of change
in media discourse**

Colleen Cotter
Revising the "journalist's bible". How news practitioners respond to language and social change

1 Introduction

In this chapter, I look at how journalists themselves think about language and language change, and respond to attitudes and opinion about style and usage that come from within the profession and from the outside world, through an examination of the Associated Press Stylebook. These responses to language issues are in the form of explicit injunctions and usage rules as well as extended, and critical, discussion about their professional (or in-group) and larger-society (external group) appropriateness.

The in-group judgments about language use and change have their own constraints (see Cotter 2010), denoted in relation to what constitutes professional practice, but very importantly also operate in tandem with the larger culture's assessments (cf. Cameron 1995) – both about correct usage and about what it means to be socially responsive and responsible as language users. In other words, journalists utilize their own profession-internal set of practice norms, the operation of which helps to constitute news practitioners as a discourse community or community of practice (cf. Lave and Wenger 1991) (and helps us as linguists identify news genres), at the same time they incorporate standard-language usage norms known to wider society and expected of public discourse in the media, education, and government (cf. Milroy and Milroy 1999).

Starting from the point-of-view that journalists are very mindful about usage and see language as the fundamental apparatus with which they operate no matter the modality – broadcast, print, online, etc. – I show the extent to which language is professionally important and in what context. Firstly, journalists self-identify as "protectors" of the language (Cotter 2010; Mencher 1997, 2006), engaging in prescriptive routines at every level of practice, and at the same time they respond to the cultural zeitgeist, promoting linguistic innovation or reacting to it. The AP Stylebook, as much as it is a tool of standardization, is also responsive to community norms and communicative necessity. I argue that both protection and promotion responses are cut from the same sociocultural cloth and show evidence of this through diachronic data from the Stylebook, drawn from editions in three different decades.

Secondly, the AP Stylebook – the self-described "journalist's bible" – identifies for linguists a key site of discussion and negotiation about language in a range of manifestations by professional journalists. It helps to answer the question about where one begins to locate journalists' explicit metatalk about language and what this might tell us (and them) about how they as a community view their social role in that regard. The examples and analysis address both the micro and macro: prescriptive usage issues – as language changes – and the ways in which journalists consciously alter their usage patterns to reflect social change in progress (a case in point being Fasold et al.'s 1990 study of gender reference in *The Washington Post*). The Stylebook over time charts these language-level and society-level changes, providing "one of the most influential language resources in changing times" (Fisher 2007). This is particularly evident through its more recent online updates, as the data will show.

The following sections describe in further detail how professional journalists are socialized to respond and react to language and social change, as well as how the ethnographic or community-of-practice-based approach provides more insider detail about what is really motivating language use and news discourse – with an aim to clarifying and "correcting" our analyses. The extent to which journalistic stylistic behavior follows from larger cultural processes of standardization and language complaint (cf. Milroy and Milroy 1999, Cameron 1995, Lippi-Green 1997), and how sociolinguists have examined the factors relevant to journalistic language attitudes, are described in Section 2. Section 3 details the degree to which the AP Stylebook is a rich repository for sociocultural information, shedding light on the concerns and metatalk about language use that occur within the profession and are behind the linguistic formulations we ultimately see in news stories.

The AP Stylebook entries, drawn from print and online editions over the past 25 years, also highlight how the "news world" and the "social world" of which it is part (cf. Schiffrin 2006) are integrated, as I will show. In this regard, the journalists in their "news world" or professional capacity tend to see usage parameters in terms of writing ability and its impacts with respect to prescriptive rules, accuracy, clarity, neutrality, and aesthetic "flow"; whereas society in its world wants to hold the journalists accountable for their discursive actions in relation to both prescriptive rules and social meaning (Milroy and Milroy 1999). I build on points I have made before about journalists and language, particularly the "prescriptive imperative" that reporters and editors follow fairly strictly within their newsroom practice (cf. Cotter 2010). Those discursive actions, supported by the articulation of a "journalistic language ideology" promoted through textbooks and professional publications, can be seen more comprehensively in an analysis of the AP Stylebook data.

1.1 The data

The data, a collection of nearly 2,000 entries or queries drawn from randomly selected print editions (in 1987, edited by French, and 1994, edited by Goldstein) as well as more recent editions from the last decade and updates online, were collated based on prescriptive and sociolinguistic variables and change, with attention to socially marked and journalistically topical contexts such as *age, race, gender, immigration, abortion*, and ongoing questions about *terms of reference*. To develop my corpus, I took systematic note of the following: *new entries*, online *updates*, and how the *tables of contents* changed. For example, "computer terminology" appears as a specific subject when the Internet was new (the 1987 edition) and disappears when it became normalized; a social media chapter was added in 2010 and updated in 2012. The broadcast media chapter was also expanded.

The Stylebook's online version provides a useful opportunity to look at more "real time" and mediated discussion about language and social change, as the Ask the Editor sub-corpus examples in Section 4 will detail. The Stylebook data can be looked at linguistically – and meaningfully with respect to language change – in terms of language ideology and the prescriptive "complaint tradition, as I discuss in Section 3. But first, Section 2 will situate journalists in relation to their own understanding of language and its role in practice.

2 Locating language in the media

In this section I briefly describe how journalists and news practitioners actively orient to or talk about usage and the extent to which prescriptive norms and pragmatic alterations come in to the equation; and how sociolinguists have accounted for language variation, discursive routine, and social dynamics in the news media particularly with respect to style. I address the significant role the Associated Press Stylebook plays within media communities in the U.S. and beyond and how it can function as a source for journalistic metatalk about language use. The processes behind audience design (Bell 1991) and the tradition of complaint about language usage (Milroy and Milroy 1999) aid in this regard. I use the terms "style" and "usage" fairly a-theoretically and interchangeably, with "style" also meaning episodic or *in situ* language choice and "usage" connoting habitual, patterned conventions. It is important to know that for journalists, use of the word "language" is often metonymic or equivalent with "usage," as examples in Section 3 will demonstrate.

2.1 Journalists and language

Journalists orient to language in two ways: 1) *implicitly* as members of the larger speech community in which they live and function, albeit as a sub-community with a particular charge, and 2) *explicitly* as self-defined news professionals. They approach language from an instrumental angle, as material with which to build and create: to tell stories and to report news. Language is part and parcel of the craft – of doing journalism – and the ability to use language in a communicatively competent journalistic manner is learned by new members and reinforced in daily practice. In this sense, appropriate language use and management of news-discourse forms marks or indexes professionalism. In neither the lay-implicit or professional-explicit sense do journalists view language as linguists would. They assume a prescriptive orientation over a descriptive one, following the language ideologies of the larger culture, and actively aim to maintain the standard variety ringfenced by dictionaries and usage guides. Nonetheless, the Stylebook editors frequently observe that language changes and evolves and usage should follow from that (as detailed in Section 3).

Journalists evaluate the salience of language in ways that pertain directly to their newswriting and reporting goals. This circumscribed and proscribed language awareness then becomes part of their everyday in-group discourse or metatalk. Firstly, reporters and editors heed prescriptive norms – in part because they provide "correct," standardized style guidelines that are on par with usage norms in other public contexts; and also because, from a professional perspective, these norms provide *consistency* across domains that cover variation in geography, topic, genre, type, modality, community focus, and reporting style. Hence a reporter in one hemisphere or stadium or parliament or premiere or protest writes stories that are stylistically and structurally consistent with a colleague elsewhere. "Consistency," like "accuracy," which are linked expository values, comes up as a rationale for usage decisions in the Stylebook, as will be discussed in Section 3.

Secondly, language is also regarded in relation to the practice or "craft" of newswriting (cf. Mencher 1997; Goldstein, quoted in Fisher 2007; Cotter 2010). "Craft" is an umbrella term used by the news community that includes reporting, writing, and editing and the activities that support them of which maintaining *consistency* and *accuracy* are part. Upholding language standards or protecting the language, as journalists would describe it (cf. Mencher 1997, 2006; Baskette, Sissors and Brooks 1996), or following a standard language ideology, as sociolinguists would describe it (cf. Lippi-Green 1997; Milroy and Milroy 1999), is a fundamental element of news craft. Appropriate language use is essential to proper craft and the Stylebook assists the reporter in that endeavor who is aware of the consequences of not doing so. As LaRocque (2011: 35) observes: "We should avoid misusing words [...] because such use can reflect badly on both skill and credibility." Thus journalists very actively manifest and manage language use, responding to, reinforcing, and initiating usage dynamics, as discussion in Section 3 will show. The AP Stylebook, providing guidance about punctuation, spelling, grammar, and general usage, as well as background on libel law and other profession-specific domains, is set up to enable consistency and correctness and thus to help promote both reporter skill on the individual, situated, everyday practice level and institutional credibility on the collective, infrastructural level.

2.2 Sociolinguistics and journalism

Sociolinguistic accounts of language in the media – whether news, advertising, film, or video, or print, broadcast, online, or social – variously approach the full range of linguistic phenomena, including the lexical, orthographic, phonological, prosodic, sociolinguistic, syntactic, pragmatic, cognitive, computer-/social-mediated, narrative, discourse-level, and macro-socio-level; and in an equally broad range of theoretical frameworks, involving variationist, socio-cultural, pragmatic, semiotic, ethnolinguistic, linguistic anthropological, multimodal, historical, media studies, and critical approaches (for a partial summary, see Cotter 2001, 2014; Johnson and Ensslin 2007; Johnson and Milani 2010).

A sub-set of scholars attempts to highlight cross-cultural variation and globalization factors in the media (from Leitner 1980 to authors in Coupland 2010), provide ethnographic explanation (Catenaccio et al. 2011), evaluate historical processes with respect to language (e.g. Jucker 2009), and investigate how the pragmatic and sociolinguistic elements of the relationship between journalist and audience play out in text and talk (starting with Verschueren 1985 and Bell 1991). Theoretically in these instances, the news community is not viewed as a monolithic or homogenous entity: local and global diversities and differences are taken into account in the analyses of sociolinguistic phenomena. That assumption is behind the analyses of language-usage metatalk in this chapter. As I have already noted, to examine the relevance and dynamics of community norms within the news media it is important to see journalists operating according to the production values of their own "community of practice" (Lave and Wenger 1991) and *concurrently* interacting with the local cultures within which they are situated (a point I establish in Cotter 2010).

With the practice-focused or "media-linguistic" orientation at the fore, two established sociolinguistic concepts and frameworks bear particular mention in the AP Stylebook cases here. Bell's audience design framework shows how the news media can both *initiate* or take the lead in presenting a language style (a function the BBC, for example, historically has done even as it has expanded its sociophonetic scope to include regional accents alongside Received Pronunciation) as well as *respond* or accommodate to its audience's language style (as local news outlets often do). From another perspective, the Milroys (1999) identify a social process in the "complaint tradition," which comprises both the ongoing public critiques of usage that date to the 18th century as well as the types of complaints that people make about language use and change. How the news media take the lead (or the moral high ground) in advancing types of usage norms, as well as respond to community complaints and requests for change by changing their own usage to accommodate to local preference, will be discussed in Sections 3 and 4. The complaint tradition, I suggest, can be seen as an underlying dimension of audience-design dynamics.

2.3 The complaint tradition and news practice

As will be relevant in understanding the AP Stylebook data, the Milroys differentiate the types of usage complaints that comprise the complaint tradition. Language complaints – those public remarks made by language "bosses" (Lakoff 2000) – fall roughly into two kinds: Type 1 or "legalistic," pertaining to rule-based errors such as those found with punctuation and prescriptive grammar (e.g. placement of the serial comma, avoiding the split infinitive), and Type 2 or "moralistic," which concern meaning and truth (e.g. accuracy of definition, obfuscation of intention, "spin"). Complaints can also come from mixtures of both types.

Journalists, who speak and write regularly about usage in professional outlets, themselves are primary movers and supporters of the complaint tradition. Its tenets are embedded in the AP Stylebook, available as it is to safeguard accuracy (Type-1-like rules) and, alongside it, clarity (Type-2-like rules). What I have called *journalistic language ideology* (Cotter 2010), which adheres to the "accuracy equals credibility" dictum as noted above, instantiates Type 1 complaints about correctness (see Stylebook examples in Section 3). Journalistic *craft ideology*, which orients to the "good writing equals clarity" dictum, leads to Type 2 complaints in which clarity is a necessary precondition for truth and which "good writing" will help to maintain. Complaint tradition correlates of *both* types follow from the journalistic *language values* of "precision" – upholding news-community norms – and "prescription" – upholding speech-community norms, language values that intersect with practice.

The complaint tradition, and its attendant metatalk about language and speakers' and writers' disfluencies with it, is essential to the perpetuation of what Milroy and Milroy (1999) term "standard language ideology," an idealized form of a language that often becomes a linguistic referent for ratifying the hierarchical relations of the status quo (cf. Hill 2007). Media language reflects this ideological dynamic in many ways because the news community considers itself guardians of prescriptive correctness and works actively within the newsroom to maintain standards. For example, larger news organizations in the US and UK have journalist "ombudsmen" who function as mediators between the public and the newsroom, responding (in part) to the public's complaints about usage. In this way, journalistic language and craft ideologies mediate with standard language ideologies and reinforce the journalistic principle: Correct language correlates with correct practice and, by extension, accurate stories, one of the gold standards. As Dvorkin 2002 (cited in Cotter 2010: 200) says: "Some of the issues raised by [radio] listeners may be considered 'picky,' but if [we get] the details right, it means that the rest of the reporting is also accurate."

In sum, Bell's audience design framework accounts for some of the variation in news-practitioner outputs, highlighting the responsive or initiative function the news media can take with language use, spoken or written. The "complaint tradition" dynamic details the type of talk and metatalk about language that occurs within the news community and as a consequence of the news community's journalistic outputs. An ethnographic orientation, and an understanding of standard language ideologies, provides an in-group accounting of what gets done discursively and why. Taken together, these foci lead to a comprehensive understanding of the discourse of the AP Stylebook.

3 The AP Stylebook as journalistic tool and sociolinguistic resource

In this section I provide a brief history of the Associated Press Stylebook, its evolution since 1953, its role in news outlets worldwide, and its orientation to language, usage, and language change. The Stylebook is known for what amounts to prescriptive advice, heading off Type 1 or "legalistic" or function-level errors as well as Type-2-like "clarity" errors (see Section 2). It is also a site for reporting guidance, decisions about socially responsive and responsible language usage, and a source of commentary about what constitutes socially relevant usage change, as the examples will detail.

3.1 Purpose and position

The Associated Press is a not-for-profit cooperative news service with bureaus and employees in more than 300 locations worldwide that provides news stories to subscribers, initially "over the wire" via satellite and now through digital technology. It has been operating since 1846. The majority of "quality journalism" news outlets – print, broadcast, and online – are subscribers; there are 1,400 daily newspaper members and numerous broadcast members in the US alone. As one of several wire-service options for the media, the AP is the primary source of most non-local editorial content (news and features stories, photos, video, etc.), as well as coverage of breaking news, for US publications.

Given the scope of the news service, the stylebook in its first iteration in 1953 was designed to establish style guidelines for AP reporters and editors writing and editing stories that were transmitted over the AP wire to subscribers in a wide range of newsrooms. As a source of copy-editing information and reporting guidance, the Stylebook deals with language on the line-editing level and the content-editing level. The Stylebook was expanded in 1977 to function as a "reference work," including some 400 pages of guidelines on usage, background information on topical issues, and media (Fisher 2007). "Far more than just a collection of rules, the book became part dictionary, part encyclopedia, part textbook – an eclectic source of information for writers and editors of any publication" (Tom Curley, quoted in 2004 Stylebook, p. vii, and AP Stylebook Online 2012).[1]

The Stylebook was significantly revised in 1986. It was updated thereafter at regular intervals and, since 2008, the Stylebook has been updated annually in print form and on an as-needed basis online. From the standpoint of responsive media language practice, "It continues to add entries that *reflect the language of our fast-changing world.*" (AP Stylebook Online 2012, emphasis added). The extent of the Stylebook's expanding reach after its 1986 revamp is also evident in testimonials on the Stylebook's front covers: "Over 700,000 copies in print" (1987); "Used by more than 1,000,000 journalists" (1994); "More than 1.6 million copies sold" (2000); "More than 1.7 million copies sold" (2002); "More than 2 million copies sold" (2004); "More than 2.5 million copies sold" (2011).

---

1 The examples in this section come from the AP Stylebook' Ask the Editor column and are all copyright Associated Press 2012.

3.2 Copy editors and the "journalist's bible"

For journalists, the AP Stylebook is an essential resource. Former Stylebook editor Nathan Goldstein (in Fisher 2007) recalls that when he started in the profession in 1963, he was told: "This is the book you have to know." Even in 2010, Globe-News copy editor Alex Chihak writes about its role and its importance for maintaining an appropriate news style in his editing blog: "What is the stylebook? It's a book on style. Journalists, writers, editors and students use it as a reference. *Its purpose is for consistency throughout copy.* It helps with word choice, spelling and usage. AP Stylebooks are called 'the journalist's bible'" (emphasis added).

Indeed, the Stylebook has long been referred to both informally within the news community and on the Stylebook's covers as "the journalist's bible." This term of reference migrated from the front to the back cover – e.g., in 2002, with additional description: "The 'journalist's bible,' an essential handbook for all writers, editors, students, and public relations specialists." – before disappearing from the covers over the last decade. It appears on the Stylebook homepage, however, in the following way (figure 1).

As a concept and metaphor, it remains active in the minds of journalists themselves, as this screenshot of Chihak's 2010 blog page shows (figure 2).

Figure 1: Screenshot of AP Stylebook homepage
http://www.apstylebook.com (accessed Feb. 27, 2013)

Figure 2: Screenshot of copy editor's blog page
http://amarillo.com/blog-post/
alex-chihak/2010-09-27/
bible-guides-me-journalists-bible

The bible guides me --
the journalist's bible

Submitted by Alex Chihak on Mon, 09/27/2010 - 12:11am

For news organizations, as Goldstein and Chihak separately observed, the Stylebook functions as one of the professional arbiters of usage. It is at the elbow (or on the screen) of every mainstream news practitioner, particularly those who work in print. (The Stylebook has a chapter on broadcast and the AP also has its own separate broadcast handbook which features style guidelines for writing and delivering news electronically.) Linguistically, the AP Stylebook is a classic tool of standardization (following Milroy and Milroy 1999), like grammar and usage guides and dictionaries, whose aim is to provide for speaker and writer consistency and eliminate optional variability in usage. Indeed, when the Stylebook was expanded in the mid-1970s, "The orders were: Make clear and simple rules, permit few exceptions to the rules, and rely heavily on the chosen dictionary [Merriam-Webster at that time] as the arbiter of conflicts" (Boccardi 1977).

This attention to stylistic consistency complements journalistic practice, which ties into journalistic language ideology as noted earlier (see also Section 4.1). Copy editor Chihak (2010) reiterates the point: "So why do we even have a stylebook? It's *so copy is consistent*. If you flip-flop (also in the stylebook), you look *unprofessional*. It's *sloppy* to have "advisor" on one day and "adviser" three days later" (emphasis added). The Stylebook, from the journalistic perspective, provides guidance and rules that help to minimize error and maximize routines that function as a hallmark of craft. What is sanctioned and to be avoided by heeding style rules, such as skipping the hyphen in "flip-flop" or forgetting to follow AP style with the non-standard "advisor" spelling, are discursive behaviors that are evaluated as "sloppy" and "unprofessional." Chihak's words emphasize the Stylebook's central role and how it operates in newsroom practice for the copy editor:

> As a copy editor, I am expected to practically memorize the stylebook. And if not memorize the hundreds of entries, one should at least know what to look up. It details specific things like when to capitalize "president" (before a name) or when to abbreviate "Boulevard" (with a numbered address).

His blog description, which gives an indication of the Stylebook's contents along Type 1 lines (e.g., capitalization and abbreviation rules) is comprehensive, and also draws attention to local style variation, which is equally important to individual newsrooms, local style guides sitting next to the ubiquitous AP Stylebook: "We use AP style at the Globe-News, but we don't follow it to the letter. For instance, our addresses are written as 1500 S.W. 26th Ave. AP style would use "SW," without the periods."

Copy editors, charged with style maintenance, with their knowledge of AP style as well as "house" style rules, also help to manage the vagaries of individual variation and reporter lapses in their stories. Reporters and editors themselves may or may not operate with the same zeal, particularly with respect to Type 1 rules, as Curley 2004 notes: "Journalists approach these style questions with varying degrees of passion. Some don't really think it's important. Some agree that basically there should be uniformity for reading ease if nothing else. Still others are prepared to duel over a wayward lower case."

Curley's point makes clear that there is variation within the profession: there are journalists who do not really care about style issues, others who see the utilitarian appeal of consistency, and others – most likely the copy (or sub) editors operating according to job description – whose commitment to upholding or determining style standards is deeply held.

4 Responding to language change

Despite the inclination toward uniformity, there are motivations for change in news language, and the Stylebook functions as a locus for their evolution. As with other standardization documents, these changes in usage are discussed, debated, and determined on explicitly articulated grounds familiar to linguists who study language ideology (cf. Milroy and Milroy 1999), especially in the case of Type 1 issues where purported logic holds sway. These rationales are also familiar to journalists for whom audience engagement is key (cf. Bell 1991; Cotter 2010), especially when the outside "social world" (cf. Schiffrin 2006) draws attention to Type 2 usage which can influence social meaning and affect a group's position in society. Behind the language standardization processes endemic to the Stylebook and to newswriting forms, the social responsiveness dimension also comes into play and this factor is a key journalistic rationale for change when it occurs.

Examining Stylebooks over time makes it clear that journalists are aware that usage evolves and "consistency" does not mean not responding to what is culturally relevant, as this excerpt from the expanded 1977 edition (and repeated in 1987's edition) shows: "We have tried to make the Stylebook current and trust it will be a lasting work. But *language changes*, and we will review entries annually, making necessary changes by wire notes during the review period" (1987 [1977]) (emphasis added). This notion of the necessity of language change is repeated more recently by a journalist commenting on the Stylebook's 2012 print edition: "In many ways, Stylebook updates reflect the evolving nature of language" (Tenore 2012).

The updates also reflect the evolving nature of society. New entries in recent years include *Tea Party* (the vocal neo-conservative anti-tax movement in the US), *illegal immigrant* and *ethnic cleansing* (see examples 11–15 and example 10 below), as well as new rulings on *hyphenation* (*e-mail* finally changed to *email* in

2012 after years of discussion). Some things do not change. The Stylebook still issues reminders about the *-person* suffix: despite numerous suggestions by AP members and journalists for a generic form, the reference to someone who chairs a meeting is still stipulated as *chairman* or *chairwoman*.

Most of the Stylebook changes I note in my corpus are ones that respond to social change, while the grammar/punctuation issues, although they take up a great deal of space (46 out of 86 recent Ask the Editor questions dealt with hyphens, capitalization, verb and plural forms, and prepositions), are more prescriptively entrenched. Questions to the Stylebook editor persist for ongoing social issues pertaining to *abortion* and *race*, and thus occupy the realm of "Type 2" or meaning-centered language use, as well as largely rule-governed technical language use like *capitalization*, which falls into the "Type 1" area. For example, the Stylebook makes clear that "identification by race is pertinent" only when the story warrants, as with the election of Barack Obama as the first black president, or coverage of civil rights. It lists other circumstances where care is meant to be taken, such as when missing persons or suspects are sought "using police or other credible, detailed descriptions. Such descriptions apply for all races. The racial reference should be removed when the individual is apprehended or found." Similarly, the Stylebook tells journalists to "not use racially derogatory terms unless they are part of a quotation that is essential to the story."

As a social document, and given its regular updating, the Stylebook shows changes to language and usage over time, and how journalists respond to them. Even the online archive is viewed as a repository of changing usage by the current Stylebook editor, responding to a user complaint as to why old entries are kept available: "It's an archive, meaning a place to keep records" (2012). The website encourages engagement: "View the entire archive – 14,980 answered questions and counting!" (2013). In this regard, the website (*Web site* in AP style until 2010) is also a source of language ephemera: "A lot of these new phrases, new words, new spellings, whatever, come in for a couple of weeks and they're gone. So they may not make it to the book, but they're online [...]" (Goldstein, quoted in Fisher 2007).

Synchronically, the Stylebook shows what is relevant at a particular moment; diachronically, it shows what does change and the internal discussions along the way. In my corpus, collated to search for usage issues and decisions, there have been changes over time both big and small – to race and ethnicity labels, gender and sexual reference, and categories like *computers* when PCs became widespread and *finance* in the wake of the 2008 banking crisis – as well as less socially divisive spelling or capitalization conventions. A more recent change (Feb. 21, 2013), reflecting changes in legal and cultural acceptance of same-sex marriage, is the new entry on *husband, wife*:

Regardless of sexual orientation, husband or wife is acceptable in all references to individuals in any legally recognized marriage. Spouse or partner may be used if requested.

The Stylebook also shows what does not change, despite entreaties by users to do so, such as the generic pronoun (use of "they" as the singular generic pronoun is still verboten – because it is the plural pronoun). What is "correct" and "logical," as the Milroys would note, prevails, following the universal mission of standardization documents. Nonetheless, change happens: "One of the most talked-about updates in recent years occurred in 2010, when the Stylebook changed the style for 'Web site' to 'website'" (Tenore 2012) – a change that many felt was significantly overdue, demonstrating the socially mediated nature of language dynamics.

4.1 Ask the Editor and usage rationales

The online version of the Stylebook, particularly as an archival document, has made it relatively easy to search for and determine what is on reporters' minds in terms of language, usage, and meaning, particularly through the "Ask the Editor" feature. The kinds of questions, similar to the Stylebook content itself, vary: From whether "etc." is "appropriate usage according to AP Style," to the plural form of "Blackberry," to a query about "front yard" as two words when "backyard" is one word, to the usage of "Third World" vs. "emerging nations." In other words, the questions include both Type 1 and Type 2 issues, although they are not situated as such. Usage rationales in the editor's answers tend to primarily fall out under the premises of *consistency*, *correctness*, and *precision* – journalistic reporting, writing, and editing values (cf. Cotter 2010). Whether it is an *AP style norm* or a *local usage* is also given credence. Less measurable are responses such as, "Assuming they are clear in the news context" and "looks fine," but these are relatively few.

The following Ask the Editor exchanges in examples (1–16), for which emphasis is added, show an illustrative range of queries and the journalistic rationales that follow, as in (1):

(1)   Q. Is etc. appropriate usage according to AP Style?
A. It is "appropriate" in some cases, but we would hope **used only with care**. It indicates some **writing laziness** and **lack of precision**. (2006)

In this example, the editor cites "writing laziness" and "lack of precision" as potential pitfalls of the catch-all summary term "etc." when it is not used judiciously. News stories are governed by space limitations, a factor that is often overlooked by outsiders, and thus every word tends to carry a higher proposi-tional weight. "Etc." can usefully indicate more in a series (likely when the word is "used only with care") but, less felicitously, it is often used in place of carefully articulated additional description, hence the claim to "writing laziness."

The rationale in the following example (2) is based on a variant of *local usage*, the brand-name norm:

(2) Q. Is the plural form of "BlackBerry" "Black-Berrys" or "BlackBerries"? We've **seen it both ways**. Thanks.
A. BlackBerrys, **per the company's usage**. AP stories tend to say BlackBerry phones. (2008)

The editor cites "the company's usage" as justification and support for the marked plural of BlackBerrys. Notably, given the plural inconsistency the lexical situation requires, the editor provides an alternate: "BlackBerry phones."

The editor also provides a "good alternative" in the case of the term "Third World" in response to this question:

(3) Q. Hello: We have a newsroom question from Pittsburgh regarding the usage of the term "Third World," as opposed to the **more modern term** "emerging nations." Doesn't Third World have **negative connotations**, denoting superiority by the Western World. Keep in mind the stylebook is composed in a western nation.
A. "Third World" is rarely used today, mostly in quoted remarks. A **good alternative** is "eco-nomically developing nations." (2007)

The questioners first situate themselves geographically and professionally, as journalists in a city newsroom, establishing their credentials. They critique "Third World" in terms of its negative valence, lack of modernity, and orient its meaning in relation to global power structure. They further situate the Stylebook in the "Western World," implying a possible deictic blind spot with respect to the term. The editor in effect agrees, noting that "Third World" is "rarely used" except in the marked – and journalistically indexed – case of a quotation. The question and response, with their references to a "more modern term" and "rarely used today," indicate that usage can and does change in relation to external judgments. The "good alternative" also shows how journalists actively "write around" problem-atic labels, producing ostensibly unproblematic and "neutral" description in the case of social disagreement ("Third World") or alternate phrasing in the case of underlying linguistic-rule conflict ("Blackberrys").

The rationale most often cited in the Ask the Editor answers tends to be *con-sistency* and lack of it as cause for usage critiques and practice judgments. As former Stylebook editor Goldstein noted: "You just need to have some reference that makes it all consistent ... it's most important to be consistent in spellings of names and usage all around" (cited in Fisher 2007). As the quote examples in this section show, "consistency" is an ideal across discursive domains. In fact, the absence of it is the reason for this question (4) about "front yard" and "backyard":

(4) Q. Why does the latest stylebook list "backyard" as one word in all instances, but "front yard" remains two words?
A. While backyard (one word) is AP usage, the stylebook doesn't rule on front yard and **Webster's** [the dictionary] unlists it. However contradictory it may seem, front yard (two words) **looks fine.** (2007)

The questioner implies that "front yard" as two words is not consistent with the Stylebook's one-word "backyard" ruling. The editor, following Stylebook practice, cites the dictionary as the primary reason for "front yard," indicates it may be "contradictory" in comparison to "backyard," and concludes that the two-word form "looks fine." (Beyond the dictionary justification, it is likely because other "front" modifiers tend not to merge with the noun, e.g. front room, front runner.) The answer also shows what might come across as eccentric, if not inconsistent, usage rulings, especially to someone outside the newsroom.

Optional variation instigates other questions, as in (5), motivated by non-standard transliteration:

(5) Q. Is AP style Hezbollah or Hizballah or two other variants I've seen. And if not Hizballah, then why not. The group is called Hiz b'Allah, or the Party of God. (Plus, the Brits spell it that way.)
A. AP style is Hezbollah. The vowel sound in question is unwritten and implied. Depending on where you are in the Arab world, the sound can be transliterated either ih (short iii sound as in it) or eh. AP decided upon the latter and that has **been our style for years.** (2006)

The questioner notes four variants, asks for a reason why Hizballah is not chosen, argues as further justification that the spelling shows a more straightforward gloss (Hiz b'Allah), and cites British usage (suggesting prestige). The editor's explanation for Hezbollah is sociophonetic, referring to Arabic spelling conventions and dialect variation "in the Arab world" as well as the longstanding tradition of that spelling for the AP.

In fact, Goldstein (in Fisher 2007) uses "Hezbollah" as an example of how emergent style decisions get made:

(6) "We'll get an e-mail, we'll get a phone call, we'll get a note or letter. A newspaper editor will **question how we spell Hezbollah,** for example, and we'll go back to our own correspondents in the Middle East and make sure that what we are using is right. And very often when the news first comes up we will have some discrepancies; we will have some differences in spelling. And so we'll go back to them and make a decision on how we want to spell it, how we think it should be spelled on a **consistent** basis. **And we'll put that online. And then we'll see when the book comes up whether that word, that spelling, is still the way it should be done.**" (Goldstein in Fisher 2007)

He cites the initial query as motivating a check with people on-site, the AP "correspondents in the Middle East." What is "right" and how to make it "consistent" are aims, although he allows that "discrepancies" and "differences" arise in the early stages of a news story. As further exemplification of the Stylebook revision process, Goldstein also notes the online version is the first repository of an agreed-upon spelling (in this case), and that the word or spelling is evaluated again before the annual print version is produced.

Despite the orientation toward consistency, there are Ask the Editor queries about exceptions to rules, like the "backyard/front yard" example (4) above. Another example (7) is when the AP style rule that stipulates the common noun of a name be lowercase in second abbreviated reference is violated, as is the case with the National Baseball Hall of Fame, which, unusually, is capitalized. The editor's explanation for the exceptional Hall reference is that it is "traditional usage rather than an inconsistency."

(7)　A. Indeed, certain highly revered institutions, such as baseball's Hall, are usually capitalized on second reference. This is **traditional usage rather than an inconsistency**. The examples you give are properly lowercase as abbreviated names in follow ups, **assuming they are clear in the news contexts**. (2010)

The Hall example is the only exception to the rule mentioned in this response. The role of baseball in the national psyche might have something to do with the Hall's "highly revered" institutional status. The questioner listed other contexts for which the lowercase rule applied in second-reference contexts – such as "party" and not "Party" for Democratic Party and "street" and not "Street" for Fleet Street – and these instances, the editor reminds us, are "properly lowercase" as long as "they are clear in news contexts" – another safeguard and potential rationale for use and one that is locally interpreted.

Precision, the companion to *consistency*, is also a common rationale, as in example (8):

(8)　Q. The Spitzer story broke as governor involved with a prostitution ring. But later references are to a call girl. **Is there an AP standard for the difference between prostitute and call girl or is the media trying to be polite since she is white and educated?** A. A call girl is defined as a prostitute who is called to assignations by telephone. The term is **precise** in this situation. Race or education aren't known to be factors. (2008)

The questioner, noting variation in terminology and suggesting a potentially biased usage in a story about a state governor, asks what the difference is between a "call girl" and "prostitute" and whether there is an "AP standard" given that both terms were used. The editor responds with the *precision* rationale, that the telephone was involved in "this situation" and thus the correct term is "call girl," answering (and dismissing) the implicit social critique on that level, as well, adding that "race or education aren't known to be factors."

4.2 Social justice issues

While the Stylebook suggests alternatives, as examples (2) and (3) show, it also makes unequivocal statements about when *not* to use a term of reference, especially in circumstances that have a social-justice dimension. For example, the *race* entry, also discussed in Section 3, has long stipulated the following:

(9) Do not use racially derogatory terms unless they are **part of a quotation** that is **essential** to the story.

The racially derogatory term's erasure (or discursive whitewashing) in a quotation – a discursive space intended to distance the reporter from the speaker and from responsibility from the speaker's words – is not sufficient; its presence must also be "essential" to the story. Determining what is "essential" relies on the reporter's and editor's news judgment, also called into play "[i]n other situations with racial overtones."

The Stylebook is also explicit about production-specific contexts when disfavored terms should not be used, as in (10), a new entry in 2012:

(10) **ethnic cleansing** Euphemism for a campaign to force a population from a region by expulsions and other violence often including killings and rapes. The term came to prominence in former Yugoslavia during the 1990s to whitewash atrocities of warring ethnic groups, then usage spread to other conflicts. **AP does not use "ethnic cleansing" on its own. It must be enclosed in quotes, attributed and explained.** Don't use the term as a keyword (slug) or in headlines. (2012)

The entry makes it clear that the term is not to be used "on its own" – where it would lose its position as a "euphemism" that obscures clarity of meaning (cf. Type 2 issues) – but with a great deal of discursive journalistic hedging: *quotes, attribution* and *explanation,* identifiable elements of news story structure that are explicitly taught to students and new reporters. In other words, its use predicates a great deal of thought and concomitant structural discursive action. That the term is explicitly prohibited in a story slug (a newsroom-internal one- or two-word story descriptor) or in headlines underscores the ruling.

A "do not use" policy is also stipulated for terms referring to immigrants – given their socially and politically contested position (in Europe and elsewhere as well as the US) – that are pejorative ("illegal alien") or inaccurate ("undocumented") terms of reference to "describe someone who has entered a country illegally [...] in violation of civil or criminal law." Until its widely reported April 2, 2013, amendment to the Stylebook "making some changes in how we describe people living in a country illegally" (Colford 2013) and making clear that the use of "illegal immigrant" except in direct quotes violated updated AP practice, the most recent entry concerning "illegal immigrant" in the Stylebook was from an online update in November 2011:

(11) **illegal immigrant** Used to describe someone who has entered a country illegally or who resides in a country **in violation of civil or criminal law**. Acceptable variations include living in the country without legal permission. Use of these terms, as with any terms implying illegalities, must be based on **reliable information** about a person's true status. Unless quoting someone, **AP does not use** the terms illegal alien, an illegal, illegals or the term undocumented. [2011]

From the news community's perspective, this rationale follows the journalistic neutrality objective (cf. Cotter 2010). It is "neutral" in the sense that the status can be externally verified and measurable through law. The point that its use "must be based on reliable information about a person's true status" refers to basic reporting norms that responsible reporters adhere to. Terms that are culturally problematic – because of what could be interpreted as derogatory – are listed as ones to avoid.

That an entry for *illegal immigrant* was in the Stylebook means that its social presence is already marked (similar to entries in the Stylebook for age, gender, and religion). Indeed, usage questions surrounding the term arose in the Ask the Editor sections in 2007 and 2008:[2]

(12) Q. Is "illegal immigrants" still current AP style? If it is, since the word "illegal" refers to human beings, **this is harsh**. Can "undocumented immigrants" be used instead?
A. AP uses illegal immigrant to describe those who have entered the country illegally. It is the preferred term, rather than illegal alien or undocumented worker or similar. [2007]

(13) Q. AP style still advises against saying "illegals" when referring to illegal immigrants, right? I've seen it come over in a few stories and headlines in the last few months and **just wanted to make sure**.
A. Correct. The stylebook entry is "illegal immigrant" [...] do not use the shortened term "illegals." [2008]

---

2 Question contributors variously self-identify in their online queries as journalists or journalism students, or the relatives or friends of one, or as outsiders. Some contributors cannot be as readily identified as members of the news community and may be interested members of the public.

The 2008 questioner (possibly a wire editor, given the use of the newsroom phrase "come over") noted a change in usage in wire stories and wanted to determine that the style rule was still in place. The concern that the use of "illegal" to refer to human beings is "harsh" (in the 2007 example) is similar to a question in 2011 in example (14), which details a rationale for the use of "undocumented" on the basis of legitimacy and utility, which, like neutrality, are very journalistic-centric rationales:

(14) Q. What is the reasoning behind the preference for **illegal instead of undocumented** when referring to immigrants? It seems to me that undocumented is a **legitimate** description and **useful** when there are multiple references in a story.
A. It's **more precise** than the euphemistic term, which seems to skirt the legalities of living or working permanently or longer-term in the U.S. without permission -- meaning in most cases illegally or unlawfully. [2011]

The reason the editor gives in his answer – *precision* – refers again to the community norm for reporting and writing (cf. Cotter 2010; Mencher 2006), and his reference to "legalities" and "permission" harkens to features that can be measured and verified. That the underlying premise, legal or otherwise, may be challenged or is inherently problematic is not considered part of the journalist's role as such – unless a case can be made, which is what eventually happened with "illegal immigrant" in the form of a new entry:[3]

(15) **illegal immigration** Entering or residing in a country in violation of civil or criminal law. Except in **direct quotes essential** to the story, use *illegal* only to **refer to an action, not a person**: *illegal immigration*, but not *illegal immigrant*. Acceptable variations include *living in* or *entering a country illegally* or *without legal permission*. [...] [2013]

The 2013 change and its journalistic and linguistic rationale is evident in the Editor's Note that accompanied the April 2 update email to AP Stylebook Online subscribers: "A new entry on illegal immigration has been added to replace the entry on illegal immigrant." The change in entry or keyword status – "illegal immigration" *replaces* "illegal immigrant" – reflects the rationale that obtained: *illegal* is to be used "only to refer to an action not a person." This refocus on action and not person, the result of "discussions on this topic [with][...] many people from many walks of life" (Kathleen Carroll quoted in Colford 2013), is made clear in the remainder of the entry, framed in accordance with journalistic reporting practice:

---

3 For an extended discussion of "illegal immigrant" by linguistic anthropologists, and their successful efforts to change AP Stylebook description and usage, see Rosa 2012.

(15) *continued*

> **Except in direct quotations,** do not use the terms *illegal alien, an illegal, illegals* or *undocumented.*
>
> Do not describe people as violating immigration laws without **attribution.**
>
> **Specify wherever possible how** someone entered the country illegally and from where. Crossed the border? Overstayed a visa? What nationality?
>
> People who were brought into the country as children should not be described as having immigrated illegally. For people granted a temporary right to remain in the U.S. under the Deferred Action for Childhood Arrivals program, use *temporary resident status*, with **details on the program lower in the story.** [2013]

The Stylebook entry, providing guidance for reporters and editors, specifies "acceptable variations" to verbally describe the action of illegal immigration (*"living in* or *entering a country illegally* or *without legal permission"*) and suggests questions to keep in mind to keep the focus on the action ("Crossed the border? Overstayed a visa?"). The entry, in its comprehensiveness, makes explicit that children and people with temporary resident status are also under the remit. Thus, reporting practice and consequent news discourse elements (attribution, quotes, position of background information in a story, focus on facts) are foregrounded, and the inherent logic – action not person – is made explicit to both cover other illegal immigration reporting contexts not specified in the entry and to provide an account that aligns with in-group newswriting and reporting norms as well as the voices of the larger culture (the "many people from many walks of life") outside the profession.

The Stylebook's senior vice president and executive editor, Kathleen Carroll, quoted in Colford's April 2 AP blog post, provides context for the change (providing for both journalists and linguists useful background). As well as the "wide-ranging" discussions on the topic that preceded the April update, Carroll cites two reasons for the change to the 2011 "illegal immigrant" entry update – cf. example (11) – that are linguistically, as well as journalistically, defensible: that language changes and that labels constrain meaning. In her words (in Colford 2013):

> A number of people felt that "illegal immigrant" was the best choice at the time. They also believed the **always-evolving English language might soon yield a different choice** and we should stay in the conversation.
>
> Also, we had in other areas been ridding the Stylebook of labels. [...]
>
> And that discussion about labeling people, instead of behavior, led us back to "illegal immigrant" again.
>
> We concluded that **to be consistent,** we needed to change our guidance.

Carroll's explanation shows how the journalistic value of *consistency* became part of the rationale to change, reinforcing a professional practice norm at the same time the "guidance" changed to reflect the larger culture's concerns. She also refers to the *accuracy* norm: "while labels may be more facile [for the ease of the writer], they are not accurate."

The larger social issues that impact on Stylebook edicts, in all their complexity, are straightforward to discern. But it is also important to see how the Stylebook as arbiter and purveyor of usage rules and social responsiveness intersect on the local level and are part of individual news communities' relationships with their coverage communities, as this example (16) shows:

(16) Q. We follow AP Style regarding African-American (use the hyphen), but recently **heard from a board member** that **using the hyphen is considered insulting to that group.** Obviously we removed it **in keeping with his preference,** but I'm wondering if you have heard this same comment in any nationality/race context?

In this case, something as seemingly innocuous as a hyphen has caused offense, a change of newsroom practice, and a query to the Stylebook Editor. The news staff were following AP style for *African-American*, but dropped the hyphen rule when they "heard from a board member" – someone with institutional clout and ostensible prestige, not just a comment on the website – because it was "considered insulting to that group." They acted on behalf of the individual and the group ("obviously we removed it") but the questioner also aims to locate the practice change in relation to the larger news community, hence the Ask the Editor query.

5 Behind the metatalk: Conclusions

The data show the degree to which there is an ongoing conversation or metatalk about language within the news profession, demonstrating how journalists think about language and language change as well as the active role the news media expect themselves to play in its linguistic and social support. Thus the news media capture a sociolinguistic reality about language in a range of social contexts as well as show how the changes they make, respond to, or influence support or work against social awareness and insight.

The Stylebook examples and editor responses, presented here and in my sub-corpus, show a journalistic attention to changing norms, linguistically and socially. Taken together, the examples indicate that journalists are more flexible with respect to social change and language than they are on the prescriptive level. In the Bell audience design sense, they are more *responsive* to linguistic issues with social applicability (but see complaints by journalists about politically correct language requirements) than they are about non-content usage, *rules* that tend to be harder to change (cf. the *e-* and *-person* examples noted in Section 4).

The examples also showed how attention to language correctness is actively pursued and evident. One can thus see news media language, on the micro level, as functioning as a bellwether for prescription, highlighting what is valued within the news community and within the larger culture. For researchers, the Stylebook also functions as a cultural artifact, articulating prescriptive patterns as well as detailing the relation of media language to practice. The Stylebook's online availability has made more transparent these patterns and practices.

The ways journalists talk about language use, in particular through a primary professional outlet such as The AP Stylebook, provides insight into the news community's attitudes toward language use, the moral judgments that attend them, and the broader dimension of society's attitudes toward its members. It also shows how and when journalists are responsive or resistant to changes. Part of the professional discourse is the anxiety or contestation that attends language change, as well as the social motivations and impacts that are behind them. The journalistic responsibility goes beyond the prescriptive, as the Stylebook examples – most recently the evolution in thinking towards the label "illegal immigrant" – make evident. As one journalist noted: "The words a journalist uses can either reinforce stereotypes or help to correct them" (LoTempio 2006).

At the same time, for the responsible journalist, precision, consistency, and accuracy are still hallmarks of good newswriting, no matter what is changing linguistically. Carroll (quoted in Colford 2013) makes explicit reference to these professional, community-of-practice factors: "Change is a part of AP Style because the English language is constantly evolving, enriched by new words, phrases and uses. Our goal always is to use the most precise and accurate words so that the meaning is clear to any reader anywhere." As the Stylebook has become more of a reference document for usage and less of a static, albeit professionally essential, prescriptive style resource, and its online component with periodic updates and the Ask the Editor feature more visible, it underscores journalistic and social responsibility. It shows how the values and practices of the "news world" and the concerns and impetus of the "social world" align or integrate as language, and the situations and propositions it instantiates, changes around them.

References

AP Stylebook (www.apstylebook.com). Accessed June 10-July 2, 2012, Jan. 20 – Feb. 28, 2013.

Baskette, Floyd K., Jack Z. Sissors and Brian S. Brooks 1996: *The Art of Editing*. (Sixth Edition). Boston: Allyn & Bacon.

Bell, Allan 1991: *The Language of News Media*. Oxford/Cambridge: Blackwell.

Boccardi, Louis D. (ed.) 1977: Forward. *The Associated Press Stylebook and Libel Manual*. New York: The Associated Press.

Cameron, Deborah 1995: *Verbal Hygiene*. London: Routledge.

Colford, Paul 2013: 'Illegal immigrant' no more. http://blog.ap.org/2013/04/02/illegal-immigrant-no-more.

Catenaccio, Paola, Colleen Cotter, Mark De Smedt, Giuliana Garzone, Geert Jacobs, Felicitas Macgilchrist, Lutgard Lams, Daniel Perrin, John E. Richardson, Tom Van Hout and Ellen Van Praet 2011: Towards a linguistics of news production. *Journal of Pragmatics* 43(7): 1843–1852.

Chihak, Alex 2010: The bible guides me – the journalist's bible. http://amarillo.com/blog-post/alex-chihak/2010-09-27/bible-guides-me-journalists-bible. Accessed Jan. 21, 2013.

Cotter, Colleen 2001: Discourse and media. In: Deborah Schiffrin, Deborah Tannen and Heidi E. Hamilton (eds.), *The Handbook of Discourse Analysis*, 416–436. Malden, MA/Oxford, UK: Blackwell.

Cotter, Colleen 2010: *News Talk: Investigating the Language of Journalism*. Cambridge: Cambridge University Press.

Cotter, Colleen in preperation: Discourse and media. In: Deborah Tannen, Heidi E. Hamilton, and Deborah Schiffrin (eds.), *The Handbook of Discourse Analysis* (Second Edition). Chinchester, UK: John Wiley & Sons.

Coupland, Nikolas (ed.) 2010: *The Handbook of Language and Globalization*. Malden, MA/Oxford UK:Wiley-Blackwell.

Dvorkin, Jeffrey A. : 2002: Details, details... http://www.npr.org/yourturn/ombudsman/2002/021114.html.

Fasold, Ralph, Haru Yamada, Steven Barish, and David Robinson 1990: The language-planning effect of newspaper editorial policy: Gender differences in the *Washington Post*. *Language in Society* 19(4): 521–539.

Fisher, Doug 2007: *Norm Goldstein, keeper of AP style*. In: Common Sense Journalism (blog). http://jour.sc.edu/news/CSJ/CSJJuly07.html.

French, Christopher W. (ed.) 1987: *The Associated Press Stylebook and Libel Manual*. Reading, MA: Addison-Wesley Publishing Company Inc.

Goldstein, Norm (ed.) 1994: *The Associated Press Stylebook and Libel Manual*. Reading, MA: Addison-Wesley Publishing Company Inc.

Hill, Jane H. 2007: Crises of meaning: personalist language ideology in US media discourse. In: Sally Johnson and Astrid Ensslin (eds.), *Language in the Media: Representations, Identities, Ideologies*, 70–88. London: Continuum.

Johnson, Sally and Astrid Ensslin (eds.) 2007: *Language in the Media: Representations, Identities, Ideologies*. London: Continuum.

Johnson, Sally and Tommaso M. Milani (eds.) 2010: *Language Ideologies and Media Discourse: Texts, Practices, Politics*. London: Continuum.

Jucker, Andreas H. 2009: Newspapers, Pamphlets and Scientific News Discourse in Early Modern Britain. In: Andreas H. Jucker (ed.), *Early Modern English News Discourse*.

Newspapers, pamphlets and scientific news discourse, 1–9. Amsterdam/Philadelphia: John Benjamins.

LaRocque, Paula 2011: Follow standards to avoid misusing words. In: *Quill* May/June: 35.

Lakoff, Robin Tolmach 2000: *The Language War*. Berkeley: University of California Press.

Lave, Jean and Etienne Wenger 1991: *Situated Learning: Legitimate Peripheral Participation*. Cambridge: Cambridge University Press.

Leitner, Gerhard 1980: BBC English and Deutsche Rundfunksprache: A comparative and historical analysis of the language on the radio. *International Journal of the Sociology of Language* 26: 75–100.

Lippi-Green, Rosina 1997: *English with an Accent: Language, Ideology, and Discrimination in the United States*. London/New York: Routledge.

LoTempio, Susan 2006 (updated 2011): Enabling coverage of disability. http://www.poynter. org/how-tos/newsgathering-storytelling/diversity-at-work/74930/enabling-coverage-of-disability/.

Mencher, Melvin 1997: *News Reporting and Writing* (Seventh Edition). Madison: Brown & Benchmark.

Mencher, Melvin 2006: *News Reporting and Writing* (Tenth Edition). New York: McGraw-Hill.

Milroy, James and Lesley Milroy 1999: *Authority in Language: Investigating Language Prescription and Standardisation* (Third Edition). London/New York: Routledge.

Rosa, Jonathan 2012: Contesting representations of immigration. *Anthropology News*. http://www.anthropology-news.org/index.php/2012/10/09/contesting-representations-of-immigration/.

Schiffrin, Deborah 2006: *In Other Words: Variation in Reference and Narrative*. Cambridge: Cambridge University Press.

Tenore, Mallary Jean 2012: AP Stylebook 2012 edition released today features new broadcast chapter. http://www.poynter.org/latest-news/mediawire/175572/ap-stylebook-2012-edition-released-today-features-new-broadcast-chapter/

Verschueren, Jef 1985: *International News Reporting: Metapragmatic Metaphors and the U-2*. Amsterdam/Philadelphia: John Benjamins.

Spiros A. Moschonas
The media on media-induced language change[1]

1 Introduction

In this paper I consider texts in the Greek print media about media language and media-induced language change. The term 'media-induced language change' should be understood in its most general sense, possibly encompassing what are often called 'folk-linguistic' conceptions of language and language change (Niedzielski and Preston 2000). In this general sense, the term should be taken to denote nothing less than any perceived alternation in oral or written language behaviour inside or outside the media. The qualification '*perceived* alternation' is necessary, since, as it will become clear from the analysis of the data, the media remain silent about many types of alternations; i.e. there are types of variation and changes that pass unnoticed or are not commented upon. It will also turn out that 'media-induced language change' has a much narrower scope in the metalinguistic discourse of the print media: in the Greek print media at least, 'media-induced language change' means, almost exclusively, any *deviation* from an established *norm* or *standard*, particularly a *written* one. The very term 'media' (Μέσα, 'Media', or MME: Μέσα Μαζικής Επικοινωνίας/Ενημέρωσης, 'Mass Media of Communication') also has a narrow scope; in the print media it is used to refer mainly to the electronic media, especially TV and internet, which are held responsible for introducing or propagating undesired linguistic changes.

'Media-induced language change' is accordingly understood as the subject, the theme or, simply, the set of references to media-induced language changes, i. e. it is here understood as a *metalinguistic* construct. In order to avoid confusion, it should be kept in mind that this paper is not about media-induced change *per se*; rather, it is about whether and how the media conceptualize the language changes they themselves possibly effect. This paper is about reflexivity: it is about language change only to the degree that language change is being observed and

1 I have profited from extensive comments and suggestions by Jürgen Spitzmüller and Jannis Androutsopoulos on earlier drafts of this chapter. Jana Tereick pointed out to me Microsoft's text strategies (section 2.2.3). I am particularly grateful to Jannis Androutsopoulos who gave me constant encouragement and put up with my delays.

talked about by possible agents of language change, i. e. by the media people or, more impersonally, 'the media'. Similarly, the opposition between scientific and non-scientific conceptions of language is also understood, in the present paper, primarily as a set of potential differences between metalinguistic constructs (and not as a difference, say, in their degree of authority, legitimacy, or plausibility).

It should be stressed at this point that the distinction between linguistic (or professional) and folk-linguistic (or non-professional) conceptions, often made in language ideology studies, cannot be readily applied to the texts considered here. In his seminal paper about language ideology, Silverstein (1979: 193) admits that "in certain areas the ideological beliefs do in fact match the scientific ones, though the two will, in general, be part of divergent larger systems of discourse and enterprise". The emphasis should be reversed: although, generally, ideological and scientific beliefs belong to different types of discourse, they do in fact match in many cases. Niedzielski and Preston (2000: viii), having first introduced the term 'folk-linguistics', hastened to caution their readers that there are no real boundaries between linguistics and 'folk linguistics': "professional linguists themselves are also a folk group, with their own rich set of beliefs". Most of the people who write about language and language change in the Greek media are not linguists, yet they cannot be considered as 'folk' or 'lay' persons either. Journalists practicing the craft of writing are professionals in their own right. They have variable access to expert opinion, one may assume. Probably they do share some of the 'folk-conceptions' of language and language change, yet it so happens that such conceptions are being propagated in and through the print media by linguists themselves (as it is the case with George Babiniotis; see *infra*). Hence, I do not assume any hierarchy of expertise on matters linguistic. My intent is to use the terms 'non-professional' and 'professional' in as neutral a way as possible in order to indicate simply where a conception comes from: the print media or a linguistic study, respectively. I will also not presume that there is an ultimate substratum of 'folk' concepts, although I wish to show that those who write about language in the print media share the same attitudes, they are guided by similar beliefs or convictions about language, and, to reverse B. L. Whorf's famous dictum, they are pointed toward *the same* types of observations and evaluations.

In all the media texts I have considered, an unequivocal belief in the reality of media-induced language change is either emphatically stated at some point or other or it is presupposed throughout. In order to document and critically analyze this and related beliefs, the present paper employs a corpus-driven approach to metalinguistic discourse. It focuses on publications about media language in the Greek print media, in the period from the mid 1980s through the early 2000s. During this period there was an upsurge of public interest concerning (electronic) media language in Greece, due to the privatization of the media sector. The first legal private radio station in Greece, Athena 9.84 FM, started broadcasting on May 31, 1987 and the first private TV channel, Mega Channel, on November 20, 1989, soon to be followed by ANT1, whose first broadcast went on the air on December 31, 1989.

In what follows, I will describe a corpus of texts about media language (Section 2.1.), I will provide relevant excerpts (Section 2.2.), and try to illustrate the conception of language change that emerges from these publications. My analysis identifies several motifs (*topoi*) that recur in the texts considered (Section 2.3.). The conception that emerges will be tested for coherence and validity against a larger corpus of metalinguistic texts and it will finally be contrasted to theories of media-induced change elaborated in the relevant linguistic literature (Section 3.). I argue that the very belief in language change might have a certain performative effect, i. e. it might manage to shape language habits through, for example, the exercise of certain linguistic controls over broadcasting. Awareness of change might change its course. The view that linguistic change can somehow be inhibited or directed towards a predetermined goal is consistent with the "non-professional" or "unscientific" view of language change, i. e. with the prescriptive attitude that seeks to prevent language change or direct it towards an accepted standard. That under certain conditions such an attitude may have the effect of a self-fulfilled prophecy is a possibility that, as far as I know, has not yet been seriously contemplated in the scientific literature. It is touched upon in the last section (3) of the present chapter.

2 The media's conception of media-induced language change

2.1 The corpus

The corpus I consider consists of 295 entries. Each entry comprises at most one page-length text published in the Greek print media, page length varying with the newspaper or the periodical; i. e. a text, as is often the case with feature articles, can extend to more than one entry. There are 16 multiple-entry texts in the corpus and there is no text extending to more than six entries (pages); only two feature articles are six-page long. The earliest text was published on 11 November 1986; the latest on 11 March 2001.

The texts were selected from a larger corpus of 6,838 texts. The earliest text in the larger corpus was published on 1 January 1964; the latest on 1 April 2001. After November 1999, the corpus was systematically compiled with the help of a press clipping agency and, for all practical reasons, it can be considered exhaus-

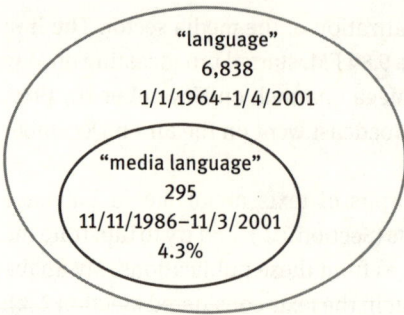

Figure 1: Smaller and larger corpus

tive, i. e. it includes all publications about language in the Greek newspapers and magazines from 15 November 1999 until 1 April 2001. While the texts of the larger corpus refer to any language issue raised in the Greek newspapers over a period of about four decades, the 295 texts selected for the purposes of this study refer, thematically or *en passant*, more specifically to 'media language' or to 'media language changes' or to 'media *and* language'. The relation between the larger corpus and the smaller one that the present chapter focuses on is depicted in Figure 1. In Section 2.3, the larger corpus is discussed as a framework, in reference to which the thematic categories attested for the smaller corpus can be understood and interpreted.

The exhaustiveness of the corpus, i. e. the fact that it comprises all relevant publications over a long period of time, is considered to be a major advantage of corpus-driven discourse analyses vis-á-vis impressionistic analyses, which usually rely on a few text excerpts and tend to read into the texts the intuitions or the presuppositions of the researchers. A corpus-driven approach also allows a wider view on the available texts, the opinions they express and their relative significance. The first thing to notice is that only 4.3 per cent of the total number of print media texts (295 out of 6,838 entries) refer specifically to media language. This measure is of course provided relative to other language issues covered in the Greek press. Since language issues in general form a very small percentage of the total coverage of a newspaper, it may be concluded that neither media language nor language in general give rise to issues that cause much concern in the Greek print media, despite the fact that language issues are usually treated in a we-are-all-very-much-concerned style.

Out of these 295 texts, 36 were published in the liberal centre-left daily newspaper *Ελευθεροτυπία* (seven out of the 36 texts appeared in its monthly magazine booklet *Infotech*); 32 were published in the rather conservative right-wing daily *Η Καθημερινή*; 21 in the centre-left newspaper *Το Βήμα*; 16 in *Ελεύθερη Ώρα* (right-wing); 14 in the conservative monthly periodical *Πολιτικά Θέματα*; 13 in

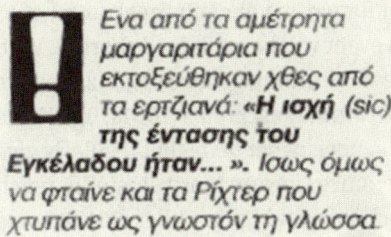

Ένα από τα αμέτρητα μαργαριτάρια που εκτοξεύθηκαν χθες από τα ερτζιανά: «**Η ισχή** (sic) της έντασης του Εγκέλαδου ήταν... ». Ίσως όμως να φταίνε και τα Ρίχτερ που χτυπάνε ως γνωστόν τη γλώσσα.

Figure 2: A short comment (*Ελευθεροτυπία* 18 September 1989, p. 9)

the daily newspaper *Έθνος* (centre-left); eight in the daily *Τα Νέα* (centre-left); eight in *Απογευματινή* (right-wing); eight in *Μακεδονία* (centre-right); eight in the financial newspaper *Ημερησία*; seven in the monthly computer magazine *RAM*; seven in the financial newspaper *ΕΞΠΡΕΣ*; six in the conservative right-wing daily *Αδέσμευτος Τύπος* (ed. D. Rizos); and five in its twin *Αδέσμευτος Τύπος* (ed. K. Mitsis). The articles in these newspapers and periodicals amount to about 65 per cent of the total number of publications. The remaining 35 per cent were published in 17 different newspapers and magazines (one to five texts in each).Dispersion seems to be another indication that media language does not attract much attention in the media. I have not detected significant differences in content on the basis of the political affiliation of the newspaper, an issue I turn to later on. (For a characterization of the political affiliation of some of these newspapers and periodicals on independent grounds, see Kollia *et al.* 2013).

The texts belong to different genres (for the definition of genre categories for metalinguistic publications, see Moschonas 2001a). One hundred and thirty-one texts are news items. There are also 66 feature articles (more precisely, 66 entries for 31 feature articles), 34 opinion articles (31 entries for 29 opinion articles), 27 letters to the editor, 24 short comments, three book reviews and ten interviews (ten entries for eight interviews). Short comments are usually anonymous and humoristic. An example of such a comment is reproduced in Figure 2; in free translation: 'One of countless blunders heard yesterday on the airwaves: "the power [= ισχή, instead of the archaistic ισχύς] (sic) of the intensity of the earthquake was ..."It is well-known that earthquakes also hit the language'.

The relatively large number of news items in the corpus may be attributed to two events that were systematically covered in the newspapers over some period of time: a) a conference on the subject of "Journalism and Language", sponsored and organized by the Athens Association of Journalists (ΕΣΗΕΑ), which took place in April 2000 (59 entries in the corpus; presumably, the large coverage is due to the fact that the conference was sponsored by Greece's most powerful journalists' association); and b) a peculiar news item referring to the inclusion into the operational system Windows 2000 of a font for writing ancient Greek (total of 43 entries in the corpus; the importance of this event will be explained shortly). With the exception of these two events, the figures concerning genre categorization are quite similar to the ones reported in our earlier study Moschonas (2001a: 99). I have not taken into account "usage columns", i. e. newspaper texts that regularly give advice on matters of (media) language usage, since I have extensively studied such texts in Moschonas (2001b, 2005) and Moschonas and Spitzmüller (2010); some results of the latter study will be summarized in the next section (2.2).

The media texts in the corpus were classified into eight thematic categories:

1. *General references* (56 entries, 19 per cent)

   In this category belong general essay-type articles with either *en passant* or thematic references to media (mostly TV) language use; for example, the publication of a public speech on Greek language by the President of the Greek Republic, with admonitions on media usage, clearly belongs here (George Stephanopoulos, «Προσοχή στη γλώσσα μας!», "Attention to our language!" *Πολιτικά Θέματα* November 2000). Texts in this category are usually critical of media language use, but, unlike the texts in the next category, they do not contain many references to particular examples. Typically, media language is referred to through definite descriptions such as "*the* language of TV", "*the* language of the internet", "*the* language of journalism", "*the* language of news", etc. Since the existential presupposition of these and similar definite descriptions is taken for granted, these texts contribute to the metalinguistic construction of such doubtful entities as "*the* language of TV", etc.

2. *Mistakes* (44 entries, 15 per cent)

   Although, as already indicated, articles on language usage in general (i. e. outside the media) were not included in the corpus, there is a considerable number of texts that refer explicitly to the alleged mistakes made by journalists, broadcasters, cinema and TV celebrities. Some of the articles in this category also lament the formulaic character of "the language of journalism" and they offer advice for its improvement. Several letters to the editor also belong here.

3. *E-communication* (38 entries, 13 per cent)

   New forms of electronic communication are discussed in a separate category of texts, with the following subcategories:

   3.1. The use of Greeklish (i. e., the representation of the Greek alphabet with the Latin script) and the danger of "latinization" of the Greek language (25 entries);

   3.2. Foreign words in information technology (nine entries);

   3.3. Effects of the electronic media on youth's language (two entries);

   3.4. E-mails and text-messages (two entries).

4. *Products and services* (26 entries, nine per cent)

These texts report on new computer/internet software products or services. Most of the products presented in this category of texts are ones that facilitate the learning or the use of the Greek language, e.g. computer software for learning Greek or for navigating in the internet (see, for example, «Φιλογλωσσία: Η ελληνική γλώσσα 'ταξιδεύει' με έναν κομπιούτερ», *"Philoglossia:* The Greek language 'travels' with a computer", *Ελευθεροτυπία* 27 May 1998). Software products and services are provided mostly for the Greek language (see,for example, «Η τεχνολογία στην υπηρεσία της ελληνικής. Η μάχη κατά της αφομοίωσης», "Technology in the service of the Greek language. The battle against assimilation", *Ελευθεροτυπία* 27 November 1999). There will be no further references to the texts in this category; most of them are reproductions of press releases circulated by manufacturing companies and agencies.

Media multilingualism (15 entries, five per cent)

There are a few texts referring to multilingualism on the internet or to multilingual radio or TV broadcasts (e.g. «Ευρωπαϊκή Ένωση: Σχέδια για ενίσχυση των πολυγλωσσικών MME», "EU: Plans for enforcing multilingual media", *ΕΞΠΡΕΣ* 3 July 2000). It is interesting to notice that multilingualism, when not seen as a "threat" to the Greek language, is understood as a platform for the promotion of Greek, for strengthening its status in the EU, etc.; more often than not, however, multilingualism is understood as an obstacle to Greek monolingualism. The texts in this category report on Greek-speaking media addressed to immigrant Greeks in Australia («Προβλήματα του ομογενειακού Τύπου», *Ώρα των Σπορ* 20 July 2000), BBC News or Euronews being broadcast in Greek («Στα ελληνικά οι ειδήσεις του Euronews», "Euronews in Greek", *Πολιτικά Θέματα* March 2000; «Πολυγλωσσικοί συνδυασμοί στα ερτζιανά. Συνεργασία ΕΡΑ και BBC», "Multilingual combinations on the air: a collaboration between the Greek State Radio and BBC", *Ραδιοτηλεόραση* 14 July 2000); Greek news in other languages («Να μιλούν αγγλικά, αν θέλουν να επιβιώσουν τα ομογενειακά MME», "Greek media abroad should speak English, if they want to survive", *Ημερησία* 18 July 2000; «Έγνοια για τη γλώσσα, μάχη για την επιβίωση». "Concern for the language, battle for survival", *Ελευθεροτυπία* 18 July 2000; «Καημός της ομογένειας για τη γλώσσα», "Expatriate Greeks' deep concern for language", *Ελευθεροτυπία* 20 July 2000); Greece's presence on the internet («Η ημετέρα παιδεία στο διαδίκτυο», "Greek culture on the internet", *Το Βήμα* 1 November 2000). The import of such publications is clear; no further analysis of their content is necessary.

5. *A conference* (59 entries, 20 per cent)

As mentioned already, a conference on "Journalism and Language" took place in Athens from 15–16 April 2000. The conference, in which both journalists

and linguists participated, was sponsored and organized by the Athens Association of Journalists (ΕΣΗΕΑ). Almost all the texts in this category report on
the event of the conference, without going into the details of the proceedings
or taking stance on the participants' views. Earlier publications simply reproduce the press release of the conference. Hence, references to the texts in this
category will be omitted. (That this is a monitored news sequence is attested
by the writer of the present paper, who was one of the organizers of the conference and one of the editors of its proceedings: Boukalas and Moschonas
2001; as well as co-author of the press releases circulated amongst journalists
in both the occasion of the conference and the occasion of the publication of
its proceedings).

6. *A Greek font* (43 entries, 14.6 per cent)
   The inclusion of a polytonic (multi-accent) font in the operational system
   Windows 2000 was hailed as a big event in the Greek print media. With this
   font, Greek language, "the language of Plato", would again be available
   worldwide through the internet. (Publications in this category may have been
   triggered in part by an advertising campaign planned by Microsoft's office in
   Greece.)

7. *"Do you speak Greek?"* (14 entries, 4.8 per cent)
   "Ομιλείτε ελληνικά;" (*Do you speak Greek?*) was a popular TV show that used
   to offer advice on issues of language usage. Participants would compete with
   each other while being tested for their knowledge of the Greek language
   and their ability to use the "correct Greek". The show ran under the advice
   of George Babiniotis, professor of linguistics at the University of Athens and
   a very well-known public persona in Greece. The launching of the show's
   new season in 2000 was announced in all major newspapers. There are three
   feature articles on the history of the show, which stress its importance for
   the cultivation of the Greek language; there is no need to discuss them here.
   Unfortunately, there is no study of the show's corrective repertoires. George

Figure 3: G. Babiniotis (right) on the pronunciation of voiced stops
(«Ομιλείτε ελληνικά;», c. 2007, source: http://
www.youtube.com/watch?v=esBeh4YYnio).

Babiniotis, who often appeared in the show, is shown in Figure 3 to provide advice on the "correct pronunciation" of voiced stops.

2.2 Examples

2.2.1 "The language of the media"

In this section I present and comment on a few examples. I will start with a text by George Babiniotis on the "quality" of TV language. Although his article is probably a transcribed telephone interview, it is nevertheless published under the interviewee's name. The text could be confidently placed in the first thematic category, which comprises general overviews of media language, often cautionary in character. Indeed, the text is prototypical in several respects: the author takes it as a matter of fact that the media affect everyday language use, he considers media (television) usage as a model for language use in general and he shows a clear preference for the scripted language over spontaneous oral communication; the latter he considers to be sloppy and full of mistakes. In addition, his views are presented in the authoritative manner of a university professor of linguistics who feels at ease with prescribing –rather than describing– language use (the views expressed by Babiniotis in this short article are expounded in Babiniotis 1994a, 1994b, which contain mostly his newspaper articles and other occasional texts of his).

Τα θετικά και αρνητικά για τη γλώσσα
Γεώργιος Μπαμπινιώτης
(Καθηγητής Πανεπιστημίου Αθηνών)

Από τη λειτουργία της ιδιωτικής τηλεόρασης σε σχέση με τη γλώσσα, έχουν προκύψει ορισμένες θετικές και αρνητικές πλευρές και ιδίως παραλείψεις.

Στις θετικές πλευρές, είναι ο λόγος που εκφωνείται και [εκ]φέρεται από ορισμένους δημοσιογράφους, καλεσμένους και παρουσιαστές. Είναι λόγος υποδειγματικός στην εκφορά του αλλά και στη δόμησή του.

Αυτό υπάρχει στα δελτία ειδήσεων, και στις εκπομπές λόγου όταν είναι προσεγμένες σε σχέση με τους καλεσμένους. Γενικά, έχουμε στιγμές πολύ καλές σε σχέση με την ελληνική γλώσσα, στην ιδιωτική τηλεόραση, που μπορεί να λειτουργήσει ως ένα πρότυπο και να καλλιεργήσει το οπτικοακουστικό αίσθημα του τηλεθεατή.

Τα αρνητικά είναι αυτά που ακούμε συνήθως στα ρεπορτάζ, από ρεπόρτερ οι οποίοι μιλούν στον τόπο των γεγονότων.

Βεβαίως οι συνθήκες δεν είναι ιδεώδεις, αλλά εν πάση περιπτώσει, φαίνεται ότι σε πολλούς από αυτούς η γλωσσική τους κατάρτιση δεν είναι η καλύτερη. Έτσι ακούγονται χοντρά λάθη τα οποία δημιουργούν πρότυπα άσχημα για τη γλώσσα.

Επίσης οι σειρές –πλην εξαιρέσεων– έχουν κατά κανόνα κακό λόγο, με την έννοια ότι τα πρότυπα που προβάλλουν έχουν συχνά ένα χυδαίο χαρακτήρα και προχειρότητα στις επιλογές προκειμένου να βγάλουν το «αστείο».

Πέρα από το ξενόγλωσσο στοιχείο που ακούγεται, δεν βοηθάει επίσης την ελληνική γλώσσα, η μεταγλώττιση των ξένων σειρών. Συχνά υπάρχουν σοβαρά λάθη και κακή απόδοση των ελληνικών τα οποία κάνουν κακό στη γλωσσική συγκρότηση του θεατή.

Στις αρνητικές πλευρές θα έβαζα και τα ριάλιτι σόου, όπου ο λόγος που εκπέμπεται είναι κατά κανόνα πολύ κακής ποιότητος.

Θα μπορούσε η ιδιωτική τηλεόραση να δώσει ένα ποσοστό χρόνου αφιερωμένο στην ελληνική γλώσσα. Υπάρχει ήδη ο Νόμος Βενιζέλου που υποχρεώνει τα κανάλια να το κάνουν, πράγμα το οποίο δεν γίνεται. Έτσι, δεν περνάει στην τηλεόραση, αυτό που εγώ λέω, πως η γλώσσα ως αξία, και ως ένα αγαθό πολιτιστικό, πρέπει να προσεχθεί και να προβληθεί. Γιατί ο λόγος στην τηλεόραση λειτουργεί ως πρότυπο και καθώς συνοδεύεται από την εικόνα αποτυπώνεται όσο τίποτε άλλο (*Έθνος* 29 November 1999).

Positive and negative aspects of [the] language
George Babiniotis
(Professor at the University of Athens)

Since the [beginning of] the operation of private television, some positive and some negative aspects of language [use] have emerged and, mostly, some omissions.

To the positive aspects one can count the speech uttered by some journalists, guests and presenters. Their speech is exemplary in its articulation [=pronunciation] as well as in its structuring.

This can be seen on the news and the talk shows, provided the guests are carefully selected. Generally, there are some very good moments for the Greek language in the private television, which can function as a model and it can cultivate the audiovisual sentiment of the viewers.

To the negative aspects one can count what is usually heard in live reporting from events.

Of course, the circumstances are not ideal, but, in any event, it seems that many of these reporters did not have the best linguistic training. Outrageous mistakes are heard which function as bad models for the language.

As a rule – there are exceptions, of course –, the discourse of TV series is also bad, in the sense that it presents models that often have a vulgar character and, in trying to force a joke, often betrays offhandedness.

Apart from the foreign language elements heard, the subtitling of foreign series is not helpful for the Greek language either. There are often serious mistakes and bad renderings in Greek, which harm the linguistic edification of the viewers.

Another negative aspect of the media, I would say, is the reality shows, which broadcast speech of a very bad quality.

Private television could devote some time to the Greek language. There is already a law that forces TV channels to do precisely that; however, the law has not been respected. As a result, television does not pass on the message that, as I say, language is a value and a cultural asset, and it should be taken care of and be projected as such, because the discourse of television functions as a model and, since it is accompanied by the picture, it is impressed in the mind more strongly than anything else.

The author keeps score of the "positive" and "negative aspects" of language use on television. Perhaps out of courtesy to the journalist interviewing him, he first mentions the "exemplary speech" of certain journalists. Their good use of language functions as a model for the viewers. The bad use of language (in live reporting, in Greek TV series, in the subtitling of foreign movies and series, in reality shows) also functions as a model, albeit a negative one. The evaluation of use as positive-negative, good-bad, vulgar or offhanded is a prerequisite for his prescriptive attitude towards language that extends beyond particular uses to whole TV genres: for example, reality shows are "bad" not only because of but also, one might say, regardless of their language use, as if they were bad in themselves; it is not only a matter of using the correct language but also a matter of being well-mannered or dignified. Language evaluation thus acquires a moral character that touches on deeper aspects of the "audiovisual sentiment".

The recurring theme in this short evaluation of media (television) discourse (λόγος) is that media language functions as a powerful model, capable of affecting the linguistic behaviour of the viewers. Complaining about loss of standards in media language and, at the same time, maintaining that media (TV) language is itself a de facto standard seems, of course, to be a paradoxical combination of views. But the paradox is resolved once we accept that the standard exists outside the media and that the media merely reproduce and propagate it. Babiniotis evaluates media language in the name of a standard; this is the reason why he shows a preference for the written norms of Standard Modern Greek; he clearly prefers the scripted, "careful" articulation of news announcements over the spontaneous use of speech in unscripted reporting or in reality shows; he adopts the widespread puristic ideology of the standard that has to be purged of "foreign elements"; he does not recognize the possibility of variation; and, certainly, he takes a prescriptive stance to language use that also allows for legislative regulation. For Babiniotis and others, media language is a battlefield for the standardization of Modern Greek. Television is judged for its pedagogical ability to cultivate the norms of the standard language. It is a means for the elaboration of a codified language, in the sense of Haugen (1966: 933). Television is considered capable of inducing either upward language change, towards the standard, or downward change, towards more "vulgar" uses of the language. Accordingly, Babiniotis' "positive" and "negative models" are evaluative terms that correspond to the opposite processes of standardization and destandardization. In either case, the media's ability to influence language change is taken for granted.

In the process of evaluating media language use on the model of a standard, the metadiscursive act of constructing "media language" should not be overlooked. Television language is always referred to by Babiniotis with the definite article in collocations such as "*the* language/discourse/speech *of/on* television". Such a metadiscursive construction of "the language of the media" belongs to the "essentialist and homogeneistic ideologies of language" (Blommaert 1999a: 18), which tend to label and rank language varieties "on the basis of criteria that have to do with the perceived 'quality' of the language or variety, or, with the degree of 'full languageness' of the language or variety" (Blommaert 1999b: 431). To this meta-discursively constructed "language" of television only maximal variation is allowed in the form of different genres or registers; minimal variation at the level of lexicon or grammar is usually stigmatized and rejected. A similar metalinguistic indexing of *the* language of the media is very common in all the articles that belong to the thematic category of general essays about media language. Usually, two types of construction are employed: "the language of (the) [medium]" or "the language in(the) [medium]", with the former being much more common; a Google search on 8 February 2013 provided 55.800 results for "'η γλώσσα της τηλεόρασης'", 'the language of television', and only four results for "'η γλώσσα στην τηλεόραση'", 'the language on television'; while "'η γλώσσα του ίντερνετ'", 'the language of the internet', gave 133.000 results, and "'η γλώσσα στο ίντερνετ'", 'the language on the internet', only two results (in view of the widespread conceptual metaphor of the internet as a –physical– space, one would expect "the language *on* the internet" to be a much more common construction).

Despite their naïveté, Babiniotis' are the views of a linguist and, clearly, they are expressed in the authoritative style of a professional. They have become very influential in Greece. Indeed, Babiniotis' views concerning the "quality of media language" are very often cited by journalists who report on linguistic topics (this is indeed the case with all publications in category eight). It should be noticed that language critique is almost exclusively addressed to the electronic media and it originates in an antagonistic medium, i. e. the newspapers; consequently, language critique may very well be the expression on the surface of an underlying conflict between the print and the electronic media, a conflict which comprises many more parameters besides the linguistic ones (such as a real competition over readership and finances).

2.2.2 Guardians and their standards
According to Vasilakis (2012), "Babiniotis is a brand name"; he represents the elite of ideology brokers (Blommaert 1999a: 9). Following Thomas (1991: 100–114), one may assume that language ideologies propagate in waves, gradually expanding to outer concentric circles: from an elite to a small circle of devotees and propagators, and from there to the general public. Letters to the editor are representative of this smaller circle of followers and devotees. Letters about media language usage clearly belong to a "complaint tradition" (Milroy and Milroy [1985] 1999: 26). They are usually written by educated people, who are, in one way or another, involved in the craft of writing (editors, proofreaders, teachers, professors, etc.). These "craft professionals" (Cameron 1995: 34) are united in

a common cause: the propagation of a standard language's norms. They belong to an army of self-appointed guardians of the language. The titles given to their letters by the journalists are often polemical in character: "They 'are killing' the language" («Δολοφονούν' τη γλώσσα», *Ελευθεροτυπία* 26 August 1997) "They are slaughtering our language"(«Κατακρεουργούν τη γλώσσα μας», *Η Καθημερινή* 7 August 1990), "Our language in front of the firing squad" («Η γλώσσα μας στο εκτελεστικό απόσπασμα», *Απογευματινή* 30 May 2000). The style of writing is often marked by the rhetoric of indignation. Here is a typical example:

«Κατακρεουργούν τη γλώσσα μας»

«Δόξα το Θεό»
Ναι, δεν διαβάσατε λάθος. Έτσι γραμμένη μεταδίνει η Κρατική Τηλεόραση (ΕΤ1) τη φράση αυτή που είναι στα χείλη όλων των Ελλήνων. [...]
Και διερωτώμαι: είναι «τόλμη» ή θεωρείται «γοητεία» η πρωτοφανής αυτή κατα-κρεούργηση της ελληνικής γλώσσας; Μα τον Θεό, δεν βρίσκεται κανείς στη ΕΤ να πει σ' αυτούς που αποδίδουν ξενόγλωσσους διαλόγους ότι όταν μεταχειριζόμαστε τυποποιημένες φράσεις της αρχαίας ή της καθαρεύουσας δεν μπορούμε να τους αλλάζουμε αυθαίρετα και ανεύθυνα την ορθογραφία.
Ένας άλλος συχνά συναντώμενος «μαργαρίτης» στις αποδόσεις ξενόγλωσσων δια-λόγων είναι το «επανέλαβέ το» (αντί «επανάλαβέ το»), «ανέπνεε» (αντί «ανάπνεε») και άλλα παρόμοια.
Πάλι κανείς δεν βρέθηκε να πληροφορήσει τους μεταφραστές ότι η προστακτική δεν παίρνει αύξηση.
Αν αφήνουμε την Κρατική Τηλεόραση να διαδίδει συστηματικά τα «τρισβάρβαρα» αυτά ελληνικά, γιατί παραπονιόμαστε για το χαμηλό μορφωτικό επίπεδο των σημερινών παιδιών;
(*Η Καθημερινή* 7 August 1990)

"They are slaughtering our language"

«Δόξα το Θεό» [instead of the archaistic Δόξα τω Θεώ, 'Thank God']
Yes, you read that right. That's how the state television (ET1) writes and broadcasts a phrase that is on the lips of all the Greeks. [...]
And I ask myself: Is this unprecedented slaughtering of the Greek language conside-red to be "daring" or "charming" or what? For God's sake [Μα τον Θεό], is there no one at ET [the state television] to tell those guys who translate the foreign language dialogues in subtitles that when we use formulaic expressions of the ancient Greek language or of *katha-revousa* [=archaistic language], we are not allowed arbitrarily and irresponsibly to change their orthography.
Another frequently encountered mistake in the rendering of the dialogues from a foreign language is the use of augmented imperative forms such as "επανέλαβε" (instead of "επανάλαβε"), "ανέπνεε" (instead of "ανάπνεε") and the like.
Again, there has been no one to inform the translators that the imperative is not aug-mented.
If we let the state television to broadcast systematically such wretched and barbarian Greek, why should we complain about the low educational attainment of today's youth?

We noticed above the metalinguistic mechanism through which "full language-ness" is assigned to such undifferentiated constructs as "the Greek language", typically denoted by definite descriptions. It is interesting to see this mechanism operating in the context of this particular letter. A few instances of rule violations, i. e. just a few "mistakes", are taken to represent a threat to "the whole language". For the writer, a mistake cannot be something local, limited, or accidental. Mistakes are always total, at least in their consequences. Hence the bombastic styles of the writer; exaggerated dignity, pomposity, irony, overstatements, an alarmist tone are characteristic of such letters to the editor. This metadiscursive strategy which constructs the "wholeness" of a language also allows the writer to speak as a representative of the whole community. Notice the us-them dichotomy: while "we" is left unspecified (the writer writing in the name of potentially every Greek speaker – or writer), "they" are clearly the journalists, the translators, the subtitle technicians – "they" are the media people. The letter is not neutral; it is polemical, like a libel. "They" are the enemies. All similar texts that fish for mistakes presuppose an unconditional belief in the linguistic influence exercised by the (electronic) media, despite the fact that such a belief is not always explicitly stated. Indeed, such letters are written in order to counter the media's influence on "our language". The publicizing of mistakes is a warning that "the Greek language is being molested by the media" («Τα ΜΜΕ κακοποιούν την ελληνική γλώσσα», *To Βήμα* 1 March 2000, letter to the editor). Letters to the editor are also written with an educational purpose in mind; the general public needs to be warned, but the young people, who are not familiar with the norms of the standard language, need to be educated.

In Moschonas (2001b, 2005) and Moschonas and Spitzmüller (2010) it is argued that letters to the editor, along with "usage columns" in the newspapers, i. e. texts by professionals that advise on common usage and correctness, provide important evidence for the language standards that prevail within a linguistic community; studied in a historical perspective, they also provide evidence for the evolution of the standards over a certain period of time (see also Tieken-Boon van Ostade 2010; Schaffer 2010). Instead of concentrating on the often extravagant rhetoric of those who prescribe language usage (see, e.g., Cameron 1995), these studies provide answers to subtler questions such as the following: What type of mistakes do the writers concentrate upon? Are there any regularities in their suggestions for correcting the presumed mistakes and do such regularities form a repertory? More generally, what are the "corrective practices" that prevail among craft professionals during a particular period of time and what do they reveal about the standards of the standard language? I will only present here a summary account of the answers to these questions given in Moschonas and Spitzmüller

(2010), a study based on a quantitative analysis of a corpus far more extensive than the one discussed here.

As it is well-known (Browning 1982), diglossia in Greece has given rise to two conflicting norms, an archaistic or puristic norm (*katharevousa*) and a demotic or vernacular one (*dimotiki*). Standard Modern Greek (Κοινή Νέα Ελληνική), the official standard in Greece after 1976, is supposedly based on the demotic norm; nevertheless a certain number of archaisms is allowed or even preferred, especially in higher registers. In recent years, while the vernacular forms have gradually become standardized, corrective instruction and guidance for properly using the archaistic forms, whose grammar is, so to speak, forgotten, has been urgently provided. Thus, a new "phraseological model" emerged in usage guides, in usage columns in the newspapers and in letters to the editor, a model which can account for constructions belonging to either variety, *dimotiki* or *katharevousa*. This new model corresponds to the mixed standards of Standard Modern Greek, which, although based on a "cultivated" demotic, encompasses nevertheless many archaisms. Archaisms have become formulaic (i. e. "phraseological") in character. The new model makes in principle no distinction between the new and the ancient language and grammar, it is preoccupied with internal rather than external purism, and its rationale is almost always based on the postulation of lexical, morphological or grammatical *conventions* that have presumably emerged out of the grammar of ancient Greek. In the example given above, «δόξα το Θεό», "glory to God", with the accusative case, is being criticized because it has replaced the formulaic archaistic expression «δόξα τω Θεώ», with the dative case (the two expressions are homophonous in Modern Greek). According to the conventionalist attitude, the original formulaic expression "should not be allowed to change", despite the fact that the dative case of the original expression is now obsolete. Similarly, compound verbs in the imperative are not allowed to have a so-called "internal augment" (the second "frequently encountered mistake" mentioned by the author of the above letter), precisely because an augmented form would violate the formation rules of ancient Greek. Conventions are like traditions: they spring from a sacred past; this is the essence of conventionalism. According to the conventionalist attitude, the norms of the modern language belong ultimately to the ancient Greek language and grammar; paradoxically, in order to be respected, the norms have to have become obsolete.

In a comparative perspective, it is interesting that, in contrast to Greek prescriptivism, which is rather 'grammatical' and 'conventional' in character, German prescriptivism is more 'semantic' and 'logical': the former concentrates on formulaic constructions under the rationale of grammatical conventions, the latter focuses on the turn of the phrase; its rationale is rather the logical soundness as well as the cohesion and clarity of the expression (Moschonas and Spitzmüller 2010: 30–31). Conventionalism is by no means a universal attitude among prescriptivists; but it is certainly dominant in the Greek print media and, more generally perhaps, in the community of Greek "craft professionals".

2.2.3 New media, new threats

Publications like the ones in category three (e-communication) have been extensively studied in the relevant sociolinguistic literature: on Greeklish and the attitudes towards the use of the Latin alphabet (the "danger of latinization [romanization] of the Greek language"), see Androutsopoulos (2000, 2009), Koutsogiannis and Mitsikopoulou (2003), Spilioti (2006). Iordanidou and Androutsopoulos (1999) and Spilioti (2006: 40–46) comment on the widespread belief that new technologies as well as the use of foreign words and foreignisms have negative effects on youth language ("youth language" being, I presume, still another metalinguistic construct that linguists share with non-professionals). Emailing and texting using the Roman alphabet are very often seen as a source for the students' low attainment in the Greek language. Conspiracy theories, which claim that "foreign centres" have laid out plans to eliminate the Greek language through the replacement of the Greek alphabet by the Roman one, often reach the press, although their favourite medium is the internet (there are now several blogs and "information" sites specializing on such theories).

How widespread such conspiracy theories are is revealed by the following incident: on 2 June 2000, the issue was brought to the Greek parliament after an interpellation by two members of the socialist party (PASOK), who seem to have accused the Greek minister of Education, also a member of the socialist party, of participating in the conspiracy against the Greek language, because he does not take measures for preserving the Greek alphabet on the internet. It is sufficient to read the relevant headlines in the newspapers:

- "Alphabet. They seek to alter the richest language, Greek, through the internet" («Αλφάβητο. Την πλουσιότερη γλώσσα, την ελληνική, επιχειρούν να αλλοιώσουν λόγω Διαδικτύου», *Αθηναϊκή* 3 June 2000);
- "Efthimiou [the Minister of Education] answers on the language of the internet" («Απάντηση Ευθυμίου για τη γλώσσα του διαδικτύου», *Αυριανή*, 3 June 2000);
- "The Greek alphabet will not be replaced" («Δεν αντικαθίσταται το ελληνικό αλφάβητο», *Εστία* 3 June 2000);
- "Shall we forget the Greek alphabet?"(«Να ξεχάσουμε το ελληνικό αλφάβητο;», *Ελεύθερη Ώρα* 3 June 2000);
- "European computers do 'read' Greek" («'Διαβάζουν' ελληνικά τα ευρωκομπιούτερ», *Έθνος* 5 June 2000);
- "The Roman alphabet in [sic] the Greek language?" («Το λατινικό αλφάβητο στην ελληνική;», *Θεσσαλονίκη* 5 June 2000);

– "Are there thoughts to abolish the Greek alphabet and apply the Roman one? The Greek people should react by employing a new strategy so that we do not reach the point of mourning a new conquest of the Greeks" («Υπάρχουν σκέψεις για κατάργησιν του ελληνικού και εφαρμογήν του λατινικού αλφαβήτου; Ο ελληνικός λαός ως αντίδρασιν πρέπει να εφαρμόσει νέα στρατηγική ώστε να μη φθάσωμεν εις το σημείον να θρηνήσωμεν και νέαν άλωσιν του ελληνισμού», *Ελεύθερη Ώρα* 11 June 2000).

It is interesting to notice that the conservative, right-wing newspapers place emphasis on the danger of latinization, while the newspapers affiliated with the socialist party or the political centre downplay the importance of the issue, following the Minister of Education's line of argument, that adequate measures have been taken to safeguard the "presence of Greek" on the internet. However, concern is expressed in all the relevant publications; also, all publications share similar presuppositions; for example, they all tend to equate language with its written norm, they all are in favour of the standard orthography, they all perceive the use of the Roman alphabet as a threat to the language and the Greek people "as a whole". The incident illustrates that sharing a common language ideology is a prerequisite for an issue to be debated; the issue of the alphabet has become the subject of political debate not because the participants in the debate favour different language ideologies but rather because they share precisely the same ideology, i. e. the same presuppositions about language, writing, the internet, etc.

There was no uptake on this issue, the reason perhaps being that at the same time that the threat of latinization was brought to the attention of the parliament, the guardians of the Greek language were already celebrating a major victory on the very same terrain of new technologies and the internet. The relevant publications in the newspapers form a category of its own: the thematic category seven (a Greek font). The 43 publications in this category (14.6 per cent of the total number of texts) spread from 12 November 1999 to 28 June 2000.

Here is the story: in December 1999, ten deputies of the Greek parliament (coming from three different parties, the right-wing, the socialist, and the centre party ΔΗΚΚΙ) address a letter to the president of the parliament with the warning that "the ancient Greek language will not be included in the polytonic languages of Microsoft's [operating system] Windows 2000, because the Greek state has not expressed the requisite interest" (literal translation). Notice how inexorably writing is interwoven with the conception of a language as a whole, as testified by such hybrid constructions as "the polytonic languages"; what is meant of course is that Windows 2000 will not have a polytonic (multi-accent) Greek *font* for the *writing* and *reading* of ancient Greek.

The newspapers picked up the issue. Here are the headlines from two newspapers that covered it:

- "Ancient Greek thrown out of the window[s] and out of the internet" («Εκ-παραθυρώνουν την αρχαία ελληνική από το Διαδίκτυο», *ΕΞΠΡΕΣ* 12 November 1999);
- "Indifference drives Ancient Greek out of the internet" («Εκτός Διαδικτύου τα αρχαία από ελληνική αδιαφορία», *Ελευθεροτυπία* 13 November 1999).

We see again that the (polytonic) writing is identified with the (ancient Greek) language. One step further, languages, through writing, are conceived to have a territorial existence, as suggested by the metaphors of space ("in and out of the internet") employed in the above headlines.

Soon after, the press returned to the issue, but now the tone was quite different:

- "We have won: Polytonic Windows" («Νενικήκαμεν: Πολυτονικά Windows», *Θεσσαλονίκη* 18 December 1999).
- "Polytonic Greek 'from birth' in Win 2000" («Πολυτονικά ελληνικά 'εκ γενετής' στα Win 2000», *Καθημερινή* 19 December 1999);
- "Windows 2000 will 'speak' ancient Greek" («Τα Windows 2000 θα 'μιλούν' αρχαία ελληνικά», *Ελεύθερος Τύπος* [ed. D. Rizos] 13 January 2000).

The last headline provides an interesting instance of a reversal: a language that exists only in written form, ancient Greek, is now conceptualized as being spoken through writing.

The "victory" was also hailed by the archbishop of Athens Christodoulos:

- "Under the blessings of Christodoulos, the Greek language enters Windows 2000"(«Με τις ευλογίες Χριστόδουλου η ελληνική γλώσσα στα Windows 2000», *Απογευματινή* 13 January 2000; similar coverage in many newspapers).

The line of publications in the press most probably follows Microsoft's advertising campaign; publications may have been prompted by press releases. There are obvious similarities in the headlines:

- "Gates opens a window to Plato" («Ο Γκέιτς ανοίγει παράθυρο στον Πλάτωνα», *Έθνος* 24/2/2000);
- "Windows 2000: Return to the language of Plato" («Windows 2000: Επιστροφή στη γλώσσα του Πλάτωνα», *Αξία* 1 April 2000);
- "Plato's language in Windows" («Η γλώσσα του Πλάτωνος στα Windows», *Η Χώρα* 24 February 2000).

In all probability, Microsoft had also used similar expressions in its advertising slogans. The story was also picked up by the international media, where similarities are also found in the way this software issue is presented. Here is a representative excerpt from *The Wall Street Journal* followed by a similar excerpt from a Greek newspaper:

Microsoft Makes Windows 2000 Support Ancient, Polytonic Greek, by K. Delaney

For the first time, a Microsoft product supports ancient Greek, a language that hasn't been spoken for centuries. Users of the 23 different versions of Windows 2000 around the world – not just those in Greece – are now able to type using the polytonic alphabet, invented roughly 2,100 years ago to codify the peculiar pronunciations of Plato's day. [...]
Even Athens' powerful prelate, Archbishop Christodoulos Paraskevaides, has weighed in, calling the new functionality a success "for the Greek language, the Greek spirit and civilization".
Outside of church circles, the move appears similarly popular. Already, TV networks and newspapers have led with headlines and editorials praising the software giant. (*The Wall Street Journal* 22 February 2000; see also "Plato's Greek is Legible at Last on Modern PCs", http://benton.org/node/12246, last accessed 15 March 2013.)

Ο Γκέιτς ανοίγει ... παράθυρο στον Πλάτωνα

Η Microsoft υποκλίνεται μπροστά στην Αρχαία Ελλάδα και κάνει ένα γιγαντιαίο βήμα στο παρελθόν των 2.100 χρόνων, περιλαμβάνοντας τη γλώσσα του Πλάτωνα στο νέο της πρόγραμμα Windows 2000. [...] Στους χρήστες των Windows 2000, σε ολόκληρο τον κόσμο, παρέχεται πλέον η δυνατότητα δακτυλογράφησης με τη χρήση πολυτονικής αλφαβήτου, η οποία επινοήθηκε πριν από δύο χιλιάδες χρόνια για την κωδικοποίηση της ιδιόμορφης προφοράς της εποχής του Πλάτωνα. [...] (*Έθνος* 24 February 2000)

Gates opens a ... window to Plato

Microsoft is bowing in front of Ancient Greece and makes a giant leap 2,100 years in the past, by including the language of Plato in its new operational system Windows 2000. [...] Users of Windows 2000, throughout the world, now have the opportunity of typing their texts in a polytonic alphabet, which was devised two thousand years ago in order to codify the peculiarities of the pronunciation in Plato's era. [...]

The last mentions of the Greek polytonic font in our smaller corpus (see Figure 1) occur in June 2000. This time, the occasion is the launching of the "Greek Windows", i. e. the Greek version of the operating system, which became available on the Greek market at about that time. If, six months before, the addition of a polytonic font had made Windows speak Ancient Greek, now, the Greek version of the operating system made it speak Greek –*just* Greek or *all* Greek. And this is exactly what the headlines portray, e.g.:

– "Windows 2000 'speaks' Greek"(«Τα Windows 2000 'μιλάνε' ελληνικά», *Μακεδονία* 9 June 2000; exact same headline in *Έθνος* 16 June 2000).

Clearly, the articles in this category form a coherent "text trajectory" (Blommaert 2001), a "communicative sequence" (Moschonas 2009: 304–306).The sequence is not based merely on a thematic coincidence; nor is it based only on advertising motifs, even if it moves to their music. The sequence follows (or constructs) a story. The story cannot be read off a single publication, nor is it developing in particular newspapers, with this or that political or cultural stance, although there are interesting nuances of attitude. The story develops in various journals of different affiliations. The narrative units are roughly the following: first, there is a threat to the language (latinization) and an enemy. Then, there is the "building of public concern", which, of course, is the media's part in the story; the letter drafted to the president of the Greek parliament is an instrument for raising public concern. And then there is an outcome, successful in our case: those who fight the good cause are victorious, even without a fight. The media narrate this story and they also participate in it.

All this sounds as the type of story referred to as a 'moral panic' (Thompson 1998: 8–9; Goode and Ben-Yehuda 1994: 33–41; Cameron 1995: 82–97). But the story is told without a passionate intensity; the increase in the number of publications and the number of persons involved (opinion-makers *and* audiences) is far from impressive. The panic recedes even before it has started. And it cannot reappear: one short-lived recurrence was the issue in category three, which we discussed earlier (interpellation in the parliament with accusations of conspiracy). One, of course, could speak of a 'minor moral panic' in cases such as these. But I think that it is precisely in cases such as these that the term 'moral panic' should not be applied: the media's response is not as intensive as in paradigmatic cases of moral panics (Cohen [1972] 2002); the issue can cause a concern only amongst those already concerned; the issue is not capable of causing a debate; it has a low 'news-value'; it can recur, but never with intensity. Indeed, there are no issues detected in the small corpus discussed here that deserve the characterization of a moral panic. All issues in this corpus are 'routine issues' (Moschonas 2009: 305). One should not be trapped by the alarmist rhetoric of the publications. The reader should also be reminded that each and every issue raised about 'media language' belongs to a corpus that does not exceed 4.3 per cent of the total number of publications about 'language issues' in general. For the media, media language itself is a routine issue.

Except for a few scarce references, I will not comment on examples from categories four, five, six and eight above. In the next section, I will mention some instances of moral panics that occur in the bigger corpus of publications about issues other than media language.

I would not have done justice to the publications about media language in the Greek press had I not mentioned, before closing this section, some popularizing articles, well-informed and solemnly written by linguists such as Jannis Androutsopoulos, on Greeklish («Από τα φραγκοχιώτικα στα Greeklish», "From frangochiotica to Greeklish", *To Βήμα* 5 September 1999); Alexandra Georgakopoulou *et al.*, on Greek language on the internet («Των Ελλήνων οι νέες ψηφιακές κοινότητες», "New Greek digital communities", *Η Καθημερινή* 14 October 2001); Panajotis Kontos, on variation («Η ποικιλία στη γλώσσα είναι ευλογία», "Variation is a blessing for the language", *Ελεύθερη Ώρα* 1 February 2000, an interview; interestingly enough, Kontos praises variation while at the same time attributing the "maltreatment" of the Greek language to "the language of the media"). I certainly respect scientific journalism; but I doubt its effectiveness. (Of my own opinion articles in the Greek press I can confidently claim that they have not been influential.)

2.3 A conceptual topology

I have defined thematic categories and discussed a few examples. The question I will now try to address is more general: Why these categories? Why the particular topics, and not others? And why the particular examples? What is it, after all, that counts as an example, i. e. as an instance in a well-defined communicative sequence?

A naïve answer to such questions could be that the press simply covers all issues that are current and relevant, including linguistic ones. Under this view, linguistic issues are happenings of some sort; they happen *now* and they are of concern to the public at large or to a smaller public. For example, a conference is taking place and it is covered in the press (category six, above); by analogy, a mistake is being made by a TV announcer and it is observed and stigmatized in a short newspaper comment (category three): this should also count as a kind of reporting. Writing media texts about media language, under this view, is just another type of journalism. The press simply responds to current "developments" concerning media language. Media language has a certain "news value".

However, not all categories in our corpus have the same news value and some do not seem to possess any "temporality" at all. Certainly, reporting on a linguistic conference (category six) does not seem to have the same relevance to the present, nor is it addressed to the same audience as spotting a linguistic mistake and writing about it (category two). The postulation of news values could not explain the existence of categories with general, untimely references to media language (such as category one, above). Also, it could not explain how thematic categories are related to each other and, possibly, differentiated from each other. For example, there seem to be routine reports on several software products (category four); but what is it that makes the use of a polytonic font in a popular computer operational system (category seven) so special? Why is this issue singled out and covered more extensively in relation to other similar "issues"? And how are 'language issues' defined in general? What is a piece of news concerning (media) language? Certainly, there is a difference between, say, a train collision and the "discovery" that some people employ Greeklish in writing their text messages and emails. Language news is certainly not like news about train-collisions, elections, or wars. "What happened yesterday, language-wise?" does not seem to be a legitimate question. But what is peculiar about it?

In what follows, I try to reconstruct the conceptual framework by means of which language issues are defined as such. I argue that there has to be a tacit agreement on what a linguistic piece of news is about and why it concerns the public. Journalists and audiences alike, in order to recognize language issues and be attuned to pieces of linguistic news, have to use some kind of mental map (Moschonas 2004: 190–193, 2009: 306–314), in which several *topoi* or conceptual areas interrelate (the notion of *topos* is drawn from the tradition of rhetorical studies; see also Spitzmüller 2005: 272–310). Agreement is not limited to what a language issue is and why it is worth reporting; it extends to general beliefs about the "nature" of the language. "News" about language presupposes a collective mentality about what 'language' is or what 'languages' are, how languages relate to each other, etc. As is probably the case in many other linguistic communities, where an official monolgossic ideology prevails, the "Greek mentality" turns out to be egocentric; the Greek language is believed to lie at the centre of the universe of languages.

In order to explain what counts as a language issue and what doesn't, reference should be made to our larger corpus, from which texts about media language were drawn for the purposes of the present study (see Figure 1, above). The conceptual topology of language issues in the larger corpus can be conveniently explained with reference to Figure 4, below. I will read Figure 4 as a classification of all issues about language in the Greek press (during the period 1 January 1964 – 1 April 2001). As will become apparent in a moment, media language issues or references (out of which the smaller corpus was constructed) tend to focus on the area in Figure 4 called the Interior.

I will now introduce some terminology that is needed in order to read Figure 4 as a conceptual map. Let us call a language an Interior. Let us call whatever does not belong to a language an Exterior. Let us imagine that a language can have within it an Exterior: an Exterior-within-the-Interior. And let us similarly imagine that an Exterior can have within it specimens of an Interior: an Interior-within-the-Exterior. Then, there are precisely four categories of language issues in the Greek press: issues concerning a) the Interior, b) the Exterior, c) the Exterior-within-the-Interior, and d) the Interior-within-the-Exterior. Let us see which issues fall in each of the four categories (the presentation follows a semi-chronological order).

First, immediately after the Language Reform of 1976, several post-diglossia issues arose in the Greek press. They all had to do with orthography, usage, standardization and they all related to often conflicting efforts, after years of divided

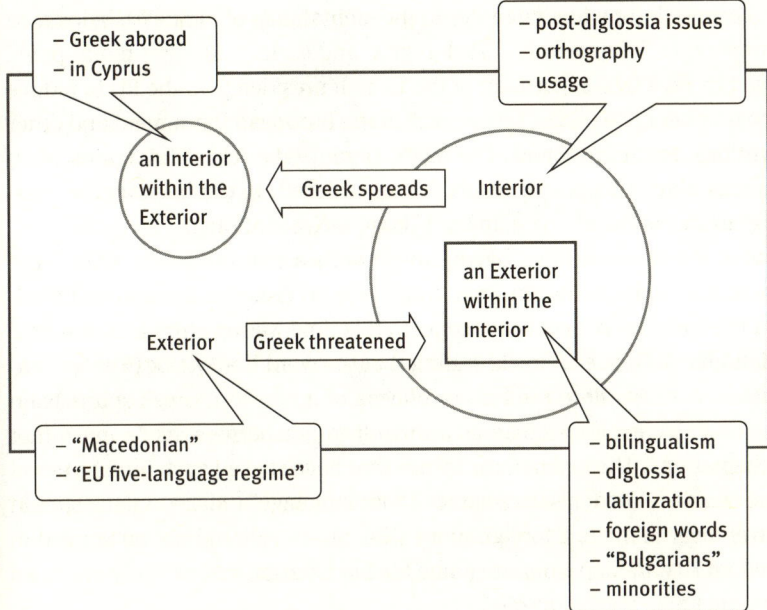

Figure 4: A territorial conception of language

usage, for the definition of a uniform, standard language (an Interior). The major issue now was not so much to arbitrate between *demotiki* and *katharevousa* – which of the two *is* the Interior (this was the issue of the Language Question); the issue was rather how much of each belongs to the Interior. The most passionate debate of the 1980s was whether ancient Greek should be taught in secondary education. The idea that prevailed during this period was that the Interior is diachronically uniform – that there is an uninterrupted continuity between ancient Greek and the modern language. Greek linguistics has not disputed this idea.

The Interior, of course, cannot be *synchronically* uniform. Remnants of diglossia, the effects of bilingualism, the use of foreign words, the existence of minority or immigrant languages all contribute to establishing an Exterior-within-the-Interior. In the early 1990s, English was identified as an enemy of the Greek language, whose purity was threatened by loan words, the Roman script, etc. The fear of latinization is an instance of this concern with the purity of the Interior.

Moral panics in the Greek press have been caused mainly by issues that relate to the Exterior of the language. One of them is a naming issue, the use of the "Greek name" 'Macedonia' as an official name for FYROM (this issue remains unresolved for the Greek foreign policy). According to a "symbolic geography" (Irvine and Gal, 2000: 63), the name 'Macedonia' cannot refer to a part of the

Exterior, because it (or what it denotes in the mental map of Figure 4), belongs to the Interior – it is the name of a Greek region and dialect. Another moral panic was caused in 1994 by a suggestion of the French presidency in the EU to reduce to five the number of "working languages" in the European Parliament and other EU institutions, excluding Greek. The media organized a "crusade" against such an "atrocious plan" that would result, it was believed, in diminishing the presence of Greek in the Exterior (i. e. in the EU and its institutions).

Another moral panic, also having to do with a naming issue, shifted the attention of the media to the "internal front", i. e. to issues relating to an Exterior-within-the-Interior. The cause for concern this time was an entry in Babiniotis' (1998) dictionary of Modern Greek, stating that the word Βούλγαρος (=Bulgarian) may be used as an insult to the fans or players of a northern Greek sports team (ΠΑΟΚ). The entry itself was read as an insult to northerners, as "a move that divided the nation". The two naming issues that have caused such intense moral panics are clearly related: just as a name of "our language" ('Macedonian') should not be given over to *them*, a foreign name ('Bulgarian') should not be applied to *us*. 'Macedonia' is an inappropriate name for the Exterior, just as 'Bulgaria' is an inappropriate name for the Interior.

The perceived "danger of latinization" also relates to other issues in the category of an-Exterior-within-the-Interior. A moral panic was caused in 2001, when the Greek Commissioner in the EU proposed to have English institutionalized as the "second official language" of the Greek state. The proposal was judged by the media to be "outrageous" or even "inconceivable".

Last, let us mention the publications in the Greek press about teaching Greek as a second language (in the Interior) or as a foreign language (in the Exterior). Greek as a second or a foreign language is a relatively new discovery (both in linguistics and the media). Teaching Greek to foreigners and immigrants is certainly seen as a means for handling the Interior's uniformity (i. e. preserving its monoglossic status). It is also a means for expanding the borders of the language; Greek itself can become an-Interior-within-the-Exterior. Of similar concern are publications about Greek-speaking media in the Exterior of the language (e.g. for immigrant Greeks) or in the Interior of the language (e.g. for immigrants in Greece); see category four, above.

The conception of the Greek language depicted in Figure 4 is a territorial conception. Figure 4 is the pictorial representation of a language as a realm, a regime, or a state. It is the representation of a language ideology that is clearly nationalistic and monoglossic. The Greek language itself is identified with the Greek state.

Having defined the conceptual topology on which language issues are raised, let us return to our smaller corpus of texts about media language and change. Most media language issues are raised from the standpoint of the Interior. Issues of orthography, usage, and standardization are vantage points from which the 'language of the media' is conceived and metadiscursively constructed as a uniform Interior. The 'language of television', the 'language of the internet' etc. belong to the Greek language, they are parts of it, like dialects are; but they are also conceived of as having their own "languageness". Standardization of a media variety is accordingly understood as the complete identification of such a variety or jargon with the Interior that the Greek language is. Error-hunting (category two) and educational broadcasts such as "Do you speak Greek?" (category eight) clearly contribute to the standardization of a media variety on the model of the Interior.

As we have seen, issues about the Interior are persistent, but they do not have the power to cause a major moral panic; they are all routine issues. Moral panics occur mostly when a threat emanates from the Exterior surrounding the Greek language; such threats can cause the Interior to diminish or they can cause an Exterior-within-the-Interior to appear. This seems then to be the reason that none of the thematic categories one through seven, above, contains any publications capable of causing a moral panic. The only possible threat is Greeklish and the latinization of the alphabet. New technologies and the Internet could, of course, pose a threat to the Greek language; but, they are also conceived of as territories in which Greek fights for its existence, and it does so successfully. Products and services (category four) are available that facilitate Greek's presence on the World Wide Web, while Greek also holds its place in the multilingual world of radio and television (according to most reports in category five). And, since Windows 2000, there are fonts that permit writing Greek in both its polytonic and in its monotonic orthography. Greek, it is believed, becomes available worldwide through the medium of writing.

If the territory of the Greek language is mainly identified with the Greek state (and even conceived of as a state), the territory of the Greek language in the print media and the internet is identified with writing. It is as if the Greek language is embodied in writing. A foreign writing (latinization) is considered as «αγλωσσία», as lack of language. A language can get as far as its writing allows it to. Accordingly, the possibility that the Roman script would facilitate the use of Greek on an international scale does not occur to anyone. It is merely inconceivable, because the Greek language *is* its script. A Roman script would also hide the language's uninterrupted continuity; it would dissociate the modern language from ancient Greek, challenging its diachronic persistence. These are recurring motifs in the texts of category three (E-communication); typically, texts in this category are critical of Greeklish, or even of texting and emailing (which they see as activities performed under the heavy influence of English). As mentioned above, because it is believed that the new media are mainly – or most confidently

– used by younger people, concern is often expressed about the effects of the electronic media on youth's language.

Media-induced language change is also realized in territorial terms. There are only two possible moves: either an expansion or a contraction of the Interior, and each one corresponds to the exact opposite move by the Exterior. Media-induced language change is thus conceived through the privileged metaphor of language policy studies: as either an increase or a decrease in a variety's fields of use or domains. Territorial concepts have their place in both the folk-linguistic and the professional discourse on language use and change.

The attitude towards language variation in the media is, of course, prescriptive. This does not mean that variation is not noticed at all; it only means that variation is not allowed. Actually, variation is a prerequisite to prescriptivism. Prescriptivists presuppose that there are at least two linguistic variants (a "correct" and a "incorrect" one), and consider it their task to try to promote language awareness of such inadmissible variation to a wider public. Accordingly, for the prescriptivists variation is always transitional, i. e. awareness of the variants is only raised with the aim of ultimately replacing a incorrect variant with the correct one (Moschonas and Spitzmüller 2010: 36).

Whether the standardization of media language or the strengthening of monologic registers could have any permanent effects on media language usage or, for that matter, on general usage, is not the aim of the present paper to decide. It remains to be seen whether standardization actually manages to eliminate variation, as prescriptivists strongly believe, or whether norms are just the prescriptivists' useless weapons in their futile war against language change, as some linguists seem to suggest.

3 Conclusions and discussion

Discourse in the Greek print media about media language and media-induced language change rests mainly on three interrelated conceptions of language, language variation and linguistic change: 1. a territorial conception of language, 2. a prescriptive approach to linguistic variation and 3. a strong belief in media-induced language change.

1. Language change is understood mostly in territorial terms. For example, norms prescribe the well-defined, delineated regions of language use that have to remain "intact"; language contact may lead to a language's "contraction" or "shrinkage" (συρρίκνωση); the internet is a often presented as a territory that has to be "conquered"; etc. The Greek language itself is an all-encompassing regime (an Interior) that has to remain unaffected by change. Language change

is ultimately a matter of shifting the borders between languages and/or language domains. One may argue that the "folk-linguistic" conception of language territories corresponds to a professional sociolinguist's conception of such processes as "language spread" or "domain loss". However, in the conceptual topology of media discourse, all domains are ultimately related to each other. If a domain is threatened, the language as a whole is placed under threat. Accordingly, change is understood as pollution; it could spread over the whole language (Delveroudi and Moschonas 2003: 18).

2. The approach to language employed in the print media is prescriptive. Prescription is based on a conventionalist understanding of a (written) standard. Variation is not tolerated; it may lead to a change away from the standard, a change that has to be reversed. 'Downward' linguistic change in particular, i. e. a divergence away from the standard, a demotization or vernacularization of the language, is precisely what those concerned about media usage are trying to prevent. Since a standard language is mainly a grapholect, language is very often identified with writing. The corrective practices adopted in the Greek print media give priority to writing, they are conventionalist and lexis-oriented, they are based on monologic conceptions of language and/or they are modeled on monologic genres (such as traditional news broadcasting). A division between the print media and the electronic ones (especially television and the internet) is presupposed throughout. Directives about language usage are issued in and through the print media and they almost always concern instances of speech or writing in the electronic media; the former regulate over the latter. Thus, the metalinguistic discourse in the Greek newspapers reproduces and reinforces an antagonistic relation between the print and the electronic media, which, to a certain degree, exists independently of any differences *in* language.

3. There is a very strong belief in media-induced language change, often expressed in voluntaristic terms. Language change – or rather the prevention of it –, is not just a possibility; it is happening all the time and the media can effect it because they are considered to be too powerful. The 'language of the media', especially television, is considered to function as a model of language usage, capable of propagating or consolidating linguistic habits and attitudes. This belief is part and parcel of an ideology of standardization. It is believed that the form and content of media discourse could and should be controlled mechanically, on the basis of linguistic conventions, by guardians of language, i. e. by agents such as proofreaders, editors, the Radio-Television Council, etc.

Expert opinion on media-induced language change, expressed by sociolinguists themselves, is not as unequivocal as the opinion of the journalists or, for that matter, of apostolic linguists appearing in the media and preaching this or that norm. Certain sociolinguists dismiss media-induced language change as yet another "language myth" (e.g. Chambers 1998, 2005). However, several studies seem to document 'upward' linguistic changes due to an increased exposure to the media (for discussion of the relevant studies, see Stuart-Smith 2007, 2011; and Section II of this volume). In other words, the scientific literature seems to corroborate the view that exposure to the media possibly induces the convergence towards a standard – which is precisely what those who prescribe media usage in Greece and, possibly in other countries as well, aspire to.

If this is the case, one should pose the question whether upward convergence is the result not only of significant exposure to media but also of a certain exposure to the *views about language* expressed in the media. It may be the case that exposure to metalanguage might have a certain *performative* effect, i. e. it might create awareness about certain language issues and manage, after all, to shape language habits and practices inside and outside the media. Could we assume then that the metalinguistic conceptions *of* language have a certain performative effect *on* language?

Studies of language ideologies have been aware of such an "affective" character of meta-linguistic conceptions. Silverstein (1979) discusses how conceptualizations of linguistic structure possibly affect language evolution. Woolard (1998: 10–11) also stresses the "active", "affective", "consequential" – in a word: *performative* – character of language ideologies; such an "affective" aspect she associates with linguistic change. Moschonas (2008) explores the possibilities for applying an appropriately modified theory of speech acts to the analysis of the "performative character" of language ideologies; he proposes "correctives", i. e. metadiscursive speech acts, as a cover category for practices mediating between metalanguage and language.

Language ideologies are not just sets of beliefs. They manage to perform their magic (Bourdieu 1991: 122) only through collective practices such as standardization, linguistic purism, domain elaboration, language learning and teaching, a certain institutionalization and regimentation of discourse, etc. Accordingly, the possible affective power of the metalinguistic discourse produced in and about the media should be measured relative to the multiplicity and strength of other standardization (or re-standardization) procedures taking place within a linguistic community. The media's conception of language and linguistic change should also be compared and contrasted to alternative rationalizations of linguistic practices, such as the ones performed by professional linguists, outside or inside the media. In this respect, the media are expected to reproduce conceptions and practices that prevail in other technologically bound and mediated forms of communication.

In standardization, several forces (administrative, educational, etc.) always unite, and they are all necessary in order for metalinguistic conceptions and/ or linguistic practices to assume efficiency and spread within the community at large. Standardization is not a multiplier just of linguistic practices, but also of their conceptualizations. The media participate in the standardization process by reproducing, on the one hand, specific instructions on language usage and, on the other hand, metalinguistic legitimations or rationalizations of such instructions. Needless to say, rationalizations of language usage also relate to other non-linguistic ideologies within a community, such as nationalism, in the case of Greece. Interestingly enough, nationalism provides the conceptual substratum for identifying and "cultivating" (or "elaborating", in Haugen's 1966 sense) standards in whole domains of language use (such as the new domains in the new media). Domains are identified through processes of "contraction" or "expansion" of a language's Interior, i. e. mostly through a language's writing system, its orthography and similar conventions. It is widely believed that the observance of such conventions in public discourse could be somehow monitored.

I have shown that the discourse in the media about "the language of the media", about language variation and linguistic change is quite systematic and coherent, in the sense that it is associated with particular genres, such as usage columns in the newspapers; it concerns issues with recognizable "news value"; it forms mass-mediated communicative sequences across different genres and media; and, above all, it is subject to a conceptual topology that is shared between sender and receiver, i. e. a mental map that is of necessity collective. The study of metalinguistic discourse in the media (what could perhaps be called *media metalinguistics*) can thus help us diagnose some of the standards by means of which (re)standardization is endeavored and possibly achieved within a community; in the media one can observe changes in standards, and subsequently form hypotheses about possible *linguistic* changes to which the *changes in standards* respond. The conceptual analysis of metalinguistic discourse can also help sociolinguists understand whether and how linguistic change is perceived and ideologized within a linguistic community and what other ideological forces it unites with.

I have tried to approach language ideologies from a practical standpoint and describe them not just as naïve, incoherent or contradictory rationalizations of language usage, exposed to the overwhelming critique of the professional linguists, but also as capable of performing certain "speech acts" at a metalinguistic level, i. e. as capable of "verifying" themselves. The "direction of fit" of such metalinguistic acts is from a (meta)language to a language or, alternatively, their perlocutionary effect is ultimately locutionary; i. e. their perlocutionary effect is none other than eventually changing collective linguistic behavior and habits – and only towards a standard. Since the metalinguistic discourse of "non-professionals" is mostly prescriptive, its illocutionary force is in essence that of a directive (according to Althusser [1970] 1971, the ultimate directive of all ideologies is simply this: "Act!"). Hence, the felicity conditions for domain specifications, for corrective instructions, for norm specifications are also conditions for linguistic change: just as the performance of a speech act may be "happy" or "unhappy" under particular circumstances, effecting a linguistic change can be successful or unsuccessful in particular periods of time under socio-cultural conditions that need to be specified and carefully studied.

To sum up: I have in this paper analyzed metalinguistic discourse in the Greek print media as a model for language ideologies. I have suggested that at least that part of media metalinguistics that is preoccupied with correcting the language and prescribing usage provides useful hints as to how media-induced language change may be effected. Corrective instructions and similar metalinguistic acts establish a link between (media) metalanguage and language. Metalinguistic acts are subject to standards, which, when effective, become integrated into what is called a standardized language.

Language ideologies, just like all ideologies, exhibit a certain social organization: they spread from an elite of intellectuals and, through a smaller group of followers and devotees, they potentially reach everyone who is literate. Media metalinguistics also follows the momentum of literacy. In the case of media linguistics, the distinction between folk and professional discourse becomes blurred and problematic.

Of course, metalinguistic acts in the media can only be felicitous under particular socio-cultural or institutional circumstances. And, of course, I have not shown whether the metalinguistic discourse is indeed successful, i. e. whether it actually affects linguistic change; I have only shown that it can possibly effect change, especially when backed up by metalinguistic acts outside the media or in other mediated linguistic practices. But then, in this respect metalinguistic acts are not different from any other category of performatives.

References

Althusser, Louis 1971: Ideology and ideological state apparatuses. In: Louis Althusser. *Lenin and Philosophy and Other Essays*, translated by Ben Brewster, 127–186. New York/ London: Monthly Review Press. First published [1970].

Androutsopoulos, Jannis 2000: Λατινο-ελληνική ορθογραφία στο ηλεκτρονικό ταχυδρομείο: Χρήση και στάσεις [Latin-Greek orthography in emails: Use and attitudes]. *Studies in Greek Linguistics* 20: 75–86.

Androutsopoulos, Jannis 2009: "Greeklish": Transliteration practice and discourse in the context of computer-mediated digraphia. In: Alexandra Georgakopoulou and Michael Silk (eds.), *Standard Languages and Language Standards: Greek, Past and Present*, 221–249. London: King's College – Centre for Hellenic Studies / Ashgate.

Babiniotis, George 1994a: *Ελληνική γλώσσα: Παρελθόν, παρόν, μέλλον [Greek language: Past, present, future]*. Athens: Gutenberg.

Babiniotis, George 1994b: *Η γλώσσα ως αξία: Το παράδειγμα της ελληνικής* [*The language as value: The case of Greek*]. Athens: Gutenberg.

Babiniotis, George 1998: *Λεξικό της Νέας Ελληνικής Γλώσσας με Σχόλια για τη σωστή χρήση των λέξεων* [*Dictionary of the Modern Greek Language with Comments on the Correct Use of Words*]. Athens: Κέντρο Λεξικολογίας.

Blommaert, Jan 1999a: The debate is open. In: Jan Blommaert (ed.), *Language Ideological Debates*, 1–38. Berlin/New York: Mouton de Gruyter.

Blommaert, Jan 1999b: The debate is closed. In: Jan Blommaert (ed.), *Language Ideological Debates*, 425–438. Berlin/New York: Mouton de Gruyter.

Blommaert, Jan 2001: Context is/as critique. *Critique of Anthropology* 21.1: 13–32.

Boukalas, Pantelis and Spiros A. Moschonas (eds.) 2001: *Δημοσιογραφία και γλώσσα* [*Journalism and language*]. Athens: ΕΣΗΕΑ.

Bourdieu, Pierre 1991: *Language and Symbolic Power*, edited and introduced by John B. Thompson, translated by Gino Raymond and Matthew Adamson: Cambridge: Polity.

Browning, Robert 1982: Greek diglossia yesterday and today. *International Journal of the Sociology of Language* 35: 49–68.

Cameron, Deborah 1995: *Verbal Hygiene*. London/New York: Routledge.

Chambers, Jack K. 1998: TV makes people sound the same. In: Laurie Bauer and Peter Trudgill (eds.), *Language Myths*, 121–131. London: Penguin Books.

Chambers, Jack K. 2005: Talk the talk? http://www.pbs.org/speak/ahead/mediapower/media/# (accessed 7 July 2013).

Cohen, Stanley 2002: *Folk Devils and Moral Panics*. London/New York: Routledge. First published London: MacGibbon and Kee [1972].

Delveroudi, Rhea and Spiros A. Moschonas 2003: Le purisme de la langue et la langue du purisme. *Philologie im Netz* 24: 1–26.

Goode, Erich and Nachman Ben-Yehuda 1994: *Moral Panics: The Social Construction of Deviance*. Oxford: Blackwell.

Haugen, Einar 1966: Dialect, language, nation. *American Anthropologist* 68.4: 922–935.

Iordanidou, Anna and Jannis Androutsopoulos 1999: «Πήρανε τη γλώσσα στο... κρανίο»: στάσεις των ΜΜΕ απέναντι στη γλώσσα των νέων ["Language ... gets on their nerves": Media attitudes towards youth language]. In: Amalia Moser (ed.) *Greek Linguistics '97: Proceedings of the 3rd International Linguistic Conference on Greek Language*, 586–595. Athens: Ελληνικά Γράμματα.

Irvine, Judith T. and Susan Gal 2000: Language ideology and linguistic differentiation. In: Paul V. Kroskrity (ed.), *Regimes of Language: Ideologies, Polities, and Identities*, 35–83. Santa Fe, New Mexico: School of American Research Press / Oxford: James Currey.

Kollia, Michaella, Artemis Sofiou, Tina Fourlari and Spiros A. Moschonas 2013: Η λόγια μορφολογία στον ελληνικό Τύπο: Δείκτης ιδεολογικής ή υφολογικής διαφοροποίησης; [Diglossic variants in the Greek press: Indexes of ideological or stylistic differentiation?]. *Ζητήματα επικοινωνίας* 16–17: 139–151.

Koutsogiannis, Dimitris and Bessie Mitsikopoulou 2003: Greeklish and greekness: Trends and discourses of "glocalness". *Journal of Computer-Mediated Communication* 9.1, http://jcmc.indiana.edu/vol9/issue1/kouts_mits.html (accessed 8 July 2013).

Milroy, James and Lesley Milroy 1999: *Authority in Language: Investigating Standard English*. London/New York: Routledge. First published London: Routledge and Kegan Paul [1985].

Moschonas, Spiros A. 2001a: Δημοσιεύματα του Τύπου για τη γλώσσα [Publications in the Greek press about language]. In: Pantelis Boukalas and Spiros A. Moschonas (eds.), *Δημοσιογραφία και γλώσσα*, 85–116. Athens: ΕΣΗΕΑ, 2001.

Moschonas, Spiros A. 2001b: Οι διορθωτικές στήλες στον ελληνικό Τύπο [Usage columns in the Greek press]. *Εφαρμοσμένη γλωσσολογία* 17: 49–68.

Moschonas, Spiros A. 2004: Relativism in language ideology: On Greece's latest language issues. *Journal of Modern Greek Studies* 22.2: 173–206.

Moschonas, Spiros A. 2005: Διορθωτικές πρακτικές [Corrective practices]. In: *Χρήσεις της γλώσσας: Επιστημονικό Συμπόσιο (3–5 Δεκεμβρίου 2004)*, 151–174. Athens: Εταιρεία Σπουδών Νεοελληνικού Πολιτισμού και Γενικής Παιδείας.

Moschonas, Spiros A. 2008: Vers une théorie performative du purisme. *Le français moderne* 76.1: 38–50.

Moschonas, Spiros A. 2009: "Language issues" after the "Language Question": On the modern standards of Standard Modern Greek. In: Alexandra Georgakopoulou and Michael Silk (eds.), *Standard Languages and Language Standards: Greek, Past and Present,* 293–320. London: King's College – Centre for Hellenic Studies / Ashgate.

Moschonas, Spiros A. and Jürgen Spitzmüller 2010: Prescriptivism in and about the media: A comparative analysis of corrective practices in Greece and Germany. In: Sally Johnson and Tommaso M. Milani (eds.), *Language Ideologies and Media Discourse: Texts, Practices, Politics,* 17–40. London: Continuum Press.

Niedzielski, Nancy A. and Dennis R. Preston 2000: *Folk Linguistics.* Berlin/New York: Mouton de Gruyter.

Schaffer, Deborah 2010: Old whine in new bottles: Mass-market prescriptivism from the '70s to the present. In: Patricia Donaher (ed.), *Barbarians at the Gate: Studies in Language Attitudes,* 44–87. Cambridge: Cambridge Scholars Publishing.

Silverstein, Michael 1979: Language structure and linguistic ideology. In: Paul R. Clyne, William F. Hanks and Carol L. Hofbauer (eds.), *The Elements: A Parasession on Linguistic Units,* 193–247. Chicago: Chicago Linguistic Society.

Spilioti, Thiresia 2006: *Text messages and social interaction: Genre, norm and sociability in Greek SMS.* Ph.D. dissertation, Department of Byzantine and Modern Greek Studies, King's College London.

Spitzmueller, Jürgen 2005: *Metasprachdiskurse: Einstellungen zu Anglizismen und ihre wissenschaftliche Rezeption.* Berlin/New York: de Gruyter.

Stuart-Smith, Jane 2007: The Influence of the media. In: Carmen Llamas, Luise Mullany and Peter Stockwell (eds.), *The Routledge Companion to Sociolinguistics,* 140–148. London/New York: Routledge.

Stuart-Smith, Jane 2011: The view from the couch: Changing perspectives on the role of television in changing language ideologies and use. In: Tore Kristiansen and Nikolas Coupland (eds.), *Standard Languages and Language Standards in a Changing Europe.* Oslo: Novus Press.

Thomas, George 1991: *Linguistic Purism.* London/New York: Longman.

Thompson, Kenneth 1998: *Moral Panics.* London/New York: Routledge.

Tieken-Boon van Ostade, Ingrid 2010: The usage guide: Its birth and popularity. *English Today* 102: 14–44.

Vasilakis, Manolis 2012: Brand name Μπαμπινιώτης [Brand name: Babiniotis]. *The Athens Review of Books* 29: 54–61.

Woolard, Kathryn A. 1998: Introduction: Language ideology as a field of inquiry. In: Bambi B. Schieffelin, Kathryn A. Woolard and Paul V. Kroskrity (eds.), *Language Ideologies: Practice and Theory,* 3–47. New York/Oxford: Oxford University Press.

Paul Kerswill

The objectification of 'Jafaican'. The discoursal embedding of Multicultural London English in the British media[1]

1 Introduction: Mediatization of new urban youth varieties

Since the 1980s, both lay commentators and academic experts have shown an intense interest in apparently new linguistic practices among young people living in multiethnic neighbourhoods in the major cities of northern Europe. Both kinds of observer note that the version of the national language used by these young people is a departure from what is 'normal' in that language. Kotsinas's work (1988a, b) is an early instantiation of academic research on the phenomenon. Having noted a number of characteristic syntactic and lexical features in the Swedish of adolescents living in a particular high-density multiethnic district of Stockholm, Kotsinas considers whether these features are a consequence of creolization or second-language learning, or whether they are part of a new dialect. The young speakers Kotsinas interviewed were highly aware that they spoke Swedish in a distinctive way, and, moreover, that this way of speaking was not to be used with adults. She states that '[t]hey [the young people] even have names for the variety, *Rinkebysvenska* 'Rinkeby-Swedish'' (Kotsinas 1988b: 135–136), named after the district she studied. At the same time as this research, newspapers began to carry reports about '*rinkebysvenska*' (Bijvoet and Fraurud 2006: 6), dealing with some of its grammatical and lexical features. Today, the term is sufficiently established that the media generally do not offer an explanation or even a gloss: the term, and its content, are assumed to be shared knowledge among the readership, and it is almost always printed without quotation marks. It is a variety that can be set up in contrast to Standard Swedish (e.g. *Dagens Nyheter* 24 August 2006) or a variety that can be heavily stigmatized: according to a blog by a notorious anti-immigration politician, anyone heard speaking *rinkebysvenska* should be shot by the police (*Dagens Nyheter* 21 November 2012).

---

1 I am very grateful to Jannis Androutsopoulos and Heike Wiese for their comments on a draft of this chapter.

This chapter explores in greater detail than the brief sketch above the way in which a similar phenomenon in London has been appropriated by the British print media over a period that began as recently as 2006. This is the multi-ethnic youth speech style which has come to be labelled 'Jafaican' by the media. The academic equivalent is 'Multicultural London English' (MLE), a term coined by linguists around 2006 (Cheshire et al. 2011). This begs the question of whether a media construction and a linguist's label are ever likely to have the same referent. As we will see shortly, there is a tension between the two. Media labels and the discourse around them evoke social stereotypes, and emphasize a handful of linguistic features – often inaccurately. Linguists are reluctant to label varieties, and the labelling they engage in is hedged and seeks to avoid essentialization. A corpus-driven analysis of the emergence of both *Jafaican* and *Multicultural London English* as *media* terms allows us to trace the development and transformation of a number of discourses surrounding them (discourses, put simply, are 'ways of talking about something', following Foucault (Irwin 2011: 104). Some of these discourses are already apparent in the sketch of *rinkebysvenska*: the reification of the variety (as opposed to its being referred to as, say, teenage slang), its non-standardness, its representation as a threat to national cohesion, and its (purported) foreignness. The sketch hints, too, at the interplay of academic and journalistic discourses: the contrast between the two will become clear in what follows.

The chapter is, then, a case study of the mediatization of a language variety in real time. I follow Jaffe's definition here: mediatization 'includes all the representational choices involved in the production and editing of text, image, and talk in the creation of media products' (Jaffe 2009: 572, cited in Androutsopoulos 2011: 106). Androutsopoulos (2011: 106) expands on this as follows:

> Die Mediatisierung eines Medienbeitrags beruht auf Transformationen vorhandener semiotischer Ressourcen, die von Journalisten neu kombiniert und rekontextualisiert werden
>
> (The mediatization of a media story relies on transformations of available semiotic resources which are recontextualized and combined in new ways by journalists [my translation])

The media, in other words, have the capacity to shape their reading or listening public's perception of phenomena which are 'out there', but not as yet conceptualized or pigeon-holed. By the same token, the media can actually create new concepts which may or may not have been perceived by the public at all. If it is a media concept, a language variety can have a discursive life of its own with only a loose relationship with a linguist's descriptive account.

The analysis will be largely restricted to print media. Although explicit mentions of 'Jafaican' are largely restricted to news and cultural reports, they often refer to other media, in particular the use of 'Jafaican'-like varieties in television dramas or soaps. Print references sometimes coincide with a radio or television interview which either immediately preceded or immediately follows it – the two media seem parasitic on one another. A YouTube search for 'Jafaican' yields a small number of videos of Jamaican or British origin, in which the notion of 'fake Jamaican' is treated, while the use of the term in the meaning 'multicultural youth language' is restricted to uploads of a British children's TV series, *Teen London*, in which characters are described as speaking 'indecipherable Jafaican patois'. However, I will discuss one piece of television coverage, one web article published by a political party and one (foreign) online magazine. The reason for including these is that they throw into relief some important, topical discourses surrounding 'Jafaican'.

On the other hand, I will not discuss readers' online comments or other online fora. These throw up a distinct set of problems and possibilities, as pointed out by O'Halloran (2010: 210):

> Many of these engagements [through online discussions] consist of commentary on a parti-
> cular text and can thus be regarded as supplements to these texts ... The larger purpose of
> this article is to flag the utility value of this electronic supplementarity for critical reading
> by highlighting how it can reveal particular meanings that the text being responded to can
> reasonably be said to marginalize and/or repress.

This area of research promises to enrich understandings of media language by dealing with its reception by readers and with the discourses often introduced by readers – discourses which may be only peripherally related to the original text or are in outright opposition to it. The focus here, then, will be on what can be found in the articles themselves through a close textual analysis.

In terms of language change, the media's construction of a language variety belongs to the history of that variety, as Androutsopoulos points out. In a paper on media representation of ethnolects in Germany, Androutsopoulos (2010: 183) sees his contribution as being to both 'language ideology research' and 'current ethnolect research' by extending 'the agenda to language-ideological issues and examin[ing] how media discourse articulates and shapes the social meaning of ethnolects in Germany'. Research on ethnolectal speech (and on 'multieth-nolects' – see below) shows that naming, both within and outside the media, forms an important part of this process: giving a variety a label serves at once to reify it as a 'real' entity and to categorize that entity as one that can be compared with others at the same level, a process often leading to derogation (as we saw in the opening paragraph; also see Androutsopoulos 2007; Jaspers 2008; Quist 2008; Wiese 2012; Kerswill 2013). Interestingly for our later discussion, neither of the terms for the London 'multiethnolect' is a vernacular label and both are largely unknown to its speakers. We can speculate whether, in the future, either of them will be appropriated by speakers (as 'Rinkebysvenska' seems to have been – though others are increasingly used) and, if so, whether this will have an effect on grassroots speakers' perceptions of themselves and their social position, and indeed on language change.

We go on now to a consideration of academic treatments of ethnolects and (by extension) multiethnolects, and their consequences for public discourse. In his 2010 paper, Androutsopoulos suggests that media presentations and representations of the language of young people in Germany generate discourses of othering: this 'language' is foreign, deficient and incorrect, while its speakers by association are un-German, uneducated and a threat. Some of this effect is achieved through explicit naming by journalists using pejorative labels ('*Kanak Sprak*'). The representation of the language through exemplification has a similar effect, by referring explicitly to phonetic, syntactic and lexical features. Androutsopoulos argues that the effect becomes entrenched through repetition – for example the use of the orthographic sequence <isch> to represent the non-standard pronunciation [ʃ] of the German palatal /ç/ – regardless of the fact that this non-standard pronunciation is found in a number of 'native' dialects of German.

The background to the naming of new, informal language varieties turns out to be varied. '*Kanak Sprak*' is, as we have seen, derogatory, though its origins lie in Feridun Zaimoğlu's 1995 book *Kanak Sprak – 24 Mißtöne vom Rande der Gesellschaft*, in which the author reproduces heavily edited recreations of interviews with young people of Turkish origin (Pfaff 2005). Zaimoğlu's intention was to present these people in a positive light, while he characterizes both their German and their Turkish as imperfect and hybrid. Berlin's *Kiezdeutsch*, on the other hand, represents the adoption by an academic – Heike Wiese – of a grassroots concept: on being asked how they would term their way of speaking, some young Berliners told her that they spoke 'as we do in the *Kiez*', or 'neighbourhood', using a Berlin dialect term. This has won acceptance in the academic world (Wiese 2012: 15). Stockholm's *rinkebysvenska* seems similarly to be a grassroots coinage adopted by an academic, though the process is not fully explained. In each case, it would be interesting to trace the subsequent fate of these terms across speaker groups – both putative speakers and non-speakers – as well as media and discourses: does the fact that a term is, or is not, a user-derived label influence later use of the term and attitudes to its use? We return briefly to this question at the end of the chapter.

The evolution of terms such as *Kanak Sprak* and *Kiezdeutsch* is one of *enregisterment*, the process by which a language variety becomes an index of a social group and, later, of a set of social characteristics (we return to this concept in more detail in Section 6.4, below).

We look now at the interaction between academics' and speakers' ideologies with regard to labelling.

Cornips, Jaspers and de Rooij (in press) look specifically at academics' naming practices in relation to that of the youth themselves. Their example, from the Netherlands, is *straattaal*, or 'street language', a term advocated by a Dutch linguist in 1999 to replace derogatory labels such as *smurfentaal* 'Smurf language'. *Straattaal* quickly became a cover term for highly derogated forms of youth language and its speakers: '*straattaal* has become available as a name for disrespectful, deviant or aggressive verbal behaviour, or seems to function as a proxy for dangerous young males and small petty-crime street gangs'. However, the authors report problems with trying to find an acceptable 'technical' label. Jaspers had suggested to some young Antwerp residents of Moroccan ancestry whose language he had been studying that he should use the term 'Moroccan Dutch'; this was not accepted because it gave the impression that the language was imperfect and 'less than normal Dutch'.

As a link back to the media practices studied by Androutsopoulos, and as a springboard for the present study, we can note that Cornips et al. (in press: 9) implicitly criticize linguists for using questionnaires and translation exercises to investigate the grammar and phonology of youth languages: 'The act of translation naturally maximizes the distance between Dutch and *straattaal*, as it also helps to reduce youthful language use to a stock of foreign or deviant words, with no attention for youths' phonological, morpho-syntactic or pragmatic exploitation of linguistic resources, and with no consideration for actual linguistic practices'. Similar accusations could also be directed against the setting up of lists contrasting (multi-)ethnolects and standard language for the purposes of education. Wiese (2012: 270–275) contains a 'Kiezdeutsch test' with solutions; however, couched as it is within a book with an explicit sociolinguistic and critical framework, the use of such a technique seems less problematic. However, such lists are very much characteristic of media treatments of these language 'styles' in Germany and Sweden (and elsewhere), as well as Great Britain, as we shall see. In this case, generally lacking any critical focus and often contained within a discourse of othering, the use of lists can serve to create the distance Cornips et al. are wary of.

2 The London multiethnolect: what it is and what people think about it

The term *multiethnolect* was first used by Clyne (2000) to refer to mixed varieties of the host language shared by immigrants of different language backgrounds.

In north-west Europe, it has been widely applied to the speech of young people (teenagers and young adults) living in multicultural and multilingual districts of large cities: here, we find what are apparently distinctive varieties of Danish, Norwegian, Swedish, Dutch and German spoken by people of various ethnicities and differing minimally between them. Researchers tend to agree that the essentializing terms 'variety' and 'dialect' are problematic in relation to multiethnolects, because these are very clearly youth styles used in various forms of identity projection, and because it is not clear whether they qualify in every case as Labovian 'vernaculars', or baseline varieties, in the way a 'dialect' is most often conceptualized. [2]

The London multiethnolect, Multicultural London English (MLE), has been studied in two ESRC projects run by Jenny Cheshire and Paul Kerswill, with research associates Sue Fox, Eivind Torgersen and Arfaan Khan.[3], [4] The projects' approach was largely variationist, in that they recorded a sample stratified by age, gender, ethnicity and borough. Linguistic features on the phonetic, morphosyntactic and discourse levels were quantified. The results showed a great deal of variation, with the multiethnic inner-city boroughs being quite distinct from the outer city. Particularly in the inner city, features on all levels tended to be shared across ethnicities, though minority ethnic speakers used more characteristically multiethnolectal variants than did their Anglo counterparts. The ethnic divides were, however, relatively fluid, with a speaker's social network being a significant predictor of the use of these features. We consider that MLE is best seen as the variable output of a 'feature pool' (Mufwene 2001: 4–6) derived from the range of language varieties in the inner city, including second-language English, African, Caribbean and Asian Englishes, local dialect ('Cockney'), London Jamaican Creole (Sebba 1993), Standard English – and also languages other than English.

In the corpus analysis to follow, I will consider which features, if any, the media have picked up upon. Here, as a reference, are the main linguistic find-

---

2 Quist (2008), Jaspers (2008), Svendsen and Røyneland (2008) and Wiese (2009) are representative of this research strand, as well of the stance described.

3 *Linguistic innovators: the English of adolescents in London* 2004–7, funded by the Economic and Social Research Council, Principal Investigator Paul Kerswill, Co-investigator Jenny Cheshire, Research Associates Susan Fox and Eivind Torgersen (ref. RES 000-23-0680). See Kerswill, Torgersen and Fox (2008) and Cheshire and Fox (2009).

4 *Multicultural London English: the emergence, acquisition and diffusion of a new variety* 2007–10, funded by the Economic and Social Research Council, Principal Investigator Paul Kerswill, Co-investigator Jenny Cheshire, Research Associates Susan Fox, Arfaan Khan and Eivind Torgersen (ref. RES-062-23-0814).

ings of the MLE projects. Only those changes which are not also characteristic of regional southeastern changes are given here:

1. Changes in the long vowel system, notably narrow diphthongs or monophthongs for vowels of the lexical sets of FACE and GOAT (Wells 1982), replacing the broad diphthongs of Cockney. Schematically, the changes are: [æɪ] → [eɪ] and [ʌʊ] → [oʊ], respectively. Importantly, the raising and backing of GOAT in MLE competes with the fronting of this vowel in levelled varieties in the South East to [əʏ].
2. Backing of /k/ before low back vowels to [q]
3. Full reinstatement of /h/ in lexical words and stressed pronouns, to an extent greater than non-MLE southeastern varieties (the region, including London, is traditionally h-dropping)
4. More syllable-timed (staccato) rhythm (Torgersen and Szakay 2012)
5. Use of a distinct levelling pattern for the past tense of BE: MLE speakers tend to level the forms to *was* and *wasn't* throughout the paradigm, instead of the widespread levelling to *was* and *weren't*.
6. Use of a new quotative: *this is* + SPEAKER, as in 'This is me: let's go now'
7. Widespread use of slang, including *blood* (friend), *cuss* (defame), *ends* (place of residence), *mandem* (Creole plural), *rude, safe, tief* (steal), *man* (as address term), *man* (as indefinite pronoun – see Cheshire 2013). Many of these are of Jamaican origin.

To anticipate: the only features which are referred to are slang terms, most of which are believed by the writers to be of Jamaican origin. Where whole utterances are represented, they are in Standard English with a heavy use of slang. Pronunciation seems never to be commented upon.

In another paper (Kerswill 2013), I used a corpus linguistic methodology to get at young speakers' own opinions and conceptualizations around identity and language. Using concordances and keyword analyses of our transcribed London youth language corpora totalling just under 1.4 million words, I examined the discourse surrounding the term 'Cockney', which was a topic introduced by the interviewer. ('Cockney' is the traditional designation for working-class Londoners from the 'East End', and their dialect.) The results showed that the speakers tended not to associate themselves with the term Cockney, either as an identity marker or, particularly, a language variety. This was stronger for the non-Anglo (minority ethnic) speakers. In the multiethnic inner city, there was little talk of race as a dividing factor, while this was more frequently a topic in the (mainly Anglo, or 'White British') outer city. In terms of their language, most people had no specific label. The majority referred to it as 'slang', and it was clear that what was being referred to was a general youth style with a large proportion of slang terms of Jamaican origin. During the interviews, the term 'Jafaican' was not discussed or even mentioned, because there was no evidence that the term was being used in any of the relevant ways – in fact, in the early phases of the research (2004–5), we were completely unaware of it, even in an earlier but still current sense of 'person pretending to be Jamaican by affecting Jamaican speech, clothing and appearance'.

Londoners in general, however, seem conscious of a style of speaking which is often labelled 'talking black', and this term was used on occasion in our interviews. They report that it is often difficult to tell the ethnicity of a speaker from language alone, and that there is a tendency to hear more people as 'black' than actually are.

This type of multiethnolectal speech is increasingly condemned by a wide range of authority figures, particularly in education, among members of Parliament, and some sections of the print and televisual media. The point often made is that young people, especially black males, are seen as unable to shift from an MLE-type variety, laden with slang, to a more standard one in situations where this is required (Robson 2011, quoting the Guyanan writer Gus John; we will return to this article later in the chapter). In 2008, a secondary school in Manchester banned the use of slang anywhere on the school premises. This was reported across the media, largely winning approval from commentators and (as witnessed by online readers' comments) sections of the public, too ('School bans youth slang and sees exam results soar'[5]). It is clear that the language that is objected to is contemporary British youth slang, which is not necessarily part of a multiethnolect. Some of the words are Jamaican in origin, to judge from the list given at the end of the article which includes *blood* and *cuss*.

A seminal event in the history of multiethnolectal speech came in August 2011, when major, spontaneous riots took place in London and other cities. In London, the perpetrators could be heard speaking in this multiethnolect, and many could be seen to be black. Media coverage was intense, and many commentators voiced their opinions. One such commentator was David Starkey, a medieval historian and successful television history presenter. He took part in a live discussion on BBC TV's *Newsnight*, during which he made an explicit link between this type of language, violence and black culture, and stated that white people had bought into it, becoming 'black' in the process. We will look in more detail at what Starkey said later in the chapter.

In what follows, I shall be using an online corpus of British newspapers to explore media awareness of this style of speech and the discourses which the

---

5 http://www.telegraph.co.uk/education/2435923/School-bans-youth-slang-and-sees-exam-results-soar.html

newspapers develop. First, we will examine the development of the multieth-nolect.

3 London's multiethnolect: A short history

The first published report of a precursor to today's multiethnolect is Hewitt's *White Talk Black Talk* (1986). In this study, he is concerned with the speech repertoires of young black and white Londoners. Writing about young Afro-Caribbeans' repertoire, he says that on the one hand there is:

> [...] strongly pronounced Caribbean Creole ... and, on the other, an everyday, vernacular language form which incorporates words from Creole ... Turkish or Punjabi into a basically English stock. ... [This is] 'Black Cockney' ... [the] primary medium of communication in the adolescent peer group in multi-ethnic areas. (Hewitt 1991/2003: 193)

Turning to the speech of both white and minority young people, he writes:

> [This is] the language of white as well as minority youth and it is the language which is switched from and back into when its users choose to move into Creole or Punjabi ... (Hewitt 1991/2003: 193)

In the 1980s, there was, it appears, a distinct, multicultural variety which young people could switch into, and out of, from their own vernaculars. Its distinguishing feature was the use of slang, mostly from Jamaican Creole. Hewitt (1986: 134) mentions only one pronunciation feature, a back and raised variant of the vowel /ʌ/ as in *come*. This is characteristic of Jamaican Creole, but *not* of today's MLE. Sebba (1993) claims that there are no obvious pronunciation differences between young black and white Londoners (his data is from 1983–1984), stating (p. 64): 'Black Londoners sound for the most part *very* London'. Yet both authors cite evidence that the ethnicity of most young Londoners *could* be identified from recordings alone. From contemporary reports, there is, then, evidence both of a nascent multiethnolect used as an in-group variety, as well as some features occasionally marking a young London speaker as black. The vernacular for most young people was a variety phonologically close to descriptions of traditional Cockney. This is corroborated by a new analysis of Sebba's 1983–1984 tapes of teenage London African Caribbean speakers: Kerswill and Sebba (2011) found that these speakers' vowel systems corresponded closely to those of white Londoners from the same period, with the phonetic changes noted above as characteristic of MLE only sporadically or incipiently present. A number of the same speakers had also been recorded using a Creole variety, with vowel formants matching those found to be characteristic of Jamaican Creole (Thomas 2001: 163) – suggesting that code-switching was a common practice.

Cheshire et al. (2011) argue that, today, the vernacular for most working-class, inner-city young speakers has moved away from a traditional Cockney-derived variety to one that contains, in varying degrees, the features listed in Section 2, above. This is the variety that is the focus of this chapter.

4 Entries referring to the multiethnolect in the *Urban Dictionary*

In deciding on a search term for London's multiethnolect, I focused on the one that (as already noted) appears to be most widespread in the media, *Jafaican* and its spelling variant *Jafaikan*. To get an initial idea of the range of dictionary meanings, and possibly discourses, which might exist, I consulted the wiki, *Urban Dictionary*. There are seven entries, as follows (slightly abridged and reformatted, but keeping the original spelling and spaces, and showing the date of posting):

1. Jafaikan (7 May 2008)

Jafaikan is the language of British people who talk in a fake jamaican accent and use words like 'bizzle' 'blad' 'shizzle' 'innit' etc etc etc
They arent always white either, theres a lot of asian and black Jafaikan speakers out there.
"chill out blad, look at them beanies cutchin over there innit tho"
"You what mate? oh right youre a fuckin Jafaikan yeah"?

1. Jafaican (20 April 2006)

Jafaican is a dialect of English becoming more common in London's West End, within the tradition boundaries of the Cockney dialect: within the sound of the Bow bells and is slowly replacing Cockney. Jafaican is a mixture of English, Jamaican, West Indian and Indian language elements.
Some Jafaican, for you reading pleasure:
Safe, man. You lookin buff in dem low batties. Dey's sick, man. Me? I'm just jammin wid me bruds. Dis my yard, innit? Is nang, you get me? No? What ends you from then?
Jafaican is the British ebonics.

2. Jafaican (13 June 2003)

A person that acts like they Jamaican ie;try talk like they jamaican, try act like they jamaican but they're not!

3. Jafaican (20 October 2009)

a person who pretends to be jamaican.
a middle class suburban white kid using patoi.

"me nah know botty ridah fa rotty bidah!"
.'wow.that kids a jafaican."

4. Jafaican (11 March 2009)

When some one is trying act getto or gangsta but with a jamaican bent.
"Tom has had his hair in dreads for months now". "Yea, he is Jafaican".

5. Jafaican (13 July 2003)

somebody, usually black whos mind leads them to believe they are jamaican but in reality they aint no jamaican
anne-marie is such a jafaican

6. Jafaican (23 November 2007)

Singer or actor who claims to be from Jamaica, trying to sound cool with fake accent.
Those two Sean guys, one a Jamaican, the other's a jafaican.
uh uh uh uh oh ooh.

7. Jafaican (13 September 2009)

Anyone with an obsession with Jamaican music, hairstyles (dreadlocks), and clothing. They tend to listen to Bob Marley and other types reggae. And occasionally they will throw on a fake accent. If you see a Jafaican don't ask them for weed. Because for some strange reason they usually don't smoke.
1. Anyone with bad dreads is jafaican.
2. Someone blasting reggae out of their car is jafaican.
3. Anyone with more than two Bob Marley pictures in their house is jafaican.
4. Someone that wishes they can be like Bob Marley might be jafaican.
5. Non-smoking Jamaicans are jafaican.

There are just two meanings here. The first two entries, 1. Jafaikan and 1. Jafaican, refer explicitly to London (or at least British) speech which is Jamaican-influenced in terms of vocabulary. While 1. Jafaikan refers to it as 'fake' Jamaican, 1. Jafaican sees it as a 'dialect of English', thereby according it a 'serious' status. The remainder all focus on 'fake Jamaican' style, appearance and musical tastes. 7. Jafaican is more concerned with Jamaican stereotypes than with wannabes. It is not obvious where the contributors come from (whether the UK, the US or the Caribbean), but it is clear that the targets of the opprobrium are mainly white, though some are black. In drawing attention to fakeness, all but the second of the definitions (1. Jafaican) are concerned with a violation of authenticity. Fakeness appears to be the only relevant discourse which can be identified here. Dates of posting are, however of interest: the two earliest, from 2003, refer to fake Jamaican style, while the sense 'London/British youth language' dates only from April 2006 – suggesting this sense had become more widely known at that time.

Since the date of the original search (July 2012), the term 'Multicultural London English' made its first appearance:

1. Multicultural London English (MLE) (6 September 2012)

> Multicultural London English is the cultural change in the English language due to influences from various cultures such as Jamaican. Originated in London (due to be such a multicultural area) and quickly spreading to other areas of the UK through use and also through grime music. It is the first time English Language in the UK has been changed nationally by the teen age group. Usually areas had their own slang words but MLE is quickly becoming the standard slang through out the UK.
>
> *Multicultural London English (MLE) example slang words: Manz, Hype, Ting, Fam, Blud (Blad), Cus, Bredrin, Nang, Dench, My Size, Famalam and various other words*

This entry reads like an expanded version of 1. Jafaican, though with a stronger focus on slang, and suggests that the writer was aware of the print media discussions which had appeared by then.

5 The multiethnolect in the newspapers: A quantitative analysis of mentions

Nexis UK is a commercial online database of English-language newspapers and other publications, going back to the early 1980s. Selecting the option 'All English Language News' I searched for occurrences of *Jafaican* and *Jafaikan*, supplementing these with a search for our own coinage, *Multicultural London English*.[6] A total of 58 different articles contained at least one occurrence of *Jafaican*, and a further 4 contained the variant, *Jafaikan*. A total of 29 contained *Multicultural London English*, of which 20 also contained *Jafaican* (and none *Jafaikan*). The next stage was to register the dates on which these articles were published. There are two reasons for doing so: first, to investigate the first mentions, and secondly to see if there are clusters which might correspond to a particular event. Figure 1 shows occurrences of *Jafaican* and *Jafaikan* in the database, including US articles.

Figure 1 excludes the single occurrence of this term before 2006: this is in fact the only non-British occurrence. It is from 2002, and refers to people dressing in a 'fake Jamaican' manner at a music festival in New York. The remainder refer to youth language in London, and date from 10 April 2006 onwards. This fact

---

6 The search was performed in early July 2012. In the period mid-July 2012 to mid-January 2013, a further 12 articles carried the term *Jafaican/Jafaikan*, and two more mentioned *Multicultural London English*.

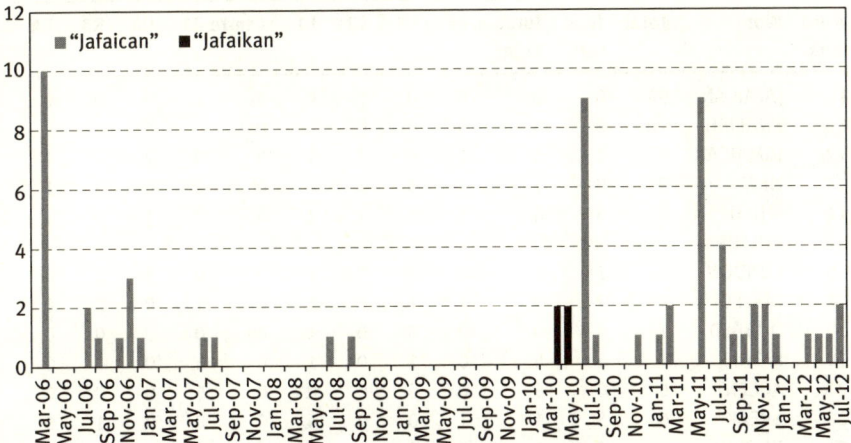

Figure 1: Occurrences of *Jafaican* and *Jafaikan* in English-language newspapers, showing monthly total of articles (Nexis UK database) and excluding a single occurrence from 2002 (see text)

suggests that the author of the first *Urban Dictionary* entry, from 20 April, was directly influenced by the media coverage in the preceding week.

What can we say about the discourses surrounding 'Jafaican'? We can begin with a quantitative methodology, using corpus linguistic methods to look for collocates of *Jafaican*. Using WordSmith Tools 5.0, we can find out which words tend to occur with *Jafaican* a specified number of places to the left (preceding the target word) and to the right (following it). (See Baker 2006 for details of this technique.) Table 1 shows the result of this analysis for 4 places to the left and right. All function words have been removed, as have words with a frequency of less than 3.

The table shows that there are 94 occurrences of *Jafaican*. To take an example, the word *English* occurs 10 times in the vicinity of *Jafaican*, up to 4 places on either side. What can we learn from this analysis? The first is that it is strongly associated with *English, Jamaican, new, multicultural* and *London*. A concordance analysis reveals that most of the tokens of *English, multicultural* and *London* in fact occur in the phrase 'Multicultural London English', which suggests that writers are aware of the equivalence of this and *Jafaican*. Likewise, *Jamaican* tends to go with *patois*. The further we go down the list of collocates, the more possible discourses reveal themselves. Jafaican is seen as a dialect or an accent, not a style or youth language. However, *dubbed*, four of whose seven occurrences are to the immediate left of *Jafaican*, suggests that the term 'Jafaican' is not quite academically acceptable – the frequently mentioned *Multicultural London English* fills

Word rank	Word	Total	Total Left	Total Right	L4	L3	L2	L1	Centre	R1	R2	R3	R4
1	JAFAICAN	94	0	0	0	0	0	0	94	0	0	0	0
10	ENGLISH	10	6	4	0	4	2	0	0	0	0	4	0
12	JAMAICAN	9	3	6	1	0	1	1	0	0	2	0	4
13	NEW	9	8	1	3	3	1	1	0	0	0	0	1
14	MULTI-CULTURAL	9	5	4	3	0	1	1	0	2	1	0	1
15	LONDON	8	7	1	3	3	0	1	0	0	1	0	0
17	DIALECT	8	7	1	1	1	4	1	0	1	0	0	0
18	DUBBED	7	7	0	0	3	0	4	0	0	0	0	0
19	PATOIS	7	2	5	0	1	0	1	0	4	0	1	0
21	ACCENT	6	0	6	0	0	0	0	0	6	0	0	0
22	SPEAK	6	5	1	1	0	0	4	0	0	0	1	0
24	KNOWN	6	5	1	0	0	5	0	0	0	1	0	0
26	CALLED	6	6	0	0	0	1	5	0	0	0	0	0
27	SLANG	6	5	1	0	4	0	1	0	0	1	0	0
31	FAKE	5	2	3	0	1	1	0	0	2	0	1	0
34	TIKKINY	4	1	3	0	0	0	1	0	0	2	0	1
36	COCKNEY	4	1	3	0	0	1	0	0	0	1	1	1
37	CARIBBEAN	4	2	2	1	0	0	1	0	0	0	0	2
40	STREET	4	3	1	2	0	1	0	0	0	0	1	0
41	MIXTURE	3	0	3	0	0	0	0	0	0	1	2	0
44	SPEECH	3	2	1	0	0	2	0	0	0	0	0	1
45	NAME	3	1	2	0	0	0	1	0	1	0	1	0
46	TERMS	3	3	0	0	0	2	1	0	0	0	0	0
52	CREPS	3	0	3	0	0	0	0	0	2	0	1	0
53	PHENO-MENON	3	3	0	0	0	0	3	0	0	0	0	0
56	LANGUAGE	3	0	3	0	0	0	0	0	0	1	1	1
57	ALI	3	1	2	1	0	0	0	0	0	0	2	0

Table 1: Collocations of *Jafaican* in Nexis UK newspaper corpus analysis (up to four places to the left and right)

this role. The relatively high frequency of *fake* reflects the inauthenticity we noted above in the *Urban Dictionary* entries. The internal morphology of 'Jafaican', suggesting both 'Jamaican' and 'fake', may well contribute to this. The fact that the Continental European terms do not have this structure may well be reflected in the lack of an association with inauthenticity, though these language varieties are regarded as both imperfect and hybrid.

So far, there is little suggestion of strongly negative or positive attitudes to Jafaican: the furthest we get is the hints of inauthenticity. An examination of the newspaper texts themselves is much more revealing, and we turn to these now.

6 The multiethnolect in the newspapers: evolving discourses and metaphors

So that we can discern the development of discourses through time, I will present the texts roughly in chronological order. It turns out, as we will see, that this development is very rapid, sometimes over a few days, while there are less active periods where the existing discourses are recycled, for the most part without reference to or (perhaps) even knowledge of previous discussions of the topic. What follows is subdivided into a number of themes which in many cases subsume particular discourses and metaphors.

6.1 Jafaican as agent: The cuckoo in the nest, pushing out the natives

By the time of the earliest print media attestations, 'Jafaican' is already a labelled language variety, set alongside others, particularly 'Cockney'. Probably the most frequently occurring theme is the notion that Jafaican is 'pushing' Cockney out of its East End heartland. Here is the very first article, from *The Evening Standard* on 10 April 2006. I cite it in full (minus the continuation of the list of slang terms) since it contains features which were to recur in later articles:

THE Cockney accent is being pushed out of its heartland by a new kind of speech.

Playgrounds and housing estates of London are alive with the sound of an accent that sounds Jamaican with flavours from West Africa and India.

The Standard can reveal that this new English variety is replacing Cockney in inner London, as more white children adopt the speech patterns and vocabulary of their black neighbours and classmates.

Teachers have dubbed the phenomenon Jafaican and TV's Ali G would understand it perfectly.

Linguistics experts from London University's Queen Mary College and Lancaster University are conducting field studies to assess the new variety of English and how widely it is spoken. Queen Mary researcher Sue Fox said: "The adolescents who use this accent are those of second- or third-generation immigrant background, followed by whites of London origin." Based on their preliminary findings, the academics are calling it "Multicultural London English".

An oldies' guide to today's yoof speak

creps: trainers
yard: home
yoot: child/children
blud/bredren/bruv: mate

ends: area/estate/neighbourhood (as in "what ends you from?")
low batties: trousers that hang low on the waist

As if aware that this is the first mention of 'Jafaican' in the print media, the journalist proclaims: 'The Standard can reveal that this new English variety is replacing Cockney ...', and goes on to introduce both 'Jafaican' and its scholarly alternative 'Multicultural London English'. The notion that '[t]eachers have dubbed the phenomenon Jafaican' is impossible to verify; the source of this notion is not clear.

As we saw at the beginning of the chapter, the naming of a style or mode of speech reifies it and allows it to be set up against other speech varieties. Descriptive linguists may well argue for this view, too, but journalists are able to deploy metaphors which presuppose the existence of entities – language varieties – which, through anthropomorphism, can be seen as having both agency and an identity. The first metaphor in the extract above is of invasion. The second is the notion that a language variety, like a people or an ethnicity, have a 'homeland'. Here, the invader is ousting Cockney from the place in which it matured and thrived and where its authenticity is guaranteed. But these metaphors are not developed: instead, Jafaican is seen as an object to be investigated. Apart from the opening, there is an air of objectivity to this article, with our research cited as a source for the information.

The article finishes with a glossary, as if this were a foreign, even exotic language. 'Foreignness' is, so far, not a major theme, however. It would very much become so in the next five years. As we shall see, glossaries containing slang are a stock-in-trade of print media treatments. Slang items also serve as defining criteria for young Londoners' constructions of their own language, as we saw earlier, with no mention of pronunciation, grammar or discourse features.

6.2 Jafaican as a problem (1): Inappropriate in formal contexts

On the same day, a similar, but longer article appeared in the same paper. This article finishes with the following:

> But Gary Philips, head of Lilian Baylis in Kennington, said it is not allowed in his classrooms.
>
> "You can speak how you want to friends in the playground – but in the classroom standard English is important because that is what they are being marked for in exams."

Here, we find the beginnings of concern with Jafaican as a 'problem' to be solved, a possible threat to educational standards. This theme, as we will see, recurs and intensifies.

6.3 Jafaican as natural linguistic development

The following day, 11 April, *The Independent*, *The Mail* and *The Sun* followed up with similar pieces, to a large extent parasitic on *The Evening Standard*'s. *The Independent* also had a word list, but found a different external commentator:

> David Roberts of the Queen's English Society said the move was part of the general development of language and should not be regarded as inferior to other codes so long as it was readily understandable to others. "The only purpose of language is to convey thoughts from inside one person's head to another as accurately and comprehensively as possible. Language must be able to adapt. If it hadn't we would all be addressing each other as thou and thee. You cannot put constraints on the development of language."

The Queen's English Society promotes 'correctness' in writing and speech. Its reaction here comes as something of a surprise: the discourse concerns language as a living and adaptable thing, and the idea that different language varieties are in some sense equal. And exactly this attitude is expressed by another Queen's English Society member in response to a further article published two days later by the Associated Press:

> And while Jafaican and other dialects may be "rather ugly on the ear," they deserve recognition as legitimate forms of proper speech, said Michael Plumbe, chairman of the Queen's English Society, a London-based institute pledged to preserve proper British English grammar, usage and pronunciation.
>
> "It's a natural progression to change language in any society," Plumbe said. "As long as its clearly enunciated, it's fine."

This rather accommodating line of reasoning turns out to be the exception, however.

6.4 The enregisterment of Jafaican by the media: Are you 'in the know'?

A different form of recognition for Jafaican comes in yet another article from *The Evening Standard* on 12 April 2006, on the rise of the 'Gruppy' ('retired groupie' – *Urban Dictionary*). The journalist invites the reader to consider the following varieties of language (which might be used by a gruppy):

> Which of these sentences/dialects are you most likely to utilize:
> a) "Raaass man, me gwan me yard see me babymother/babyfather" (Jafaican for "I'm off home to my better half").
> b) "Issa paw show orroun', yarsk muy" (Estuary for "What a disappointment, on every count, in my opinion").

c) "Orright geeeezaaaah/treacle, owzit gan, 'en?" (Mockney for "How do you do?").
d) "Air hellair, hi yu? Beck f'm Yurp? (Home Counties for "Good morning. Have you just returned from your continental holiday?").

Here, 'Jafaican' is for the first time embedded within a national culture where language varieties can legitimately be made fun of. Jafaican is set alongside other stereotyped language varieties: Estuary English (a levelled south-eastern variety), mock, or affected Cockney, and a version of Received Pronunciation. Jafaican has gained recognition and can now be stereotyped, not (only) presented as new and exotic. Readers are supposed to recognize the four language varieties through a combination of common-sense knowledge and a close awareness of recent media stories; here, I would suggest, the recognition of the 'Jafaican' extract – both the name and the linguistic form – is heavily reliant on media interdiscursivity, since of the four varieties it is the most recent to enter public discourse – only two days before in the case of the print media!

Whereas the articles we have already mentioned deal with 'Jafaican' as a threatening agent or a problem, we are dealing here with a stage in the full enregisterment of Jafaican. *Enregisterment* refers to the social perception of a language variety as a register, or style, where both of these terms refer to the recognition of a relationship between the linguistic forms and social characteristics or social situations. Johnstone (2010: 34), summarising Agha (2003), states: 'A register emerges when a number of indexical relationships begin to be seen as related; a particular linguistic form (or non-linguistic sign) is 'enregistered' when it becomes included in a register'. She cites the example of 'Pittsburghese', a working-class accent which only became noticed by local people in the 1960s when 'the right historical, geographical and ideological conditions were in place' (2010: 34). 'Pittsburghese' became associated with a small set of linguistic forms and also local identities, and hence 'enregistered'. In the Jafaican case, enregisterment appears to be rapid (perhaps over as little as a few days), but so far much less firmly entrenched and, unlike Pittsburghese, existing only in media discourse and readers' online comments (almost always negative): arguably the appearance of Jafaican terms in advertising, printed *en masse* on t-shirts, etc., has the potential to give offence and to incite hatred, given the low, even marginal, social status of many of its speakers. This is despite the fact that young people explicitly claim the variety ('slang') as their own (Kerswill 2013), and despite the strong presence of a multiethnolect in locally-targeted advertising in other cities, such as the Belgian city of Genk (Marzo and Ceuleers 2011).

The enregisterment of 'Jafaican' is essential to the following extract from a much later *Daily Mail* article on sources of supposed waste of public money (30 July 2012):

Thank you for calling the Equality Hotline. Please hold. All our operators are busy squabbling among themselves.

Hello.

Our services are available in 207 different languages. Please choose from the following menu. For Urdu, press 1. For Jafaican, press 2. For Scribble, press 3...

The (real) Equality Commission hotline, which reportedly had only received 73 calls, is lampooned for its multiculturalism, in line with the newspaper's anti-political correctness agenda. However, as so often, we are none the wiser as to the precise referent of 'Jafaican'.

6.5 Jafaican as 'foreign', but not (yet) a threat

The version of Jafaican depicted in the 2006 *Evening Standard* extract above is clearly not Standard or dialectal English, nor even MLE as outlined earlier: the subject form 'me', /gwɑn/ for 'going' and 'yard' for 'home' are Jamaican, while *babymother* and *babyfather* are originally Jamaican words for 'unmarried mother/father' now found as British slang terms. Earlier, I referred to the idea of Jafaican as 'foreign'; here, we see it represented by an utterance that is Jamaican in grammar, lexis and phonology. Importantly, Sebba (1993) showed that the version of Jamaican Creole spoken by young Afro-Caribbean Londoners emerged in London, and was also used by young black people who did not have Jamaican ancestry. Whether the representation above betokens 'foreignness' is therefore open to dispute, yet (as we shall see) the later emphasis on the 'Jamaicanness' of Jafaican/MLE suggests a shift in this direction. 'Foreignness' is taken up a couple of years later by right-wing organizations, as we shall see.

6.6 Jafaican as a problem (2): A cultural threat to gender equality

Already on 14 April we see Jafaican portrayed for the first time as representing an undesirable culture. The left-of-centre *Independent* ran a feature entitled 'Conservative to the core: To celebrate today's street slang as fun and trendy is to ignore its deep-rooted misogyny':

> There is a new language on the streets of London and other British cities, according to academic research: "Jafaican", supposedly derived from Jamaican and African slang, is now way more prevalent than Cockney. Despite the name, there is in reality no racial demarcation and a good deal more Ali G posturing here than genuine Jamaican roots, and the chief uniting feature of Jafaican speakers is age (very young).

But when you read the newspaper reports, you can smell the benign neutrality wafting off the page. "Listen here, chaps. When youngsters today say 'jamming', they mean hanging around! 'Nang' might not sound like a word to you and me, but it means good. 'Sket' is a loose woman, and 'bitch' continues to mean girlfriend – but sket seems to have replaced 'ho', which is now woefully out of date and used only by the rap community because it rhymes with so many things. 'Babymamma' has come and gone, to be overtaken by the old-fashioned sounding 'wifey'."

What all these words in fact have in common is that they define women by sexual function – denigrating them if they show any interest in sex themselves, ranging them according to their physical attributes and dismissing them once their physical peak has passed.

After an objective-sounding introductory paragraph, though with disdain contained in the words 'supposedly' and 'posturing', the writer goes on to condemn the Jafaican word lists which had been published that week on the grounds of their misogyny. The language variety may be cool, but it is also deeply conservative and oppressive to women. There is an intimation here of what will come in 2011: the direct association of Jafaican with unacceptable behaviour. The fact that there is no explicit link made between Jafaican, its apparently misogynous vocabulary and the culture from which both might be considered to spring does not obscure the fact that this link is being made implicitly: perhaps to make the association with Jamaica or another non-British, developing country could be seen as too racist or at best illiberal for this newspaper.

6.7 Jafaican as norm: The British music industry

The London music scene was heavily influenced by Jamaican music in the 1950s to 1970s, due to the influence of such people as Smiley Culture (David Emmanuel). In a famous video, *Cockney Translation* (1984), Smiley Culture can be heard contrasting the Jamaican of the immigrants with the local Cockney of the host population. Nowadays, Jamaican Creole has merged with strongly slang-laden Jafaican to form the mainstream accent in hip-hop, at least in London, in later decades. *The Daily Telegraph* comments on this on 23 December 2006:

> It's significant that the message-board of the new Englishness is MySpace, the social networking website that somehow flattens out the traditional nuances of class differentiation. It's there, too, in the magpie lexicon from which the lyrics are drawn, with many of them delivered in the fertile hybrid of Cockney, the Queen's English and pretend Jamaican – what's it called? Jafaican? – that is the lingua franca of young southern England.

The tone here is objective, approving even. Jafaican joins the mainstream as part of the 'new Englishness', which strives for classlessness.

6.8 Cockney as a museum piece

The years up to mid-2011 see 'more of the same' with opinions and journalistic approaches being recycled with modifications – often in apparent ignorance of previous media reports. In 2010, we find an initiative by the King's Place arts centre in London to have Londoners record their elderly relatives for posterity, intended to form an archive. A motivation for this was the encroachment of Jafaican, reported as follows in the *Mail* on 2 July 2010:

> Paul Kerswill, professor of sociolinguistics at Lancaster University, said: 'In much of the East End of London, the Cockney dialect that we hear now spoken by older people will have disappeared within another generation.
>
> 'People in their 40s will be the last generation to speak it and it will be gone within 30 years.' He said East Enders had for decades been moving into Essex and Hertfordshire and their traditional accent was being 'transplanted' with them.
>
> 'Cockney in the East End is transforming itself into multi-cultural London English, a new, melting-pot mixture of all those people living here who learnt English as a second language,' he added.
>
> Now the dwindling ranks of Cockney speakers are being asked to record their voices for posterity. The Kings Place arts centre in central London also plans to post a downloadable recording of Bow Bells on its website so that Cockneys who have moved away can still let their children be born within the sound of its chimes.

For the first time, the potential loss of Cockney (though I was careful to talk about its 'transformation') is now seen as a problem, to be addressed by the archival preservation of what is seen here as a disappearing dialect. In fact, this initiative came to virtually nothing: according to the organizer, only one person submitted material – suggesting that the media's and (some) intellectuals' concern is not shared by speakers themselves (in this case, working-class Londoners). Below, we will see a different reaction to the reported replacement of Cockney by Jafaican as revealed in the writings of some other public institutions: right-wing political parties and organizations.

6.9 Enregisterment – again

Increasing recognition of Jafaican as a cultural phenomenon that people 'in the know' should be aware of comes in an end-of-year quiz in *The Evening Standard* on 24 December 2010. Among the questions was:

How did Nang, Greezy and Butters triumph in 2010?

a)   They are the producers who work on the X Factor winner's recordings.
b)   They are the stars of a new CBeebies show.
c)   They are "street" or "Jafaican" expressions which have overtaken Cockney slang terms.
d)   They are ingredients popularised by Delia Smith in her last Waitrose promotion.

– the answer being (c). However, this is of course an act of journalistic amnesia: 'Jafaican' is being hailed as a news item in 2010, with no regard to its appearance in the 2006 quiz in the very same paper.

The predicted demise of Cockney continues to be referred to with some alarm, with some journalists claiming that it is 650 years old and will disappear in just a few years.

6.10 Jafaican as a problem (3):
Bad language, challenging dress style and bad behaviour

We now come to the first example of Jafaican being associated specifically with modes of dress and problematic behaviour, from a review of television in the *Mirror* on 23rd March 2011, five years after the first journalistic mention of the term. The review is of an episode of Midsomer Murders, set in genteel rural England:

> One of the star guests is a DJ called Dave Doggy Day – complete with loud hoodie and Jafaican accent. Somebody is about to give him the message that his sort just aren't welcome round these parts.

The producers have rather self-consciously 'othered' this character – but he is not 'foreign', just not from 'these parts'. For the first time, we read a reference to Jafaican as an 'accent', by implication 'of English'. There is no mention this time of slang; as a result, any link with Jamaican Creole is not present, though (most likely) not consciously avoided.

Similar comments can be made about a review of a sitcom intended for children, which appeared in *The Independent on Sunday* on 5 June 2011:

> Although it dealt with teenage sex – or the lack of it – drugs, and parental rebellion, it steered clear of any real issues, so there was no "Jafaican" spoken, no stabbings or gun crime, no teenage abortion.

There is an explicit link here between Jafaican and bad behaviour. Jafaican is an 'issue', according to this journalist.

The idea of Jafaican as 'bad' was made particularly forcefully by David Starkey in his BBC TV *Newsnight* appearance after the summer 2011 riots. He didn't use the term, but he did say:

> The whites have become black. A particular sort of violent, destructive, nihilistic, gangster culture has become the fashion, and black and white, boy and girl, operate in this language together, this language which is wholly false, which is this Jamaican patois that has been intruded in England, and that is why so many of us have this sense of, literally, a foreign country. (David Starkey, *Newsnight*, 13 August 2011)

This statement sparked powerful reactions in the print media as well as on air. There was controversy on all levels, ranging from issues of multiculturalism, integration, immigration and race to the role of language. Starkey talks about a foreign, black, Jamaican culture and language which young Londoners are buying into. According to Sebba and Dray (2013), Starkey's statement 'highlights a public preoccupation with the ownership of language varieties and accents in their 'pure' form'. Regardless of their political stance and their opinions about the cause of the riots, few commentators defended Starkey's claim that this language was foreign. A telling case is that of Katharine Birbalsingh, a well-known blogger for the conservative broadsheet newspaper *The Daily Telegraph*. Like Starkey, she sees what she calls 'gangsta culture' as the root of the riot problem. But her linguistic analysis of London's youth differs sharply:

> Lastly, Starkey's claim that he feels like a foreigner in his own country because Jamaican patois rules the streets is laughable. Has David Starkey ever been to Jamaica? My mother is Jamaican, and I can assure you that she sounds nothing like our out-of-control kids! For one, the accent Starkey is talking about is specific to London ... Two, that accent ... is uniquely ENGLISH. It is a kind of fusion of many cultures, including Cockney East End speech. One can also hear some Jamaican influence, general working-class London influence and so on. Does Starkey really believe that Jamaicans go around saying "innit"? "Innit" has a Cockney glottal stop in it! ... [T]his accent not only is not Jamaican, but neither is it in American gangster culture. What MTV rapper sounds like our kids?
>
> (*Daily Telegraph* blog, 15th August 2011)

Birbalsingh does not make a link between black speech, or 'that accent' as she puts it, and the riots, in the way Starkey does. Unusually for journalistic treatments, her focus is on pronunciation; as we saw above, discussing 'accent' and not slang allows the writer to emphasize that this is a home-grown variety of English.

We should briefly look at the web pages of one of a number of avowedly anti-immigration political organizations and their treatment of the same discourse of 'foreignness' and 'threat'. The following appeared on the British National Party site in February 2011 (http://www.bnp.org.uk/news/cockneys-have-become-first-british-group-be-ethnically-cleansed):

Cockneys Have Become First British Group to be Ethnically Cleansed

The Cockney culture and language has been ethnically cleansed from London's East End as mass Third World immigration has pushed white people into minority status and destroyed the world-famous accent.

According to an analysis of demographic figures — which are already several years out of date — white British people make up as less than 40 percent of the population in the areas of London traditionally associated with Cockneys.

Furthermore, the world famous Cockney accent and rhyming slang has already been completely replaced amongst the younger age groups in the region as they form the over-whelming majority of that population.

True Cockney, a dialect more than 500 years old, is now spoken only by the elderly in London and will, a study recently showed, be completely extinct within 30 years.

Cockney is being replaced by what is politely called "Multicultural London English" or LME for short. LME is also known as "Jafaican" which is a combination of Jamacian, African and Asian.

Traditionally, people born within earshot of the bells of the church of St. Mary-le-Bow in Cheapside, London, were classified as true Cockneys.

…

'Foreignness' and nationalism are to the fore here and in the remainder of the article, but the writer nowhere links 'Jafaican' with bad behaviour. The writer takes a much stronger view of the idea of 'heartland' (as *The Evening Standard* put it in its 10 April 2006 article) by writing at length about the history of the area since the Middle Ages. And the notion of 'pushing out' is now transformed into 'ethnic cleansing', a euphemism from the atrocities of the Yugoslav war of the mid-90s. The metaphors, however, remain the same as *The Evening Standard*'s.

6.11 Jafaican as a problem (3):
Hindering educational achievement and social mobility

As we noted earlier, there is a widespread belief that the consistent use of Jafaican/MLE in a more extreme form including a high rate of slang could be educationally harmful and socially excluding. The school in Manchester acted on this belief, at least in relation to slang. In an online article I mentioned earlier, the American sociologist Garry Robson writes:

All of this, of course, has reignited a popular British debate about the "dumbing down" of English. But this time round, in the aftermath of riots, the stakes are high. Arguments about the coarsening of language and imprisoning effects of "restricted" language codes are emerging from unlikely sources. For example Lindsay Johns, a self-defined hip-hop intellectual, argues that the youths he mentors in south London are trapped – linguistically, educationally, socially – by "ghetto grammar" and cannot "code switch" their way out. He describes a key issue from a linguistic point of view: the inability of some young people to navigate between different languages, dialects or registers of speech. Lindsay's fear is that young people who cannot do so may be psychologically trapped with a restrictive language that is more for performance than reflection.

(*YaleGlobal*, 23rd December 2011)

Robson's position is very close to that of Bernstein (1971), echoing the latter's vocabulary in talking about 'restricted language'. Unlike Birbalsingh, he focuses on linguistic areas other than pronunciation: he sees grammar, language, dialect and register as the problem, or rather, the apparent inability to be flexible in these areas and to 'code switch'. Language, and not social conditions more generally, is seen as a root cause of the problem.

6.12 'Jamaican' (or Jamaican slang) as fashion

In March 2011, the *Guardian* blogger David Hill wrote:

"Suddenly [in the 80s] our slang was cool and it didn't seem that alien anymore. It became the done thing to mix Cockney with Jamaican slang.

"Now [i. e. 2011] you hear even people from the best private schools and universities speaking the now universal London accent – a Solicitor in a major city law firm calling to his friends saying 'Yo' (instead of Oi) and its not because he has Caribbean friends. I have heard Asian, White and Polish (oh yes) refer to their house as their 'Yard'."

Hill does not use the term 'Jafaican'. Instead, he refers to well-educated people using 'the now universal London accent'. Despite his terminology, it is clear that he is referring to the adoption of a small number of slang items of supposedly Jamaican origin and not a shift to a new language variety, in this case MLE/'Jafaican'. The use of certain words from London slang is a 'safe' way of appearing cool: excessive use of these words, and probably the appropriation of MLE phonetic features, would cross unbridgeable boundaries of identity and class. These are examples of crossing, in Rampton's (1995) sense.

7 Conclusion

In this chapter, I have traced the surprisingly short history of the term 'Jafaican' in the British print media, supplemented with some online sources. There is a clear

evolution of the discourses over just 4–5 years, with occasional intense developments occurring over just a few days. The progression of the discourses can be
summarized schematically like this:

'Jafaican' as:

as a language variety: exotic, new, interesting → but a threat to a variety which exists in the
same geographical space, Cockney → a natural development arising out of social and demographic conditions → an educational problem → a well-known variety whose existence is a
matter of common sense (i. e. enregistered) → a normal variety → a foreign variety → a threat
to liberal values → a foreign variety threatening social cohesion → a threat to nationhood
→ a variety associated with bad behaviour à cool

The arrows in this schema imply transition between discourses, but in fact the
transitions cut across a number of strands, or perhaps metadiscourses. The most
pervasive discourse utilizes the metaphor of 'threat', and within this we can
discern two strands. The first is the threat of displacement (of Cockney, of 'true'
British people, of 'British' cultural values) and involves discourses originating in
the political right. The second strand is the threat to liberal values (gender equality, but also (in hip-hop lyrics) homosexual equality).

Many of the discussions of 'Jafaican' insist on its foreignness, and many of
these in turn see this not only as a threat (as we've just seen), but also as inextricably linked to bad behaviour and social unrest. But at the same time some
commentators, such as those from the Queen's English Society, take a non-com-
mitted, neutral stance, seeing it as a natural development.

The discourse of 'Jafaican' as fashionable or 'cool' is dependent on a number
of others: exoticism, oppositionality through its association with subcultures,
and youthfulness. It is seen by the media as being freely adopted by people of
all classes. This construction of 'Jafaican' differs sharply from the analysis which
(socio)linguists place on it. The latter see, on the one hand, young, middle-class
people as buying into limited aspects of it by borrowing slang and professing a
preference for certain musical styles. On the other hand, for the speakers themselves, who are young, working class and multicultural, it is their everyday way
of speaking incorporating distinctive phonological, grammatical, lexical and discourse patterns.

To what extent have the media contributed to the various constructions
of 'Jafaican' which exist? An important point to note is that the term 'Jafaican'
remains outside the vast majority of people's experience. This is in contrast to
either *rinkebysvenska* or *Kiezdeutsch*, which by all accounts have a much stronger
presence in everyday discourse – at least educated discourse – and it is claimed
that these terms are derived from grassroots labels, as we saw at the beginning
of the chapter. The origin of the current sense of 'Jafaican' remains unknown to

us. To the extent that the media mentions any features of this variety, they are, as we have seen, mainly limited to slang. It is conceivable that this is so because the London-based journalists will be familiar with the 'crossing' use of these slang terms from their own mainly middle-class social and professional circles.

At the time of writing (January 2013), frequency of mention has remained at around two per month for the past three years. There was no spike following the August 2011 riots, though mentions have increased slightly since then. This means that it is not possible to isolate a causal effect between external events and mentions. During 2011 and 2012, Heike Wiese, the academic who has written most about *Kiezdeutsch*, was frequently interviewed on the radio and television, as well as receiving a large amount of correspondence objecting both to the language variety and her research (Wiese, pers. comm. 2012). The authors of the London study (Cheshire et al. 2011) have been interviewed a number of times by a range of newspapers, magazines and radio stations, as well receiving contacts from other media outlets. A TEDx talk was given in London by one of the authors shortly after the riots. However, none of the authors received any mail at all of the kind Wiese received. There is no space here to speculate about the reasons for these differences: suffice it to say that a number of German newspapers and puristic organizations see the German language itself as under threat, not only from English, but also from disruptive forces within, such as immigrants and their descendents (Wiese 2012: 220–223). By contrast, British newspapers are largely unconcerned about the fate of the English language as such, but focus instead on the local dialect, Cockney, as a symbol of Englishness – apparently oblivious to the low esteem this variety is normally held in. Parts of the British press concentrate their energies on what they see as the social consequences of the use of multiethnic language varieties. This is a concern they share with German commentators, though they display much less concern for the *linguistic* consequences of this language and dialect contact.

If the media reports have contributed to the (as yet modest) familiarity of 'Jafaican' among the population at large, we do not have any evidence yet of its take-up among its prototypical users, working-class adolescent Londoners. This chapter, however, has shown how a new term spreads across the media, and through the media is circulated among different types of populations. Crucially, its relative popularity is firmly embedded in wider public and political discourses of the present time. When these subside, the term 'Jafaican' may subside regardless of whether Multicultural London English continues to exist. Alternatively, 'Jafaican' may stay, but it will be modified in meaning and social connotations.

References

Agha, Asif 2003: The social life of a cultural value. *Language and Communication* 23: 231–73.

Androutsopoulos, Jannis 2007: Ethnolekte in der Mediengesellschaft. Stilisierung und Sprachideologie in Performance, Fiktion und Metasprachdiskurs. In: Christian Fandrych and Reinier Salverda (eds.), *Standard, Variation und Sprachwandel in germanischen Sprachen /Standard, Variation and Language Change in Germanic Languages*, 113–155. Tübingen: Narr.

Androutsopoulos, Jannis 2010: Ideologizing ethnolectal German. In: Sally Johnson and Tommaso Milani (eds.), *Language ideologies and media discourse*, 162–181. London: Continuum.

Androutsopoulos, Jannis 2011: Die Erfindung >des< Ethnolekts. *Zeitschrift für Literaturwissenschaft und Linguistik 41:164: Ethnizität*, 93–120.

Baker, Paul 2006: *Using corpora in discourse analysis*. London: Continuum.

Bernstein, Basil 1971: *Class, codes and control*, Vol. 1. London: Routledge and Kegan Paul.

Bijvoet, Ellen and Kari Fraurud 2006: "Svenska med något utländskt". *Språkvård* 2006/3: 4–10.

Cheshire, Jenny and Sue Fox 2009: *Was/were* variation: A perspective from London. *Language Variation and Change* 21: 1–38.

Cheshire, Jenny 2013: Grammaticalisation in social context: the emergence of a new English pronoun. *Journal of Sociolinguistics* 17: 608-633.

Cheshire, Jenny, Paul Kerswill, Susan Fox and Eivind Torgersen 2011: Contact, the feature pool and the speech community: The emergence of Multicultural London English. *Journal of Sociolinguistics* 15/2: 151–196.

Clyne, Michael 2000: Lingua franca and ethnolects in Europe and beyond. *Sociolinguistica* 14: 83–89.

Cornips, Leonie, Jürgen Jaspers and Vincent de Rooij (in press): The Politics of Labelling Youth Vernaculars in the Netherlands and Belgium. In: *Jacomine Nortier and Bente A. Svendsen (eds.), Language, youth and identity in the 21st century. Linguistic practices across urban spaces*. Cambridge: Cambridge University Press.

Hewitt, Roger 1986: *White talk black talk. Inter-racial friendship and communication amongst adolescents*. Cambridge: Cambridge University Press.

Hewitt, Roger 1991/2003: Language, youth and the destabilization of ethnicity. In: C. Palmgren et al. (eds.), *Ethnicity and youth culture*, 27–41. Stockholm: Stockholm University. Also in: R. Harris and B. Rampton (eds.) 2003, *The language, ethnicity and race reader*, 188–198. London: Routledge.

Irwin, Anthea 2011: Social constructionism. In: Ruth Wodak, Barbara Johnstone and Paul Kerswill (eds.), *The SAGE handbook of sociolinguistics*, 100–112. London: Sage.

Jaffe, Alexandra: 2009: Entextualization, mediatization and authentication: orthographic choice in media transcripts. *Text & Talk* 29–5: 571–594.

Jaspers, Jürgen 2008: Problematizing ethnolects: naming linguistic practices in an Antwerp secondary school. *International Journal of Bilingualism* 12: 85–103.

Johnstone, Barbara 2011: Locating language in identity. In: Carmen Llamas and Dominic Watt (eds.), *Language and identities*, 29–38. Edinburgh: Edinburgh University Press.

Kerswill, Paul 2013: Identity, ethnicity and place: the construction of youth language in London. In: Peter Auer et al. (eds.), *Space in Language and Linguistics: geographical, interactional, and cognitive perspectives. linguae and litterae*, vol. 24, 128–164 Berlin/Boston: de Gruyter.

Kerswill, Paul, Eivind Torgersen and Susan Fox 2008: Reversing 'drift': Innovation and diffusion in the London diphthong system. *Language Variation and Change* 20: 451–491.

Kerswill, Paul and Mark Sebba 2011: From London Jamaican to British youth language: The transformation of a Caribbean post-creole repertoire into a new Multicultural London English. Paper given at the 2011 Summer Conference of the Society for Pidgin and Creole Linguistics, July–August, University of Ghana, Accra.

Kotsinas, Ulla-Britt 1988a: Rinkebysvenska – en dialekt? [Rinkeby Swedish – a dialect?] In: Per Linell, Viveka Adelswärd, Torbjörn Nilsson and Per A. Petersson (eds.), *Svenskans beskrivning* 16, 264–278. Linköping: Universitetet i Linköping.

Kotsinas, Ulla-Britt 1988b: Immigrant children's Swedish – a new variety? *Journal of Multilingual and Multicultural Development* 9: 129–140.

Marzo, Stefania and Evy Ceuleers 2011: The use of Citétaal among adolescents in Limburg. The role of space appropriation in language variation and change. *Journal of Multilingual and Multicultural Development* 32: 451–460.

Mufwene, Salikoko 2001: *The Ecology of Language Evolution.* Cambridge: Cambridge University Press.

O'Halloran, Kieran.A. 2010: Critical reading of a text through its electronic supplement. *Digital Culture & Education* 2:2, 210–229.

Pfaff, Carol. W. 2005: Kanaken in Alemannistan. Feridun Zaimoğlu's representation of migrant language". In: Volker Hinnenkamp and Katharina Meng (eds.), *Sprachgrenzen überspringen. Sprachliche Hybridität und polykulturelles Selbstverständnis,* 195–225. Tübingen: Narr.

Quist, Pia 2008: Sociolinguistic approaches to multiethnolect: language variety and stylistic practice. *International Journal of Bilingualism* 12: 43–61.

Rampton, Ben 1995: *Crossing: Language and Ethnicity among Adolescents.* London: Longman.

Robson, Garry 2011: Riots, language, and Britain's globalized underclass. *Yale Global Online,* 22 December 2011.

Sebba, Mark 1993: *London Jamaican.* London: Arnold.

Sebba, Mark and Susan Dray 2013: Making it real: 'Jamaican', 'Jafaican' and authenticity in the language of British youth. *Zeitschrift für Anglistik und Amerikanistik,* vol 60, no. 3, 255–273.

Torgersen, Eivind and Andrea Szakay 2012: An investigation of speech rhythm in London English. *Lingua* 122 (7): 822–840.

Svendsen, Bente Ailin and Unn Røyneland 2008: Multiethnolectal facts and functions in Oslo, Norway. *International Journal of Bilingualism* 12: 63–83.

Thomas, Erik 2001: *An acoustic analysis of vowel variation in New World English. Publications of the American Dialect Society* 85. Durham, North Carolina: Duke University Press.

Wells, John C. 1982: *Accents of English,* Vols. I–III. Cambridge: Cambridge University Press.

Wiese, Heike 2009: Grammatical innovation in multiethnic urban Europe: New linguistic practices among adolescents. *Lingua* 119: 782–80.

Wiese, Heike 2012: *Kiezdeutsch. Ein neuer Dialekt entsteht.* München: C. H. Beck.

Barbara Johnstone
Commentary: Sociolinguists and the news media

As the chapters in this section show, there is a difference between how the news media construct the categories and meanings of linguistic variation and how linguists do. Many sociolinguists have found this out for ourselves: we take the time and energy to talk to journalists about our work only to find our accounts twisted or ignored in the resulting reports, which often seem to be more about confirming what laypeople already thought they knew than about challenging it. There was a time in the history of linguistics when it was possible to say, simply, that linguists were the experts about language and other people were not, that we were right and they were unenlightened, and if they could just be persuaded to listen carefully they would change their minds. Now, post-Foucault, we no longer talk this way. We now acknowledge, with these chapter authors, that different ways of talking about linguistic variation arise from different "discourses," different meaning systems with different internal logics, embedded in different material and ideological worlds and different social practices. Colleen Cotter shows us how journalists talk about language variation in the context of their own work; Spiros Moschonas and Paul Kerswill contrast journalists' representations of variation in Modern Greek and London youth language, respectively, with those of "academic" or "scientific" linguists.

Kerswill and Moschonas describe some recurring characteristics of journalistic accounts of linguistic variation. For one thing, journalists tend to reify varieties, giving them essentializing labels like "Jafaican" or "The Greek Language," or, in the case I am most familiar with (Johnstone, Andrus and Danielson 2006; Johnstone et al. 2006; Johnstone and Baumgardt 2004; Johnstone 2009, 2011a, 2011b, 2013), "Pittsburghese," as if there were no differences from speaker to speaker or from situation to situation. (Of course, linguists do this too, via labels like "Multicultural London English" or "Pittsburgh speech," even by talking about "languages" and "varieties," and we must take pains to guard against the essentialization this can lead to.) The entities that are created by labels like these are sometimes treated as agents, as Moschonas points out: media language causes bad things to happen to Greek. Second, journalistic accounts of language variation often highlight what is non-standard about non-standard varieties at the expense of what is standard about them, their internal logic, or their usefulness and appropriateness in the right context. Reports about Jafaican focus on slang; reports about Greek television usage focus on mistakes. Newspaper and TV reports about Pittsburghese note that Pittsburghers have a funny way of saying *downtown*, but they do not note that this is the result of a systematic pattern of monophthongization in certain contexts that is arguably related in a systematic way to other aspects of (some) Pittsburghers' phonology. Third, journalists sometimes treat variation in language as a potential threat to social cohesion: people are becoming unable to understand each other, standards are falling, how can democracy work in such circumstances? Closely related is the attribution of foreignness to varieties like Jafaican (linked with Jamaica via its name, not even called English). And, finally, Moschonas points out that journalistic accounts tend to treat all language as writing, focusing, for example, on orthographic differences that have no effect on how words are pronounced, and on the variants associated with the almost-archaic katharevousa register for written Greek rather than with the contemporary demotic register that is closer to speech.

In part, journalists' discourse about linguistic variation is shaped by widely circulating ideologies about language, such as the idea that language is a "conduit" through which ideas flow from one brain to another (Harris 1981; Reddy 1993). I have learned in my own fieldwork that Pittsburghers think language consists of words, so that the way to describe a variety is to provide a glossary. Grammar (in the sense of recurring patterns at any level) tends to get short shrift from news reporters. Other ideas that shape how people talk about Pittsburghese include the idea that language varieties are naturally linked to places and the idea that there is a single, describable, correct way of speaking and writing and that other ways are incorrect. Cotter shows, however, that journalists' own professional identity brings with it a language ideology. Journalists perceive themselves as language experts and as guardians of better language, and they care about getting the words right. They care about correct usage, but also about the social loadings of words, and the questions they pose on the website of their style guide often have to do with choosing the most "neutral" word in controversial cases. They care not only about national matters but also about local norms, and these concerns are sometimes what leads them to sociolinguists. Words are serious matters for journalists. It is hard to forget the valiant effort of one newswriter at a Linguistic Society of America convention to describe the American Dialect Society's "Word of the Year" election as a serious scientific endeavor, when the linguists were, as usual, cracking wise and making end runs around the voting procedure. Words are tangential to what many of us are centrally interested in, and, to the linguists, the idea that it would make any difference which word we chose, or that we had any idea which new words would persist and which would die out, was funny. To the journalist, if linguists weren't serious about words, what were they serious about?

Why should we care what journalists, or anybody else, think language is like? For one thing, the media's construction of a language variety is part of the history of that variety, as Kerswill points out (paraphrasing Jannis Androutsopoulos). Media accounts of linguistic variation are, in this view, an aspect of our research object, the thing we task ourselves, as linguists, to describe thoroughly. Perhaps more importantly, though, media representations of variation can have implications for language change and for ideological and social change. For example, as Moschonas points out, belief in language change can have a performative effect. Even if stopping or reversing change is more difficult than prescriptivist non-linguists think, it can happen, and, when it does, media attention is often part of the reason it does. This is because media representations of language can lead to what Labov called linguistic stereotyping, the widespread awareness of the social meaning of language forms that can cause people not to use them or to use them more. Media representations of language are among the sites where linguistic forms or sets of forms are enregistered with social meanings such as correctness or incorrectness, class, gender, place, and so on.

Another reason why we should care about journalists' accounts of language variation is that we help create them. Reports in the news media do quote linguists, and sometimes they pick up linguists' ideas, or at least our words. Kerswill notes that the linguists' term *Multicultural London English* does appear in the media accounts, even if not very often. Not all reporters are the same: even if some do not appear to hear what we tell them, others do get it and report on it clearly and fairly. In Pittsburgh, linguists have been primarily responsible for legitimizing Pittsburgh speech in the eyes of journalists and at least some of the public at large, in part by giving it a history and in part simply by taking it seriously (Johnstone 2011b; Johnstone et al. 2006). Until 1967, newspaper articles about Pittsburgh speech were based on casual personal observations by reporters and their acqaintances. But they began to cite designated language experts as soon as a dialectologist arrived on the scene that year and offered to talk to reporters. Every media report about Pittsburgh speech since 1967 has quoted or paraphrased at least one expert, even if they misunderstand or reject the expert's account, and linguists have been the go-to experts.

Finally, as Moschonas notes in a slightly different context, when it comes down to it, the news media actually pay relatively little attention to language. If we think our work is important, it is in our interest that they should. As many of us know, bringing sociolinguistic research to the attention of the media carries with it the risk of misrepresentation, and both Moschonas and Kerswill are skeptical about the possibility that linguists can make any difference in the public's understanding of language variation, no matter how "well-informed and solemnly written" our popularizing attempts may be (Moschonas, p. 414). Cotter reminds us, however, that journalists care about language, probably more than the general public does. To think that our intervention is pointless is to confuse the news audience at large with its most ideologically entrenched, resistant members. We need to remember that there are more than just two ways of understanding language, linguists' and non-linguists'. There are many types and levels of expertise in the language-understanding endeavor. The discourses that enable and constrain how journalists think about language and those that enable and constrain how linguists think about language are, to be sure, different, but that is not the same as saying that they are incommensurable.

Refererences

Harris, Roy. 1981: *The language myth*. New York: St. Martin's Press.

Johnstone, Barbara 2009: Pittsburghese shirts: Commodification and the enregisterment of an urban dialect. *American speech*, *84*(2), 157–175.

Johnstone, Barbara 2011a: Dialect enregisterment in performance. *Journal of sociolinguistics*, *15*(5), 657–679.

Johnstone, Barbara 2011b: Making Pittsburghese: Communication technology, expertise, and the discursive construction of a regional dialect. *Language and communication*, *31*, 3–15.

Johnstone, Barbara 2013: *Speaking Pittsburghese: The story of a dialect*. Oxford UK/Cambridge USA: Oxford University Press.

Johnstone, Barbara, Jennifer Andrus, and Andrew E. Danielson 2006: Mobility, indexicality, and the enregisterment of "Pittsburghese." *Journal of English linguistics*, *34*(2), 77–104.

Johnstone, Barbara and Dan Baumgardt 2004: "Pittsburghese" online: Vernacular norming in conversation. *American speech*, *79*, 115–145.

Reddy, Michael J. 1993: The conduit metaphor: A case of frame conflict in our language about language. In: Andrew Ortony (ed.), *Metaphor and thought* (2nd. ed., pp. 164–201). Cambridge: Cambridge University Press.

Section VI: **Mediatized spaces for minoritized languages**

Mairéad Moriarty

Súil Eile.
Media, sociolinguistic change and the Irish Language

1 Introduction

Súil Eile is an Irish language expression which means 'a different view', and the aim of this chapter is to offer a difference perspective on the nature of the relationship between media, minority languages and sociolinguistic change. The chapter shares with recent research the idea that the media is a site for the (re) production of language ideologies through it's valorization of alternative and/ or new linguistic practice (Androutsopoulos 2009). It will address the gap in minority language studies in this regard by focusing on the consequences for language revitalization. In exploring this relationship the chapter engages with a number of theories including language planning and policy (LPP), sociolinguistic scales and language mobility. The chapter is based on the premise that minority language media perform an important eco-linguistic function enabled by micro-level acts of LPP which are often up-taken by macro- level actors. It is this fusion of LPP levels which can be seen to provide the best opportunity for language revitalization and normalization. On the whole, outlining how this is the case is the principal concern of this chapter.

In so doing, the present chapter will outline how minority language media contribute toward challenging and changing the ideology(s) that surround minority languages and how such media provide innovative contexts and practices through which new sociolinguistic practices and ideologies are harnessed. This will be achieved through the examination of two specific case studies relating to one minority language context, namely Irish. The first case study examines how TG4, the Irish-language television channel, impacts on the language ideologies and language practices of young Irish adults. The second case study examines the effect the presence of Irish in the performative genres of comedy and Rap has on language ideologies. In this way, the present study addresses one of the pitfalls in the scholarship on minority-language media, that is the lack of evidence to support the claim that such media do impact positively on language practices and ideologies (cf. Cormack and Hourigan 2007). The structure of the chapter is as follows: The next section provides the theoretical underpinning for the study by accounting for the relationship between media, minority language planning and policy, and sociolinguistic change. The following section contextualizes the study by providing an account of the current sociolinguistic situation of the Irish language. Following that, two separate case studies are discussed. Firstly, a description of how the Irish-language television channel, TG4, impacts on language ideologies and language practices is discussed. Secondly, an account of how the Irish-American comedian Des Bishops functions as an agent of LPP is provided. A number of avenues for further research are outlined in the concluding discussion.

2 Media, minority language LPP and sociolinguistic change

Mobility and the mobile nature of today's society and hence of language resources is what concerns much of the thinking on the relationship between language and globalization. As languages become more mobile it is not so easy to predict the value of linguistic resources. Languages, like Irish, which traditionally carried little symbolic capital (Bourdieu 1991) outside of its importance as a marker of ethnic identity, have gained new forms of capital as a result of global processes. For example, as a response to a globalized popular culture, niche Irish-language media offerings have increased, in the form the television channel under discussion here for example, which in turn increases the symbolic capital attached to the language. Makoni and Pennycook (2007) argue that globalization has stimulated and mobilized a greater response in support of minority languages. Indeed, the recognition of globalization as a force that has the potential to expand the possibilities for both majority and minority languages has become the subject of recent research within sociolinguistics (cf. Androutsopoulos 2009; Blommaert 2010; Coupland 2010a; Heller 2003; Kelly-Holmes 2011; Moriarty 2011; Pennycook 2007, 2010; Pietikäinen 2010). Such research highlights the fact that the phenomenon of globalization has an impact on language ideologies, practices and regimes. The concept of localization is an important aspect of this change. Localization is described by Androutsopoulos as: "discourse process by which globally available media content is modified in a local manner involving some linguistic transformation to a local code and an orientation to a specific audience defined by means of language choice" (Androutsopoulos 2010: 205). Through linguistic localization local linguistic forms gain new ideological value. Johnstone's (2010) work on Pittesburgese illustrates this as a case in point. Similarly, Pennycook (2010) argues that globalization enables new forms of localization which lead to novel usages for minority languages which in turn can impact on language ideologies and practices. However, this is not to deny that aspects of the global/

local divide are not problematic, indeed, many of the problems with respect to the so-called digital divide are well documented (cf. Joseph and Ramani 2012).

Appadurai's (1996) notion of mediascape is useful in capturing the significance of the media's role in this regard. Appadurai's (1990) described globalization as a complex, overlapping and disjunctive order made up of five types of forces and flows which are captured through a collection of overlapping landscapes. Mediascape is one such landscape and it has come to mean the globalization of media industries resulting in a rapidly changing media environment. The flexibility of today's mediascape is what has allowed for the growth in the availability of media in minority languages. Today's mediascape is in stark contrast to those of years gone by where media, particularly news media, were agents of linguistic homogeneity enacting relatively stable and fixed language practices. In the case of Ireland, the lack of Irish language media offerings meant that the language was de-capitalized which had a negative impact on the perceived value and function of the language. However, recent advancements in media technologies has allowed the media to transform in to agents of linguistic heterogeneity. While, the media remains a powerful agent of linguistic homogeneity helping to solidify notions of language purism, it is now also "changing the terms of our engagement with language and social semiosis in late modernity" (Coupland 2010b: 69). This in turn poses powerful challenges and opportunities to traditional sociolinguistic orders.

While, traditionally, the relationship between language and the media has focused on the role of news media in promoting monolingualism and standard languages in attempt to promote the idea of nationhood (cf. Anderson 1983), the flexibility of today's mediscapes allows for a more varied linguistic presence. For example, as Androutsopoulos (2010a) points out, there has been a widespread increase in the visibility of diasporic languages in new media sites. Similarly, Busch (2006) argues that as a result of the changes in global flows, linguistic diversity has become more visible, societies are more tolerant of linguistic creativity and there is evidence of the emergence of hybrid and mixed codes such as youth languages and secret languages, which have been given market recognition through their use in radio and television programming (cf. Makoni, Brutt-Griffler and Mashari 2007). Arguably, the media have the potential to alter existing language regimes. Such changes allow for fluidity, hybridity and mobility, which in turn provide many opportunities for minority language revitalization and normalization. Androutsopoulos (2009, 2010a; 2010b) states that the increase in linguistic heterogeneity and the visibility of vernacular linguistic practices in public discourse is one outcome of global media changes. This in turn has consequences for ideologies that surround minority languages and their potential social uses. Similarly, Cotter (2001: 308) argues it is the combination of familiar structures and practices of the dominant language and use of minority language of a once-stigmatized, politically powerless community in the public legitimizing sphere that makes minority language media agents of linguistic normalization[1]. A language cannot be considered to be outdated or lacking relevance if it is present in media. Minority language media help to: (1) raise the status of the relevant language, (2) aid corpus planning through the dissemination of new terminology, (3) encourage language acquisition by increasing language contact in both the public and private domains, (4) create fashionable domains of language use, and, (5) help to transfer linguistic skills in to attractive job opportunities (cf. Cormack and Hourigan 2007; Honeycutt and Cunliffe 2010; Lenihan 2011; Moriarty 2011; Pietikäinen 2010; Riggins 1992). The developments provide many new opportunities for minority language planning and policy.

Language planning and policy are established, resisted and modified in the daily practices of minority language media as they function in a terrain of contact negotiation and struggle for an improved position for the relevant language in both national and global terms (cf. Kelly-Holmes, Moriarty and Pietikäinen 2009). Although referred to collectively in the literature there are some important differences between language planning and language policy. Grin (2003) describes language policy as the intention to modify the linguistic features of an environment, that is a society taking steps to influence the linguistic environment, while language planning is the functional realization of these steps. A frequently cited definition of language planning is that by Cooper (1989), where language planning is defined as: "deliberate efforts to influence the behaviour of others with respect to the acquisition, structure, and the functional allocation of their language codes" (Copper 1989: 45). Language planning is enacted at the levels of status, acquisition and corpus. In the majority of cases language planning refers to the macro-level initiatives as it is generally only those in power who can intervene at these levels. In describing language policy Shohamy (2006) and Spolsky (2004, 2009) use a tripartite distinction noting that language policy is shaped by three main factors. These include: (1) language management, which refers in any deliberate attempt to intervene in the language situation, (2) language practices which refers to the patterns and language use, and, (3) language ideology which refers to common-sense ideas that speakers have about their language(s).

Several studies show that language ideology is a useful framework for understanding issues of importance to the present study including language change,

---

1 A process to be understood here as in the case of Catalan (Bastardes 1987), as the attempt to normalize the relations between languages and to eradicate the position of linguistic inferiority traditionally associated with the minority language.

language policy and planning etc (e.g. Irvine and Gal 2000; Kroskrity 2000; Milani 2010; Woolard and Schieffelin 1994). Irvine and Gal's (2000) theoretical model for language ideology forms the background for the understanding of the concept in this study. In their model they propose that language ideology works through three semiotic processes of iconization, fractal recursivity and erasure that provide a framework for understanding and interpreting linguistic differences. Irvine and Gal define iconization as "a transformation of the sign relationship between linguistic features (or varieties) and the social images with which they are linked" (2000: 37). They define fractal recursivity as "the projection of an opposition, salient at some level of relationship, onto some other level. For example, intra-group oppositions might be projected outward onto intergroup relations or vice versa" (2000: 38). Erasure is defined as "the process by which ideology, in simplifying the sociolinguistic field, renders some persons or activities invisible" (2000: 38). Erasure is an important concept in the context of the present study when one considers that the historical lack of media offerings in the Irish language effectively erased the language from this domain which had a negative impact on the perceived value and function of the language.

Traditional approaches to LPP had a habit of looking back to the "preshift society that existed before the economic, ideological and educational pressures led to language shift" (Jaffe 2006: 53), which is why, particularly in the past, more emphasis has been placed on macro-level LPP agents such as governments and educational systems. However, this emphasis gets called in to question in the global era. According to Blommaert *et al* (2009), the state is no longer the main LPP agent or disseminator of language norms. Haarmann (1990) put forward the notion that the reality of LPP initiatives means there are different levels of agency involved both at the macro and micro-levels. In recent times, there has been a growth in the literature which addresses the role of micro-level LPP (Baldauf 2006; Liddicoat and Baldauf 2008; Hogan-Brun 2010). These scholars argue that local contexts and/or agents provide unique sites for LPP particularly given the fact that language is experienced at the local level. As Hogan-Brun (2010: 91) argues "language planning needs to acknowledge the relationships of the social world in its complexity and consider localized settings in order to fully take account of language issues at stake". It is here that minority-language media play an important role as agents of micro-level LPP.

It is possible to measure the potential for minority-language media to function as agents of micro-level LPP by drawing on the notion of language as a mobile resource (cf. Pietikainen, 2010). The view of language as a mobile resource focuses on the situated nature of language, an idea that can be further elaborated by drawing on the theoretical notion of sociolinguistic scale (cf. Blommaert, Collins and Slembrouck 2005). The concept of sociolinguistic scaling put forward by Blommaert (2007) draws on much of the current thinking in social geography, in particular on Wallerstein's (2004) notion of 'World System Analysis'. Here the notion of scale is seen as a dual metaphor for capturing the vertical and horizontal ordering of social space as well as understanding its communion of time and space. With respect to language, scalar shifts are defined as interpretive changes in the value and validity of linguistic competence and their concomitant socio-spatial identities (Blommaert 2007). In this way the concept of sociolinguistic scaling refers to exchangeability of language resources across places, situations and groups. In everyday contexts this means that different scaled orders or regimes are negotiated, imposed or resisted in daily linguistic practices where linguistic and semiotic resources have different values on differing scale levels. Over time these changes can trigger shifts in the scalar orientation of speakers encompassing new regimes of value, which in turn have the potential to transform the dominant linguistic regime. Such scale shifts can be triggered by a number of factors. For example, the Irish language has been 'upscaled' through its presence on the Irish language television TG4 and its subsequent use in performative genres such as Rap (cf. Moriarty 2011). Similarly, as is evident through Pietikäinen's (2010) work on Sámi language, mobility alters existing language relations and hierarchies and the movement across scales has created new language environments, domains and users. The data presented in the two case studies addresses these issues with regard to the Irish context.

3 The Irish language context

The Irish language is the first official language of the Republic of Ireland. The language is an important marker of identity, yet after more than 80 years of LPP there are no monolingual Irish speakers, there are limited significant levels of intergenerational transmission both within and outside of the Gaeltacht, and the use of the language in contemporary Irish society remains low (cf. Ó Laoire 2007; MacGiolla Chríost 2006). There is a clear need for Irish-language LPP to tap in to the ideological goodwill that supports the language in order to increase the actual use of the language. Edwards (2005) argues that one of the challenges for minority languages is that often they seem old fashioned and unglamorous particularly when compared to the higher status languages. Yet in spite of the wide support for Irish as an important marker of ethnic identity, the language has traditionally been a stigmatized resource associated with the label of backward and, as a result, speaking Irish has been afforded little indexical value in Irish society.

The preliminary results of the 2011 Census show that even though 41.1 per cent of the population reported an ability to speak Irish, one in four people reported they never spoke Irish. If one examines these figures further, they show that the actual daily use of the language outside of the educational system is limited to just 1.8 per cent. Daily use of the language within the Irish language stronghold of the Gaeltacht is also low with only 24 per cent of the Gaeltacht population using Irish on a daily basis. As such, as Walsh (2011) argues, active use of the language is limited to a small per cent of the Gaeltacht population. One of the more concerning trends within the Gaeltacht is the declining use of the language by young people. The results of the *The Comprehensive Linguistic Study* of the use of Irish in the Gaeltacht conducted in 2007 states that Irish will cease to be a community language within the Gaeltact within 20–25 years if the current rate of language shift among young adults continues (Ó Giollagáin et al. 2007: 27). Similarly Ó Rian (2009: 43) argues "The continuing decrease in the use of Irish by young people in the Gaeltacht (Irish speaking regions), due to the unrelenting pressure of English, is a matter for deep concern, as is the failure of the authorities over many years to appreciate that language use, and not just language learning, needs to be planned". MacGréil and Rhatigan (2009) conducted a comprehensive survey of the use of and attitudes towards Irish. They found that while 93 % of those surveyed had a positive attitude to the Irish language this was not translating in to use: "This raises a central issue with regard to the future of the Irish language as a vital part of the culture of the people, namely how to translate competence into use" (2009: 114).

Many scholars would argue that as a result of many of the processes of globalization the position of the Irish language has further declined. For example, Ó Riagáin (2007: 388) argues: "in the Republic of Ireland the perceived relationship between the Irish language and national (or ethnic) identity is weakening". However, I argue, that while globalization processes have had some negative impact of the situation of the Irish language, the potential to improve the situation of the Irish language has also arisen. During the period of economic advancement known as the Celtic Tiger, the Irish language became an important tool in promoting a new more confident Ireland. The Irish language was seen as key in preserving a sense of national distinctiveness and a new found energy could be found in the language. Globalization has also impacted positively on minority languages like Irish by providing new spaces for Irish language use. This is discussed with respect to media in section 4.

The results from the various surveys show that there is a need for Irish LPP research to address approaches to Irish-language revitalization which have the potential to impact on the L1 Gaeltacht community, but also on the L2 speech community who live outside these areas. The State's most recent intervention in Irish- language LPP issues is the 20 year strategy for the Irish-language 2010–2030. In the strategy the importance of fostering LPP activities that are in line with the lived reality of the language are evident. Media is identified as a strategic area for aiding the increases in language use demanded by the strategy.

Overall, it can be argued that the limited space for the Irish language in the public domain has increased the association of the language with schooling, with individuals seeing little purpose for the language outside of the educational domain. Recent changes to how the Irish language is perceived and to a lesser extent to how the Irish language is used can be linked to the significant improvement in the portrayal of the language due to its presence in media and popular culture domains.

4 Irish language mobility in media domains

The data presented in this chapter stems from two separate studies, a wider Ph.D project on Irish and Basque language media and from a wider project on minority language media which falls under the remit of the Northern Multilingualism and the Peripheral Multilingualism projects. A number of research methods have been employed to gather the data including questionnaires (N = 130), diaries (N= 12), focus groups (N = 10) as well as content and discourse analysis. The data pertaining to the first study on TG4 was gathered amongst a cohort of university students, aged between eighteen and twenty-four. Thus the data gathered reflects the language attitudes and language practices of young, educated Irish adults, for whom the Irish language does not form a major part of their day-to-day lives. In the second case study, the data was elicited from a corpus of television and stand-up comedy transcripts, Rap lyrics, blog and social networking comments with respect to the artist under discussion.

4.1 TG4

As is argued elsewhere (Moriarty 2007, 2009; Ó hIfearnáin 2000), traditionally there was limited space for the Irish language on the State broadcaster RTÉ. In the late 1980s *Feachtas Náisiúnta Teilifíse* (National Television Campaign), which lobbied the government for a national channel for the Irish language was established. As is the case for the majority of campaigns that call for the establishment of media in minority languages, the campaign for an Irish-language television channel involved an imperfect synergy between macro-level language planning agents and micro-level initiatives and practices by communities and speakers (cf. Shohamy 2006). Such pressure from the micro-level was certainly a contributory factor to the establishment of *Teilifís na Gaeilge* (TnaG). Following a relatively unsuccessful initial period marked by low audience figures, TnaG rebranded itself as TG4 in 1999. This rebranding was significant in allowing TG4 secure its place as the fourth national channel. Included in the rebranding was the slogan *Suil Eile,* which emphasizes the channel's desire to offer a different perspective and to service a niche audience. TG4 is marketed as an Irish-language channel even though it broadcasts programmes both in Irish and English; the inclusion of English-language programming is vital to the channel's survival. TG4 has no formal language policy, but through its Irish language broadcasts the channel does mix between local dialects and the standard form of the Irish language.

TG4 has a role to play in the three main facets of LPP previously outlined. Firstly, the presence of the language on television and existence of a service dedicated to its promotion may help to raise the status of the language. Ó Laoire (2000: 152) says that by being present on television, minority languages are: "no longer confined to the rurality and staid backwardness in the minds of 'people' who live outside these languages". The Irish language cannot be considered 'dead' when it is reaching the homes of Irish people on a daily basis. In terms of corpus planning, TG4 has led to linguistic innovation. For example, following the decision to broadcast the Wimbledon Tennis Championships, the channel had to set about coining words for ace and other tennis terminology. The channel also contributes to the circulation and valorization of standard phrases, key words and ready-made phrases in popular culture, the example presented in Extract 4 illustrates this point. In relation to acquisition planning, the channel provides an excellent language-learning tool. For example, many popular children's cartoons such as 'Sponge Bob Square Pants' are screened on TG4 which benefits child acquisition of Irish. Similarly, the use of English subtitles in Irish-language programming aids language acquisition amongst viewers more generally. Ironically, there are no subtitles in Irish, which perhaps reinforces the reality that no monolingual speaker of the Irish language remains. Another point of note is how TG4 has been recognized as a catalyst for the increased associations of the language with modernity and youth (cf. for example, Kelly-Holmes 2006, 2011; Moriarty 2009, 2011). The discussion of the "Hector Factor" in section 4.1 illustrates this point.

As was mentioned previously, the data presented here stems from a study of how TG4 impacts on the language ideologies and language practices of university students. These students represent a significant cohort to investigate the potential of TG4 as regards language revitalization for a number of reasons. For example, one of the major obstacles to Irish language revitalization is the lack of contact with the language once compulsory education has been completed (cf. Ó Laoire 2005). The limited space for the Irish language in the public domain has increased the association of the language with schooling, with individuals seeing little purpose for the language outside of the educational domain. Indeed an analysis of the questionnaire item, which asked students (N = 130) to describe their level of Irish language use since coming to University, revealed that the majority of students rarely (48.5 %) or never (36.1 %) use the language. Only 4.6 % reported using Irish on a daily basis and 10.8 % on a weekly basis. A further examination of the respondents who reported never using Irish revealed that their lack of use of the language relates directly to a decline in their language competence as a result of not having any contact with the Irish language since completing second level education. For example, one student commented that: *"Since secondary school I rarely hear Irish being spoken, never speak it and never read it"*. In what follows we examine the extent to which TG4 has impacted language ideologies and language practices.

4.1.1 TG4 and Language ideology

The evidence to show that TG4 positively impacts on the ideology students ascribed to the Irish language and how it should be used, manifests itself both quantitatively and qualitatively in the data. Firstly, in all 94.5 % agreed that TG4 was a positive promoter of the Irish language. Secondly, an analysis of the mean score of the ideological items revealed that the statement 'The presence of Irish on television is important for Irish people' was one of the more favourable attitudinal statements, receiving a score of 4.65 on a Likert scale. The qualitative data further enhances the symbolic role that the presence of Irish on television plays. The answers to qualitative questionnaire items presented in Excerpt 1 reveal that from the participants' point of view the presence of the language on TG4 has improved their overall perception of the usefulness of the language. It would seem that by becoming a daily reality within the homes of these young people, the Irish language has gained important symbolic capital amongst the student cohort.

Thirdly, the participants also identified TG4 as being responsible for the promotion of a more positive image for the language and identified certain media personalities as particularly influential in changing the perception of the language as being backward, a perception which has been dominant within Irish society. The "Hector factor" is one example of this. Hector presented a travel series called Amú on TG4 from 2002–2008. Hector, through his off-beat and whacky programming, was largely accredited by the press in successfully attracting young people to the Irish-language:

> Tá ag éirí ag Hector Ó hEochagáin, láithreoir an chláir 'Amu Amigos' ar TG4, daoine a mhealladh i dtreo na Gaelige nár chuir suim sa teanga rima cheana (Editorial, Beo 05/01/03).

> (Hector Ó hEochagáin, presentor of the programme Amu Amigos on TG4, is attracting people to the Irish language who never had an interest in it previously)

- Being made a daily living reality it reminds people that the language is still in existence.
- It has made the language accessible to all people and has helped to initiate people's interest in the language again.
- The usage of Irish on the channel has killed rumours of an imminent death of Irish.
- It may not work wonders over night by turning us all into Irish speakers. But the image of the language before TG4 was of a dying backward language. It can hardly be considered that now.

Excerpt 1: TG4 and impact of language ideology

For the cohort presented in this study, Hector was reported to have had a significant influence on the readjustment of their relationship with the Irish language, with one student commenting: *"(...) using people like that Hector guy creates an awareness of the language being 'cool'.* Similarly Kelly-Holmes (2011) outlines how the channels use of good-looking, youthful presenters has led to what she describes as the discourse of 'sexy Irish'. In the data from the focus group presented in Excerpt 2 participants outline how the youthful presenters on TG4 are serving to address the image of an Irish-language speaker as old-fashioned. The acknowledgement of a 'cool factor' coming to the fore due to the onset of TG4 is particularly of note.

- Do you think that TG4 has changed the image of the Irish language?
- Yeah
- How has it changed it?
- Well, it promotes the language in a different way to what we are used to. Like when I was in school it was the oldest teachers that taught the language and they were obsessed with Irish music and dancing and weren't really in tune with what we considered cool.
- I think that is exactly what TG4 has done though, **it has made the language cool again.** If you tune into the channel for whatever reason you are going to see a young presenter, who is also pretty good looking, who speaks in Irish. As a result the language is no longer seen to be associated with just Irish traditions; it also has a place in Celtic Tiger Ireland.

Excerpt 2: TG4's cool factor

4.1.2 TG4 and language practices

With respect to the influence of TG4 on actual language practices, it is important to first re-emphasize the fact that the levels of Irish-language attrition are high amongst the studied cohort. For example, 29.2% of those who reported a decline in their language ability citied 'no opportunity to use Irish' as the predominant factor, while a further 22.5 % felt that the 'lack of contact' with the language had a negative impact on their language ability. However, 3.2 % of students did claim their Irish language ability had improved since coming to university, with a total 2.4 % reporting that their increase in language ability was a direct result of watching TG4. A further 5 % reported no change to their level of language ability and said that this was because of their contact with the language via TG4. The data presented in Excerpt 3 is drawn from a qualitative questionnaire item where students were asked to outline a reason for the increase or decrease in their Irish-language ability. The data provide qualitative backup to the claim that TG4 is impacting on students' language ability, albeit to a limited degree.

– I continue watching TnaG (TG4) and listen to the commentary for matches **as Gaelige**
– By frequently watching programmes on TG4, I think my Irish has improved since I left school

---

Excerpt 3: TG4 and language ability

As well as providing a domain of contact with the Irish language, a further analysis of questionnaire data reveals that students either speak more Irish (12.5 %) or would like to speak more Irish (46.4 %) as a result of watching TG4. In establishing that watching TG4 has a moderately positive impact with respect to increases in the use of Irish, a Pearsons correlation analysis was carried out on the following two questionnaire items: (1) domains of use and (2) interlocutor, in order to determine where and with whom these increases in Irish-language use occurred. The results reveal that for those who watch TG4 the most frequent domain of Irish-language use was the social domain ($r = 0.84$) and friends was the interlocutor with whom Irish language was most frequent ($r = 0.93$). Although a limited percentage of the Irish participants reported a direct increase in their Irish-language use as a direct result of watching TG4, the results are indicative of sporadic use of the language in domains in which the use of the Irish language is not typical for these young adults. A more longitudinal study is required in order to discover if this change to language practices is long term or simply associated with the period of their life.

In addition to the direct effects the presence of Irish on television is having on the reported language practices of the research participants, the data also shows how TG4 impacts on the students' ability in the language through the dissemination of new terminology. The following excerpt from the focus group study is indicative of one such example:

– Most of you said that you use Irish more as a result of watching TG4, what do you mean by this?
– I suppose for me, its just that it reminds me that I can speak it, I wouldn't say that I use it everyday or anything.
– I think it can help you learn new words like the other day I was watching Pop TG4 with Sharon, my flatmate, when describing how to enter a competition they were running the presenter used the word **fón poca** (pocket phone). We had never heard it before and we thought it was hilarious, a pocket phone! And now we keep saying that we'll call each other on the **fón poca**. It's such a great word

Excerpt 4: TG4 and language use

Historically the burden of Irish language revitalization has been placed on the educational system, which has done little to promote the use of the language outside of this setting. The data presented here points to the important role of media in Irish in overcoming some of the problems associated with over-emphasizing the role of education in language revitalization. TG4 provides a forum for the language outside of the educational setting, thereby allowing for the normalization of Irish in pop-culture domains such as music, comedy, television and radio, the long terms consequences of which shall be interesting to observe. Thus, from a language revitalization point of view it can be argued that the onset of TG4 has altered the relationship of the studied cohort with the Irish language. With respect to Irish society at large, there has been a considerable change in attitude and perception of the Irish language over the last fifteen years. To what extent TG4 has been the catalyst behind this change and/or a creative reaction to the increasing popularity of the language is an issue that demands further attention. However, as the data shows, TG4 has been the main driving force behind the change in the perception of the language for this particular cohort of young Irish adults. Indeed to return to Blommaert's (2007) notion of 'scaling', the onset of TG4 has meant that in the eyes of these young adults the Irish language has been upscaled. It has been exported from its traditional setting to television screens, which has had positive consequences for how they perceive the language. The language is also upscaled by the fact that the language has the potential to reach more people both in the context of Ireland but also in terms of a more global reach through the channel's digital platform.

Overall, it is argued that the impact the presence of minority languages on the media has on actual language practices is indirect and is mediated through language ideologies (cf. Cormack and Hourigan 2007). However, the future of languages such as Irish depends on first and foremost a positive attitude to the language in everyday society. As a result of TG4, the Irish language has become more fashionable, which carries an indexical value of 'coolness'. This change in

the ideology surrounding the language is indicative of a new process of iconization (Irvine and Gal 2000) which may help to further the endeavour to revitalize
and normalize the Irish language. Another outcome of TG4 has been the creative
use of Irish in novel domains. For example, this has inspired advertisers and their
agencies to innovate with Irish-language advertising in highly creative ways (cf.
Kelly-Holmes 2010). Similarly, the Irish language has a wide presence on the Web
and there are a number of social networking sites available in the medium of Irish
(cf. Lenihan 2011 for an account of the Irish language on Facebook). There is also a
marked increase in the presence of Irish in mediated performative genres such as
comedy and Rap. Such domains have generally been the preserve of the English
language within the Irish context, therefore this is representative of a scale jump
(Blommaert 2010). The consequences of which are experienced through a change
in the assumed value and the function of the language.

4.2 Performative genres

Performance has been examined from a number of perspectives in sociolinguistics (cf. Bauman and Briggs 1990; Bell and Gibson 2011; Coupland 2011, 2007;
Johnstone 2011). These studies have shown that highly performative data can
be useful in examining many issues pertinent to this study such as: language
practices, language ideologies and issues of identity. In context of the present
study issues of performance are examined through an analysis of performative
genres which are understood to include aspects of media and popular culture
that are performance-orientated (cf. Moriarty 2011). Such genres constitute what
Coupland (2007) describes as 'high performance events' which are typically pre-
planned. Such performances are staged and are intended for an audience, be that
a live audience in the case of stand-up comedy and live music performances, or
a more fragmented performer/audience relationship in mediatized genres. Examples of such genres include stand-up comedy, Rap music and Hip-hop, radio
and television broadcasts etc. Performance genres of this kind make languages
visible, analysable and mobile. Moreover, by drawing on the work of Pietikäinen
and Kelly-Holmes (2011: 61) it can be argued that such performance genres can
lead to "a reorganizing and changing of performative resources resulting in new
discursive and linguistic combinations and a refashioning of identities". A key
feature of performative genres which make them available for an examination of
issues pertaining to LPP research stems from the fact that: "performances move
the use of heterogeneous stylistic resources, context-sensitive meanings and conflicting ideologies in to a reflexive arena where they can be examined critically"
(Bauman and Briggs 1990: 6).

The concept of enregisterment (Agha 2003) is an important in further unpacking how the presence of minority languages in performative genres impacts on language policy and planning. Enregisterment as defined by Agha (2007: 81) is "processes and practise whereby performabale signs become recognized (and regrouped) as belonging to distinct, differentially valorized semiotic registers by a population". Agha uses the example of the association of received pronunciation with Queen Elizabeth 2 to illustrate his point. Media is one site where enreisgterment takes place and allows for linguistic features to become linked to certain ideological schemes which give some languages high symbolic value and erase such value from others. As the account of TG4 outlined, the lack of media provision for the Irish language in the past meant the language had little value. While the existence of TG4 has led to the construction of a new indexical value for Irish, the presence of Irish in performative genres further promotes this change in the value of the language. Here the focus is on one performer, Des Bishop, who has contributed to change in the indexical value of Irish through his use of the language in the performative genres of comedy and Rap.

Des Bishop is an American born comedian living in Ireland for almost twenty years. His comic effectiveness is drawn from his unique position of perceived marginality, he is simultaneously one of 'us' and one of 'them'. Bishop's comedy largely focuses on observing "peculiar Irish idiosyncrasy then crafting a monologue of sustained humour and we laugh at the insight and punch line" (O'Dywer, quoted in Moynihan, 2008). In 2007, Bishop moved to Leitir Mór, a small town in the Connemara Gaeltacht, where he set himself the challenge of gaining enough fluency in the Irish language that he would be able to perform a stand-up comedy routine through the medium of Irish. His experience was recorded as a six-part mini television series entitled 'In the Name of the Fada', a clever play on the American English pronunciation of Father, but also on the name given to the accents used in the Irish language. The television series was aired from March 13th to April 17th 2008. It charted his experience as an Irish-language learner; his attempts to integrate in to the local community; his challenges with learning the language and his struggles in creating a comedy routine in Irish. Following the television series Bishop toured with his comedy routine Tongues/Teanga. Through his comedy Bishop addressed a number of problems with the traditional approach to Irish-language LPP enacted at the macro-level of the State. Bishop bridged a number of divides. Firstly, he created a television series which represented Gaeltacht life in a fun way, which was beneficial to both the local community and to those who stand outside these communities. As I have argued elsewhere, throughout his various routines Bishop mocked the tensions that exist between L1 and the L2 speech communities and highlighted the failure of the educational system to create active Irish-language users (cf. Moriarty 2011). In many ways he transcends the boundary of where the use of the Irish language is acceptable through his creative use of Irish in these performative genres. By using a multimodal methodological framework to analyse data from Bishop's stand-up comedy routines and television series, as well as data from blogs which discuss Bishop's comedy and Rap, the flowing section will demonstrate how Bishop has contributed to a revaluing of the ideology attached to the Irish language.

4.2.1 Des Bishop as an agent of sociolinguistic change

Throughout the television series, and in his subsequent media appearances, Bishop has been highly critical of the how the educational system has approached the teaching of Irish, arguing that the overt emphasis on the acquisition of the complex grammatical rules has not lend itself to the adoption of Irish as a language for use in everyday society.

By making these criticisms one aspect of the comic gaze, Bishop has triggered an ideological shift. This scalar shift has the potential to result in a realignment of dominant discourses that surround the language, where the Irish language gains a new indexical value of being cool. In order to trace this realignment a corpus of data from blogs, on-line discussion boards and you-tube comments was complied. Bishop's use of the Irish-language in his comedy and Rap is subject to interpretation by the local community and these on-line forums where seen as an ideal site in which to investigate the impact on local language ideologies. The data presented in Excerpt 5 is taken from on-line discussion board (www. boards.ie). The thread was entitled 'Des Bishop: is making learning Irish look cool?'. Throughout the thread there are a number of incidences where the local reaction to Bishop's performances has led to a change in the indexical value of the Irish language. Of particular note is the value the participants in the thread place on Bishop's role in addressing the problems with the manner in which Irish is taught in school.

As has been previously mentioned the overemphasis on the educational system to revitalize the Irish language amongst the L2 community has had limited success. It has impacted negatively on the status of the language in the eyes of many Irish people who have typically viewed the language as a stigmatized resource. Bishop has highlighted this both within the television show and in his comedy routines, but also in a number of subsequent television and radio interviews. But rather than simply mock this reality, Bishop developed a number of different methods to aid the acquisition of some of the more problematic aspects of the grammar. Episode 3 of *In the Name of the Fada,* Bishop is having difficulty getting to grips with the some of the grammatical idiosyncrasies of the Irish language. He turns to rap for help and adapts the popular House of Fame rap song

Dún do chlab, dún do bhéal, éist le mo scéal
Má cheapann tú go dtuigeann tú tá tú cur i géill
Tá mé ag dul thú a bhomhradh, ceangail mé le slabhra
Guile a mhac, ná bí caint cac anseo i lár an samhradh
Súistín búistín buile beaga shúistín
Ná bí a phlaidhca no gheobhaidh tú a leice
Níl mé ag iarraidh éisteacht le do chac bó
Damhsa damhsa gan aon stró
Buachaillí gránna, cailíní beaga dána
Ní thugann mise áird ar na Gárdaí síochána
Ar an gCeathrú Rua, amuigh anseo faoin tuath
Léim anois, léim anois, léim anois go luath
Má tá sé mí-cheart, má tá sé mí cheart
Is cuma liom is cuma liom, léimigí thart
Léim thart
Éirigh as do pholl is léim thart
Léim (x12)

Figure 1: Lyrics of *Leim Thart*

Jump Around, to the Irish language giving it the title *Leim Thart*. The lyrics of the first verse and chorus are presented in Figure 1.

Through his Rap, Bishop performs a scale jump and is involved in a process of localization. He has taken the globalized popular culture domain of Rap and adopted it to fit with the needs of the local audience. Of particular note in the lyrics is how Bishop localizes the song with reference to *Gárdaí Síochána* (Police) and *an gCeathrú* Rua (the Gaeltacht area where he was living). The following

– I've the highest of respect for Des for learning the language and adding to making the language fashionable. This can only help the revival of the language
– personally I think des is amazing 😊😊
  he's definitely made me ALOT more interested in Irish
  I've had arguments with my Irish Teacher over how **** we're thought it cause of him😊
  And he's the only thing I talked about in my Irish oral
  I don't care if people don't like him
  He's done more for Irish than ye have!
– Des Bishop is an important part of the Gaeilge revival, whether you like it or not. If it takes a foreigner to come over here to outline our failed curriculum, then I'll take it! The man is passionate about the language and is doing all he can to help it's revival. He's a true Irishman and a great asset to this Island
– Maith thú! I totally agree with you. Des Bishop is a Legend[2]

Excerpt 5: Selection of comments from the thread: Des Bishop: Is he making Irish cool?

---

2 http://www.boards.ie/vbulletin/showthread.php?p=55672281 (Accesssed 12.05.12)

selection of comments taken from corpus of comments posted on a You Tube clip of Bishop performing the Rap highlight some of the ways this has impacted on Irish-language ideologies and practices.

The comments present in Excerpt 6 show that Bishop's transcendence of existing expectations regarding where Irish should be used is addressing the language's capability of functioning in a globalized world. Indeed, the indexical value of the Irish language being trendy is something Bishop has tapped in to and subsequently has created an Irish-language web course available on his website www.desbishop.com. The use of hybrid mixing in the *mo abhail-ies* (Homies) is an example of one instance of creative language use which was a common feature of Bishop's Irish-language routines. This further exemplifies the process of localization, where a phrase associated with the global genre of Rap and Hip-hop has been adapted to suit the local linguistic code. Also, the domain of Rap provides a novel language-learning tool for the classroom which contests the typical approach to the learning of grammar. The learning of *Leim Thart* in schools was frequently reported in the media and the inclusion of Rap competitions in the annual *Oireachtas na Gaelige*[3] competitions is indicative of a knock-on effect. A further example of how Bishop's Rap gets recontextualized is through the merchandize available displaying some of the lyrics from *Leim Thart*, such as T-shirts, hoodies, a very clear example of the commodification of the language. Bishop was also been invited to take part in a re-structuring of the school curricula, which is indicative of a potential knock on effect when micro and macro LPP agents can work in tandem with one another. However, due to the economic crisis Ireland has been experiencing since September 2008, the language issue has been placed on the back burner.

– Mad props to Des for keeping the language alive through music
– That is great. I love mo abhaile-ies my homies
– Haha we are learning this in school and rapping as gaelige (in Irish) is surprisingly easy[3]

Excerpt 6: Selection of You Tube comments on Des Bishop's Leim Thart

The presence of minority languages in performative genres offers the possibility of triggering an ideological shift, which in turn can have consequences for

---

3 Oireachtas na Gaelige is an annual Irish-language arts festival which celebrates literature, music, media etc.
4 http://www.youtube.com/watch?v=zmIy8VfXPhU (Accessed 24/08/12)

minority language use. While there has been a change in the status of the language, it is as yet unclear if changes to how the language is perceived are being translated into increases in the actual use of the language. This is where the challenge for language planning and policy scholarship lies. There is a need for further research to examine how the potential for increased use offered by the presence of minority languages in performative genres can be translated into the actual usage of minority languages, particularly amongst young members of the given speech community. However, the analysis of Bishop's comedy and Rap signifies that the movement of the Irish-language from a local resource to a mediated space has resulted in a new process of enregisterment. By challenging many of the stereotypes that surround the notion of Irish-language speaker and language's 'fit for purpose' as regards media presence, Bishop activated a process of re-valorization. Bishop has opened up a new space for Irish and allows the local community to recontextualize their identities and relationship with the language.

5 Discussion

The data presented in the preceding section makes clear the importance of minority language media to LPP. Such media provide powerful arenas for language production and they contributed towards challenging and changing the sociolinguistic reality of the Irish language. Both TG4 and the use of Irish by Bishop in the performative genres of comedy and Rap offer platforms for innovative Irish language practice which can lead to further development of the language and a restructuring of the sociolinguistic order. The two case studies under discussion here show that in these globalizing times the Irish language has been mobilized and (re) appropriated for new purposes, which brings with it its own set of opportunities and threats. The data presented identify how TG4 and the comedy and music of Des Bishop have added new value to the Irish language in terms of its ideological standing. The findings show that both TG4 and Bishop's comedy and Rap have helped to alleviate the stigmatized out-dated image of the Irish language. These changes to the Irish-language mediascape have helped to confer on new legitimacy on the language for these students as it becomes associated with positive and desirable role models. Television and music personalities show young people that they are willing to stand up and be counted as speakers of minority languages in a very public way, thus sending a very strong message with regard to how a given language can and should be valued. Thus helping to confer a real-world status where minority languages are seen as hip, trendy and cool. For speakers of minority languages the availability of mass media in one's own language makes it harder for some of the more extreme stereotypes about the particular language to survive. Furthermore, minority-language media in general permit speakers or learners who may live in areas where the geographical base of the language has been eroded to maximize their connection with and participation in the particular speech community. Increasingly, as media develop their global reach by means of such devices as digital television, languages such as Irish are no longer invisible and have the potential to reach members of the speech community all around the world. This in turn brings long term benefits in terms of the availability of attractive job opportunities and the overall economic viability of languages like Irish. It would however, by naïve to assume that the provision for minority languages in media and pop-culture domains and performative genres does not raise other language revitalization issues. Often the unconventional manner in which minority languages are used in media and popular culture domains are criticized by so-called 'language purists' as it is sometimes the case that a language is used incorrectly in terms of its grammar or syntax in media and pop-culture domains. Similarly it can lead to contestation over who counts as a legitimate speaker, which in turn brings its own challenges as regards authenticity.

It can be argued that these results point to the fact that minority-language media may be powerful resources in promoting and disseminating a type of sociolinguistic change. Coupland (2012 and this volume) identifies five interrelated dimensions to sociolinguistic change. These include: (1) social norms; (2) discursive practices; (3) language ideologies; (4) cultural reflexivity and (5) media(tis) ation. The results of the combined case studies would indicate that the changes to the Irish-language mediascape have influenced each of these dimensions. The use of Irish on TG4 and in Bishop's performances has opened up a new space for Irish and has allowed the local community to recontextualize their relationship with the Irish language. The data shows that new indexical relationships have been constructed as a result of these media. There has been a significant change at the level of language ideology and more limited change on the level of language practice. The reflexivity in Bishop's comedy and Rap drew awareness to alternative spaces for Irish-language learning and acquisition and has had the lasting effect of encouraging more individuals to transcend typical boundaries of Irish language use. In my opinion this is indicative of sociolinguistic change, where a response to social changes brought about by globalization and localization has blended with linguistic change.

The results pose new questions for language planning and policy. Media puts huge pressure on minority-language revitalization, but it has the potential to also function as a powerful mechanism of language policy (cf. Moriarty 2007). Indeed it is often the case the media and pop-culture have powerful effects in shaping a micro-level LPP that can be in line with or at odds with that envisaged by formal state language planning (cf. Kelly-Holmes, Moriarty and Pietikäinen 2009). While media alone cannot revitalize a minority language, they are important catalysts in changing the ideological and functional value attached to lesser-used minority languages. Future research needs to examine how the kaleidoscope of available media can fruitfully combine with LPP agents in an attempt to bring about more dynamic LPP activities which will have the potential to influence a process approaching what one could call sociolinguistic change.

References

Agha, Asif 2003: The social life of a cultural value. *Language and Communication* 23(3–4): 231–273.

Agha, Asif 2007: The object called "language" and the subject of linguistics. *Journal of English Linguistics* 35(3): 217–235

Anderson, Benedikt 1983: *Imagined communities: Reflections on the origins and spread of nationalism*. London: Verso.

Androutsopoulos Jannis 2010b: The study of language and space in media discourse. In: Peter Auer and Jürgen E. Schmidt (eds.), *Language and Space: An International Handbook of Linguistic Variation. Volume I: Theory and Methods,* 740–758. Berlin/New York: de Gruyter.

Androutsopoulos, Jannis2009: Policing practices in heteroglossic mediascapes: a commentary on interfaces. *Language Policy* 8(3): 285–289.

Androutsopoulos, Jannis2010a: Localizing the Global on the Participatory Web: Vernacular spectacles as local responses to global media flows. In: Nikolas Coupland (ed.), *The Handbook of Language and Globalization*, 201–231. Oxford: Wiley-Blackwell.

Appadurai, Arjun 1990: Disjuncture and difference in the global cultural economy. *Theory, Culture and Society* 7: 295- 310.

Appadurai, Arjun 1996: *Modernity at Large: Cultural Dimensions of Globalization* . Minneapolis: University of Minnesota Press.

Baldauf, Richard B. 2006: Micro language planning. *Current Issues in Language Planning,* 7 (2 and 3).

Bastardes, Albert 1987: La planification linguistique en Catalogne au XXe siècle. In: J. Maurais (ed.), *Politique et Aménagement Linguistiques,* 121–158. Quebec/Paris: Conseil de la Langue Française.

Bauman, Richard. and Charles Briggs 1990: Poetics and performance as critical perspectives on language and social life. *Annual Review of Anthropology* 19: 59–88.

Bell, Alan. and Andy Gibson 2011: Staging language: An introduction to the sociolinguistics of performance. *Journal of Sociolinguistics* 15(5): 555–572.

Bishop, Des 2008a: *In the Name of the Fada*. DVD RTE 2008.

Bishop, Des 2008b: *Tongues* Stand-up Comedy Show Vicar Street Dublin Febuary 2008.

Blommaert, Jan 2007: Sociolinguistics scales. *Intercultural Pragmatics* 4(1): 1–19.

Blommaert, Jan, J. Collins and Stef. Slembrouck 2005: Spaces of multilingualism. *Language & Communication* 25: 197–216.

Blommaert, Jan, Helen Kelly-Holmes, Pia Lane, Sirpa Leppänen, Máiréad Moriarty, Sari Pietikäinen and Arja Piirainen-Marsh 2009: Media, multilingualism and language policing: An Introduction. *Language Policy* 8 (3): 203–207.

Bloomaert, Jan 2010: *The Sociolinguistics of Globalisation*. Cambridge: Cambridge University Press.

Bourdieu, Pierre 1991: *Language and Symbolic Power*. Cambridge: Cambridge University Press.

Busch, Brigitta 2006: Changing media spaces: The transformative power of heteroglossic practices. In: Clar Mar-Molinero and Patrick Stevenson (eds.), *Language ideologies, policies and practices,* 206–219. Basingstoke: Palgrave Macmillan.

Cooper, Robert 1989: *Language planning and social change*. Cambridge: Cambridge University Press.

Cormack, Mike and Niamh Hourigan 2007: *Minority language media: Concepts, critiques and criticism*. Clevedon, UK: Multilingual Matters

Cotter, Colleen 2001: Raidio´ na life: Innovations in the use of media for language revitalisation. *International Journal of the Sociology of Language* 140: 136–147.

Coupland, Nikolas 2007: *Style: Language Variation and Identity*. Cambridge: Cambridge University Press.

Coupland, Nikolas (ed.) 2010a: *Handbook of Language and Globalization*. Great Britain: Wiley-Blackwell.

Coupland, Nikolas 2010b: Language, ideology, media and social change. In: K. Junod and D. Maillat (eds.), *Performing the Self*, 127–151. Tübingen: Narr.

Coupland, Nikolas 2011: Dialect style, social class and metacultural performance: The pantomime Dame. In: Nikolas Coupland and Adam Jaworski (eds.), *The New Sociolinguistic Reader*, 311–325 Basingstoke: Palgrave Macmillan.

Coupland, Nikolas 2012: Welsh tea: The centring and decentring of Wales and the Welsh language. In: Sari Pietikäinen and Helen Kelly-Holmes (eds.), *Peripheral Multilingualism*, 133–153. Oxford: Oxford University Press.

Edwards, Viv 2005: When school is not enough: New initiatives in intergenerational language transmission in Wales *International Journal of Bilingual Education and Bilingualism* 8(4): 298–312.

Grin, François 2003: *Language Policy Evaluation and the European Charter for Regional or Minority Languages* London: Palgrave MacMillan.

Haarmann, Harald 1990: Language planning in the light of a general theory of language: A methodological framework. *International Journal of the Sociology of Language* 95: 109–129.

Heller, Monica 2003: Globalization, the new economy and the commodification of Language. *Journal of Sociolinguistics* 74: 473–492.

Hogan-Brun, Gabrielle 2010: Contextualising language planning from below. *Current Issues in Language Planning*, 11(20): 91–94.

Honeycutt, Courtenay and Daniel Cunliffe 2010: The use of the Welsh language on Facebook. *Information,Communication & Society* 13(2): 226–248.

Irvine, Judith and Susan Gal 2000: Language ideology and linguistic differntiation. In: Paul Kroskrity (ed.), *2000 Regimes of language: Ideologies, polities and identities*, 35–83. Santa Fe: School of American Research Press.

Jaffe, Alexandra 2006: Minority language movements. In: Monica Heller (ed.), *Bilingualism: A social approach,* 50–70. Palgrave: Hampshire.

Johnstone, Barbara 2010: Pittsburghese shirts: Commodification and Enregisterment of an urban dialect. *American Speech* 84 (2): 157–175

Johnstone, Barbara 2011: *Dialect Enregisterment in Performance Journal of sociolinguistics* 15(5): 657–679.

Joseph, Micheal and Ester Ramani 2012: "Glocalization": Going beyond the dichotomy of global versus local through additive multilingualism. *Journal of Multilingual Research*, 6 (1): 22–34.

Kelly-Holmes, Helen 2010: Rethinking the macro-micro relationship: Some insights from the marketing domain. *The International Journal of the Sociology of Language* 202: 25–40.

Kelly-Holmes, Helen 2006: Multilingualism and commercial language practices on the Internet. *Journal of Sociolinguistics* 10(5): 507–519.

Kelly-Holmes, Helen 2011: Sex, lies and thematising Irish: New media, old discourses? *Journal of Language and Politics* 10(4): 511–534.

Kelly-Holmes, Helen, Máiréad Moriarty Sari and Pietikäinen 2009: Convergence and divergence in Basque, Irish and Sámi media language policing, *Language & Policy* 8(3): 227–208.

Kroskrity, Paul V. 2000: Regimenting Languages. Language Ideological Perspectives. In: Paul V. Kroskrity (ed.), *Regimes of Language*, 1–34. Santa Fe: School of American Research Press.

Lenihan, Aoife 2011: 'Join our community of translators' Language ideologies & *Facebook*. In: Crispin Thurlow and Kristine Mroczek (eds.), *Digital Discourse: Language in the New Media*. New York/London: Oxford University Press.

Liddicoat, Anthony J. and Richard B. Baldauf (eds.) 2008: *Language planning in local contexts*. Clevedon: Multilingual Matters.

Mac Giolla Chríost, Diarmuid 2006: Micro-level language planning in Ireland. *Current Issues in Language Planning 7* (2and3): 230–250.

Mac Gréil, M. and F. Rhatigan 2009: *The Irish Language and the Irish People*. National University of Ireland Maynooth: Survey and Research Unit, Department of Sociology.

Makoni, Sinfree and Alastir Pennycook (eds.) 2007: *Disinventing and Reconstituting Languages* Clevedon: Multilingual Matters.

Makoni, Sinfree, Janina Brutt-Griffler and Pedzisai Mashari 2007: The use of 'indigenous' and urban vernaculars in Zimbabwe. *Language in Society* 36 (1): 25–49.

McCubbin, Justin 2010: 'Irish-Language Policy in a Multiethnic State: Competing Discourses on Ethnocultural Membership and Language Ownership'. *Journal of Multilingual and Multicultural Discourses* 31(5): 457–478.

Milani, Tomasso 2010: What's in a name? Language ideology and social differentiation in a Swedish print-mediated debate. *Journal of Sociolinguistics* 14(1): 116–142.

Moriarty, Máiréad 2007: *Minority language television and language policy: A comparative account of the Irish and Basque sociolinguistic contexts*. PhD thesis, University of Limerick.

Moriarty, Máiréad 2009: Normalising language through television: The case of TG4. *Journal of Multicultural Discourses* 42: 137–149.

Moriarty, Máiréad 2011: Minority languages and performative genres: The case of Irish-language stand-up comedy. *Journal of Multilingual and Multicultural Development* 32(6): 547–559.

Moynihan, Sarah 2008: Stand(ing) up for the immigrants: The work of comedian Des Bishop. *Irish Studies Review* 16(4): 403–413.

Ó Giollagáin, Conchúr, Seosamh Mac Donncha, Fiona Ní Chualáin, Aoife Ní Shéaghdha and Mary O'Brien 2007: *Comprehensive linguistic study of the use of Irish in the Gaeltacht: Principle findings and recommendations*. Dublin: Stationery Office.

Ó hIfearnáin, Tadhg 2000: Majority and Minority in Language Policy in Ireland. In: Elmara Vēbers (ed.), *Integrācija un Etnopolitika*. Vēbers, 251–267. Rīga: Jumava: Latvijas Universitātes Filozofijas un socioloģijas institūts.

Ó Laoire, Muiris 2000: Learning Irish for Participation in the Irish Language Speech Community Outside the Gaeltacht. *Journal of Celtic Language Learning* 5: 20–33.

Ó Laoire, Muiris 2005: The language planning situation in Ireland. *Current Issues in Language Planning* 6 (3): 251–314

Ó Laoire, Muiris 2007: Language use and attitudes in Ireland. In: David Lasagabaster and Ángel Huguet (eds.), *Multilingualism in European Contexts: Language use and attitudes*, 164–183. Clevedon: Multilingual Matters.

Ó Riagáin, Padraig 2007 : Relationships between Attitudes to Irish, Social Class, Religion and National Identity in the Republic of Ireland and Northern Ireland. *International Journal of Bilingual Education and Bilingualism* 10, 4: 369–393.

Pennycook, Alastair 2007: *Global Englishes and transcultural flows*. London: Routledge.

Pennycook, Alastair 2010: *Language as a local practice*. London: Routledge

Pietikäinen, Sari and Helen Kelly-Holmes 2011: The local political economy of languages in a Sami tourism destination; Authenticity, mobility in the labelling of souvenirs. *Journal of Sociolinguistics* 15(3): 323–346.

Pietikäinen, Sari 2010: Sámi language mobility: scales and discourses of multilingualism in a polycentric environment. *International Journal of the Sociology of Language* 20(2): 79–101.

Riggins, Steve. H. 1992: *Ethnic Minority Media: An International Perspective*. London: Sage.

Shohamy, Elana 2006: *Language policy: Hidden agendas and new approaches*. London: Routledge.

Spolsky, Bernard 2009: *Language Management*. Cambridge. Cambridge University Press.

Spolsky, Bernard 2004: *Language Policy*. Cambridge. Cambridge University Press.

Wallerstein, Immanuel 2004: *World-systems Analysis: An introduction*. Durham NC: Duke University Press.

Walsh, John 2011: *Contests and Contexts: The Irish Language and Ireland's Socio-Economic Development*. Oxford: Peter Lang.

Woolard, Kathlyn and Bambi Schieffelin 1994: Language ideology. *Annual Review of Anthropology* 23: 55–82.

Ana Deumert

Sites of struggle and possibility in cyberspace.
Wikipedia and *Facebook* in Africa[1]

1 Introduction – empowerment through technology?

In February 2012, *Mozilla* announced its plans to translate the popular web browser *Firefox* into Quechua, a South American language (with about 10 million speakers).[2] The initiative is linked to *runasimipi.org*, a collaborative project which aims to create open software in Quechua. Its webpage frames efforts towards software localization in overtly revolutionary and political language, drawing on concepts such as modernity, culture and freedom.

> The very act of using software in Quechua is a political statement that Quechua has cultural value and a future in modernity. (Introduction)

> Our dream is that any Andean child who goes to a cyber-cafe in the future will have the option to see everything in his native language. (Manifesto)

> Together we can create a freer future! (Manifesto)

Can digital technology – its historical English bias notwithstanding – become a tool for the political empowerment of hitherto marginalized languages and their speakers? The American linguist David Harrison has called this the "flipside of globalization": rather than assimilation to a dominant – typically English-speaking – global culture, we now see a myriad of activities in which marginalized communities use digital media in order to gain visibility for their voices in the global arena.[3] Examples of such initiatives are plentiful:

- The establishment of *IndigiTube*, as a dedicated space for media produced by Australian indigenous communities (http://indigitube.com.au);

---

1 The work reported in this paper was supported by the *National Research Foundation* (South Africa), the *South African Netherlands Programme for Alternatives in Development* (SANPAD), and the University of Cape Town. My thinking on the issues discussed has benefited from conversations with friends and colleagues. I would like to acknowledge, in particular, Jannis Androutsopoulos, Nkululeko Mabandla and Marion Walton.
2 All demographics cited in this article comes from the *Ethnologue* data base (Lewis 2009).
3 http://www.bbc.co.uk/news/science-environment-17081573.

- A *FirstVoices* chat app for *iPhone* which allows users to replace the QWERTY keypad with a First Nations language keypad (http://www.firstvoices.com);
- An on-line translator for Hmong which is meant to help Diaspora youth to maintain, and/or acquire, their heritage language (http://www.mercedsunstar.com/2012/03/26/2283667/online-tool-aims-to-save-hmong.html#storylink=cpy);
- The internet publication and dissemination of Indian poetry using Devanagari Unicode fonts (http://www.indianexpress.com/news/Verse-by-Verse/938068/);
- Dedicated web-sites such as www.ojibwe.net to provide access to texts, dictionaries, audio files, and language lessons (http://www.healthcanal.com/life-style-fitness/26778-How-social-media-help-save-endangered-language.html).[4]

As noted by Daniel Prado in his preface to the recently published volume *Net. Lang – Towards the Multilingual Cyberspace* (2012: 27), the digital world offers both opportunity and threat to non-dominant languages:

> A threat, because the most highly equipped languages, and those spoken in dominant states, impose themselves over others and are supported by the network's technicality. An opportunity, because cyberspace's accessibility and universality allows it to give voice to languages that have been unable to make themselves heard via other recording and knowledge dissemination tools.

Thus, technology itself is neither bad nor good, "not a destiny but a scene of struggle" as well as possibility (Feenberg 1991: 14). Public institutions – be it classrooms, libraries, theatres or the internet – always reflect, and are shaped by, larger societal inequalities. At the same time, there is contestation of – as well as resistance against – these inequalities (and the power structures that create them), and change is possible (Giroux and Simon 1988). This paper approaches the digital domain as an important site of struggle over questions of representation, authority and voice. The focus of the analysis is on African languages which show a severe "online language deficit" (Prado 2012: 39) on the internet; a deficit which mirrors their marginalization in formal literacy domains such as book publishing or higher education.

---

4 Efforts to use digital media to strengthen indigenous languages go back to the *Leokï* ('Powerful Voice') bulletin board service which was established for the teaching and learning of Hawai'ian in the mid-1990s (see Warschauer 1998).

It is important to state from the outset that – as a result of early missionary efforts as well as colonial and post-colonial language policy – most larger African languages have fairly standardized orthographies, are used in print, the school system, and by local governments. On-going efforts by SIL (*Summer Institute of Linguistics*, a global Christian, non-profit organization) continue to expand the number of written, standardized African languages. In addition, UNESCO's literacy indicators show an upward trend across African countries, with the average literacy rate now estimated to be around 72 percent for youth literacy in Sub-Saharan Africa (63 percent for adult literacy). However, Africa remains the only continent with countries (particular in the West African interior) showing literacy rates of below 50 percent.[5] Although the former colonial languages continue to be central resources in the education system, local languages are increasingly taught and supported. The focus in this chapter is on African languages (isiXhosa, Kiswahili, Malagasy and Yorùbá as well as Afrikaans) which have (a) a large speaker base, (b) a literate tradition, and (c) are used as an official language (which requires a certain degree of *Ausbau* or elaboration, although not necessarily, yet, in the digital domain; see Androutsopoulos 2011). These languages are thus strong compared to many other languages on the continent, but their position remains nevertheless weak on the global stage.

The article is structured as follows: the first section looks at the question of access from a global perspective; who has access to communication technologies in today's world? Having access – personal or shared – to digital media is a pre-requisite for their use, and language communities which lack access do not have "writing-rights" in the digital sphere (Walton and Donner 2011). Section (3) analyzes the presence of African languages on the internet, and discusses the measures that have been used to estimate online multilingualism: user profiles, web-presence and user activity. Sections (4) and (5) provide case studies and discuss in detail two very different examples of user-generated digital content: *Wikipedia*, an educational, relatively formal environment, and *Facebook*, a social networking application which is deeply embedded in popular culture.

---

5 UNESCO statistics: http://www.uis.unesco.org/literacy/Pages/adult-youth-literacy-data-viz.aspx.

2 Who has access to digital technology? Who can speak and act in cyberspace?

In October 2003, UNESCO member states adopted the *Cyberspace Recommendation*, which affirms the importance of cultural and linguistic diversity on the internet. The resolution states:

> The public and private sectors and the civil society at local, national, regional and international levels should work to provide the necessary resources and take the necessary measures to alleviate language barriers and promote human interaction on the Internet by encouraging the creation and processing of, and access to, educational, cultural and scientific content in digital form, so as to ensure that all cultures can express themselves and have access to cyberspace in all languages, including indigenous ones.[6]

This formulation raises important questions: who are these private and public sectors that should ensure the multilingual nature of the internet? Who are the envisaged actors, that is, the producers of digital content? And who regulates and supports them? There is no president of the internet, and although national governments can shut it down (as has happened, for example, during the Arab Spring), they can hardly control what goes on it once they support and permit its presence.

Obviously governments can contribute directly to some form of digital multilingualism by providing information about their services in multiple languages. Software companies are important role-players as well. They have developed, for example, search engines which allow users to do searches in multiple languages, have provided support for different scripts and engaged in the linguistic localization of text processing software. But what about the "civil society" evoked by UNESCO? The speakers and writers who – in the context of Web 2.0 – have become a major force in shaping the internet and its linguistic ecology?

An important constraint for UNESCO's vision is the uneven access that exists with regard to technology. The main source for information on global access to digital media is the *International Telecommunication Union* (www.itu.int) which is affiliated to the United Nations. Two types of statistics are relevant in this context: internet access (including mobile access) and mobile phone penetration. The latter provides a stepping stone towards telecommunication access and con-

---

6 Full title: 'Promotion and Use of Multilingualism and Universal Access to Cyberspace'; available at http://www.unesco.org/new/en/communication-and-information/about-us/how-we-work/strategy-and-programme/promotion-and-use-of-multilingualism-and-universal-access-to-cyberspace/.

stitutes, in the words of Goggin (2011: 4), 'an important part of the contemporary global media system'.

However, there remain deep global inequalities with regard to internet access: the majority of people in the Global South are still not in a position to use the internet as a communication tool.[7] Internet access is typically concentrated among the educational elite who are well-to-do and able to afford computers and/or internet-capable mobile phones. Moreover, bandwidth is expensive in the Global South and usually paid for per megabyte (unlike the all-you-can-surf contracts which are common in the Global North). At the same time, it is important not to over-generalize as the Global South is highly heterogeneous: it includes Singapore with an internet penetration rate of 71%, Brazil with an estimated 41%, but also Cuba with 16%, India with 8%, and Cameroon with 4% (ITU data for 2010; the estimate for the United States was 74% in 2010).

It is, however, possible that current ITU statistics, which are based on broadband subscriptions, under-estimate digital access: internet access can also be via mobile phones and/or shared computers. A recent study by *Basis Research* (www. insightsafrica.com) looked at internet usage in urban Ghana, Kenya, Nigeria, Senegal, South Africa and Uganda (data collection 2010/2011, 13,000 interviews conducted). The results show that about 50% of urban residents in these countries have used the internet in the past (with the familiar pattern of highest use in the younger age groups), and usage is regular and growing. Cyber-cafés are a common point of access in the West and East African countries, whereas mobile access is pervasive in South Africa. Each national context thus offers different challenges and opportunities for those who look at the internet as a tool to promote, preserve, or simply use, indigenous languages. Careful techno-ethnographies are needed to understand local challenges, and to contextualize observed practices.

In addition to the access divide, we also need to consider the usage divide: what matters is not only ownership of, or access to, a given technology, but also what people can do with this technology (Hargittai 2003). Thus, writing/reading skills (literacy) and technical skills (sometimes referred to as computer literacy) matter: not only do we need to be able to read and write in the language we wish to use, we also need to know how to operate the technology (Van Dijk 2005). Modes of access also affect our use of the technology. Cyber-cafés, for example, raise issues about privacy and data storage, lack of control over network settings,

---

7 The following countries and geographical regions are commonly considered to form part of the Global North: Europe, North America, Australia, New Zealand, Japan. The rest of the world is grouped under 'developing world' or Global South.

outdated equipment and inadequate software as well as limited opportunities for spontaneous and experimental use (see Lim, 2009, for a review of the literature). Similarly, mobile-access can limit digital practices: many websites are not developed with mobile users in mind, and specially designed mobi-sites (mobile websites) frequently offer limited functionality. The mobile version of *Wikipedia*, for example, only allows one to search, but not to edit and contribute. It also does not allow access to the discussion pages which are an integral part of the full web version, and necessary for a critical reading of the information provided.

Given these material conditions: who are the producers of web content in African languages? Rivon (2012) provides an instructive discussion of the use of Eton on *Facebook*. Eton is a Cameroonian language with a population of around 50,000 speakers. Cameroon, as noted above, has very low levels of internet access. Eton is one of Cameroon's many smaller-to-medium-sized languages, and – unlike larger African languages – does not exist in a standardized, written form. These unfavourable conditions notwithstanding, Eton has a noticeable web presence on cultural heritage sites, blogs and social networking sites (especially *Facebook*). Although French is the dominant language on these sites, Eton material occurs in the form of emblematic, socially-symbolic code-switching. Who are the actors who have created these virtual spaces in which Eton is digitally represented in a written form? Rivon refers to them as "cosmopolitan literati, if not expatriates" and stresses the "decisive role of cosmopolitan elites" in establishing digital spaces for indigenous languages. Thus, in the case of the Eton *Facebook* groups the founders and moderators were "a white Cameroonian, a Cameroonian expatriate in the United States, and a Cameroonian Intellectual" (Rivon 2012: 165). The Diaspora, as well as bilingual outsiders, thus emerge as an important group of actors.

Consider another case: texting in N'ko, an indigenous West African script which is used for Mande, a family of closely related languages spoken across West Africa (estimates of speaker numbers vary, but 'range in the tens of millions', Wyrod 2008: 30). The N'ko script was created in the 1940s. However, typewriters using N'ko orthographic symbols were never produced *en masse* and texts were often copied by hand. Using DOS, a first digital font was produced at Cairo University, and in 2006 N'ko was added to Unicode, a character set which allows text production in a wide range of scripts, and thus helps to overcome the constraints of ASCII (which includes only Latin letters). Similarly to Eton, N'ko websites are mainly produced by "cosmopolitan elites": Ibrahima Traore, who left Guinea in the 1980s to move to New York, runs the website *kourousaba.com* (which has an associated *Facebook* site); Mamady Doumbouya, a retired software engineer from Philadelphia, coordinates the *N'ko Institute of America* (fakoli.net); Baba Mamdadi Diané, who established an N'ko studies programme at the University of Cairo, runs *kanjamadi.com* and was actively involved in the development of the Unicode standard for N'ko (Wyrod 2008; Rosenberg 2011). The involvement of Diaspora elites has thus been important in making indigenous languages visible in the digital space and such elites can be agents of change.

3 Measuring the multilingual internet – where are we now?

According to Crystal (2011: 78), the most notable development of the internet since its inception in the early 1990s has been its diversification, its move from an English-dominant space to an increasingly multilingual space (see also Danet and Herring 2007; Goggin and McLelland 2009). However, there remains disagreement as to the magnitude of the transformation. One the one hand, Prado (2012: 39) notes that the relative presence of English has declined from about 75 percent in 1998 to an estimated 30 percent in 2012 (see also Pimienta at el. 2009). On the other hand, Gerrand (2010) maintains that "all circumstantial evidence points to English remaining the statistically, as well as culturally, dominant written language of web presence on the Internet up to the present" (see also Paolillo 2007).

Reliable statistics are hard to come by. Frequently assessments are based on user profiles, that is, "the number or proportion of active internet users in each language group" (Gerrand 2007). In other words, how many speakers of Russian are online, how many speakers of Akan, how many speakers of Hindi, and so forth? To rely on such user profiles is problematic as it is quite possible that these individuals may not use Russian, Akan or Hindi online, but English as a global lingua franca. In other words, we cannot assume *a priori* that off-line language choices are the same as on-line language choices. Such limitations notwithstanding, these statistics show unequivocally that the user base is becoming ever more diverse in terms of its geographic and linguistic origins, and this creates the *potential* for the diversification of digital practices. The growing presence of China, especially, is clearly visible in the Alexa global rankings[8]: among the top ten web sites are not only the usual global suspects (*Google, Twitter, Facebook, YouTube, Wikipedia*), but also more localized sites such as *Baido* (a Chinese search engine) and *QQ* (a Chinese social networking portal; September 2012). If the geographical location of users is at best an approximate measure of the internet's diversity, what other options are available to estimate the degree of multilingualism on the internet?

A second option is to analyze what Gerrand (2007) has called web-presence, that is, to calculate the overall proportion of webpages that are available in differ-

---

8 http://www.alexa.com/topsites.

ent languages. Daniel Pimienta and his colleagues (2009) studied the representation of English, German and the Romance languages on the internet. They used a set of 57 key words, measured their occurrence using search engines, and, finally, calculated a combined index for each language using the full set of key words. Although useful for obtaining a broad estimate of a given language's representation on the internet, this approach has serious limitations because current search engine behaviour is far from ideal. Pimienta et al. (2009: 20ff; also Gerrand 2007) list the following constraints:

(a) No search engine is able to search the entire web (the current estimate is that search engines cover about 30 percent of the web);
(b) Different search engines use different algorithms and results across search engines are therefore inconsistent;
(c) Search engines tend to be biased towards English and other languages, especially those using a non-Roman script, tend to be marginalized.

The methodology, and its pitfalls, can be illustrated with a simple example using one of the words in Piemento et al.'s set: the adverb *today*. Table (1) gives word page counts for *today* in languages of my own repertoire: English, German, Afrikaans and isiXhosa. The overall linguistic hierarchy (English > German > Afrikaans > isiXhosa) is likely to be reliable, given the large and consistent differences in numbers (from billions to millions to thousands). However, the actual page numbers need to be taken with several pinches of salt. For example, the very first *Google* entry for isiXhosa *namhlanje* comes from the English-speaking site wiki.answers: *What does 'namhlanje' mean in Xhosa?* The second entry directs me to *Namhlanje Travel Agency,* followed a few entries down by a video for Abdullah Ibrahim's song *Siyahamba namhlanje* ('we are leaving today'). Moreover, *namhlanje* is also used in isiZulu, a closely related language, and the count thus includes pages in both languages. Similarly, for *vandag, Yahoo!* immediately includes the Dutch spelling *vandaag*, and lists sites with both spelling variants (even when preferences are set to 'search exact phrase').

While best seen as a crude approximation, search engine-based approaches are useful. The data summarized in Table 1 shows clearly that isiXhosa material is present on the internet, even though frequencies remain low. Moreover, a longitudinal analysis (using the custom range 1/1/1992 to 15/5/2012) shows that this presence has grown since the early 1990s when only one webpage containing the word *namhlanje* could be located via *Google* (on the on-line growth of African languages see also De Schryver 2002; Osborn 2010).

Growth notwithstanding, African languages remain severely underrepresented on the internet. The *Language Observatory* in Japan collected a set of almost forty million webpages from African domains, and determined the lan-

Key words	English		German		Afrikaans		isiXhosa	
	Google	Yahoo!	Google	Yahoo!	Google	Yahoo!	Google	Yahoo!
today/heute/ *vandag/* *namhlanje*	6800 million	2600 million	110 million	100 million	5 million	228 thousand	43 thousand	8 thousand

Table 1: English, German, Afrikaans, and isiXhosa: web presence estimation (Date of search: 15 May 2012; search engines: google.com/yahoo.com; results are rounded)

Language	Number of pages	%
English	30,327,396	78.40
French	2,737,455	7.08
Afrikaans	660,510	1.71
Arabic	592,746	1.53
Chinese	391,745	1.01
Portuguese	348,131	0.90
Russian	307,178	0.79
Spanish	276,126	0.71
Japanese	158,992	0.41
Others	2,884,916	5.10
TOTAL	38,685,195	100.00

Table 2: Language composition in the African web domain (Yoshiki and Kodama 2012: 136)

guage of each using a specially developed language identification programme (Yoshiki and Kodama 2012).[9] English was found to dominate African-domain web content with 80 percent. Surprising in their data is the low representation of French and Portuguese, which – like English – are ex-colonial languages and continue to be used as official languages on the continent.

The biggest challenge for understanding digital multilingualism is user-generated content. Gerrand (2007) terms this third, and perhaps most important measure, user activity. However, while we can search public webpages for key words in different languages, we cannot easily search user-generated content in the form of, for example, instant messaging chats, blogs, emails, *YouTube* video comments, *Facebook* wall postings, and tweets. Privacy and ethical issues loom large for many of these genres, and as noted somewhat tongue-in-cheek by Gerrand: "The only organizations known to have the resources to do this are the

---

9 The identifier is available from http://gii2.nagaokaut.ac.jp:8080/g2liWebHome/index.jsp, and currently supports just under 200 languages.

national security agencies, and they have yet to publish their results" (ibid). User activity is typically approached through case studies and frequently limited to a specific genre (e.g. email or chatting) and a specific population (e.g. university students). The following two sections will provide an analysis of user-generated content on two popular sites: *Wikipedia* and *Facebook*.

Wikipedia – the popular, collaboratively-edited, online encyclopedia – is well-suited for both quantitative and qualitative analysis: it provides detailed longitudinal statistics on each language version, all entries can be dated, their creators can be identified, and subsequent edits to texts can be traced.[10] Although misspellings and ungrammatical constructions occur, they usually get corrected over time, and the style for *Wikipedia* entries approaches formal academic prose (Baron 2008: 124).

Facebook does not offer the same ease of access and data (such as wall posts) have to be manually collected and quantified. Stylistically, *Facebook* – as a social network(ing) site – exhibits primarily relational and interactive language use. The focus is on forming and maintaining social relationships, not on exchanging information. However, the informal, interactive genres of *Facebook* deserve close attention from digital researchers: it is the top site on the internet, both globally and on the African continent (Table 3). *Wikipedia*, while important, clearly plays second fiddle.

Country	Facebook	Wikipedia
Algeria	1	20
Cote d'Ivoire	1	12
Egypt	1	23
Ghana	1	11
Kenya	1	8
Libya	1	13
Madagascar	2	9
Nigeria	1	11
Senegal	1	19
South Africa	2	9
Sudan	1	17
Tunisia	1	10
AVERAGE AFRICA[11]	1.2	13.5
GLOBAL RANKING	1	6

Table 3: Top-sites per country, rank number (http://www.alexa.com/topsites/countries, September 2012)

---

10 http://stats.wikimedia.org/EN/Sitemap.htm. Unless otherwise indicated, data presented in the following sections is based on the statistics available on this site. All quantitative data was updated in September 2012.
11 Google is the number one site in Madagascar and South Africa.

4 Wikipedia – "one of online multilingualism's greatest successes"?

Wikipedia has received considerable praise for its multilingual ethos and design. Bortzmeyer (2012:381), for example, describes it enthusiastically as one of "online multilingualism's greatest successes". The encyclopaedia is not only meant to be collaborative, free and comprehensive, but also multilingual. In the words of *Wikipedia*'s founder Jimmy Wales:

> Wikipedia is first and foremost an effort to create and distribute a free encyclopedia of the highest possible quality to every single person on the planet in their own language (2005).[12]

As noted by Petzhold (2011: 29), *Wikipedia* can be seen as representing a "benchmark [project] of Anglo-based efforts for a more multilingual web". The basic ideological premise is one of parallel monolingualisms and separate versions are available for different languages (for a critical discussion of Wikipedia's linguistic ideologies see Ensslin 2011). They are created through the so-called community model, that is, (unpaid) volunteers translate and write new articles. Their motivations are varied and include altruism, fun, wanting to learn new things, and showing off (Nov 2007). At the time of writing, *Wikipedia* was available in over 280 active language versions, the majority of which were created between 2002 and 2004 (Figure 1).

African languages remain a minority group on *Wikipedia*: they account for only 13 percent of the total number of editions, and a mere 1.83 percent of the

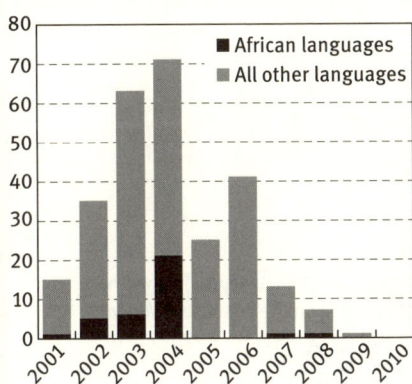

Figure 1: Number of *Wikipedia* language editions created per year, 2001–2009

---

12 http://en.wikipedia.org/wiki/Wikipedia:The_rules_are_principles.

total article count. In the following two sections, I will take a closer look at five different *Wikipedias*: the isiXhosa *Wikipedia* (established 2004), one of the least successful projects; as well as the Afrikaans, Kiswahili, Malagasy and Yorùbá *Wikipedias* (established in 2001, 2002, and 2003 respectively) which are currently the most successful African language projects.

4.1 The isiXhosa *Wikipedia*

The isiXhosa Wikipedia has been a 'problem child' for many years: in September 2012 the official article count was a mere 148 – only Twi, Tumbuka and Kashmiri had fewer articles at the time.[13] IsiXhosa is a south-eastern Bantu language, spoken by around eight million speakers in South Africa, where it has co-official status and is used in education, government publications, print media, TV and radio. It has a well-established standard form and a literary tradition which dates back to the 1820s. As I show in detail elsewhere (Deumert in preparation), the isiXhosa version of *Wikipedia* is marred by serious problems of quality and would hardly be an attractive reading choice for native speakers, who are usually bilingual in English and would thus have access to the high-quality English version.

The growth of the isiXhosa *Wikipedia* shows three spurts in content production: in 2005, there was a growth from 3 articles to 25; in 2007, 51 articles were produced; and in the first five months of 2012, 25 new articles were added (Figure 2).

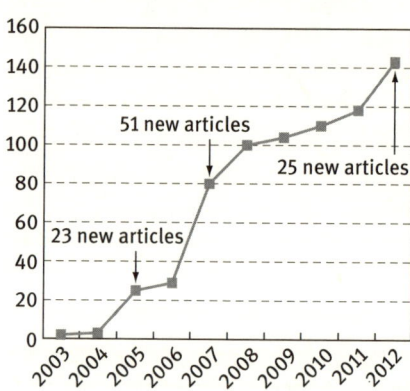

Figure 2: Cumulative article growth (number of articles) on the isiXhosa *Wikipedia*, 2003 to May 2012

---

13 Two other projects, *Wikibooks* and *Wiktionary* in isiXhosa, have been closed due to lack of activity.

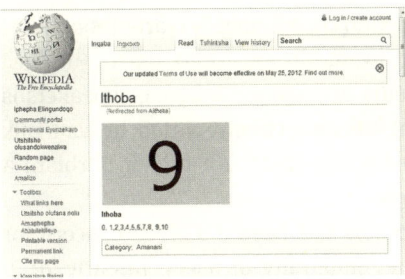

Figure 3: Article 'nine' in the isiXhosa *Wikipedia*. Created by user Pandinosauria in 2007

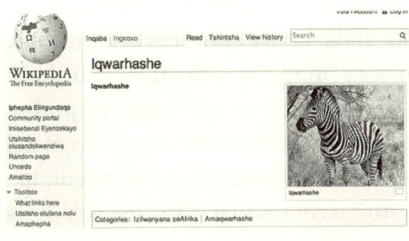

Figure 4: Article for 'zebra' in the isiXhosa *Wikipedia*. Created in 2007 from an IP address in New South Wales, Australia

In 2005, all but one entry were created by the same user in the month of June. Although he or she did not register a name, the IP address can be traced to a computer in Phoenix, Arizona, United States. The writer's knowledge of isiXhosa is limited and the entries produced are linguistically problematic and, at times, entirely incomprehensible.

The growth in 2007 was possibly a response to *Wikipedia's* 2006/2007 publicity drive to support African languages. This created a fair amount of interest and press-coverage.[14] As a result, contributions are no longer the work of a lone language enthusiast, but of a more diverse and varied group of authors. However, the majority are again second language speakers, with very limited language skills: from the United States, Germany, Australia, New Zealand, Spain and Turkey. The articles are frequently mechanically constructed. For example, user *Pandinosauria* (Spain) added ten articles which – in the fashion of word lists – simply give the isiXhosa equivalent for the numbers one to ten (Figure 3). Other pages are reminiscent of illustrated dictionaries: they give the isiXhosa word in the title, repeat it in the text and illustrate its meaning with an image (i. e. they do not provide a text definition as required by the encyclopedic format; Figure 4). In 2007, there

---

14 Examples include: http://www.nytimes.com/2006/08/26/arts/26wiki.html; http://news.bbc.co.uk/2/hi/africa/5072596.stm; http://wikimediafoundation.org/wiki/Press_releases/Wikipedia_Academies; http://www.ethanzuckerman.com/blog/2007/05/16/the-survival-of-languages-in-a-digital-age/.

was also one isiXhosa-speaking user, Xola, who contributed two articles on local topics. However, his involvement was short-lived.

Active engagement of language amateurs and second language speakers is not limited to the isiXhosa *Wikipedia*, but has also been reported by Van Dijk (2009) for Kiswahili (see below), and by Petzold (2011: 106 ff.) for Sorbian, a Slavic minority language spoken in Germany.

The lack of isiXhosa-speaking contributors has been a serious concern for *Wikipedia* and its vision of establishing a community of users. In early 2012, Douglas Scott, an English-speaking South African *Wikipedian*, organized a number of workshops in Cape Town to encourage native speakers to contribute to the isiXhosa *Wikipedia*. He targeted African language departments at local universities and introduced academics, as well as students and language professionals, to *Wikipedia*. There was an immediate benefit in terms of growth: at the workshops each participant would create at least one new article. As a result, the overwhelming majority of new articles in 2012 were created – for the first time – by native speakers: they were substantial in terms of volume and appropriate in terms of language use. However, non-native language enthusiasts remained a strong feature of the isiXhosa *Wikipedia*: *MirkoS18*, a nineteen year-old speaker of Serbian, and *Midnight Green*, a speaker of Russian, joined in early 2012 and contributed content. According to their Babel Box – an image on their user page which indicates their knowledge of, and proficiency in, different languages (see Figure 6 for an example) – neither of them had any knowledge of isiXhosa.

The Cape Town workshops did not lead to the hoped for community of editors and user activity declined immediately after completing the workshops. The reasons for this are multifaceted, ranging from limited computer skills to lack of interest, motivation and/or time. Ian Gilfillan (see above) reflected on the experience in his blog (April 2012; http://www.greenman.co.za/blog/?p=953):

> Particularly disappointing has been Xhosa. I know of at least three Xhosa Wikipedia workshops that have taken place, at the University of Cape Town, the University of the Western Cape and with the provincial government, and yet it still remains as the smallest of the official South African language Wikipedias.

4.2 *Wikipedia*'s African successes – Malagasy, Yorùbá, Kiswahili and Afrikaans

It is not difficult to understand *Wikipedians* disappointment regarding the encyclopedia's performance on the African continent: although there are more than 30 editions of *Wikipedia* in African languages, the vast majority of them are very small and contain only a handful of articles (Figure 5). As a point of comparison:

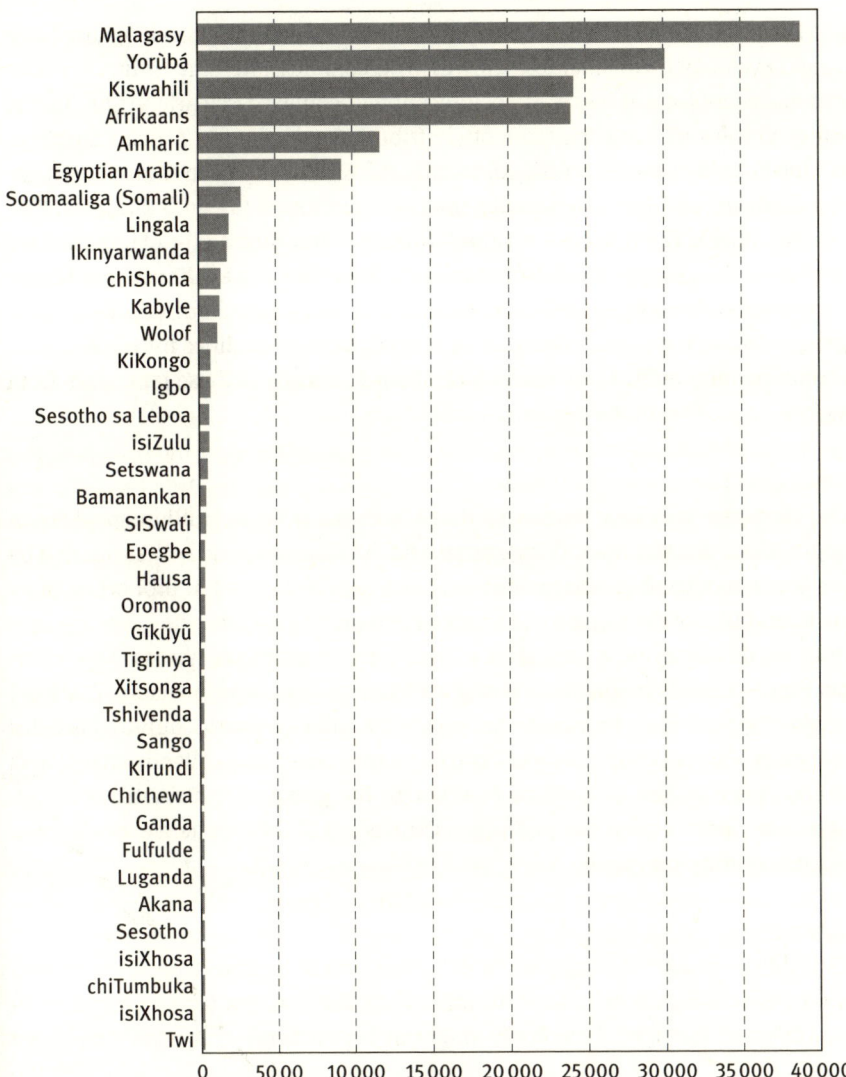

Figure 5: African language Wikipedias, number of articles per language(as of 18 September 2012; http://meta.wikimedia.org/wiki/List_of_Wikipedias)

the English *Wikipedia* has close to 14 million articles; the German and French *Wikipedias* well over one million; Italian and Russian are approaching the one million article mark; Vietnamese and Catalan have more than 300,000 articles; Basque, Hindi and Malay over 100,000.

However, the picture is not altogether bleak and some African languages editions have shown considerable growth. The complex interplay of literacy/education, technology access and socio-economic context is clearly visible in the editor profiles of – and patterns of contribution to – the top African language *Wikipedias:* Malagasy, Yorùbá, Kiswahili and Afrikaans. All four languages are standardized and have well-established written norms (as does isiXhosa, discussed above). The presence of standardization and *Ausbau* (or elaboration) is important. Languages which lack standardization face quite different challenges compared to those discussed here. Focusing on large, standardized African languages throws the fundamental social and political inequalities into relief: there is nothing inherently 'linguistic' which should stop any of these languages from succeeding in the digital domain.

Afrikaans
The language is closely related to Dutch and has over six million speakers in South Africa and Namibia. During apartheid, Afrikaans was heavily supported by the government and language-activism has a long history. A fair proportion of its speakers fall into the top income brackets in South Africa, and the language continues to be supported by cultural and political organizations. Access to the internet is not a serious problem, and most contributors are native speakers. There are several high-profile editors who have each contributed several hundred articles (between 200 and 1700). The work can be characterized as a collaborative project in the best tradition of *Wikipedia*: although the group of contributors is small (which is typical across *Wikipedia*, see Panciera et al. 2009), there exists a sense of a community among them.[15]

Kiswahili
Kiswahili is a north-eastern Bantu language which is used as a lingua franca across East Africa. It has about 40 million speakers and is usually acquired in childhood. Kiswahili is commonly taught in Departments of African Languages across Europe and North America, and non-native speakers who engage with the Kiswahili *Wikipedia* frequently come from these educational backgrounds (Van Dijk 2009). In contrast to the non-native contributors of the isiXhosa Wikipedia, their proficiency levels allow for meaningful text production. The Kiswahili *Wikipedia* has three highly active contributors: *Baba_Tabita* (2,573 articles, German L1 speaker and a member of the *Summer Institute of Linguistics;* has lived in East Africa for many years), *Kipala* (1,936 articles, German L1 speaker; has also lived in

---

15 http://meta.wikimedia.org/wiki/Tell_us_about_Afrikaans_Wikipedia.

East Africa for many years), and *Muddy_Blast_Producer* (3,208 articles; a native speaker of Kiswahili from Dar es Salaam). It is this mix of native and high proficiency non-native contributors which has come to characterize the Kiswahili *Wikipedia*.[16]

Malagasy/Yorùbá

These are currently the top two *Wikipedias* on the continent. Both editions were created by and large by single individuals, albeit assisted by technology.

Malagasy is an Austronesian language spoken on the island of Madagascar by about 15 million people. Over 90 % of the entries in this edition were created by user *Jagwar*, often – it appears – with the assistance of a bot (*Jagwar-bot*) which would help to create short stubby articles and thus boost the overall article count. *Jagwar* – an expatriate, native speaker who lives in France – notes in his response to the 'Tell us about your Wikipedia' project that there are many barriers to local content production: many Malagasy cannot read and write, internet connections are slow and expensive, computers costly, and content production is not remunerated ("as there is no wage given").[17] The latter is a serious concern in countries where there are no, or minimal, social welfare provisions and people struggle to maintain their livelihoods. The 'community model' of collaborative content generation requires contributors who are sufficiently affluent so that they can 'gift' their time and skills without serious socio-economic repercussions.

Yorùbá belongs to the western Volta-Niger group and is spoken by about 20 million people in Nigeria, Benin and Togo. The Yorùbá *Wikipedia* was dormant until 2007 when user *Demmy*, a native speaker of Yorùbá from Nigeria, began to contribute. As in the case of the Malagasy *Wikipedia*, his activism was technologically aided by a bot which helped to create pages.[18] Similar one-person efforts are also evident for some smaller editions. An example is the Northern Sotho *Wikipedia* where Mohau Monaledi, a South African software developer and native speaker of the language, created over 80 percent of articles. Thus, rather than harnessing the 'wisdom of crowds', realizing *Wikipedia*'s vision in the context of restricted access relies very much on dedicated individuals, who are not only motivated to contribute, but who are also in a position to 'gift' their time.

With over 280 separate language editions, *Wikipedia* certainly looks like a successful example of user-generated multilingual content. However, as argued

---

16 http://meta.wikimedia.org/wiki/Tell_us_about_Swahili_Wikipedia.
17 http://meta.wikimedia.org/wiki/Tell_us_about_Malagasy_Wikipedia.
18 http://wikipediocracy.com/2013/01/16/whos-the-best-yoruban-wikipedian-of-them-all/.

above, the majority of these editions are very small and, because of the involvement of language enthusiasts rather than proficient speakers, frequently of
dubious quality.

Successful African language *Wikipedias* require the involvement of native
speakers. Yet, issues of access are a concern. Only the Afrikaans *Wikipedia* –
which serves a socio-economically advantaged community – shows consistent
and collaborative native speaker involvement. In the case of, especially, the Malagasy and Yorùbá *Wikipedias*, success is the result of individual activism. Efforts
to encourage native speaker contribution have not shown much success for the
isiXhosa *Wikipedia* – and since the language is not commonly taught in the
Global North – contributions from well-meaning non-native contributors are best
interpreted as symbolic. They are a visible affirmation of *Wikipedia*'s multilingual
ethos. However, they do not produce usable content.

Native speakers of isiXhosa might only rarely be found on Wikipedia, but
they are prolific contributors on various social networking applications (see
Deumert forthc. a for examples and discussion). The crowds, which are absent
from *Wikipedia* (Deumert 2014), are found here.

5 Facebook – Indlu ka Xhosa ('the house of Xhosa')?

A recent study of two remote villages in southern Africa (Macha in Zambia, and
Dwesa in South Africa), found *Facebook* to be the main application accessed via
wireless networks which had been installed as part of a development project
(Johnson et al. 2010). In a 2010/2011 study of internet use among Cape Town's
youth (aged 15 to 20, N = 553) over 90 % were on *Facebook*, with some variations
depending on socio-economic status. Since 2008, the number of South Africans
on *Facebook* has increased from 700,000 to over 5.4 million (September 2012).

An important aspect of *Facebook* is that it is easily accessible via mobile phones,
which – as noted in Section (2) – are an important mode of digital access in South
Africa. In terms of language choice on *Facebook* two levels can be distinguished:

(a) the language of the interface (which has been available in languages-oth-
er-than-English since 2008), and
(b) the language of interaction (wall postings, messages, chats).

Looking at data from Tunisia and Egypt, El Zaim (2012) found that these two
choices rarely match: overall users opted more frequently for the non-local/global
default in the interface, but would use mainly local languages in their interactions (Table 4). However, online language choices are striking in their diversity

		Tunisia	Egypt
Interface	Arabic	1.56	48.88
	English	2.72	48.98
	French	95.60	0.39
Interaction	Arabic	51.53	75.40
	English	0.95	25.60
	French	47.62	0.00

Table 4: *Facebook* language choices: interface vs. interaction (based on El Zaim 2012: 332; 2011 data is self-reported; in percentages).

and generalizations are difficult. In the case of older bulletin board services, for example, local language use was found to be rare: even dedicated discussion groups for specific languages (Gaelic, Krio, Basque) showed dominant use of the majority language (English and Spanish respectively; Danet and Herring 2007: 21). In such contexts the use of the non-dominant language is typically limited to emblematic functions, such as greetings, culturally specific genres, or code-switching is used as a contextualization cue (Androutsopoulos forthc.). This is particular pronounced for languages such as Yiddish or Ladino which can be described as 'post-vernacular', i. e. they are no longer used regularly in everyday spoken interactions, but continue to have strong symbolic value and cultural significance (Benor 2011).

Although isiXhosa is listed as one of *Facebook*'s interface language options, its selection does not create an isiXhosa environment: the interface remains predominantly English, with just one isiXhosa word (*thanda* for 'like'), and a number of isolated phrases in (!) Turkish (for a critical discussion of *Facebook*'s approach to interface translation via volunteers, see Lenihan 2011). IsiXhosa speakers thus experience *Facebook* generally through the English interface. However, use of isiXhosa occurs on private walls and is common in *Facebook* groups dedicated to Xhosa-ness. A simple group search lists a myriad of such groups:

Xhosalite
Jokes in Xhosa
99 % Xhosa Comedy
Proudly Xhosa
Xhosanostra
INDLU KA XHOSA ('the house of Xhosa')
Xhosa's are beautiful
Xhosa Boyz
Jokes in Xhosa Lingo
Xhosa People Rock!!!
how many xhosa's are there on facebook
FACEBOOK XHOSA IS DA FUTURE

In these groups, meaningful participation in wall discussions is not possible without solid knowledge of isiXhosa. The remainder of this section will focus on two groups which have been around for several years: *Xhosa People Rock!!!* was established in 2007; *how many xhosa's are on facebook* in 2008.[19] Their respective mottos/descriptions are:

> *Siluhlang' oluhle! Vumani bo!* ('We are a beautiful nation! Agree to that!')
> *Amaxhosa amahle* ('the beautiful Xhosas')

Apart from the identity-affirming 'we are beautiful', the first motto also includes the phrase *vumani bo!* The literal translation of this imperative ('agree to that!') does, however, not capture its emotional meaning and deep imagery. The phrase is used in spiritual contexts of ancestor veneration when the diviner (*isangoma* or *igqirha*) requests affirmation from those seeking his or her help. The requested answer would be *siyavuma* ('we agree'). Its use in the digital context is marked and purposely establishes a link between traditional oratory practices and the new, emerging digital world. The symbolism of *vumani bo!* is echoed on the group's photo page: images of people dressed in traditional attire, engaging in the performance of ritual practices (see Figure 6 for an example).

On the walls of the two groups, three language choices can be observed: isiXhosa-only, English-only, and mixed language use, involving alternational as well as insertional code-switching between isiXhosa and English (a style which broadly mirrors the colloquial language use of many bilingual speakers; see Deumert and Masinyana 2008). Use of isiXhosa-only is by far the dominant

Figure 6: Image of an *isangoma* from the photo page of *Xhosa People Rock!!!*[20]

---

19 Both groups were reconstituted in the new group format in 2011. However, they lost a large number of their followers. They are still active, but much less so than in 2008.

20 Source: https://www.facebook.com/photo.php?fbid=15045376887&set=o.2462736951&type=3

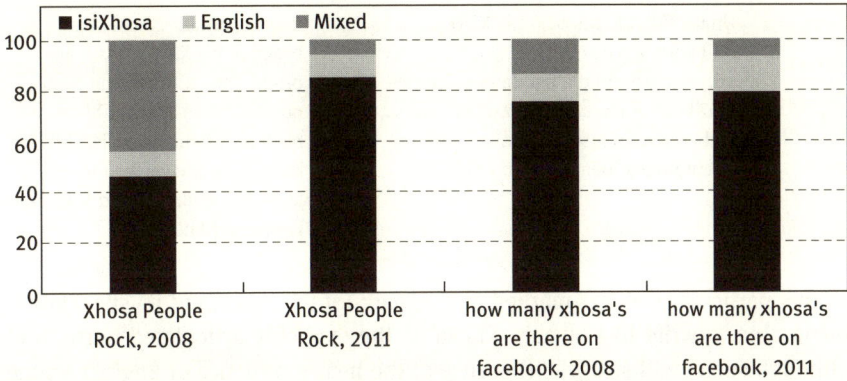

Figure 7: Language choices on *Xhosa People Rock!!!* and *how many xhosa's are on facebook*, 2008 and 2011; in percentages. (Based on random sample of 100 wall postings plus comments, October 2008/2011)

choice in both groups in 2011, and has replaced the use of a mixed English-isiXhosa style on *Xhosa People Rock!!!* (Figure 7).

In 2008, when it was still relatively early days on South African *Facebook*, language choices were a topic of overt discussion. Examples (1) and (2) come from *how many xhosa's are there on facebook?*, and show the expression of normative linguistic ideologies in dialogic action. Unlike in the earlier discussed cases of Eton and N'ko, the Diaspora is being sidelined in the case of isiXhosa. In (2), Babalo, who resides in Australia, is admonished for her limited skills. This is not a group which encourages the symbolic and emblematic use of isiXhosa, but which demands full use of the language.

(1)   Siyabonga: bekufanele into yokuba sithetha isixhosa sodwa apha,nanjengamaxhosa. Kaloku akufuneki siliyeke ifuthe lasentshona lide lingene nzulu apha kuthi

'As Xhosas we're supposed to be talking isiXhosa only here. Because we must not let the Western influence sink deeply on us'

Sonwabo: KWEKHU!!! wathetha ngengomXhosa nyani ngoku.
Lusuko: ewe yazi ndicing'ba nam masithethe isiXhosa apha, nangona ke abanye bethu bezokusokola

'WOW! You really speak like a pure Xhosa now'
'Yes, you know, I also think we must speak only isiXhosa here, although some of us will struggle'

(2)   Babalo: is it ok if i speak english! i am not very talented on writing ma language
Sonwabo: please try writing in the beautiful clicking language. do for us Xhosas

Unati: Ndigum Xhosa othi "XHO"
ndinebhongo ne qhayiya ngobu Xhosa bam,
ndiyazingca, ndidla ngodana xa omnye
umXhosa ofana nam, exakwa sisiXhosa,
kodwa ulwimi lase mzini ulzai mhlope!
Phambili ngolwimi lethu maXhosa!!!

'I am a genuine Xhosa, I am
proud of my Xhosaness, I am
proud, I usually become disap-
pointed when another Xhosa like
me has difficulty with isiXhosa,
but he/she knows the foreign
language well! Forward with our
language Xhosas!!!!'

In this particular *space* – marked as a *place*[21] for isiXhosa (and its speakers) – being able to write like 'a pure Xhosa' is the explicitly articulated norm, and although some 'will struggle' (because of the heavy influence of English on the language, especially in the lexicon), everyone must at least try. The style tends to be formal, rather than colloquial, and there is a sense of 'showing-off': wall postings are generally in full standard orthography, and mistakes are rare (in the above extracts, for example, there is only one misspelling: *ulzai* for *ulazi*). And it is not just about purging the language from English influence and to write accord-ing to the (monolingual) standard norm, equally important is it to have knowl-edge of traditional ways of speaking.

A long-standing concern of Anglo linguists has been to locate digital com-munication in relation to spoken and written language (see, for example, Baron 2008; Crystal 2006). In many ways, however, this has been a prototypical red herring, intellectually indebted to the old idea of a 'great divide' between orality and literacy (a perspective which goes back to the work of Eric Havelock, Walter Goody and Jack Ong). This divide, however, is culturally contingent and the isiX-hosa data is a case in point. Orality in isiXhosa cannot be equated with informal-ity, and formal oratory skills are greatly valued. These oratory skills find their rep-resentation on *Facebook* in the form of elaborated greetings and introductions.

Greeting and salutation rituals are an important aspect of on-line language use (see, for example, Rintel et al. 2001; also Androutsopoulos 2013), and are found regularly on the walls of these *Facebook* groups. Greetings, as noted by Duranti (1986), are central to communication as they allow participants to frame their social relationships in particular ways – as friendly or formal, as local or global –, and evoke a shared tradition and history. Traditional isiXhosa greetings do not merely salute, but also include the clan name and clan praises of the indi-

---

21 *Space* and *place* are not synonyms. In this context, *space* refers to a kind of geographical and virtual 'container', a backdrop against which human behaviour is played out. Space can be transformed into *place*, i. e. belonging, lived and experienced intimacy and emotion, through discursive action (see Deumert 2013, for a detailed discussion).

vidual. Clan names (*iziduko*) are based on the name of a male ancestor and reflect shared descent, history and kinship. It is possible to use one's clan name as an alternative name, and such usage is a sign of respect to the lineage. Thus, Nelson Mandela is affectionately known as Madiba, the name of one of his ancestors. In addition, every clan has so-called clan praises attached to it. These praises trace the lineage of the clan sequentially, from the most distant (male) ancestor to the most recent one. They are recited in ceremonial contexts, can form part of personal introductions, and are used in contexts where one wishes to honour the person one addresses (Opland 1983: 43 ff.).

Examples of such salutations are given in (3) and (4). Both examples come from the group *Xhosa People Rock!!!* (2008). In (3), Vuyokazi introduces herself by reference to her historical ancestor Mpinga; in (4), Zolani recites the clan praises of his family, and refers to his fellow Xhosas in traditional style as 'Phalo's children, those of Zanzolo'. Phalo is a direct descendant of Xhosa (the common ancestor of the ethnic group); Zanzolo is his great-grandson.

(3) Vuyokazi: Maqobo nani maqoboka-   'Young men and women, the Mpinga's
zana, owase mampingeni umntana   child is greeting'
uyazibulelisela.

(5) Zolani: Ngukhwalo lo uNcuthu,   'This is Kwahlo, Ncuthu, Mlanjane,
umlanjane, usohopeza, uNkuma,   Sohopeza, Nkuma, Ndikelo of Mazang-
Ndikelo wase Mazangweni, Kwa Sinxo   weni. From Sinxo in Xesi at Njwaxa, let
Exesi Enjwaxa, Mandingene Ndizi-   me get in and greet for myself beautiful
bulisele kuni MaXhosa amahle Nto   Xhosas, Phalo's children, those of
zikaPhalo uZanZolo. Ndimtsha Apha   Zanzolo. I am new here, I hope it will
Ndiyathemba kuzobamnandi apha.   be pleasurable here.'

Not knowing one's clan name and the ancestors that form one's lineage can be seen as a sign of cultural dislocation. Thus, in the acclaimed novel *Coconut* (Matlwa 2007), the sixteenth birthday of Ofilwe – a young Black middle-class woman – is spoiled when her friends connect to one another by sharing 'their clan names and the histories behind them' (p.59). Ofilwe, however, is left out of this process of social and emotional bonding. Her schooling has placed her in an English-only environment and she knows too little about her African roots to participate: 'how foolish must I have looked, sitting there silently with not a thing to share' (ibid.). Similarly, Sibulele Magini, a South African blogger, writes: 'Knowing your "Isiduko" is vital to the Xhosas and it is considered a shame and "Uburhanuka" (lack-of-identity) if one doesn't know one's clan.' (http://fubustyle.blogspot.com/2010/09/clan-names-of-xhosas.html).

Elaborate traditional greetings were not a fad of the early isiXhosa *Facebook*. Examples (6) and (7) are 2011 postings from *how many xhosa's are on facebook* and *Xhosa People Rock!!!*. In addition, traditional salutations continue to occur on private walls, for example, in the context of wishing someone a happy birthday; and are performed by both men and women. In oral discourse, on the other hand, they are primarily the domain of men. In this creative, digital recontextualization of existing oral practices (Bauman and Briggs 1990), we see the reshuffling of traditional hierarchies and boundaries, and thus a redefinition of who constitutes the 'legitimate speaker' for this genre.

(6)   Alizwa: molweni bethuna.. ithi intombi yakwa Xhosa, intombi yakwa Tshezi, ooJalamba, OoFakade mayikhe izbulisele kule ntsasa nje... ndinethemba nani maXhosa amahle niphilile... Eish simnandi isixhosa inene!!!   'Hello folks, says the Xhosa girl, the girl from the Tshezis, the Jalambas, the Fakades, let her pass a greeting in this morning, I hope that you too beautiful Xhosas are well, Eish Xhosa is really nice'.

(7)   Ziyanda: baphi ooNxuba, OWashota ooNgcengane OoZwelibhangile ....LiRhudulu Lase Mthatha eli Molweni zino zakuthi   'Where are the Nxubas, Washotas, the Ngcengane, the Zelibhangile ... This one is the Rhudulu from Mthatha: Greetings to you'

These are examples of performance or 'verbal art' in the sense of Bauman (1977), that is, moments within communicative encounters where speakers/writers show 'special attention to and heightened awareness of the act of expression' (p.11). In addition, such acts of performance are 'capable of evoking pleasure in the participants' (Bauman 1972: 331), that is, they elicit an aesthetic response. This is clearly visible with regard to example (7), where a fellow member of the group responds: 'im impressed!!!!!!'. To this Ziyanda answers: 'i might be living a mordern lifestyle bt i know my roots u see'.

The *Facebook* data suggest that social networking sites are emerging as an important space for the use – and, especially, creative performance – of indigenous languages. Paolillo (2007: 426) has suggested that indigenous languages have 'an expressive advantage' in modes of digital communication where there is a sense of real interaction between participants. *Wikipedia*, on the other hand, is a lonely space: although discussion pages allow for some interaction, the general mode of participation is far removed from the lively, and often playful, face-to-face encounters in which African languages thrive in everyday life.

6 Conclusion

This volume deals with the theme of sociolinguistic change as well as, by implication, continuity. How does the data discussed in this chapter relate to the larger
theme? There certainly has been change in terms of access over the last ten or so
years: many more people, speakers of many different languages, have now access
to the internet. This has led to the internet becoming a more diverse, more multilingual space. However, diversity remains skewed and, as discussed in Section
(3), the African continent and its over 2000 languages remain only marginally
represented. The digital space thus continues to be a site of struggle, i. e. a space
where existing power structures – reflected for example in unequal access to
digital technology – entrench imbalances and inequalities. These imbalances
apply to all three measures of internet diversity: user profiles, web-presence and
user activity (Gerrand 2007).

Wikipedia is an important example of user-generated, multi-lingual content;
yet, it has fared badly with respect to African languages. Lack of access remains
a serious stumbling block and it is not surprising that minority languages of
the North fare considerably better than even large community languages, such
as isiXhosa, in the South. For African languages, there are less than 0.5 active
editors[22] per million speakers; for Cree, Navajo and Pennsylvania German there
are more than 10 editors per million speakers. The importance of access is further
exemplified by the case of Afrikaans, a language whose history is unlike that of
other African languages: many of its speakers have been privileged (in terms of
education, socio-economic status and political power) and the language received
strong state support from 1948 to the 1990s. The fact that access to digital media
is greatly easier in the North – or, more generally, for those who live in socio-economically privileged contexts – also contributes to the type of actors we see: many
are expatriates in the Diaspora, or language enthusiasts with widely varying
levels of proficiency in the language(s) they wish to support.

However, access alone does not explain the current failure of *Wikipedia* to
attract African editors. The problems go deeper: they are located within *Wikipedia*'s knowledge project which claims to be universal, yet, constitutes a particularly Western view of knowledge, and ultimately asks speakers of other languages
(and cultures) to assimilate to this view. The list of 'articles every Wikipedia
should have' is an odd collection from an African perspective: no African script
is deemed important enough for inclusion; African philosophical traditions are
absent; African political structures such as 'chieftainship' are not listed; among

---

22 Defined as those who have contributed 5 or more edits.

the 120 people, for whom biographies should be written, only Nelson Mandela is mentioned for sub-Saharan Africa; and among the five social issues deemed important (abortion, capital punishment, human rights, racism and slavery), 'poverty' is conspicuous by its absence.[23]

In 2012, a South African user who participated in one of the local isiXhosa *Wikipedia* workshops established a page titled *Iziduko zethu* ('our clan praises'), and listed the praises for the Bamba, Bangula, Bhayi, Bhedla and Bhele clans. It was – to my knowledge – the only page created during the workshops which did not simply translate material from the English *Wikipedia*, but instead provided locally meaningful content. Ironically perhaps, this desire had long before found its expression on *Facebook* walls where speakers have been actively engaged, freely creating locally meaningful content in isiXhosa. The popular social networking site is thus transformed into a treasure chest of traditional knowledge, complete with the performance of writer's identities in interaction, creating the communities of users *Wikipedia* wishes to establish. This is not the 'neutral point of view' (NPOV) embraced by *Wikipedia*, but a performance which is simultaneously playful and serious, boldly partial and passionate, unapologetically affirming local, indigenous identities and knowledges.

References

Androutsopoulos, J. 2011: Language change and digital media: A review of conceptions and evidence. In: K. Tore and N. Coupland (eds.), *Standard languages and language standards in a changing Europe*, 145–161. Oslo: Novus

Androutsopoulos, J. 2013: Code-switching in computer-mediated communication. In: S. C. Herring, D. Stein and T. Virtanen (eds.), *Handbook of the Pragmatics of CMC*, 667–694. Berlin/Boston: Mouton de Gruyter.

Baron, N. 2008: *Always On. Language in an Online and Mobile World*. Oxford: Oxford University Press.

Bauman, R. 1972: The La Have Island General Store: Sociability and Verbal Art in a Nova Scotia Community. *The Journal of American Folklore* 85: 330–343.

Bauman, R.1977: *Verbal Art as Performance*. Prospect Heights, Illinois:Waveland.

Bauman, R. and C. L. Briggs 1990: Poetics and Performance as Critical Perspectives on Language and Social Life. *Annual Review of Anthropology* 190: 59–88.

Benor, S.B. 2011: Jewish Languages in the Age of the Internet: An Introduction. *Language & Communication* 31: 95–98.

Bortzmeyer, S. 2012: Multilingualism and the Internet's Standardisation. In: L. Vannini and H. Le Crosnier (eds.), *NET.LANG. Towards the Multilingual Cyberspace*, 105–118. Caen: C&F éditions.

---

23 http://meta.wikimedia.org/wiki/List_of_articles_all_languages_should_have.

Cystal, D. 2006: *Language and the Internet.* Second Edition. Cambridge: Cambridge University Press.

Crystal, D. 2011: *Internet Linguistics. A Student Guide.* London/New York: Routledge.

Danet, B. and S. C. Herring (eds.) 2007: *The Multilingual Internet. Language, Culture and Communication Online.* New York: Oxford University Press.

Deumert, A. in preparation: *Sociolinguistics and Mobile Communication.* Edinburgh: Edinburgh University Press.

Deumert, A. 2014: The Performance of a Ludic Self of Social Network(ing) Sites. In: Philip Seargeant and Caroline Tagg (eds.), *The Language of Social Media: Communication and Community on the Internet,* 23–45. London/New York: Palgrave/MacMillan.

Deumert, A. 2013: Xhosa in Town (Revisited) –Space, Place and Language. *International Journal of the Sociology of Language* 222: 51–75.

Deumert, A. and O. S. Masinyana 2008: Mobile Language Choices – The Use of English and isiXhosa in Text Messages (SMS), Evidence from a Bilingual South African Sample. *English World-Wide* 29: 117–148.

De Schrywer, G.-M. 2002: The Web for/as Corpus: A Perspective for the African Languages. *Nordic Journal of African Studies* 11: 266–282.

Duranti, A. 1986: Framing Discourse in a New Medium: Openings in Electronic Mail. *The Quarterly Newsletter of the Laboratory of Human Cognition* 8: 64–70.

El Zaim, A. 2012: Cyberactivism and Regional Languages in the 2011 Arab Spring. In: L. Vannini and H. Le Crosnier (eds.), *NET.LANG. Towards the Multilingual Cyberspace,* 325–336. Caen: C&F éditions.

Ensslin, A. 2011: "What an Un-wiki Way of Doing Things": Wikipedia's Multilingual Policy and Metalinguistic Practice'. *Journal of Language and Politics* 10: 535–61.

Feenberg, A. 1991: *Critical theory of technology.* New York: Oxford University Press.

Gerrand, P. 2007: Estimating linguistic diversity on the Internet: a taxonomy to avoid pitfalls and paradoxes. *Journal of Computer-Mediated Communication* 12: 1298–1321.

Gerrand, P. 2010: The Multicultural Internet – Parallel Worlds? Review of Gerard Goggin and Mark McLelland (Eds.), Internationalizing Internet Studies. In: *Telecommunications Journal of Australia* 60. (http://www.tja.org.au/index.php/tja/article/view/82/html).

Gireoux, H.A.and R. I. Simon 1988: Schooling, Popular Culture, and a Pedagogy of Possibility. *Journal of Education* 170: 9–26.

Goggin, G. 2011: *Global Mobile Media.* London/New York: Routledge.

Goggin, G.and M. McLelland (eds.) 2009: *Internationalizing Internet Studies. Beyond Anglophone Paradigms.* London/ New York: Routledge.

Hargittai, E. 2003: The digital divide and what to do about it. In: D.C. Jones (ed.), *New Economy Handbook,* 822–841. San Diego: CA: Academic Press.

Johnson, D.L., E.M. Belding, K. Almeroth and G. Van Stam 2010: Internet usage and performance analysis of a rural wireless network in Macha, Zambia. In: ACM Workshop on Networked Systems for Developing Regions (NSDR'10), June 15, 2010, San Francisco, CA, USA. 2010. Available from: http://portal.acm.org/citation.cfm?id=1836001.1836008.

Lenihan, A. 2011: 'Join Our Community of Translators': Language Ideologies and/in Facebook. In: C. Thurlow and K. Mroczek (eds.), *Digital Discourse. Language in the New Media,* 48–66. Oxford: Oxford University Press.

Lewis, M. P. (ed.) 2009: *Ethnologue: Languages of the World.* Sixteenth edition. Dallas, Tex.: SIL International. (Online version: http://www.ethnologue.com/).

Lim, S.S. 2009: Home, School, Borrowed, Public or Mobile:Variations in Young Singaporeans' InternetAccess and Their Implications. *Journal of Computer-Mediated Communication* 14: 1228–1256.

Matlwa, K. 2007: *Coconut. A Novel.* Auckland Park: Jacana.

Nov, O. 2007: What Motivates Wikipedians? *Communications of the ACM* 50: 60–64.

Opland, J. 1983: *Xhosa Oral Poetry. Aspects of a Black South African Tradition.* Johannesburg: Ravan Press.

Osborn, D. 2010: *African Languages in a Digital Age. Challenges and Opportunities for Indigenous Language Computing.* Cape Town: HSRC Press.

Panciera, K., A. Halfaker L. and Terveen 2009: Wikipedians Are Born Not Made. A Study of Power Editors on Wikipedia. *GROUP '09: Proceedings of the ACM 2009 international conference on Supporting group work.* Available at: http://grouplens.org/system/files/Group09WikipediansPanciera.pdf.

Paolillo, J.C. 2007: How much Multilingualism? Language Diversity on the Internet. In: Danet and S.C. Herring (eds.), *The Multilingual Internet. Language, Culture and Communication Online,* 408–430. New York: Oxford University Press.

Petzhold, T. 2011: *The Uses of Multilingualism in Digital Culture: The Case of Inter-Language Linking.* Unpublished PhD Thesis, Queensland University of Technology, Australia.

Pimienta, D., D. Prado. and A. Blanco 2009: *Twelve Years of Measuring Linguistic Diversity on the Internet: Balance and Perspectives.* Paris: UNESCO.

Prado, D. 2012: Language Presence in the Real World and in Cyber Space. In: L. Vannini and H. Le Crosnier (eds.), *NET.LANG. Towards the Multilingual Cyberspace,* 35–52. Caen: C&F éditions.

Rintel, E.S., J. Mulhollandand J. Pittam 2001: First Things First: Internet Relay Chat Openings. *Journal of Computer-Mediated Communication* 6. http://jcmc.indiana.edu/vol6/issue3/rintel.html.

Rivon, V. 2012: The Use of Facebook by the Eton in Cameroon. In: L. Vannini and H. Le Crosnier (eds.), *NET.LANG. Towards the Multilingual Cyberspace,* 161–168. Caen: C&F éditions.

Rosenberg, T. 2011: Everyone Here Speaks Text Message. *New York Times,* 11 December 2011.

Van Dijk, J. 2005: *The Deepening Divide.* London: Sage.

Van Dijk, Z. 2009: Wikipedia and Lesser-Resourced Languages. *Language Problems and Language Planning* 33: 234–250.

Warschauer, M. 1998: Technology and indigenous language revitalization: Analyzing the experience of Hawai'i. *Canadian Modern Language Review,* 55(1): 140–161.

Walton, M., and J. Donner 2011: Read-Write-Erase: Mobile-mediated publics in South Africa's 2009 elections. In: J. E. Katz (ed.), *Mobile Communication: Dimensions of Social Policy,* 117–132. New Brunswick, NJ: Transaction Publishers.

Wyrod, C. 2008: A Social Orthography of Identity: The N'ko Literacy Movement in West Africa. *International Journal of the Sociology of Language* 192: 27–44.

Yoshiki, M. and S. Kodama 2012: Measuring Linguistic Diversity on the Net. In: L. Vannini and H. Le Crosnier (eds.), *NET.LANG. Towards the Multilingual Cyberspace,* 35–52. Caen: C&F éditions.

All webpages cited were live as of 11 September 2012.

Sari Pietikäinen
Circulation of indigenous Sámi resources across media spaces.
A rhizomatic discourse approach

The dynamic nature of many contemporary media spaces creates novel and potentially contested ways of using, mixing, and moulding languages. The circulation of minoritized languages, such as the indigenous Sámi languages, across media spaces stirs up existing language practices, categories, and hierarchies. Such processes of transition also highlight the tensions between various constructions and understandings of language change. At the same time, discursive innovations, and the creative use of a variety of meaning-making resources, indigenous language included, result in new types of crossings, mixtures, and norms for mediated indigenous language practices. These transitions underscore the need to examine circulation as a complex, rhizomatic sociolinguistic process, and it is this perspective that is addressed in this article.

Looking at the circulation of Sámi resources across media spaces as a sociolinguistic process provides, as I will argue below, a fruitful perspective for examining language change in media. This is particularly the case with minoritized language contexts like the indigenous Sámi languages, where media is given an important role in community building, in increasing language prestige, and in language revitalization. Circulation is a term often used to refer to fluid and dynamic movement in a circle or in other form of system. However, in this article I draw on work by philosophers Deleuze and Guattari ([1980] 1987) in understanding circulation as a perspective to explore shifting and multiple (re)configurations and conflation of language resources in a complex, rhizomatic network of spaces. This understanding of circulation is helpful in my attempt to examine multiplicity of mobility of Sámi resources across already inhabited and connected media spaces. I will return to this rhizomatic discourse approach below.

In this article, I will draw on my longitudinal discursive and ethnographic research[1] on Sámi in media (Pietikäinen 2003, 2008) and on language change in Sámiland in terms of multilingualism (Pietikäinen 2010, 2013a; Pietikäinen et al. 2008). The data come from a range of media spaces, including Sámi television

1 This article is based on the *Peripheral Multilingualism* research project (www.peripheralmultilingualism.fi), funded by the Academy of Finland.

news, Sámi television comedies, press coverage on Sámi programmes, and social media discussions of these programmes. This data is complemented by ethnographic data, including interviews with and written mission statements by Sámi journalists and ethnographic observations of journalistic working practices in Sámi media as well as various informal discussions about the comedy show with its viewers. With a rhizomatic discourse analysis of this data (Pietikäinen 2013a), I will explore what happens to Sámi languages in this circulation across media spaces. I will next give a brief description of the sociolinguistics of Sámiland, with an emphasis on the Finnish part of this transnational area, before moving on to discuss the rhizomatic discourse approach applied here to examine Sámi circulation in media spaces. I will then present an analysis of two cases of Sámi circulation, and conclude with a discussion of the conditions and consequences of this circulation.

1 Sociolinguistic transitions in Sámiland

Sámiland is often regarded as a "periphery" from the perspective of the southern urban "heartlands" of the nation states concerned (Finland, Norway, Sweden, and Russia). However, this geographical periphery has a long history as a central nexus of the Sámi people, as well as of mobility, multilingualism, and mixed ways of making a living, now intensified by globalization. The Sámi, who number approximately 60,000–80,000, are an indigenous people living in Scandinavia and northwest Russia. There are nine Sámi languages in all. The language with the highest number of speakers is Northern Sámi (c. 30,000 speakers), whereas other Sámi languages have as few as 250 to 400 speakers each (Aikio-Puoskari 2005; Kulonen, Seurujärvi-Kari and Pulkkinen 2005). Today, it is estimated that only half of the Sámi people speak the language, while almost 70 per cent of Sámi people live in urban areas outside of the traditional Sámi domicile area. This transition has increased the significance of the role of Sámi media spaces as sites for practicing and experiencing Sámi languages (cf. Pietikäinen 2008).

Sámi communities have gone through several changes, many familiar from accounts of other minority and indigenous language contexts. Resulting from a language shift within a relatively short period of time of two generations (Aikio 1988; Lindgren 2010), the role of a Sámi language varies among its speakers: for some, the language is a daily resource, for others it is a school subject, and for still others it is a resource used only for ritual purposes. Currently there are no monolingual Sámi speakers, and Sámi languages are a part of the multilingual repertoire of speakers and a part of multilingual practices in the communities. Before the Second World War, Sámi languages were regularly learned as mother tongues, and were widely used as primary means of daily interaction in the community. However even then, many people were multilingual and knew, in addition to their own language, other Sámi languages, Finnish, and other national languages (Lehtola 1997; 2000; Lindgren 2000). The postwar years after 1945 and the modernization process that has swept across the world have had deep effects on Finnish society, and at the same time on Sámi communities. One crucial factor is development of an educational system. With minor exceptions, Finnish-only education marked the beginning of a large-scale language shift from the Sámi languages to Finnish (Aikio 1988), and had drastic effects in narrowing down the domains of Sámi language use. Also, as the attitudes of the majority population towards Sámi culture and language were largely negative, the languages became increasingly marginalized, and the number of speakers decreased (Aikio-Puoskari 2001). Furthermore, while the postwar generation was educated in Finnish, they were frequently trained in jobs and professions that required majority language skills. Yet during these years of language shift, Sámi activism also began to strengthen. By the 1970s, it was evident that the language issue had to be reconsidered. The Sámi community was now working actively for its civil and linguistic rights. Today, the Sámi languages have a regional official status in three northern municipalities of Finland (for a review in the Nordic context, see Pietikäinen et al. 2010). The Sámi Language Act (1991), along with certain constitutional amendments, acts, and laws have made Sámi-language services possible in many areas of everyday life, including education and media (see Aikio-Puoskari 2001).

Sámi media have developed in this politically and linguistically changing and complex space of Sámiland. Nowadays the Sámi media—along with Sámi media, film, and journalism studies—is a significant local employer and a site for Sámi language practices and development. However, the historical trajectory of the Sámi in media tells a story familiar from many other minority language media. The written history of Sámi languages is relatively long, though very scarce, and consists mainly of very few, mainly religious texts in Northern Sámi language (Lehtola 1997). Yet the lack of resources restricts the activity of newspapers published in Sámi languages. There are no daily Sámi newspapers in Finland; only one magazine, *Anarâš*, is published quarterly in Inari Sámi. The broadcast history of Sámi began in the early twentieth century. The first broadcasted Sámi event was a church service in Northern Sámi. More regular radio programmes started in the middle of the twentieth century. Sámi radio has a long tradition in the Sámi revitalization movement, and has served as one of the instruments of language revitalization and maintenance (Sara 2004). The development of Sámi radio within the Finnish public broadcasting company YLE is often considered the result of persistent, long-term work by the Sámi to bring Sámi radio into existence (Lehtola 1997). The language policy—to make programmes for the Sámi, in Sámi and by the Sámi—has always been a key element and a driving force in Sámi radio development and programming (Pietikäinen 2008; Sara 2004). Today, the Sámi radio on the Finnish side of Sámiland produces approximately 11 hours of programming daily, mainly in Northern Sámi, and a few hours weekly in Inari and Skolts Sámi each. TV programmes in Sámi or made by the Sámi are still a rarity, although new developments have taken place in the past 15 years: following years of preparation, joint Sámi television news broadcasts were launched in 2001. A 15-minute television news programme, *tv-Oddasat*, is broadcast nationwide on weekdays in Norway, Sweden, and Finland, with subtitles in majority languages. It is also available on the internet. Sámi children's television programmes, subtitled in Finnish, also began in the autumn of 2007. The latest development in Sámi television is a comedy programme, which began broadcasting in 2012, and is also accessible through social media. On the whole, the use of Sámi languages in the social media and internet started relatively late, and with some linguistic ideological tensions: Sámi languages have special characters and letters, and debates occurred regarding whether the standard written version would be the only acceptable version for use on the internet, or whether it would also be acceptable to use a slightly modified version to overcome some technical obstacles. Now new technological development has removed most of these problems, and the standard written form can be used without any serious issues.

2 A rhizomatic discourse approach

This article takes up a discursive understanding of media as a space produced and experienced in human interaction (cf. Pietikäinen 2013a; Scollon and Scollon 2003). This has two implications relevant to the aim of this article. Firstly, it puts forward a view of space as a complex and dynamic social construction (Jaworski and Thurlow 2010; Lefebvre 1991; Pennycook 2010). This means that what is understood as a particular space—say, the space related to Sámi languages—is an object of constant negotiation and (re)defining. A space is not empty, but is carved out and performed in a complex and changing system of semiotic practices and circulating discourses. For example, Pennycook (2010: 56) argues that we can see space as a process. This means that a particular space, such as the Sámi media space, is not developed in isolation, but rather in relation to other spaces. What becomes interesting, then, is the ways in which spaces are organized, and the question of what logic lies behind a particular kind of structuring of available resources within a particular space. Thus, the reformulation of multilingual Sámi media spaces as set of relations is accomplished by confronting both creative and normative dimensions. Mediated Sámi spaces can thus be understood as a complex set of spaces and their relationships.

This definition comes close to what other key spatial thinkers have suggested about how space might be understood. For example, Foucault (1984, see also 1994) argues that we live in a heterogeneous space in which various relations, orders, and logics can be juxtaposed, in "a network that connects points and intersects with its own skein" (Foucault 1994: 22). Foucault introduces the concept of heterotopia to refer to other spaces and their relationships. This view moves away from understanding space as fixed and unchanging, as a kind of vacuum within which we locate individuals and objects. It rather encompasses temporal and spatial aspects of space, and the ways in which space is produced in interactions and through language practices (cf. also Pennycook 2010: 55–56). Thus, in any particular space – such as the space of Sámi media, or even of one particular television programme – there is potentially a juxtaposing of several different spaces, typically linked to cycles of time. For example, as we will shortly see, the Sámi television news broadcast connects with the spaces of national television news broadcasts in Norway, Sweden and Finland, rooted in the historical development of these nation states and media development therein. From this perspective, any space refers to real places or sites in which the social structuring is simultaneously represented, contested, and inverted. Thus heterotopia highlights that we are living in heteroglossic spaces, where structures and counterstructures, logics and regimes all coexist.

The argument that I wish to develop in this article is that, if the spaces are viewed as a result of social structuring with their own rationalities and with rhizomatic links to other spaces, then the circulations of Sámi languages across these various spaces stir up existing language relations and hierarchies, and potentially create new language practices, and even users. Also, the particular media spaces through which Sámi languages circulate impact on their perceived value and function; this is because, as Pennycook (2010) reminds us, spaces, just like places, are already constituted by previous uses, norms, and histories. Moreover, we need, I believe, to develop a complex understanding of circulation and trajectories of resources across spaces, one that allows for multiple entry and exit points as well as multiplicity of trajectories. To analyse heteroglossic spaces and multiplicity of circulation of Sámi resources across complex networks of these spaces call for, I would argue, an approach that takes this multiplicity and connectivity as a starting point. In my view, rhizomatic discourse approach offers some promising steps towards this. This conceptual move makes use of the conceptualisation of *rhizome* by Deleuze and Guattari as a construct that sees the processes and events to be observed in terms of *flow* and *dis/connections* (Deleuze and Guattari 1987; Honan 2004). Deleuze and Guattari (1987: 23) ague that "the rhizome is an acentered, nonhierarchical, nonsignifying system without a General and without an organizing memory or central automation, defined solely by a circulation of states".

Thus a rhizomatic discourse approach to language circulation in a particular time and space is not a closed or unchanging unit, but is rather an open system, emerging and transforming in the course of interaction. Consequently, relationships between language practices and their networked characteristics are implied and are seen in connection with historical, social, economic, and political practices and processes. As Honan (2007) explains in talking about applications of the rhizomatic approach in education research, discourses about languages operate in rhizomatic ways – they are not linear or separate, but instead, any text, sign, or speech act potentially includes several interlinked discourses, which are connected to and across each other. Thus a rhizomatic discourse analysis traces the lines of trajectories that connect different language practices and discourses (Pietikäinen 2013a). In this approach, the researcher becomes a map maker, who instead of perfect duplication, maps out alternative routes, trajectories and crossroads (cf. Foucault 1994).

In language research, rhizomatic approaches, such as multisided ethnography or nexus analysis in discourse studies aim to trace the changing trajectories and circuits of language resources. Such approaches also make it possible to capture the connectivity and interaction between and across resources—the end result of which is often contestation and creativity. As Appadurai (1996: 5) argues, it is only through the analysis of these trajectories that we can interpret the human transactions and calculations that enliven things. Languages move along trajectories of cycles of change from language into material products or practices, and back to languages (Scollon and Scollon 2004). To give an example, endangered Sámi languages, used as community and identity resources among Sámi communities, can be turned into a part of tourist souvenirs in the labelling practices of Sámi tourism products, such as t-shirts, mugs, hats, dishes etc. Potentially, these products and their labelling practices provide a contact zone (Pratt 1987) for the tourists to encounter Sámi languages (Pietikäinen, 2013b; Pietikäinen and Kelly-Holmes 2011). Tracing the trajectory of particular languages helps to explain the shifting meanings and values of particular languages and the various historical, political and economic processes underpinning them.

Language circulation results in a particular kind of polycentric environment, where people have a range of overlapping navigation points to choose from, and where traces of various languages can be found inscribed on the landscape (Pietikäinen 2010). To investigate this kind of multilayered and polycentric multilingualism, a conceptual move taken in this article is to see Sámi media as spaces, albeit linked to a geographical place, but always constructed situationally in interaction, and hence emerging (possibly) differently in different contexts. The media spaces under scrutiny here can hence be seen as a nexus point, where different Sámi resources and their trajectories, along with discourses about them, come together. This conceptualization is an application of the work by Scollon and Scollon (2001, 2004), whereby a nexus can be understood as a point at which historical trajectories of people, discourses, practices, experiences, and objects come together to enable some action which itself alters those historical trajectories (Scollon and Scollon 2004: 159).

To map out the circulation of Sámi resources and the rhizomatic connections between this mobility and the media spaces, I draw on my long-standing discourse analytic and ethnographic research on Sámi in media, including newspapers, Sámi Radio and Sámi television programmes (cf. Pietikäinen 2003, 2008, 2010). These previous studies provide an understanding of the diachronic processes taking place in media environment, as regards Sámi resources. Secondly, I have mapped out the current key media sites for Sámi resources, and chosen two sites that are crucial for Sámi languages in terms of circulation and potential for language change. These two sites are the multilingual Sámi television news program, *tv-Oddasat*, and a multilingual Sámi television comedy, *Märät Säpikkäät/Njuoska Bittut*. In the current Sámi media environment, these two programmes have the widest circulation in terms of audience and in term of various media spaces, including social media. These two programmes must also negotiate their language policies (e.g. on subtitling) and make use of various language resources, Sámi languages being one of them. Potentially then, these two programmes provide an interesting nexus for examining language change. For both programmes, the data includes the programme itself, its website and social media presence (e.g. Facebook, Youtube, comments, "likes"). In addition, the journalists working at Sámi Radio in Finland (which also produces the Sámi television news from the Finnish part of Sámiland) have been interviewed, and an ethnographic study of their working practices has been carried out (Pietikäinen 2008, 2010). As a part of the ethnographic study, these journalists have also written mission papers on the role and future of Sámi media. For the Sámi comedy, the data also includes media coverage of the programme and its producers from the time of the programme's broadcast period (January–April 2012). To analyse this multidimensional data, I will develop and make use of the rhizomatic discourse approach described above. In this work, I will draw on ideas of rhizome and circulation as discussed by Deleuze and Guattari (1987) and others applying these ideas (Honan 2004, 2007; Wallin 2010). In addition, I will apply some aspects of the discourse analysis called nexus analysis (Scollon and Scollon 2004). This is a form of transdisciplinary, multidimensional discourse analysis that emphasises the simultaneous coming-together of experiences of participants, circulating discourses, and interactional normativities in any moment of language use. Adapted to current study, this can be seen as bringing together the research strategies of ethnography, discourse analysis, and genre analysis (Pietikäinen 2013a). Against this backdrop, I next turn to the two media spaces: the television news programme *tv-Ođđasat*, and the multilingual Sámi television comedy, *Märät Säpikkäät/Njuoska Bittut*.

3 Circulation across Sámi media spaces

3.1 Space 1: Superfixed multilingual space: tv-Ođđasat

The Sámi television news broadcast *tv-Ođđasat* was launched in 2001, and is often considered a real breakthrough in Sámi media efforts. This relates to the value given to the visibility of television in minority media planning and prestige. *TV-Ođđasat* is jointly produced by Sámi newsrooms in Norway, Sweden, and Finland. The three newsrooms were brought together for economic reasons, as their collaboration was the only way to make this news production economically viable. For over 10 years now, 15 minutes of television news have been broadcast nationwide on weekdays in Norway, Sweden, and Finland, using mostly Northern Sámi as the lingua franca, and with subtitles in the majority languages. The programme can also be viewed on the internet for a few days after the broadcast.

Both Sámi radio and *tv-Ođđasat* are profiled as designated Sámi programmes. When talking about their work in research interviews, the Sámi journalists involved emphasized three aspects in particular. First, they said that their mission is to be the voice of Sámiland, bringing a Sámi perspective to news world. In the words of one of the news editors: *"the most important task is, obviously, is to tell the Sámi people about issues relevant to Sámi people"*, (interview 6.10.2003). The constant ambivalence here is, of course, the heterogeneity in Sámi communities regarding boundaries between Sámi and non-Sámi, and regarding multilingual practices. Secondly, they argued that it is important to make news about events and hot topics in Sámiland, and in that way to strengthen the idea of one Sámiland and one Sámi nation—very much in the sense of Benedict Anderson's (1983) classic notion of imagined communities and the role of media in nation-building. This is, however, now made more complicated by the audience beyond the geographical area of Sámiland. A further complication related to the choice of news topics: while the journalists agree that the Sámi topics to be covered in *tv-Ođđasat* include reindeers, land rights, and cultural issues, the different news criteria in respective countries also bring in other topics, such as crime and conflict in Sámiland. This kind of tabloidization of *tv-Ođđasat* was not perceived well by all journalists, as one of the news editors comments in the mission text written in August: "As *tv-Oḍḍasat* is jointly produced by YLE, NRK, and SVT, we have three different models of news. And this makes prioritization difficult. NRK's emphasis regarding news topics is different from ours". What can be seen emerging here, I would like to suggest, are tensions caused by attempts to localize – or better, to indigenize – the national order, related to what is perceived to be nationwide news media and the genre norms of television news related to what is perceived to be newsworthy and good journalism.

In the sociolinguistic context of the indigenous Sámi languages, the television news programme creates a media space that is economically and ideologically heavily invested. This investment has created, I would like to argue, a super-fixed multilingual space where languages and their boundaries are regulated and policed by explicated norms regulating language practices, and by a monolingual ideological orientation (cf. Jaffe 2007). To begin with, the official language policy of *tv-Oḍḍasat*, and more generally that of YLE Sámi radio, is a Sámi-only language policy. This means that everything that is aired, music included, is in Sámi languages—most often in Northern Sámi, and occasionally in other Sámi languages. In practice, this means that interviews or clips from other news broadcasts in any other language than Sámi (such as Finnish) are translated and dubbed into Northern Sámi, the largest Sámi language in terms of number of speakers and domains of use (cf. Pietikäinen and Kelly-Holmes, 2013). Occasionally, other Sámi languages are aired without dubbing. As less than half of the Sámi people speak any of the Sámi languages, and since it is extremely rare that any of the majority-speaking interviewees (municipality officials, politicians, local people, etc.) speak any Sámi language, dubbing is used on a regular basis on *tv-Oḍḍasat*.

Dubbing is very seldom used in the Scandinavian context, with subtitles typically being preferred. In the case of *tv-Oḍḍasat*, the reason for dubbing is clearly language-ideological: while dubbing is one method of facilitating understanding and overcoming language barriers, in the case of *tv-Oḍḍasat* there are no practical reasons for dubbing in Sámi. Both the journalists and the audience would fully understand interviews in the appropriate majority language, regardless of whether they belong to the Sámi or the majority community. Yet for language-ideological reasons, linked to revitalization and language planning of Sámi languages, dubbing is required in the creation of a Sámi-language media space – even though it is expensive and time-consuming. In fact, given the position of the Sámi languages in people's repertoires, the dubbing of majority language voices in Sámi creates a language barrier for more than half of the Sámi people, and to almost every viewer of the majority community. Consequently, subtitles in the original majority language are now needed to overcome the language barrier created by dubbing in Sámi. Thus, there is a circuit of translation and mode transitions: first, a voice in the majority language is voiced-over in Sámi, and simultaneously the original majority voice is given in subtitles in the majority language in question. This language-ideological desire to have a Sámi-language-only space also creates a shift in modalities: in the first instance, the spoken majority language (e.g. Finnish) is translated and dubbed over in Sámi, and at the same time subtitles are provided in the original majority language (i. e. Finnish). This is a case where the language-ideological reasons override the economic reasoning of cost-effectiveness.

What we see here, I would argue, is the emergence of a superfixed Sámi media space. This is analogous to what Bucholtz (2001: 88) describes as a linguistic superstandard. She argues that, "a linguistic superstandard is a variety that surpasses the prescriptive norm established by the standard (...) It may also go beyond these norms, to the point of occasionally over-applying prescriptive rules and producing hypercorrect forms". If this idea of a superstandard is applied to the context of *tv-Oðdasat*, the norm of using only the (Northern) Sámi language and its most recent standard variant in the broadcasts erases (Irvine and Gal 2000) the multilingualism present in the community, in the working environment, and in the audience. This official language policy rather creates superfixed multilingual practices in a situation where the standard itself is constantly evolving due to the endangerment of the languages, the various variants of Sámi, and the fact that multilingual repertoires and practices are a part of everyday language use (cf. Lehtola 1997). The practices are superfixed in the sense that an extra effort is made on a daily basis to keep the Sámi languages apart from other languages and to police the boundaries with explicit norms and rules (see below). Within the context of language endangerment, the establishment of clear linguistic boundaries and the foregrounding of monolingual language practices can play a critical role in the work of identification, differentiation, and political and cultural legitimation for speakers. However, the superfixed multilingual Sámi practices exemplified in *tv-Oðdasat* conflict with the multilingual and diverse language practices which exist among the journalists themselves and in the audience. This leads to language-ideological tensions, as many Sámi speakers struggle with the ambivalences brought about by the contrast between their own dynamic language practices and the dominant (boundary-oriented) ideologies of language.

This tension is illustrated in the data related to the multilingual practices of the Sámi journalists working in radio- and television programmes. As a part of research on language policy in Sámi Radio, the journalists were asked to reflect in writing on the possibility to use multilingual practices in their programmes, for example by using both Sámi and Finnish (without voice-over). The next two extracts come from two journalists who are very experienced in Sámi radio and television programmes. What follows are their responses to the question of multilingual practices on Sámi programmes:

Example 1a. Journalist 1. Extract from a written document 13. 12. 2006.

Ainakin pohjoissaamessa meillä on (kirjoittamattomana) sääntönä, että kaikki suomen tai muun kieliset jutut käännetään. Minusta se on ihan hyvä käytäntö tällä hetkellä. (...) Itse henkilökohtaisesti en haluaisi tehdä täysin sekakielisiä lähetyksiä, joissa ei käännetä. Se tuntuisi vähän kuin periksi antamiselta: "no okei, ei saamen kielellä pärjää, vaihdetaan sitten kieltä" tai "no saamen kieli on niin huono, että sillä ei pysty sanomaan sitä tai tätä asiaa". Käsitemaailmamme jopa saattaisi kaventua. Itse kannatan vahvasti kääntämistä.

'At least in the Northern Sámi programmes, we have an (unwritten) rule that all reports in other languages are translated. I think this is quite good practice for the moment. (...) Personally I would not like a mixed language programme in which there are no translations. It would feel a bit like giving in: "Well Okay, we do not manage with Sámi, so let's switch language" or "well, Sámi language is so bad that one cannot say this or that with it ". Ever our world of concepts might get narrower. I strongly support translating.'

Example 1b. Journalist 2, extract from a written document, 13. 12. 2006.

En usko että siinä nyt niin paljon olisi haittaa jos lähetyksissä puhuttaisiin eri kieliä. Minun lähetyksissä sitä tapahtuu jo nyt aika paljon eikä niitä aina käännetä. Huom: laiska toimittaja! Ja sen olen kans huomannut et ihmiset ovat tulleet rohkeammaksi kun huomaavat, että ei radiossa tarvitse puhua puhdasta kieltä, ei haittaa vaikka tulee virheitä. Kuvittelisin, että tulevaisuudessa tullaan käyttämään kieltä enemmän "sekaisin".

'I don't believe it would harm anyone that much if different languages were used in the programmes. In my programmes, that happens quite often already. Note: lazy journalist! And I have also noticed that people have become braver when they notice that one does not need to speak pure language on the radio, it does not matter if one makes mistakes. I would imagine that in the future, there will be more mixed language practices used.'

These two examples illustrate how the journalists manage the competing frameworks for understanding the value and meaning of both specific indigenous language and multilingual practices and identities in the Sámi context. The first example illustrates the powerful ideological framework, in which languages are conceptualized primarily as bounded, autonomous formal linguistic codes with an "essential" or natural relationship to collective identities and territories—a framework which structures many minority and indigenous language revitalization strategies (see e.g. Jaffe 2007; Pietikäinen 2010). The journalist's account echoes the traditional task of Sámi media to serve Sámi community in their own languages. The language policy of the Sámi media has been governed by this mission. It entails, however, an essentialist view of identity (being Sámi means speaking Sámi) and a monolingual standard towards language (Sámi-only language policy) echoing the modernist processes of the homogeneous construction of nation and national identity (Pietikäinen and Kelly-Holmes 2013). Minority languages are represented in a multilingual context as under threat, needing protection, often articulated through a discourse of endangerment and revitalization (Heller and Duchêne 2007; Pietikäinen, 2013a), explicated in the example by the journalist's feeling of "giving in" and a fear that use of multilingual practices would indicate that Sámi languages are not good enough.

In the second example, we can see the reflection of an alternative ideological formation—a heteroglossic perspective in which the emphasis is on language practice, as opposed to linguistic form. The emphasis on multilingual practices is seen potentially to enable audience members to find their voice and agency in media space, regardless of their language skills. Consequently, the focus moved from the languages (and skills) towards the speakers and their voice and experiences. The alternative reflection, however, is mitigated by the acknowledgement of the journalist of the dominant norm, as she refers to herself as a "lazy journalist" for not translating everything in her programme.

3.2 Space 2: Strategically hybrid Sámi space: television comedy

At the other extreme, we have the latest development in the Sámi media environment: the Sámi television comedy. The multilingual Sámi-language comedy *Märät Säpikkäät/Njuoska Bittut* represents several shifts in Sámi circulation across media spaces. The first shift relates to changes in media spaces. The vast majority of programmes in Sámi or by Sámi are broadcast on a special radio channel, *Radio Sámi*, under the umbrella of the Finnish national broadcasting company YLE. It is also distributed online. *TV-Ođđasat*, on the other hand, is broadcast on the national television channel YLE TV2, nationwide, though in a very marginal broadcasting slot—either early in the morning or very late in the evening. The Sámi television comedy represents an extremely rare exception, in that it is broadcast on the national television channel YLE TV2 during prime time, on Thursdays at 8 pm. This shift triggers another shift, this time in audience. The prime-time broadcast on a nationwide channel permits a nationwide audience, and indeed many took the opportunity to watch the new show: for example, the first episode had an audience of 250,000 viewers – a large number in Finland, which has about 5.4 million inhabitants. Furthermore, the reach and circulation of the comedy series were enhanced by an effective social-media presence. From the beginning, the programme had its own Facebook page with regular postings, clips, and discussion areas. In addition, there are also several clips from the programme available on YouTube, often accompanied by people's comments. These production conditions created the possibility of creating a new type of media space, one that has not been seen before for Sámi.

The novelty of this particular programme was further enhanced by the shift in genre. The comedy series is the first Sámi comedy on the Finnish media scene, where programmes about Sámi, in Sámi, and made by Sámi most often fall within the news and documentary genres. There is also a niche market for Sámi music—varying from traditional Joik (Northern Sámi throat singing) to Sámi rap (see Pietikäinen 2010)—but humour or parody are seldom utilized in these genres. The final shift relates to the age and gender of both the producers/presenters and the target audience. In contrast with the more typical case where the producers are middle-aged and male, the producers and presenters of this comedy series are two young bilingual Sámi women. They are both also experienced and acknowledged Sámi journalists with experience working in Sámi radio and Sámi documentaries. They have also worked at various cultural events in Sámiland, typically as presenters and interpreters, making them well known within the community and beyond.

I would like to suggest that these production and circulation conditions enabled the creation of a transformative Sámi media programme. Here "trans" is used not only in meaning of "crossing over", but also in the sense of displaying a potential to dislocate and problematize existing, often fixed, ontologies of language, gender, and ethnicity (cf. Pennycook 2007). The comedy genre, with its resources of humour and parody, can be regarded as transformative in the sense that shared laughter is a way to make stereotypes and fixed categories visible, perhaps to shake them, and to potentially to open a space for creativity and reflection. In this sense, the genre of comedy comes close to what Bahktin (1968) says about the carnival. He (1968: 10) argues that, "carnival can be seen as a temporal liberation from the prevailing truth and from the established order". In the context of Sámi television comedy, this kind of carnivalization circulates novel ways of contextualizing and materializing Sámi languages and resources, beyond the existing traditional categories, practices, genres, and modalities (for carnivalization in the tourism context, see Pietikäinen, 2013a). The carnival television comedy includes multimodal designs, humour, irony, and language play, as we shall see below.

This playful potential between various resources is visible already in the programme's name, logo (Example 2), and blurb.

Example 2. The logo for the comedy *Märät Säpikkäät/Njuoska Bittut*[2]

The Finnish-Sámi name *Märät Säpikkäät/Njuoska Bittut* literally refers to wet reindeer-fur gaiters (shown on the legs of the presenters in the logo). In various media interviews, the presenters are repeatedly asked about the name of the programme, and they repeatedly provide the same explanation. In the Sámi context, apart from the meaning of wet reindeer-fur gaiters, the name of the programme can also refer to "lustful, aroused women" or to "loose women". The story behind this meaning is said to be explained by a some 100-year-old Joik, which tells the story of a cheating wife and her husband's reaction. These multiple meanings of the name are evoked in discussions of the series and its gendered aspects, now also foregrounded in the multimodality of the logo.

The bilingual name of the programme forms the backdrop to the logo, with the Finnish title written in pink with a white wave at the bottom—mostly likely indexing the fells of Sámiland. The Northern Sámi title appears below this in blue. The pink colour is interesting here, in the sense that it does not belong to the traditional Sámi colours (bright colours of red, blue, yellow, green) used in Sámi handicrafts, dresses, and the Sámi flag, and neither is it one of the typically Finnish colours of blue and white (as in the national flag, for example). The colour pink is rather a gendered colour, indexing the relationship with femininity seen in, e.g. practices of differentiating baby girls and baby boys, some feminist movements, and some social movements connected with female diseases, such as the breast-cancer awareness movement. In addition, the colour pink also indexes post-feminist femininity, as well as the gay community and movements (see e.g. Johnson, Milani and Upton 2010; Koller 2008). Koller (2008) suggests that the

2   http://www.facebook.com/pages/M%C3%A4r%C3%A4t-s%C3%A4pikk%C3%A4%C3%A4t-Njuoska-bittut/265936423453929?sk=photos. Accessed 20.9.2012

colour pink functions as a marker of gender and sexuality in cultural models and in the multimodal texts they inform. As a result, the colour pink in the context of a Sámi television programme simultaneously expresses, complements, and extends conventional and countercultural associations of pink, resulting in an ambivalent meaning related to creativity and contestation. The two presenters of the programme are presented in the logo as dressed in stylized Sámi dresses, pink in colour, with *"märät säpikkäät/njuoska bittut"* on their legs, capturing and playing with the stereotypes and categories linking to ethnicity, age, gender, and sexuality.

This kind of strategic hybridization with a carnival touch seems to be characteristic of this programme. This is visible, for example, in the blurb of the programme (Example 3), released 16 December, 2011, and circulated and cited in many other media texts.

Example 3. The blurb from the comedy show *Märät Säpikkäät/Njuoska Bittu*

> *Mystinen ja kaunis Saamenmaa, jossa revontulet valaisevat kaamoksen tummentaman taivaan ja yksinäinen poropaimen voi kuulla suden ulvovan yössä... Vai jotain muuta? Kuinka hyvin sinä tunnet Saamenmaan ja saamelaiset?*
>
> *Märät Säpikkäät –ohjelmassa Lapin omat pocahontakset Suvi West ja Anne Anne Kirste Aikio, nuo häpeämättömät, suorasanaiset – ja flirtit – nuoret naiset, valloittavat Helsingin ja pistävät pääkaupunkimme sekaisin. Samalla he uudistavat kuvaamme Saamenmaasta ja saamelaisten kulttuurista.*
>
> *Tässä uudessa hybridiohjelmaformaatissa sekoitetaan sujuvasti faktaa ja fiktiota ja nauretaan tasapuolisesti saamelaisille, suomalaisille, helsinkiläisille, vähemmistöille, enemmistöille ja ennen kaikkea itselle. Rovaniemi on Keski-Suomea ja sillä linjalla pysytään! Märät Säpikkäät Yle TV2:lla torstaisin 21:00, 12. tammikuuta alkaen.*

'The mystical and beautiful Sámiland, where the northern lights illuminate the sky, darkened by the Kaamos... where a lonely reindeer herder can hear the howling of wolves in the night... or is it something else? How well do you know Sámiland and the Sámi people?

In Märät Säpikkäät, Lapland's own Pocahontas Suvi West and Anne Anne Kirste Aikio—a pair of shameless, outspoken, and flirtatious young women—conquer Helsinki and mess up the capital. At the same time, they give us a fresh image of Sámiland and Sámi culture.

In this hybrid programme, fact and fiction are mixed fluently and everybody is laughed at equally, be they Sámi, Finns, Helsinki people, minority, majority, and above all, ourselves. Rovaniemi is located in central Finland, and this is an argument we will stick with. Märät Säpikkäät will appear on YLE TV2 Thursdays at 9 pm, starting this January.'

In this promotional text, the hybridization with carnival is created by bringing together the traditional, stereotypical view of Sámiland and the Sámi people—presumably held by the potential Finnish viewers—with the playful, lighter tone of the comedy and the promise of laugher, facilitated by the hybrid genre and crossing of typically bipolar categories, such as minority–majority, Sámi–Finn, and periphery–centre (both geographical and political). The two presenters are portrayed with intertextual links to both the Virginia Indian girl Pocahontas (whose story has been circulated, e.g. in the Disney film)—presumably making use of indigenous and gender connections—and to flirting and sexuality, an undertone of the whole programme. Finally, laughing is foregrounded as a central activity of the programme. The marking of the programme seems to centre on bringing together ethnicity, geographical centre and periphery, gender, and sexuality, all wrapped together using laughter.

This deliberate attempt at hybridization is further reinforced by genre decisions. Each programme includes various mixed genres, e.g. celebrity interviews, Finnish music-video parodies, sketches of stereotypical characters in Sámiland (e.g. a tourist, a super-Sámi, a wannabe-Sámi etc), street polls on Sámi issues, a mock "current events in Sámiland" report, discussions between the two presenters, mock nature and anthropological documentaries on both the Sámi people and the "Helsinki tribe". However, each genre used in the programme is united by a tongue-in-cheek style linked to the programme's overarching genre of comedy and parody. Indeed, the whole programme can be seen as consisting of genre parodies and utilizing intertextual links, not only between the various uses of these genres, but also the between typical ways of representing Sámi in the media. Humour is used as a resource for reflecting on ethnic, sexual, gender, and geographical stereotypes and categories, as well as a resource for legitimating this type of ironic stirring-up of ideological relationships and categorization (cf. Hutcheon 2000). With laughter, the viewer can decide whether to interpret the programme as merely entertainment, or to see some critical undertones in it.

This kind of genre hybridity within the programme brings in multilingual practices and facilitates mixed language practices. The programme employs a mixture of predominantly Finnish and Northern Sámi languages, but Swedish and English are used occasionally, and subtitling also figures. Whenever another language than Finnish is used, subtitling in Finnish is provided with exception of occasional temporal crossings to Northern Sámi (see the example below). The Northern Sámi language is a designated language for music-video parodies, in which popular Finnish songs are turned into Sámi versions, with multimodal contextualization in the Sámi context. For example, a famous Finnish punk-rock song, "I want to make love to you", is transformed into a song sung in Northern Sámi called "I want to be a Norwegian Sámi". In the parody, the song describes how everything is better with Norwegian Sámi, referring to the better economic and legal conditions of the Sámi in Norway than elsewhere. Northern Sámi is also the sole language of a character called *John Fire Stone*, a Sámi man who unbendingly keeps his cultural habits (such as sleeping in a "laavu", a kind of outside tent, making an open fire, lassoing moving objects, etc.) even in the Helsinki environment, and thus running into various kinds of conflicts with the authorities, etc. In the mock anthropological documentaries about "the Helsinki tribe", the narrator's voice also speaks in Northern Sámi. The presenters also use both Northern Sámi and Finnish when talking to each other in commenting on events and people, and in the mock current-event report on Sámiland. Finnish is often used with celebrity interviews, with exceptions of one Northern Sámi speaking celebrity and one Swedish speaking celebrity. Also, street polls are performed in Finnish, and international tourists are interviewed in English. The mock nature documentaries on the Sámi people are in Finnish, narrated by a voice familiar from other nature documentaries on Finnish television.

In the interactional flow of the events—particularly in the interviews and in discussions between the presenters—there are temporal crossings and borrowings between Northern Sámi, Finnish, and English. The following extract from a celebrity interview illustrates the temporal, almost casual crossings between linguistic resources in the show. In the extract, the two presenters, Suvi and Anne Anne Kirste, are interviewing a Finnish MP, named Jani, who is also a well known media persona, dancer and actor. He has also publicly stated that he is gay, and on his father's side, he also belongs to a Kenyan tribe that he himself labels *Luja* in the interview. These various linguistic, ethnic and gender categories are evoked and discussed during the interview, accompanied with temporal crossings between Finnish, English and Northern Sámi.

Example 4: Temporal crossings between Finnish, English (bold) and Northern Sámi (italics)[3].

Visual story	Media talk	Translation
A shot of Jani arriving, shaking hands with Anne Anne Kirste and Suvi, hugging them. In the background is a bench and a park on a sunny, summer day.	Anne Kirste: Hei. Anne Kirste Jani: No niin hei, hauska tavata. Suvi: Hei. Mä oon Suvi Jani: Hei, moi	Anne Kirste: Hello. Anne Kirste Jani: Well yes hello, nice to meet you Suvi: Hello, I am Suvi Jani: Hello hello

---

3 Representation of talk in written form invariably means change in modality and consequently choices as regards what is represented and how. Here I have focused on what was said and provided only an overview of the visual story.

Visual story	Media talk	Translation
A close shot showing the faces of Suvi, Jani and Anne Kirste looking at each other. At the bottom of the picture, a text emerges: "Jani Toivola: indigenous brother." A close shot, Jani is putting his hand on his chest. Suvi and Kriste are patting Jani on the back and massaging his shoulders gently. A close shot, zooming in on the faces of Suvi and Jani looking at each other. A shot showing Suvi, Jani and Anne Kirste seated on the bench looking at each other. Camera zooms in on Jani showing him laughing; Suvi is patting him on the shoulder. A shot showing Suvi, Jani and Anne Kirste sitting on the bench.	Suvi: Jani tiiäksää mitä musta oli niin kiva kun sinä halusit tavata meiät Jani: No minusta on ihan mielettömän kiva tavata teidät. Mua vähän jännittää Suvi: Oh ei se mitään **Relax, Relax** Anne Kirste: Oh **Relax Relax** Suvi: Säkin oot vähemmistöö, sä oot tuplavähemmistöö. Jani: Joo Suvi: Mekin tunnetaan yks saamelainen homo. Jani: Joo Suvi: Voisikää soittaa sille? Jani: (purskahtaa nauruun) Suvi: Se on vähän yksinäinen. Voisitko näyttää hänelle vähän mestoja jos hän muuttaa tänne Jani: Ai mun pitää näyttää sille mestoja Suvi: (Niin)	Suvi: Jani, you know what, I think it was great that you wanted to meet us. Jani: Well, I thought it would be really great to meet you. I am a bit nervous. Suvi: Oh, it´s all right. Relax, relax. Anne Kirste: Oh Relax, relax. Suvi: You, too, are a minority person, you are a double minority person. Jani: Yeah Suvi: We also know one other gay Sámi. Jani: Yeah Suvi: Could you call him? Jani: (bursts out laughing) Suvi: He is bit lonely. Could you show him around, if he moves here? Jani: Oh, so I should show him around? Suvi: (Yes)
A close shot showing Jani and Anne Kirste. Camera zooms in to show Suvi´s profile and Jani´s face A shot first focused on Jani and then panning to Jani´s and Anne Kirste´s faces A close shot of Jani´s face	Anne Kirste: Vai meet sää mieluummin sit sinne sen luo sinne pohjoseen Jani: Mä ehkä mieluummin voisin tulla sinne Anne Kirste: Entä jos me muutettais tänne Helsinkiin Suvi (niin) Anne Kirste: Erottaisko että me ollaan niinku vähemmistöjä Jani: No mä ehkä luulen että ne kiinnitäis enemmän huomiota teidän persooniin Te vaikutatte niinku aika mielenkiintoisilta hahmoilta	Kriste: Or would you rather go up there to visit him, to the north? Jani: Perhaps I would rather go up there. Anne Kirste: What if we moved to Helsinki. Suvi: (yeah) Anne Kirste: Would people notice that we belong to a minority? Jani: Well I think that perhaps people would rather pay attention to your personalities. You seem to be pretty interesting characters.

Visual story	Media talk	Translation
A close shot of Suvi, who is smiling and laughing. The camera pans to show Suvi hugging Jani and then back to Suvi´s face.	Suvi: (laughing) Ahhh, *Árvidin, ahte son liiko midjiide.*	Suvi: (laughing) I knew he likes us.
	Jani: (laughing)	Jani: (laughing)
	Anne Kirste: (laughing)	Anne Kirste: (laughing)
	Suvi: Haluatko olla meidän kanssa?	Suvi: Do you want to be with us?
	Jani: No mulle heti tuli semmoinen olo että haluaisin olla teidän kanssa niiku pitemmän aikaakin	Jani: Well, I immediately felt that I would want to be with you, sort of, for a longer time.

In this example, labelling the guest, Jani Toivola, as *indigenous brother* in English and only textually, at the beginning of the programme, can be seen as potentially indexing and making links with various spaces and organization of relations: the indigenous people´s networks in which Sámi people belong, the tribal relationships or other kinds of close relationships of belonging, etc. At the same time, we can see this label is filled with the carnival spirit (Bahktin 1984:179), transformed from its original functions, having acquired a general tone of laughter through this movement and serves as an extension of its original meaning. Thus this labelling can be seen as making a joke about this very same categorization system. The lexical borrowing of the English word *relax* can be seen as functioning as a shared resource for mutual support in an attempt to reduce the potential nervousness and thus to secure the flow of interaction among the three participants. This function is further reinforced by a Finnish pronunciation of the word, accompanied with shared laughter and the encouraging patting and massaging of Jani´s shoulders by both presenters. A vernacular, localized use of an English word (cf. e.g. Androutsopoulos 2010), combined with supportive gestures contribute to an understanding of this interview as non-threatening and non-serious. Instead, the use of the Northern Sámi clause (*I knew he likes us*) seems to be an informative resource between the two presenters, enabling them to comment on events at the local level of interaction without including the non-Sámi speaking Jani. However, the Finnish speaking viewers are included with the help of Finnish subtitles.

4 Discussion: Circulation across modern and postmodern Sámi media spaces

Circulation of Sámi resources in and through diverse and networked media spaces shows how language change is a rhizomatic sociolinguistic process with various, even contradictory orientations and practices. This relates, at least partly, to an understanding of space as already inhabited and situated, with its own history and links to other spaces and their norms and practices. For example, *tv-Oðða-sat* can be seen as an example of a modernist media space with its preference on unity, fixed boundaries and centrally distributed norms. In terms of language change, the emphasis is on managing multilingualism, prioritization of standard variants of Sámi languages as well as on policing fixed language boundaries. What we have then, is a carefully planned and heavily invested Sámi only or Sámi only plus regulated multilingualism media space. What becomes critical– and politicized – is the alignment with the language revitalization goals regarding language prestige, visibility and homogeneity. A counter example is provided by the Sámi TV-comedy *Märät säpikkäät/Njuoska bittut*, which can be seen as constituting a postmodern media space. In this space of multiplicity, fluid and fleeting moments of contact are embraced, and temporal echoes and recircula-tion of resources are celebrated. This ambivalent comedy show marks a point of carnivalism and laughter. In a Bakhtinian sense of the carnival world, the laugh-ter pushes aside the seriousness and the hierarchies of real life. It shakes up the authoritative notion of language and values, making room for multiplicity of voices and meanings. In the Sámi television comedy show we can see and expe-rience Bakhtinian carnival creating a space where pregiven and accepted catego-ries and conventions are broken, reversed and subverted, e.g. through mockery, parody, and humour (cf. Abduran 2011). The Sámi comedy show is a playful, but carefully planned strategic performance that purposefully moulds the require-ment of ownership and appropriation of Sámi languages with the need for enter-tainment into a performance that gives license to laughter and play, as well as to temporal crossings between categories and positions with potential of more serious, political implications. In terms of language change, in this space Sámi becomes part of a multilingual practice, used also casually in interchange and combined with other languages. This kind of use of endangered indigenous Sámi language comes close to the everyday "messy" language practices among many Sámi speakers.

Language change in minority language contexts is always ideologically invested process. For example, Benor (2011) notes that media discourse on and by minority languages leads to an increase of language-ideological discourse and debates. Especially in the case of endangered languages such as Sámi languages, language change is often viewed through the recent historical developments which have lead to the very situation of endangerment. At the same time, change can also be perceived as holding a potential for improvement. Especially change in media language practices is seen as having a potentially important role in lan-guage revitalization and profiling, bypassing the challenges related to territorialized view on minority language community and overcoming the potential status of minority languages as resources located in the past.

It seems to me that language change in minority media spaces leads to an increase in linguistic, discursive and social reflexivity. Both examples of Sámi media spaces discussed in this article are characterized by linguistic reflexivity, be it in the practices of dubbing or in language choices and policy in the programmes. Discursive reflexivity is manifested in careful and strategic use of genres, for example in enhancing the status of Sámi language as informative resources (news genre) or using genre to create an alternative, counter space of Sámi media representations (TV comedy show). Social reflexivity with regard to position of Sámi languages can be seen in the appropriation of Sámi resources in the programmes. Furthermore, in the comedy show, testing and teasing the linguistic, ethnic and gender categorization system is a central theme. These two media spaces and their rhizomatic links to other spaces together create a kind of heterotopia (Foucault 1984), governed by multiplicity and connectivity. A rhizomatic discourse approach, adopted in this article, taps into this multiplicity and connectivity. It allows the mapping and tracing of the circulation of recourses, such as languages, genres, discourses, across various spaces, including spaces of production as well as spaces of consumption, and the examination of the conditions and consequences of this circulation. Moreover, the rhizomatic approach may help in finding and in imagining novel routes and ways to validate and revitalize Sámi language engagements with multilingual practices that are becoming increasingly relevant for heterogeneous communities of indigenous language speakers.

References

Abrudan, Elena 2011: The dynamics of postmodern identity. *Journal of Media Research* 1: 3–14.
Aikio, Marjut 1988: *Saamelaiset kielenvaihdon kierteessä: kielisosiologinen tutkimus viiden saamelaiskylän kielenvaihdosta 1910–1980* [The Cycle of Language Shift among the Sámi: A Sociolinguistic Study of Linguistic Change in Five Sámi Villages 1910–1980]. Helsinki: Suomalaisen Kirjallisuuden Seura.
Aikio-Puoskari, Ulla 2001: About the Saami and the domestic legislation on their language rights. In: Ulla Aikio-Puoskari and Merja Pentikäinen (eds.), *The Language Rights of the Indigenous Saami in Finland: Under Domestic and International Law*, 3–70. Rovaniemi: University of Lapland, Northern Institute for Environmental and Minority Law.
Aikio-Puoskari, Ulla 2005: The education of the Sámi in the comprehensive schooling of three nordic countries: Norway, Finland and Sweden. *Gáldu čála – Journal of Indigenous Peoples Rights* 2/2005.
Anderson, Benedict 1983: *Imagined Communities: Reflections on the Origin and Spread of Nationalism*. London: Verso.

Androutsopoulos, Jannis 2010: The study of language and space in media discourse. In: Peter Auer and Jürgen E. Schmidt (eds.), *Language and Space: An International Handbook of Linguistic Variation. Volume I: Theory and Methods*, 740–758. Berlin/New York: Mouton de Gruyter.

Appadurai, Arjun 1996: *Modernity at Large: Cultural Dimensions of Globalization*. Minneapolis: University of Minnesota Press.

Bakhtin, Mihail 1968: *Rabelais and His World*. Translated by Helene Iswosky. Bloomington: Indiana University Press.

Bakhtin, Mihail 1984: *Problems of Dostoevsky*. Edited by Caryl Emerson. Minneapolis, MN: University of Minnesota Press.

Bucholtz, Mary 2001: The whiteness of nerds: Superstandard English and racial markedness. *Journal of Linguistic Anthropology* 11: 84–100.

Benor, Sarah Bunin 2011: Jewish languages in the age of the Internet: An introduction. *Language & Communication* 31: 95–98.

Deleuze, Gilles and Felix Guattari 1987: *A Thousand Plateaus*. Minneapolis: University of Minnesota Press.

Foucault, Michel [1967] 1984: Of Other Spaces, Heterotopias. Translated by Jay Miskowiec. Lecture published 1984. Des espaces autres, Hétérotopies. *Architecture, Mouvement, Continuité* 5: 46–49. English translation available at http://foucault.info/documents/heteroTopia/foucault.heteroTopia.en.html, accessed 18.6.2012.

Foucault, Michel [1966] 1994: *The Order of Things. An Archaeology of the Human Sciences*. New York: Vintage Books.

Heller, Monica and Alexandre Duchêne 2007: Discourses of endangerment: Sociolinguistics, globalisation and social order. In: Alexandre Duchêne and Monica Heller (eds.), *Discourses of endangerment: Ideology and Interest is the Defence of Languages*, 1–13. London: Continuum.

Honan, Eileen M. 2004: (Im)plausibilities: A rhizo-textual analysis of policy texts and teachers' work. *Educational Philosophy and Theory* 36: 267–281.

Honan, Eileen M. 2007: Writing a rhizome: An (im)plausible methodology. *International Journal of Qualitative Studies in Education* 20: 531–546.

Hutcheon, Linda 2000: *A Theory of Parody: The Teachings of Twentieth-century Art Forms*. New York: University of Illinois Press.

Irvine, Judith and Susan Gal 2000: Language ideology and linguistic differentiation. In: Paul V. Kroskrity (ed.), *Regimes of Language. Ideologies, Polities, and Identities*, 35–83. Santa Fe: School of American Research Press.

Jaffe, Alexandra 2007: Minority language movements. In: Monica Heller (ed.), *Bilingualism: A Social Approach*, 50–70. Hampshire: Palgrave.

Jaworski, Adam and Crispin Thurlow (eds.) 2010: *Semiotic Landscapes: Language, Image, Space*. London: Continuum.

Johnson, Sally, Tommaso Milani and Clive Upton 2010: Language ideologies on the BBC Voices website: Hypermodality in theory and practice. In: Sally Johnson and Tommaso Milani (eds), *Language Ideologies and Media Discourse: Texts, Practices, Politics*, 223–251. London: Continuum.

Koller, Veronica 2008: 'Not just a colour': Pink as a gender and sexuality marker in visual communication. *Visual Communication* 7: 394–423.

Kulonen, Ulla-Maija, Irja Seurujärvi-Kari and Risto Pulkkinen (eds.) 2005: *The Sámi: A Cultural Encyclopaedia*. Helsinki: Suomalaisen Kirjallisuuden Seura.

Lefebvre, Henri 1991: *The Production of Space*. Oxford: Blackwell.

Lehtola, Veli-Pekka 1997: *Saamelaiset: Historia, yhteiskunta, taide* [The Sámi: History, Society, Arts]. Jyväskylä: Gummerus.

Lindgren, Anna-Riitta 2000: *Helsingin saamelaiset ja oma kieli* [The Sámi in Helsinki and their language]. Helsinki: Suomalaisen Kirjallisuuden Seura.

Lindgren, Anna-Riitta 2010: Modernisation and small languages: fatal language sociological delay? In: Helena Sulkala and Harri Mantila (eds.), *Planning a New Standard Language. Finnic Minority Languages Meet the New Millennium*, 74–94. Helsinki: Suomalaisen Kirjallisuuden Seura.

Pennycook, Alastair 2007: *Global Englishes and transcultural flows*. London: Routledge.

Pennycook, Alastair 2010: *Language as a Local Practice*. London: Routledge.

Pietikäinen, Sari 2003: Indigenous identity in print. Representations of the Sami in news discourse. *Discourse and Society* 14: 581–610.

Pietikäinen, Sari 2008: Broadcasting indigenous voices: Sami minority media production. *European Journal of Communication* 22: 173–192.

Pietikäinen, Sari 2010: Sámi language mobility: Scales and discourses of multilingualism in polycentric environment. *International Journal of Sociology of Language* 202 (2010): 79–101.

Pietikäinen, Sari 2013a: Multilingual dynamics in Sámiland: A rhizomatic discourse approach to changing language. *International Journal of Bilingualism*. DOI 1367006913489199, first published on June 4, 2013

Pietikäinen, Sari 2013b: Heteroglossic Authenticity in Sámi heritage tourism. In: Sari Pietikäinen and Helen Kelly-Holmes (eds.), *Multilingualism and the Periphery*, 77–94. New York: Oxford University Press.

Pietikäinen, Sari and Helen Kelly-Holmes 2011: The local political economy of languages in a Sámi tourism destination: Authenticity and mobility in the labelling of souvenirs. *Journal of Sociolinguistics* 15: 323–349.

Pietikäinen, Sari, Riikka Alanen, Hannele Dufva, Paula Kalaja, Sirpa Leppänen and Anne Pitkänen-Huhta 2008: Languaging in Ultima Thule: Multilingualism in the life of a Sami boy. *International Journal of Multilingualism* 5: 77–89.

Pietikäinen, Sari, Leena Huss, Sirkka Laihiala-Kankainen, Ulla Aikio-Puoskari and Pia Lane 2010: Regulating multilingualism in the North Calotte: The case of Kven, Meänkieli and Sámi Languages. *Acta Borealia* 27: 1–23.

Pietikäinen, Sari and Helen Kelly-Holmes 2013: The Dangers of Normativity. The case of minority language media. In: Jan Blommaert, Päivi Pahta and Sirpa Leppänen (eds.), *Dangerous Multilingualism: Northern Perspectives on Order, Purity and Normality*, 194–206. Palgrave McMillan.

Pratt, Mary Louise 1987: Linguistic Utopias. In: Nigel Fabb, Derek Attridge, Alan Durant and Colin MacCabe (eds.), *The Linguistics of Writing: Arguments between Language and Literature*, 48–66. Manchester: Manchester University Press.

Sara, Inker-Anni 2004: Saamelaisuutta vahvistamassa. Sámi Radion toimittajien käsitykset saamelaismedian tehtävistä [The Sámi radio journalists' views on the role of the Sámi media]. MA thesis, Department of Communication, University of Jyväskylä.

Scollon, Ron 2001: *Mediated Discourse: The Nexus of Practice*. London: Routledge.

Scollon, Ron and Suzie Wong Scollon 2003: *Discourse in Place: Language in the Material World*. London: Routledge.

Scollon, Ron and Suzie Wong Scollon 2004: *Nexus Analysis: Discourse and the Emerging Internet*. London/New York: Routledge.

Wallin, Jason 2010: Rhizomania: Five provocations on a concept. *Complicity: An International Journal of Complexity and Education* 7: 83–89.

Helen Kelly-Holmes
Commentary: Mediatized spaces for minoritized languages. Challenges and opportunities

The mediatized spaces that have opened up as a result of the contemporary era of globalized digital media are evident in all three contributions to this section: Máiréad Moriarty highlights how Irish can become a resource in the repertoire of a comedian, who learned it as an adult, as well as a 'rehabilitated' identity resource for those who learned the language in school to various degrees of fluency; Ana Deumart's case shows how the technoscape (Appadurai 1996) provides the tools for individuals to localize resources for themselves away from the restrictions of normative institutions; and Sari Pietikäinen's rhizomatic analysis of spaces, both fixed and fluid, for mediatizing the Sámi languages, provides us with a way to analyse the complexities of new mediatized spaces for minority languages. All three contributions highlight the interdependencies between technology, agency, language practices and wider ideologies that are involved in the creation, maintenance and usage of mediatized spaces for minority languages. Performance is a keyword that permeates all of the contributions, and perhaps best illustrates the particular constellations of technology, agency, practice and ideology that we are currently experiencing.

The cases in this section can be seen to illustrate three eras or paradigms (cf. Pietikäinen and Kelly-Holmes 2011) in the evolution of mediatized spaces for minority languages. In the first era, the gifting era (Pietikäinen and Kelly-Holmes 2011), scarce media resources and spaces are gifted by the centre (a national/regional authority) to peripheral / minoritised language communities. The state is the key agent and actor with the ultimate power. The speech community is perceived as demarcated, monolingual, internally unified; and language is conceived as an objective, isolated system with material properties which can be fixed, kept pure, maintained, etc. These are the 'superfixed spaces' which Sari Pietikäinen identifies in her contribution. Media communication is primarily monologic with authoritative, ideal speakers being heard. From the sociolinguists' point of view also, media presence is seen as a guarantor of life and existence for the minority language (cf. Dorian 1991). Media presence guarantees credibility and existence and would automatically bring revitalization and revival, and the opinions of Máiréad Moriarty's respondents certainly appear to bear out this contention.

In the next era, the 'service' era or paradigm (Pietikäinen and Kelly-Holmes 2011), simply being present is not enough; the drive is for 'functional completeness' (Moring 2007), to be all things to all speakers, even as fragmentation with media and within the speech community starts to occur. Media spaces are seen as a resource for corpus, status and acquisition planning, as Máiréad Moriarty points out in relation to the Irish language television station. Writing about Irish, Ó Laoire (2008) identifies this as the era of the 'mega-policy'. In the Irish context, this was the time of the campaign for Irish-language television and launch of Teilifís na Gaeilge (although, as Máiréad Moriarty points out, its successor, its rebranding and relaunch as TG4 belongs much more to the current 'performance' era). Communication is still primarily monologic, although there is limited dialogic communication. Media actors – community-based organizations and channels – along with the state are the key agents.

In the gifting phase, the primary actor with the greatest agency is, not surprisingly, the state; in the service era, agency is extended to media professionals and associated companies; in the third era, the performance era, we can see the individual as the primary actor, in line with Friedman's (2006) view of the individual's role in globalization 3.0, as a result of digital technology. Whilst participation and practices change somewhat between the gifting and service eras, the performance era or paradigm, the predominant one in the current climate, represents a very significant change, not only in agency and technology, but also in terms of language practices and associated ideologies. Firstly, there is a challenge to territorially-defined speech and media communities with the emergence of speech and media communities based on linguistic competence and interest in a language or activity rather than location (e.g. isiXhosa speakers and learners online). This era both results from and in a general decline in the role of the professional linguist and media professional in favour of a gift economy model of media multilingualism and minority language media. For example, Facebook has used a crowd-sourcing model to localize for all languages other than English (Lenihan 2011). In this model, language communities are formed from the bottom-up by volunteers who put themselves forward as part of a translation community, with no verification of competence, qualifications etc. (cf. Ana Deumert's discussion of Wikipedia). The Web is becoming a vast multilingual corpus created by users rather than by producers; it is a linguistic (and by extension a sociolinguistic) machine, fed by users: Google translate, for example, uses the linguistic choices and renderings of individuals on the Web to 'feed' Google Translation, rather than relying on a team of professionals to translate and localize content.

The second main feature is the evolution of the resource/performance paradigm in sociolinguistics (e.g. Pennycook 2010; Rampton 2006) in response to changing practices and participation in digital and social media. This paradigm shift argues for a view of languages as resources which make up an individual's repertoire, and thus can be used by speakers acting in an agentive way in performing identity work. A resource paradigm allows for the opening up and creation of 'strategically hybrid spaces' as Sari Pietikäinen terms them. Languages become 'detached' from their established geographical 'habitat', becoming 'mobile' resources in individual repertoires, as highlighted by Máiréad Moriarty and Sari Pietikäinen in their chapters. A 'circulation perspective', Sari Pietkiäinen tells us, provides a more appropriate insight into the everyday life of indigenous, minoritized languages, than, for example, a quantification or competence approach might. In all of the cases presented, we can see evidence of the valuing of play, humour and hybridity, as well as the recognition and exploitation of mixed, 'truncated' (Jacquemet 2005) repertoires, which were previously hidden and/or not deemed suitable for mediatization or commodification. This phenomenon is dependent on a language-ideological shift in relation to minority languages, whereby a previous 'deficit' model (Jaffe 2007), focussed on the decline of the language, the lack of competence, and disappearance of monolingual speakers has gradually given way to an 'added value' model in which a little bit of language is enough (Jaffe 2007) and even limited competence is to be celebrated alongside an acceptance of 'imperfect' bilingualism and language mixing. TV presenter Hector's imperfect practices, described in Máiréad Moriarty's chapter, exemplify this trend, and, as Ana Deumert shows, many contemporary practices on Web 2.0 defy categorization in terms of received norms about code-switching and mixing and the written-spoken dichotomy. Such spaces enable play with language as just one resource for various types of performance, for example, voicing the self in online interactions (Ana Deumert) and voicing/styling others in comedy sketches (Máiréad Moriarty and Sari Pietikäinen). Humour and play are a common thread in these cases and are something new in terms of mediatized spaces for minority languages. Certainly, humour and play were never part of the gifting or even the service eras, when the stakes were too high, the power too imbalanced, the need for homogeneity and an agreed narrative too urgent to risk humour and play.

Linked to a shift away from territorially-based speech communities, has been an increasing commodification in relation to minority languages in the media. Here we can see a move from a rights based model to a lifestyle/consumption based model – Ó Laoire (2008), for example, uses the term 'speakers of choice' to refer to the Irish context. Minority language media communities are self-selecting and characterized less by location than by competence, interest, a desire for self-actualization and performance, and political ideology – this being understood as a commitment to maintaining the minority language. Speakers are now also primarily consumers, and new technology makes it possible to serve their needs, since the Web breaks down the traditional economies of scale that favour publishing media in big languages. Speakers of Irish and other minority languages have become niche consumers in long tail markets (Anderson 2006), with a type of hyperlingualism developing in new media, as Ana Deumert's contribution shows. There has also been a commodification of (some not all) minority languages and identities, which can add distinction (Bourdieu 1991), especially in an English-speaking context (Kelly-Holmes 2010). The emergence of the 'Sexy Irish' phenomenon, which has many parallels in similar context such as Welsh, can be seen to be part of this (Kelly-Holmes 2011). Globalized genres have become acceptable for minority language media, representing a move away from a cultural nationalist, Whorfian model; likewise, minority languages such as Irish and Sámi are now seen as fit for such genres, representing what Máiréad Moriarty and Sari Pietikäinen identify in their respective cases as a scalar shift for these languages. In addition, this shift from a concern with geographic fixity implies, as Sari Pietikäinen points out in her chapter, a shift in our understanding of mediatized spaces, from ones that are gifted and fixed to ones that are created as required and constantly reconfigured and renegotiated. In such a context, circulation becomes key and all three chapters are focussed in one way or another on tracing or mapping these circulations of language resources. We can also see in the three chapters how sociolinguistic change is both the driver and the product of these different types of circulations and the resulting creation of new mediatized spaces for minority languages.

These three eras or paradigms, while being chronological are also concurrent – this relates to Sari Pietikäinen's argument about the heterotopic nature of mediatized spaces. Just because performance is now dominant does not mean that gifting and service paradigms cease to exist or do not form part of the current context – either synchronically or diachronically. This is why new mediatized spaces create particular challenges and also opportunities for minority languages, as all of the cases studied illustrate. Máiréad Moriarty argues strongly that globalization has not only been bad but also good for Irish, with the balance in the current phase coming down on the positive side. Likewise, Sari Pietikäinen shows how change can lead to improvement in the context of a minority language and its speakers. Ana Deumert's chapter shows how the development of digital media and the participation possibilities afforded by Web 2.0 mean that languages and speech communities can skip the gifting and service eras and move straight to the performance era without having to rely on state or traditional media institutions and resources. All three contributions raise issues about participation and agency in this brave new era. While there is hybridity and fluidity, there is still a concern with quantification and demarcation, for example, in terms of measuring multilingualism on the Web. Such tensions and challenges highlight the importance of approaches such as that advocated by Sari Pietikäinen's rhizomatic model, which allow for the chronology and simultaneity of gifting, service, and performance paradigms to be uncovered in the new mediatized spaces.

Helen Kelly-Holmes would like to acknowledge support of 'Peripheral Multilingualism' Project, funded by the Academy of Finland.

References

Anderson, Chris 2006: *The Long Tail: Why the Future of Business is Selling Less of More.* New York: Hyperion.

Appadurai, Arjun 1996: *Modernity at large: Cultural dimensions of globalization.* Minneapolis: University of Minnesota Press.

Bourdieu, Pierre 1991: *Language and Symbolic Power* (edited with an introduction by J. B. Thompson). Cambridge, UK: Polity Press.

Dorian, Nancy 1991: Surviving the Broadcast Media in Small Language Communities. *Education Media International* 28(3): 134–137.

Friedman, Thomas 2006: *The World is Flat: The Globalized World in the Twenty-First Century.* London: Penguin.

Jacquemet, Marco 2005: Transidiomatic practices: Language and power in the age of globalisation. *Language and Communication* 25: 257–277.

Jaffe, Alexandra 2007: Minority language movements. In: Monica Heller (ed.), *Bilingualism: A social approach,* 50–70. Basingstoke/New York: Palgrave Macmillan.

Kelly-Holmes, Helen 2010: Rethinking the macro–micro relationship: some insights from the marketing domain". *International Journal of the Sociology of Language* 202: 25–40.

Kelly-Holmes, Helen 2011: Sex, lies and thematising Irish: New media, old discourses? *Journal of Language and Politics* 10(4): 511–534.

Lenihan, Aoife 2011: 'Join our community of translators': Language ideologies in/on Facebook. In: Crispin Thurlow and Kristine Mroczek (eds.), *Digital Discourse: Language in the New Media,* 48–65. New York/Oxford: Oxford University Press.

Moring, Tom 2007: Functional completeness in minority language media. In: Mike Cormack and Niamh Hourigan (eds.), *Minority Language Media: Concepts, Critiques and Case Studies,* 17–33. Clevedon UK: Multilingual Matters.

Ó Laoire, Muiris 2008: The language situation in Ireland. In: Robert Kaplan and Richard Baldauf (eds.), *Language Planning and Policy Europe Vol. 3. The Baltic States, Ireland and Italy,* 193–255. Clevedon, UK: Multilingual Matters.

Pennycook, Alastair 2010: *Language as a Local Practice.* London/New York: Routledge.

Pietikäinen, Sari and Helen Kelly-Holmes 2011: Gifting, service, and performance: three eras in minority-language media policy and practice. *International Journal of Applied Linguistics* 21(1): 51–70.

Rampton, Ben 2006: *Language in Late Modernity: Interaction in an Urban School.* Cambridge: Cambridge University Press.

Notes on contributors

Jannis Androutsopoulos is Professor in German and Media Linguistics at the University of Hamburg. His research interests are at the intersection of sociolinguistics and media discourse studies. He has published on sociolinguistic style, language and identity, the language and discourse of youth cultures, linguistic heterogeneity in the media, computer-mediated communication, and metalinguistic discourse on language and ethnicity in Europe. His recent publications include *Language and society in cinematic discourse* (Special Issue of *Multilingua*, ed. 2012) and *Orthography as Social Action* (co-ed., 2012).

Isabelle Buchstaller is Professor for varieties of English at Leipzig University. Her research focuses on language variation and change at the level of morpho-syntax and discourse. She is particularly interested in contact scenarios, including globalisation, mediation, linguistic borders and language ideologies. Her recent publications include *Quotatives: New Trends and Sociolinguistic Implications* (2014, Wiley-Blackwell) as well as "Localized globalization: A multi-local, multivariate investigation of quotative *like*" (with Alex D'Arcy, *Journal of Sociolinguistics* 2009).

Colleen Cotter is a Reader in Media Linguistics at Queen Mary, University of London. Her research areas include news media language, endangered languages (Irish), language in use, and the ethnographic and performative dimensions of institutional discourse and language style. She was a daily newspaper reporter and editor in the US before studying Linguistics at the University of Sussex (MA) and University of California-Berkeley (Ph.D). She taught full-time in Linguistics and Journalism departments in California and Washington, DC, before relocating to London. Her book, *News Talk: Investigating the Language of Journalism* (Cambridge), was published in 2010.

Nikolas Coupland AcSS, FAHA is Research Professor both at the Department of Scandinivian Research, University of Copenhagen and at Cardiff University, and Distinguished Professor of Sociolinguistics at the University of Technology Sydney. He is founding co-editor (with Allan Bell) of the *Journal of Sociolinguistics*, and co-editor (with Adam Jaworski) of the OUP book series *Oxford Studies in Sociolinguistics*. His research interests include the sociolinguistics of style and performance in spoken interaction and in media contexts, sociolinguistic theory, and the sociolinguistics of Wales. His books include *Style: Language Variation* *and Identity* (Cambridge University Press, 2007); the *Handbook of Language and Globalization* (Wiley-Blackwell, ed. 2010); and *Standard Languages and Language Standards in a Changing Europe* (Novus Press, ed. with Tore Kristiansen, 2011).

Ana Deumert is Associate Professor and former Head of Linguistics at the University of Cape Town, South Africa. She has studied, worked, taught and researched on three continents, Africa, Europe and Australia. Her research programme is located within the broad field of African sociolinguistics and has a strong interdisciplinary focus (with particular attention to anthropology, sociology and economics). Her most recent book is 'Sociolinguistics and Mobile Communication' (forthc. EUP). Ana Deumert is editor of *IMPACT – Studies in Language and Society* (Amsterdam/New York: John Benjamins), co-editor of *Cambridge Approaches to Language Contact* (with Salikoko Mufwene) and an NRF-rated scientist.

Alexandra Georgakopoulou is Professor of Discourse Analysis & Sociolinguistics at King's College London. She has published extensively on everyday life storytelling (both face-to-face and on new/social media) and identities construction with a focus on youth and gender identities. Her books include *Analyzing narrative. Discourse and sociolinguistic perspectives* (with A. De Fina, 2011, Cambridge University Press) and *Small stories, interaction and identities* (2007, John Benjamins). She is currently co-editing (with A. De Fina) a *Handbook of Narrative Analysis* (Wiley-Blackwell) and a *Handbook of Digital Language & Communication* (with T. Spilioti, Routledge).

Andreas Hepp is Professor of Media and Communication Studies at ZeMKI (Centre for Media, Communication and Information Research), University of Bremen, Germany. His research interests are media and communication theory, media sociology, mediatization research, transnational and transcultural communication, media change, and methods of media culture research. His most recent publications include *Mediatized Worlds* (Palgrave 2014, edited with F. Krotz), *Cultures of Mediatization* (Polity Press 2013), *Media Events in a Global Age* (Routledge 2010, edited with N. Couldry and F. Krotz) and a special issue of *Communication Theory* on *Conceptualizing Mediatization* (2013, 23:3).

Josh Iorio is an adjunct professor in the Myers-Lawson School of Construction and a senior researcher in the Civil Engineering Network Dynamics Lab at Virginia Tech. His research examines the interplay between language variation, cultural diversity and computer mediation in the global virtual architecture, engineering and construction industry. He leads development of and research in the *CyberGRID*, a virtual world that supports globally distributed, cross-disciplinary design and planning projects. His research has been funded by the National Science Foundation, the Alfred P. Sloan Foundation and the National Institute of Health.

Barbara Johnstone is Professor of Rhetoric and Linguistics at Carnegie Mellon University and former editor of *Language in Society* (2005–2013). She is the author of *Repetition in Arabic Discourse* (Benjamins, 1990), *Stories, Community, and Place: Narratives from Middle America* (Indiana UP, 1990), *The Linguistic Individual* (Oxford, 1996), *Speaking Pittsbughese: The Story of a Dialect* (Oxford, 2013) and two popular textbooks, *Qualitative Methods in Sociolinguistics* (Oxford, 2001), and *Discourse Analysis* (Blackwell, 2002, 2008), in addition to many articles and book chapters. Her recurrent interests have to do with how people evoke and shape places in talk and with what can be learned by taking the perspective of the individual on language and discourse. Since 2000, Johnstone has been conducting research on Pittsburgh speech in its social and historical context.

Helen Kelly-Holmes is Senior Lecturer in Sociolinguistics and New Media at the University of Limerick, Ireland. She has published widely in a range of journals on the economic aspects of multilingualism, and on media and multilingualism, particularly in relation to minority languages. Publications include: *Multilingualism and the Periphery* (edited with Sari Pietikäinen, Oxford, 2013), *Thematising Multilingualism in the Media* (edited with Tommaso Milani, Benjamins, 2013), *Language and the Market* (edited with Gerlinde Mautner, Palgrave, 2010) and *Advertising as Multilingual Communication* (Palgrave, 2005).

Paul Kerswill is Professor of Sociolinguistics at the University of York. His research is in language variation and change, with a strong focus on dialect contact. His doctoral research is reported in his 1994 book *Dialects converging: rural speech in urban Norway*, published by Oxford University Press. He has directed major research projects funded by the UK Economic and Social Research Council on dialect change in the south of England, the first dealing with dialect formation in the New Town of Milton Keynes, followed by a study of dialect levelling across England. Most recently, he has worked on projects investigating Multicultural London English with Professor Jenny Cheshire as collaborator. He is co-editor (with Ruth Wodak and Barbara Johnstone) of the *SAGE Handbook of Sociolinguistics* (2011).

Tore Kristiansen is Professor of Sociolinguistics at the Department of Scandinavian Research, Copenhagen University and member of the leader team of the Danish National Research Foundation's LANCHART Centre ('Language Change in Real Time') at Copenhagen University. The central theme of his research is the role of social psychological processes (representations, attitudes, ideology) in language variation and change, including a focus on how these processes are shaped by, and shape, mediatizations of language. Recent publications include a co-edited volume (with Nikolas Coupland) on *Standard Languages and Language Standards in a Changing Europe* (Novus, 2011), and book chapters on "Attitudes, ideology and awareness" (in *The SAGE Handbook of Sociolinguistics*, SAGE, 2011) and "Language attitudes in the Nordic countries" (in *The Social Meanings of Language, Dialect and Accent*, Peter Lang, 2013).

Martin Luginbühl is full professor in German Linguistic at the University of Neuchâtel, Switzerland. His current research interests include contrastive textology in media discourse, genre history, cultural genre analysis and oral communication in school. Among his recent publications is a co-authored article (together with Carol Berkenkotter) on "Producing genres. Pattern variation and genre development" (to appear in *Handbook of Writing and Text production*, de Gruyter, 2014), an edited volume (together with Stefan Hauser) on *Contrastive media analysis – approaches to linguistic and cultural aspects of mass media communication* (Benjamins 2012) and a book on contrastive genre history of TV news (*Medienkultur – Medienlinguistik. Komparative Textsortengeschichte(n) der amerikanischen 'CBS Evening News' und der Schweizer 'Tagesschau'*, Peter Lang, 2014).

Vally Lytra is Lecturer in the Department of Educational Studies at Goldsmiths, University of London. She studies multilingualism, language use, language ideologies and social identities in schools, homes and communities in cross-cultural urban contexts. She is the author of *Play Frames and Social Identities: Contact Encounters in a Greek Primary School* (John Benjamins, 2007). She has edited *Multilingualism and Identities across Contexts: Cross-disciplinary Perspectives on Turkish-speaking Youth in Europe* (with Jens Normann Jørgensen, Copenhagen Studies in Bilingualism, 2008), *Sites of Multilingualism Complementary Schools in Britain Today* (with Peter Martin, Trentham, 2010) and *When Greeks and Turks Meet: Interdisciplinary Perspectives on the Relationship since 1923* (Ashgate, 2014). She is currently working on a new edited book, *Navigating Languages, Literacies and Identities: Religion in Young Lives*, with Dinah Volk and Eve Gregory (Routledge).

Máiréad Moriarty lectures in sociolinguistics at the University of Limerick in Ireland. Her specific research interests lie in the field of minority language policy and planning. She has a particular interest in the role media, popular culture and tourism play in the maintenance, revival and revitalization of minority languages. The majority of her work to date has focused on the Irish language, but she has also worked on Catalan and Basque. More recently, through her involvement in the *Peripheral Multilingualism* project (Funded by the Finnish Academy, 2011–2014) she has worked on the context of Inari Sami.

Spiros A. Moschonas is an associate professor of linguistics and the philosophy of language at the Department of Communication and Media of the University of Athens, Greece. His current research interests are in language ideologies and standardization.

Ichiro Ota is Professor of Sociolinguistics at Kagoshima University, Kagoshima, Japan. His main research interests are language variation and change, dialectology and interaction via digital networking services. For several years, he has been working on phonological and sociophonetic variations observed in Japanese dialects with particular focus on the impact of the media.

Sari Pietikäinen is a professor of discourse studies at the department of languages, university of Jyväskylä, Finland. Her research interests are discourse studies, media studies, multilingualism, minority and indigenous languages. Among her recent publications are *Multilingualism and the periphery* (2013, Oxford University Press) edited together with Helen Kelly-Holmes and "Multilingual dynamics in Sámiland: A rhizomatic discourse approach to changing language" (in *International Journal of Bilingualism*, 2013).

Ben Rampton is Professor of Applied & Sociolinguistics and Director of the Centre for Language Discourse and Communication at King's College London (www.kcl.ac.uk/ldc). He does interactional sociolinguistics, and his interests cover urban multilingualism, ethnicity, class, youth and education. He is the author of *Crossing: Language & Ethnicity among Adolescents* (Longman 1995/St Jerome 2005) and *Language in Late Modernity: Interaction in an Urban School* (CUP 2006), and a co-author of *Researching Language: Issues of Power and Method* (Routledge 1992). He co-edited *The Language, Ethnicity & Race Reader* (Routledge 2003) and edits *Working Papers in Urban Language and Literacy*. He was founding convener of the UK Linguistic Ethnography Forum (www.uklef.net), and is currently the Director of the King's ESRC Interdisciplinary Social Science Doctoral Training Centre (www.kcl.ac.uk/kissdtc).

Ulrich Schmitz is Full Professor of Linguistics, German Language and Language Teaching at the University of Duisburg-Essen, Germany. His research focuses on contemporary German language, language in mass media and digital media.

Recently, he has worked on multimodality with special regard to relations between text and image. Among his recent publications are a book on language and money (*Sprache und Geld*, with P. Vosskamp, ed. 2012), an article on „Multimodality and Globalization" (in C. Chapelle (ed.): *The Encyclopedia of Applied Linguistics*, 2013) and an article on „Monolingual and bilingual electronic dictionaries on the Internet" (in R. H. Gouws et al. (eds.): *Dictionaries*, HSK 5.4, 2013).

Jürgen Spitzmüller is a senior research assistant in Germanic Linguistics at the University of Zurich. His main research interests are located in the fields of interpretive sociolinguistics, visual and scriptal communication as well as discourse analysis. His latest publications cover a monograph presenting a sociolinguistic theory of graphic variation (*Graphische Variation als soziale Praxis. Eine soziolinguistische Theorie skripturaler 'Sichtbarkeit'*, de Gruyter, 2013), a textbook introducing to linguistic discourse analysis (*Diskurslinguistik. Eine Einführung in Theorien und Methoden der transtextuellen Sprachanalyse*, de Gruyter, 2011) and several articles on discourse theory and multimodal scriptality.

Lauren Squires is assistant professor in the English department at The Ohio State University. Her research investigates language variation across contexts, including the mass media and digital media. Much of her work investigates ideologies regarding "standard" English, and sources of tension between standard and vernacular practice. She also conducts experimental research into the perception of grammatical and lexical variation, and the perceptual correlates of social meaning.

Jane Stuart-Smith is Professor of Phonetics and Sociolinguistics at the University of Glasgow. Her research interests are in social and regional accents, especially Scottish English, and ethnic varities of English, such as British Asian accents. She has worked on the social and linguistic factors involved in phonological variation and change, especially the influence of the broadcast media, as well as on developing methods of articulatory phonetic analysis, such as ultrasound tongue imaging, for use in sociolinguistic investigations.

Shoji Takano is a professor in sociolinguistics at Hokusei Gakuen University, Sapporo, Japan. His research interest includes sociolinguistic theories, sociophonetics, and language and identity. For the past few years, he has been working on the linguistic impact of rapid globalisation on a small rural community in Hokkaido, and real-time studies (both trend and panel) of variation and change in Hokkaido Japanese.

Index